ILLUSTRATED HISTORY OF

GREAT BRITAIN

ILLUSTRATED HISTORY OF

GREAT BRITAIN

by Sir George Clark

edited and with additional material
by Dr J.N. Westwood

Cathay Books

An Accurate Map of GREAT BRITAIN and IRELAND from the Best Authorities
British Statute Miles
20 50 100 150
References to the Scotch Shires
A. Cathness
B. Sutherland
C. Ross
D. Inverness
E. Murray
F. Bamff
G. Aberdeen
H. Mernis
I. Angus
K. Perth
L. Argile
M. Sterling
N. Fife
O. Renfrew
P. Clydesdale
Q. Lothian
R. Berwick
S. Peebles
T. Roxburg
V. Twiotdale
U. Annandale
W. Dumfries
X. Aire
Y. Kirkoudbright
Z. Wigton
References to the English Counties
1. Cornwall
2. Devonshire
3. Dorsetshire
4. Hampshire
5. Somersetshire
6. Wiltshire
7. Berkshire
8. Oxfordshire
9. Glocestershire
10. Monmouthshire
11. Herefordshire
12. Worcestershire
13. Staffordshire
14. Shropshire
15. Essex
16. Hartfordshire
17. Kent
18. Surrey
19. Sussex
20. Norfolk
21. Suffolk
22. Cambridgeshire
23. Huntingdonshire
24. Bedfordshire
25. Buckinghamshire
26. Lincolnshire
27. Nottinghamshire
28. Derbyshire
29. Rutlandshire
30. Leicestershire
31. Warwickshire
32. Northamptonshire
33. Yorkshire
34. Durham
35. Northumberland
36. Lancashire
37. Westmoreland
38. Cumberland
39. Middlesex
40. Cheshire
Western Circuit
Oxford Circuit
Home Circuit
Norfolk Circuit
Midland Circuit
North Circuit
No Circuit
References to the Welch Counties
a. Denbighshire
b. Flintshire
c. Montgomeryshire
d. Anglesey
e. Carnarvonshire
f. Merionethshire
North Wales
g. Cardiganshire
h. Carmarthenshire
i. Pembrokeshire
k. Radnorshire
l. Brecknockshire
m. Glamorganshire
South Wales
N. East Circuit
N. West Circuit
S. West Circuit
S. East Circuit
References to the Irish Counties
1. Dublin
2. Louth
3. Wicklow
4. Wexford
5. Longford
6. Eastmeath
7. Westmeath
8. King's
9. Queen's
10. Kilkenny
11. Kildare
12. Catherlagh
13. Down
14. Ardmagh
15. Monaghan
16. Cavan
17. Antrim
18. Londonderry
19. Tyrone
20. Fermanagh
21. Dunnagall
22. Leitrim
23. Roscommon
24. Mayo
25. Sligo
26. Gallway
27. Clare
28. Cork
29. Kerry
30. Limerick
31. Tipperary
32. Waterford
Shetland Islands
Orkney Islands
WESTERN ISLANDS
OCEAN
GERMAN
IRISH SEA
St. GEORGES CHAN
Bristol Channel
ENGLISH CHANNEL
Long.de East from London
West Longitude from London
J. Gibson Sculp.

Contents

This illustrated edition first Published 1982
by Octopus Books Limited
59 Grosvenor Street, London W1

Reprinted 1985
This edition Published in 1987
by Cathay Books Limited
59 Grosvenor Street, London W1

ISBN 0 86178 503 7

Printed in Hong Kong

1 CIRCULAR ROUTE 1
INGERSOLL WATCH C° LD
B 2569
A·37
LF 9681

Preface

This book was originally published by Oxford University Press with the title *English History: a Survey*. In the preface its author, the late Sir George Clark, explained his aims as follows:

'The purpose of this book is to show how the English people came to form a community; what kind of community it has been in its successive stages of development; and what have been its relations with the other communities to which English people have belonged, or with which they have had dealings. There are communities within England, such as villages, towns and counties. Around it, and separate from it in varying degrees, are such neighbouring communities as Wales, Scotland, Ireland, and France, and many others further away. There are international communities, like the churches, and the many political or other associations in which England has shared. I have not surveyed the histories of any of these other communities except in as far as they explain the growth and action of England . . .'

This new edition, because it is illustrated, looks very different from the original version, but in fact the text remains substantially as it was written by Sir George Clark. His original opening chapter, dealing mainly with geography, has been excluded, and certain passages and sentences throughout the book, dealing typically with events in foreign countries, have also been omitted or abbreviated. The last five chapters of this edition were not written by Sir George Clark, and have been added so as to take the narrative up to date, and to give greater detail for the 1914–1945 period than he was able to give. Here and there throughout the book extra passages have been inserted to provide fuller information about developments in Scotland and Wales.

Another new feature in this edition is the tables of dates provided for each chapter. These are intended to assist those who use this book for study purposes, but they will also help to clarify the order of events for the general reader. It should be realised, however, that many major historical developments do not appear in these tables, simply because processes (like the Renaissance or the Industrial Revolution) did not occur in one particular year.

In the preface to the original edition Sir George Clark listed several persons who had helped with the book. To these should now be added the name of his son, Dr Martin Clark, who offered perceptive advice for this present edition.

J.N. Westwood
Bristol, 1982

Britons and Romans
55BC–446AD

BC

5000 At about this time Britain becomes an island as melting ice overwhelms the connection with the continent.

55 Julius Caesar's first brief expedition to Kent.

54 Julius Caesar invades Kent, but is forced to retire to the continent.

AD

43 The emperor Claudius sends legions to invade Britain, thereby beginning the Roman occupation.

60 The beginning of Boadicea's initially successful revolt against the Romans in Britain.

81 The governor Agricola, after mastering Wales, conquers Scotland as far as the Clyde.

122 The building of Hadrian's Wall.

208 The emperor Severus drives barbarian invaders from northern England and then advances beyond Aberdeen.

410 Emperor Honorius tells Britain that Rome can no longer send help against northern invaders.

432 In about this year St Patrick begins his Irish mission.

From the time when civilized men first wrote about the country and its inhabitants, British history covers more than two thousand years, or seventy generations of mankind. In comparison with the whole length of time during which men have lived here this period is short. Around three thousand years ago there were people with domestic animals, horses, cattle, and pigs; and if we try to fix the time when men and women first lived here, we have to think in terms of tens of thousands of years. The beginning of written evidence means not only that from this point we know more about the past, but also that we have a different and a richer kind of knowledge. What we know of Britain before the Romans came is like what we know of the Caribbean islands before Columbus. We do not know the names of any of the inhabitants. We cannot tell a connected story of what any of them did, or when, or why.

In the first century before the Birth of Christ most of the inhabitants of the British islands were alike in speaking one or other of two Celtic languages. There were out-of-the-way places, especially in Scotland, where earlier and unrelated languages lingered on such as that of the Picts in the south-west; but they have left no trace to which we can assign a meaning even in the names of places or hills or rivers. The two Celtic languages, each of which no doubt had various dialects, were British and Gaelic. The older of the two seems to have been British, the ancestor of modern Welsh, and Gaelic most likely originated in Ireland. The boundaries between the two languages had not settled down yet into permanent positions: movements were still to come of people who took their language with them. Within the Celtic-speaking area the differences from one language to another were great enough to make foreign speech hard to understand, or impossible for most people to understand without being taught; but the resemblances were close enough to make interpreting easy all over the British Isles, and even over the wide area of the Continent where Celtic languages were spoken, as they were in Gaul, north Italy and Spain. In Wales the Celtic tongue, vitalized and re-vitalized by bards who created and sang their own narrative poetry, would for two thousand years remain the essence of Welsh national consciousness even though the Celts themselves were destined to be only a part of Welsh ancestry.

Language was by no means the only characteristic that most of the inhabitants had in common. They had, roughly speaking, the same sort of religion. In its everyday aspects no doubt it was local religion, with village or regional gods and goddesses and with holy places, such as groves, wells, and big stones, which had no connection with other deities or other holy places; but there were some sacred monuments to which pilgrims came from great distances. The most impressive of them, then as now, was Stonehenge even though its original use and purposes had been forgotten long before. Everywhere at stated seasons there were sacrifices to the gods. Some of the priests who performed these

Stonehenge, by far the biggest of the stone circles erected in prehistoric Britain. The photograph shows the surviving stones, and the diagram reconstructs the original design. The upright stones are of sandstone, and weigh about 80 tons. Smaller, 4-ton, stones used in the inner sanctum were brought from Wales. The greatest engineering achievement of prehistoric Europe, Stonehenge was built and rebuilt between 3000 and 2000 B.C. Its layout is based on astronomy, presumably for a religious purpose.

rites belonged to an order of priesthood called Druids, and this order also existed in parts of Gaul. On some occasions, including occasions of crisis, they sacrificed human victims.

In many ways life in one region differed from life in others, and the reasons are sometimes obscure. The most striking remains of this period are the earthworks of many shapes and sizes which were used for various purposes. Some of them were already ancient, others of recent construction. Most of them were defensive, ranging from simple banks and ditches around a single homestead or a small village to huge systems of concentric fortifications, faced with stonework or timber, which we must imagine to have been regional capitals where many men with their cattle were congregated around some chieftain. Some seem to have been places of refuge, but others were permanently occupied. Not only were there many types of defensible settlements, on hill-tops where there were hills; but they were distributed very unevenly over the country. They were scarce in the wild north, numerous and elaborate in some of the southern parts such as Dorset, and this seems to result not from physical geography but from human conflicts and authority and organized co-operation.

At a more commonplace level the varieties of ways of life depended on the lie of the land and the nature of the soil. Except for objects made of metal, for salt (if they got it), and for pottery, most people lived on the produce of their own farms or their own neighbourhoods. Wheat and barley were grown in the more suitable parts of South Britain, as they had been for a very long time; and recently a good deal of new land in the Midlands, East Anglia, and the south-east had been cleared of trees and brought into use for cereal cultivation. Oats and rye were grown where wheat would not ripen, but over most of the hills, especially in the rainy north and west of Britain, animal husbandry was the main means of livelihood. There were good farmers and bad farmers, in what proportions we cannot guess; but the best standards were high. We happen to know that some men were very skilful in breeding and managing horses, and we may be sure that they were not the only experts.

The reason why we know about their horses is that they still used war-chariots, which survived nowhere else west of Asia and impressed foreigners as curiosities. Nor was this the only way in which they were old-fashioned in comparison with their nearest continental neighbours. Some of them were beginning to strike coins, but others used metal bars as currency. They seem to have had few, if any, settlements that deserve to be called towns. There was indeed some foreign trade, and there were ports where merchants as well as shipmasters congregated, perhaps seasonally. In later times London was the most notable port because it was near the Continent and deep in the country. Its tidal, fordable river gave access to the Midlands, and to all the country north and south of the long estuary. Strangely enough, however, there is no evidence that there was a port of London before the coming of the Romans. There was inland trade, and, although there were no metalled roads, there were practicable trackways on which it was easy to find the way for hundreds of miles. Except for the tin-mining of Cornwall there was no industry so concentrated as to create an industrial district; but the best industrial products travelled far. The metal-workers made serviceable tools in considerable variety, and also ornaments for the person, for animals, and for articles of use. These last were works of art, with distinctive styles which had undergone development in Britain itself.

British and Irish civilization was illiterate. Laws and customs were handed down by word of mouth and that tradition is lost; but we can reconstruct some of it from the surviving remains and the few statements written down by travellers from abroad. There were many communities, each controlling its own territory, which are often called tribes. Some occupied much larger areas than others, and we may be sure that they were by no means uniform in their habits and institutions. We know little about the links which bound them together. The strictly tribal element, the element of kinship or what was believed to be kinship, may have been more dominant in some than in others. There may have been contrasts between those which had preserved the same organization since they conquered their territory and others which had altered their system to suit the peculiarities of the country where they settled. For some, and perhaps for all of them, warfare against their neighbours, defensive or aggressive, was something for which they normally had to be prepared, and warlike preparedness implied arrangements for internal order and for justice in matters of ownership. Each community had a king, a leader in war chosen in some way from a royal family, and head of the community in all the matters for which it needed a head. Next to the kings were members of rich and powerful families. The kings needed their support. Their wealth consisted of land, or of dues paid in labour or in kind by the agriculturalists in the next stratum below them. This enabled them to assemble men and equipment for war. It also enabled them to keep the peace and to dispense justice. Whether the life of the community ran smoothly or broke up into quarrels and feuds depended in the first place on the relations of the kings and their powerful subjects. Below that level there were differences of wealth and freedom; but we know little about the functions and standards of life of the descending strata. Nor do we know how rigid the structure of the communities was. Sometimes life was turbulent, and that is a reason for thinking that there were chances for useful men or ambitious men to make their way up to wealth and responsibility. It is not likely that the importance of families and kinship amounted anywhere to a system of caste.

Some of the most powerful of these communities, holding the east and north of Kent, and parts of Hertfordshire and Essex, went by the name of Belgae. They had come as invaders within living memory, from north-eastern Gaul. At first Diviciacus, the king of the Gaulish Belgae, had been their ruler too; later they separated, but they kept up relations with their continental kindred. There is no reason to suppose that these newcomers constituted the bulk of the population in their territory. The ruling elements and their fighting men most probably spread over the country and took charge of all the inhabitants whom they could force or persuade to stay and obey their orders. They seem to have been able organizers and to have extended their dominions at the expense of their island neighbours. Their pottery, made on the wheel, is said to have been technically much superior to anything hitherto made in Britain, but at this time they were not distinguished for any kind of artistic production.

The first event in the history of the British Isles to which we can assign a date happened in the year 55 B.C. It was then that Britain for the first time came into the line of view of a mature and highly articulate civilization. Julius Caesar, the most victorious general of the Roman republic in his time, had been operating for four years in Gaul. He had subdued many Gallic communities, the Belgae among them. He had done something to steady the restless barbarians to the north-east of Gaul, for instance by raiding across the Rhine. He made inquiries about Britain. His chief informant was Commius, whom he had put in as king of the Belgic community of the Atrebates, a name which survives in that of Arras. He also questioned merchants. Although he learned disappointingly little, in the late summer of 55 he assembled a force, probably at Boulogne. They were troops of a quality such as had never been seen in Britain, either for discipline or administration or armament. There were two legions of infantry, each above four thousand strong, besides archers and slingers and machines for hurling stones, *catapultae*, the artillery of the time. A smaller force of cavalry was to embark probably at Ambleteuse.

The Britons heard about these preparations and some of them sent emissaries to make terms. Caesar sent Commius over. He also sent an oared warship to reconnoitre for landing-places. In July or August the expedition put out to sea. The cavalry-transports were unlucky in their navigation and never made the landing. The main force sailed at night but had to anchor near Dover, losing the chance of tactical surprise. There was no opposition by sea, but when Caesar sailed eastwards next morning there were British cavalry and chariots dogging his movements by land. Somewhere beyond the North Foreland he ran his transports aground, and in spite of opposition his legionaries landed and held their ground. The invaders spent about a month in Kent, an uneasy time. They cut corn for their own use, and were harassed by the Britons as they worked. There were comings and goings between the two sides: Commius had the risky task of bringing them together. When a gale at high tide damaged the transports on the beach, the only thing Caesar could do was to evacuate his beachhead. Whatever the purpose of his expedition may have been, it was a failure.

In the next year Caesar came again, earlier in the season and with a much stronger force, five or six legions instead of two, and Gaulish cavalry. He landed somewhere near the same place as before, but this time his opponents did not dispute the landing. Many Kentish chieftains had united against him, but he advanced across the River Stour and carried by storm a fortified position, probably Bigbury. Resistance was broken for the moment, but again his ships were damaged by storm on the beach, and he had to deal with the emergency in person. When he took the offensive again he met the most powerful of the Belgic kings, Cassivellaunus. The latter ruled the Catuvellauni, who had the same name as the Gallic tribe whose centre was Châlons-sur-Marne. His own main fortress is thought to have been at Wheathampstead in Hertfordshire. Cassivellaunus and his charioteers were skilful enough to make things difficult, but not to stop Caesar's advance when he kept his troops tightly together in close order. Some communities submitted to Caesar and some were willing to collaborate, at least to the extent of supplying victuals and allowing him to march through their territory. Among these were the Trinovantes of Essex, in Cassivellaunus's rear. They were the latter's enemies already and Caesar had brought with him an exiled prince of theirs, Mandubracius, a useful ally. Caesar now forced a crossing of the Thames and made short work of capturing the Wheathampstead hill-fort. But fighting flared up behind him in Kent and there was bad news of disturbances in Gaul. Cassivellaunus might have gone on with guerrilla fighting, but Commius took a hand and Caesar granted peace. He led his prisoners away with him, to be sold as slaves and pay for the campaign. Cassivellaunus gave hostages and promised to pay an annual tribute to Rome. He also promised to refrain from molesting Mandubracius and his Trinovantes. Caesar sailed away after this second failure which, being one of the most convincing military historians of all time, he was able to represent as a success.

Nearly a hundred years went by before any other Roman commander attacked the island. The Roman empire already had more than five thousand miles of frontier to defend, and Britain was no threat. But Britain and Ireland did not stagnate. Roman civilization leaked in, especially in the east. The use of coinage gradually increased. There was trade with Gaul, and even with the barbarians of Germany and the North. Wheat, cattle, perhaps slaves, iron, tin, and lead were exported in sufficient quantities to pay for wine, fine pottery, and metal wares. But outside the range of Roman influence there were other stimuli to change. In the west and north the craftsmen who worked for the rich made metal mirrors, scabbards, and personal ornaments in purely Celtic traditions which astonish and satisfy us by their beauty. And the Roman influence did not extend to social organization of any kind. For instance, neither in the East, nor in the West did any of their enemies ever form an army like the Roman army, for the simple reason that the Roman army was an expression of Roman society. In Britain the rivalries of the little communities went on. New units appeared, to vanish by absorption into the others. At first the successors of Cassivellaunus left Caesar's protégés the Trinovantes in peace and changed the direction of their own advance. They built a new, unfortified town at Verulamium, near the modern St. Albans, a few miles from their old hill-fort. They extended their territory by way of the Chilterns and the Dunstable Downs to the upper basin of the Great Ouse. Cunobelin, who appears in Shakespeare's play as Cymbeline, was probably a descendant of Cassivallaunus. During his long and prosperous rule he acquired fresh territories, including that of the Trinovantes. Here at Colchester (Camulodunum) he made his principal seat, and such was his pre-eminence that a Roman historian a generation later referred to him, not accurately, as king of Britain. South of the Thames a new Belgic community arose. Commius, Caesar's old ally, broke away to fight in the last stand for Gallic independence. He and other survivors from the débâcle settled in parts of Hampshire. From there they spread widely to the east, west, and south-west, carrying more or less diluted Roman ways.

The upshot of it all was that South Britain was divided into more than a score of communities to which we can give names, each with a character and history of its own. The successors of Commius, of Cassivellaunus, and of Mandubracius ruled over a wide belt from the Channel to Suffolk and the Wash. The Iceni were in possession of Norfolk; Kent was independent but perhaps divided; three other partially Romanized kingdoms to the west of all these covered a large area from Dorset to the Humber. One northern kingdom was comparatively advanced, that of the Parisi or Parisii, relations of the people who gave their name to Paris. They seem to have come up the Humber and taken possession of Holderness and the Yorkshire Wolds, with a frontier roughly corresponding to that of the present East Riding of Yorkshire. West of all these again were half a dozen kingdoms.

The most northerly, that of the Brigantes, spread over most of Yorkshire and Lancashire and further north. Beyond it were the kingdoms of North Britain, which seem to have had little intercourse with their southern neighbours.

For reasons of which we know little, the minds of Roman statesmen gradually turned towards the idea of invading Britain. Whatever others reasons they may have had it seems that they knew much more about the resources of the island than Caesar, who never heard of its mineral wealth, and therefore they probably considered that the venture would be profitable. They may have supposed that the British Isles presented some danger to their empire. If they did it is hard to believe they were right. The imperial navy policed the narrow seas so well that we hear scarcely anything about it, and no one could imagine that the British kinglets could have invaded Gaul by sea. Whatever his reasons may have been, the emperor Claudius decided on invasion. This time, much of the island was conquered and the Romans held it for nearly 400 years. We may doubt whether the history of their whole empire would have been materially different if they had never come at all; but in Britain a new era began.

In the year A.D. 43 Aulus Plautius, who had been commanding in what is now Hungary, made an unopposed landing in East Kent, very likely at Richborough near Ramsgate, a much safer and more commodious beach-head than Julius Caesar's. His army was of the same order of magnitude as that of Caesar on his second visit, though stronger in cavalry. This time the defenders began by evading battle, and there was never any properly concerted defence. The ablest of Cymbeline's sons, Caractacus or Caradoc, was defeated in Kent. Such forces as remained tried to stop Aulus at the River Medway and they failed. The Romans advanced westwards until they reached a point where the Thames could be forded. The emperor came over to take command in person, with a suitable escort, including elephants. The army crossed the Thames and marched to Colchester, perhaps without casualties. There Claudius received the submission of about a dozen kings. After sixteen days he returned to Rome to celebrate his triumph. Four years later when Aulus Plautius gave up the British command he had pretty well finished the conquest of the easily accessible lowland country. A frontier line, running from the Bristol Channel to the Humber, was fixed in the regular Roman way. Forts were built in the occupied area and a metalled military road was built from end to end of it, so that troops could move quickly to any point. Its long straight stretches are still in use: we call it the Fosse Way, or more officially A46.

The Fosse Way frontier was temporary. It was very long and it did not follow any easily defensible natural features. On the map it looks more like a take-off than a destination. On the left it has open access to the south Welsh coast; in the centre it is only a few days' march from the gap of the Dee, the way to North Wales. The Welsh mountains were difficult, but not prohibitive to veterans who knew the Alps, the Pyrenees, and the Balkans. Physically the north of England was easier than Wales. The high, wet moorlands stretched interminably away into the unknown, but there were practicable ways round them both on the east and the west, to say nothing of the sea, and there were ways across them at short enough intervals. In the whole island the only insuperable obstacles were some of the fens and marshes, and here too there was always a way round. Yet the conquest of Britain was a slow process. Roman Britain did not enter on a long period of unbroken peace until the third century. Even so the Romans never conquered the whole of the island. They scarcely set foot in the Scottish Highlands and they never attacked Ireland or even the Isle of Man, though they could see them plainly from their forts and farms. They had nothing to fear from these thinly peopled lands, which had no riches, natural or man-made, to tempt them. Yet, in the parts which they did set out to control, one sequence of events was repeated time after time: a massive advance was followed by rebellions of those already subjected, sometimes far in the rear. For all their military superiority and for all their experience of successful empire-building, the Romans seem never to have found the secret of stabilizing the northerly part of this new province.

Their problem was to exact tribute, not so much in money as in money's worth, and it was complicated by the efforts of their private citizens to do the same. Their merchants might drive hard bargains. Their capitalists invested money to develop the resources of the country but expected a high return. The Romans are commonly credited with the maxim 'Divide and rule'. They offered physical protection to friendly communities. They did not offer material aid in the forms of gifts, but they did offer the advantages of their civilization.

In particular they promoted the growth of towns as they had already done in Gaul. These were adorned with dignified stone buildings, town halls, temples, market squares, theatres for plays and concerts, amphitheatres for circuses and gladiatorial shows. This was the setting for a way of life, with a corresponding structure of ranks and privileges which fitted the personal relationships of the subjects for subordination to the empire. The towns grew gradually, and each had its own character and purpose. Four of them, Colchester, Gloucester, Lincoln, and York, were associated with settlements for veteran soldiers, to whom agricultural holdings were assigned. They were called *coloniae*. The others were not founded by official acts, but guided and fostered. There were the capitals of *civitates*, perpetuating more or less the communities which the Romans found in existence. The larger of these, Cirencester, St. Albans, Wroxeter, Canterbury, and Winchester, covered from half to a quarter of a square mile; the smallest measured well under three hundred yards on its longer face. They were regularly planned and not overcrowded. As time went on they were provided with walls. In each of them officers and citizens had gratifying titles and social standing. The Romans did not suppress the British ways of life. They allowed the existing religious cults to go on side by side with the official worship of the emperor and with the rites of temples and altars to the Roman or other gods which private individuals could set up. Some kings who accepted Roman rule were allowed for a short while to keep their royal titles and were called allies. The lack of real self-government and the reality of subjection were agreeably disguised.

When the Fosse Way frontier was made the friendly population beyond it in the Midlands was apt to be plundered by raiders from free Wales and also from the Brigantes, although their queen, Cartimandua, had made peace with the Romans. We do not know how much communication there was at this time between the various Celtic communities, beaten and unbeaten; but Caractacus, whom Aulus Plautius defeated, had gone off to Wales, and he may have been in touch with all the British enemies of Rome. Ostorius Scapula, the successor of Aulus,

The remains of the theatre at Verulamium, an unfortified Roman town built in the first century A.D., near the present-day St. Albans in Hertfordshire. Verulamium was one of three towns destroyed in A.D. 60 by The Iceni, led by Boadicea, in a rebellion against Roman oppression. Most information about Roman Britain comes from the excavation of sites like this, rather than from documents.

decided to advance towards Wales, and took the precaution of disarming the population in his rear. The Iceni of Norfolk, a nominally independent client-state, resisted, but Ostorius put them down and they kept their allied status. Ostorius went forward almost to the Irish Sea. He had to break off to quell a movement of the Brigantes, and then for some years Caractacus and his guerrillas gave trouble in South Wales. In the end finally beaten, Caractacus fled to Cartimandua and she betrayed him. He was led through Rome in triumph, but his life was honourably spared. Ostorius probably established the legionary fortress at Caerleon on Usk and he made the *colonia* at Colchester; but when he died in the year 52 he still had trouble on his hands both in Wales and in the North. In the occupied part of the country there were deceptive signs of progress. Three earlier legionary stations were at Wroxeter, Chester, and Lincoln. Prosperous towns of the Roman type were Colchester, St. Albans, and London. In 59 the energetic Suetonius Paulinus took over the British command. In his first two years he made headway in North Wales and forced a landing on Anglesey. Once on shore he massacred soldiers, Druids, and women.

In the country he had left behind him there was discontent. The Roman rule was hated, no doubt both because it was alien and because it was oppressive. One of the old communities had new and burning grievances. The king of the Iceni died. The Romans stretched the law to declare his line extinct, to annex the kingdom, and to confiscate the property of the king and all his nobles. When the imperial financial officials took over they flogged the widowed queen Boadicea and raped her daughters.

Boadicea raised her Iceni in arms, and the rebellion spread from the Wash to the Thames. The new towns at Colchester and Verulamium went up in flames. The legion stationed at Lincoln was cut to pieces. Suetonius heard the news in Anglesey. With only his cavalry, leaving the infantry to follow, he raced southward down Watling Street. He reached London, but with too few troops to save it. It too was burnt. But Suetonius made his way back to his infantry. The rebels threw themselves at him and the legionaries won. Boadicea died: perhaps she took poison. After a burst of military vengeance, civilian officials, some of them specially commissioned from Rome, settled the ruined province by clemency and reconstruction.

Ten years went by before the Romans pressed forward again. They worked their way northwards through Yorkshire and Lancashire and fixed the headquarters of one of their legions in York. In 77 or 78 the command fell to Julius Agricola, a strong man with a record of long service in Britain, whose biography was written by his son-in-law Tacitus, one of the best prose-writers of all time. In one campaign Agricola finished the conquest of Wales. Then he turned north. Supplied by his fleet and methodically building roads and forts, he advanced year by year into what is now Scotland until he won a victory which he regarded as decisive. He may have intended to occupy the whole of the Highlands and have contemplated invading Ireland. In 83 or 84 he was recalled to Rome, and the forward policy in Britain was abandoned. Troops were needed on the Danube and the Rhine, and the garrison in Britain was permanently reduced to three legions. What followed in the north is uncertain. Agricola's forts, spread out from the Lothians to north of the Tay, were held against attacks for some years, but not for many. The Romans kept effective control as far north as the Tweed. About the year 117 a great northern rising rolled them back to the short line between the Tyne and the Solway Firth.

In 122 the emperor Hadrian came over to supervise or inspect the new fortifications on this frontier. His famous wall is the mightiest ancient edifice in Britain. It is longer and more monumental than the earlier walls which the Romans had built on the Continent. No other geographical situation could seem more suitable for a fortified frontier than a line of only three or four days' march, with harbours at each end on which a fleet could be based. But it is hard to define the purposes of the wall, military and psychological. It never marked the absolute limit of the Roman forces: they had outposts beyond it, largely for obtaining intelligence. When it had stood for some twenty years, they made another push northwards and built another wall between the Firth of Forth and the Firth of Clyde. This was only about half as long, only thirty-six modern miles; it was built more quickly and less expensively. It was held for thirty years or so; but then came another great rising. The advanced wall was temporarily evacuated. Another twenty years brought a third and worse rebellion, and the permanent loss of the further wall. In the last decade of the first century A.D. came the worst of all the northern risings: the main wall was partly destroyed. Some years of confusion followed. The Romans restored the position and rebuilt the wall and their fortifications. The last phase of this crisis brought Severus to Britain in 209–11, the third emperor to visit it. He advanced beyond Aberdeen, and the defenders, without ever risking a battle, obliged him by formally submitting. There was no serious fighting on the frontier for the next eighty years or so.

LEFT **A view of Hadrian's Wall near Housesteads in Northumberland. This enormous undertaking expresses Roman competence and confidence in engineering and organization. Here as elsewhere the Roman surveyors have taken full advantage of the contours. Built between A.D. 122 and 127 it was manned by some 10,000 men. Hadrian (inset) was Roman emperor until 138 and was in Britain in 122.**

BELOW **The Romans proved themselves to be more than highly competent civil engineers: they were also very accomplished at designing and making mosaics. This example is the head of Autumn and forms part of a mosaic of the seasons found at Corinium (now Cirencester, Gloucestershire). It dates from the second century A.D. and can be seen in the Corinium museum.**

The Roman armies were already going outside their primary business, but their bloodstained interferences in politics did not concern most of the inhabitants of Britain. The army was self-contained, but not cut off from the civilian population. Its commander was a high official, the pro-praetor, the emperor's representative. The troops were not Roman or even Italian: they were recruited in various parts of Europe, chiefly in Germany and the countries around it. By the third century many were probably recruited from Britain itself. They were long-service men, enlisted for fifteen to twenty years, and every year or so something approaching 1,000 of them earned their discharge. Most of them went home to their native countries; few seem to have settled in Britain, and those few left the frontier to settle in the south. Naturally towns and villages of British and immigrant civilians grew up around their quarters to supply their needs, including the need for female companionship. Many of these had a recognized place in local government as *vici*, wards or villages.

Behind the army were the roads. Some of these date back to the early days of the conquest; but some which were built by and for the army were still useful when they were no longer much needed for movements of troops. The Fosse Way, for instance, was the route between Bath, the great watering-place, with several towns in its neighbourhood, and the populous centres Leicester, Lincoln, and York. Ultimately the whole occupied area had a road-system, well planned, well surveyed, and well built. The great highways radiated from London, to Dover, Colchester, Newcastle-on-Tyne, Carlisle, Chester, Gloucester, Bath, Exeter, Chichester, and so on, much as they and the railways have done ever since. This general lay-out was not a Roman invention. In parts its followed the course of older tracks. To a great extent it conformed to the obvious economic needs of the country. No one had to decide that London was to be the focal point: it simply was so. What was Roman in the system was the engineering and the execution.

Britain was governed by a section of the immense imperial administration. One of its departments, the most detested, was independent of the emperor's local representative and reported direct to Rome; this was the corps of tax-gatherers and paymasters under the procurator. The remainder all worked together. Besides the roads they carried out some large public works. They drained, or directed those who drained, tracts of the fens to the north-east of Cambridge, and wet land in other parts of the country. They increased the production of the mines. A lead ingot has been found in the Mendips which bears a stamped date of only six years after the landing of Claudius. Besides lead (from the west and also the north) there was a little silver extracted from it. Near Pumsaint in South Wales remains can still be seen of well-engineered shafts driven into the hillside for gold and supplied with water by a seven-mile artificial channel. Copper came from Anglesey, and iron from Sussex, the Forest of Dean, and elsewhere. Less attention was paid to Cornish tin than in more ancient times, because Spain could now produce more cheaply and was nearer to the centres of demand. Cornwall has scarcely any Roman remains. With this exception all the metal-winning and metal-working industries were stimulated. The pottery and textile manufacturers were active and their best products reached high standards.

We have no figures relating to the economic life of the country, neither for civilian populations, nor for industry nor for trade. We may, however, safely infer that all these were growing under

the Roman occupation. We can be sure that in some parts of the country the Romans improved agriculture, probably more on the side of organization than on that of farming handiwork. Here again we have no figures, and changes of this kind were probably uncommon. Over most of the lowland zone the face of the country was altered by the putting up of substantial buildings. Hundreds of these were built wholly or partly of stone or brick. There were simple farm-buildings, and there were habitations usually with farm-buildings about them, from modest home-steads to comfortable bungalows, large and ornate. Little is left of their carved stonework, but from the ground-plans and fragments it is clear that they were Italian buildings on British soil. In two things only were they adapted to the climate. As in northern Gaul they had good systems of under-floor heating, and glass was used for the windows more often than in Italy. Many of them had mosaic pavements, richly coloured in classical designs, with figures from mythology which still bring memories of the Latin poets into English fields.

There is not one of these 'villas' in England of which we know who built it or who lived in it, whether it was an expatriate official who settled here or a native landowner who appreciated Roman ideas and ways. Just as we cannot draw a line between military and civilian activities, so we cannot draw a line between the immigrants and the native population. Some of the newcomers must have picked up something from the Britons. A large proportion of the Britons underwent a process of Romanization, but inevitably it cut deeper in some places and in some social strata than in others. The simplest example is that of language. Daily meetings in the law-courts and markets must have made some Romans understand some Celtic words, but none was absorbed into any Latin that survives in writing. On the other hand, there are a few words scribbled on surfaces when they were wet which make it probable that some native tilers and plasterers knew a little Latin. There is no positive evidence of the bilingual Britons whom we must suppose to have existed among the upper elements of the towns: there is only the negative evidence that, while there are many Latin inscriptions on stone which concern Britons there are none in their own language. And there is a surprising fact about the Latin words which survive at the present day in the English language. When, later, the Anglo-

Saxon invaders came over from the Continent, although most of them and their ancestors had never lived under Roman rule, they had already picked up a good many Latin words, and it is from this source that we have derived our familiar names for wine, butter, pepper, cheese, silk, copper, a pound, an inch, a mile, and a mint, in the sense of a place where money is made. The other Latin words which the Anglo-Saxons incorporated in their language after they arrived, finding them current here, are much fewer, and such as they would hear in the towns. One such word was the Latin *castra* which became the Old English word for a fortified town. It survives in the place-names Chester, Caister, and Caistor and in the ending of many other names such as Winchester, Doncaster, Leicester, and Exeter.

One aspect of Romanization has a unique kind of meaning for us: Christianity came to Roman Britain. We do not know when or how it first appeared, but it came early, in a simple guise, when it had scarcely begun to gather around it a literature of theological interpretation. There were other religions from the Near East which also had their followers among the military and civil immigrants. In the first phase Christianity touched only the towns. In the early years of the third century Christians were persecuted: the names of three English martyrs have been preserved. Of these Alban counts as the first, after whom the new town which succeeded Verulamium was named. The last official persecution was that of Diocletian nearly a century later. The emperor Constantine first tolerated Christianity and then himself became a Christian. Finally Theodosius I made Christianity the established religion of the empire.

Other religions survived beside it in Britain, but British Christianity was now a regular part of an organization which extended over the whole empire. Its framework was partly imitated from that of the imperial civil service; its languages were Latin and Greek. Among its immediate tasks was defining its beliefs, soon with the ominous implication that heretics, those who held beliefs contrary to its doctrines, were to be expelled and coerced. To do all this there had to be ecclesiastical officers and assemblies. Early in the fourth century three English bishops attended a council at Arles in southern Gaul. We know little about the building of churches. Were it not for one thing we might suppose that the British converts were all among the humbler people, but several mosaic pavements with unmistakable Christian symbols belonged to great houses.

Christianity, by unrecorded ways, reached parts of the British Isles where the Romans had never been, and reached them early. Towards the end of the fourth century St. Ninian, a Briton educated in Rome and trained as a monk by St. Martin of Tours, returned as a missionary to Galloway and founded a monastery at Whithorn. Another pupil of St. Martin was St. Patrick. He was the son of a fully Romanized Briton, a man of position and a Christian; but he was kidnapped and carried off to Ireland as a slave. Sent to Gaul as handler with a consignment of wolfhounds, he escaped and came back to revivify such Christianity as there was already in Ireland. Later came St. Illtyd, a disciple of St. Germanus, the bishop of Auxerre, who himself visited St. Albans. Illtyd set up his monastery at Llantwit Major in Glamorgan, to become the teacher of St. David and of the Breton St. Pol de Léon. So Irish and Welsh Christianity became strongholds of Latin traditions, not only spiritual but intellectual, and not only strongholds but bases for missionary sorties. Their life and scholarship was not interrupted by the upheavals of the following age. Besides their skill, they maintained their own exclusive communication with the Mediterranean world.

In glancing at the growth of Christianity we have moved ahead from the time when the Romans held Britain firmly to the time they let go their grasp. Now we must go back to look at the events which followed the visit of the emperor Severus, who died in York in 211. He had pacified the north to such effect that it remained quiet for more than eighty years; but two-thirds of the way through that interval, the defences had to be reorganized to face in new directions. Raiding reached inconvenient proportions both on the eastern and the western coasts of occupied Britain. On the east and south-east coasts Saxons appeared, originating probably from the barren lands around the lower Weser. They would certainly be attracted to Britain by the hope of plunder, and they probably discovered that they could make room for themselves as settlers. A new official appeared, with the title 'Count of the Saxon Shore', and he seems to have had charge of the defences from East Anglia to Sussex and also of Saxons already established there. The fleet was redistributed and new fortifications were provided for its harbours. On the west coast similar measures were taken. The Scots (that is the peoples, or the eastern and northern peoples, of Ireland) were giving trouble. They too were settling as well as raiding, and they too were met by forts of the new type and by new naval methods.

These were the local examples of a mounting pressure from the overcrowded barbarians which ended by overwhelming the imperial frontiers along the whole length of the Rhine and the Danube. But the decline of the Roman Empire was a double process, the thrusts from outside went home because there was decay and dissension within. Britain experienced these in its own insular way towards the end of the third century. Carausius, by birth one of the Menapii who lived around the estuary of the Scheldt, in command of naval forces on both sides of the Channel, used the opportunity to land in Britain and declare himself emperor. He maintained himself for several years, until his treasurer Allectus murdered him and took his place. The lawful emperor Constantius came with a fleet, sailing in two divisions from Boulogne and Havre. They evaded Allectus's fleet in fog and his army was destroyed.

During the last phase of his gamble Allectus had left the wall undefended, and the barbarians poured over it, ravaging the country. It may well be that, quite independently of the confusion caused by the usurpers, there was already economic decline in the south and east, as there was in various parts of Europe, but imperial policy could do nothing to remedy that. In the administrative and military spheres there were vast reforms and reconstructions. Not long after the rebellion of Carausius, Diocletian, the persecutor, divided Britain into four provinces, subdivided into dioceses, with a reformed administrative system in which the military and civil spheres were separated. His successor, the great Constantine, completed the reforms with the most startling of all, the removal of the capital from Rome to Byzantium, renamed Constantinople.

Whether the reforms were beneficial or detrimental to Britain no one can say. Picts and Scots continued to attack the wall and the west coast to the south of it, while the Saxons and Franks came in across the Channel and the North Sea. The whole country was in confusion and London was besieged until a

A page from the Lindisfarne Gospels, now in the British Museum. This illuminated manuscript dates from about 700, and its rich, elaborate and well-planned detail is characteristic of this period.

Anglo-Saxon valuables. The ring (below), now in the British Museum, was found by accident in a field in 1870. Its inscription indicates that it belonged to Aethelwulf, King Alfred's father. Like the gold buckle (left), it was the kind of jewellery which was often buried with its owner. The coin (bottom left) is a penny; King Offa popularized this denomination, and it remained for centuries afterwards the basic English coin. Edward the Confessor, to meet the demand as money became more widely used as a medium of exchange, set up several new mints to produce pennies. Even in Harold's brief reign, three types of penny were produced, one of which is shown (bottom right). Such coins were hammered; that is, each was struck by means of a hand-held hammer, so no two were exactly alike. But, as these enlarged pictures show the dies used were already quite intricate.

capable general, Theodosius, cleared it of enemies in 369 and restored the wall as Severus and Constantius had done before him, if less completely. In 383 a third usurper, the Spaniard Magnus Maximus, marched away the troops from the wall and took them off to the Continent. That ends the military history of the wall. Once more and for the last time the imperial power was restored in Britain, but local recovery could not save it now. Early in the fifth century Roman authorities took troops away. The centre of gravity of the empire had shifted far to the east. Gaul and Italy itself were in imminent danger. In 410 Alaric the Goth sacked the city of Rome. The last appeal to Rome for military assistance appears to have been sent by some of the *civitates* in Britain in 446. It was unsuccessful. By that date at the latest the Romans ceased to defend Britain and to control it.

If we knew precisely in what ways and to what extent Britain was Romanized, it would still be very difficult to estimate how much survived from this Romanization through later centuries. The survivals were disguised by layer upon layer of later civilizations; some were untraceable because they were assimilated into what was there before. Some things were imported later by roundabout ways but ultimately from Roman sources, and these have been mistaken for survivals. Antiquarians have believed that they could trace Roman measurements in the lay-out of fields, or Roman institutions in the medieval organization of estates and legal relationships, only to find their conclusions rejected by other scholars. Little by little the Roman ways of life disappeared like the Roman buildings, sometimes by the cartload, sometimes by the slow action of wind and rain.

Starting at ground level it seems to be proved that the Roman time was favourable to the spread of weeds, the seeds of which were carried with loads of crops. The road-system, the movements and supply of troops, and the growth of towns all contributed to this, and about fifty common species of weeds are thought to have spread widely. Two plants which seem to have been introduced by the Romans from abroad are the opium poppy and a kind of chervil. There are more than a dozen edible plants which were certainly used in Roman Britain and may have come in then for the first time, including radishes, cultivated plums, medlars, mulberries, peas, and walnuts. It is almost certain that the Romans introduced the vine. As to farming practices we can say nothing for certain. Roman methods of draining, on the larger and the smaller scale, seem to have gone out of use early. There seems to be no evidence that any agricultural estate was held together as a unit throughout the period of confusion and invasions. In some parts of the country upland settlements were deserted and villages were settled in the valleys; but this process has gone on intermittently until our own time, and we do not know when or exactly why it began.

The central question about the survival of Roman civilization is, what happened to the towns? In the last century of Roman rule there was a decay of town-life throughout the western provinces. Business was less prosperous; defences were neglected; civic activity decayed. Two hundred years after the Roman army departed most of the towns were more or less deserted and more or less in ruins. How far these two kinds of deterioration went in each town by any given date is a complicated problem, and it has not yet been solved in any single instance. Some Roman towns have kept their names – London, Gloucester, Cirencester, and so on – but that does not prove them to be more continuous in other ways. Little or nothing is known about the numbers of inhabitants from time to time in towns like York where some sort of occupation has probably gone on from Roman times until now. Nor do we know definitely when the last family left the ruins which were completely deserted, as at Silchester. But we do know the main facts about the decline of Roman civilization in Britain. In some respects there was an absolute breach of continuity. No person now living can trace his pedigree back to any Romanized Briton. There was an end to the distinctively Roman elements of urban life, the theatres, the temples, the public buildings, the statuary, the local government. Something of Christianity may have survived but not its administrative system, centred on the bishops of the towns. Even before the Romans went away Celtic art was reviving, and after they left, many of the Mediterranean motifs went out of fashion. In the main the Roman civilization in Britain came to an end and such of its elements as kept alive were what the botanists call ruderals, plants growing among stone-rubbish.

The Anglo-Saxons 446–865

577 West Saxons defeat the Britons at Dyrham.
597 Augustine begins his Roman Christian mission at Canterbury.
613 Northumbrians defeat the Britons at Chester.
664 The Synod of Whitby decides in favour of Roman, rather than Celtic, Christianity.
735 The death of Bede, the scholar-monk of Jarrow.
793 The sacking of Lindisfarne marks the beginning of Viking attacks.
796 The death of King Offa marks the end of Mercian predominance in England.
825 Wessex under King Egbert defeats Mercia and becomes the dominant kingdom.
843 The kingdoms of the Picts and the Scots unite, later becoming the kingdom of Scotia.

English history made two false starts, one with Julius Caesar and the second with the Roman occupation. After that comes another century and a half of prehistory before the story begins again, to run on without a break until the present day. The light comes on at an advanced stage of a fresh conquest of part of Britain. This Anglo-Saxon conquest was very different from the Roman conquest. Instead of being co-ordinated by an imperial power, it was the work of independent raiding-parties which pounced wherever they chose, from the Humber to Southampton Water. This time it was the defenders who were civilized and the aggressors who were barbarians. The terrain was the same and so, as before, Kent took the first shock and the lowland zone submitted earlier than the more difficult country. But the result was more decisive and more lasting. All over the conquered parts people came to speak Old English, the language from which our present English is derived. They not only spoke this language but they renamed most of the places and natural features. These processes continued far into historic times as the newcomers pressed forward. In the end only a few Celtic names survived among the many thousands of English names, and most of these are the names of rivers, forests, hills, and hill-forts. A few Celtic elements like *tor*, a hill, *comb*, a valley, *carr*, a rock, and *brock*, a badger appear in place-names far back in the lowland zone; but apart from such rare exceptions, language changed, and the change of language was an index of deep changes in ways of life. In the north and west, however, and especially in Wales and Scotland, the old language and the old civilization lived on. The Anglo-Saxons did not influence them as the Romans had done, and so, though this conquest cut deeper than the Roman conquest, it was geographically much more restricted.

It was an episode in a great complex of migrations, often called *the* wandering of peoples, which rolled over every part of Europe, Romanized or not, from the fourth century to the sixth, wrecking the western Roman empire and setting a new course for European history.

The Romans left Britain at a time when attacks from overseas were already frequent and severe. They left it in the hands of the *civitates*, which had experience in administering their own local affairs, but not in the higher responsibilities of government. The *civitates* may have combined to organize defence at sea, on the coast, and inland; but if they attempted this they never mustered the necessary forces at the right times and places. There may have been old animosities between neighbouring regions, though we know nothing of them, and there may not have been enough sense of common danger to overcome differences of local interest. At any rate no one showed the political knowledge and skill that were needed. Even in Roman times it seems that a beginning had been made, on the Saxon shore, in relying on an alternative possibility, that is on calling in some of the raiders as allies. This would have been a dangerous course for a united state, but it was

Anglo-Saxon conviviality. The participation of women as equals reflects the circumstance that in many ways women had higher status in Saxon times than they had in later centuries. They normally held the key of the storeroom, a vital role in an age of scarcity, symbolising their authority inside the household. Some owned substantial property and were regarded as the senior partner in their marriages.

far more so for the British communities. They fell to fighting one another. Here again we do not know what may have caused them to take up arms, nor what they thought about their comrades and their enemies, but we do know that internal war was endemic during the period of invasion and that the leaders of the Britons came to be called kings.

In what is now Scotland the Romans left, in the lowlands, a collection of British tribes. Some of these were Romanized and a few professed Christianity. To the north, the Picts still dominated. Little is known about the Picts, but it seems that the succession of their kings was passed down through the female line, and that at some period the centre of their society came to be Perthshire and Strathmore. At Scone they had a religious or ceremonial centre. Meanwhile, from the north of Ireland the Scots were infiltrating into the western parts of the land which would eventually bear their name. Anglians were beginning to invade the lowlands.

These Anglian invasions were just part of the long process by which Britain was largely taken over by peoples from across the North Sea. This process had begun with raids during the final years of the Roman occupation, but about the middle of the fifth century it became more intense, taking on the character of conquest. The newcomers came from the wide region of northern and central Europe which the Romans called Germania. From this great reservoir of men came some of the migrants who moved furthest and in the most widely different directions. It seems likely that they began to move because the poorer lands of the northern European plain became overcrowded; but the booty of richer and ill-defended countries was another motive, and some of them moved on again even after they found homes in countries where life was easier. When they learnt the use of writing the newcomers to Britain called themselves Anglo-Saxons, but they distinguished two local groups, one in Kent and the other in the Isle of Wight and the adjacent mainland, as Jutes. Procopius, a good sixth-century historian, states that there were Frisians in Britain. There were Saxons in Germany and the Low Countries; there was a Jutland in Denmark, and also a district called Anglia in Schleswig. The Frisian language, still spoken in the Netherlands and some of the German islands, is more closely allied to English than any other. Somehow these facts must fit together; but the more facts we consider, the harder the dovetailing becomes. The origin of the name of Saxon cannot be pinned down to any one region, nor even to any one kind of society, whether tribal or made up of shifting warrior-federations. Old English was written in clearly marked dialects, but these seem to have grown apart after the invasion, not before. Archaeologists are inclined to map out four types of culture: Jutish, in the places mentioned above; Anglian, to the north of the Welland and the Warwickshire Avon, and again in East Anglia; Saxon, in the Thames basin and southwards from there to the Channel coast; Anglo-Saxon, around the Welland and the Great Ouse. All the invaders came by sea, and probably from the opposite shore of the North Sea, but to name their homelands more precisely is to run into uncertainties.

This matters less for British history than might appear. Once settled in Britain the invaders did not keep up much communication with their old homes. They traded across the sea, but not to any great extent, and there is nothing to indicate that their own relatives meant anything more to them than the other inhabitants of shores where there were prospects of business. Much more important than their origin are the character of their civilization and their relations as settlers with the British population. Although some of them may have spent at least a time in countries comparatively advanced in knowledge and the arts, they were all illiterate and they built with wood, not with stone or brick. They were countrymen, setting no store by town life. They were heathens, worshipping the gods and goddesses of Germania; but we know little about what their religion meant to them. They had priests, idols, and sacred buildings. The names of some of their deities survive in our names for the days of the week, as they do in the continental countries with Teutonic languages. In later times much literary tradition gathered around these deities on the mainland and came to be known in Britain; but it seems that the beliefs of the Anglo-Saxon invaders were crude and unadorned. In a couple of instances local landowners are found appointing their local priests; in others a king is attended by a higher priest, but there was presumably nothing like priestly domination. Whether any of the invaders came to Britain with kings as their leaders we do not know. It seems unlikely, but kingship was already rooted here at an early stage of the conquests. Compared with monarchy in the tradition of the Near East it was informal and not majestic. The kings were leaders in war. Their followers were warlike, but not military in the sense in which the Romans were military; they were fighting men, not builders of professional armies.

In the nature of the case we have no detailed knowledge of their social institutions. We cannot even say for certain whether the bond of kinship was the strongest force in holding them together, or whether the war-bands were of mixed origins and united by such rules and ideas as followed from their being together in hazardous adventures. We do not know what proportion brought women with them, or how early they began to bring them. Arguing back from the institutions of their later descendants, we can be sure that there were dissimilarities between different parts of the country, and that the outstanding exceptional group were the Jutes. They had unusual arrangements for the rights and duties of men of different ranks, and also for the inheritance of property. In the long run and in combination with many other factors these may have led to a divergent type of society, with a more even distribution of wealth and a more numerous body of men capable of standing up against authority. There were times in later history, even as late as the eighteenth century, when Kent took the lead in struggles for freedom, but it would be irresponsible to connect this with a social difference, let alone a racial difference, between Jutes and

Anglo-Saxons. For one thing it would be impossible to make similar claims for the other Jutish settlement round the Isle of Wight; for another it would be easy to argue from geography, that whatever sort of men had lived in Kent, its natural wealth and its position on the main routes from London to the Continent would in any case have made it a home of freedom. The Jutes seem to have come from comparatively highly developed countries about the lower Rhine, and this may account for their distinctive institutions.

The landing which has always been regarded as the beginning of the invasion took place in the middle of the fifth century, probably in the Isle of Thanet. Very likely the local potentate called some Jutish force to his assistance, only to find that they came to stay. The other Jutish area around Southampton Water was probably settled later on from Kent. There was a separate early settlement by the South Saxons, whose territory was named after them, Sussex. At first they extended further north than the modern county; but their main seat came to be hemmed in by more powerful peoples and they played only a modest part in subsequent history. The kingdom of Wessex, which grew up to the west of them, proved in the end to be the most powerful of all. Its chief town was Winchester, the name of which is half Celtic and half Roman, and it included the southern group of Jutes; but there are strong reasons for believing that the West Saxons themselves came overland, probably along the high ground of the Icknield Way and across the Wiltshire Downs, from somewhere around Cambridge. If so they passed on their left other colonies, Angles in East Anglia, Saxons in Essex and the lower Thames valley. The estuaries and rivers of the east coast were the main entries from which the invaders fanned out over these parts and also over the Midlands. The Humber was a broad highway from which it was easy to overrun the country east of York and almost as easy to master the country around Lincoln. So a second route led into the northern Midlands, and a kingdom called Deira, largely of Frisian people, grew up round York. From there adventurers sailed northwards along the coast and fortified themselves in positions like Bamborough and St. Abb's Head. They were the founders of the kingdom of the north-east, Bernicia, which was afterwards joined to Deira to form Northumbria, the kingdom north of the Humber.

Bit by bit, research is correcting and adjusting our knowledge of these movements, which together make up the retreat of the Britons and the solidifying of the fluid invading forces into settled unities. In the last paragraph we have summarized the events of about a century. The advance was slow, and it was not uninterrupted. Somewhere about 520 the West Saxons were defeated at the siege of a fortress called Mons Badonicus by a great leader, presumably a Briton with a good deal of the Roman about him, called Ambrosius Aurelianus. This battle did fairly certainly give a respite from war for more than forty years to some larger or smaller area; but we do not know where the hill-fort Badonicus was, nor which side were the besiegers and which the besieged, nor whether there is any reason to identify Ambrosius as the King Arthur of later legend. We do not know whether this battle was fought on foot, or whether horsemen on one side or the other were important in any of these wars. Neither do we know how to relate this event to an emigration across the Channel, for which the dates 511 and 519 are suggested. In this movement many Britons from the south-west went over to Armorica, the Celtic-speaking peninsula which is still called Brittany. We know that some others followed them in later years; but we have no grounds for supposing that anywhere, let alone throughout the conquered districts, the whole indigenous population was driven out or put to the sword. No doubt the proportion of those who died or fled to those who stayed and submitted varied from one part of the country to another. There are places, such as the upper Thames valley, where place-names, archaeological finds, and even words in modern dialects concur to suggest surviving pockets of British people. For the whole country which was under Anglo-Saxon control in the sixth century, it appears that the bulk of the population were descendants of the people who were there before the troubles. A naturalist has remarked that invaders do not kill good-looking women. Nor do they kill peasants who will collaborate. A seaborne mass-transference of entire peoples was beyond the capacity of sixth-century transport.

Two famous battles marked the end of the invasion of the lowland zone and defined the objectives for future advances. In 577 the West Saxons defeated the Britons at Dyrham, on the southern end of the Cotswolds, and slew three kings. Then they occupied Gloucester, Cirencester, and Bath, clearing their way to the Severn valley and cutting off the Britons of Wales from the Britons of Devon and Cornwall. In 613 the Northumbrians defeated their British neighbours at Chester, cutting the Welsh off from the British kingdom of Cumbria. Henceforth instead of one long, narrow Celtic-speaking strip from Land's End to the Roman wall there were three detached regions which could not combine in defence except by using the sea, which they never effectively did. The physical isolation of Wales marks in a real sense the beginning of the history of Wales as a nation. It coincided with the vigorous spread of Christianity. There had been scattered Christians in Roman settlements in Wales, but in the sixth century the creed was effectively propagated by missionaries from outside the Roman establishment. St. David [Saint Dewi] became the best-known of these.

In the interval between the battles of Dyrham and Chester came the stride from pre-history into the dawning light of history, and it was brought about by the progress of events outside our island. Romanized Gaul, like the rest of the western world, had its share of the wandering of the peoples; but the Franks, who took possession of the parts facing the Channel, spared and assimilated much that they found there. There was some trade between Britain and this Christian Francia, and in 584 Ethelbert, king of Kent, married Bertha, daughter of the king of the Franks. With her came Liudhard, bishop of Senlis, north of Paris. They restored the ruined Romano-British church of St. Martin at Canterbury and worshipped in it. They probably corresponded with the pope, Gregory I, called the Great.

Gregory, who worked hard to rescue the western world from its confusion, in 596 commissioned the prior of a monastery in Rome to go as a missionary to Kent. After various hesitations Augustine arrived in the following year with forty monks. King Ethelbert, though not at first converted, gave them leave to preach, and in Canterbury they founded a monastery on the site where the Cathedral stands. They made converts rapidly, their procedure being first to baptize and after that to instruct. Augustine went to France to be consecrated as a bishop; then in 601 Pope Gregory made him the first archbishop of Canterbury. This step was part of a complete plan for the ecclesiastical

The tombs of the Scottish kings at Iona, western Scotland. The Scots came here from Ireland, and their Saint Columba founded a monastery in Iona during the 6th century. This became the centre of the Celtic church in Scotland; ruins of the subsequent Iona cathedral can be seen in the background.

administration of England as two provinces. Augustine was to be bishop of London and head of the southern province, with twelve bishops under him. He was to send a bishop to York as head of the northern province with authority equal to his own. Gregory sent instructions on matters which the missionaries were finding it difficult to decide. They needed to know how far they must insist on the Christian view of marriage; how church property was to be legally protected; what forms and rituals they were to follow; what was to be their relation to the bishops in France. The pope ruled that the church in England was to be neither over nor under the church in France. On the other points he allowed the missionaries much freedom to accommodate their rules to the prejudices of their converts. He sent a new body of missionaries as reinforcements, and he urged Ethelbert to use his influence in spreading Christianity among the other English kingdoms.

It took only about sixty years for those kingdoms to become Christian, at least in the sense that the kings received baptism and put down the public practice of heathenism. Laws against devil worship were still made until the late seventh century, and remnants of it lingered on as village superstitions long after that; but along with the official conversion there went a real and general change of faith and morals. It could not have been otherwise. The new religion brought coherent ethical standards, and gave access through books and writings to fundamental philosophy and science. It implied contact with continental Christianity. Its representatives, the monks, set a new kind of example in their regulated lives. Very early they brought with them builders and other craftsmen. The kings made use of literate men: Ethelbert himself was the first Anglo-Saxon ruler who committed laws to writing. In short, a mature civilization came to the Anglo-Saxons in the form of Christianity.

Although it prevailed quickly it did not follow the course that Pope Gregory laid down. For one thing, as we shall see later, its progress became entangled with the wars between the newly established kingdoms; and there was another problem. Cornwall, Wales, Cumbria, and Ireland were Christian already. For many years they had little communication with the Continent, but in their isolation they had developed intense religious traditions of their own. They had been led by ascetic evangelists whom they regarded as saints. In everything essential they were at one with the Roman Church, but there were matters in which they had drifted apart. Of these the knottiest was the calculation of the correct dates for Easter and the other variable feasts of the church. The pope had intended that the Welsh should come under the authority of Augustine, who therefore, with Ethelbert's support, proceeded to the west. The Welsh clergy came to his summons and there were two conferences, probably beside the river Severn. At the first conference the difference over Easter was raised; the second broke up without any discussion at all.

The building of churches, the planting of bishops, the demarcation of dioceses, and modifications to suit changes of circumstances, all went on in the conquered areas without any further attempt at co-operation with the Welsh. In 627 Paulinus, a Roman and one of Gregory's second party of missionaries, presented himself to Edwin, the victorious king of Northumbria. In an assembly mentioned in the earliest report of a debate in England, he won his point: Edwin accepted baptism. As the first archbishop of York he preached in the plain and the dales and in Lindsay, south of the Humber. Another landmark was the baptism of Cynegils, king of the West Saxons, in 635, in the river Thame. Birinus, who performed the ceremony, was sent from Rome, but made his own plans independently of Canterbury.

By this time a new band of missionaries from overseas was at work in the north. When Augustine came there were no Irish monks on the mainland of Britain; but in 563 Columba, from Donegal, had founded a community in the Hebridean island of Iona, on the boundary between the nominally Christian Scots and the heathen Picts. Columba, a descendant of kings, had followers in the next generation who carried Irish Christianity into far distant fields. They carried its monastic system, its rules of penitence, and with it their own special Latin scholarship, and their artistry in sculpture and in illuminating manuscripts. In 635 St. Aidan came to Northumbria. There, as we shall see in a moment, the Christianity of Paulinus had been overwhelmed by a return of paganism; but Aidan restored it. Soon the two influences in the conversion, Roman and Irish, were inextricably intermixed. The Irish and their followers were not restricted by dioceses and plans of campaign. In East Anglia the Irish visionary author Fursa worked in his monastery and the Burgundian Felix organized the diocese and founded a school, leaving his name in Felixstowe. There were, of course, the disputed questions which had helped to frustrate Augustine's approach to the Welsh, but they were settled at a synod at Whitby in 664. The decision was in favour of the Roman practices; but it was not followed by any exodus of Irish monks. In spite of personal quarrels and differences of principle, the diverse elements worked together in the end.

The period of the conversion was virtually ended when Theodore of Tarsus was appointed as the sixth successor of St. Augustine in 668. He at last established the organization of the church among the Anglo-Saxons, and his career symbolizes the significance of this fact. He was born, like the Apostle Paul, at Tarsus. He was a student, the last whose name has been preserved, in the schools of Athens, which traced their history back, four centuries beyond St. Paul, to the greatest days of Greek philosophy and science and letters. During the century after Theodore the vitality of the English church was proved by the missionaries who went out to convert the heathen Frisians and Germans. They represented both strains of English Christianity. Several of them, such as St. Willibrord of Utrecht and the martyr St. Boniface of Mainz, are remembered as founders of sees.

A casket dating from about 750, and assumed to be from Northumbria. The whalebone carving depicts the taking of Jerusalem. The explanatory inscription is in the Nordic alphabet (Runic).

The course of the conversion was troubled by the rough and tumble of wars and politics. It could not have been carried out in the earlier days of utter confusion, and now that there were coming to be kingdoms, with definite territory and a fair degree of control, they were still perpetually shaken by mutual warfare. Each of them had its own character, and some may have been more aggressive than others; but, so far as we can tell, they fought mainly for territory. When a king acquired more land it gave him greater opportunities of display, of raising troops, and of rewarding his followers. Whether there were quarrels at lower levels over rights of pasturage and the like, we do not know. Nor do we know whether the people of any separate kingdom thought of it as deserving loyalty and devotion resembling the devotion which they rendered, in the spirit of their ethics and their poetry, to the king as a person. If there was any such sentiment it has left no memorial. Whatever local or regional feeling a modern Englishman may feel, it is not a feeling for Northumbria or Mercia or Wessex. The hostility of pagans to Christians added a new factor to these wars; but the old motives still operated as before. When pagans fought Christians they were not fighting wars of religion, and they did not decide on religious grounds alone whom to choose as allies or enemies.

From time to time, as often happens among petty rulers, one of the kings asserted a vague superiority over some, or even all, of the rest. They promised to respect his frontiers and to make war on his enemies. These agreements were often upset by changes in the fortunes of the kings; but they seem to point forward to the time when all the kingdoms were united into a single legally constituted organism. That, however, came about in conditions very different from those of the eighth, ninth, and tenth centuries. In those centuries the main institutions of government were still unstable. The power of a monarchy depended on the personality of the monarchs. There were no cut-and-dried rules of hereditary succession, and so the right to a throne was often disputed. It was not a rarity for a king to abdicate or to be murdered, or for an exiled prince to reappear as a claimant. The noblemen who surrounded a king played their parts in giving advice and putting decisions into practice, but they too derived their authority not only from legal powers, but largely from their own wealth and personal strength. If there were reasons for thinking that the merging of kingdoms into larger units would bring about a more peaceful and a more prosperous life, neither kings nor nobles appear to have acted on them. Scotland was exceptional in achieving unity as early as 863. This happened when the Scots king, Kenneth McAlpin, obtained the throne of the Picts. The name Scotia, originally used to describe the part of Ireland from which the Scots had first come, was soon used instead to describe the new united kingdom of Picts, Scots, British lowlanders and Anglian settlers north of the Forth. In England the churchmen, while not exempt from competitive jealousies, were in advance of the lay rulers in overcoming the local and regional spirits. They may not have consciously thought of the whole Anglo-Saxon area as a community; but they took advantage of the opportunities for acting as though it was a single whole. This was the attitude of Theodore of Tarsus. In 672 a synod was held at Hertford which represented all the English-speaking dioceses.

The history of the wars may be passed over quickly. Ethelbert

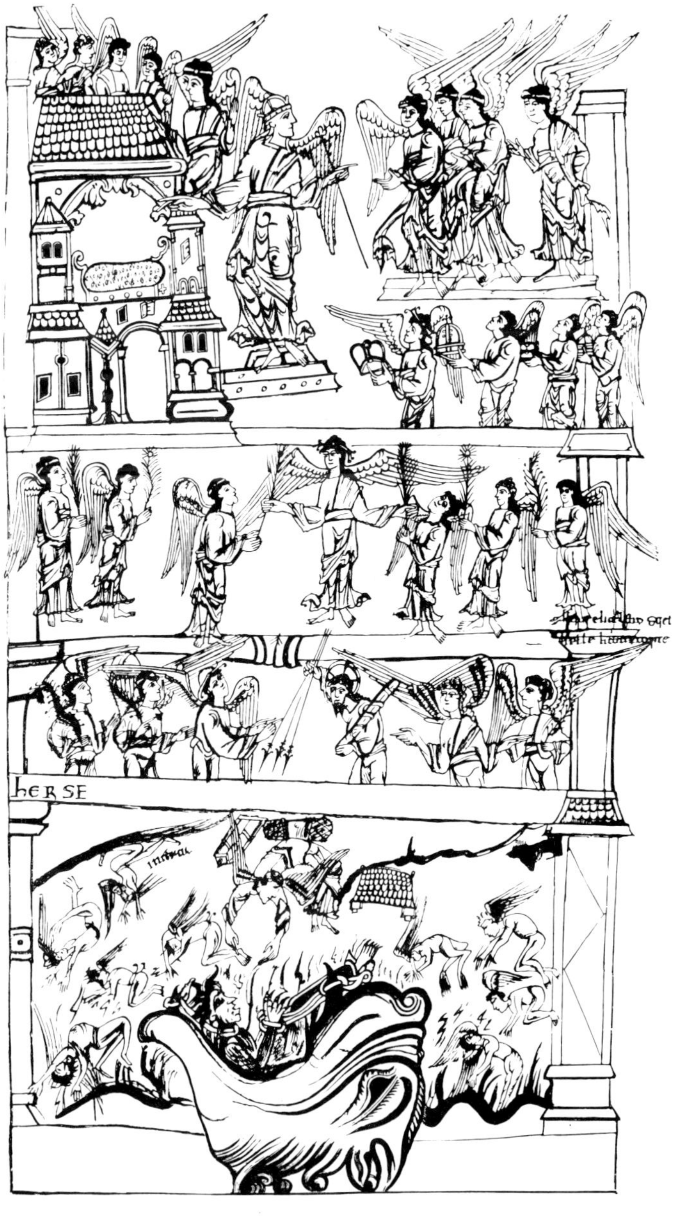

An illustration from a 10th century Anglo-Saxon manuscript now preserved in the Bodleian Library at Oxford. It shows the defeat of a 'bad angel', who can be seen among the torments of hell in the bottom of the picture.

of Kent, the king who received St. Augustine, had fought against Surrey and was an overlord, but after his time Kent subsided into the second rank of kingdoms as Sussex had done before it. The Northumbrians took the first place from the time of their victory over the Welsh at Chester. Edwin, the convert of Paulinus, was more powerful and more regal than any earlier Anglo-Saxon king. He annexed the district of Elmet, running up from the plain of York into the Pennines. He conquered Anglesey and the Isle of Man, and near his northern boundary he founded Edinburgh, which perpetuates his name. His authority was recognized in some sense in East Anglia. But the Northumbrian supremacy was brief. Edwin invaded North Wales. He had underrated his opponents. Cadwallon, king of Gwynedd, found a Saxon and heathen ally on Edwin's left flank, by name Penda, a warlike noble of the Mercian royal house. Together they invaded Northumbria. Edwin was killed in battle near the marshes of Hatfield Chase. The victors deliberately devastated Northumbria. It fell apart into its two components, Deira and Bernicia. Edwin's immediate family lost the throne.

This was the most notable success of any Welsh counter-attack, but it was to Mercia that the prizes fell. Penda became king of Mercia, and as the champion of heathen conservatism he enlarged his kingdom from its nucleus about the Trent, pressing out both to the south-east and the south-west. He extinguished the Hwicce people of the Cotswold country; he fought against Cynegils of Wessex; he set up his eldest son as under-king of East Anglia. But his family was linked by marriage to Christian dynasties; in the later years of his long reign he tolerated Christianity in his own dominions. When he in his turn was defeated and killed by a Northumbrian king, there was a brief revival of Northumbrian power. With the support of a fleet King Ecgfrith advanced to the north so effectively that he was recognized as overlord by the Irish colonists of Argyll and the Britons of Strathclyde; but he advanced too far, and in 685 at the Battle of Nechtansmere, somewhere near Forfar, the Picts won a victory which weakened Northumbria for good. Border warfare, with longer or shorter intervals of peace, persisted north and south of the line of the River Tweed. The chief beneficiary from the decline of Northumbria was the now Christian Mercia. The conversion of Sussex, a few years earlier, had eliminated the last official heathenism among the Anglo-Saxons, but the same rhythm went on well into the ninth century: one after another kingdoms grew strong in fighting, or threatening to fight, both against the Britons and against their Anglo-Saxon neighbours. Around 600 Cadwaladr had been the last king in Wales to claim suzerainty over all Britain. On the other hand, the Anglo-Saxons made little headway in conquering Wales. They made incursions, and sometimes occupied small territories. But in turn they were themselves threatened by counterattacks. Offa, king of Mercia from 757 to 796, created the greatest public work of the Anglo-Saxon period. This was Offa's Dyke, an earthwork which runs from the Dee to the Severn, marking the eastern frontiers of two of the great Welsh kingdoms, Gwynedd and Powys.

Mercia reached its highest point under Offa. He annexed Kent and Sussex and East Anglia. He defeated the West Saxons and drove them back from Oxfordshire and Buckinghamshire to the south of the Thames. His entourage, which from time to time included his under-kings, had the apparatus of a royal court. Offa gave himself high-sounding titles, one of which was *Rex Anglorum*. This rise in status and maturity of kingship was similar, in origin and form, to the far greater ascent of Offa's contemporary Charlemagne, king of the Franks, who in 800 revived the title of emperor and began the long history of the Holy Roman Empire of the West. Offa was the only western ruler with whom Charlemagne corresponded as an equal. In their diplomatic correspondence, the first in our history, they discussed pressing European problems. They failed to agree on a marriage alliance; but, after some friction they made the first English commercial agreement. English traders in Gaul or Gaulish traders in England were to have the protection of the public authorities, and Offa was to see to it that in future cloths or cloaks exported from England were to be of the accustomed length.

In Offa's correspondence the ecclesiastical element bulked large. One of his successes, short-lived like most of them, was that his bishop of Lichfield was made archbishop of a province which was intended to rank with Canterbury and York. He granted an annual payment to the Roman see; some have traced in this the origin of the permanent tax called Peter's pence.

The Saxon church at Escomb, near Durham, built in 682. Most Saxon churches, especially those built of wood, were rebuilt in Norman times but a few, like this one, have survived with little change.

Anglo-Saxon society was, of course, based on working the land, in the sense that most of the population were occupied in raising crops and animals. Over most of the fertile lowland plains there were villages, though in the hillier parts and in some exceptional regions, such as Kent and East Anglia, hamlets and isolated farms were common. Villages were safer from robbers and the like. Able-bodied men were liable for military service, and there was some rudimentary collective responsibility for protecting persons and property. There were graded social distinctions. These were quite unlike the Roman distinctions of rank. A man of higher rank carried greater weight in the law-courts, and was entitled to higher compensation for offences done against him. If he were killed the slayers had to pay a greater sum to his kindred than was paid for a man lower in the scale. The wealthier men had larger houses than the rest. They had some men, slaves and others, directly under them and had power and authority over the rest.

The one sharp contrast of civilization, however, was that between this main body of the population and the slowly growing minority, with the churchmen as their instructors and guides, who could apply systematic knowledge and skill in their daily activities. This difference is seen most sharply in the arts and letters. In the seventh century there were stone churches not only in Kent and the adjacent parts, but in Northumbria and Mercia. The large church at Brixworth, near Northampton, is the most imposing seventh-century building north of the Alps. In many places which had no churches there were tall and richly sculptured crosses in the open air, blending together in their sculptured decoration the Mediterranean, Celtic, and northern traditions. These things everyone could see, and many people attended Mass and listened to sermons. Few could appreciate the rapid rise of literary culture. The monks bought and copied many books, and they gathered pupils round them. One of these, the Venerable Bede, a monk of Jarrow who died in 735, was the greatest scholar of his time in all Europe. He knew Greek and Latin and some Hebrew, and in his books he wrote about all the sciences that were studied in his time. His masterpiece, The Ecclesiastical History of the English People (*Gentis Anglorum*), is still often read and still makes excellent reading.

The English monasteries handsomely repaid part of their debt to the Continent. Alcuin, who had been taught in the cloister school at York and became the head of it, took service with Charlemagne himself and for more than twenty years was at the head of the educational revival in his dominions. The literary movement in England, however, was not merely a foreign importation. Even in Bede's Latin history some readers believe they catch echoes of the old northern heroic tales. Another Northumbrian, Caedmon, a generation older than Bede, certainly wrote religious poetry, trying to adapt the idiom of the orally transmitted heathen epics for this purpose. Later poets improved on his example, but, for reasons which will appear shortly, this progress was checked before any notable English poetry was written. For the same reasons architecture and sculpture fell from the high standard they had reached. The most obscure period of their history runs from the early eighth century to the middle of the ninth. The artistic and intellectual achievements of the seventh century were as precariously based as the supremacy of the Northumbrian and Mercian kings.

The Anglo-Saxons and the Scandinavians 865–1066

865	The Danes land in strength in East Anglia.	957	Edgar becomes king of all England.
878	King Alfred of Wessex defeats the Danes at Edington, near Westbury.	991	The Vikings defeat the East Anglians at Maldon and advance into southern England, until bought off with Danegeld.
891	King Alfred sponsors compilation of the Anglo-Saxon Chronicle, a history of England.	1016	Canute, a Dane, becomes king of England.
937	King Athelstan's combined Wessex and Mercian army wins the Battle of Brunaburh, bringing most of England under one king.	1065	King Edward the Confessor's newly-built Westminster Abbey is consecrated.

Not long after Offa's death new waves of raiders began to harass the coasts. These were Danes, ruthless fighters on land and sea, robbers and heathens. They were not savages, although there were variations in their acquaintance with the arts and letters. Many objects inscribed with their Runic alphabet have been found in Britain. They came at this time in consequence of changes on the European mainland. The Franks had worn down the Frisians so that the Danes succeeded to their dominant place in the North Sea, but Frankish power reduced the opportunities for small forces operating against the mainland and so they and their northern neighbours, the Norsemen, turned against the British islands. They did not come with the support or even the goodwill of their own rulers. Only a weak king would tolerate pirates who disturbed their own country and offended neighbouring kings; but as it happened their kings were weak. It is hard to estimate the raiders' strength, but until 865 they seem to have been operating with forces of less than a thousand men. None the less they went where they chose and did as they pleased. Against them there were no fortifications worth mentioning at the ports or river-mouths and there was no military system except that each king had a personal following, to which his nobles might add their personal followings, and each peasant was bound to turn out to defend his own neighbourhood. The kings were still fighting among themselves, or they had been fighting very recently. Wessex had won first place. It had fought the Britons both in Wales and in Cornwall, and before the North Welsh submitted, Egbert, king of Wessex, was accepted by Kent, Surrey, Essex, and East Anglia as their overlord. The Danish wars began in his time, and they developed in such a way that his descendants became kings of England.

In about thirty years the raids amounted to more than a dozen Danish descents, several of them very destructive. On one occasion raiders operated in the country round the Wrekin; on another they killed a king of Northumbria. They sacked Canterbury and London. At least twice, instead of going home for the winter, they settled into winter quarters by the coast. There were one or two signs that the English might stop all this. The under-king of Kent won the first sea-fight in English history, off Sandwich. The local levies of Devon and Somerset combined to beat a Danish force on the Parret. But the danger became grave in 865 when a great Danish army landed in East Anglia, intending to stay for an indefinite length of time, not so much to conquer the country as to pillage it. They would seize some strategic point, and fortify it, whether by repairing the old Roman walls of a city or by throwing up earthworks. This was their base, and they did not need to think about lines of communication with any other point. They lived on what they could take from the surrounding countryside, and if supplies were not forthcoming they massacred the people and harried the land. In any case they demanded money and looted everything

A Saxon warrior. The spear, usually of ash, was about 2 m (7 ft) long, with an iron head. The shield was also wooden, though it was covered with leather and sometimes had a metal boss in the centre to protect the hand. The sword was already a sign of rank, being normally carried only by the wealthier warriors.

that was portable. Their political procedure was simple: if a king resisted them they killed him and put in a puppet who stayed in office as long as he worked for them. Five years after they landed, this method had made them masters of Northumbria, Mercia, and East Anglia. They had learnt some lessons. In military matters the most important change was that they took to using horses, on which, of course, they moved more quickly from place to place, though they did not fight in the saddle.

So things stood when the Danes invaded Wessex in 871. The fighting went on until 878, and for most of the time it was a continuation of the experiences of the other kingdoms, the Danes on the whole having the upper hand. For a time the Danes were drawn off to deal with a revolt against them in Northumbria; but when they reappeared in force King Alfred, their opponent, left the field and for a few months took refuge in the Isle of Athelney among the marshes of the Parret. He had been chosen king seven years before when his elder brother was mortally wounded, and in preference to that brother's sons. In his refuge he kept the war alive by organizing raids, and when he emerged from it he defeated the Danish army near Westbury. In the resulting peace agreement the Danish king Guthrum agreed to be baptised and to leave Wessex. By this time the Danes had decided to settle, and this agreement did not prevent their settlement in East Anglia, Northumbria, and eastern Mercia. Nineteenth-century historians invented a convenient name for this region, which they called the Danelaw. The English in the Danelaw, Alfred had stipulated, were not to be treated as a subject people or as a subject majority with special rights; rank by rank they were to be equal with the Danes.

After a peaceful interval of about ten years a new host invaded Kent. When he died in 899 Alfred handed on an unfinished war of liberation. It may seem surprising that he should be regarded as the most effective ninth-century monarch after Charlemagne; but this claim is not seriously disputed. His long endurance and final success in the defence of Wessex were due not only to the qualities of a fighting commander, but to far-sighted reforms. Alfred built or reconditioned fortresses at fairly close intervals. He organized the manning of these defences. He increased the range of movement of his peasant infantry by dividing each local contingent into two parts which should alternately fight and stay in their villages. He built some warships to a new design, and he was the first king in England since Ecgfrith of Northumbria to have a fleet of his own. He probably improved the characteristic administrative arrangements of Wessex which we shall notice shortly. And Alfred in the end established a suzerainty, political control, over all non-Danish England.

These and other military and political services amounted to putting Wessex in the way of collecting and using its resources better than any English kingdom had ever done; but Alfred did far more. He consciously aimed at raising the level of civilization in England. He had been to Rome twice as a child; he had men of learning about him; but he was not a mere promoter of educational reforms. He learnt to read; he learnt Latin; he founded a palace school as Charlemagne had done. In addition to all this he promoted the translation of useful and important books into English: Bede's history, the history of Orosius, and a religious text, the Pastoral Care of Pope Gregory the Great. Some of these he translated himself.

A few years after Alfred died, his son and daughter, Edward the Elder and Ethelfleda, 'the lady of the Mercians', pushed on against the Danes, fortifying towns as they went. The Danish armies showed no capacity for common action, and perhaps the resistance of the Danes was weakened by the spread of Christianity among them. In 909 Edward, at Tettenhall in Staffordshire, defeated an incursion of Northumbrian Danes so soundly that he altered the whole balance of forces. There was no longer a strong kingdom north of the Humber. Edward, having northing to fear from this direction, subdued every Danish army south of that estuary; bringing the Danish settlements under his own rule. In the north, however, new invaders came from a new direction. Norsemen, vikings from Norway, who regarded the Danes as foreigners, had set up kingdoms of their own in the Shetlands, the Orkneys, the Hebrides, the Isle of Man, and on the east coast of Ireland. From these bases, they raided the country between the Pennines and the Irish Sea. They settled on the Wirral peninsula between the Dee and the Mersey, and northwards from there at intervals all the way up to the Solway Firth. The north and north-west fell into chaos. In 919–20 a viking force marched down from the Tyne and captured York,

The Vikings' ships were the technological advance which made possible their success as marauders and colonisers. This example was unearthed in Norway and exemplifies the fine lines of these ships. A single square sail was used but, as can be seen, there was provision for about 16 oars along each side for use in unfavourable winds.

and an army from Ireland invaded north-west Mercia. Edward then moved north into the Peak district of Derbyshire and there secured the submission of the established states of the north, the English, Danes and Norsemen of Northumbria, and the king and people of Strathclyde.

Edward's son Athelstan was a successful soldier like his father. All the enemies who had been injured or alarmed by the recent English advances joined in a formidable offensive against him. First was Olaf, king of Dublin, who seems to have been the leader of all the Norsemen of Ireland. He was the son of the viking who had been ousted from York, and he sailed across in 937 with a large fleet to join the king of the Scots and the king of Strathclyde. Athelstan's crushing victory over this alliance marks a stage in the decline of heathenism in Britain. It was celebrated in a poem of savage rejoicing, which names the battlefield as Brunanburh. The location of Brunanburh is unknown, so this is the last important battle on English soil whose site cannot be identified. In the years which followed, Athelstan and his successors did away with some of the obstacles to unity in England. The last remaining Danish resistance in Mercia, in the five boroughs of Derby, Nottingham, Leicester, Stamford, and Lincoln, was eliminated. Northumbria ceased to be a kingdom and became an earldom. In 957 Edgar the Peaceful became king of all England. This was not the beginning of the continuous history of the English realm. That came later. But this was a sign that the conditions necessary for bringing all the peoples of England under one king had now been brought into existence. After Brunanburh came years of comparative safety in which intercourse with continental kingdoms became a regular part of the business of kings. For the time being this did not involve the English directly in continental affairs. There were friendships and even alliances, including marriage alliances, but no English soldiers served on the Continent, nor did any continental soldiers cross to England. Where increasing intercourse made a lasting mark was in the ecclesiastical sphere.

In Anglo-Saxon times no one drew a distinction between this sphere and the secular sphere. It was not until centuries later that people at all commonly contrasted church and state as we do now. Church gatherings made rules for laymen about marriage, property, inheritance, and morals, and kings promulgated laws about church property and offices in the church. Churchmen sat with the nobility in royal councils. Laymen took part in ecclesiastical synods and appointed priests to churches. But the priesthood and the laity were two distinct kinds of men, and they now became more distinct in England, as they were becoming on the Continent. Here the great name is that of St. Dunstan. He

was a man of noble birth, educated partly at Glastonbury, where Irish learning had a foothold, and partly at the royal court of Wessex. His life was chequered, but he was always a fearless advocate of reforms, on the one hand restoring the obedience to Christian morality which had been undermined by the Danish wars, and on the other improving education and tightening discipline among the churchmen. When he began his work, the clergy in the English monasteries had virtually ceased to be monks: they married and followed no fixed rules of common life.

Dunstan reversed these two tendencies where he could. As an exile in Flanders he came into contact with the current interpretations of the Rule of St. Benedict, the sixth-century Italian founder of western monasticism. In the last period of his life he was archbishop of Canterbury and the principal adviser of King Edgar the Peaceful. The Benedictine system won much ground. Dunstan also supported Edgar's policy of effacing the differences between the Anglo-Saxons and the Danes, for instance by employing Danes in responsible positions in the Anglo-Saxon regions. It is typical of his work, and of the character of the monarchy in his time, that the archbishop of York and all the bishops of both provinces, Canterbury and York, took part in the coronation of Edgar.

Although there were so many favourable omens for the formation of a national unity, there were still fissures that could reopen widely. Among them were disputes between the monks and the secular clergy, as the other clergy of the parishes and some of the cathedrals were called. Above all, there was still danger from overseas. Before Dunstan died small parties of Scandinavians made hit-and-run raids on various parts of the coast. They may have taken to the sea partly because Denmark, Norway, and Sweden were then united in a short-lived Christian kingdom. They received countenance and support from Normandy, where a Norse line of Dukes, now in its third generation, ruled with an aristocracy of the same origin. Then, in 991, came a larger force which effected a landing at Maldon in Essex. The poem of the Battle of Maldon tells how Byrtnoth, the 'alderman' (that is, the king's viceroy) of East Anglia, died fighting against impossible odds: it expresses memorably that central theme of heroic poetry. This Danish army ravaged the country as far as Kent, Hampshire, and western Wessex until the king levied a heavy tax to buy it off: the first instance of Danegeld, which was a recurrent misery in England until, long after the last Danish raid, it remained as the first regular direct tax. In its early days Danegeld was an inducement to the Danes to go away, and likewise to come back again for more.

The attacks, now annual events, very soon entered a new stage: in 994 an army, probably more than two thousand in number, landed in Kent under the command of the most famous Norse viking then living, Olaf Trygvason, and of Sweyn, a son of the king of Denmark. Two significantly new features of this invasion were that Olaf was already a baptized Christian and that some of the Anglo-Saxon nobles plotted to submit to Sweyn as king. The army finally departed in a friendly manner at the enormous price of £16,000; but the respite only lasted for two years. And then the defence collapsed. The king, Ethelred the Redeless, could not command or control his aldermen. Even traitors among them were too strong to punish. When Ethelred died two rival kings were chosen, in London Edmund who rallied southern England and earned the name of Ironside, and in Southampton Canute the Dane, the son of Sweyn. They fought one summer campaign to and fro, but in October 1016 Edmund was soundly beaten at Ashingdon in Essex. The two kings made a peace-treaty under which Edmund was to rule Wessex and Canute everything north of the Thames. The terms left openings for future trouble, but they were never put to the test. Edmund Ironside died six weeks after his defeat. Wessex accepted Canute as its king and so as king of all England.

Canute reigned over England for nineteen years, and after him for seven years two of his sons. This foreign rule was utterly unlike what it would have been if it had come in the days of King Alfred a century before. Canute was a Christian, not exemplary in his conjugal arrangements nor in his treatment of enemies, but enthusiastically on the side of the monks when they set about restoring ecclesiastical authority after a whole generation of war. He not only advanced the interests of the church; he governed England in accordance with the churchmen's teaching about the duties of a Christian king. Within a very short time he made his rule acceptable to his new subjects, so much so that between 1019 and 1028 he felt safe enough to leave England three times to lead successful warlike expeditions to Scandinavia. As king of Denmark and conqueror of Norway, he wisely made no attempt to unite his Scandinavian and English possessions into one kingdom. But his strength and wise behaviour brought Scandinavia a long stage nearer to being an integral part of Europe. He was the first viking to be admitted into the civilized fraternity of Christian kings. So far as England was concerned he renewed and widened relations with the Continent. He corresponded with the duke of Aquitaine. In 1027 he attended the coronation of the new emperor, Conrad II, by the pope in Rome. He used the opportunity to do some useful pieces of business, for instance on behalf of traders and pilgrims who followed the same route.

After his return from Rome Canute marched an army into Scotland. The northern frontier of England had naturally been poorly defended during the Danish invasion. King Malcolm II ruled a territory virtually identical with present-day Scotland; moreover the 'union of the four peoples' of 843 had succeeded in creating a distinct Scottish nation. In 1006 Malcolm, not content with the cession of the Lothians a generation before, advanced as far south as Durham only to be thrown back again; but a few years later, in alliance with Owen the Bald, king of Strathclyde, he won a battle at the border village of Carham on the Tweed. Canute secured recognition as their overlord from Malcolm and two lesser kings, and afterwards the earl of Northumbria, letting the Lothians wait, recovered for his earldom the lands between the Solway Firth and the Lake District which had been lost a century before.

So at the end of Canute's time the affairs of England seemed to be well ordered. The sequel showed how much still turned on the personalities of kings. Canute was succeeded by his elder and illegitimate son Harold Harefoot, whose title was disputed by the legitimate Hardecanute. Harold's five years reign was uneventful, and when he died Hardecanute succeeded peaceably. The latter seems to have been generally hated. One incident of his reign is worth noting. Two of his house-carls, or personal troops, out on tax-collecting duty in Worcester, were murdered by men from the city and the shire. As a punishment Hardecanute sent a strong force which burnt the city and harried the countryside for five days. The villagers kept out of the way, and the townspeople held out in a field fortification on Bevere island in the Severn.

The seal of King Edward the Confessor, last-but-one-monarch of Anglo-Saxon England. He died in 1066 and was canonised as Saint Edward in 1161. Among other things, his piety was expressed by Westminster Abbey, whose early structures were built at his command.

Hardecanute, still in his early twenties, died after reigning for two years. His death put an end to the male line of Canute's family. The great English nobles, the magnates, with the support of the people of London, immediately chose a king from the old English royal family: namely Edward, the elder and only surviving son of Ethelred the Redeless. He must have been in his late thirties, older than any other king who had come to the throne for many years past. He is known as Edward the Confessor, on account of his personal piety and virtuous life. One of the important events of his reign was his founding of Westminster Abbey, a mile higher up the river from London. He was Hardecanute's half-brother, for Canute had married Ethelred's widow, but his accession automatically cut England off from Canute's other possessions. Fortunately for the English those other possessions plunged into fighting among themselves, and all through Edward's reign of twenty-four years there was no invasion from Scandinavia. But instead of freeing England from continental entanglements, Edward drew it further in. Under the Danish kings he had been a fugitive and a pretender to the English throne. For family reasons he found his refuge at the court of Normandy, where he was educated and lived for nearly thirty years. His mother was the daughter of Richard I, duke of Normandy. Until Edward succeeded to the throne this family connection was of no importance to England; he had indeed Norman help in some unsuccessful attempts to assert his claim, but the Normans were not in a position to do more in that direction for his interests or their own. It may indeed be said that sooner or later Normandy was certain to count for a great deal in English affairs. It was separated only by the short crossing of the Channel, and in soil and climate and landscape it was, more than any other part of the Continent, like southern England. Politically it was the most solidly compacted of all the settlements left behind by the southward advances of the Scandinavians in the tenth century. It has been called a continental Danelaw; but it was unlike the Danelaw in England in three cardinal ways. Its language was not Norse but French. It had a single, strong ruler in its duke, and the duke was a vassal of the Frankish kingdom, virtually independent but in contact with its full civilization. Edward, being almost a stranger among the English, not unwisely kept some Normans and other Frenchmen about his person, and set up others in influential ecclesiastical offices.

In home affairs he had to steer his way through a rocky channel. His three most prominent subjects were Godwin, Leofric, and Siward, earls whose authority centred on Wessex, Mercia, and Northumbria respectively. Siward the Strong, born in Denmark, was content to govern his turbulent frontier province. Leofric, the husband of the legendary Lady Godiva, had succeeded his father and also seems to have been an able man without inordinate ambition. The third and most powerful, Godwin, had risen by the favour of Canute, and he had married a sister of Canute's brother-in-law, the Danish earl Ulf. Godwin had sons. The two elder, Sweyn and Harold (both Danish names), were grown men, and Godwin was ambitious not merely for himself but for his family. The king had a reason for working against Godwin. In Canute's time, in one of Edward's unsuccessful attempts on the throne the latter's brother Alfred was captured and died after torture. Godwin was responsible for this. Nevertheless the king married his daughter Edith, and, in spite of untoward incidents, it was not until 1051 that there was a breach. This was connected with the favours shown to the Normans and their like. When Edward came to England he was accompanied by his friend Robert, abbot of Jumièges, whom he made successively bishop of London and archbishop of Canterbury. The court and many people outside it were divided between two parties led by Godwin and Robert. In 1051 Eustace, count of Boulogne, was on his way home to France from a visit to King Edward. His retinue demanded billets in Dover; a riot broke out and about twenty people were killed. The king ordered Godwin, as the earl in charge of the district, to carry out a military execution of the usual kind, such as Hardecanute had let loose on Worcester. Godwin refused, and not only refused but rebelled. He and his sons collected troops from all their territories and converged on the king, who was at Gloucester. Siward and Leofric stood firm and another army gathered on the king's side. Civil war was averted by an agreement that a meeting of the *witan* (see p. 33) of the whole kingdom should meet in London to settle the issues; but Godwin and his family first made difficulties about coming, then fled the realm and were banished.

For about a year King Edward was free from opposition at the centre, and there is little or no evidence of any widespread

LEFT The end of the agricultural year: in December, inside the barns, the Anglo-Saxon peasants would beat out the wheat grains (centre) and then sift the grain from the chaff (right).

BELOW A Saxon king and his *witan*. On the right, a man has been hanged, presumably following sentence by the king and his advisers. Stoning, burning, and drowning were alternative capital punishments.

English national feeling against French influence. Godwin himself was much linked by marriage and otherwise with Danes. With his son Sweyn and a younger son, Tostig, he now found a refuge in Bruges, under his wife's kinsman the count of Flanders. Harold and another younger son went to Ireland. But there were two grave weaknesses in the king's position. For twelve years or more a strong power had been growing up among the Welsh. Gruffydd ap Llewellyn, king of Gwynedd and Powys, had defeated a Mercian army and then mastered all the princes of South Wales: he was dangerous. Even more serious was the state of the naval defences. There was a communal duty to provide ships, parallel to the personal duty to serve in the army. In both the coastal and the inland counties this liability seems to have been spread over the districts by a system of levying ship money. In addition to this, however, since 1012 every king had a permanent force of large warships of the contemporary Scandinavian type, a nucleus round which the ship-money fleet could be assembled for war. In 1049 this force consisted of forty-nine vessels. Chiefly for reasons of economy their crews were discharged. So great was the king's false sense of security that he abolished the army-tax, *heregeld*, which, also from 1012, had been raised annually to pay troops in the king's service. Meanwhile, Edward appointed more Normans to offices. He received a visit from his cousin the duke of Normandy, and it is highly probable that, being childless, he promised that his visitor should succeed him on the throne.

Meanwhile Godwin collected a few ships in Flemish waters, evaded some English ships off Sandwich, and landed at Dungeness. He found friends about the coast, but he went back to Flanders, and in his absence the crews of the royal navy deserted *en masse*. Then he sailed again and Harold sailed from Ireland. After a successful junction somewhere between Portland and the Land's End, they sailed up the Channel, collecting ships from the harbours which were afterwards called the Cinque Ports. They surrounded the king's ships at their moorings above London Bridge, and entered the city as conquerors. Robert, the Norman archbishop of Canterbury and other prominent Normans fled. The bishop of Winchester, Stigand, arranged a suitable settlement. The *witan* met outside London to discuss the old charges against Godwin which had never been heard. Of course, they acquitted him and punished the more unpopular of the Normans with banishment and confiscation of their goods. With a foolish disregard of ecclesiastical formalities the archiepiscopal throne informally vacated by Robert was handed over to Stigand. Godwin's line was now firmly reestablished in the succession. The Duke of Normandy would be unlikely to obtain the English crown by peaceful means on the death of Edward the Confessor.

Godwin did not live seven months after his triumph, but the king lived on for eleven years. His own authority was diminished; but for several years none of the impending dangers came to a head. On the contrary, the Welsh frontier problem was, for the time being, solved. It seems to have been the king's nephew Ralph who as earl fortified Hereford and encouraged various Frenchmen to build castles at points where Welsh raiders could be checked. To check King Gruffydd needed more than this. It was a sign of his power that an earl, Aelfgar, son of Leofric, justly or unjustly outlawed for treason, raised eighteen ships' companies among the Irish vikings, and led them with Gruffydd's army against Hereford. They defeated the local soldiers, burnt the town, and plundered the cathedral. Godwin's son Harold moved against the Welsh and settled terms without a battle. There were several years of confused negotiations and probably some fighting. At one point Magnus, the son of Harold

Anglo-Saxon costumes. The top three are churchmen, with the archbishop at the left, a bishop centre, and a monk at the right. The lower trio are well-to-do laymen, shown from left to right in descending order of wealth.

The cloak was fastened at the shoulder with a brooch clasp. Many such brooches, often colourful and finely-worked pieces of jewelry, have survived to the present day.

Hardrada king of Norway, came to the help of Gruffydd and Aelfgar with a fleet; but Aelfgar died and Harold crushed the Welsh in a merciless campaign. First he marched from Gloucester to attack Rhuddlan; then he worked round the coast northwards, landing and devastating at intervals. Gwynedd and Powys were given as tributary provinces to two puppet rulers. In the south the heirs of old ruling families were restored, and the English took Gruffydd's conquests back.

In the other frontier region, the north, things went badly. Siward defeated the Scottish king Macbeth, but his son was killed. When Siward died the house of Godwin had obvious reasons for putting in as his successor Harold's younger brother and comrade in arms, Tostig. Tostig, however, did not know the north and after he had tried to govern it for ten years it rebelled, not against the king, but against him. An army of Northumbrians, Mercians, and Welsh marched down and occupied Northampton. Tostig was dismissed and, as before, retired to Flanders; Morcar, the brother of Edwin earl of Mercia, took his place. Then, in January 1066, the king fell ill and died.

The monarchy in Edward's time was still unstable, but it was much more mature than the monarchy of Alfred the Great. The kingdom still had no capital: the king could not hope to control it from one fixed point, and, even in quiet times, he had to appear in person wherever his decisions were needed. At the centre of his mobile court were the *witan*, wise men or councillors, who advised the king and whose names appeared in the more important of the documents which he approved. This association of the king and the *witan* did not mean that the king presided in a national assembly. It was the public expression of the fact that decisions could not be either well-weighed, or generally known or effective without the participation of a good proportion of those who could answer for the general population, that is of those who could foresee how the decisions would work and who would themselves have to put them into effect. The numbers who were called upon varied with the occasion: most of them were often kept away from the court by their duties. The largest recorded number was 107. Bishops and latterly some abbots were comparatively regular in their attendance, as were the few princes and ladies of the royal family. Then came the royal officials who had authority in the different regions, earls and sheriffs, and finally, if they were summoned, some of the king's thanes. The latter became more numerous as their position glided over from that of royal servants endowed with lands to that of a land-owning nobility. There was no rigid definition of the matters which the *witans* might discuss, and there was not even any distinction between constitutional functions which they might lawfully fulfil and political or even revolutionary acts which they took it upon themselves to do. They chose kings; perhaps on occasion they deposed kings. The earliest written laws were selected from a floating body of customs, but by the eleventh century legislation was approaching the stage of being specially enacted. Taxation, such as Danegeld and Ship Money, was obviously imposed by new enacted law. The king and his *witan* dealt with major judicial business, as in the case of Godwin, with church affairs, and with grants of land. Generally speaking the stronger the king, the less he needed to rely on advice.

The business that had to be done at the centre increased steadily in quantity as the kingdom grew in area and became more unified. It also came to be more fully recorded as more of it came to be done in writing. Documents, such as charters in which the king granted lands or privileges to persons or monasteries, were copied and indexed and, to prevent confusion, set forms for them were standardized. The king came to have a staff of clerks, clerics, either priests or of lower ecclesiastical ranks; and in some ways the English king's chancery was more efficient than those of neighbouring continental rulers. The official letters called writs, in which royal orders were communicated to subjects, were an English invention in secretarial science, and very useful. But most of the daily work of government depended on the regional and local powers. The highest regional officers, in the last century, had become fewer, more powerful, and less closely attached to their regions. Instead of a score or more of aldermen there were now less than half a dozen earls, whose provinces were often changed by the addition or subtraction of large areas. We have seen how the earls in Edward the Confessor's time were occupied in national affairs. A new office grew up as a link between the centre and the regions, that of sheriff, or shire-reeve.

The whole country was an aggregate of about a score of shires, which came to be called counties in later times. They had grown up not at haphazard, but in several different ways. North of the Trent the divisions still to this day embalm some of the history of the old kingdoms of Northumbria and Strathclyde. Kent, Sussex, Essex, and some other counties have equally venerable antecedents. Some of the Midland counties seem to have begun from the territories assigned to Danish armies. But in Wessex the counties seem to coincide with the military districts marked out for recruiting, fortification, and defence in King Alfred's time; and it is to the domination of Wessex that we have to ascribe the extension of the shire-system to the whole country. Each shire had its court, meeting twice a year in the same place, usually a town. The public officers and landowners had a duty to attend,

An Anglo-Saxon brooch of the 9th century. In the centre are depicted the five senses. Most such brooches were of iron or bronze, but wealthy people had silver and sometimes gold jewelry. This brooch is of silver, with black resin in the engraved lines.

and, nominally at any rate, the reeve and four best men from every township. The court tried cases, the real judges being twelve thanes. The king's representative, the sheriff, who presided, laid the king's financial, legal, and military business before it. No doubt the county families knew how to keep control of the outcome.

Each county had subdivisions called hundreds, which were known by other names in some parts of the country, for instance in the northern Danelaw where they are still called wapentakes. Because of their varying origins the counties are very unequal in size, and except in Wessex there are great irregularities both in the names and in the areas of hundreds. Attempts have been made to trace back the origin of the hundreds to some primitive numerical unit such as a hundred warriors; but in the historic period the hundred is an administrative and judicial unit intermediate between the shire and the village. In this sense the hundred may be West Saxon, like the shire. The hundred court was the important court for the ordinary rural population. It decided cases of all kinds, and those which it could not decide went to a higher court. All freemen were entitled or expected to attend and each township to be represented by the reeve and four best men. The actual judges were a smaller number, sometimes twelve. The court met once a month, probably always on the same day of the week, and usually its own executive officer presided, but twice a year the sheriff came for the more important business. Sometimes the hundred was used as the area assessed to pay some fixed sum in taxation.

The smallest unit of administration was the township, the same area which was afterwards called the parish both for ecclesiastical and for civil purposes. If townships ever had courts of their own, by this time they had vanished. The civil township was a unit for taxation and for police. The police-system was rudimentary, but it suited the state of society. Any man who was any sort of lord or master was responsible for the good behaviour of his employees and dependants. All other men belonged to small groups who were collectively or mutually responsible, that is, the whole group was liable to pay the fine for any crime of which any member of the group was convicted. This gave the other members a motive for keeping an eye on potential offenders.

Most historians believe that the central course of social development in Anglo-Saxon times was the gradual loss of economic and personal independence. For several kinds of reasons there came to be landlords on whom the king conferred powers over the cultivators of the soil, powers which enabled the landlords to render services to the king or, to look at it from another point of view, rewarded them for their services. The earliest instances of which we have clear records are grants by which a king, as an act of piety, granted to some religious house some of the payments due to him. Sometimes, in addition to their prayers, the ecclesiastical landlords had to provide the military services, and so they in turn granted land to mass-thanes. These military tenant-landlords were free to serve in the king's army because the villagers were bound to put in work on the demesne, the landlord's own land. When the king promoted or rewarded one of his followers the same system was followed, and down at the level of the village there were other reasons for its development. Even the chief man of a single village might have a moated and defensible hall; he had able-bodied men about him, and he could offer protection against rogues and ruffians. When a peasant was ruined by flood or fire or a bad harvest he might have nothing to fall back on. The lord had his barns and cattle. It would suit him to put the peasant on his feet again if he undertook regular work on the demesne, and so the peasant exchanged his freedom for bread.

Thus there grew up the system of relations called feudalism, in which the economic and political control of the country was assigned to landlords, one above another, all of them subject to the highest landlord, the king. All the tendencies in this direction were strengthened by the Danish invasions. Military needs were pressing. There was a need for mounted troops, and they were quartered on the land as military landholders. Money was needed for the royal household troops, and for ships and crews. The Danegeld and *heregeld* were taxes which some of the peasants could not afford to pay. For one reason or another the men of rank acquired many-sided power. If fresh land was broken in for cultivation, some of it was added to the demesne. Sometimes the king granted the right to hold a village court, so that the landlord took the profits of justice, the fines, in return for keeping down rural crimes, especially theft. In many places the lord had the sole right to keep a windmill or water-mill for grinding the village corn, and to take a customary share of the resulting flour.

No doubt it would be an anachronism to think of these arrangements as neatly defined and punctiliously carried out; but it would be equally wrong to think of them as uncouth efforts of our rude forefathers. We know that their agricultural implements were well made and well suited to their needs. The yields which they obtained from the land seem to have been as good as could be expected. There is one piece of evidence which shows that they were skilful in country planning. Although they had no maps, they divided up much of the country into parishes, taking permanent natural features for the lines and turning-points, and beating the bounds *en masse* once a year. It was important to keep the correct line because on one side of it one person and on the other side another had the right to collect tithes and fees for marriages and burials. But if we examine these lines we find that they were drawn to allow to each village a reasonable share of whatever water and good land were available.

We know very little about the standards of living of the village people; but we can say of the country as a whole that it had reached such a level of production as to support a considerable number of people who consumed food and clothing but did not produce the materials for them. Besides the kings, nobles, full-time soldiers, and ecclesiastics, there were townsfolk. With one exception the towns were scarcely urban in size or ways of life: they were like large villages distinguished from other villages by

The arrival of the Normans did not mean a sharp change in architectural styles. Norman architecture only gradually modified Saxon styles, and in some cases its influence had been felt before 1066. For example, at St. Mary-in-the-Castle at Dover (above) the Saxon structure includes a tower supported on arches, built before the Conquest but incorporating Norman technique.

At All Saints Church in Bradbourne, Derbyshire, the doorway of the tower (left) is plainly Norman with its arch wedges and moulded columns, but the lower stonework is Saxon.

The ruins of Tintern Abbey, one of the great Cistercian foundations. The structure was started in 1131, but almost all the ruins date from the 13th and 14th centuries. Enough remains to demonstrate the architectural advance represented by walls which have largely shed their load-bearing function and have become, almost, frames for large expanses of stained glass.

two things, a market and some sort of defence by walls and gates. York may well have had more than 8,000 people, Norwich and Lincoln more than 6,000, but probably not more than five other towns had more than 3,500. Some were on the coast or up the rivers, and there sea-fish could be had and perhaps imported goods, of which none were essential to ordinary daily life. In both ports and inland towns there were probably some small concentrations of craftsmen, such as smiths, potters, and wheelwrights; and there were also dealers, whom historians dignify with the name of merchants. Some of the houses in towns were owned by country landowners, with the duty of repairing the town-walls when required to do so. In practice this meant that they provided money, materials, and labour. But the business of keeping up the walls and manning them in emergencies, of watch and ward, was in the care of the townsmen themselves, as was the management of the market. More than that, they might by charter obtain the right to be exempt from the jurisdiction of the hundred court and hold a court of their own. Policing was tighter in the boroughs than outside them: in Dover, for instance, there were specially strict rules for keeping the peace in the herring season. A borough, it has been well said, was a walled hundred. It paid a regular fee for its privileges, usually to some lord who passed it on to the king.

The one exceptional town was London, by far the most populous, the richest, and constitutionally the most developed. It was regularly visited by traders from France, the Low Countries, and Scandinavia. It had its own shipmen, mostly of Danish extraction. Its leading men, ranking as thanes, probably had rights as a civic aristocracy. Instead of one court London had a system, a higher and a lower court for the whole city and a court for each ward, presided over by its aldermen. In Athelstan's time there was an elaborately organized guild, an unofficial association for keeping the peace, in which the landowners who had responsibilities for the defence of London were members along with the countrymen of a surrounding region, perhaps larger than Middlesex. It had religious observances and feasts. How long it continued to be needed or whether there were other guilds in London we do not know. The earliest recorded guild in England was in Canterbury in the ninth century. Very little is known about its purposes or its membership; but these signs of a capacity for voluntary association show at least the promise of civic life. On the other hand, we must not yet think of London as a great city or anything like it. Its population cannot be estimated even approximately. One fact seems to prove that it was not in the first rank of trading-towns: it had not, like all the major towns in the western kingdoms, a Jewish community. It had only one major ecclesiastical foundation besides St. Paul's Cathedral, the collegiate church called St. Martin's le Grand.

From about the time of Charlemagne trade had been growing all over Europe, and well-governed states, England among them, made agreements to suppress piracy and to protect peaceful commercial comings and goings; but, in the absence of any figures for the movements of ships and goods, historians are liable to exaggerate the volume of trade. If we consider the remarkably scanty records of industry in Anglo-Saxon England we shall have to conclude that both imports and exports were very small in quantity. Lead-mining seems to have gone on continuously from Roman times in Derbyshire and Gloucestershire. The Cornish tin was probably worked, but very little is known about it. The Romans dug coal, but there is no reference to it in Anglo-Saxon times. Nor is there any reference to iron-mining after the Romans until the time of Edward the Confessor, when it seems to have been practised in the Forest of Dean, in Sussex and in one or two other parts. From the time of St. Dunstan there were skilled metal-workers in many places, but there is no reason to suppose that their goods were sent abroad. Bricks were not made, and if there were tiles, they were probably made for local use. There is nothing to suggest that leather-goods were sold abroad. Nor do we know of any manufactures on the Continent which were sufficiently developed to need raw materials from England.

There is indeed a contrast between the backwardness of industrial development and the advancement of the arts and letters. None of the greater Anglo-Saxon buildings has survived, but we know from descriptions and from their excavated remains that there were very large and splendid churches, for instance in Canterbury, Winchester, and Westminster. There are hundreds of parish churches scattered over the country in which some larger or smaller portions of Anglo-Saxon masonry still stand. There are a good many in which we can see a tower or a wall or even a whole church substantially as it was first built. The active period of building which began in the middle of the ninth century is called Carolingian, and continental influences in style and construction were strong enough to justify us in regarding it as a part of the western revival which began with Charlemagne; but there are enough insular and even regional characteristics to justify us also in saying that this was native architecture and sculpture. It is not all primitive: the best of it shows a feeling for proportion and a skill in managing surfaces and shadows which belong not to the instinctive craftsman but to the finished artist. There are reminders that the times were rude. There are church buildings, such as the round towers in Suffolk and Sussex, which were very likely intended as places of refuge from sea-rovers. But it seems strange that the Anglo-Saxon art should have been created in an age of violence.

The surprise seems greater when we turn from the outdoor works of art to the indoor arts. One outstanding result of the monastic reformation of the tenth century was the rise of a new religious literature written in Old English prose, and intended not only to be read by ecclesiastics but to be read by, or at least read aloud to, laymen and women. Another was a new wave of English missionary journeys to the Continent, especially to Scandinavia. In this period, as in the earlier age in which the arts reached their highest point in Northumbria, some of the most treasured works of art were illuminated manuscripts. Those which are still preserved astonish us first by the infinite pains that were spent on them, and then by their mere beauty. Much is still uncertain about the origin of the old Northumbrian school; but in minuteness of formal design and in glowing mosaic colour its masterpieces, such as the Lindisfarne gospels, represent a high culmination. Three centuries later the Winchester painters had advanced from the Carolingian tradition to an entirely different kind. They drew in outline men and women, animals and scenes, life and movement in the light and air. Yet both schools had this in common, that very few people could ever touch and open their treasured books. There was slowly growing knowledge with widening order and prosperity in the realm. In sheltered seclusion there was refinement.

The Norman Conquest and its Sequel 1066–1216

1066 (January 6) The funeral of Edward the Confessor, cousin of the Duke of Normandy, and crowning of Harold, Earl of Wessex.
1066 (September 25) King Harold defeats the Norwegians at Stamford Bridge.
1066 (September 28) William, Duke of Normandy, leads his army ashore after crossing the Channel overnight and captures Pevensey.
1066 (October 14) King Harold is defeated and killed at the Battle of Hastings.
1066 (December 25) William is crowned as king of England in Westminster Abbey.
1086 The compilation of Domesday Book, a detailed survey of the kingdom.
1087 The first crusade to reverse Islamic gains in the Middle East begins.
1107 King Henry I and the pope agree that the former should invest bishops with their temporal authority, and the latter with spiritual authority.
1135 The death of Henry I and the coronation of his nephew Stephen.
1139 Empress Matilda lands to claim the throne. Civil war begins.
1154 Henry II, Matilda's son and the first Plantagenet king, succeeds Stephen by agreement.
1170 Thomas Becket is murdered at Canterbury.
1189 The death of Henry II and succession of his son Richard I.

Edward the Confessor did not die suddenly. The magnates had time enough to prepare. They chose a successor on the day of the king's death, and next day he was crowned. The one possible candidate from the royal family, Edmund Ironside's grandson Edgar 'the atheling' (the prince), was too young; so the new king was the successful soldier Harold, Godwin's son and Tostig's brother. It was foreseen that he would be attacked from more sides than one; but for the first four months of the year 1066 no enemy appeared. Harold was able to assemble the militia of the whole country at places round the coast, and collect a large fleet. The first would-be invader was Tostig. Who was backing him is not certain, but he had both English and foreign supporters. At one time he had sixty ships. He landed first in Sussex, then in Kent and in Norfolk, and finally on the south bank of the Humber, where he was heavily defeated by Earl Edwin. While he was being efficiently dealt with, a far more powerful enemy, William, duke of Normandy, was openly bringing together an army and a fleet. It was not until September that his preparations were complete and he moved to St. Valéry, at the mouth of the Somme, where he lay ready to invade. Until a few days before he reached this port it seemed as if he might very well fare no better than Tostig. The English fleet was watching him, and the militia were in their positions. But they had been on duty all through the summer. It was not easy to keep up either their supplies or their morale. When harvest-time came Harold sent the militiamen back to their homes, and ordered the ships to make for London. The Channel was left unguarded.

Then came the news that Harold Hardrada, king of Norway, had sailed up the Humber with 300 ships or more, and landed within ten miles of York. As soon as he heard this, Harold set out for the north. He found that the Norsemen, who had Tostig with them, had beaten Edwin and Morcar and their regional forces in a hard fight on the road to York. York had surrendered, its citizens and some of the Yorkshire thanes promising to join the invaders, and the invading army was a few miles to the east of York, where Stamford Bridge crosses the little river Derwent. Here Harold at once attacked them. Tostig and the king of Norway were both killed; their army was shattered and the survivors sailed home under promise never to make war on England again.

Three days after Harold's great victory William of Normandy disembarked his army unopposed in Pevensey Bay. Hastings, a few miles to the east, was a better place to get away from by land or by sea, so William moved thither after a few days and had a wooden castle built. He cannot have known much about the state of Harold's fortunes; but in any event his best course was to wait by his base. The wait was astonishingly short. On 13 October his outposts reported a large English army approaching from London. At dawn on the 14th William marched out and his patrols sighted their enemy. The English were taking up a

The coronation of King Harold, perhaps the best moment of his brief reign. Archbishop Stigand officiates on his left. Based on the Bayeux Tapestry, this drawing shows that the coronation ceremony was already taking its modern form.

defensive position seven miles from Hastings across the uneven ridge along which William was advancing. He drew up his force unmolested on lower ground and then attacked uphill.

The English army may have numbered some 6,000 or 7,000 men, and William's was probably smaller. Probably also it was fresher and in better order after a fortnight on shore, with no fighting and no forced marches. But these were trifles. There were far greater differences between the two armies. The English, especially Harold's housecarls, fought on foot in close order with spears, battle-axes, and hand missiles, as both sides had fought at Stamford Bridge. The Normans had three arms, archers and cross-bowmen being the first, heavily armed infantry the second, and the third heavy cavalry. Of knights there were three divisions, Bretons on the left, Normans in the centre, and French mercenaries on the right. It was the first appearance on British soil of the armoured knights, who rode over the battlefields of Europe for the next four centuries. Their skill and discipline were even more formidable than their equipment, but in this battle there was little for them to do: it was the archers and the foot-soldiers who fought it out. The hacking and hewing went on all day: but Harold and two of his brothers were killed; at dusk the remnant of the English made their last stand, and by night the war was over.

William of Normandy now had to use his victory as a statesman. He was about forty years old. In an adventurous life he had established his authority as duke of Normandy by showing equal skill in fighting and in diplomacy. He had defeated rebellious subjects and aggressive neighbours; he was a firm ally of the powerful count of Flanders and, after twice successfully resisting it, of the crown of France. He was on good terms with the Church, and with the best element in it, a reforming party in Rome. He had submitted his claim to the English crown to the pope, Alexander II, and the pope, deciding in his favour, had sent him a consecrated banner. This, no doubt, was an advantage to him in recruiting the foreign knights, especially from France and Flanders, who joined his expedition in the hope of plunder or grants of land. In England it made no impression. William's claim was not contemptible, but it was not convincing. Edward the Confessor had probably promised him the succession, which, strictly speaking, was not his to give, and in 1064 Harold had promised his support, but under duress, when he was William's guest after being shipwrecked on the coast of Ponthieu. William had scarcely any supporters in England. He not only had to gain control of the country, but he had to satisfy his own followers and allies. Fortunately for himself and his Normans he lived on for rather more than twenty years.

The first objective was London. William approached it by way of Dover and Canterbury, but it was hostile, or at least the party in control intended to have Edgar the atheling as king. William's advance guard beat back a sortie from London Bridge, but he knew better than to storm, damage, and alienate the city. He marched on westwards, and crossed the Thames at Wallingford. There Archbishop Stigand, the atheling's chief supporter, came in and surrendered. A few days later, at Berkhamstead, only twenty-five miles from London, the city authorities followed suit. William was crowned in Westminster Abbey on Christmas Day. He immediately began to build a castle, probably on the site where he afterwards built the Tower of London, fortress, residence, and prison. The next phase of the Norman Conquest consisted of two operations. First was the raising of money to pay for the war, partly from the confiscated lands of those who had fought and died at Hastings, then from penalties paid by landowners who had favoured Harold or the atheling and thirdly from a heavy tax levied on the whole country. Simultaneous with this was the planting of castles to hold the country down. William himself, while his London castle was building, went out settling garrisons, and his principal followers spread out over the country, taking possession of the estates and earldoms that he had assigned to them. The first castles were quickly built and simple in construction, either natural strong points or artificial mounds with wooden stockades and buildings. Many of them were improved and strengthened as time went on. They were never impregnable. Siege-warfare was not altogether primitive; but it was slow, and it required expensive equipment. Only kings or very rich subjects could count on subduing castles that were held against them. For the next four hundred years and even longer the castles stood as symbols of military domination.

By the end of March 1067 William was sufficiently sure of his grip on England to leave the country and spend eight months in Normandy. He took with him Stigand, Edgar the atheling, Edwin, Morcar and Waltheof, the son of Siward, the five most dangerous of his new subjects; but, in spite of that, there were disturbances in England, the most serious being in Kent. There Eustace of Boulogne, who had fought as an independent ally at Hastings, attacked Dover Castle. He failed and went back to his own country; but this and other incidents showed that no deputies could fill William's place. On the other hand, if he had stayed in England, everything would have gone wrong in Normandy. Military rule was never safe from military rebellion. The knights and their leaders were schooled to courage, to discipline in fighting, and to command; but they were proud, ambitious, and violent. Many of them, Waltheof for instance, still believed it was their duty to pursue a blood-feud from generation to generation. Some restraints, such as loyalty to a feudal superior or to an oath, were lightly evaded, it being easy to find a justification for asserting a claim by force of arms, whether it was a claim to land, or to some office or to respect and consideration.

Except in the northern and western frontier districts, Norman England did not, like the continental monarchies, recognize a legal right, given just cause, to wage private war; but in practice it was not until the late thirteenth century, when this feudal right was becoming obsolete everywhere, that English practice and sentiment came over to the side of the law. Levying war even against the king was not commonly interpreted as high treason until the time of King Edward I.

If men often fought, singly or in conspiracy, at the prompting of uncontrolled impulse, they also often obeyed unreasoned impulses to surrender or to forgive. William was a prudent man who sometimes preferred receiving or even giving a cash payment to insisting on a bloody revenge. The only one of his innumerable traitors who paid the death penalty was Waltheof, and that may have been because Waltheof was believed to have plotted with foreign enemies. In 1067 the city of Exeter held out against William for eighteen days, but he allowed it to make tolerable terms of surrender. Only in the harrying of the North did he go to the extreme of severity. After subduing Devonshire he appeared in force at York where many of the Yorkshire landowners submitted and the king of Scots agreed not to make war on behalf of the atheling. William left a chain of castles from Warwick to Nottingham and Cambridge; but the whole of the north broke into disorder. William put in a Norman as earl, who was defeated and killed at Durham by an English rising. At the invitation of the rebels Sweyn Estrithson, king of Denmark, sent a fleet of perhaps 240 ships, and a mixed force of Danes and Norwegians landed from the Humber. York fell and there were risings all the way from Cornwall to Lincolnshire, the real danger-points being in Mercia. The castles held firm. William won a battle against the English and bought off the Danes. It seems certain that he then deliberately devastated a large area. It included Cheshire, Shropshire, Staffordshire, and Derbyshire; but the worst damage was in Yorkshire. This can only be explained as providing against further resistance by terrorism; but that leaves an unsolved puzzle, for this was not foreign territory, but land from which William might have drawn men and revenue. The English resistance movement ended with the desperate defence of the Isle of Ely by Hereward the Wake.

Whatever the explanation may be, no doubt the devastations policy had some connection with the position of the north as a frontier area and with the Danish aid. It may be reckoned as William's greatest good fortune that he never had to face a full-scale invasion from the sea. Eustace of Boulogne amounted to very little; Sweyn, although he came over to join his army in person, wanted to limit his risks. He died in 1074 and his son Canute, an unsuccessful competitor for the succession, brought over a strong fleet to support a rebellion raised by Waltheof and two other earls, one a Norman and the other an Englishman with Breton relations. But he came too late and went away without doing any serious harm. Eleven years later, in 1085, came the last threat of a Danish invasion, far worse than this. Canute had become king of Denmark, had revived his family's claim to the English throne, and had formed alliances with the king of Norway and with William's former ally Flanders. William prepared for an invasion, and hired troops from France, Brittany, and Maine; but Canute's fleet never came. His affairs went awry at home and next year he was murdered. No invading fleet has ever come to England from Scandinavia since then. The main reasons for this immunity are to be found on the side of the Danes and Norwegians, who no longer took to this hazardous outlet; but the English kingdom became stronger and more compact, which contributed to the same result.

In many respects the wars and rebellions of William's reign resembled those of the last Anglo-Saxon kings. Up to a point they were continuations; but the continuity of English life was broken very sharply. William, indeed, regarded himself as the lawful successor to the Crown, and it emphasized his royal status to keep the main institutions as they were. Formally there was little change in the consultation with the *witan*. There were still earls and sheriffs. A good many of the earls were troublesome and consequently the sheriffs grew in importance as agents of the royal will, reaching their zenith a few years after William died. By then there were about twenty of them, nearly all feudal tenants-in-chief. Their tenures of office were long, but son very seldom succeeded father. Their position at the head of the system of law-courts was the central fact of Norman local government. But the Normans were organizers: in all the states which they established, in Normandy itself, in Italy and beyond it, they braced institutions together by their legal rules and administrative practices. In England this work was done partly by some of the leaders and partly by the little-known clerks who came over to take charge of the financial, military, and judicial machinery. In the process they destroyed or misunderstood some of the best of the Anglo-Saxon arrangements. Generally speaking they based their system as much as possible on feudal practices. No one appeared among the *witan* except the king's tenants-in-chief. The country was parcelled out into knights' fees, and the knightly sub-tenants were responsible for providing the services which the tenants-in-chief owed to the king. The right to hold local courts of law was brought into the same system: it became a feudal right, though in theory the feudal lord was not as such a judge. Even the village police customs were tightened: the villagers were grouped in tens, with a headman for each, and these 'frankpledge' groups were inspected once a year by the sheriff or his subordinates.

One of the Conqueror's laws grimly recognized that the Normans were a conquering minority. If a man were found slain and the slayer not produced, the hundred collectively had to pay a fine called *murdrum*, a murder-fine, unless it could prove that the victim was an Englishman. While people were alive of course it was easy to tell the difference. They spoke different languages.

Part of the Bayeux Tapestry, made to celebrate the Norman conquest of England. The completed tapestry depicts 72 scenes, and takes the form of a very long (70 m, 231 ft) and narrow (0·5 m, 20 in) strip executed in yellow, blue, red and green Although it is embroidered, in more than one sense perhaps, it is a good source for studying the styles and techniques of war and society of that time.

The results of the importation of French were quite unlike the results of the earlier importations of Latin, Old English, and Danish. To explain, it will be necessary to look forward into history far later than the conquest. The reason for this is that the importing continued for a long time, changing its character when the Norman dynasty ended in 1154, to be succeeded by kings who spoke, not the language of the Normans, but the rather different French of Anjou. We have no space to distinguish the different influences of those two waves, but only to glance at the influence of French as a whole. Until some time in the fourteenth century French was the language of the royal court, of the aristocracy, of many immigrant monks and other clergy, and to a great extent of the army and the law. Many lesser people who had to do with the governing classes understood or spoke more or less of it. It has left some place-names behind it, especially names of castles and abbeys, such as Belvoir and Beaulieu. Like these two, a remarkable proportion of these names draw attention to the beauty of the places, as does one of the much fewer purely geographical names, Beachy Head.

There was also a large deposit of French words in the English language. In his novel *Ivanhoe* Sir Walter Scott quite rightly pointed out that the names of animal foods – beef, mutton, veal, pork, bacon, venison – are derived from French, the animals themselves – oxen, sheep, calves, swine, and deer – have native names. The moral of this has been reinforced by the remark that we owe to the French the names of master, servant, butler, buttery, bottle, dinner, supper, and banquet. A great many of our ordinary words relating to property, law, government were taken over from French before the end of the thirteenth century. It is one of the curiosities of our legal history that Law French, a degenerate Norman French, was the special language of the English common law, not done away with until the eighteenth century. French military words were taken over. A few craftsmen, such as the smith, the baker, the skinner, and the salter kept their Old English names, most of the others, like the butcher, the barber, the carpenter, the draper, the grocer, the mason, and the tailor, took theirs from French. This may be a sign that the division of labour was more advanced among the invaders, and social anthropologists can make something of the curious fact that all the now current terms for family relationships outside the circle of the household – uncle, aunt, nephew, niece, cousin, and so on – come from French. It was, however, in literary and not in spoken language that the conquest had it greatest effects. The knowledge of French gave access to the literature of the Continent, and there was a great influx of French words and of words adopted from Latin. The educated clergy came to read and write in Latin for many purposes which English had served, and so no more was added to the Old English literature in prose. The poetry had already ended.

William the Conqueror had no language-policy and, notwithstanding such practical measures as the *murdrum* law, his intention in regard to the national differences among his subjects was not to keep them distinct but to merge them. The effect of his strong government was to reduce the importance of regional customs and laws, such as those of the Danish and Norwegian settlers. He needed on his side all the men he could win over, and as early as 1068, when he marched against Exeter, there were English militiamen in his army. As the successor of the Anglo-Saxon kings, he began employing Englishmen in places of the highest trust. This policy did not succeed. By the end of William's reign the defence of the country needed foreign mercenaries, and Englishmen had little influence in decision-making. The insubordination of powerful individuals like Waltheof was not the only cause of this. All William's acts of repression and all his financial exactions made life harder for smaller men, even down to the cultivators of the soil. Many men who might have been useful had gone abroad to seek their fortunes. Among those who remained, hatred of foreign rule must have sharpened their resentment at material grievances. We cannot say whether there was a developed or developing national feeling, with an ideal of a free England: such a feeling could scarcely have left memorials for us to read. Nor can we trace the early steps by which the Normans and the English came together, as the history of language shows that they did. Some of the intruders married English wives, including the heiresses to estates. William's own youngest and ablest son, afterwards King Henry I, was born in Yorkshire, spoke English easily, and in due time married the sister of Edgar the atheling.

The consecrated banner which William flew at Hastings implied that if he won he would reorganize the English church in conjunction with the papacy. The active life of William the Conqueror coincided with the first successes and the severe tribulations of the reforming party in the Church. Their purpose was to raise the level of the clergy in character and in devotion to their work, and they set out to do this by liberating the clergy from control by laymen. They put an end to the system by which the aristocracy of Rome elected the popes, transferring that function to the cardinal bishops. Next they tried to stop the appointment of bishops by kings and other rulers, who commonly regarded the bishop's office as part of the machinery of government. A further item in their programme was to end the system by which landowners appointed priests to their local churches. All these kinds of patronage led to the appointment of

A page from the Domesday Book. In fact, there were two volumes. This is from the so-called Little Domesday, an economic survey of Essex, Norfolk, and Suffolk consisting of 384 vellum pages. Both this and the Great Domesday (450 pages) are preserved at the Public Record Office.

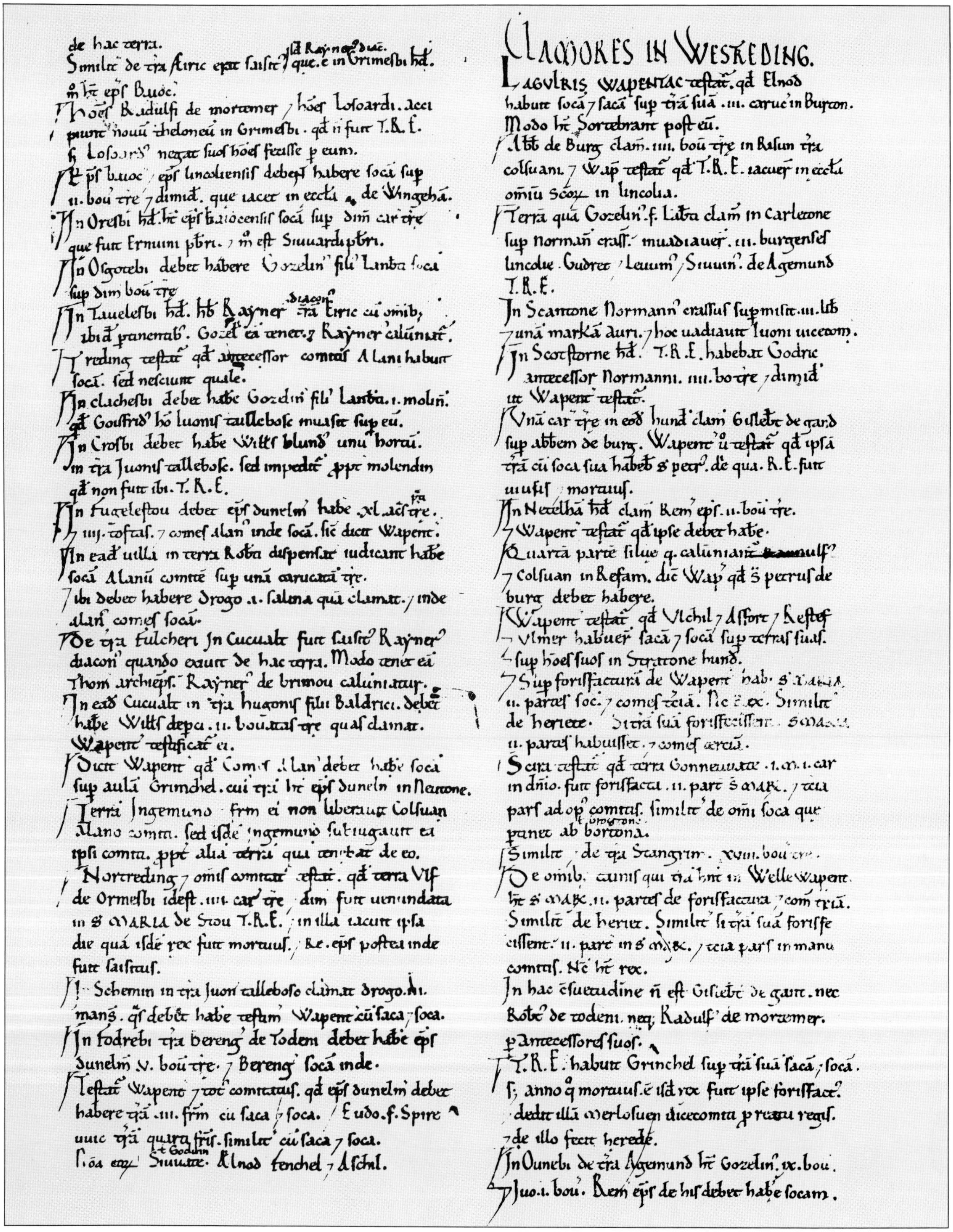
de hac terra.
Similit de tra Siric epat saisit' que e in Grimesbi hd.
m ht eps Baioc.
Hoes Radulfi de mortemer 7 hoes Losoardi . acce
perunt nouu theloneu in Grimesbi . qd n fuit T.R.E.
S; Losoard' negat suos hoes fecisse p eum.
Eps baioc 7 eps lincoliensis debent habere soca sup
ii. bou tre 7 dimid . que iacet in eccta de Wingeha.
In Oresbi hd. ht eps baiocensis soca sup dim car tre
que fuit Ernuini pbri . 7 m est Siuuardi pbri.
In Osgotebi debet habere Gozelin' fili' Lanba soca
sup dim bou tre
In Lauelesbi hd. hb Rayner diacon' tra Eiric cu omib,
ibid ptinentib'. Gozel ea tenet. 7 Rayner caluniat.
Treding testat qd antecessor comitis Alani habuit
soca. sed nesciunt quale.
In clachesbi debet habe Gozelin' fili' Lanba . i. molin.
qd Goisfrid' ho Iuonis taillebosc inuasit sup eu.
In Crosbi debet habe Witts blund' unu hortu.
in tra Iuonis tallebosc. sed impedit ppt molendin
qd non fuit ibi. T.R.E.
In Fugelestou debet eps dunelm habe .xl. acs pa tre.
7 iiij. toftas. 7 comes Alan' inde soca. sic dicit Wapent.
In ead uilli in terra Robti dispensat iudicant habe
soca Alanu comite sup una carucata tre.
7 ibi debet habere Drogo .i. salina qua clamat. 7 inde
alan' comes soca.
De tra Fulcheri In Cucualt fuit saisit' Rayner
diacon' quando exiuit de hac terra. Modo tenet ea
Thom archieps. Rayner' de brimou caluniat.
In ead Cucualt in tra hugonis filii Baldrici. debet
habe Witts depc . ii. bouatas tre quas clamat.
Wapent testificat ei.
Dicit Wapent qd Comes Alan' debet habe soca
sup aula Grimchel. cui tra ht eps duneln in Nettone.
Terra Ingemund frm ei non liberauit Colsuan
Alano comiti. sed isde Ingemund subiugauit ea
ipsi comiti. ppt alia terra qua tenebat de eo.
Nortreding 7 omis comitat testat. qd terra Ulf
de Ormesbi idest . iiii. car tre dim fuit uenundata
in S MARIA de Stou T.R.E. in illa iacuit ipsa
die qua isde rex fuit mortuus. 7 Re. eps postea inde
fuit saisitus.
In Schemin in tra Iuon tallebosc clamat Drogo . iii.
mans . qs debet habe testim Wapent cu saca 7 soca.
In Fodrebi tra bereng de Todeni debet habe eps
dunelm .v. bou tre. 7 Bereng soca inde.
Testat Wapent 7 tot comitatus. qd eps dunelm debet
habere tra . iii. frm cu saca 7 soca. Eudo . f. Spire
uuic tra quarta fris. similit cu saca 7 soca.
Sioa tra Siuuate . Elnod fenchel 7 Aschil.

CLAMORES IN WESTREDING.
LAGULRIS WAPENTAC testat. qd Elnod
habuit soca 7 saca sup tra sua . iii. carue in Burton.
Modo ht Sortebrant post eu.
Abb de Burg clam . iii. bou tre in Rasun tra
Colsuani. 7 Wap testat qd T.R.E. iacuer in eccta
omiu scor in lincolia.
Terra qua Gozelin'. f. Lanba clam in Carletone
sup Norman crass. inuadiauer . iii. burgenses
lincolie . Gudret 7 Leuuin' 7 Siuuin'. de Agemund
T.R.E.
In Scantone Normann' crassus supmisit . iii. lib
7 una marka auri. 7 hoc uadiauit Iuoni uicecom.
In Scotstorne hd. T.R.E. habebat Godric
antecessor Normanni . iiii. bo tre 7 dimid
ut Wapent testat.
Una car tre in eod hund clam Gislebt de gand
sup abbem de burg. Wapent u testat qd ipsa
tra cu soca sua habet S petr'. de qua. R.E. fuit
uiuus 7 mortuus.
In Netelha hd clam Rem eps . ii. bou tre.
7 Wapent testat qd ipse debet habe.
Quarta parte silue q. caluniant ulf
7 Colsuan in Resam. dic Wap qd S petrus de
burg debet habere.
Wapent testat qd Ulchil 7 Asfort 7 Restef
7 Ulmer habuer saca 7 soca sup terras suas.
7 sup hoes suos in Strattone hund.
7 Sup forisfactura de Wapent hab . S MARIA
ii. partes soc. 7 comes tcia. Nec rex. Similit
de heriete. Si tra sua forisfecissent. S MARIA
ii. partes habuisset. 7 comes tercia.
Scira testat qd terra Gonneuuate . i. car
in dnio. fuit forisfacta . ii. part S MARIA. 7 tcia
pars ad op' comitis. similit de omi soca que
ptinet ab bortona.
Similit de tra Stangrim . xviii. bou tre.
De omib, tainis qui tra hnt in Welle Wapent.
ht S MAR . ii. partes de forisfactura 7 com tcia.
Similit de heriet. Similit si tra sua forisfe
cissent . ii. part in S MAR. 7 tcia pars in manu
comitis. Nec ht rex.
In hac csuetudine n est Gislebt de gant . nec
Robt de todeni . neq; Radulf' de mortemer.
p antecessores suos.
T.R.E. habuit Grinchel sup tra sua saca 7 soca.
S; anno q mortuus e isd rex fuit ipse forisfact.
dedit illa Merlosuen uicecomiti p rectu regis.
7 de illo fecit herede.
In Ounebi de tra Agemund ht Gozelin'. ix. bou.
7 Iuo . i . bou. Rem eps de his debet habe socam.

unsuitable men, and often to corrupt and undesirable practices by those who sought appointment. Finally the reformers took up the related question of clerical celibacy. The monks were celibate, but some of the bishops and many of the parish clergy were not. They married and gave their children in marriage, and so they were entangled in the worldly affairs of property and the quarrels that arose from it. William's attitude to this reforming movement was consistent but peculiar to himself. He was a religious man, a great founder of abbeys, and a friend to the reformers in their spiritual aims. As duke of Normandy, however, he had inherited from his ancestors a more complete control of ecclesiastical appointments than any other continental ruler enjoyed. He extended this control to England and the popes, understanding his good intentions towards the church, did not object.

Two successive popes did indeed put forward the erroneous argument that England had formerly been subject to the Roman see and that Peter's Pence was a proof of it. William promised to pay up some arrears of Peter's Pence but he flatly and successfully refused to do homage. He went even further in asserting England's independence; for example he forbade his bishops to go to Rome without his own leave, even if they were summoned by the pope. Of his own motion, however, he carried out reforms which strengthened not only the church but the papacy. Stigand was allowed to stay as archbishop of Canterbury for four years; but then the pope sent two cardinals who took the necessary steps. Stigand was turned out, and also some other delinquent bishops.

The king made a great constitutional change by establishing separate courts of law for the church. The new courts not only tried offences by the clergy, and offences of laymen against church law; but also dealt with all matters relating to the government of souls and these included many which would not be regarded as spiritual now. The law of marriage was among them. It was still not well developed, but it was the only body of rules to decide who might marry whom and what constituted a valid marriage. The law of wills and inheritance also belonged to the ecclesiastical courts; and in a society based on property and the family these two branches of law were of high importance.

From 1070 William had an admirable associate in his reforms, his friend Lanfranc, who followed Stigand at Canterbury. Lanfranc was an Italian, learned in the civil law, who had been a famous teacher and abbot in Normandy, a man who combined an instinct for order and regularity with a realist's eye for what was practicable. For the time being he settled in favour of the province of Canterbury some of the uncertainties about its relations with York. Even before this settlement he began a series of councils which dealt with most of the major problems of the church in England. He gradually improved its organization in such matters as the layout of dioceses, and their staffing with archdeacons, travelling officers with authority over the clergy. He made regulations tending towards clerical celibacy. He supervised the working of dioceses and monasteries, and he stood up for the church where its affairs concerned the king or the nobility.

In his time the church showed signs of vitality, one of which, uniquely impressive, remains until this day. Very soon after the conquest, and throughout the country, even into the turbulent north, there began an immense rebuilding of cathedrals and monasteries and parish churches. It seems that in places, especially in the south-east, Norman masons came over to work. Everywhere, though the change was slower in the smaller buildings, the formed Romanesque style of Normandy overpowered the native traditions. Long, high, dominating edifices towered above the roofs of houses and even above the castles. Internally they were plain and austere. No later buildings in England express such strength, and few express such majesty. In the twelfth century, the style grew ornate, and sculpture was supplemented by wall-paintings and painted glass. But the more delicate arts, manuscript illumination and the like, were slow to recover from the shocks of war and social change.

From this time onwards, our knowledge of economic life and social relations becomes much fuller and more precise from this time onwards. This is symbolized by two huge manuscript volumes called Domesday Book, the greatest treasure of our public records. King William decided in his council at Christmas 1085 that the whole of his kingdom should be surveyed. Commissioners were sent down to the shires and hundreds. There they collected information by taking sworn evidence from juries on which both Normans and Englishmen sat. Clerks in London digested this accumulation of facts into the book, which gives with many details, manor by manor, the area, the ownership, the numbers of different classes of men and the annual value both at that time, at the date of the Conquest twenty years before, and in the time of Edward the Confessor. The returns were brought in before the end of 1086, and there is no doubt of their general correctness. This was an unequalled feat of administration. No other European ruler could command such knowledge of his dominions until the fifteenth century. It is true that it fell far short of the standards that we expect of modern statistics. We do not know exactly what the king wanted from it. It was a survey of his own and other men's rights, connected in some way with finance and disputes over legal rights; but it was essentially a list of separate local facts, not a collection of facts on which national or regional totals were to be based. Even so it was not complete. The four northern counties, part of Lancashire, besides London, Winchester, Bristol, and some other towns are omitted. The survey did not directly include all kinds of people: it mentions women and the clergy only incidentally and children not at all. But in itself, and still more in conjunction with other documents, Domesday Book gives a new depth to English history. It enables historians to make estimates of the population of England; something near, probably below, two millions seems to be a good working hypothesis. It also indicates that the Conquest was followed by recovery and, at least in trade, industry, and the towns, by economic progress.

It is an accepted opinion among historians that the hundred and thirty years which separate Domesday Book from Magna Carta witnessed the emergence of the English nation. The twelfth-century sovereigns addressed their subjects in official documents as 'French and English', but the distinction was worn away, with royal encouragement, by intermarriage and by daily sharing in every kind of activity. In the latter part of the century it was almost impossible to distinguish the two peoples among the free population, and long before the *murdrum* fine was limited in 1259 and abolished in 1340 it ceased to depend on the nationality of the victim. The growth of the nation was part of a process, spreading over most if not all of Europe, in which the diversities of speech and customs were becoming polarized so that many a man's place in the world was indicated more by his nationality and less by his kinship or his allegiance to a master than of old. Patriotism was beginning to bind people together, at first as a scarcely separable ingredient of personal loyalty to superiors, but afterwards independent and capable of turning against even a king. It was still to take long centuries before the national sentiment of populations became the driving force of armies and of tyrannies. That resulted from fundamental changes in the structure of communities; but in the twelfth century we can trace some of the preliminary steps. In England we find some of them in the frontier warfare which, in the end, was to fix the geographical limits of the nation; we can find others in the economic and constitutional developments which dictated the nature and degree of its internal cohesion; but first we may look at England's relations with the Continent, for these made the framework within which at each time the national organism was cramped in some directions but left free to expand in others.

Military comings and goings across the Channel were a normal part of the lives of the kings and their followers. Although he kept a tight hold on both England and Normandy, William the Conqueror never had any intention of uniting them into a single kingdom. In Normandy he was only duke, a vassal of the king of France: to have made himself king would have been legally rebellion and in practice very dangerous indeed. His eldest son Robert had to inherit in Normandy; but in England the kingship was still elective, and as he lay dying William saw to it that Archbishop Lanfranc should fix the election in favour of his second son, William Rufus. The separation, however, was only at the highest level. There were still landowners, both barons and abbeys, with possessions in both countries. They were apt to assert rights against their neighbours and against their superiors. Normandy was separated by a long land frontier from a ring of equally restless vassals of the French monarchy, some of them with more powerful vassals behind them, such as the counts of Brittany and Flanders. The quarrels of great men and their families expressed themselves in feudal rivalries and rebellions running across boundaries and frontiers. In William's reign there were several outbreaks in Normandy. In one, Philip I of France sought to take part of the county of Vexin from Normandy. After capturing the local town of Mantes, William was injured there by accident, and died.

After William's death in 1087, frontier questions were still disputed, and a three-cornered rivalry between William's sons was added to them. Robert, now Duke of Normandy, was the only amiable character among the three but he was incurably incompetent; William was a vigorous and cunning brute; Henry, the ablest all round, was cruel and treacherous. First of all, barons in both England and Normandy rose against William Rufus, ostensibly in order to place Robert on the English throne. It took Rufus three years to win control of the situation, but it needed little fighting. In England he was firm but lenient. He mobilized a large English force for service in Normandy; but at Hastings his agents collected from them their subsistence-money and sent them back to their homes. With this money Rufus bribed his way into the keeps of the rebellious Norman barons, and then he joined with Robert to fight their brother Henry who, in breach of an agreement, was holding on to Mont St. Michel and the Cotentin Peninsula.

Henry's turn came in 1100. Rufus, hunting in the New Forest, was shot dead in highly suspicious circumstances by an arrow. Except for one thing Henry I succeeded auspiciously to the English throne: the one obstacle was that the throne was claimed by his elder brother Robert. So Henry's reign began like that of Rufus with a rebellion of English and Norman barons in Robert's favour. The English militia was solidly behind Henry, but there were traitors at sea, and Robert landed a considerable force of horse, foot, and archers right up in Portsmouth harbour. The brothers met at Alton in Hampshire, and Robert was talked into a treaty of peace. This gave Henry time for thorough preparations. In 1104 he invaded Normandy with a powerful force and won a complete victory at Tinchebrai. On 28 September 1106, forty years to the day after his father's landing at Pevensey, the king of England conquered Normandy. Duke Robert was kept prisoner for the remaining seven and twenty years of his life. Told in outline this story so far seems to have much the same plot, if with different actors and scenery, as countless earlie stories of rebellion and aggression; but a new element had appeared which could not have existed in any earlier time. In 1095 the news had come that the Roman emperor, successor to those eastern Roman emperors who had once ruled over Britain

Mont St Michel, an ecclesiastical fortress in Britanny which frequently figured in the history of Norman England. In 1066 it contributed ships to William's invasion fleet. Henry II held court here to receive homage from his Bretons. Its monastery was formed by the Benedictines, who came in 966. St Michael's Mount in Cornwall, which is similar though smaller, was one of the dependencies of this monastery.

A crusaders' castle, Krak de Chevaliers, in Syria. These castles served as forward bases for attacking the Moslems. Though similar to castles in the crusaders' homelands, they did include Byzantine features. They were unusually large, because they had to accommodate many soldiers and supplies. This castle even had its own windmill for producing flour.

from their capital at Constantinople, had appealed to Pope Urban II for help against the Mahommedans. The latter, centuries earlier, had swept out from Arabia to the north and east. They had even reached Poitiers in 732. That, however, had been their highwater mark. Christianity was gradually pushing them back to where they had come from. In doing so, it made the eastern Mediterranean more inviting, especially for merchants and pilgrims from western Europe. Now, fortified by the emperor's plea, the pope wanted to increase the pressure, and made no secret of his wish to direct the energies of the fighting men from their feudal anarchy to a crusade for the common cause of Christendom. Knights and nobles took the cross. Priests used their diplomacy, for instance by reconciling Robert of Normandy with William Rufus. In 1096 a composite army arrived at Constantinople. Among its leaders was Robert, who to raise the necessary money had pawned his Norman duchy to William Rufus for five years.

In the first years, of course, the crusades did not alter much in England except that the places of the absentees had to be filled. Nothing altered the conditions which caused the perpetual fighting at home except the firmness of a strong king when such there was. Henry I was a strong king; but by his own ambitious policy he prepared a calamitous future. He was the last male in the direct line of descent from the Conqueror. His only legitimate son was drowned in the Channel, leaving a sister, called Matilda in Latin, Maud in French, who was over thirty when her father died in 1135. She had two political marriages behind her. When she was eight years old she had been crowned as the wife of Henry V, the western emperor. In her twenties she came back to England as a childless widowed empress, and Henry of England treated her as though she was to succeed him; but against her own wishes she was married to Geoffrey Plantagenet, a boy of fifteen, son of the count of Anjou. Anjou, between the River Loire and Maine, which it had absorbed, was apt to take part in

A 12th century English knight's armour. Mail was still the basic protection, despite its great weight. However, an early role for plate armour, in the form of an articulated joint over the knee, can be seen. The cloth surcoat was a characteristic of English knights and in later years bore the heraldic emblem of the wearer.

combinations against Normandy. The Normans disliked Anjou, and no one except the Germans seems to have liked the empress. When Henry I died in 1135 one of his nephews, the son of his sister, hurriedly crossed over to England and was crowned before anyone could stop him. This was Stephen, the younger brother of the count of Blois on the Loire, between Orleans and Tours. He was brave, well-endowed with lands in both England and Normandy, and effectively supported by his younger brother Henry, who was bishop of Winchester. He put down local resistance in some parts of the kingdom, and then he had to go to Normandy where the empress Matilda was claiming the duchy and her Angevin husband had backed her up with cruel violence. Stephen made the mistake of taking with him Flemish mercenaries who were disliked in Normandy. He quarrelled with his supporters, and left the duchy to its own devices.

England collapsed into chaos. Not only some of the barons but highly placed ecclesiastics fortified their castles and made ominous preparations. Stephen put them down, but by so doing he provided the empress with a party, and when she landed in 1139 she began a civil war. In a battle at Lincoln Stephen was taken prisoner. Ruffianly barons robbed and burnt and murdered in villages and abbeys. After six or seven years of this, settled government was restored. The empress, having made herself impossible, left the country. Two young men were growing up whose antagonism might have prolonged the confusion. One was Eustace, the son of King Stephen; but the churchmen seemed likely to refuse to crown him as the successor. The other was his cousin Henry, the son of the empress and of Geoffrey of Anjou. Henry came to England and renewed the war; but Eustace died. Stephen agreed to a peace by which he was to reign for his lifetime. Henry was to succeed, and even before that to carry out the work of government as Stephen's adopted son. Less than a year later King Stephen died.

King Henry II brought Normandy back into effective personal union with England. His father Geoffrey had conquered it for Anjou after Stephen's unlucky visit. He had administered it with a view to Henry's succession, which came about there in 1151. With Normandy came, as a matter of course, Maine, Anjou, and Touraine. Two years before he became king Henry made a daring marriage which brought him, in right of his wife, an even greater assemblage of French fiefs. His bride was Eleanor, the wife of Henry VII of France. Her father had left her Poitou, Saintonge, the Limousin, and Gascony, that is the whole coast from the Loire to Bayonne with all the towns and countryside as far inland as the *massif central*. Altogether Henry's fiefs amounted to more than half the French king's dominions. He was the first king of England who commanded greater wealth and power on the Continent than in Britain. He became a party to the high diplomatic combinations of Europe, with interests beyond the Rhine and beyond the Pyrenees. Englishmen could gain wide military or administrative experience in Henry's service, and some of his French subjects came over to serve in England.

The agglomeration of lands has been called the Angevin Empire, or even the English Empire; but its structure was still essentially the same as that of the Anglo-Norman combination. Henry set up no common organs of government even for adjacent countries. Like William the Conqueror he intended that after his time his territories should be divided among his sons. For himself he had old-fashioned ambitions. He claimed the county of Toulouse as his wife's. But western Europe was changing. Henry himself was one of several rulers who became stronger in relation to their vassals. New kinds of wealth were growing up among humbler people, especially in the towns. The initiative would soon pass from the great feudal lords to the kings. This change was masked by the feudal and family wars of Henry's reign. His sons were able, pugnacious, and disloyal, never satisfied with their actual and prospective portions. In 1173 the youngest, John, was still a child. The three adults were Henry, who was meant to succeed in England, Richard Lion Heart, and Geoffrey, count of Brittany. They formed alliances, which appeared formidable, with France, Flanders, and Scotland, and they rebelled. King Henry was a match for them all. Ten years later the young Henry and Geoffrey rebelled again; but as fate would have it they both died before their father. The end of his long reign was gloomy. Richard was doing well as governor of the southern provinces; but Henry unwisely and unfairly intended to supplant him in the succession to the Angevin lands in France by his favourite son John. For the first time after many years France had a king who was capable of using to the full the resources which Louis VII had quietly improved. This young man, Philip II, called Augustus, induced Richard to join him in war against Henry. Henry led English and Welsh troops across the Channel, but he lost Tours and he was losing the war when, in 1189, he died.

The succession and reign of Richard I were scenes in the great historical drama of the age, the crusades. The victories of the first

Fountains Abbey, one of the great 12th century abbeys in the north of England. Its ruins still exemplify, by their absence of ornament, the austere tradition of the Cistercian monks.

crusaders left behind them in the Holy Land occupying forces under many masters, a kingdom of Jerusalem, other feudal principalities, and military orders of knights dedicated to religion. As time went on and the political immaturity of Europe reproduced itself among them, their Moslem enemies grew more united. The crusaders never received as much support as they needed from the West, and in 1147–9 the Second Crusade was a failure. In 1187 the sultan Saladin won the battle of Hattin, west of the Sea of Galilee. Jerusalem and the other Holy Places were lost, with every inch of the conquered lands except Tyre. The pope proclaimed the Third Crusade, and the last war of Henry II was fought while all the great western monarchs were preparing for this crusade. In 1189 Philip Augustus and the newly crowned Richard I of England both set out with their contingents of volunteers. Richard had 180 ships with him when he embarked, the first English naval force that sailed beyond the Narrow Seas. Until a truce was made with Saladin in 1192 all the operations of the crusaders were supplied from the sea, another innovation in warfare; and from this the English gained no inconsiderable training. The crusaders achieved something. Richard himself on the outward voyage conquered Cyprus (a nominal and neglected possession of the eastern empire) and set it up as an independent kingdom and naval base. He did dazzling personal feats of arms. But the leaders quarrelled; they won battles but they could not hold positions inland, and all they gained when they evacuated their beach-heads was a promise from Saladin that Christian pilgrims should come and go unmolested. On his way home Richard was shipwrecked in the Adriatic and fell into the hands of one of the leaders whom he had offended, the emperor Henry VI. After many uncertainties he was ransomed and released in 1194. He spent two months in England and then, for the rest of his life, grappled with his affairs in France. At his accession he had come from France for two months before setting out for Syria, and so, in his reign of eleven years he spent just a few months in his kingdom.

That England never deserted him is a proof that, as we shall see, Henry II had given it new cohesion. It is the more remarkable because the envious John, unlike the Norman barons who were true to the absent crusader, acted with Philip Augustus. The French king seized the Vexin and began a siege of Rouen. John did homage to him for all the possessions in France and perhaps for England too. He was making ready to meet an English rebellion, with very doubtful chance of success, when Richard returned. Richard spent his last four years in hard, but intermittent fighting against Philip Augustus. These wars had a wider scope, at least in their diplomatic aspects, than any earlier English wars. Flanders, previously an ally of France, changed sides. But Richard, besieging the castle of a disobedient baron, was mortally wounded by an arrow. John succeeded and bought recognition from Philip by surrendering many lordships and paying a heavy indemnity. Philip took an early opportunity of picking a feudal quarrel with him, and caught him unawares.

John had not cultivated the new friendships that Richard had made. Philip's aim was to take Normandy for himself and to make use of John's nephew, Arthur of Brittany. John, by a lightning stroke, took his nephew prisoner. By cruelty and in the end by murdering Arthur, John threw his advantage away. The Norman barons would not fight for him and in 1204 he had to surrender the duchy to the king of France. The personal union of England and Normandy was ended. (Except for the Channel Islands, where the British monarch still reigns as duke.)

In the crusading movement the church influenced the world of action; and not in the crusading movement alone. It tried to mitigate the damage and confusion of feudal warfare. One of its methods for doing this, the proclaiming of a special truce or suspension of hostilities on church festivals, was of little or no importance in England; but the complex of ideas and customs which we call chivalry made its mark on English life for centuries to come. Chivalry means knightliness, the ethics of the feudal cavalry. It included the formal side of knighthood, who might confer it, upon whom, after what proofs of merit, and by what ceremonies. These ethical notions grew steadily into a code of fidelity, endurance, and generosity. Some of these had come down from the traditions of the heathen Saxons and Northmen, but in its mature forms chivalry was Christian. Originally it was the distinguishing code of an upper class, perhaps too wide to be called aristocratic, a system of obligations interwoven with privileges. As time went on it was elaborated and specialized. One branch was a set of laws for war on land, rules about fair fighting, courts martial, heralds, flags of truce, prisoners, and ransoms. It regulated coats of arms, rank, and precedence. When, long afterwards, the character of armies altered and they became organized multitudes of infantry, artillery, engineers, and what not, chivalry in the old sense lost its central place. Knights in armour were relegated to romances and all the various kinds of rules were reduced to prosaic system; but the spirit which grew strong in the eleventh century lived on. It may be recognized in the traditions of regular armies, and in such perversions as the formalities of duelling.

Durham Cathedral, the outstanding creation of early Norman architects. Begun in 1093, its massive pillars and round arches are characteristically Norman, though the pointed arches which form the roof were a 12th century innovation, marking the introduction of the pointed arch to European architecture.

That it flourished was one sign that the twelfth century was a period of vitality in the western church. Not only among the crusaders but also among those who stayed at home there were many who made sacrifices for religion. If their motives were sometimes mixed, and tinged both by penitence and a desire to insure their own eternal future, at any rate their belief was genuine. In the early years after the Conquest most of the major benefactions were gifts of land to existing monasteries in England and Normandy; but by the last decade of the eleventh century there began a series of new foundations in England. The donors joined hands with the reforming movement of the churchmen and new orders of regular clergy made their homes here. The Cistercians, ardent and ascetic, had more than fifty houses by the end of Stephen's reign. Their rule prescribed that they should settle in remote and not populous places, and so their best-known monuments are the abbeys of the Yorkshire dales, Rievaulx, Fountains, and Kirkstall. Each house, most of all in the newer orders, was a unit in an international congregation and might well take its instructions from a foreign superior, or look to Rome for guidance and for protection against the claims of nearer authorities.

Each house also, to a higher or lower degree as its rule and circumstances decided, was a home of thought and learning, and this was the time of the wonderful intellectual revival which is called the twelfth-century renaissance. It was a revival in the sense that it brought back into circulation in the West the basic ideas of philosophy and the sciences as they had been known to Greek and Roman thinkers. They had been neglected largely because the West was in no condition to need or maintain philosophers and scientists. The Greek-speaking governing classes of the Eastern Empire were aware of their existence; but the alienation of East and West in theology and politics and the lack of intercourse prevented the imparting of this knowledge. Now it came in by a more roundabout channel. The Moslem world which the crusaders attacked had already for centuries been more advanced than the West in many literary and intellectual accomplishments. From the eleventh century a new flow of ancient Greek ideas came from Arabic translations retranslated into Latin. The learned Jews of Spain were among the most active intermediaries, and so the revival of ancient learning was mingled with elements of Moslem and Jewish thought. It was not a mere coincidence that the new content of scholarship went along with a change in the scholars' ways of life. The first Moslem university was founded in Baghdad in the year before the Norman conquest of England, and others soon after it. In Italy and France secular clergy, priests who were not monks, began to figure as teachers, and the earliest universities appeared in Italy. England came into touch with the movement. The Italian Anselm of Aosta, a theologian of the first rank, became

A carving in the 12th century Temple Church in the City of London. It shows a crusader-knight of the Order of Knights Templar, whose church this was. Members of this Order captured by the Saracens were usually beheaded rather than ransomed; they were such effective fighters that their release was not worthwhile at any price.

archbishop of Canterbury. His admirer John of Salisbury, who was probably born between 1115 and 1120, represented the broadening interests of his time in classical philosophy and in political thought. An earlier philosopher, the much-travelled Adelard of Bath, worked in mathematics and science. Students were attracted to various places by the reputation of teachers, and a good many of the more fortunate went to the university of Paris. Two centres of learning, Oxford and Cambridge, attained the status of universities, not by any act of foundation and not even at any date that we can fix, but partly in imitation of Paris and partly because they were conveniently placed.

In the sphere of the church there was one kind of division from which England was free. On the Continent the ecclesiastical authorities faced organized bodies of heretics, and the old belief that they should be put down by force became fused with the crusaders' idea of the holy war. In Italy, Germany, and France there were terrible persecutions. In England the only victims were some thirty German Catharans in 1166 and a single Albigensian in 1206: heresy did not disturb the country until late in the fourteenth century. But in many ways the affairs of the church were disorderly. The early Norman kings brought over bishops and other clerks from France who pressed forward the plans of the reforming party, but were often unjust to the English clergy and their traditions. The old contest between Canterbury and York revived. It was settled sensibly enough by a compromise which left Canterbury superior in status but not in authority. The Norman Thurstan, archbishop of York, who saved his province from subordination, was brave and intelligent. Towards the end of his life, when a Scottish army had overrun the bishopric of Durham and King Stephen could send no help, he rallied the hesitating lords of Yorkshire, and sent his clergy to lead their parishioners to victory in the Battle of the Standard (1138).

It is no wonder that this was a crucial period in the relations, as we should say, of church and state. That phrase is modern. In the twelfth century there was no developed idea of 'the state', and churchmen sought to define their relations with this or that king or prince or, in a few instances such as Venice, republic. But everywhere the whole population were subjects of the king or republic and, from another point of view, the same entire population constituted the church. There were problems which could be stated in general terms: what kind of authority did each power enjoy; where did it come from, and what were its limits. Some ideas were generally accepted. Kings ought not to be tyrants; the two authorities ought to be distinct. As lawyers and ecclesiastics worked out these ideas in detail, making use of biblical texts, and of the recovered thoughts of ancient Greece, they produced a body of political theory, diversified by disagreements about the respective boundaries of the two powers. At every level, but most of all at the highest level, there were matters which needed adjustment, or something more drastic, between the two systems of authority. In England the archbishops, the bishops, and the greater abbots, besides their spiritual attributes, had rights and duties in the feudal system like those of the lay barons, and equally likely to engender disputes. When a baron died and his heir was a minor the king, as guardian, took charge of the estate and made sure that during the minority the military and other services of the fief were duly rendered. When a bishop died, the king in a similar way received the revenues of the see until a successor was appointed. William Rufus raised a great deal of money by the simple method of leaving the sees and abbeys vacant year after year. Other kings both on the Continent and in England practised this and other much less justifiable methods of extortion; but Rufus went so far that the normally mild and reasonable Anselm stood up to him. There were several points at issue in their quarrel. At that time there was a dispute between two rivals who both claimed the papacy, and this raised the question whether Anselm had the right to choose for himself, without the king's permission, which of the two he should obey in spiritual matters. At the other extreme were purely secular matters: for instance, the king complained that the Canterbury contingent sent to the Welsh war in 1097 was badly trained and equipped. This latter difference led Anselm to leave the country without permission and go to Rome. Three years later Rufus died, with nothing settled, and the new king invited Anselm to return. Henry I began his reign with a charter which granted an indefinite freedom to the church (*sanctam dei ecclesiam . . . liberam facio*) and explicitly promised to end the abuses of Rufus's time. But Anselm came back determined to carry out the full programme of the church reformers and so he brought to a head the dispute round which all the subsidiary disagreements revolved. This dispute, hitherto evaded, is known as the investiture contest.

On the Continent this dispute took a different and stormier course; but in England it was conducted with ability and dignity on both sides. It was a dispute about ceremonies, or rather it was a dispute about the relations of lay and ecclesiastical authority as they were typified in certain ceremonies. Before Anselm's time no one became a bishop or abbot until he had done homage to the king and received his amethyst ring and his pastoral staff from the king's hand. When Anselm returned from exile Henry demanded homage; but Anselm, although he had accorded it to Rufus, refused now on the ground that this custom was against the rules of the church, as indeed it had been since 1075. He went to Rome at the king's instance to negotiate for an agreement, and when this failed he remained abroad with the king's approval. He refused to recognize the bishops whom Henry had invested; the pope excommunicated them and threatened to excommunicate the king; but the pope, Paschal II, was prepared to compromise. In 1107 a reasonable agreement was reached. Kings must not presume to confer spiritual authority on a bishop, but it was their right to invest him with his worldly possessions and authority, receiving homage. And in fact, though this was not committed to writing, the choice of the man who was to become a bishop remained with the king.

At this time the monastic revival was beginning, and it reached its full strength in the turbulent days of Stephen. So did the pretensions of the church in matters of jurisdiction. The separation of the lay and ecclesiastical courts by William I was a rough-and-ready measure, and it needed more definition. In the intellectual activity of the time church law was developing into a rigid and detailed system. The church courts claimed more and more cases as belonging to them. They claimed the exclusive right to judge and punish the clergy. They could not inflict the death penalty and they seldom exercised their right to imprison (prisons cost money), so they were ineffective as well as grasping. For all these reasons King Henry II, a strong upholder of law and order, decided to restrain them. As an obvious step towards this, he chose as archbishop of Canterbury his right-hand man, the chancellor Thomas Becket. Becket was a Londoner born, the son of a Norman merchant settled there. He had risen rapidly in the notably able household of Theobald, who was archbishop from 1139 to 1161. In the first eight years of Henry's reign Becket had been a courtier and minister, and even in ecclesiastical affairs no more of a churchman than was necessary for anyone in official employment. As Theobald's successor he unexpectedly became a champion of ecclesiastical claims and he opposed the king in ordinary business. Henry, provoked by several errors of justice, or worse, in the church courts, claimed the right to punish clerical criminals, after they had been duly tried and degraded by their bishop's court. Becket opposed this, and for a short time carried the bishops with him; but neither they nor the pope were willing to go to all lengths and Becket gave way. Henry, however, put forward a document, the Constitutions of Clarendon, consisting of moderate and reasonable rules on this and related points but, for all that, defining them. The quarrel broke out again. At a council held in Northampton Castle Henry set about his opponent with fines and prosecutions for alleged offences in his personal and ministerial doings. Becket staged a scene in which, wielding his pastoral staff, he denied that the king in council had any right to judge him. That night he fled to the Continent in disguise.

For six years Becket remained abroad doing all he could to press his cause, while the pope and the kings of France and England manœuvred in vain to weaken him. A new and more dangerous quarrel came on when Henry insisted on having his son and heir, the young Henry, crowned by the archbishop of York; but one of those surprising medieval reconciliations followed and the two antagonists met in La Vendée. As soon as he could get the pope's authority Becket renewed the struggle. He crossed to Sandwich and went to Canterbury where he denounced and excommunicated his enemies. Not only they but his former friends were against him for this. This was defiance, and the king, in his fury, uttered words which were enough to set four knights of his household on the way to England. A royal messenger followed to restrain them; but he was sent too late. The four knights murdered the archbishop in his cathedral.

St. Thomas of Canterbury was venerated from that moment, and in foreign countries his martyrdom remained for centuries the best-known event in English history. It was one of those symbolic acts which colour and fortify the convictions of the many. The few who were closely involved had to extricate themselves. The penance of the four knights was fourteen years' service with the Knights Templars in the Holy Land. The king had to provide 200 knights for a year for the defence of Jerusalem and to make a vow, from which the pope excused him, to spend three years on crusade. He had to make the major concession of allowing appeals to Rome. On the dispute about jurisdiction he agreed to an ambiguous formula, which in practice worked out favourably for the royal courts. The immunity of clerical offenders continued, but the judges interpreted it in such ways that it became rather an anomaly than an abuse. Otherwise the royal control over the church went on as before.

The next great struggle between the lay and the ecclesiastical powers formed one of the main threads in the tumultuous reign of King John. In 1205 Hubert Walter, archbishop of Canterbury and chancellor of the realm, having died, two bodies, each of which believed it had the right to do it, elected a successor. One was the bishops of the province, the other the monks of the cathedral priory, who corresponded to the chapter of a cathedral. It was for the pope to decide between them, and the pope, Innocent III, was one of the strongest and most successful of all the assertors of papal rights. He quashed both elections and in his presence a deputation of the monks elected the most eminent living English churchman, Cardinal Stephen Langton. John refused to confirm the appointment and the pope put England under an interdict. This meant in principle that no priest could do his duties. The principle allowed for some exceptions, and its enforcement was no more rigid than that of other medieval laws; but church services, Christian burial, and other rites were practically suspended. John tried hard to negotiate and he put pressure on the church; but the pope excommunicated him, which shook the loyalty of his subjects and made it harder for him to cope with his mounting problems in the north, in Ireland, and in Wales. Finally, after six years of interdict, Innocent threatened to depose him, and at the same time the king of France decided to invade the country. John played his last trump, surrender. He resigned the kingdom of England and the lordship of Ireland (the latter of which was already a papl fief) to Innocent and received them back after rendering fealty and homage and promising a substantial annual tribute, which was sometimes paid until the fourteenth century and not formally repudiated until 1366. This may sound like humiliation; but it only put England in the same feudal subordination as Sicily, Sweden, Denmark, Aragon, and Poland. And if John became the pope's man, he gained the pope as his protector. Innocent not only proved a staunch ally against France; he did not interfere between the Crown and the English church. John issued a charter granting freedom of election to all the ecclesiastical electing bodies.

Consolidation in Britain and Ireland 1066–1216

1092 King William Rufus establishes an Anglo-Scottish frontier between the Tweed and the Solway Firth.
1170 Anglo-Norman rule in Ireland is initiated by Richard Strongbow.
1176 The first recorded Welsh eisteddfod is held at Cardigan.
1193 A new land-tax, with elected assessors, is introduced.
1204 King John surrenders Normandy to the French king.
1215 The barons force King John to sign Magna Carta, which asserts their rights and privileges and confirms the rule of law. John allows London to elect its mayors.

Scotland

England and Scotland faced one another across a region of fells and moors where frontier conditions prevailed, such as thieving, abductions, and blood feuds. Up to a point the frontier problem was the same for each of the two kings. To protect their law-abiding subjects they had to rely on authorities, local lords or royal officers, strong enough to stand above the mêlée and put down the self-appointed protectors who led the forces of disorder. The more powerful the lawful authorities became, the harder they were to control. Beyond this point the problem was not alike for the two kings. For the king of Scotland it was very near home. On the eastern side the border country adjoined the richest part of his dominions, the partly English-speaking Lothian, which had once been part of Northumbria. This was the core of the 'governed' part, roughly the eastern Lowlands, as contrasted with the greater Gaelic-speaking area of mountains and western coasts, where royal authority counted for little. To the west the border country adjoined the Celtic Galloway. Cumbria, which belonged to the king of Scots as far south as the Lake District, had a Celtic-speaking population with Norse, not Anglo-Saxon, settlements well established in the valleys. For the king of England all this was a long way from his principal towns and his most prosperous agriculture.

For both kings the crux of the frontier-problem was their own personal relation, friendly or hostile. If they were at peace their efforts to control the borderers were mutually supplementary; but if they were at war each of them could offer shelter to the other's enemies and fugitives. The king of Scots might lead a destructive raid at very short notice. The king of England commanded more men and ships and money; he could move an army and something of a fleet; but this took time. He might well be distracted by some crisis in Normandy or Wales. An earl of Northumberland or Lancaster, once he became strong, might prove a feudal rebel. There was the further complication that the king of Scotland was not a mere foreign neighbour, but involved in feudal and dynastic relationships with England. After the failure of resistance to the Conqueror in the north of England, Edgar the atheling took refuge with Malcolm Canmore, who had become king when he defeated Macbeth. Malcolm married the atheling's sister Margaret and took up her cause. In 1073 William came with sea and land forces and Malcolm, not venturing to fight, met him at Abernethy on the southern shore of the Firth of Tay. There Malcolm did homage. It seems to have been at the same time that he was granted some estates in England. William on his way home built a castle for the bishop of Durham. A few years later there were similar movements. Malcolm had been raiding as far south as the Tyne and William sent his son Robert, who pushed as far as Falkirk, received Malcolm's homage again, and founded or restored another castle, at Newcastle on Tyne. When William Rufus became king he gave Malcolm a new pretext by depriving the atheling of his estates in

Pembroke Castle, one of the big Norman castles in Wales. A massive round keep is its most notable feature. In the 12th century round keeps began to replace square ones; the latter provided too uneven a field of fire, encouraging besiegers to concentrate on the weak points. In 1457, in one of the towers adjoining the gatehouse, the future King Henry VII was born to his widowed 13-year old mother.

Normandy. Malcolm penetrated as far as Chester-le-Street, and Rufus's first attempt at a punitive expedition was not a success; but a second, in 1092, made a lasting change. Rufus captured and fortified Carlisle, so that the frontier now ran from the Solway Firth to the Tweed. At the outset of his fifth invasion of England Malcolm was murdered.

In spite of all the hostilities his reign, partly through his wife's influence, saw a rise in the standard of comfort at the Scottish court and the beginning of reforms which brought the church into line with the general western practices. After Malcolm's death there was a short interval of reaction and disorder; but early in the twelfth century the English language became the common speech of the people of the south of Scotland. Lothian and Cumbria were progressively anglicized. David I, who reigned from 1124 to 1153, had lived long in England and had inherited the earldom of Huntingdon in the right of his wife, the daughter of Waltheof. In his time Scottish, English and Norman-French lordships were being integrated in a single aristocratic society. King David and his successors had Norman, Flemish, and English vassals, and by the middle of the thirteenth century most of the Scottish magnates held lands in England.

Unfortunately for everyone David inherited a claim to the earldom of Northumbria and this feudal stimulus led him to plunge into the civil war of Stephen's reign. Like his father Malcolm he bought off the revenge of the English king by doing homage but also renewed his invasion. It was more devastating and it was carried further south than any of Malcolm's; but, when Stephen could not face it, and the Scots were deep in Lancashire and had crossed the Tees, it aroused a new sort of resistance, something like a crusade. Even after the Battle of the Standard, near Northallerton, in 1138, Stephen had to grant favourable terms. They were both in the field again after that; but David, for the rest of his reign, developed Scotland and consolidated it on the lines of Norman or Anglo-Norman land-tenure, ranks, and justice. Church reform and the foundation of monasteries went forward.

David, as an English feudatory, held a fief round Wark in Northumberland besides Carlisle, and, for a time, the whole honour (large estate) of Lancaster. After his death, however, King Henry II of England easily took the northern counties back in exchange for the harmless earldom of Huntingdon. But, except for the claim to Northumberland, all the old elements of warfare were still there. In 1173–4 William the Lion joined the rebellion of the Young Henry. His ragged army was plundering in the west when he took Norman knights and Flemish mercenaries to attack Alnwick. He was taken prisoner and the rebellion collapsed. The price of his release was homage for Scotland as well as for his English lands. He did not behave as an obedient vassal, and his chance came when Richard I, before setting out on his crusade, placated everyone who might have taken a mean advantage of his absence. The two kings met at Canterbury and the Scots, at the price of 10,000 marks, recovered all that they had lost in status, besides the castles of Berwick and Roxburgh. For the rest of Richard's reign relations were cordial, and the influence of English law continued.

When King John succeeded, William the Lion grasped another opportunity, and there were years of trouble, which boiled up into warlike preparations in 1209. But when John appeared before Norham on the Tweed, once more there was no battle. William had to pay 15,000 marks and gained nothing except that the English castle at Tweedmouth, facing Berwick, was destroyed. For some years he depended on England for his own security, but he still waited for an opportunity. When John was at odds with the barons William raided across the border, only to provoke a savage counter-raid. He tried again in vain and had to surrender Carlisle after holding it for a few months. For twenty years or so the English and Scottish courts were friendly, to the advantage of both; but, apparently for no urgent reason, the Scottish claim was mentioned again. This time there was no conflict, and in 1237 it was finally abandoned in exchange for lands in England. Thus the two kingdoms accepted the frontier which William Rufus had established in 1092, and it lasted, in spite of many wars, until the crowns were united in 1603.

Wales

Wales had not much more than a quarter of the area of Scotland, but its frontier with England was half as long again. This frontier was also more accessible than that of Scotland; there were the rivers Dee, Severn and Wye, and most of the frontier passed by the cultivated lands of the English Midlands. There were three ancient divisions, Gwynedd in the north, Deheubarth in the south, and Powys between them. For long periods a king of one of these was recognized as supreme, and thereby supervised what was virtually a federation of the three big kingdoms. Each kingdom was itself a federation of several territorial units; such a division was inevitable because it was the Welsh custom for all sons, including royal sons, to inherit an equal share of their father's estate. But marriage alliances between princes for the most part kept Wales united. Welsh law, which had been codified in the tenth century by Prince Hywel Dda, recognized no blood privileges for nobles, but discriminated strongly against residents who were not Welsh. The distinct form of Welsh society, with its emphasis on kinship and community, persisted after the Norman conquest. Wales's mountainous interior was perfect guerilla country. English kings could march around the valleys without ever getting to grips with the people. The language frontier seems all through the Middle Ages to have gradually receded from the Severn Valley into the mountains, as the links of the farmers with English neighbours and English traders turned their interest to the east.

As in England, William the Conqueror's method of subjugation was to let his enterprising Normans have their heads. In Chester, Shrewsbury, and Hereford he set up three earls over against the old kingdoms and under these were dozens of marcher lords, each with his castle, to control as much country as he could manage. In a good many places towns were founded and chartered beside the castles, where craftsmen and traders could settle in safety. Most of the lowlands were easily occupied and, after some checks, in 1094 it seemed as if even Snowdonia had been conquered. In that year, however, the Welsh of Gwynedd and Powys drove the Normans back. In two campaigns William Rufus failed to restore the position. The earls of Chester and Shrewsbury, with the added obstacle of a chance intervention by the king of Norway's fleet, failed again. In 1114 King Henry I and King Alexander I of Scotland made a three-pronged attack, which resulted, without a battle, in homage and a money fine; but from then until the time of Edward I, Snowdonia was not seriously disturbed by the English.

Further south the progress of the Normans was entangled in the feudal ambitions of the great lords. In the Conqueror's time

the earl of Hereford joined the rebellion of 1075, and under Henry I the earl of Shrewsbury's ambitions cost him his earldom; but, although each of these great positions was left vacant for years, lesser men were able to profit from the endless feuds and rivalries of the Welsh princes. The revolt of 1096 had some effects in central and southern Wales, but they were less permanent than in the north. By the end of Henry I's reign the Anglo-Norman power was firmly established in Gwent, Glamorgan, and Brecknock. Pembrokeshire, where Pembroke Castle had held out when everything else was overrun, was also organized, like Glamorgan, as an English county, with a sheriff, who rendered his accounts to the English exchequer. It had a special source of strength: about 1108 a body of Flemings, farmers, sheep-breeders, and traders, settled there and anglicized many of its ways and even many of the place-names. This 'little England beyond Wales' sometimes needed support from the sea, for it was cut off on the east by a strip of Welsh territory roughly corresponding to the later counties of Cardigan and Carmarthen. The Normans had edged their way into Kidwelly and the Gower. In 1136, at the beginning of Stephen's reign, and before his troubles in England began, there was a spontaneous rising in Wales. It began with a battle near Swansea in which some 500 Anglo-Norman colonists were killed. By the end of Stephen's reign two leaders, Owain Gwynedd and Rhys ap Gruffyd, had liberated all South Wales except Pembrokeshire, and in the north Owain was threatening Chester from the captured castles of Mold and Rhuddlan. It was not until 1157 that Henry II was able to lead a well-equipped army and fleet from Chester. He had losses both of troops and seamen, and had to be content when Rhys did homage, gave hostages, and withdrew beyond Rhuddlan. Against the south he sent out an even stronger army, with Flemish mercenaries and a fleet hired from the Danes of Dublin. No battle was fought, but Henry could not supply his troops across the bogs and mountains. He retreated ignominiously. The two princes went on with their work. Rhuddlan fell again to Owain. Rhys, who captured the isolated castle of Cardigan, dominated all Wales from the death of Owain almost until the end of the century. He became the trusted ally of Henry II, and for a generation the English, not unsuccessfully, co-operated with him and his people.

It is pleasant to remember that at Cardigan in 1176 the Lord Rhys promoted the first recorded eisteddfod. There was a contest between bards and a contest between poets, the winning bard came from Gwynedd, and the winning poet from the south. But the culture over which the Welsh princes and chieftains presided was not shut off from the outer world. The ecclesiastical revival knew no boundaries of race and language. English and Norman monasteries were endowed with cells in Wales, and great Cistercian abbeys, such as Whitland, were founded in the valleys. After long but quite dignified disputes, the Welsh gave up the claim of St. David's to be an independent archbishopric: from 1198 until the early twentieth century it acknowledged the supremacy of Canterbury. Among the contestants in these disputes the best-remembered is the brilliant Latin writer, historian, and observer of the contemporary world, Gerald of Wales. He was born in Pembrokeshire of royal descent and made his mark in Paris, Rome, and Ireland as well as in England. Another Welshman, Geoffrey of Monmouth, made a gift to the literature of the whole western world which can still be traced today. He was probably of Breton parentage; he was closely connected with Oxford learning before the university emerged; but he was brought up in South Wales, and towards the end of his life was consecrated bishop of Llandaff where also he had lived and taught. He wrote the history of the Britons, and, if his lavish admixture of myth misled and puzzled subsequent historians for centuries, he was the main transmitter of the Arthurian legend. This became one of the cycles of romance, one of the stocks from which the poetry and prose of chivalry and courtly love flowered in many languages.

Strife began again when the newly-crowned Richard I personally slighted the Lord Rhys by refusing to meet him. Both Wales and the border were fought over, in spite of which John, both before and after his accession, recruited a steady supply of Welsh mercenaries for service in England. From this confusion Llywelyn ap Iorwerth, grandson of Owain Gwynedd, emerged as the master of the north. In return for his homage John accorded him friendship and even indulgence of his local proceedings; Llywelyn in his turn led a contingent of Welshmen in the war against William the Lion of Scotland in 1209. In 1210 there was a rupture. John concentrated an army, largely Welsh, at Chester, advanced into the mountains, met no enemy and retreated. He advanced again from Oswestry, and scored a momentary triumph. One of his barons built a castle at Aberystwyth, which raised the chieftains against John at the moment when he was in danger from his English barons. Llywelyn and his allies fought their way forward, and, with statesmanship that was rare in the thirteenth century, Llywelyn kept Wales together by subordinating his own interests to the common cause. When he died in 1240 as a liegeman of King Henry III, only the district around Pembroke remained under the authority of the English Crown.

Ireland

The Norman lords of this district around Pembroke had done far more than hold this last bridgehead. The Lord Rhys found the road to power easier, and King John's attempts at reconquest were hindered, because these Pembrokeshire lords, with truly Norman energy, had embarked on a conquest which even the Romans had never undertaken. Ireland had not attracted the attention of either of the two comparatively stable monarchies which, in spite of many set-backs, were pressing against the old Celtic civilization of Britain. The kings of England were ceaselessly occupied elsewhere. For the kings of Scotland the distance was less, and there was little difference between their immediate neighbours in the west and the related people of Ulster, but the kings of Scotland never relinquished their ambitions for conquering English territory to the south. Since the beginning of the twelfth century, when the Norsemen conquered the western Isles, Norse sea-based power was interposed between the two large islands; but it never intruded on the Irish mainland. The last of Scandinavian power there had been scattered at the Battle of Clontarf in 1014, the last fight of Brian Boru. A century later the Danish settlements on the estuaries, Dublin, Wexford, Cork, and Limerick, were quiet and not very prosperous trading-posts. There was little trade by sea, only some exporting of hides and other cattle products to England and some importing of luxuries. Inland there was endemic warfare between kings, and irrepressible fighting between their subjects.

King Henry II of England inherited more possessions than he could manage, but he wanted still more. Early in his reign he sent

A surgeon extracting an arrow. This is part of a manuscript, dating from about the end of the 12th century, which is preserved at Cambridge. Other parts of this manuscript indicate that surgeons also acted as pharmacists, stocking and manufacturing a range of herbal medicines.

John of Salisbury to Rome. There the church in Ireland was known to be largely isolated from the recent reforming influences, and to have degenerated from the good order and high civilization of its missionary era. For this reason the pope, Adrian IV, the one English pope of all time, granted a document called the Bull Laudabiliter. This authorized Henry to conquer Ireland, and at the same time he was virtually invested with this new lordship. He was, however, dissuaded from taking any action at that time. In 1166 he was asked to intervene in an Irish quarrel. Dermot, the refugee king of Leinster, a bad man deservedly expelled from his kingdom by the high king of Ireland, sought out King Henry and swore fealty to him. Henry, deep in the Becket contest, could not act; but he gave leave to any of his barons to aid Dermot to recover his kingdom. In 1169 a small mixed force of knights and light-armed Welsh troops crossed from Pembroke. In spite of quarrels among themselves they won Leinster back for Dermot as under-king. Reinforcements landed, followed in 1170 by a considerable force under an able commander, Richard, earl of Pembroke, called Strongbow. Strongbow captured Waterford and Dublin. His reward for coming had been the hand of Dermot's daughter, and when Dermot died in the following year Strongbow became titular king of the fair land of Leinster. This was too good to be true. The Irish did not like it. Nor did King Henry, who had been jealous of the adventurers all along, and now ordered them to return to England. Strongbow refused politely, stood a siege in Dublin, won a battle and slipped over to England to meet Henry, who had meanwhile raised a large army and assembled 400 ships in Milford Haven. He had to agree to give up Dublin, Wexford, Waterford and all the fortresses to the king, but the rest of Leinster became his fief, thereby making him lord of Ireland's best farmland in return for the obligation to provide one hundred knights for the king's service. When Henry took his impressive army to Ireland all the kings except those of remote Connaught, Tyrone, and Tyrconnel acknowledged him as their overlord. A papal legate presided over a council at Cashel which brought the church more into line with the Roman principles. This settlement could not last. There were new outbreaks of fighting. The barons made trouble. Anglo-Norman immigrants who adopted Irish wives and customs formed a new element, the Anglo-Irish, which for centuries would complicate the Irish problem. In 1177 Henry made his young son John lord of Ireland. John's rule was at first disastrous, but after he became king the colonization was

Milk and butter in the 12th century. Cows, goats, and sheep provided milk, which was stored in the form of butter and cheese. Because root crops for winter feed were not grown, most livestock was slaughtered in the autumn. Compared to modern breeds, the sheep, pigs, and cows were small and wiry.

consolidated and was extended westwards. He favoured the Irish princes at the expense of the English barons in Ireland, thereby strengthening his own position. A new castle in the emerging capital of Dublin was the centre from which two thirds of Ireland was ruled in relative peace and justice.

Economic Growth in England

Notwithstanding the incessant fighting the twelfth century was a period of advancing economic development. In some directions warfare itself promoted development. Smiths had to deliver large quantities of horseshoes at fixed times and places; there was work from armourers, bowyers and fletchers (arrow-makers), and many others. It is impossible to guess whether this activity furthered or hindered the general prosperity of the country; but there seems no doubt that industries grew. One indication of this is the rise of the towns. Many of them received charters which gave considerable instalments of self-government. They had their own courts, their own officers, their own control of police and defence. There were many variations: some had privileges copied from those of English or Norman towns which were taken as models, in others the arrangements were home-grown. The core of it all was the market, a regular centre for supervised trading, and a special kind of market was the fair, held at longer intervals, often only once a year, for special kinds of goods or goods from wider areas. In many towns the embryonic local authority was the market guild, an association of those who had the right to sell in the market. These were not all town dwellers: neighbouring landowners might be the most influential sellers and sometimes took their places in such guilds. The rise of the towns depended on the productiveness of the countryside, and in some places new rural resources were opened up. Some landowners, both noblemen and religious houses, were rich in sheep. Newcomers, especially the Cistercians, greatly extended the sheep-walks in the hillier country. There was probably no corresponding increase of the land under crops; but in some places such as Romney Marsh fresh ground was won by drainage.

One strange innovation of the time may appear to have set agriculture back. This was the forest law. William the Conqueror introduced this law, unknown in Anglo-Saxon England, to protect his hunting. In any part of the country declared to be forest there were savage penalties for poaching or damaging the woods. The protected game included not only deer, but other creatures down to hares and partridges. William mapped-out his New Forest. Under his successors the area of forest steadily grew to a maximum in Henry II's time, when it was not far short of a third of the whole kingdom, and a man might travel from the Solent to the Wash and not be out of the forest for more than twenty or thirty miles. After that it diminished as one king after another gave or sold his forest rights to the landowners; but, as we shall see, the forest law was not finally abolished until the reign of Charles II. All this does not mean that a vast area was kept out of cultivation. Even in the New Forest it is hard to say how many human settlements were displaced to increase the waste; perhaps about twenty villages and twelve hamlets. When the entire county of Essex was in the forest that did not mean that it was entirely given over to the greenwood tree and the king's hunting lodges: there were villages and towns. The woods themselves, largely on poor land, were managed; they produced timber for ships and houses, or copsewood for humbler uses. The forest courts and the forest officers were not mere instruments of tyranny; they watched over production.

The best-attested and no doubt the most important instance of economic growth is that of London. We know it from the increasing independence and complexity of the municipal constitution. Henry I relieved the citizens from various taxes and tolls throughout the realm, gave them the right to appoint their own sheriff and to try various cases previously reserved for his own courts. They did not retain these rights without interruption; the examples of revolutionary municipalities on the Continent were enough to make the kings suspicious of their towns; but in the ups and downs of public affairs the kings needed money and the Londoners could often bargain with it. Twice, in 1191 and 1194, they asserted themselves with almost revolutionary vigour. In 1215 King John gave them the right to elect a mayor annually, which they have done ever since. It is not only from these events

that we can infer that London was becoming richer and more powerful. It was becoming a capital city. Government depended more and more on officials who were tied to their papers and their staffs of subordinates. They and the lawyers and law-courts settled in Westminster, which was now continuous with the original London, so that the seat of government was at the greatest seaport. There is a record of the duties paid on imports and exports in each of the ports on the east and south coasts in 1203–4. From this it appears that London accounted for nearly an eighth of the total. Four other ports have figures which are lower, but within the same order of magnitude, namely Lincoln, Boston, King's Lynn, and Southampton. The ports of the Humber taken together also come within this limit; but those of Sussex, Kent, and the north-west are far below it. We know that the imports were various: not only wine from France and Germany, costly articles of luxury, fine cloth from the Low Countries, but timber from Scandinavia.

But medieval trade was on a very small scale indeed. Three things which were to contribute to its later growth were active in limited spheres. Of the first, improvement in technology, there were as yet few signs. The first rude windmills appeared, welcome for grinding corn where there was no stream adequate to turn a water mill. There was some progress in inland transport: the comparatively large trade of Lincoln has been explained as due to the reconditioning of the old Roman drainage channel, the Fosse Dyke, as a link between the Trent and the Humber. The third factor, business organization, is best represented by the coming of the Jews. Their first settlement in England was in London during the reign of William the Conqueror, and they enjoyed the special protection of the king. As elsewhere in Europe they formed a separate community, with their own street or quarter in the City, preserving their own religion and customs. They had widely ramifying international connections among themselves, and they were, as we have seen in the matters of translations from Arabic, valuable intermediaries in the circulation of knowledge and ideas. They undertook many kinds of business, and they specialized in finance. To the kings this meant that the Jews could provide loans and that their wealth, being in the form of money, could easily be tapped by taxation. Their numbers increased and there came to be Jewries in six or seven of the larger provincial towns. How high they had risen is shown by the career of Aaron of Lincoln, who died in 1185. Among his clients, who spread over twenty-five counties, were the king of Scotland and the archbishop of Canterbury. He helped to finance the building of Lincoln Cathedral and of at least eleven of the great monasteries. The position of the Jews was, however, precarious. They charged very high rates of interest: $43\frac{1}{2}$ per cent was the legal maximum in 1233. These rates were not disproportionate to the risks of lending money in an unbusinesslike and undisciplined society; but that did not reconcile the borrowers to paying what they had promised. About the middle of the twelfth century a new and horrible phenomenon arose in England, as it did abroad. Anti-Semitism acquired a mythology, with untrue stories of boy-martyrs, victims of Jewish ritual murders. The Crusades had made men used to avenging slaughtered saints. On the day of the coronation of Richard I, although the king tried to stop it, there was a pogrom in London. One after another towns from Norwich to York massacred their Jews. The communities survived until in 1290 they were expelled by an act of royal prerogative from a country which no longer needed their services; but from the time of the massacres their history was one of decline. The kings extorted money for charters which had little value; the barons were equally hostile. In Magna Carta there are two clauses each of which prohibits malpractices by creditors, both of which are so worded as to imply that it is first and foremost against the Jews that debtors needed to be protected.

English Law and the Constitution

On the whole the twelfth century was a time of economic progress, largely because society was still loosely-knit. Local and functional interests could cooperate while remaining free from excessive control and interference. Up to a point this also explains the facts that this was a period of progress in the law and that in it some fundamentals of the constitution were established. There were many courts, royal, feudal, municipal, ecclesiastical, and what not. The judges, litigants, and advocates, however pertinaciously they quarrelled, all had an interest in reducing their proceedings to predictable and intelligible regularity. And in the matter of law the king had a more direct and visible interest than he had in economic progress. Two kings of the period, Henry I and Henry II, especially the latter, have a good name as legislators; but even the much-abused King John took a personal part, and it seems not an unenlightened part, in judicial work. More, however, was needed than the king's will. He directed an organization which, as it grew more complex, helped to create the principles of its own progress.

By the end of Henry II's reign the Crown had become simply hereditary: the coronation of the young Henry during his father's lifetime showed that this could not be reckoned on as a matter of course, but there was never afterwards any semblance of election. The king's great council still dealt with all manner of business and there was still no formal list of its members; but it had given rise to various special courts. From 1107 officers of the king's court went down from time to time to the shire courts to deal with all judicial and financial matters that concerned the king. By stages their duties were defined until the country was divided into six circuits round which judges travelled, as they do now, to hear cases brought before them by twelve senior thanes in each assize-town, the predecessors of the grand jury. Local government soon developed new organs. In 1193 a new carucage, or land-tax, was imposed and the juries which assessed it were chosen by the coroner and four knights in each shire, a regular form of election. Individual knights received commissions to

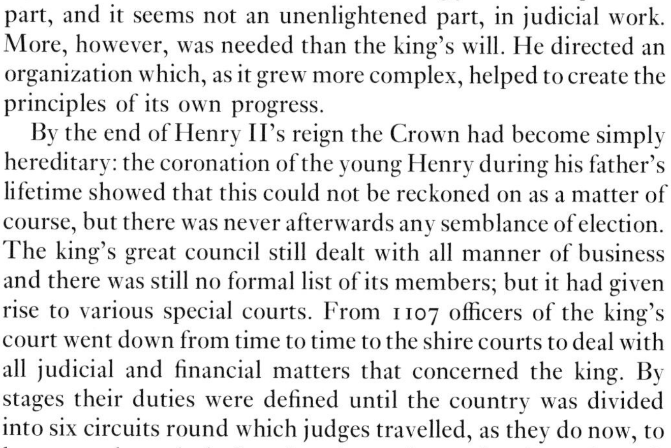

Weaving in the 12th century. In medieval times households were largely self-sufficient, with their womenfolk entrusted with the production of blankets and cloth from local wool. But commercial clothmaking developed in the towns quite early; town weavers had organized themselves into guilds by the 12th century.

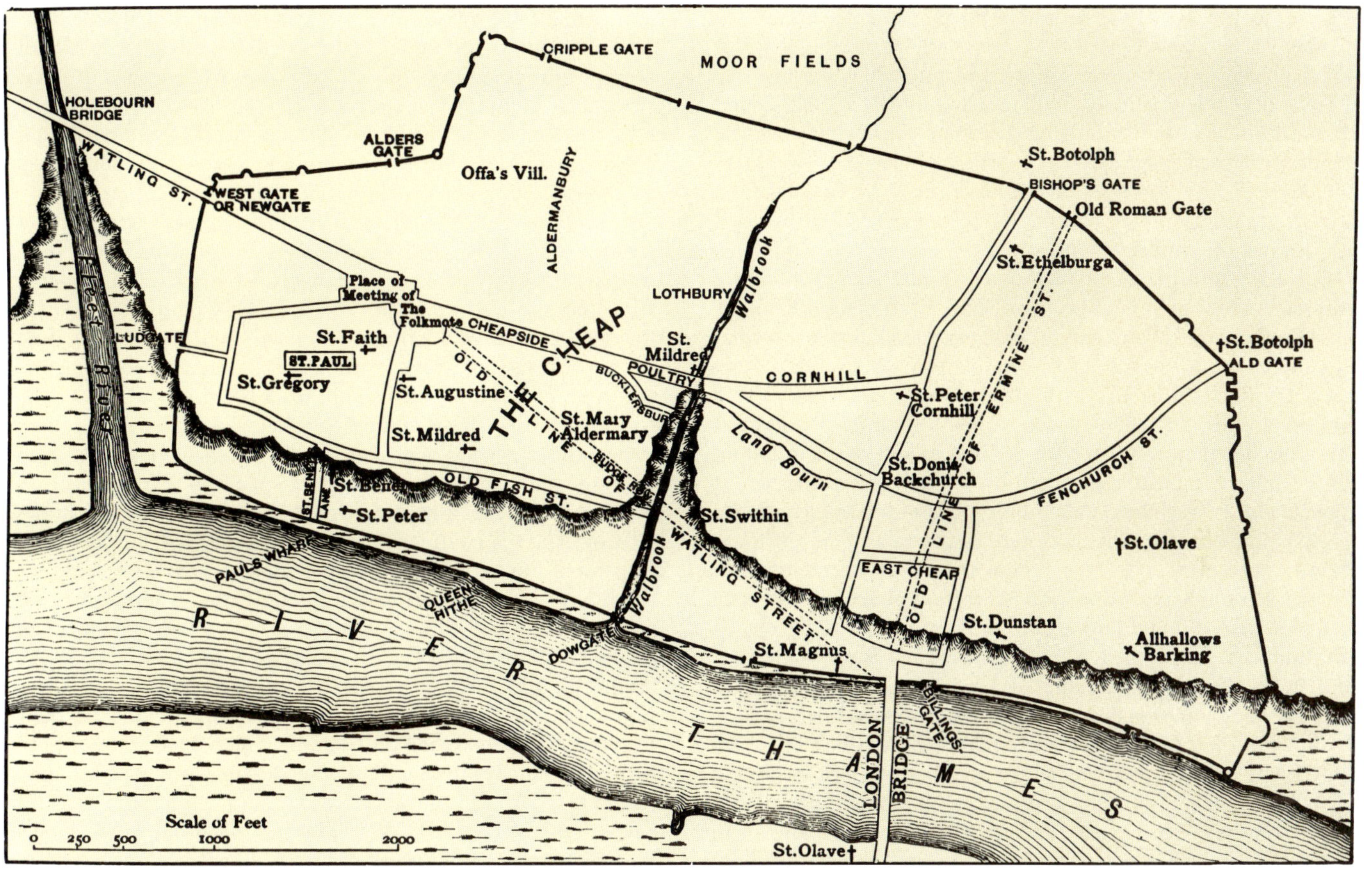

The City of London in the 12th century. At this period it was enclosed in a defensive wall, with seven gates. Beyond the walls to the north were meadows and pastures. To the west were suburban dwellings and, two miles away, the king's palace. A contemporary described London's sole drawbacks as 'immoderate Drinking of idle Fellows, and often Fires'.

hold courts and take police action as officers of the king, the small beginning of the system of justices of the peace. At the centre judges were appointed to sit as the king's court, and this developed into three more or less specialized branches which remained in existence until the year 1873. First was the court of king's bench, the royal court for trying criminal cases and all others that concerned the king's peace, second the court of common pleas, which at first travelled with the king and dealt with cases between individuals and corrected mistakes of lower courts, and third the court of exchequer for business relating to taxation and other branches of finance.

These distinctions were of no interest except to the lawyers and their clients; but lawsuits were an important element in the business affairs of most of the wealthy and many of the rest. Quarrels or uncertainties about the respective powers and functions of the courts affected many people's interests. The Normans introduced trial by combat, a kind of formalized duel, and in certain eventualities it was used for centuries to come. The Anglo-Saxon trial by ordeal, which rested on a basis of superstition, was forbidden by the great pope Innocent III in the fourth Lateran Council of 1215. This cleared the way for an advance of the jury system. Bodies resembling juries had existed for a long time, but, as in many primitive countries, to begin with they spoke for what was common knowledge about a person or about an event, and it was only gradually that they were expected to hear evidence impartially or to confine themselves to matters of fact as distinguished from law. These changes were still incomplete in the seventeenth century; but the first steps towards them date from the twelfth.

The changes in the structure and procedure of the courts went along with changes in the law that they administered, especially in the law relating to the land, which, in feudal times, was the basis of most social relations. The legislation of Henry II laid down definite rules where there had been vagueness and uncertainty as to what constituted a right to own or occupy land and what were the obligations of each superior and inferior in the feudal ladder of tenure. This legislation was influenced by ideas from various sources, including Roman law. It was a manifestation of the intellectual movement of the time, and towards the end of Henry II's reign two famous practical books were written in Latin which surveyed the law and much of the constitution. One was the Dialogue on the Exchequer, a detailed guide to the work of that department; the other was a book called 'Glanvill' on the royal court. They show that this law, largely home-grown and insular, was doing much to regularize English life; but they also show that innumerable people must have been offended, if not positively injured, by the reforms, to say nothing of illegalities and abuses.

The Crisis of King John's Reign

From this state of affairs there arose a crisis of a new kind, which decided questions for the future. To explain it we must go back for a moment to the events following the loss of Normandy in 1204. This loss made a permanent change in the international position of England. From being one part of a combination of territories with a sea-channel between them it was turned into an island with associated lands in western France, but facing a hostile coast. From the time of the Conquest there had been no need for a navy. The suppression of piracy was entrusted to the Cinque Ports, which earned their privileges by providing ships. These privileges were now extended, but much more was needed. A royal fleet was organized and stationed in fifteen British and Irish ports. In 1205 it numbered fifty-one oared galleys, and a regular system of supply and dockyards supported it. Round this nucleus a larger force could be built up by requisitioning merchant ships, and the manning of fleets was ensured by good pay and also by impressment.

But King John did not intend to withdraw to a defensive posture. As soon as he could extricate himself from his difficulties with Scotland and Wales and prepare to end the pope's interdict by submission, his first concern was the war with France. There was a prospect of a French invasion, and the English fleet, based on Portsmouth, carried out successful raids on French ports and shipping. The count of Flanders refused to join in the invasion; King Philip Augustus invaded his county, and the count appealed for English help. A combined fleet of 500 ships with 700 English and Flemish knights rowed up the narrow waterway to Damme, the port of Bruges. There the French fleet, lying at anchor, was totally destroyed. The naval part of the war had gone well; but it was not followed up, and many of the barons in England were dissatisfied. King John had the nature of a tyrant, and, in his efforts to raise money and crush opposition, he gave it rein. Stephen Langton did what he could to reconcile the parties. He did not bring new ideas to bear on the dispute. The intellectual movement had given rise to the first systematic political thought of the Middle Ages, in acutely argued treatises on the nature of monarchy, royal and papal, and such thinking was known in England. The archbishop represented the intellectual movement not in the sense that he brought such thought to bear on practical politics, but in standing for regularly formulated principles of justice, for that aspect of the intellectual movement which was embodied in the legal and administrative institutions of Henry II. He announced his position two months after the Battle of Damme to an assembly at St. Paul's Cathedral, when he read aloud and commended the charter of liberties granted by King Henry I. Thus he virtually provided the outline of a programme for opposition. The barons were familiar with the justifications for feudal rebellion which were current both at home and abroad. In England feudal law had never admitted, as it did in many parts of the Continent, that, in some eventualities, the barons had a right to make war on the king; but everyone knew that rebellions had often ended in a king's giving way to the rebels. The idea of an opposition programme was itself not altogether new: in 1201, for instance, a number of earls made a collective demand for the restoration of certain rights which had been transferred from them to the sheriffs. The movement of 1213 was novel because its aims were comprehensive and coherently put together.

When Langton the mediator made his announcement the king was still dangerous to all his enemies. For the following year, 1214, he brought into an alliance against France the emperor Otto, and the leading rulers of the Low Countries, those of Brabant, Limburg, Flanders, Holland, and Boulogne. The fighting began badly. John, with his base at La Rochelle, opened what was meant to be a diversion from the south-west; but the barons of Poitou deserted and the diversion failed. The allied army in the north was then shattered by Philip at Bouvines, with the commander of the English contingent clubbed from his horse by a French bishop. This Battle of Bouvines ended John's hopes of recovering his continental possessions and left him defeated and ruined, no match for his opposition at home.

It took nearly a year before the contest with the barons reached the point when both sides accepted the famous agreement called Magna Carta, the great charter. John tried and failed to buy the support of the Church by making separate concessions in a charter granted to it. The barons armed and renounced their allegiance. They marched on London, which opened its gates to them. In the meadow at Runnymede they presented a long statement of all their grievances, and this was the basis of a week's bargaining which ended, after some modifications in the king's favour, with the sealing of the charter. This was not the end of civil strife, nor even of the amazing personal vicissitudes of John. There were still barons under arms, and John appealed to his suzerain the pope against them. Innocent III responded by quashing the charter, and his representatives suspended Langton. The barons in their turn appealed to the king of France. John captured Rochester after a siege and subdued resistance everywhere except around London. The ships of twenty-one ports were concentrated at the mouth of the Thames to meet a French invasion, but a storm dispersed them. Louis, the French king's son and heir, landed at Thanet and joined the barons in London. From June 1216 there was widespread civil war, with John leading his forces on swift cross-country campaigns. By

An incident in the Battle of Bouvines; the king of France is unhorsed, but rescued. Chain mail was still favoured, but was soon to be supplemented and then replaced by plates. Chain mail was flexible but could not prevent bruises and broken bones. Moreover, a hard blow could drive the links into the body, causing a septic and perhaps fatal wound.

The royal seal of King John, as affixed to the Magna Carta.

October his fatigue had developed into dysentery, but he carried on. A freak tide carried away for ever his baggage train in the Wash. On October 18, still attending to royal business on his sickbed, he died. Magna Carta survived.

For the times it was a long document: with more than sixty clauses. Originally, probably, its unofficial Latin name only meant the big charter, in comparison with other charters before and after it which were much shorter. Most of the clauses deal with specific grievances. A few of them are temporary, such as the promises to release Welsh hostages and to send out of the country all foreign mercenaries; but the rest are intended as permanent rules. Some confirm or amplify the privileges of particular bodies of subjects, notably the church and the citizens of London. Most deal with the grievances of the barons in their capacity as tenants-in-chief. They almost amount to a list of all the different payments and services which were due to the king, with detailed undertakings on his part that he and his officers would not stretch his rights to cover cases which they did not cover in law or established custom. Except for a little more in some clauses and a little less in others, the king promised to restore the government by law as Henry II had left it. For the most part it was the barons who stood to benefit, and to that extent their policy was selfish; but there were some clauses which protected sub-tenants against the tenants-in-chief. There was nothing to upset the generally accepted principle that in feudal matters the king did not interfere between a lord and his man; but there were some general expressions repudiating arbitrary government and these were understood in later times to grant a basic freedom to all men except slaves. They are still household words: 'No free man shall be arrested or imprisoned or dispossessed or outlawed or banished or in any wise ruined . . . save by the lawful judgement of his peers or by the law of the land'; 'To none will we sell, or deny, or delay right or justice.'

It must be admitted that these clauses, and some others which are impracticable, could not well be enforced by courts of law: they have been described as platitudes of good government. But the charter was meant to affect the constitution as well as the courts and the administrative officers. It asserts in a rudimentary form the principle that was afterwards expressed in the battle-cry 'No taxation without representation'. The king may impose taxes of reasonable amounts on his tenants-in-chief or on the City of London for three recognized occasions, to ransom him from captivity, to provide for the knighting and marriage of his eldest son; but all others are to be laid 'by the common council of our realm'. Rules are laid down for the summoning and membership of this common council of tenants-in-chief, baronial and other. This vaguely foreshadows the approach of a national assembly more articulated than the previous royal court, if narrower than the parliaments which did ultimately arise to authorize taxation and much else; but the barons relied on a very different constitutional device to ensure that King John carried out his promises. They were to elect twenty-five of their own number, and any four of these twenty-five were to have the right to ask the king to remedy any abuse that they detected. If he did not comply within forty days, it was to be lawful for them to make war on him. The 'twenty-five kings' were to decide on action by a majority, and they themselves were to fill any vacancies that occurred in their number. There were similar provisions in other countries, but they had the effect of legalizing anarchy. The twenty-five were elected, and, as we have seen, anarchy ensued.

Magna Carta survived because at times of conflict and negotiation it was useful to have a comprehensive statement of the issues, and all the ground was covered in the document which John had granted and Innocent annulled. So in 1216, 1217, and 1225 it was reissued, and each new edition was amended to suit the changes of circumstance. What remained was an indispensable working document for lawyers and officials, but it was more than that. Its history and some of its phrases made it a rallying-point for those who suspected kings of placing themselves above the law, and as late as 1297 its confirmation was a major event. After that, for a long time, it was taken for granted and seldom studied; but when the Stuart kings fell out with their subjects it was brought forward as a sacred text, and reverenced, as it still is today by thousands who have never read it.

The Growth of Community 1216–1307

1258 Provisions of Oxford are exacted from King Henry III, establishing a body to examine grievances and providing for the summoning of the Oxford parliament.
1264 Simon de Montfort defeats royalists at the Battle of Lewes.
1265 The defeat and death of Simon de Montfort at the Battle of Evesham.
1284 King Edward I completes the conquest of Wales.
1290 The Jews are expelled from England. Edward begins his campaign to subjugate Scotland.
1290 Calling of the 'Model Parliament', a stage in the development of representative assemblies.
1301 King Edward's heir is invested as Prince of Wales at Caernarvon Castle.
1306 Robert Bruce is crowned as king of Scotland.

From about the middle of the tenth century until some years after the beginning of the fourteenth the population of western and central Europe increased. The increase was not spread uniformly over the map; it was not steady and regular; but it was general. The demand for food, clothing, buildings, and services increased. To satisfy it economic life was more highly organized. The functions of various kinds of producers and traders became more specialized. When the increase slowed down and stopped England probably had about 3½ million inhabitants. Very few of them manufactured anything for export; but the wool-export had grown, and had come to occupy an important place in the new map of European commerce. Across the North Sea, in Flanders and Brabant, there was now a textile industry with wide markets. English wool merchants had to deliver to it the necessary number of sacks by known routes to safe destinations at fixed times. This led to changes in the management of sheep walks and markets at home. For this and other reasons English agriculture underwent many changes. There was a brisk trade in buying and selling land. There were manuscript handbooks of estate management, and they appeared here earlier than anywhere else in Europe. More business came to be dealt with by contracts for money-payments. In various matters of detail, such as the hiring of soldiers and the government taxation of the wool-trade, we shall see that some of these tendencies extended beyond the economic into the political sphere and, indeed, affected all contemporary life.

The period of French dominance, established at the Battle of Bouvines in 1214 and ended by the Battle of Crécy in 1346, corresponds roughly with the reign of three English kings, which between them filled more than a century, from 1216 to 1327. The three kings were so unlike, and the course of political and constitutional events depended so closely on the characters of the kings, that each reign seems to be a separate drama, complete in itself. King John's son, Henry III, succeeded as a boy of nine and lived to be sixty-five. He was deeply religious. This side of his life is commemorated by the main buildings of Westminster Abbey. He watched over the reconstruction of the abbey for many years and saw it completed. He lacked neither intelligence nor physical courage, but in public affairs he failed miserably. He was excitable, erratic, and untrustworthy, and it was mainly for this reason that the country was distracted again by civil war. Henry's son Edward rescued his father from humiliating captivity, and upheld him for the last seven years of his reign. Throughout his own long reign as successor, from 1272 to 1307, Edward I carried on his work as an outstanding military organizer and commander, statesman, and legislator. Yet his son Edward II, who came to the throne at the age of twenty-three, stumbled along from one calamity to another for twenty years, which ended with his deposition and murder.

It is easy to think of all the sound and fury of these three reigns as essentially futile. The history of the preceding reigns seemed

Caernarvon (Carnavon) Castle in north Wales. Edward I, to secure Wales, built a series of powerful castles, with royal boroughs of English settlers alongside. This castle was begun in 1285 and completed in 1322. There is no keep in the traditional sense; the castle is essentially a highly fortified wall with very generous provision of slits for archers, and carefully sited towers enabling archers to shoot along the outside faces of the walls.

to repeat itself. Magna Carta had to be confirmed four or five times. Edward I, as prince, went on crusade like Richard I and won fruitless battles in the Holy Land. It would indeed be an error to look here for far-sighted schemes of policy, for permanent solutions to great problems or even for well-laid foundations for constitution-building in the future. The task of the statesman was to deal with the emergencies of each year or day. The kings were in a central position, not a stronghold, but a point at which forces could be gathered.

From whatever quarter emergencies came up, there was a limit to their dislocating effect. The main directions were the same as they had been for long before and were to remain for long afterwards, but the emergencies were new because in each direction there were independent centres of growing or receding power. The English barons were many in number, differing in their ideas and ambitions, sometimes combining and sometimes at variance. In dealing with them the kings, like all feudal superiors, had always to balance the need for strong support against the danger of allowing rival powers to grow up. There was a similar problem of balance in the two large matters of Wales and Scotland. Likewise in relation to the Church, with its different but never negligible authority, whether near at hand or away in Rome, all the kings and their ministers were restrained by a network of interests. And it was still the paradox of the multicellular feudal society that crude and mindless passions cancelled one another out and held men back from going to extremes. There were innumerable murders and treasons, but there were no republicans and no dictators.

For the first eleven years of his reign King Henry III was a minor; but, for once, this did not leave the country at the mercy of ungovernable subjects. The two successive regents were William the marshal, earl of Pembroke, and, after his death in 1219, Hubert de Burgh, who had held the chief ministerial office under him. Both were firm and loyal. William the marshal was an old crusader who had seen fighting and gathered wisdom ever since King Stephen's time. He cleared away the most obvious dragon in the new king's path by beating the French king in a fight at Lincoln. Then a French fleet was defeated off Sandwich. Louis pocketed an indemnity and went home to France. The unsettled constitutional difficulties were dealt with reasonably. Magna Carta was reissued twice. The first of the revised versions omitted the clause against taxation without the consent of the great council, and that which appointed the 'twenty-five kings'. The second had further modifications. Some of them were favourable to the king, such as one which directed the immediate destruction of all castles built or rebuilt since the beginning of the barons' war against King John. Some of the others appear to favour feudal against royal jurisdiction. A new and separate charter dealt with the oppressions of the forest law. But this detailed legislation on subjects of dispute was not merely agreed

Jousting in the 14th century. Jousting was a ritualistic sport originally intended to provide useful training for war. The two contestants, carrying blunted lances, would charge and attempt to unhorse each other.

between the king's council and the barons. There was a third party who had to be satisfied, the papal legate, an Italian cardinal named Guala. He represented the overlord to whom Henry had done homage like his father before him, and the popes acted as conscientious guardians.

During Henry's minority, Guala was succeeded by another Italian, Pandulf Masca, who obtained the bishopric of Norwich; but the archbishops of Canterbury were natural legates, *legati nati* as they were called, of the popes and Stephen Langton was promised that during his own lifetime no legate should be sent from the pope. Pandulf therefore retired abroad; but he retained his bishopric for several years, and there was still ample room for disagreements over the exercise of papal power in England. In two different ways the papacy pressed its acknowledged powers. It collected heavy taxation from the beneficed clergy, to which they assented in their assemblies, and it arranged for foreigners to be appointed to bishoprics and other benefices.

The king himself and many of the barons were neither quite Englishmen nor quite Frenchmen. French was the language of the court and for the first time in English history the court was a centre of the arts and of cultivated manners. Not only was French literature known there; but the ideas and the techniques of the newly rising English literature were stimulated and guided by French examples. Throughout the nation, however, there was a growing will to be independent of foreign interference, and a growing feeling that what was French was foreign. During Henry's minority, there were powerful men who held castles and collected revenues from estates for which they did no homage to the new king. They forcibly resisted Hubert de Burgh when he demanded submission to the sovereign. Enough of them were Frenchmen to give this feudal party a foreign look. Two who rose to great power were Peter des Roches, a native of Poitou who started as a knight and was bishop of Winchester for more than thirty years, and Falkes de Bréauté, a Norman upstart who, at his zenith, was described by a chronicler as 'something more than king in England'. Hubert de Burgh frustrated them both, but after his fall from office Peter des Roches again enjoyed a few years of power, and used it as before.

King Henry's relations with the king of France as overlord of Poitou and Gascony intensified the friction over foreigners in England. When he came to the throne hostilities had been suspended by a truce, and until 1259 the course of Anglo-French

relations was that observance of one truce after another was interrupted by open but inconclusive war. The first breach came when Louis VIII moved against both Poitou and Gascony, clearing the English out of the latter. In 1230 it was Henry's turn to invade: he received homage in Poitou and desisted. Six years later he married Eleanor, daughter of the count of Provence. She and her entourage did add to the civilization of the court; but she, and still more her rapacious uncles, were unpopular and distrusted. One needy uncle, her mother's brother Boniface of Savoy, became archbishop of Canterbury. He made enemies right and left, not only by his irruptions into baronial politics, but also by insolence and bullying in standing up for his diocese and his archiepiscopal authority. The foreigners whom he thrust into office were joined in 1243 by a number of Poitevins who came back to England with the king when he lost Poitou to the king of France. In that year a new pope, Innocent IV, began his reign. In many things, such as the improvement of the canon law, he did a great work; but he had expensive plans for advancing the papal power over the affairs of kings. His ultimate aims were those which everyone accepted as commendable, such as crusading; but his immediate purpose was to prevail over the brilliant and successful emperor Frederick II. Thus it was that Henry III became involved in unrealistic plans, of which the most fantastic was that he accepted the pope's offer of the crown of Sicily to his son, a papal fief of which the emperor was the excommunicated occupant. There seemed to be a connection between the extravagance of the king's foreign dependants and the crushing papal taxation of the clergy, against which the best of the English bishops protested.

This was the setting of a new baronial opposition, which aimed at bridling the monarchy as the barons had almost succeeded in doing a generation before. By a set of chances characteristic of the age, this opposition, which may fairly be called nationalist, took a revolutionary turn and was led by a near relation of the king who was a Frenchman by birth. This was Simon de Montfort, earl of Leicester, a man of strong will and a well-trained military commander. He had married the widow of William the marshal, and she was the new king's sister. There were quarrels and reconciliations between the two brothers-in-law; but in 1248 Simon became governor of Gascony and governed the undisciplined province well. He was badly supported from England, accused of malpractices, acquitted, reinstated and then superseded. By 1257 he was openly at odds with the foreigners, though he was employed on diplomatic missions by the king.

In 1258 the discontented barons put two demands before the king, to which he yielded. A body of twenty-four bishops and barons, twelve chosen by himself and twelve by the earls and barons, was to inquire into grievances and a parliament was to be summoned. The parliament met in Oxford, and the twenty-four were named, Simon being one of the nominees of the peers. The parliament chose another twenty-four to treat with the king over a grant of money. It agreed on many clauses about such purely feudal concerns as inheritance, jurisdiction and the like, and about Jewish and Christian usurers and the grievances of London and the boroughs, and even about the accommodation of the king and queen. But the Provisions of Oxford became famous, and a few years later this parliament came to be called the Mad Parliament but not on account of any of these reforming laws. Its measures included several, following up the appointment of the first twenty-four, which were intended to give permanent control of the administration and of the high officers of state to baronial elements. None of the other western kingdoms had anything like this. But its original and amended forms do not deserve to be called paper constitutions. They were attempts to settle immediate, practical differences, and in the five years after the Mad Parliament they were sworn to and repudiated. In the course of the disputes a new peace-treaty, not merely a truce, was made with France, in which Henry dropped the empty title of duke of Normandy. The pope absolved him from his oath to keep the Provisions; the opposition barons rebelled; the king of France mediated and decided in favour of the king, whereupon the barons renewed their war.

It was a civil war, but of a peculiar character. On Simon's side there was, as we know for certain from the popular songs of the time, an element of hatred of foreigners. He drew some of his support from various social strata below the baronage. His greatest initial advantage was that he held the Tower of London and the armed commonalty of the city sent troops with him. But this did not imply that he was a social reformer. England was an armed nation, and it had no unarmed subject class. It was accepted law that all men, including villeins, must provide the arms proper to their several ranks, and, in the summer months, take their turns at watch and ward and join in the hue and cry after marauders. Civil war was not reserved for the gentry.

Simon established himself in country friendly to him south-east of London. The king and his son Edward marched south from Northampton, which they had captured. Their army lay in and about the seaport town of Lewes, on the Sussex Ouse. Simon approached along the high chalk downs and won an outright victory, making prisoners of the king and the prince. A sort of peace was patched up, and a sort of parliament agreed to another set of articles about the appointment of councillors and ministers. Nothing was settled. When Simon de Montfort summoned a parliament of his own it included burgesses from the boroughs that he controlled, but only five earls and eighteen barons. The pope once more backed the king. Simon discovered that he could not trust the promises of his defeated opponents. He moved against the loyal lords of the Welsh marches, and took Prince Edward with him. The prisoner escaped and took command of the western forces. At Evesham in Worcestershire Simon was defeated and killed.

The rebellions left no permanent results except that, for the future, foreign fortune-hunters found no careers except in the Church. Henry III reigned for six more years, with his authority restored; the Welsh border was pacified by the recognition of Llywelyn ap Gruffydd as prince, or overlord of Wales; Magna Carta and the Forest Charter were reaffirmed as usual; and Prince Edward, the mainstay of the government, felt free to go away on crusade. In Sicily, on his way home, he heard of his father's death. Lawyers had not yet invented the maxim that the king never dies, but for the first time the reign of an English sovereign was dated from the funeral of his predecessor: the barons and bishops swore fealty to Edward while he was still abroad. The new king was a man of purpose, rich in military and civil experience, and the administrative machinery of the kingdom, when properly manned, was equal to his demands. He spent almost two years after his accession on the Continent, settling his relations with France, the internal affairs of Aquitaine and other business, such as a stoppage in the export of wool to

Flanders. Later, he went abroad twice, on the first occasion staying for three years. He also spent many months campaigning against the Welsh and the Scots; but these distractions did not prevent him from enacting a long series of measures, partly original and partly codifying existing law, which amounted to a general framework for government.

The old system of feudal obligations was braced together. Every owner of land worth £20 a year was to become a knight, which obliged him to render personal service in the wars or to buy exemption with a payment of money. The qualifying sum was sometimes raised and at other times lowered. Every landowner who received a writ asking by what warrant did he hold his land ('Quo Warranto') had to furnish particulars of all jurisdiction and other rights that he claimed. The practice of subinfeudation, by which a landlord granted land to new lords beneath him, was limited. The Statute of Mortmain, the dead hand, forbade all ecclesiastics to acquire or part with land. It may perhaps have been intended to limit the wealth of the Church; but it did not prevent the king from making exceptions on occasion, and most likely it was mainly intended to check certain kinds of fraud, such as escaping liabilities by passing off estates as church land. On the other hand the hereditary ownership of land was made firmer by the system of entails: even treason or felony by the owner, if his land had been granted to him by a private donor, was not to deprive his heirs of their rights. The police regulations and those about arms and armour were renewed. Besides these laws there were equally important permanent administrative measures. The system of customs duties became a regular part of the national finances when Edward raised some of the money for his first war by an export duty on wool. The summoning of parliaments, after various experiments, reached the main outlines which it has retained ever since.

The first war for which Edward needed money was the first of his two Welsh wars. After the death of Llywelyn ab Iorwerth, Llywelyn the Great, in 1240, there was some confusion in Wales, with English royal power working outwards from the recaptured castles of Cardigan and Builth, as it also did from Carmarthen and Montgomery; but from 1255 a new phase of national resistance began, and Llywelyn ap Gruffyd took full advantage of the divided state of England. Simon de Montfort bargained for his support, offering a high price in money and in recognition of his overlordship as prince of Wales and his gains of land and castles. The marcher lords, however, whose record of loyalty had recently not been unimpeachable, saw that their own future must depend on that of the Crown. Prince Edward had begun his public career in 1254 as the lord of many castles from Chester to Upper Gwent; but the Welsh had pressed him back both in the north and in the south. It was the marchers, under his leadership, who overthrew Simon; but he was not in a position then to renew the war, and as part of the general pacification he made peace with Llywelyn on the terms to which Simon had agreed.

The terms left opportunities for local disputes about rights and boundaries; but it was not from them that war originated in 1276. One of Llywelyn's brothers, David, conspired against him, was detected and fled to England. Edward judged that it was time for the prince to swear allegiance as his vassal. Llywelyn refused to come to England for the purpose and insisted, as vassals of the French king had sometimes done, that the ceremony should take place at some place on his frontier. Edward declared him a rebel and immediately moved forward paid troops (which stiffened the garrisons) and new local levies, English and Welsh, in three theatres, north, midland, and west. Next year the archbishop of Canterbury gave orders for Llywelyn's excommunication. The feudal army was mobilized, and Edward had at his disposal probably the best-organized force that had operated in Britain since the Norman Conquest. Counting in the miscellaneous services behind the lines there were some 15,600 foot, about 9,000 of them Welsh. Edward, in the north, commanded the whole methodical summer campaign, building castles, and cutting off the enemy's food supplies.

A late 13th century manor house, at Acton Burnell. By this time manors were beginning to look less like small castles and more like homes, though in this example the design is obviously influenced by defence considerations. As in earlier manor houses the great hall, and the main living rooms, were on the first floor.

Llywelyn, hemmed in in Snowdonia, wisely sought terms and the king agreed to the Treaty of Conway. Llywelyn did homage at Rhuddlan Castle, but the homage of nearly all his own vassals was transferred to the king, and the important area called the Four Cantreds was annexed to England. There were other hard terms, from some of which Llywelyn was excused when Edward took him into favour. He repeated his homage in full parliament in London. Neither he nor his people were satisfied with the fulfilment of the treaty, but in two directions there were collisions that could have been avoided. By the letter of the treaty Edward was bound to respect the Welsh laws when they were reasonable; but the English judicial system was introduced in North and Central Wales and Edward's subordinates ruthlessly enforced their own interpretation of rights in deciding the many claims left over from the years of encroachments and invasions. These differences could not be separated from those which arose when the archbishop of Canterbury set about restoring order and obedience in the bishoprics of Bangor and St. Asaph. There were already misgivings in 1278 when Llywelyn, in the presence of the kings of England and Scotland, was married to Edward's cousin Eleanor, the daughter of Simon de Montfort, at the door of Worcester Cathedral.

Four years later Llywelyn's brother David was goaded, it seems mainly by Church grievances, into throwing away all that he had gained from his original defection. He and Llywelyn together formed the desperate design of raising the country against the king. This began with a night attack on Hawarden Castle in March 1282 and ended with the surrender of Harlech Castle on 25 April 1283. King Edward gathered all his resources from England and Gascony. He did not need so much strength. Although the rebels took castles and collected followers across the north from Aberystwyth to Ruthin, and stirred up the central Marches, they never had a co-ordinated plan. Llywelyn was killed, perhaps in a skirmish, near the upper waters of the Severn.

David fought on till he was hunted down after the fall of Harlech. The sequel was the long Statute of Wales, which extended the English system of administration by counties, the judicial system, and the exchequer. Criminal law was anglicized, but civil law remained essentially Welsh. The long-established policy of building castles and establishing boroughs was carefully planned and carried on at great expense.

Although these measures were, for the times, enlightened, they could easily be upset by bad management, and the English had to cope with two more risings. In 1287 Rhys ap Maredudd, a prospering but restless baron in central Wales, captured three minor castles at the head of his own neighbours, but the country as a whole was indifferent, and the authorites put him down by a movement which involved many troops but was no more than a police operation. In 1294 there was an insurrection prepared in all parts of Wales and timed to coincide with the preparations, some of which involved Welshmen, for an expedition to Gascony. In North Wales the local leader, Madog ap Llywelyn, gained some early successes. At Carnarvon the sheriff was killed and the castle partly destroyed. The king gave Wales priority over all his other concerns. Again he assembled large forces, took command and supplied his coastal castles from the sea. Madog checked him in an advance from Conway, but then unwisely took the offensive in Powys, where he was defeated. The king promenaded through the country with a small, picked force and all resistance faded away. Madog surrendered on terms and was allowed to live. The success of Edward's conquest and laws was celebrated in 1301 by the investiture of his son at his birthplace, Carnarvon Castle, as Prince of Wales. It was not an empty pageant: this boy of sixteen also received the earldom of Chester, which was inseparable from the Crown and included the Four Cantreds. He was marked out as the future ruler of a great lordship of his own and as overlord of all Wales.

Neither the attacking nor the defending soldiers who plodded beside the mountain streams of Snowdonia had eyes for scenic beauty, and most likely none of their commanders on either side supposed that their wars would influence, let alone decide, the future of the Welsh language and Welsh ways of life. There were Welshmen fighting on both sides; King Edward and many of his followers were bilingual in French and English, and no one supposed that language contributed anything of moment to the causes or the prosecution of wars. The contrast between the institutions of England and those of pastoral Wales was plain enough; but the Welsh princes themselves tried, perhaps without much energy, to modify their old laws, reducing tribal responsibility and bringing individuals into graded feudal subordination to themselves.

To the opposing commanders and to such mediators as the papal emissaries, the Welsh wars appeared as feudal contests of the familiar type, and there was nothing inconsistent in Edward's two roles, as the stern exactor of what was due to him from his vassals, and as the recalcitrant vassal of the French king, his superior in the duchy of Aquitaine. As duke he governed Aquitaine well, laying the foundations of order on principles which have a generic resemblance to those he followed in Wales, with the castle and the market as the centres of control and prosperity. He succeeded so well that on three occasions he was able to summon help from Aquitaine to Britain. But, as in the times of his predecessors, there was no attempt to unite the two chief blocks of his territory. The French monarchy was growing stronger, and pressing outwards as Edward was doing in Britain, and so Aquitaine and England were at war with France for four years from 1294, and then only in a state of truce until they made peace in 1303. Even before the truce there was no fighting on a large scale; but throughout the ten campaigning seasons the French were in occupation of Gascony, depriving England of its wine-trade and harbours.

For another reason this French war presented King Edward with the greatest difficulties of his reign. To the French an alliance with Scotland seemed both desirable and easy to compass. They had experience of it in the time of King John. Under Henry III, however, English relations with Scotland were on the whole friendly and sometimes cordial. In 1237 a treaty was made at York in which the Scottish king Alexander II abandoned the claim to the three northern counties of England: he was turning his attention to the unsubdued country to the north and west. He and his son Alexander III both married English princesses, but they each married a second time and both the second wives were French. The Scottish court and aristocracy were even less national than the English, and there were many ties of which France could take advantage. In 1295 the alliance was made, and in circumstances which tangled up the conflict of the states with the internal affairs of Scotland. Five years earlier the direct royal line died out: after the death of Alexander III, his granddaughter Margaret, the Maid of Norway, was queen for a few years and died a child. The succession was disputed, and it was evident that the best, indeed the only, way to avoid civil war was to refer the issue to the English king.

Edward could have acted as a mere arbitrator between the claimants, and that was certainly the wish of some part of the Scottish nobility; but when Edward came to the border-castle of Norham to decide the case, he insisted that he must act as the superior or direct lord of the kingdom. His arguments were perhaps weak, and his decision would not have gone for much unless someone had the right to enforce it, and no one except himself could assume that right. At any rate he had his way. After elaborate discussions the questions of law and fact were referred to twenty-four of Edward's counsellors, assisted by eighty assessors. Half of these were chosen by the partisans of each of the two claimants who remained on what might be called the short list out of twelve who put in petitions. These were two descendants of the brother of William the Lion: Robert Bruce, the son of his second daughter, and John Baliol, the grandson of his eldest. Neither of them represented any principle nor any element of the governing class which was not equally represented by the other. The decision of the twenty-four and the eighty went unanimously in favour of Baliol, who duly became king and did homage.

The years of discussion only sharpened the differences of interpretation about Edward's duties on the one hand to respect the good laws of Scotland and on the other to see that justice and order were preserved there and, more particularly, his right to decide appeals from judgments of the Scottish king sitting in his parliament. Over this the two kings broke, and when the breach was completed Baliol was an ally of France. Edward put his military machine in motion. The earl of Warenne won a battle at Dunbar. The castles surrendered, including that of Edinburgh where siege-engines were used. Baliol surrendered his kingdom to spend the rest of his life in captivity and then in exile. King

Edward travelled through the kingdom, establishing peace. He carried away the Stone of Scone, on which the kings of Scotland were seated at their coronation. In Berwick, which he refortified, he held a Scottish parliament and appointed Warenne governor. When he went south again in 1296 Scotland seemed to be provided for.

Already, however, there were signs that intermittent warfare on three fronts was straining the resources of England. The aged Pope Boniface VIII, defending the rights of the papacy against the surrounding kings in the vain hope that this would enable him to pacify Europe, issued a Bull forbidding them to levy any taxation on the clergy. Neither Edward nor Philip the Fair obeyed it. Archbishop Winchelsey refused to pay. Edward, at the last minute, obtained a clerical subsidy by the plea of necessity but without carrying his point of principle. The clergy were not alone in their resentment. Merchants were aggrieved, not only by a heavy increase in the export-tax on wool, but by orders to confine their trade to fixed channels, where it could on occasion be laid under contribution in new and arbitrary ways.

The barons had legal justification for questioning some of the king's demands. Their dissatisfaction came to a head when the two great earls who, as constable and marshal, were the hereditary heads of the army, refused to sail for Gascony because the king was not to lead his army in person. He was about to do something of greater importance for the war, to concert measures with the count of Flanders. An offensive from the north would be even more powerful than it could have been when King John lost his great opportunity: Flanders was richer, more warlike, and more closely bound to England by its commerce. But when Edward was negotiating in Ghent in 1297 England was mutinous. It was in Ghent that he had to grant the confirmation of the charters. His son had already agreed to it in council in London, in exchange for a grant of money. It was not the last of the many confirmations, but it was rightly regarded as the greatest. Along with it there went the annulling of illegalities committed in the last few years in the raising of money. And even with such support as he received, this crisis ended Edward's grandiose continental plans. He left his Flemish ally in the lurch. Edward, with the help of Pope Boniface, made a new truce with France. Two years later he married his second wife, Margaret, the youngest daughter of Philip III, king of France. Then he made peace. He kept Aquitaine, but with it there went a labyrinth of unsettled litigation about lordships and boundaries.

In Scotland none of the nobles had stirred, but there was a new kind of resistance, led by men of more modest station, of whom the heroic William Wallace was the chief. He defeated Warenne in a battle at Stirling. Unhappily for him the truce with France followed soon afterwards, and the chances of support from the pope disappeared in consequence. The English sent up greatly superior forces. At Falkirk they had already destroyed Wallace's army. Later he was betrayed and taken to London to be executed as a traitor. King Edward invaded the country, and had no difficulty in recapturing the castles and the formal allegiance of its leaders. For the country he planned such a status as fitted all his ideas. Scottish law was to be revised and preserved; but there was to be a lieutenant, as in Ireland, and with his council he was to have legislative power. In addition Scotland was to send representatives to the English parliament, and, like Ireland and Wales, to be subject to such laws made in England as were intended to have this effect. It was expected that Scotsmen would be employed along with Englishmen in the administration. All this contrivance went for nothing. Robert Bruce, a baron of Norman descent, powerful in the south-west, and the grandson of that Robert who was competitor to the throne, was working secretly. In 1306 his only possible rival as a pretender to the throne, Baliol's nephew John Comyn, was murdered in Bruce's presence. Six weeks later Bruce was crowned as king at Scone. Edward was an old man, and he was ill; but once more he went north. He spent the next winter at Lanercost Priory near Carlisle, and in the summer he set out to lead his army; but he never crossed the Solway Firth. He died at Burgh on Sands.

Although Edward I is remembered in Scotland and Wales as a ruthless warrior, English historians dwell on another aspect of his rule even there, an aspect which is clearer in England. Here he presided over a decisive stage in constitutional development. In literature and politics and in dealings with the Church there was a growing consciousness that Englishmen had common concerns and were becoming a community. This was helped by the changes in the administrative system. A sworn body of the king's ministers developed and, with it, rules about the nature and

The Scottish 'Stone of Destiny' (or Stone of Scone), resting in the coronation chair at Westminster Abbey. Edward I's subjugation of Scotland was cruel and thorough, and the removal of the Stone to England both symbolised the fact of conquest and made it hard for the Scots to instal another King of Scotland, for the Stone was the traditional throne of Scottish kings at their coronation and there could be no real substitute.

A castle besieged in the 14th century. Sieges were protracted and tedious, the main enemy of the defenders being time, the begetter of disease and hunger. Guns, like the early example shown her, were no more effective than the older techniques of undermining and battering, and for centuries were only of marginal significance. As late as the Civil War of the 17th century, castles could still resist sieges for several weeks.

limits of their responsibilities. But this process was quieter and less in the public eye than the growth of representative institutions. Before Edward I came to the throne the old feudal assemblies of tenants-in-chief were being superseded by bodies with a wider variety of members. They were known, at first informally and then, from as early as 1236 in official documents, by the French name of parliaments.

It suited the kings to call these wider assemblies together because they wanted to broaden the basis of support in the country for their government. In particular they wanted to strengthen their machinery for raising money, increasingly indispensable for their many wars. The only credentials which the new representatives had to bring to their sessions consisted of a power of attorney authorizing them to agree to taxation on behalf of those who would be bound to pay. In early days it was not uncommon for members to come reluctantly; but even from early days the shire courts and boroughs which sent members could see advantages in the plan. They had experience which prepared them for it. Assessors of taxes were elected in full shire court, and there also boroughs did some of their inland revenue business. Sometimes if only through the sheriffs, counties could make their wishes known to the king, and now they soon found that parliaments, like most assemblies that have any life in them, tended to widen the scope of their discussions. They did not confine themselves to finance; they legislated and they dealt with plaints. Under Henry III they imitated the barons before them by refusing to grant money before their grievances were redressed and by interfering with the king's choice of councillors. The clash of rival ambitions hastened these processes: Simon de Montfort tried to increase his resources for civil war by summoning a parliament. Edward I needed parliamentary support; and he knew that weak parliaments were useless.

All this was part of the European development of representative institutions. Representation of some sort is an essential of all organized social life, even the most primitive. By the year 1200 the Church had accumulated much experience of assemblies, whether of dioceses or international religious orders, or of the whole western communion. In the course of the century that followed, the European kingdoms provided themselves with bodies, more or less like the English parliaments, which are known as assemblies of estates. As things then were it was impossible to mix up the whole population in an electorate like that of a modern republic. It was necessary to follow the social structure of each country. Every man belonged to some station, standing, or rank, some estate, and the only kind of assembly that could represent the whole of a country was one that represented each of these estates.

For the effectiveness, and still more for the permanence, of these assemblies the defining of the estates was of primary importance. In England there were various bodies of freemen which might have become separate estates but failed to do so. In some countries the peasantry formed an estate of their own, separate from the landlords: in England there was never any question of this. One powerful body which might have become a constitutional unit was that of the lawyers; but they were so much involved with other classes in their work and interests and personal lives that they contented themselves with functions within the other estates. The merchants would have liked a place of their own in the assemblies. It suited the kings better to negotiate separately with the merchants for taxes on their commerce, but on occasion the other estates were jealous of being circumvented; so the merchants became an element, growing in influence as time went on, in the general body.

This general body was divided according to the three main divisions of society, lay and clerical, town and country, lords and liege men; but the division worked out in a special way to produce the three estates of which parliament still consists, lords spiritual, lords temporal, and commons. The definition of the estates reached its final form, which has been maintained ever since, in the time of Edward I: the parliament of 1295 fixed the result of the experiments of his reign and his predecessor's, and for this reason it is called the Model Parliament.

The lords spiritual, the bishops and the greater abbots, had a double right to be there, as great landlords and as spiritual heads. King Edward wanted to have the whole of the clergy represented in parliament, and he summoned them accordingly; but they preferred to meet in assemblies of their own for transacting the business which they would have done in parliament and so they disregarded the summons. The English clerical assemblies had grown up side by side with the lay assemblies, for much the same reasons and consequently in similar shapes. Both the Crown and the papacy claimed the right to tax the beneficed clergy, and for this and other purposes the assemblies called convocations were held. Like parliaments they consisted of the higher dignitaries along with elected representatives called 'proctors' (procurators or persons empowered to act for the lower clergy whom they represented). One difference which weakened the convocations was that, instead of one for the whole country, there was one for each of the still incompletely reconciled provinces of Canterbury and York. They were, however, strong enough to keep the taxation of the clergy in their own hands. The clergy were taxed separately from the laity until, as we shall see, the reign of Charles II, and none of them were allowed to sit in parliament except the few lords spiritual.

It took some time for the composition of the second estate, the lords temporal, to become fixed. In the earlier assemblies the great lords attended as a matter of course, and the sheriffs summoned the minor barons of each county, the feudal tenants of estates which counted as baronies. Later the king's ministers summoned each individual by a writ, and so a small body of barons was defined. The minor barons as such dropped out of the representative system, and joined with the third estate, the commons, to the advantage of both. The name of the commons had nothing to do with the common man. They were the 'community of the communities', the representatives of the county courts and boroughs. Whether all freeholders voted in electing them is not certain, but it is unimportant: the major fact is that all the kinds of landowners above the villeins were united. Still more noteworthy is it that along with these electors, the sheriff summoned the boroughs to send representatives. The system of taxation was the same in the country and in the corporate towns (so much on land, so much on all other possessions), and so it came about that the knights of the shire, as the county members were called, sat together with the burgesses as a single estate. This union was not fully accomplished by the time of the Model Parliament. It was not until the middle of the fourteenth century that the parliamentary assembly divided into an upper and a lower house; but when it did so, the lower and larger house represented both town and country, and within it were members who came from all the various strata of wealth and influence except the very highest. And of all assemblies of estates in Europe this became the strongest and proved to be the most enduring.

A Turbulent Society 1307–1399

1314 Bruce routs Edward II's army at the Battle of Bannockburn, thereby ensuring Scottish independence.
1338 The Hundred Years' War with France begins.
1340 The English navy defeats the French at Sluys.
1346 The English army defeats the French at Crécy.
1349 The Black Death epidemic spreads to England, and to Scotland the following year.
1356 The Black Prince wins the Battle of Poiters, capturing the French king.
1380 The first English translation of the whole Bible.
1381 Wycliffe writes his heretical *Confessio*. The Peasants' Revolt is suppressed.
1399 The Lancastrian Henry IV succeeds the deposed King Richard II.

When King Edward I died he still had the problems of Gascony and Scotland on his hands. The compromise by which he had restored co-operation with the barons had lasted, not seriously shaken, for ten years; but he already had trouble with his son, on whom these responsibilities now devolved. Edward II was twenty-three, and he had been apprenticed to war and policy, but without acquiring either soldierly or kingly qualities. He showed abnormal affection for his foster-brother Piers Gaveston, a Gascon knight, and the old king, as he lay ill at Lanercost, ordered Gaveston's banishment. No sooner was Edward II king than he recalled his favourite, made him earl of Cornwall and did much more to advance him. Gaveston immediately alienated most of the magnates by his arrogance and alienated them for good. Edward went to France for a few days to marry, in accordance with the peace-treaty, the daughter of Philip the Fair. He foolishly left Gaveston as regent, and on his return the barons, headed by the king's cousin Thomas earl of Lancaster, demanded that Gaveston should be banished anew. Banished he was, but only to be lieutenant of Ireland, and only to be recalled again after a year.

Then, as early as 1310, came a revolutionary step, reminiscent of the days of Simon de Montfort. Parliament appointed twenty-one lords ordainers, Archbishop Winchelsey among them, and they drew up their ordinances to rectify the abuses which had come in with the new reign. Gaveston was to be banished from all the king's dominions. The Italian financier Angelo Frescobaldi was to be arrested and his goods seized pending an examination of his accounts: his family firm had made loans to Edward I on the security of the customs, but it was a different matter when they financed a king who was spending nothing on war and far too much on extravagant gifts. There were several clauses of constitutional import. The great officers of state were to be nominated with the consent of the barons and sworn in parliament. The king was not to engage in any war without the consent of the baronage in parliament. Parliament was to meet at least once a year. These ordinances never came into full effect, if only because political conditions went from bad to worse. Gaveston went away for the third time, but three months later he was in England again, at first secretly and then with the king's public approval. Lancaster and other barons set out against them in arms and Archbishop Winchelsey excommunicated Gaveston. He surrendered on a promise of his personal safety, but another baron who had given no promise seized him, and by agreement of four of the principal magnates, he was executed.

The king patched up terms with the barons, but years of calamity followed. Edward decided to resume the war against Scotland. He had made attempts at preparations in earlier years, but they had led to nothing, and Bruce had gone on step by step overcoming his Scottish enemies and occupying their castles. In 1313 his brother Edward appeared before Stirling. The castle

Robert Bruce. Unscrupulous, violent, and ambitious, Bruce succeeded in having himself crowned as King Robert I of Scotland. Though he was the subjugator and frequently murderer of many Scots, he nevertheless had the support of the population, which was developing a primitive nationalism. This national spirit was both a cause and beneficiary of Robert's great victory over the English at Bannockburn.

was built on the rock there by Edward I when he captured it from a small garrison in 1288. It commanded the lowest crossing of the Forth, which was the most important way between the Highlands and the Lowlands. At that moment it was in no condition to stand a siege, and the English commander made the promise, in line with medieval custom, that if no English army appeared within three leagues of it before Midsummer Day in 1314 it was to surrender. The strategy of the campaign which followed was therefore as simple as could be: it was one straight march to relieve Stirling. Edward disregarded the ordinance about baronial consent for waging war. He got together a good army, perhaps of some 20,000, including cavalry, archers from Wales and the Marches, militia infantry from the Midlands and north-west, and possibly some Irish. A good many of them had seen fighting. They did not start in good time. They reached Edinburgh on 21 June only three days before the appointed day, Falkirk on the evening of the 22nd, tired after a twenty-mile march. On the 23rd they came to a stream called Bannock. There they were within their three leagues of the castle. Bruce was there too, with an army perhaps half the size of theirs, and they made contact that evening.

The first encounters did not go well for the English. Even the next day they need not have fought a battle; they needed rest, and Bruce's four dense oblongs of pikemen were hard nuts for any force to crack. King Edward foolishly ordered his cavalry to attack. The English infantry and archers were never properly in action; the Scottish light horse came in effectively on a flank and after a ferocious mêlée the English broke in pieces. This was the decisive Battle of Bannockburn. Scotland was now an independent kingdom, and remained so as long as England did: the two ended on the same day in 1707 when they were united.

The Treaty of Northampton, which set down the new fact on paper, was not concluded until 1328. For the time being there was nominally war, and even after the treaty, as after most treaties, there were disputable questions; but in terms of realities Bannockburn ended the Scottish question. In 1318 Bruce captured Berwick and a truce was made in 1323; but the divisions of England, which were only briefly suspended when Berwick fell, rolled on towards catastrophe. In the year after the battle Edward Bruce accepted an invitation from an Irish faction to take over an army and become king of Ireland. For three years he pillaged until he was defeated and killed. In 1316 there was a revolt in Wales, comparatively a minor affair, which was put down. But the king prepared new troubles for himself by raising new favourites to power. These were the two Despensers, father and son, of whom the son became the more prominent. They were experienced in office, but the king ensured unpopularity for them by raising them far above their station. In 1321 a parliament banished them; but, immediately after this parliament, the king raised troops to put down the opposition of discontented barons, and, as civil disturbances began again, he recalled the Despensers.

The greatest and most active of the earls opposed to the king was Lancaster. In the north he organized his territorial power and held assemblies of his supporters. The king marched north against him and at Boroughbridge, on the Great North Road at the crossing of the river Ure, Lancaster was trapped between the royal army and the militia of Cumberland and Westmorland. He was taken prisoner, adjudged guilty of treason by a few magnates in the presence of the king, and beheaded. A parliament at York revoked the Ordinances and made constitutional declarations which had no effect. The Despensers made the truce with Scotland. The new king of France, Charles IV, chose this time to summon Edward to do homage. Open war had already begun in Aquitaine, but, as so often before, it was easily converted into truce. In the diplomatic preliminaries one point was soon settled: Edward was excused from going in person to do homage but was represented by his son, a boy of twelve. It was also thought advisable to send his mother, Queen Isabella, who might well smooth away difficulties at her brother's court.

In raising the younger Despenser to wealth and position Edward had made the mistake of granting him lands and lordships in South Wales which were already the subjects of disputes among the war-like barons of Wales and the Marches. Among the enemies this made for him the most formidable was Roger Mortimer, lord of Chirk, who fought against him and the king before marching north against Lancaster. Mortimer had to surrender, but he escaped from the Tower of London and now, an exile, he met the queen in Paris. What followed was pure melodrama. The queen and Mortimer equally hated the Despensers. The French king was not rash enough to support their plans, especially when the queen became Mortimer's paramour. The pair crossed the frontier into Hainault, where the count, who was also count of Holland and Zeeland, was less fastidious. In exchange for the promise that the young prince should marry his daughter, he provided some adventurous young noblemen, some hundreds of troops, and the ships in which they sailed from Dordrecht. Landing at Orwell in Suffolk, they marched on London. The City was on their side. The king fled to the west, the queen pursuing. The London mob murdered Walter Stapledon, the bishop of Exeter, who was guilty of nothing except devotion to duty and generous gifts to education. Sir Hugh Despenser was behind the walls of Bristol, but the citizens would not fight. He was tried by such magnates as were at hand, and executed. The king could not defend the castle of Kenilworth. Parliament met at Westminster to carry out the rebels' will. Edward was browbeaten into abdication. Mortimer had him taken away to Berkeley Castle and murdered.

A Dominican monk, or 'black friar'. The different orders of monks were very distinct in their work and outlook. Dominicans, like Franciscans, specialized in preaching, whereas Cistercians were noted for their intelligent farming and their persistence in bringing unused land under cultivation, while the Benedictines took a large share in preserving civilized styles of living during violent times.

For three years Mortimer tyrannized in the name of the youthful Edward III. He made peace with France and Scotland, on the lines already prepared. He had learnt nothing from the fate of Gaveston and the Despensers: he proclaimed it aloud by taking the newly invented title of earl of March, or in other words earl over all the Welsh marchers. He tricked the earl of Kent, the brother of the murdered king, into joining in an imaginary plot and on this pretext murdered him too.

In 1330 King Edward was eighteen, ruthless and confident. One night, with a handful of trusted young nobles, he entered Mortimer's apparently secure retreat, Nottingham Castle, by a secret passage. Mortimer was seized, condemned by his peers in parliament, and hanged in infamy at Tyburn. Queen Isabella survived for thirty years in becoming grandeur.

We have seen that ecclesiastics did what they could to curb the ferocity of international and civil strife; but there were no heroic or inspiring incidents, and in these matters the popes and archbishops were beginning to lose their authority. They still did not shrink from using their weapons, especially excommunication; but they often used them in concert with one or other of the quarrelling lay powers. Scandalous churchmen in high places, like Boniface of Savoy, were few; but the best of the ecclesiastics who ventured into politics did not rise above the level of well-intentioned advisers. Yet this century is remembered both for reforms and for wonderful new beginnings in English church life. The impulse to establish monasteries, which had changed the face of England in the previous century, slackened, and the monasteries themselves, after their pioneering

days, as settled institutions, appealed less strongly to the lay imagination. It was ordered that all monks should become priests. The one kind of ecclesiastical taxation which was abolished unopposed was the taxing of English monastic houses for the benefit of continental houses of the same orders. In England the founders of abbeys and priories for monks and nuns, being themselves the lawful recipients of tithe from their properties, had endowed their new foundations not only with land but also, to a very great extent, with tithes. Reforming bishops now carried out the great and delicate task of making sure that such allocation, or appropriation as it was called, of tithes did not deprive the parishes of the clerical services which they needed. Parish by parish they drew up agreements, which subsisted until the Reformation, by which the monastery or other great church which received the tithe, was bound to leave a specified amount for a representative, called a vicar, who was to be a resident parish priest. In most cases the parish church also had glebe land for the use of the vicar. There was something like a standard amount, double that of a villein's holding. Thus, with an assured living and under the authority of the bishop, the parish clergy had the chance of rising from the status of villagers. The universities sent out some of their well-taught graduates to parish work. The parishioners received more attention than before. They gained as individuals; and the Church came to figure more in their social duties and enjoyments.

Changes like these were more noticeable in the towns than in the country, and a new church activity which came in from the Continent was centred in the towns, the activity of the friars. The friars were bound to poverty, chastity, and obedience like monks, but unlike monks they were not tied to the cloister. They were also unlike the monks in accepting no endowments; they built churches and shelter for themselves; but for their subsistence they depended on alms from day to day. St. Francis, their first founder, was a product of the thriving, adventurous Italy of his day: he was unconventional, high spirited, and irresistibly in earnest. The great pope Innocent III gave the movement full recognition, and did the same for the slightly younger movement of St. Dominic, whose followers were intended to do their missionary work not, like the Franciscans, among the poor, but among the educated and influential. The Dominicans, who arrived in England in 1221, three years before the Franciscans, were and are officially called the Friars Preachers, but both orders preached and soon every considerable town had at least one large church with a nave for a congregation. Ultimately there were four orders of friars, but these two, grey friars and black friars, remained the most influential. They mingled with all kinds of people from the lowest to the highest. Both orders, with houses in the university towns, took a full share in the impressive intellectual activity which carried forward what the twelfth-century renaissance had begun. Oxford became known throughout Europe as a centre of scientific study, where new knowledge was added especially to optics, mechanics, and physics in general.

In the world of thought as in the world of law and administration there was a tendency to elaboration and definition. In architecture and in the subordinate arts, such as illumination, an elegant harmony was sought. Perhaps the deeply cut mouldings and acute-angled arches of early Gothic may symbolize the unresolved contrasts of thirteenth-century Christianity. Among these are to be reckoned not only the ambiguities of ecclesiastical statesmanship but even darker failures. As we have seen there were purely secular and economic reasons for anti-Semitism, but they were reinforced by pseudo-religious feelings, and the churchmen must bear some of the blame for the expulsion of the Jews from England in 1290. On paper it was intended to be humane, but in practice it was accompanied by cruelty and robbery.

The economic stagnation that seems to have affected much of Europe from about 1350 may or may not have been felt in Britain. But signs of increasing productivity are easily visible at least throughout the fourteenth century. The draining of fens and marshes added to the amount of arable and pasture land; it cost much labour and those who undertook it often had to wait for years before their expense was repaid: it implies plenty of hands and a demand for food. It went on here and there all through the fourteenth century, round the Kentish coast, in Sussex and Somerset, in Nottinghamshire, Lincolnshire, and Yorkshire. In mining there was perhaps nothing comparable to the great increase in tin-mining between 1200 and 1300; but the northern coalfields were developing. Vertical pits were now dug as well as surface-workings, and sea-going ships, capable of crossing to the Netherlands and further, carried the coal coastwise, even to London.

The fourteenth century, besides making headway in pure science, had some technological improvements to its credit. One, already known on the Continent, was that of the fulling-mill, with tilt-hammers worked by water-wheels. This assisted a change of course which permanently altered the character of the chief English export industry. By degrees England ceased to export her wool as a raw material for foreign spinners and weavers. First one industrial process and then another was carried out in England: spinning by women as a home by-industry, weaving by the guildsmen in the towns, who had to face more or less illicit competition from country weavers, and now fulling, one of the finishing processes. Until this time the whole of the British Isles had been industrially undeveloped. That is to say they exported agricultural and mineral raw materials, receiving in exchange the finished products of industries in which they themselves produced only on a very small scale for their own needs, and consequently for the most part without reaching high levels of quality. Early in the fourteenth century, however, most of the English textile-market was supplied by English industry. In this early industrialization under the old craftsmen's technology, the first long stride was the rise of textile manufacture for export. In the fourteenth and fifteenth centuries this did not go beyond the exporting of unfinished cloth. Finishing processes, including dyeing, had still to be done in the Netherlands, and they were more profitable than the basic processes. But the export of raw wool dropped to a third of what it had been, and the counterpart of that was the concentration of

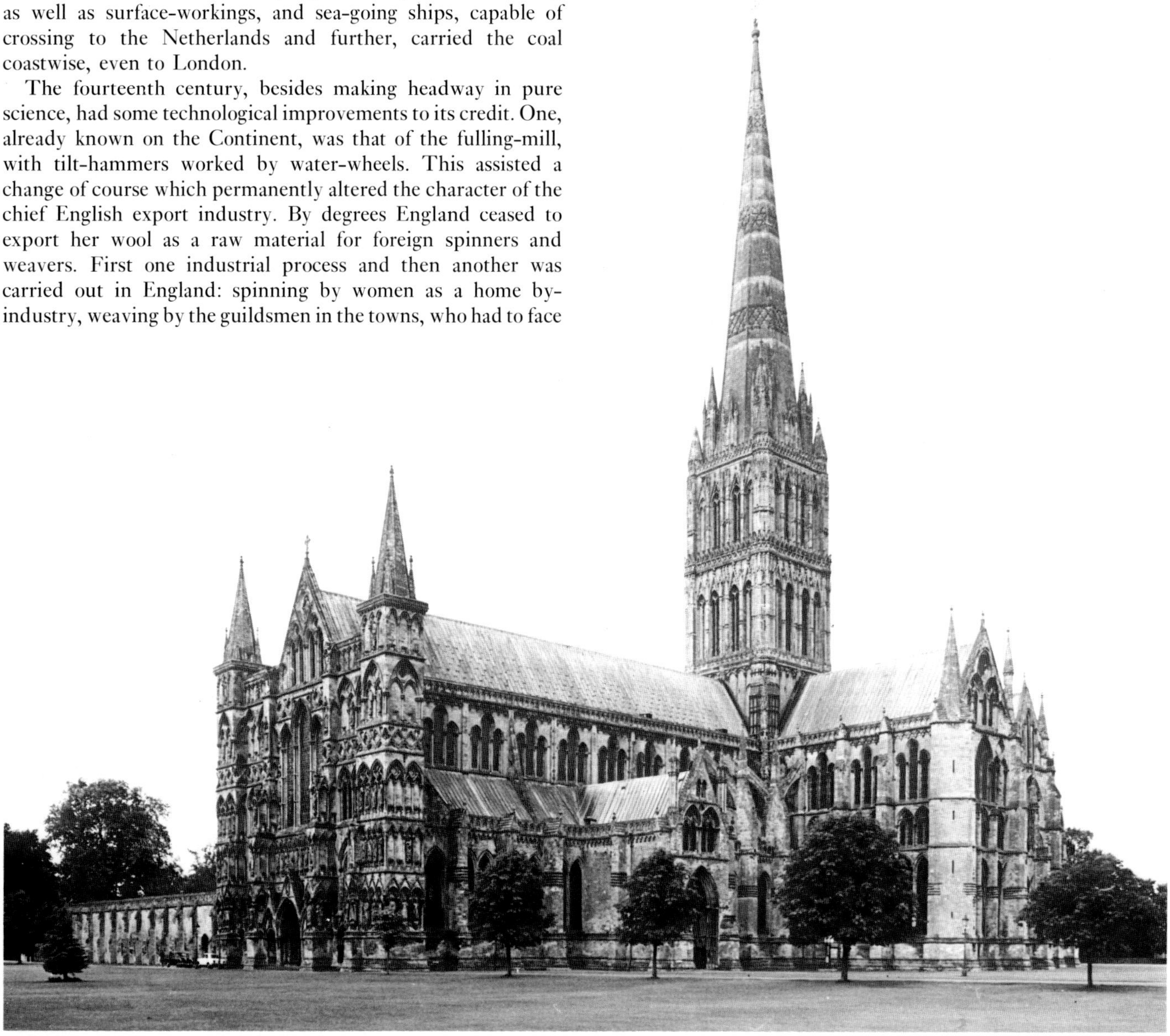

Salisbury Cathedral which, because it was built in an exceptionally short period, from 1220 to 1258, is largely in one style. However, the tower and spire, at 123 m (404 ft) the highest in Britain, were added in 1334. The cathedral was built before the city of Salisbury itself, being the first building of a medieval 'new town' planned by a bishop to replace the existing town of Old Sarum as a religious centre.

Daily life in England on the eve of the Black Death. These scenes are derived from the Luttrell Psalter, a work believed to have been drawn and written for a knight named Sir Geoffrey Luttrell, and now preserved. Numerous sketches, like those shown here, make this psalter a detailed source of information about how the English lived in the 14th century.

manufacture in districts where such conditions as water-power and communications were specially favourable. This came about in Wiltshire, the Cotswolds, Devonshire, East Anglia, and later in the West Riding of Yorkshire. The economic map of England changed, as may still be seen from the large and expensive new churches and additions to old parish churches which the rich clothiers built.

England's modest seaborne commerce grew and became more diversified. Late in the thirteenth century Italian merchants began to appear regularly in English ports, especially Southampton, Sandwich, London, Bristol, and even Hull. The members of the German trading federation called the Hanse already had, like the Flemings, their own organized settlements in London. The Italians, as we have seen already, provided financial support for merchants and for the government; but in these spheres, though less clearly than in manufacturing, there were signs of a growing English capacity to take over activities from which the foreigners profited.

Economic development did not run smoothly. As always it was subject to shocks from outside, and it is hard to tell how far these deflected the flow of buying and selling, saving and spending. The sharpest disturbances came from the Black Death, the epidemic which ravaged Europe from about 1347. It struck England in 1349, then again, but less heavily, in 1361–2 and in 1369. It was a sort, or more than one sort, of plague. No one had the slightest idea how it was caused or transmitted, or whether any sanitary measures or any treatment could give protection against it, so it ran its course. The mortality was enormous; and many facts about this mortality have been gathered by research; but at present it is useless to combine them in general statistics. The three visitations may have reduced the population of England by a third, or a quarter, perhaps even by half: no one knows. Still less does anyone know what proportion of loss was made good in subsequent years, or what the relation of these facts about the total population (if we could know them) would be to the facts about the numbers of people available for different kinds of work or requiring goods and services.

After a temporary dislocation in 1349 the wool-trade was normal again in 1357. On the other hand there was a shortage of agricultural labour for many years. The pestilence was not the only cause of this; but it suddenly hastened a tendency which was already beginning. Under the old system the lord had a first claim on the peasant's work. There might be conditions as to the hours of labour due and the subsistence which the lord had to provide. These varied from place to place, and sometimes there were disputes about them followed by agreements; but, however much or little attention his own holding needed, the peasant owed his service on the lord's demesne. This system was never universal. It was not suitable for animal husbandry, and it did not cover all the people employed in the ploughed areas: in these there were larger or smaller numbers of landless labourers who worked, when they were needed, for wages in money or kind.

Gradually, according to the local conditions of soil and markets, alternative arrangements were tried which hinged on more rational calculation, and involved either the use of money or at least a more commercial attitude to commodities and labour-services. A land-owner might let off some or all of his demesne to a tenant who took over the whole work of

The Black Death spared no social class, even though the rich may have died between clean sheets. It may have killed a third of England's estimated 3 million inhabitants in the course of one year. It was transmitted from person to person by fleas from the common black rat. It would reappear, notably in the Great Plague of London, in later centuries.

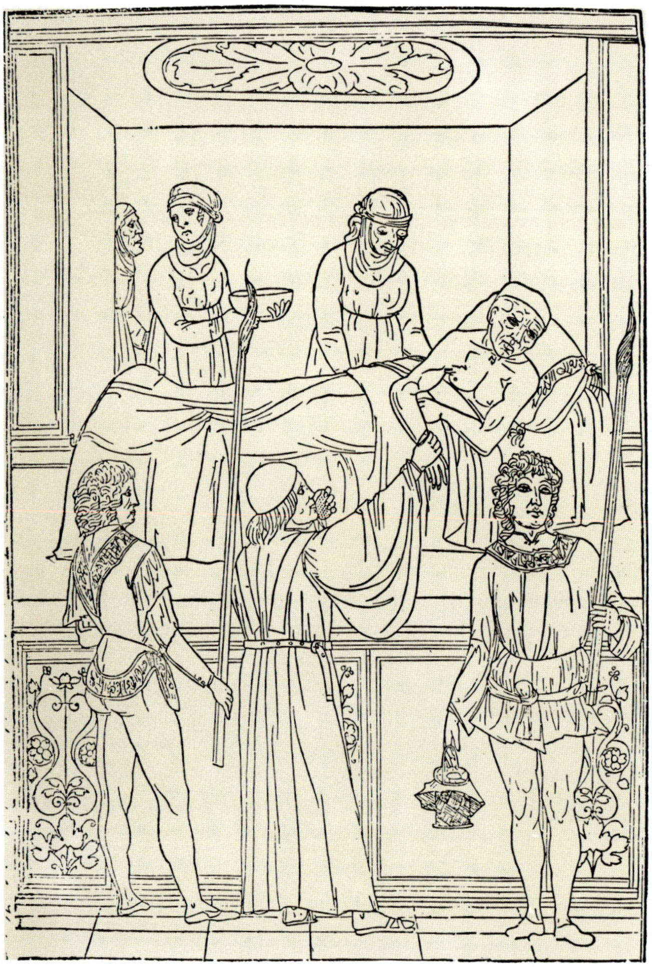

management and owned the crops, making his own arrangements for marketing them, and, of course, hoping for profits and risking losses. Many landowners did this before the Black Death and were satisfied with the results. Barons could bargain for rents with which they could recruit, equip, and pay mercenary soldiers. Cathedral chapters could raise money for buildings. Simple squires could go away on crusade and leave their lessees in charge of the land. There were experiments in the details: for how long a term should the leases run, how and when should the tenants pay for them, and so on. But in the period of development the inland corn-trade and other trades became better organized, more specialized, and more efficient, so that opportunities for profit multiplied, and the old feudal practices began to look archaic. By the end of the fourteenth century there were still very substantial survivals of these superseded social relationships and the corresponding agricultural methods; but the newer plan was becoming predominant over most of the country. The social structure of rural England congealed in the shape which it kept until the nineteenth century. Between the landowners and the agricultural workers there was a rural middle class, not very different from the various kinds of farmers as we still know them, who paid out both rent and wages. The Black Death came at an early stage of this transition. Suddenly the great mortality created a scarcity of workers.

This led to an entirely new kind of action by the king in parliament: labour legislation applied to the whole realm. It was not based on any concept of national economic welfare: its purpose was to remedy immediate maladjustments of the existing organization in the localities where it jammed. The initiative in parliament came from the commons. The policy was the natural reaction of the bulk of the propertied classes. An ineffective ordinance of 1349 was followed by the first Statute of Labourers in 1351. This simply fixed the rates of wages at the pre-plague rates, and ordered all landless men up to the age of sixty to accept employment at these rates, their own lords having the first claim on them. There were other restrictions on the free movement of labour, besides a feeble gesture towards the regulation of prices; but the first purpose was to prevent the labourers from standing out for higher wages. The machinery of local justice might have been adequate for enforcing this. It was controlled by the landowners, and the penalties were to be applied to reducing the taxation, to which the labourers were not liable. But the provision that no master was to offer wages above the rates was hard to enforce. Wages went up, the labourers were unruly, and discontent spread from them to villeins who were still bound to their customary services. The Statute became a dead letter; agriculture and landownership became less prosperous; but the governing classes did not relinquish the notion that economic ills might be cured by coercive Acts of Parliament. It was a long time, nearly two centuries, before the state was strong enough, or the economy sufficiently mature, for putting this into practice on the largest scale; but in one particular sphere after another, parliament tried to apply it. In 1363 it was enacted that no man should belong to more than one craft guild. In the same year, as in 1336, there were laws regulating, according to rank, the food and clothing of the population.

There were other signs, as we shall see shortly, that new social relationships were bringing about new forms of action by the state; but in their outward appearances the main lines of political and constitutional history were little more than continuations of the wars and domestic struggles of the thirteenth century. There was fighting in Scotland and Ireland. There were wars against the French, in which both sides had allies who seldom counted for much in the outcome. There were quarrels with parliaments about the kings' rights of taxation and about their ministers. The disagreements over papal taxation and appointments to benefices dragged on. Promises were broken and concessions were revoked: nothing seemed to be settled finally. We may pass lightly over the day-to-day events in these matters, and over the careers of individuals. The peace with France which was made in Mortimer's time lasted for ten years, and when it ended Scottish affairs were involved as well as the traditional quarrels between England and France. When Robert Bruce died in 1329 the succession was disputed again: his son David, a boy of five, was duly crowned. Edward Baliol, the son of the John Baliol who made his brief appearance as king in the time of Edward I, set up a claim, formed a party, and invaded the country from France. He also was crowned. He did homage to the young English king and ceded the ancient Lothian to England. For this price he had the support of an English army which won a victory at Halidon Hill and captured Berwick near by. But he could not maintain himself in Scotland; he came back with the English invader Edward III. At this point David Bruce received assurances of support from Philip VI, the first French king of the house of

A stone river bridge at Bradford-on-Avon. Although rivers were a frequent means of communication, most travellers regarded them as obstacles, for bridges were few. This bridge has two surviving arches from the 14th century, and it carries a small chapel intended for the use of pilgrims travelling to Glastonbury.

Valois. Philip invaded Gascony, and the alternate wars and truces began again. As before the English had allies in the Netherlands and Germany, the most useful, from their strategic position, being the burghers of the Flemish towns, our trading customers, who for the time being had the upper hand in their struggle with the nobility. Their alliance was accompanied by a promise to transfer the English staple, or centre of distribution, from Antwerp to Bruges. They concerned themselves with the politics of the neighbouring counts and sovereigns, and they egged Edward on to a step which committed him to a new kind of belligerency. Philip VI of France was the grandson of King Philip III in the male line, and Edward III was a grandson of King Philip IV, but only through his mother, the queen of Edward II. The law of succession was obscure enough to suggest the idea that a claim might be made on Edward's behalf; but for twelve years after the accession of Philip VI it was not made. Then, in 1340, Edward assumed the title and arms of king of France. The stakes of the war were multiplied many times.

This is commonly taken as the beginning of the Hundred Years War against France. There was nothing like a hundred years of actual hostilities: the age which ended with the expulsion of the English from all France except Calais in 1453 was as much punctuated by truces and treaties of peace as the age before it. Nor did that expulsion put an end to French wars. The claim to the French throne lingered as an heraldic fantasy until the reign of George III. By then symbolism had far less meaning for the world in general than it had in the days of Edward III, the most decorative period of English history. Edward promoted display as an expression of kingship and chivalry. For instance, he was the founder of the Order of the Garter, with its robes and jewels, and processions, and the vows of the knights. Many modern writers have thought that there was something spurious in these trappings for the realities of war. The king could cloak very ordinary ambitions under the pretext of vindicating his feudal rights. His nobles might obey a code of knightly conduct and insist on loyalty as a primary virtue; but they were business men, making a profit on their contracts to supply the king with troops, and, if they were lucky, making capital gains by the ransoms of any prisoners they might take. Their system has been called, too harshly, a bastard feudalism. Lordship was indeed taking on new forms. Landowners were no longer allowed to require military service for new grants of land, but more than ever, in peace as in war, they aimed at a style of living in which a retinue of knights and men-at-arms was a means to power and an end in itself. This they acquired by making contracts, for life or for a term of years, with all whose services they required, and these men drew their wages and wore their liveries. Military service and aristocratic dignity were drawn further into the network of money-transactions; but this does not mean that they were commercialized in any derogatory sense. We have seen that the pure-bred feudalism of the Conqueror's time gave ample opportunities for bullying and swindling.

In the first eight years of King Edward's war only one thing happened which had no parallel in the earlier wars. In 1340 a strong French fleet was anchored in the Zwin, the estuary leading up to the port of Sluys, where it threatened all the movements of English trading and naval ships in the Narrow Seas. The king himself attacked it, commanding a smaller force, well manned, well marshalled, and skilfully navigated. He destroyed it almost totally, but this was not only a well-managed naval victory. It was the first success outside Britain of a new mode of fighting in which the English, without any foreign examples, had trained themselves. This was the combined use of masses of bowmen and ordinary infantry. It had nothing to do with technological progress; indeed from that point of view it was backward. Cross-bows were already in use, and deadly. Edward III himself had already used primitive artillery in the siege of Berwick. The English long bow was perfect in its kind, but making it was a craftsman's job. The secret of its successes was in the skill and discipline of the bowmen. Every village had its butts, where boys and men trained hard. It is permissible to believe that the long bow was never adopted on the Continent because no other country had a social system capable of producing well-drilled soldiers who did not cease to be free men. The first proof of what their accurate, concentrated, and swiftly repeated fire could do came at Halidon Hill; the ships at Sluys, where the tactics were a variant of land-tactics, gave the next.

The third proof came at the Battle of Crécy in 1346. Crécy is about ten miles out of Abbeville, which has the lowest bridge over the Somme. Edward was engaged in a bold but hazardous operation. He landed his army in the Cotentin and set out to march eastwards the whole length of Normandy to join hands with his Flemish allies. He dodged the French king's army and crossed the Seine at Poissy, close to Paris; but he was lucky to ford the Somme before the French overtook him. He turned to bay, with the forest of Crécy behind him and the little river Maie in front. The right wing of his forward line was commanded by his son and heir, the Black Prince, who was sixteen years old. In the evening of 26 August the knighthood of France tried to overrun the English, and was destroyed. After his victory Edward captured Calais, and cleared out the inhabitants to make way for English colonists. Late in the autumn King David of Scotland invaded the north, only to be defeated and taken prisoner at Neville's Cross, near Durham. But it was Crécy which won for Edward and his captains momentary wealth and lasting glory.

The next ten years indeed brought no further instalment of either. From 1347 to 1355 there was a truce. When it ran out, the Scots captured Berwick and the Black Prince plundered Gascony. Then came the Battle of Poitiers. In 1356 he led a raid from Bordeaux into the valley of the Loire. John II, king of France, thinking to avoid the fatal error of Crécy, attacked with most of his army on foot. It was a close-run affair, but a Gascon officer led a small mounted force in a flank attack which decided it. The French losses were heavy. King John himself, with many of his greatest subjects, was taken prisoner. France was in a very bad way, and needed urgently to ransom her king. Scotland set the example and King David was released. At Brétigny, a little south of Paris, France and England agreed on what looked like the terms of a true settlement: Edward was to renounce his claim to the French throne and to all provinces north of the Loire except Calais and Ponthieu. When it came to ratifying the treaty quibbling began about the legal details, and, whether because of cunning or bad faith or pride and stupidity on one side or the other, some of the terms were left ambiguous.

For nine years there was peace, and Edward did not use the title of king of France. Then the Black Prince, governor of Gascony, was unwisely authorized to cross the Pyrenees to support Edward's ally, the deposed king of Castile, Peter the Cruel. The Prince won a great victory, lost many men, and so alienated the Gascon frontier lords by his demands for war-finance that they appealed to the French king, who summoned the prince to Paris to answer. War between England and France began again. Edward resumed his claim to the Crown. He was now inferior at sea. He had neglected his naval preparations, and the French had Castilian galleys to help them. Also the French had learnt the true lesson of their defeats. They had found the English invincible, but only twice, and these two occasions had been pitched battles, in both of which the English had held strong defensive positions. The new French leaders avoided battle. Whether the English commanders followed coherent strategic plans is uncertain. They marched far and wide, doing great havoc, but their position deteriorated. The Black Prince returned to England in 1371, broken in health. All war is cruel, and he had not overstepped the limits permitted by the laws of war; but his conduct, especially at the storming of Limoges, had been inhumane. After his return, when a truce was made at Bruges for two years, the English had no firm hold on any places in France except Calais, Bordeaux, and Bayonne. Yet they fought again, never winning. The Black Prince died in 1376, and in the next year King Edward died, having lost nearly all that he had conquered, nearly all that he had inherited, and nearly all of the good feeling between Frenchmen and Englishmen which had outlasted the earlier wars. Under his successor, Richard II, in 1388 there was another sputter on the border, a Scottish victory at Otterburn, barren except that it was followed by a three-year truce between England and France. Even in 1396, when the English king and his ministers had good reasons for aiming at a solid peace, they stopped short at a truce for twenty-eight years, and the marriage of the widower King Richard II to the French king's daughter Isabella, who had reached the age of seven.

Edward III reigned for fifty years and was the only sovereign between Canute and George III who was never troubled by rebellion or treason or plots. This extraordinary good fortune must have resulted from many favouring circumstances, but very likely the French war contributed to it by drawing off ambitious men who might otherwise have made disturbances at home. The war did arouse discontent; but parliaments had become so much a normal stage for national business that there was no opposition except in them. When the war began Edward promised that no tallage or aid, that is no direct tax on feudal tenants, should be imposed without parliamentary consent. A statute was passed that England was not subject to him in his capacity as king of

Harlech Castle, one of the massive fortresses planted by King Edward I to hold down the people of north Wales in the late 13th century. Despite its strength and lofty situation, it was captured by Owen Glendower's Welshmen in the early 15th century. However, in the Civil War it was the last of the Royalist castles to surrender to Cromwell's forces.

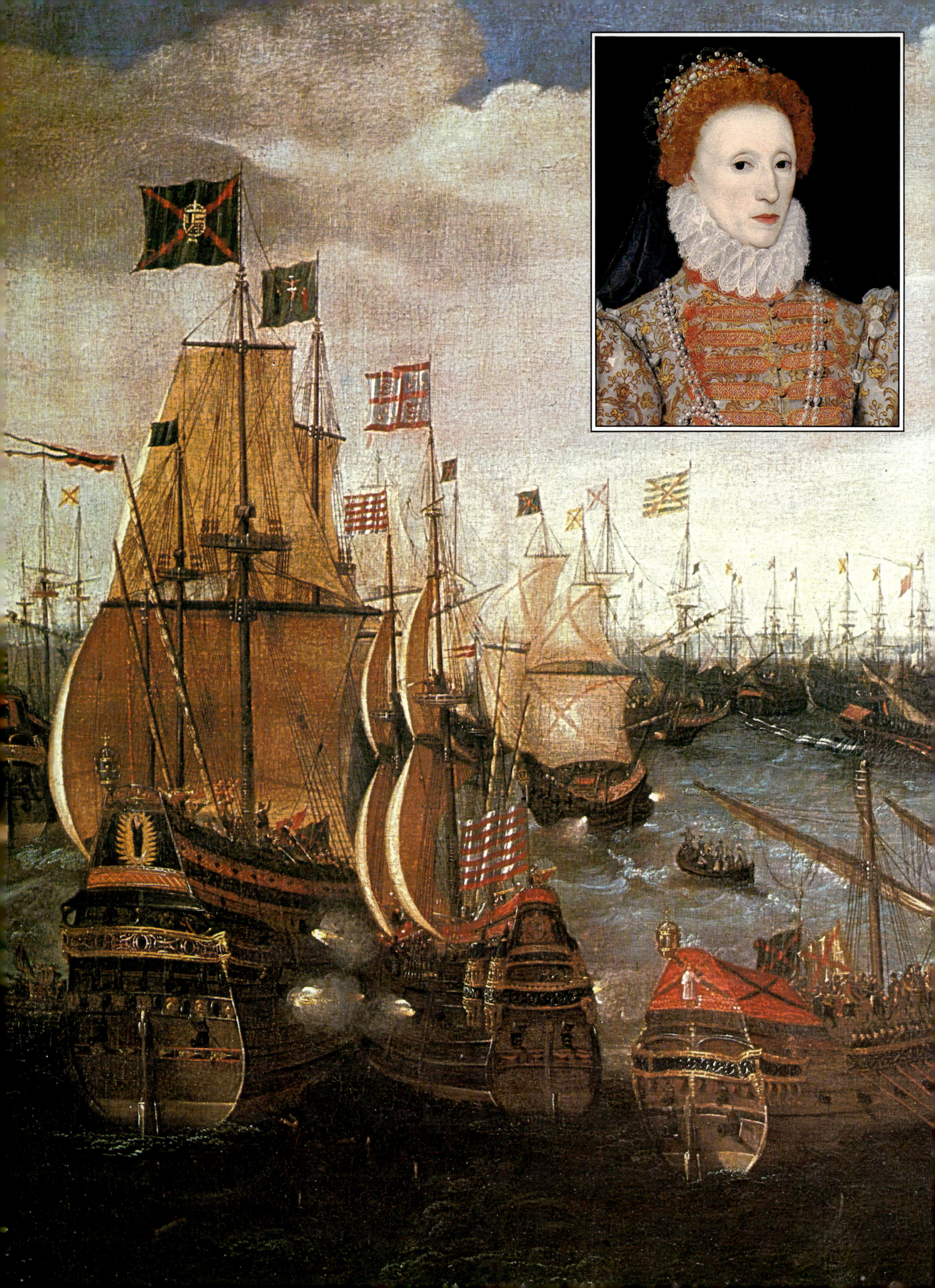

Despite achievements in other fields, especially in the arts, for many the reign of Queen Elizabeth I (inset left) is the age of Drake (inset right) and the Armada (below). Sir Francis Drake was a Devon seafarer who found that bold attacks on Spanish shipping were a quick though not easy way of gaining glory and riches. Having helped to incite the Spaniards' attack on England, he won further glory in the fight against their Armada. In a series of battles he commanded a division of the English fleet. Most successful of these actions was the attack by fireships against the anchored Armada, shown here.

Gawsworth Hall, near Macclesfield. This timber-framed house was built in the late 15th century, but has some later additions. Inside, the rooms are numerous but small, and its most imposing feature is the three-storey bay window.

France. Soon afterwards he made several far-reaching concessions, which he very quickly revoked in council; but he co-operated with his parliaments all through the period of his great victories, although it was also a period with misfortunes, including the Black Death. Two Acts restricted the pope's powers of interfering with the English church. One, the Statute of Provisors, dealt with papal appointments ('provisions') to benefices (church offices) and with the freedom of elections to offices in the church, the other, the Statute of Praemunire, with the trying of ecclesiastical lawsuits in foreign, including papal, courts. The Statute of Treasons, of 1352, defined what offences amounted to treason and what did not. In spite of many subsequent modifications it is still the basis of the law of treason, and its enactment is notable because it seems not to have been aimed against dangers that were feared, but simply against defects in the existing law.

So long as the war went on, however, Edward used all possible means of raising money, and parliaments repeatedly raised objections of two kinds. They objected to some of the methods of taxation, such as taxing the wool-merchants outside parliament, which involved granting monopolies or other advantages to the merchants or financiers who paid. They also protested against corruption and wasteful expenditure. For much of this the king's ministers were blamed, especially some of the bishops and other highly placed ecclesiastics. In 1371 some of these were dismissed to placate the parliament, but five years later the Good Parliament, as it was called, attacked another group of extortioners and embezzlers, of whom the most prominent were Lord Latimer, the merchant Richard Lyons, and Alice Perrers, the ageing king's grasping and meddlesome concubine. In order to act judicially the parliament invented a procedure (impeachment), which became a regular method of prosecuting political, and indeed other, offenders, and remained so until the eighteenth century. The commons collectively acted as accusers and the peers as judges. This first attempt had a brief success: the accused were found guilty. But a great council promptly declared the Good Parliament to be no parliament. The citizens of London, led by John Philipot and Nicholas Brembre, sided against the court and when a new and more submissive parliament met, John of Gaunt proposed to abolish some of the principal liberties of the City. John of Gaunt, the eldest surviving son of Edward III, as duke of Lancaster was the richest and most influential of his subjects. In action he was seldom or never masterful, but his collision with London constituted a national crisis. It was still unresolved when, in 1377, the king died.

This was the lamentable state of the kingdom when war began again with both France and Scotland. The new king was a boy. By something resembling a miracle the contestants reconciled themselves. Philipot led a deputation to the king and his mother, assuring them of his loyalty. A new parliament voted money for the war and made Philipot and another City man, William Walworth, treasurers of the moneys granted. They and other London merchants lent a large sum on the security of the crown jewels. French ships came raiding on the coast: Rye and Hastings were burnt, the Isle of Wight was ravaged, and the Yarmouth herring-fisheries were attacked. With French and Spanish ships in company a Scots corsair seized merchant ships at Scarborough. Philipot fitted out and manned a squadron at his own expense, recovered the prizes, and took fifteen Spanish ships as well. There were few other successes. John of Gaunt worked with his former opponents and held important commands, and the Channel coast was protected, but no serious damage was done to the French. John was appointed special envoy to Scotland to treat for peace. In 1381 he took command on the Border.

Then a thunderbolt fell. In the spring villagers in Essex refused to pay their taxes. A judge was sent down to quell what had become a general mutiny of the county, but he was seized. In June the trouble spread to Kent. Crowds assembled at Dartford and marched by Rochester to Maidstone, gathering numbers as they went, capturing a castle and defying authority. They chose as their leader Wat Tyler (Walter the roofer), a man who, at least, could lead. At Canterbury they crowded into the cathedral, and released from prison an excommunicated priest and preacher John Ball, famous for his text,

When Adam dalf and Evë span
Who was then a gentleman?

Canterbury is 55 miles from London, but it is said, improbably, that the rebels in a march of two days reached Blackheath. Essex men had already marched as far as Mile End, outside Aldgate, the eastern gate of the City. The fourteen-year-old king rode up from Windsor to his home in the Tower. On the morning of Thursday, 13 June, with his chancellor, Simon Sudbury archbishop of Canterbury, besides the treasurer and others of his council, he set out by water for Greenwich, no doubt intending to parley. When the ministers saw the mob they took fright and would not land; but when the royal barge turned back, Tyler led his men westwards along the south bank. In Southwark they opened the Marshalsea prison; at Lambeth they burnt the house of the archbishop. They met with no resistance at London Bridge, and London rioters joined them once they were across. Along Thames-side the lawyers' quarters in the Temple and John of Gaunt's magnificent Savoy Palace were wrecked.

Next day the outrages went on. The king with the mayor, William Walworth, and a handful of lords and knights went to meet the rebels at Mile End. The rebels presented a petition, and Richard replied that he would grant what they wished, that all should be free and that they might go through the realm and seize traitors, who were to be brought to him. The Essex men began to disperse, but the worst was to come. Rebels broke into the Tower, seized the archbishop and two others, and beheaded them on Tower Hill. The king and his mother took refuge in his defensible house Baynard's Castle. On the Saturday he and the mayor again faced the rebels, this time at Smithfield. The turning-point had come. Tyler was insolent and touched his weapon. The mayor stabbed him in anticipation, and another hand wounded him mortally. The mayor was knighted on the spot, and four other aldermen with him, of whom one was Philipot.

In London the rebellion collapsed at once. It had spread widely in the provinces, as far as Hampshire and Yorkshire. The worst outbreaks were in East Anglia, where there were murders and fighting besides destruction. There too it took only a matter of days to restore order. The repression was severe but it was kept pretty well within the bounds of the law; and it was soon over. In August arrests and executions were stopped, and all outstanding trials were transferred to the king's bench, which virtually meant that there would be no more capital sentences.

What had happened? It is difficult to understand the simple facts of the revolt, especially in London. We do not know even

The Battle of Crécy, Edward III's great victory over the French. Although this picture is hardly an accurate representation of what really happened, it does show in good detail the military equipment of that time, with the longbows on the right contrasting with the French crossbows on the left.

approximately how many men marched from Essex and from Kent. We do not know what elements in London sympathized with them, nor whether it was from fear of these that the City was not defended. We do not know why the garrison of the Tower let the rebels in when the king went to Mile End. However we may interpret his attitude and that of the rioters, it is hard to understand how he was able to ride or walk freely about the City on the Friday.

Probably, but not certainly, the rising was the culmination of long-gathering discontent. There had been disturbances in the countryside after the Statute of Labourers. The rebels of 1381 were not all workers on the land. Wat Tyler, presumably, was a master-craftsman. In East Anglia some townsmen and even one or two knights took their side. But it seems that the main body were tillers of the soil. That there were many villeins among those from Essex is proved by the undoubted fact that the king gave out charters of manumission, granting them their freedom from customary services, which he afterwards revoked. In Kent conditions were different, and the demands put forward there seem to be those of landless labourers. The list of demands which have come down to us are summaries made by hostile witnesses, and we do not know what literate or illiterate forms they were expressed in. They certainly show a detestation of lawyers and the law, and the rebels destroyed legal documents in many places. This shows that lawyers and the law were familiar and disliked in everyday life; but it does not prove that the rebels knew much about the nature and contents of the documents.

When the trouble started the authorities believed, no doubt rightly, that it was touched off by the poll-tax of 1380. This form of tax was new and simple: every one, whether he had property or

John Wycliffe, who lived from about 1320 to 1384. A religious reformer who yet died a natural death, he emphasized the importance of the inward piety of individuals, which he thought was becoming submerged by the emphasis the church placed on ritual and mechanical practices.

not, must pay. After experiments in taxing the clergy in this way, it was extended to the laity in 1377. In 1380 the rate was trebled: *1s.* for every man and woman of fourteen and over. The tax itself was oppressive; the collectors often behaved harshly; the tax was a failure before resistance became violent. After the revolt nothing more was heard of poll-taxes, and the idea of taxing the whole population directly did not emerge until the twentieth century. To that extent, no trifling extent, the revolt succeeded, and this may help to account for the calm which followed. But once violence began many other local or general grievances were brought up and the rebels shouted for a nightmare version of the policy of the Good Parliament. This accounts for the political murders of the archbishop, Richard Lyons, and others. So far from being the unenfranchised but politically conscious outer fringe of the nation, this shows them to have been politically infantile, and the same may be said of the cryptic threats which have been held to prove that they were to some degree organized. After that one summer there is no whisper of anything resembling an organization. Nor did the rising create a legend among the disobedient or the miserable. It was a grim and perplexing episode, not suitable for fitting into that mythology in which the outlaws Robin Hood and Little John were already celebrated as romantic champions of the oppressed.

There is, however, one aspect in which this first popular insurrection is typical of a deep-seated change in the mind of the whole people. The revolutionary period which began in the last years of Edward III is the first period in English history which cannot be understood without reference to the workings of academic thought. The rebels of 1381 were anti-clerical. They flouted the monks of Canterbury and killed the archbishop. At St. Albans they contented themselves with obtaining a charter of liberation from the lord abbot, and with doing comparatively minor material damage. At Bury St. Edmunds they set up the severed head of the prior beside that of a neighbour, the chief justice of the king's bench. At Cambridge they burnt books and papers belonging to the scholars. These excesses and others in other places were extreme examples of something which had happened here and there in earlier years. The best known was the bloody battle between town and gown, with countrymen helping the town, in Oxford on St. Scholastica's Day, 1356.

The conflicts over clerical taxation and papal claims had sometimes seemed to imply that the clergy as such had interests contrary to those of national policy. They had not been carried to extremes. During the French war the popes were at Avignon, nominally independent of the French king, but within reach of his power: it was natural that the king in parliament should repudiate the pope's right to tax the English clergy, as he did in 1366. It was equally natural that Edward III, like Edward I before him, should take into his own hands the revenues of the alien priories, or even their property; but this was done in a conciliatory manner, for instance by allowing some of the proceeds to go to new foundations of religion and learning, such as the two colleges founded by William of Wykeham, at one time chancellor, Winchester and New College, Oxford. All these practical matters raised questions of principle, and around these questions there was intense and specialized discussion among men of learning. On the Continent, especially at the imperial court, bold anti-papal writers had worked out doctrines of the nature of ecclesiastical and secular powers, from which they concluded that the Church, being not of this world, ought to leave many most important functions to the secular rulers. One of the foremost was William of Ockham, an English Franciscan, educated at Oxford. A parallel controversy among churchmen themselves raised many of the same fundamental questions from a different point of view. Among the friars there were some who upheld their original ideal and practice of poverty; but others, under the pressure of popularity and benefactions, found expedients to justify them in accepting material possessions. The question whether rich endowments were compatible with the purposes of the Church led on to the demarcation of the lay and the spiritual spheres. The parliament of 1371 debated the question whether ecclesiastical endowments should be taxed. Two friars supported the project, and there was also present an Oxford theologian, of great reputation, who was known as an upholder of the rights of the secular power.

This was John Wycliffe, the first Englishman who became a figure of national importance as a champion of dissident beliefs. In Oxford he was the leading theological teacher and thinker of his time. Since he supported the anti-clerical view in the questions of taxation and papal powers, he was employed by the government in business connected with these matters. He was favoured by John of Gaunt. In his writings and preaching he attacked one abuse after another, not only the familiar objects of criticism, but others which came to notice in the course of events, such as the right to take sanctuary in a church. He rejected the current justifications for monasticism, for penances, indulgences, images, and many other things. His weapons were not only academic and intellectual: what drove him forward was a deep desire to make religion sincere, simple, and evangelical. This made him value preaching above all other clerical functions; but his life of teaching and study led him to value the Scriptures more highly than the other sources of religious knowledge.

He argued against the accepted interpretations of the nature of priesthood. After the Good Parliament he was summoned before the archbishop of Canterbury on a charge of heresy; but John of Gaunt protected him, crowds of London citizens demonstrated in his favour, and two attempts to try his case broke down. He pushed on to a final challenge. In Oxford he denied the doctrine of transubstantiation (the key doctrine that Communion bread and wine miraculously became the body and blood of Christ). For this undoubted heresy he was condemned in Rome. A majority in Oxford backed him up as far as it dared; but the archbishop was stronger than the university, and Wycliffe was banished to his rectory of Lutterworth. Even then he had so many followers that no one ventured to molest him further and he died a natural death after several years. Unhappily for him the crisis of his career chanced to coincide closely with the revolt of 1381. There were scarcely any Wycliffites among the rebels, and scarcely any rebels among the Wycliffites; but it was inevitable that indignation against the rebels should spill over against the heretics. In his late years, however, Wycliffe planted two enduring growths. Without any systematic organization, followers of his went out as poor preachers and started a spiritual underground movement. A group of scholars, at least some of them in Oxford, made the first translation of the whole Bible into English.

The number of manuscript copies of this book which survive to the present day proves that it was widely read and known. It was not a great work of scholarship or literature. It was translated from the Latin, not from Greek and Hebrew, which were virtually unknown in England, and it was too literal to be understood. A revised version was made after a very few years. None the less it expresses a change in the status of the English language which may be called the beginning of modern English literature. The gradual social changes among the upper classes had gone so far that French was no longer the only language fit for an English gentleman. Philologists distinguish Modern English from the Middle English which was spoken from about 1150 to about 1500; but this Middle English had become a remarkably serviceable and adaptable language, with a rich vocabulary and with grammatical forms much simpler than those of Old English, as Anglo-Saxons wrote it. Although Latin was still used for many purposes, English literary prose was coming in. In verse until this time the aim of English poets had been to follow the French system of versification and arrangement; and it was now that they reached perfection in this aim. A new river of inspiration flowed in through the later works of Geoffrey Chaucer, the earliest poet whose works are still part of the daily reading of the English-speaking world. Chaucer was the son of a prosperous London wine-merchant, and for most of his life he lived in comfortable circumstances, in touch with official business and court circles. He acquired wide knowledge in the sciences and learning, and he mastered the writing of prose and verse. In 1372–3 he went on a commercial mission to Genoa and to Florence, in that century the throbbing heart of European culture. He came back not merely to translate and to imitate, but to infuse the new Italian vitality into the blood-stream of English literature. He had many moods, humorous, moralizing, lyrical, satiric, and he drew speaking likenesses of an astonishing variety of English men and women; but even he did not cover the whole range of English characters. His contemporary Langland, a poor clerk from the Welsh border, using the unfashionable old technique of alliterative verse ('fair field full of folk' etc.) in the poem Piers Plowman gave poignant expression to the sufferings of the poor. Richard II, said to be the first English king to possess a handkerchief, numbered among his courtiers men of refinement who appreciated the arts. He was himself a reader, a connoisseur of pageantry, and he commissioned buildings, in the new insular perpendicular style, though he was an admirer of all the French accomplishments.

These tastes and his character were not such as to recommend him to the warlike aristocracy, especially his uncles, the Black Prince's younger brothers. He was emotional, unreliable, and self-assertive. He had no enthusiasm for the French war, but it dragged miserably on. As before it ramified in strange directions. Richard himself made a marriage alliance which brought Englishmen into contact with the Czech nation. His wife was Anne of Bohemia, the daughter of the emperor Charles IV. Charles IV, the founder of the university at Prague, was a missionary of French culture, but an enemy to French policy. His alliance, however, proved to be useless. So did an expedition to Spain on which John of Gaunt wasted three years and much money.

Even more futile was the 1383 crusade of the bishop of Norwich in support of the Flanders rebellion. The latter was in favour of Pope Urban VI; Richard II recognized Pope Urban and opposed the rival Pope Clement VII, elected at Avignon and recognized by the French, Spanish, and Scots. Meanwhile the war against France went drearily on. The young king only once took a hand in it. The French, as a preliminary to invasion in the south, sent a force to Scotland. Richard marched against the Scots into Lothian, but he made no contact with the enemy, who took the other main road and did damage in Cumberland. With matters in that position, the king turned back to Berwick.

There had already been trouble between the king and his officers, and he soon had to face baronial opposition. In addition to their war-policy the malcontents were personally hostile to the king's ministers and entourage. Some of these were aristocratic enough, but unmilitary. The ablest and probably the least self-seeking was Michael de la Pole, the son of a merchant of Hull, whom Richard made chancellor and earl of Suffolk. The king's uncles had been raised above all earls with the new-fangled title of dukes; but the old nobility were jealous of this upstart. In a parliament in 1386 the weapon of impeachment was aimed against him, and, though not condemned to death, he was dismissed, imprisoned, and deprived of his estates. Partly because it began in this way with parliamentary proceedings, the opposition to Richard has been thought more constitutional in spirit than the opposition to Edward II, and it is true that throughout the revolutions and counter-revolutions which began with the impeachment of Pole, both sides were at pains to follow legal forms as far as they could. They had at their disposal a more developed theory of the king's prerogative, and a more settled parliamentary procedure; but in essence there was once again a naked struggle for power between the king and his opponents. After the fall of Pole a great and continual council of fourteen was appointed for one year, with powers over all matters of state and the king's household. Besides the duke of Gloucester, the most capable of the king's uncles, and others of his party it contained some ecclesiastics and others of moderate views. While the king was thus set aside, there came the one success of his war. The opposition earls of Arundel and Nottingham won a naval victory over the French and Castilians off Margate, and captured the naval port of Brest.

The king obtained an opinion from the judges, as he had a perfect right to do, that all the proceedings of the parliament, including the impeachment, were illegal. Then five lords, led by Gloucester, began civil war. They formed an army and marched on London to bring an appeal (before what tribunal is not known) against the king's intimates: from this they are called the Lords Appellant. The king promised that his closest friend Robert de Vere, duke of Ireland, should stand trial for treason in the next parliament, but the duke slipped away to the loyal county of Chester and led an army back to the south. He tried to pass to the westward of the appellants' force; but at Radcot Bridge on the upper Thames he was hemmed in behind and before. His troops broke up; he escaped overseas and was killed in the hunting field a few years later. In the subsequent 'Merciless Parliament' of 1388 the appellants secured the execution of several of Richard's advisers. In the same year the Scots won the Battle of Otterburn near Durham, which was followed by the four years' truce with France. In the next, King Richard lawfully declared himself of age and dismissed Gloucester from the council.

For five years Richard was in control, and on the surface it seemed as if normal conditions had returned. There was new legislation about provisors, and an important statute of Praemunire (see p. 81). Another statute, although it was ineffective, showed that the council knew of one possible way of mitigating disorder: it forbade all below the rank of banneret (next above a knight) to retain others, and all above the rank of esquire to be retained; it prohibited the wearing of liveries except in war or in a lord's service. Two measures were taken which, to any judgement free from fourteenth-century prejudices, must appear salutary. The French war was wound up, not indeed by a treaty of peace but by a truce made for twenty-eight years and intended to last. Richard, two years a widower, married his child-wife, Isabella, daughter of the French king.

The other step was badly needed: Richard went in person to Ireland. The devastation of Edward Bruce had been followed not by general economic and political recovery, but by a Gaelic revival. Large areas of Ulster and Connaught reverted to Irish law and customs; the authority of the government in Dublin was confined to the east-central area afterwards known as the Pale; the government itself was slipping from English control to that of the great Irish feudatories, and these feudatories, by intermarriage and by insulation from England, were ceasing to be foreigners among the Irish. Edward III had done as much as his preoccupation with the French war permitted. Shortly after the peace of 1360 he appointed his young son Lionel, duke of Clarence, to the office of lieutenant. In administration Clarence was a failure, but the Statute of Kilkenny, passed by the Irish parliament in 1366, did something to preserve the English and colonial social customs of the Pale, thereby upholding English ways of life as an instrument of power. In 1394–5 Richard spent more than six months in Ireland receiving homages and submissions, and planning pacification. He came back to England when Thomas Arundel, the archbishop of Canterbury and brother of one of the Lords Appellant, asked him to deal with the growing menace of Wycliffite heresy.

In that matter he did little, for the rest of his reign was dominated by his revenge for Radcot Bridge. In the parliament of 1397 the archbishop and his brother, and Gloucester himself, were impeached. The archbishop was banished and his brother was executed; Gloucester was murdered in prison. In 1398 a parliament at Shrewsbury annulled the proceedings of the Merciless Parliament; the king's friends who had escaped execution were restored to their estates. The king was granted customs for life, a revenue sufficient to make him independent of parliament. It also appointed a committee of eighteen to wind up its business after its dissolution. Some have thought that by means of such committees Richard planned to dispense with parliaments altogether. Of this there is no proof; but there is no doubt that he was acting as a tyrant, without respect for any law. Two of the Lords Appellant, Hereford and Norfolk, had come to terms with him and escaped the fate of Arundel and Gloucester. Now they quarrelled, and a magnificent scene was set at Coventry for them to meet in a trial by combat, with the king presiding over the lists. Before a blow was struck the king countermanded the fight and banished both the contenders. The greater of the two was Henry, earl of Hereford, the son and heir of John of Gaunt. He withdrew to Paris, where other English exiles, including the archbishop, gathered about him. King Richard received bad news. His able, if dangerous, lieutenant in Ireland, Roger Mortimer earl of March, the grandson of Clarence and heir to the throne, was killed in some petty skirmish. The king needed money and recklessly extorted fines from supporters of the Appellants, including fines on whole counties to the number of seventeen. Then John of Gaunt died. Richard confiscated his property, which was Hereford's due. Then he set out against Art McMurrough, who had proclaimed himself king of Ireland when March died. But he was less than two months in Ireland. Henry of Hereford and Lancaster had landed at Ravenspur in Yorkshire and gone to his family castle of Pontefract. The whole of the north rose in his favour, and when Richard landed at Haverfordwest in Pembrokeshire he could be sure of no part of his realm. He made for Chester but Henry was there before him. He offered terms which the king accepted; but then he took the king prisoner. A parliament, summoned in Richard's name, met at Westminster, and was told that Richard had resigned the throne. Henry then claimed the Crown on the grounds of his descent from Henry III and of his victory over Richard. The parliament accepted his claim. Archbishop Arundel led him to the throne. Decorum was so far observed that Richard was allowed four more months of life, and was disposed of so quietly that it has never been proved whether he was starved or stabbed to death.

Wars and Lack of Governance 1399–1485

1400 Chaucer dies, leaving his Canterbury Tales unfinished. Owen Glendower begins the Welsh revolt.
1401 *Statute de Heretico Comburendo* confirms the punishment of burning for heretics.
1415 King Henry V defeats the French at Agincourt.
1431 Joan of Arc is burned by the English.
1450 Jack Cade's unsuccessful rebellion demonstrates the unpopularity of the government.
1453 Final English defeats bring the Hundred Years' War to a close.
1455 The 'Wars of the Roses' begin with a battle at St. Albans.
1471 King Edward IV returns after dethronement and defeats the Lancastrians at Barnet and Tewkesbury.
1476 Caxton demonstrates his printing press at Westminster.
1485 The Battle of Bosworth Field results in the succession of King Henry VII, the first Tudor monarch.

Throughout almost the whole of the fifteenth century English soldiers were fighting either at home or abroad, and, apart from the burden of taxation to pay the expenses of the kings, there were economic maladjustments which caused depression and poverty in some regions and some occupations. By the end of the century, however, foreign visitors commonly described England as a rich country, in which the few lived expensively and the many were well fed and well clad. They were generally better off than people of similar stations on the Continent except for the most favoured parts, such as the cities of the Netherlands and southern Germany. This was due not to any sudden change in economic relationships but to gradual gains in many directions. Population probably took an upward turn. There were improvements in industrial and commercial technique, though not to any notable extent in agriculture. At the beginning of the century northern Europe still used square-rigged ships with a single mast, but by the end of it there were bigger ships, with three masts, lateen-rigged so that they could sail closer to the wind. In spite of their mutual destructiveness the states gave better protection to their traders, and this also came about step by step. In 1496 there was a commercial treaty between England and Burgundy, which was famous for a long time as the Magnus Intercursus. Probably, like Magna Carta, it first earned this name simply from its size: it had nearly forty clauses, considerably more than any previous commercial treaty. But fourteen of these clauses, in substance and in part verbally, are to be found in a treaty of 1446 with Brabant, Flanders, and Malines; others were joined to them in later treaties, and the Magnus Intercursus marked not a new beginning but the end of an evolution. The social and legal framework of international trade was becoming more adequate and more stable. One consequence of this was that the idea of a national economic interest found clear expression. The first English economic classic is the mid-fifteenth century rhymed pamphlet called *The Lybelle of English Polycye*, which advocates sea power as a means to bring seaborne commerce into English hands.

It seems that the national community was growing together into something more uniform and more compact, even though prose and poetry after Chaucer inspired piety and chivalry rather than a feeling of nationhood. The number of boys and youths who were taught in schools and universities seems to have grown, and to have been larger than in most of the continental countries. One tendency, which was alive on the Continent, emerged in England in the fourteenth century and continued in the fifteenth, the tendency to mysticism, to spiritual illumination of the believer through personal experience. The Church guided this movement sympathetically and wisely, making provision, for instance, for women who renounced the world as solitary anchoresses; but there was a frontier where mysticism might easily slide over into heresy. Wycliffe had set the bishops on the alert for heresy, and this was practically a new division in the national community.

Possibly art and architecture reflected these developments. English architecture diverged more sharply than ever before from French architecture in the later years of Edward III, and the divergence became more complete as time went on. While the French passed on from the grace of curvilinear structure to the flamboyant and the extravagant, the English worked out the perpendicular style, with its emphatic vertical lines and its use of stained glass as the main decoration of churches. They reduced much of their ornamentation to the conventional, and repetitive. They retreated from elegance, preferring the monumental, even the ponderous.

In the last phase of King Richard II it was evident that someone would have to take his place; but when the duke of Lancaster became King Henry IV it was necessary to publish an explanation of what had happened. He was a usurper, but the men of law persuaded him not to claim the throne by right of conquest. The legal learning of the time did not deny that such a right might well exist; but it almost invited a challenge. It was vaguely announced that parliament and the people were concerned in recognizing Henry; but he did not accept the Crown from parliament: if parliament could give, it could take away. Nobody took Henry's hereditary claim seriously: the earl of March, the boy whose father had lately been killed in Ireland, had a better claim through his great-grandfather Clarence, the elder brother of John of Gaunt. So Henry's constitutional position was never properly defined. In practice he and the Lancastrian dynasty which he founded, three kings all named Henry, raised a façade of correctness by working with parliament and the church. It was their plain interest to win support from these two institutions.

For more than twenty years at the beginning of the Lancastrian regime parliaments met annually except for two interruptions: the government needed to levy taxes which only parliaments could impose. The parliaments neither pressed nor altogether forgot the claims, which they had put forward in the previous reigns, for greater powers over finance and over the choice of the king's officials and advisers. The Speakers of the House of Commons were allowed to represent the house collectively and were no longer held personally responsible for the requests they made to the king; though a Speaker, Thomas Chaucer, the poet's son, found that Henry IV set limits to this privilege. On one occasion, in 1406, Henry IV conceded the demand for an audit of his accounts, not as a general principle but for a new land-tax granted two years before. One source of complaint was that the action taken by the council to carry out the king's practice in granting parliamentary petitions did not always coincide with the desires or expectations of the Commons. This was finally settled when the procedure by Bill was introduced in the time of Henry VI: instead of merely petitioning the king to deal with a matter, parliament submitted for his assent a document in the exact form of the enactment which they required.

There were limits to the ambition of parliaments. They continued to avoid direct responsibility for wars and treaties. The influence of the Commons continued to grow, no doubt partly because they carried out their indispensable duties without becoming involved in the greater political disputes. Several Acts were passed for regulating parliamentary elections. They did nothing to promote uniformity in the borough franchise: the charter of each separate borough determined which of the burgesses should vote for members of parliament, and these charters conformed to the wishes of the town rather than to any national policy. The borough constitutions became less democratic as time went on, and the fifteenth-century charters, either originally or by subsequent interpretation, for the most part limited the franchise to a narrow urban oligarchy. In the counties the franchise had never been defined. Nominally it included all the suitors in the county court. Which of them attended and voted was partly a matter of chance, and partly a matter decided by persons of influence. A series of statutes now regularized the system. The sheriffs were made to hold the elections at stated times, and to present correct returns of the results. Electing and being elected were confined to residents in the county. Then in 1432 came an important statute which professed to remedy the evil of voting by 'very great, outrageous and excessive number of people, of which most part was people of small substance and of no value'. It restricted the franchise to the owners of freeholds worth at least 40*s*. per annum net. This excluded, however rich they might be, all tenant-farmers without freehold and copyholders (those whose title to their land was a copy of a manorial court second entry, and who had almost superseded the villeins by 1500). At that time a 40*s*. freeholder was a substantial man, perhaps owning one or two hundred acres. But it must be remembered that the people of small substance probably voted far more often as bigger men told them to vote than as their own free judgement dictated. This statute was probably intended to bring order into gatherings which had been tumultuous and chaotic, and it probably had some success. Its later history was strange. It remained in force for four hundred years, and during that time the value of money fell so steeply that the electors were numbered in thousands.

Parliament was an ally worth having, and the Church also had much to offer to the dynasty. Archbishop Arundel's approval from the moment of Henry IV's accession, and the coronation ceremonies, did more than constitutional theory could do to invest him with the royal prerogative. All the three Lancastrian kings were spontaneously obedient churchmen, and it was not through any bargain or calculation that they seconded the bishops in their measures against heresy. The followers of Wycliffe were already known as Lollards, a word meaning mutterers or mumblers, which had been used as a term of disparagement for earlier, not heretical, religious innovators. The bishops took strong measures against them in the universties, but needed help from the government. In 1401 the Statute de Heretico Comburendo confirmed the existing law, by which an obstinate or relapsed heretic, after condemnation by the bishop's court, was to be handed over to the secular arm, to be punished by burning to death. It had seldom been enforced in the past; nor was anything done now to strengthen its operation by setting up special courts such as existed under the name of Inquisition in other countries. Nor did the enforcement in Lancastrian times reach the level of a severe persecution. From 1414 to 1520, apart from those who died in the former year for reasons which, as we shall see, were not purely religious, the number of Lollards who are certainly known to have been burnt is 74. There were others now unknown, but there is no reason to suppose that these executions caused widespread indignation or weakened the respect in which churchmen were held.

King Henry V. He succeeded his father in 1422 while he was in his mid-20s. But he died after only a nine-year reign; his victory over the French at Agincourt was his greatest moment.

That respect, however, was by no means unquestioning. Something was done to remove the defects of the ecclesiastical institutions: the schism in the papacy was ended, after many misadventures, by a General Council in 1415. But nothing was done to remove the main disability which made the co-operation of the government with the great ecclesiastics a source of weakness and danger. They were closely involved in the faction strife of the royal family and the nobility. Archbishop Arundel was the brother and political ally of one of the Lords Appellant. One of the richest and most powerful politicians in the reign of Henry VI was Cardinal Beaufort, bishop of Winchester, one of the legitimized, not originally legitimate, sons of John of Gaunt.

Whatever allies the Lancastrian usurper might attract to his side, the main political reality of his time was that in England power was distributed among a small number of magnates, more or less closely grouped by family connections, accustomed to form temporary combinations to further their own aims, and apt to back up their demands by resorting to force. Henry IV himself was the greatest of these magnates. The palatine duchy of Lancaster, created for John of Gaunt, gave him revenues and followers in a wide area of the north-west. His kinsmen the Beauforts also had possessions in that direction as well as in Somerset, Gloucestershire, and elsewhere. As king, Henry acquired the lands of the principality of Wales, mainly on the western side, and the county palatine of Chester, in addition to estates and castles scattered over the whole of the country from Cornwall to Hertfordshire, Essex, Sussex, Lincolnshire, and Yorkshire. The other great noble families also had their possessions widely extended, and even those which were mainly associated with special regions had outlying castles, nominally the king's, but effectively their own.

The uncertainties of Henry's constitutional position increased the chances of success for those who combined against him, and in the first nine years of his reign he put down five hostile movements. While Richard II was still alive a small number of his supporters, peers, and others made an attempt to restore him. They seized Windsor Castle, but the new king had left it. London supported him and he sent troops to round up the conspirators. Some of them were lynched, others tried and executed. One, Thomas Merke, was a bishop, and the pope did not give permission for him to be degraded. He was pardoned and survived for several years at liberty.

Henry could not be secure on his throne unless he could obtain some degree of recognition from his foreign neighbours. The king of France did recognize him, to the extent that he negotiated for the return of Queen Isabella to France and for the repayment of her dowry. When other matters were touched on, the French showed no wish for a new marriage-alliance or indeed for peaceful relations. Robert III, king of Scotland, refused to do homage, and Henry had no alternative but to force him to it. He had some hopes of support within Scotland; but he moved north in 1400 with a strong military and naval force. The Scots, however, avoided battle and Henry withdrew after spending only ten days on their soil. It seems to have been after this withdrawal that he heard bad news from the Welsh border. A feud had broken out between Lord Grey of Ruthin and a Welsh neighbour, Owen Glendower [Owen Glyn Dŵr]. Grey was not only a marcher lord, with his castle at Ruthin, but a large landowner in England, a peer, and a member of the king's council. Glendower was one of the very few Welshmen who were rich landowners; he had widely ramifying family connections, and he claimed, with at least some justification, to be descended from the old line of the princes of North Wales. He had studied law and had been in the service of Henry IV.

Glendower's squabble with Grey became a private war; the fighting spread; Welshmen assembled and attacked castles and boroughs with startling successes. Welsh scholars and workmen streamed back from England to join what was becoming a national revolt. There was no concerted English defence: the marcher lords did not co-operate with one another, or with the officers of Henry as Prince of Wales. Owen declared himself Prince of Wales. Welsh national feeling burnt high, and the bards fanned it with their traditional art; but it was not a mere renewal of the resistance which Edward I had crushed. Owen Glendower was not anglicized, but he knew England, and he was competent to take his place in the politics of the English magnates. King Henry took the crisis seriously. He sent orders summoning the levies of ten counties of the border and Midlands, which checked the Welsh on the Severn at Welshpool, and in the autumn of 1400 he marched his army round North Wales, as far as Anglesey, in person. But the Welsh national movement grew stronger and spread over the whole country. The king made a second expedition in 1401; but in 1402 Glendower took Grey of Ruthin prisoner, and also Sir Edmund Mortimer, the uncle of the earl of March. A third royal expedition failed to rescue them and kept the field only for three weeks of cold and storms. After that the revolt widened out into a crisis affecting all Britain.

Edmund Mortimer married his captor's daughter and made an alliance with him, at the same time declaring that they would restore King Richard if, as some believed, he were still alive, but if not they would place March on the throne to which he was the rightful heir. This was the first assertion of March's hereditary claim. There was worse to come. The Scots invaded England; but they were heavily defeated by the Percys, father and son, the one earl of Northumberland and the other personally famous as Harry Hotspur. Their family was the most powerful in the far north of England, and it had great estates in places further south, including Wales and the border. The father had helped Henry IV to gain the Crown, and to withstand Glendower. After they had crushingly defeated the Scots at Homildon Hill they fell out with the king in a dispute, typical of the times, about ransoms and money lent. Now they and theirs joined Glendower. The king defeated them in battle at Shrewsbury. Hotspur was killed and Northumberland was pardoned; but the crisis was still to come. Glendower found a new ally in the king of France. In 1405 the earl of March broke away from Windsor and was recaptured; but the north rose and its leaders denounced the government as law-breaking and inefficient. The king had wind of the plans formed by Northumberland and his fellow conspirators, and reached their country before they were ready. Northumberland fled to Scotland. One of three leaders executed at York was the archbishop, Richard le Scrope, who had appeared in armour. That part of the rebellion was ended; but a French force landed at Haverfordwest in Pembrokeshire and joined hands with Glendower in the capture of Carmarthen, town and castle.

There were no more battles between English and Welsh; but the English sent considerable forces and blocked any further advance. Early in 1406 the French went home disappointed, and the English applied themselves methodically to recovering the

castles and the lands around them. Three years later only Harlech held out and when it fell English rule was undisputed. Glendower never surrendered: how, when, or where he died among the hills of central Wales cannot be known. The war of Owen Glendower had kept alive Welsh national feeling. But it had devastated much of Wales. Towns had been ruined, lands abandoned, manors broken up. Henry and his parliament introduced laws making Welshmen second class citizens in their own country. They could no longer carry arms. They could not own land in the boroughs. They could not hold municipal office. In court they could not seek justice against Englishmen except before a jury of Englishmen. They could not assemble without leave. Soon there grew up an unpopular class of Welshmen, men who became officials and stewards of the crown or of English lords and obtained 'letters of denizenship' giving them the rights of Englishmen. Rich Welsh families of later generations were often the descendants of these denizens, whose offices had provided good pickings off their fellow-countrymen.

In the north of England the rebellion flared up again when Welsh resistance was in its last throes. Northumberland, unable to raise the Scots, came back to be defeated by the sheriff of Yorkshire, and killed, at Bramham Moor. Among those of his small force taken prisoner was the bishop of Bangor; but the Welsh bishops who took up arms may perhaps have had less selfish motives than those of the worldly clergy in general.

Henry IV was a man of one achievement: he set his family on the throne. He used such advantages as he had, and, although he had no opportunity of conducting bold or striking campaigns, he undoubtedly owed much to his own military skill. In one respect he owed much to fortune. France was unable to take advantage of his difficulties. Full-scale French help to either Wales or Scotland or both might have overwhelmed him; but Charles VI of France, who had reigned since 1380, was subject to intermittent mental disease, and his kingdom was as badly divided as England by faction or worse. The chief opponent of the English, the duke of Orléans, was murdered in 1407, and from that time French efforts in the war dwindled to nothing. In 1411 and 1412 there was confused English intervention, at first for but later against John of Burgundy, who was by far the most powerful of the French king's vassals.

Henry IV died in 1413, leaving relations with France and internal politics almost equally confused. The Prince of Wales was still a young man and unmarried. He was devout, and had taken part both in measures against the Lollards and in defending church property against confiscation for military purposes. From boyhood he had seen fighting in Wales and on the Scottish border. In recent years, however, he had been neither generally popular nor on good terms with his father. The first two years of his reign as Henry V seemed like an uneasy prolongation of the last. Beaufort, the bishop of Winchester, succeeded Archbishop Arundel as chancellor. The earl of March and other political prisoners were released. The Lollards were more openly active. One of the new king's soldier-friends, Sir John Oldcastle, was found to be in their counsels; stood his trial and would not recant; but escaped from the Tower. In the meantime Lollards in London tried to make plans for a rising against the government. Negotiations were begun for peace with France and the marriage of Henry to Catherine, daughter of Charles VI.

Henry's third year, however, saw an astonishing change. The English ambassadors presented the French with impossible demands, and in April 1415 it was no secret that Henry was making ready to invade France to recover his inheritance. In August his expedition sailed from Portsmouth and landed unopposed on the north bank of the Seine. Harfleur surrendered after a five days' siege. The English army was suffering heavily from disease; but with those who were fit Henry set off for Calais. The French were in force on the line of the Somme and Henry had to march as high as Béthancourt to ford it. The French fell back before him until 25 October, when they joined battle. Agincourt was the third victory on the classical English plan, a defensive position with the wings protected by woods. The French attack was pressed hard. The bowmen had to fight hand-to-hand, and at the end of the day the French cavalry reserve was intact, for which reason Henry gave the order to kill all prisoners except those of the highest rank. On the English side the casualties were extremely few; but on the French side they were enormous. The campaign yielded definite material gains, Harfleur and some ransoms, but the gain in glory was unbounded. To it may be ascribed the absence of any notable disloyalty in England for the rest of Henry's reign. At the very time when he was making ready for his expedition there was a conspiracy to put the earl of March on the throne. When it was detected three ringleaders, one of them the brother of Archbishop Scrope, were executed; but that was all, and there was no sequel.

It is impossible to give a simple answer to the question whether this military revival was due to King Henry V in person. No event in English history is more widely known, because Shakespeare's play about this king represents him with all the resources of language and imagination as the embodiment of medieval valour and kingly leadership. In strategy, Henry did better in at least one way than Edward III and the Black Prince. From 1417 to 1420 he set out to reconquer Normandy without any brilliant battles but by besieging and occupying the castles and walled towns. For this wise choice of method Henry must personally receive much credit. It was his driving-force that made the whole military machine efficient, and his dominant will that united the magnates and the parliaments behind him.

In 1419 a political crime in France opened new prospects for Henry. In revenge for the death of Orléans long before, John of Burgundy was murdered. The new duke, Philip the Good, broke away from the pro-French policy and began a new, Burgundian, aggrandisement. He offered his support to Henry: Henry was to act as regent for the imbecile Charles VI, to marry his daughter Catherine, and to succeed to the throne on Charles's death. The Burgundians had control of most of France north of the Loire. The French queen was with them. Paris was on their side. From the military point of view they could count on the communications with their own provinces in the Netherlands, and with the English both in Calais and in Normandy, where Henry was organizing his gains as the first stage of a conquest which he intended should be permanent. In the Treaty of Troyes in 1420 he committed himself to this bold project. The allies immediately carried out as much of it as was in their power. Henry married Catherine and she was crowned as queen in Westminster Abbey. The war was no easy matter. The Scots took a hand, even sending troops to help France; there were reverses; but Henry and his generals did well. In 1421, as in previous years, a strong secondary force went out from the neighbourhood of Paris to the

Knights' armour of the late medieval period. The best armour was reputed to come from Milan, but ordinary knights relied on their local armourers; the latter's technique had so improved that during the 14th century mail was superseded by plate armour. In the right-hand figure shown here, mail is retained only for the inside joints at elbow and armpit.

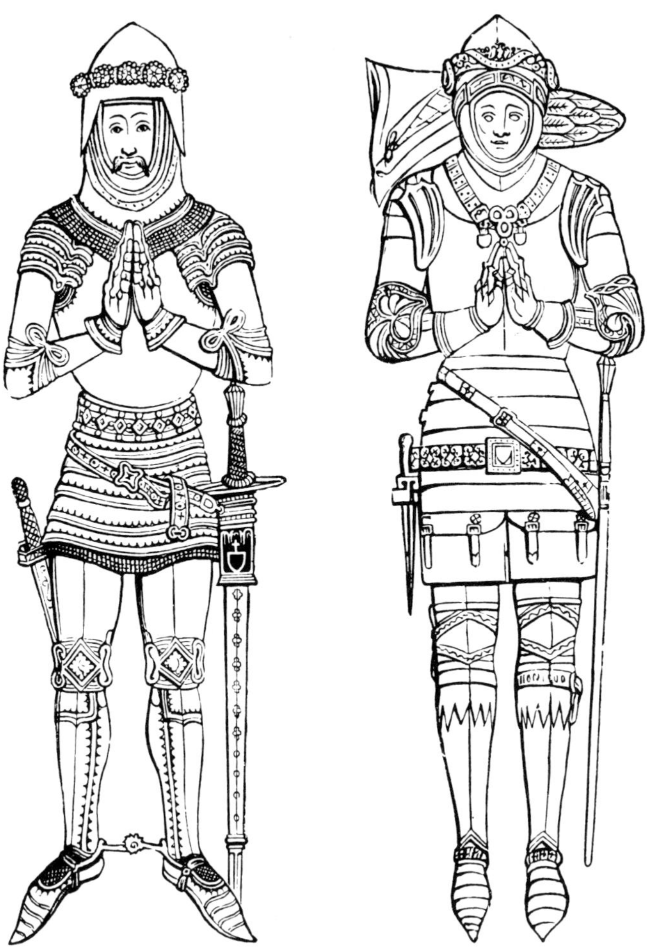

east. Henry drove back the French from Chartres to the Loire. He was using all his resources, and he had to call on his allies in Germany and Portugal for men-at-arms and archers; but in the spring he took Meaux in spite of a tough defence. The duke of Burgundy was hard pressed on the Loire and Henry started out to reinforce him; but fell ill, handed over his command and died.

If Henry had lived and reconciled the French factions as he had reconciled those of England, he might, just might, have satisfied his ambition of ruling over both kingdoms. The war dragged on for another thirty years, and more than once the English archers showed their old superiority in defence; but, as the French artillery grew stronger and more efficient, this superiority was worn away. All through this period the significant gains and losses were decided by sieges, as they had been before in spite of the shining victories in pitched battles, and in siege-craft gunnery was now the main factor. To begin with there was no sign that the military balance would change. The English had good generals in France; Burgundy was attached more firmly to their cause by new political marriages; the Scots made peace when their king, James I, was released after nineteen years as a prisoner. The Anglo-Burgundian power became supreme everywhere north of the Loire. Then came a change in France. Charles VI had died in the same year as Henry V. His successor Charles VII was weak in character; surrounded by intriguers and incompetents, and wretchedly short of money. At Orleans, the key-crossing of the Loire, an insufficient English force in 1428 was beginning a desultory siege, when the situation began to be transformed. Joan of Arc, the illiterate, visionary, peasant-girl, fired the new king and some of his ministers and generals with a new belief in France and action. A new army was raised for the relief of Orleans and Joan fought with it in armour. After the relief, the English saw her again at Jargeau, where the earl of Suffolk was taken prisoner, and at Patay where John Talbot was taken. She brought about the coronation of Charles VII at Rheims, the historic crowning-place, and this ceremony symbolized the resurrection of France.

In the loathsome catastrophe of Joan's end the Burgundians had a share: they took her prisoner fairly enough, then sold her to the English. The English called in the ecclesiastics, who condemned her as a sorceress and heretic. But Philip the Good of Burgundy saw that the French revival took away his need for the English alliance. Moreover he had grievances, for instance against John of Lancaster, duke of Bedford, the most important English soldier and statesman of his time.

The revival of France and the secession of Burgundy helped to aggravate the disagreements in England. Five years of truce were followed by a disastrous renewal of the war: Normandy was lost. There were further defeats, and some of the magnates began to arm. Two of the ministers who were blamed for the ill-managed fighting came to violent ends at the hands of the populace, William de la Pole, earl of Suffolk, and the bishop of Chichester.

Whatever other causes may have contributed to the outbreak of a rebellion in 1450, dissatisfaction with the conduct of government was the chief, or at least was the point on which the rebels concentrated most of their attention. Their rising is known as Jack Cade's rebellion, from the adventurer, perhaps of Irish origin, who was its leader during its brief duration of a little more than two months. Cade, whoever he was, had no previous political career and no known status except what he had acquired from marriage with the daughter of a country squire. He may have had some military experience; but there is little evidence that his followers were less ignorant of discipline and military operations than the rebels of 1381. No part of the country rose except Kent, Surrey, Sussex, and, later, Wiltshire. Although they demanded the repeal of the Statute of Labourers, the rebels seem to have been unlike the men of 1381 in their social origins. There was no nobleman among them and only one knight; but it is said that a great part of the gentry, the mayors of the towns, and the constables of the different hundreds took their part. In Kent and east Sussex, all men capable of bearing arms were summoned in proper form to join the rising. On 1 June they made a defensible camp on Blackheath. Henry VI came to London and sent a deputation to learn their demands. The reply was that they desired the removal of certain traitors who had too much influence in his council. In a written document they called for administrative reform, the ending of corruption in the law courts, and a change of ministry. Among the particular evils mentioned were the transfer of royal property (which the king had already promised should cease), the non-payment of royal debts, the tyranny and corruption of underlings of the court, the interference of 'estates' with county elections, and the loss of the possessions in France by treason. The king did not enter into any palaver but prepared to fight. The rebels withdrew by night as far as Sevenoaks. There on 18 May they defeated a force which advanced against them, killing its two commanders. When the news reached the royal camp at Blackheath, the troops mutinied: many of them were at heart with the rebels. The king hurried back to London. Some of the nobles immediately about him were hostile to his old advisers, one of whom, Lord Saye and Sele, he had promised to imprison. Saye and Sele was one of the 'guilty men' of the loss of Normandy, and he was also accused of extortion, as was his son-in-law William Crowner, the sheriff of Kent. The king tried to conciliate the accusers, or to protect the

An early example of Caxton's printing: 'If it please any man spiritual or temporal . . .'. This is original sales literature, advertising Caxton's services. A former wool merchant, Caxton had commercial as well as scholarly and technical talents. One of his earliest publishing successes was a chess manual.

If it plese ony man spirituel or temporel to bye ony pyes of two and thre comemoraciōs of salisburi vse enpryntid after the forme of this presēt lettre whiche ben wel and truly correct, late hym come to westmo-nester in to the almonesrye at the reed pale and he shal haue them good chepe

Supplico stet cedula

accused, or both, by putting them in the Tower. The mayor and common council begged him to stay in London, and offered not only to die for him but to pay half the cost of his household; but he betook himself to Kenilworth.

The rebels returned to Blackheath on 29 June and two days later they moved to Southwark, where a party in the common council negotiated with them. This party carried its motions in the common council, apparently with most of the citizens behind it, and the rebels were allowed to cross London Bridge. Saye and Sele was arraigned before the mayor and other justices at the Guildhall, but not tried: Cade's followers carried him off and beheaded him. William Crowner and another victim were also beheaded and there was some looting and robbing. The mayor took counsel with Lord Scales and the keeper of the Tower; on the following day Cade stayed in Southwark and in the evening troops took up a position on London Bridge. There was a long and bloody fight until nine in the morning, when the assailants gave way and agreed to a few hours of truce. The leading members of the king's council, including the two archbishops, met Cade in Southwark and offered a general amnesty, which was accepted. The rebels dispersed to their homes. Cade stayed in Southwark about a week, and then went away by water into Kent. There he raised fresh disturbances, but, seeing he was beaten, he went into hiding. On 12 July he was found in a garden in Sussex and mortally wounded as he was taken. Quiet was restored there by executions. A preliminary outburst in Wiltshire ended without any punishments. On this occasion the bishop of Salisbury, William Ayscough, the king's confessor, was dragged away from Edington church in his alb and stole, and butchered.

The events of 1450 showed that the whole structure of government at the centre and from the centre was on the edge of collapse. Many men of all ranks in society were angry at the loss of Normandy, and, even those who had not lost their employments or their hopes of enrichment, looked for scapegoats. Public finance was chaotic. In spite of heavy taxation approved by parliament the judges were unpaid and it was believed that they accepted bribes to pervert justice. Soldiers were ill paid and they could not be relied on. But the court and those about it lived lavishly. Some of the high officers were founders or benefactors of costly churches or colleges. All of them, irrespective of their responsibilities, incurred hatred and distrust in one quarter or another. Legally and in fact the ultimate responsibility lay with the king in council. Only they could remedy this 'lack of governance'. The lawyers taught that the king's authority was not despotic, not merely royal like that of the king of France, but royal and 'politicum' or, as we should say, constitutional. The king could do no wrong, in the sense that he could not be called to account for his acts; but for every one of those acts there was some minister who could be called to account. Someone was responsible at each stage for carrying out promises which the king made to parliament. Someone was accountable for errors of policy, someone who had given bad advice. But the king insisted on keeping councillors whom parliament tried to impeach, and officers of state who were notoriously incompetent or tyrannical. A point had been reached at which the Crown could no longer shield itself behind subordinate authorities, and when the king's personal acts could not be distinguished from those he did in his capacity as king.

For the rest of the century, or almost as long as that, those with political power struggled to end this embroilment, and it did end at last, but they had all grown up with their own selfish interests, and nearly all of them were prone to violence. The course of events was charted by their past experiences, and most of all by the Lancastrian usurpation. The Lancastrians were not barbarous despots and, to their credit, they had not rooted out the line of the earls of March, who had the better genealogical descent from Edward III. Jack Cade as a rebel leader claimed the name of Mortimer, the family name of the earls of March, and people about the court asked one another whether he might have some link or understanding with the contemporary representative of that family, Richard duke of York.

Besides being heir presumptive to the throne, York was a man with brains and energy, in the prime of life. With vast estates in England, the Welsh Marches, and Ireland, he had a good record in the French war. He never made any secret of his desire for a high place in the king's counsels, nor of his antipathy to the

Beauforts, especially to two brothers who were successively dukes of Somerset. In 1447 his career was checked. His enemies engineered his appointment for ten years as the king's lieutenant in Ireland, an honour which was equivalent to banishment. He carried out his duties well, though he was inadequately supported from home. In 1450, a few weeks after Cade's rebellion, he crossed to Wales without leave, and the council excusably tried to waylay him. With 4,000 men, mostly raised from his estates in the Marches, he made his way to the king, who accepted his protestations of loyalty, and promised to make him one of the members of a new council. This promise was not kept: the younger of the two Somersets, returning after disastrous failures in France, retained the king's favour. The new council, belatedly appointed, imprisoned Somerset to await trial on charges arising from the war. Two events in the royal family created a new situation. The king's mind gave way and he became incapable of doing any business. His queen, Margaret of Anjou, after eight years of marriage, gave birth to an heir. She demanded the whole government of the realm during the king's illness; but the lords appointed York protector, or, as we should say, regent. He behaved well, though he and his opponents were in arms and he had to march to the city of York to put down northern disturbances; but neither party showed undeviating respect for the law. They faced one another in what had become, step by step, a civil war.

The Wars of the Roses are commonly described as having lasted from 1455 to 1485, and in those thirty-one years sixteen or more armed encounters are counted as battles. This gives too much the impression of a continuous contest between York and Lancaster. The roses were not worn as badges in the wars and nobody seems to have used the phrase 'Wars of the Roses' before Sir Walter Scott. They were contests fought by professional soldiers, usually not in very large numbers. The high commanders were territorial magnates, which meant that they could raise recruits and pay them; they were also adventurers and politicians. There was remarkably little destruction of buildings in town or country; these campaigns were not devastating like the wars in France. By humanitarian standards the fighting was merciless; but its ill effects do not seem to have spread far beyond the soldiers and their families. For the first five or six years there was a principle at stake: the cause of York, which was the same as it had been when York was in opposition but not in rebellion, a demand for a voice in policy, with something like a national policy, and even, if possible a return to the glories of Henry V or Edward III. By 1461 that cause triumphed; but the old ingredients of disorder remained, and the old poison was mixed again. Fighting went on, from that time, as unmitigated faction-strife. Each renewal was made possible by some shift in the alliances of the magnates, and even on the field of battle, even in the last battle which ended all this misery, victory was decided because one of them changed sides. The Wars of the Roses were an expression of social forces only in the sense that the nobility wore itself out in a multiple blood-feud.

Fighting began at St. Albans in 1455. York, who believed himself threatened, barred the road to Leicester against the king and queen. Somerset was killed. For a short time the Yorkists were in the ascendant; but nothing was changed in essence; again the king was ill. York was protector; the king recovered and the queen drove the Yorkists out of office again. Then came more fighting. York and his friends betook themselves to Calais, which was in their control, and used it as a base. They returned in force, landing at Sandwich, and at Northampton they won a victory, taking the king prisoner. Then at last York declared himself: he claimed the throne by hereditary right. A parliament agreed to a compromise by which he was recognized as heir apparent, to succeed on Henry's death. By his own misjudgement York threw his chance away: he went north to chastise Lancastrian barons, but he went with insufficient force. At Wakefield he was defeated and killed. But his cause remained victorious. In 1461 the new duke of York and heir apparent won a battle at Mortimer's Cross on the Welsh border, and the queen, after winning a fight at St. Albans, had to retire to the north. Edward, duke of York, entered London, and was acclaimed as king.

Edward IV was not a usurper, or not quite. His pedigree was as good as could be; but everyone knew that he had won the throne by force, and in the course of sixty years the Lancastrians had accumulated loyalties which could not be cancelled quickly. Edward was an able man and an efficient soldier. He had the gifts which win popularity. He began his reign with military successes, among which was the Battle of Towton, the largest and most murderous engagement of them all. He mastered the north, but then he began to make mistakes. He married beneath his station. His beautiful wife, Elizabeth Woodville, was the daughter of Lord Rivers, a deserving soldier, only recently ennobled, and surrounded by relations who were unpopular as pushing upstarts.

King Edward then made a mistake which perhaps he could not have avoided: he alienated the earl of Warwick, known as the king-maker. Warwick, 'the last of the barons', was the head of a strong younger branch of the great house of Neville, and in right of his wife successor of the Beauchamps, earls of Warwick. He had been the mainstay of Edward's father's operations from Calais and elsewhere, and now he was the most powerful of Edward's supporters. But they crossed one another's plans for advancing their relatives by rich marriages, and disagreed about foreign relations. In 1469 Warwick started an old-style rebellion and succeeded only too well. He took the king prisoner and had the queen's father and brother, among others, beheaded. He had to release the king to prevent the rise of Lancastrian resistance in the north. A year later, the king's strength, after he had suppressed another rebellion, was menacing enough for Warwick to seek safety in France. The king's younger brother, the duke of

One of the earliest printed book illustrations, accompanying one of Aesop's Fables, *The Fox and the Grapes*, printed at Caxton's press. Caxton published almost 100 titles in England. At the age of 48 he had decided to learn printing in Germany, and it was only in 1476, at the age of 54, that he set up his press in Westminster.

Clarence, went with him. There Warwick was reconciled with Queen Margaret. Warwick and Clarence returned and the king fled, his destination being Burgundian Flanders. The unhappy Henry VI was brought from his captivity in the Tower and reinstated as king; but his second reign was very short. The duke of Burgundy found money and ships for Edward, who landed with an army at the same Ravenspur where Henry IV had landed. He marched on London. Clarence was the most influential of the many who came over to his side. At Barnet Warwick tried to block the way, but posted his army wrongly, lost his battle, and was killed. Too late Queen Margaret landed at Weymouth, with her young son Prince Edward, and set off to assemble the Lancastrian supporters in the south-west and Wales. Edward overtook her at Tewkesbury on the Severn, and destroyed her force. The prince was killed. The battle and the executions after it accounted for a dozen or so of the Lancastrian leaders. The Kentish men were stirred up to rise in sympathy; and once more they camped on Blackheath. But this time London stood firm. King Edward re-entered his capital in triumph and knighted twelve of the aldermen. King Henry was quietly murdered in the Tower. Edward reigned for twelve more years without having to repress any armed movement. The only person of high rank whom he sent to impeachment and execution was his brother Clarence in 1478; their relations had deteriorated after Edward had rejected a plan for Clarence to marry a daughter of the Duke Charles of Burgundy.

Burgundy, which was destined to disappear as a separate European power on the death of Duke Charles, at this time actually seemed likely to become a kingdom as big as France. For England, the two fixed points were that Calais was the one English possession on the Continent, giving access to the Netherlands on one side and to France on the other, and that England and the Burgundian Netherlands depended on one another for their mutual trade in wool and cloth. In 1475 Edward, whose sister Margaret of York had married Duke Charles, after a diplomatic preparation which consisted mainly of unfounded hopes, transferred a large and expensive army to Calais, only to find that, if he wanted to reconquer the lost territories in France he would have to do it with little or no Burgundian help. In the Treaty of Picquigny with Louis XI of France he therefore agreed to take his army home and accept a seven years' truce in exchange for cash and an annual payment.

Except for this bloodless expedition all the foreign affairs of the Yorkists and the Lancastrians were peripheral, both from their points of view and from those of their neighbours. This is true even of relations with Scotland, to which France gave help at the beginning of the civil war and again towards the end of Edward's reign. The solid progress of the cloth-trade, and of its legal scaffolding of commercial treaties, was indeed in tune with Edward's personal inclinations. He worked closely with London. He traded in wool and cloth. His success in establishing order, such as it was, depended in the first place on his military victories; but these were followed up by good management on a new line. In 1471, when Queen Margaret was a refugee in France, she was accompanied by a splendid veteran, Sir John Fortescue, the greatest English jurist of his time, and there he wrote his *Governance of England*. The final moral that he drew from the country's miseries was not that parliamentary government should be restored, but that no realm may prosper or be worshipful or noble if the king is poor. This lesson Edward IV too had learnt. There were parliaments in only nine of his twenty-three years. They passed no laws to strengthen the liberty of the subject but they paid attention to the cloth trade and to currency, to fulling-mills, the price of bowstaves and fish. Edward raised money without consent of parliament, by compulsory levies called benevolences, and by compulsory loans. These impositions did not rest on the already obsolete assessments and apportioning of parliamentary taxes. They probably fell most heavily on those who could best afford to pay. It does not appear that their arbitrariness caused resentment. Edward's time, for a variety of reasons, seems to have been comparatively prosperous for the lower and middling classes. In the country wages were high and prices low. In the towns great buildings rose, such as St. George's Chapel at Windsor and the collegiate church at Fotheringay. William Caxton, employed in the household of Margaret, duchess of Burgundy, learnt the new art of printing, which he demonstrated to the king and queen in the cloister of Westminster Abbey.

King Edward IV died in his bed and was succeeded by his son Edward, a boy of twelve, who had been born in sanctuary in that same abbey when his father was in exile. Two great evils were still not uprooted, the power of overmighty subjects and the savage cruelty of the ruling few. The boy king had one surviving uncle, Richard duke of Gloucester. In a matter of weeks he seized the king and his younger brother, became protector, did away with three great noblemen who might have resisted, had the late king's marriage declared invalid and accepted for himself an offer of the Crown. With him the monarchy reached its lowest depth. Even if he had not procured the murder of the two young princes in the Tower, of which his guilt is almost certain, he would have been the type of a tyrant. He did meet a parliament, which declared benevolences illegal and passed other useful Acts. It took two years for nemesis to overtake him; but his hopes of winning over the country dissolved very early and most of his reign was spent in defending himself and making ready to defend himself again. One rebellion was crushed, and one more duke executed. Then Henry Tudor, earl of Richmond, an exile with high dynastic connections, who had never seen an arrow shot in anger, landed in a remote village in Wales, Milford Haven. With him were two thousand men, some supplied by the French king; but he rightly trusted to his fellow Welshmen and to the English magnates who would join him on the march. In mid-August, at the Long Mountain near Welshpool, Henry was joined by Rhys ap Thomas with a strong force from mid-Wales, as well as by forces sent from south-east Wales and by the tribes of north Wales. Little more than a week later Henry confronted the royal army at Bosworth in Leicestershire. As his banner he unfurled the red dragon which had been the standard of Cadwaladr, whom he regarded as the last Welsh king of Britain. King Richard, wearing his crown, attacked. His old comrade-in-arms Sir William Stanley, with his redcoats, did not move. He waited for the decisive moment and then came in on the other side. Richard was killed and Stanley put the crown on Henry's head.

Henry VII and Tudor Government 1485–1603

1487 The attempt to instal Lambert Simnel as king fails.
1489 Act to prevent the conversion of arable land to pasture is passed.
1495 Poyning's Law brings Ireland into the English structure of government.
1497 Cabot discovers Newfoundland. The Cornish rising is suppressed: Pretender Perkin Warbeck is captured.
1536 The Statute of Wales strengthens the Anglo-Welsh connection.
1543 Further laws are passed to cement the union of England and Wales.
1569 Unsuccessful rebellion of northern earls.

King Henry VII was a Welshman. He was born in Pembroke Castle and spent most of his boyhood in Wales. His victorious army had a Welsh nucleus. He belonged to the great family of Tudor, one of whom had died for Owen Glendower. His grandfather, Sir Owen Tudor, had served Catherine of Valois, the widow of King Henry V, as clerk of the wardrobe and had married the great lady, so that the Tudors came into the front rank in the Wars of the Roses and Henry had at his back the old Lancastrian domains, Pembroke and Glamorgan. His mother, a Beaufort, had gained by a later marriage something of the power and influence of the Yorkist marcher lords, and now, as king, he acquired the 'principality' formed by Edward I, divided into the shires of Anglesey, Caernarvon, Merioneth, Flintshire, Cardigan and Carmarthen. He gave his eldest son the legend-charged name of Arthur and sent him, as a boy, to hold court at Ludlow.

Henry's Welsh supporters were rewarded with offices. Rhys ap Thomas received so many appointments that he became the virtual ruler of southern Wales. This interrupted the customary Anglo-Norman domination of south Wales. So many Welshmen followed Henry to London that their presence was resented by the English at court. Welsh bishops were appointed to Welsh bishoprics. One Welsh supporter, David Seisyllt, rose to become sergeant of Henry's guard, a wealthy landowner, and ancestor of a family, the Cecils, which produced a great Elizabethan statesman and the earls of Salisbury.

But despite his sincere intention of doing much for Wales, the new king soon found his attention occupied by more pressing matters. The Welsh bards began to sing their disappointment. But towards the end of his reign Henry sold charters to various lordships, and finally to the principality of North Wales, which freed Welshmen in those lands from the low status imposed on them after the defeat of Owen Glendower. They could hold land and offices without restraint, and became equal with Englishmen before the law.

Tradition has it that on his deathbed Henry charged his son and successor with special care of his fellow-countrymen. Be that as it may, King Henry VIII did little for Wales in his early years, contenting himself with acquiring various Welsh lordships for himself and putting down lords who seemed too powerful to be tolerated. Nevertheless, in the final years of his reign the union of Wales with England was accomplished. One motive for this was the need to impose order in Wales, where those entrusted with the administration of the law had become themselves the biggest law-breakers. Another impulsion was the requirement for a stable and effective administration in the face of possible dissaffection arising from Henry's break with the Roman Catholic church. But, in broader terms, the union was part of a process in which monarchs sought to end feudal survivals which limited their sovereignty, and to establish a centralized government over the whole of their dominions. The union with Wales

King Henry VII handing to the abbot his instruction for the foundation of the King's Chapel in Westminster Abbey. This chapel, with King's College at Cambridge and Bath Abbey Church, represents the flowering of native English architecture in the early 16th century.

was a first step for English monarchs, and would be followed eventually by unions with Ireland and Scotland.

The Statute of Wales of 1536 laid down, somewhat tentatively, the broad line of approach, while the Act of 1543 was more confident and detailed. The 1536 legislation divided Wales into English-style shires. Some new shires were created, like Brecon and Montgomery. Some lordships were incorporated into existing shires. The absorption of lordships of the Marches by Shropshire, Herefordshire and Gloucestershire in effect determined the frontier of Wales; this frontier marked neither the edge of the Welsh-speaking lands nor of the Welsh dioceses, but this was not felt to matter since the new union would make the frontier irrelevant. The new county of Monmouth, because it was close to London, was made subject to the Westminster courts in legal matters. Henceforth it was in the anomolous position of being part of England for some purposes, and part of Wales for others. Because the intention was to win the hearts and minds of Welshmen, the whole approach of the 1536 and 1543 acts was conciliatory. Welshmen, if they were to become part of England, had to have the same rights as Englishmen. So they were to send their own representatives to parliament. They were given the English common law and the English judicial system. Their own justices of the peace were to administer the law. Welshmen acquired full citizenship rights. The old Welsh laws of Hywel Dda were superseded, and by this time there were few who regretted their disappearance.

The 1543 Act, among other things, gave statutory authority to the council of the Marches, which already existed at Ludlow, and became, in close touch with the privy council, a central administrative body with some judicial functions. Its president was responsible for defence and the preservation of the peace. The same Act completed the structure of the law-courts and brought land-tenure under the English common law, which meant, among other things, that primogeniture, the succession of the eldest, became the rule instead of the division of inheritances. On this basis Wales came to be a land where increasingly Anglicized squires, who were also justices of the peace, formed part of the ground floor of the constitution. While equality of all before the law was the paramount consideration, the 1536 stipulation that the courts' business would be only in English meant that the Welsh tended to regard the new laws, fair though they were, as alien and even hostile. Yet the imposition of English was not with the worst of intentions, even if not quite with the best either. It was simply a means of establishing the uniformity which the new forms of government required. Efforts were indeed made to ensure that Welsh-speakers would not be at a disadvantage; provision was made for court interpreters, and later it was recommended that at least one assize judge should have some command of Welsh. Yet the fact remains that, starting with the class of officials, an ever-increasing number of Welshmen found it more rewarding to speak English. Insofar as it is in its language that a nation demonstrates that it is still a nation, this process could only be at the expense of Welshness. However, in later decades and centuries the Welsh language continued to flourish as the language of religion. Starting with the Reformation, which most Welshmen neither resisted nor welcomed, the spokesmen of new religious movements realized that, to make headway, they needed to address the Welsh in their own language. The first Welsh-language book to be printed, dated 1546, contained the Creed, the Lord's Prayer, and the Commandments. For some reason it lacked the Eighth Commandment, and a title too; so it was called *In This Book*, these being its first words [*Yny lhyvyr hwnn*].

In their main purpose of establishing order and law, the acts were successful. Nor was this the only benefit to Wales. The new order deserved some of the credit for an improvement in the cattle-trade and in the Welsh woollen industry. This migrated from the south and west to the six counties of North Wales, where, with Oswestry as its staple-town, it flourished. The Tudors were the most exalted of the Welsh families who rose to power in England; but there were others below them in gradation from the next highest, the Herberts (originally Norman but almost wholly Welsh in blood), through the Cecils, to merchants, lawyers, barber-surgeons, and craftsmen who made fortunes in London or Shrewsbury or Chester which they could not have hoped for in Wales.

Not only was there more coming and going between England and Wales, England itself was being opened up and it was becoming both easier and more useful to think of it geographically. Until this time maps of England were rarities. Now several causes joined together to make them familiar possessions for men of affairs. Surveying, with better instruments and a better scientific basis, produced more accurate maps. Landowners ordered maps of their estates. Printing made it possible to produce maps of wider areas in many copies. About 1574 Queen Elizabeth authorized Christopher Saxton to draw maps of every county in England and Wales. Her minister William Cecil, Lord Burleigh, a man for figures and calculations, carried a map of England about with him. A rudimentary postal system appeared, perhaps copied from that introduced in France by Louis XI. An Act of Parliament in Queen Mary's time imposed on parishes the duty of providing labour and materials to keep in repair the main roads which ran through them. In the first year of Queen Elizabeth there came a change in the customs system which, for the first time, made it possible to know with some degree of accuracy what quantities of goods were exported and imported.

One of Christopher Saxton's county maps. Good maps were a prerequisite of good rule. This example shows Northumbria, and although it shows considerably less detail than modern maps, and is less exact, it was a great advance.

This was the provision that no goods should be loaded or discharged except in daylight and at open places designated for the purpose, which afterwards came to be called the lawful quays. The possibility of analysing and estimating the customs revenue helped statesmen to regard it not as an item of public income earmarked, like the other items, for special purposes, but as a contribution to a public revenue which could be estimated as a whole and distributed among all public purposes. Thinking topographically led to thinking of the king's revenues not only as the dues which his subjects rendered to him, but as his share of the wealth of all his people, and so to the inference that the surest way to enrich the king was to husband the wealth of his realm. This attitude of mind was essential to the main endeavour of the Tudors, to bring about social peace through the establishment of their dynasty.

The council of the Marches of Wales was one of three regional councils. Their purpose was not devolution of functions from the centre, but more effective transmission of central purposes to the circumference. The council of the west, was short lived and unimportant. But the council of the north dealt successfully with a major problem. The north was comparatively poor and thinly populated as it had always been. In the border country and a good way south of it society was predominantly military, and there was no middle class worth mentioning. The city of York was the most northerly urban centre of the lowland zone, and Hull was a thriving port; but there were less than a dozen municipal corporations north of the Trent. All the evils of fifteenth-century England were deeply rooted there. The kings normally governed through the Percys, and the only alternative, when the Percys were out of hand, was to build up the Nevilles. From time to time experiments were made with new arrangements of functions. The border country kept its division into three marches, west, middle, and east, each with its warden, one being sometimes set over the other two. Yorkshire, the base area, where troops and supplies for operations against Scotland were assembled, had its separate authorities. In both areas but especially towards the border, justice was impeded by the surviving powers of feudal lords, and most of all by immunities, such as that of the bishop of Durham, where the king's writ did not run. The royal servants used such means as they could to extend their control, and sometimes their opportunities were very great, as for instance when Cardinal Wolsey, the all-powerful minister, was both bishop of Durham and archbishop of York. After his fall the Crown boldly ousted the Percys and

The checking of weights and measures in Henry VII's Exchequer. While the first duty of a monarch was the maintenance of law and order, the establishment and upholding of standards was another important function. Standard weights and measures were especially important for the development of trade at home and abroad. Under the Tudors standardization became more scientific.

others from their privileged positions, and parliament ratified the action. But in 1536, as we shall see, the problems of the north came to a head in a rebellion called the Pilgrimage of Grace. The council sitting at York then received its constitution, and settled down to a century of effective work, partly judicial and partly administrative.

The regional councils were instruments of the central authority, and few of the potential breeding-grounds of local resistance escaped notice. In 1504, for instance, an Act of Parliament ordered all guilds and fraternities in the towns to submit their by-laws to the king's judges before enacting them. In all these measures, however, there were very few new ideas: what was novel was that they were firmly enforced. King Henry VII himself repaired the two defects that Sir John Fortescue had pointed out. He began his reign with debts; but towards the end of it he had annual surpluses and a substantial 'treasure' of plate and jewels guarded in the Tower of London. He had pressed his legal rights against encroachments, and he had firmly confiscated the lands of unruly subjects. His parliament granted him the customs for life, as Richard II's had done in 1398, and he made the most of the gift by presiding over a policy of encouraging seaborne trade. Parliament provided for his occasional special expenditure. He did not reform the system of taxation, although it needed reform, and his agents were hated as tax-gatherers usually had been; but he was a financier and a reader of account-books. He was the first English sovereign to enjoy the advantages of solvency, and we may say that posterity, in spite of outrageous lapses, never entirely disregarded the lesson.

Henry in person was also the leader of the body of counsellors and office-holders who coped with aristocratic contempt for the law. They renewed, strengthened, and carried out the prohibitions of livery and maintenance. Landowners no longer organized retainers in para-military formations. They no longer openly thwarted the regular administration of justice. The last time a nobleman fortified a castle in the old manner came when the earl of Leicester bought cannon for Kenilworth in the fifteen-seventies. Naturally it took time for this great reform to work its way through the body politic. Great lords, generations later than this, could still call their tenants to arms in a crisis, and their dependants still had unfair advantages with juries or even with judges; but in Tudor times the process made a notable advance. The feudal system of service for all purposes faded away. There were still rebellions and noblemen who led them; but they lost their feudal character. There were new causes for civil strife, among them bitter disputes about religion, and disturbers of the peace were often actuated by principle. Governments were less troubled by overmighty subjects, but more troubled by popular disturbances, and they used all the available resources of propaganda, such as the pulpit, to denounce the sin of wilful rebellion. At the same time the governments could attract young men to their service who, in earlier times, would have sought activity and adventure on horseback with their lords.

The Tudor dynasty as a whole maintained its systems of government for more than a century, and by its means made the English into a more united community so far as the old regional and feudal divisions were concerned, though new fissures were opening. Tudor rule was despotic in the methods by which it dealt with emergencies, of which there were many; but it was not despotic in the normal conduct of affairs. Essentially it was government by the sovereign in council. The church, the civil and criminal courts of law, and parliaments when they assembled, stood half outside the system, with rights of their own, not clearly defined. They were not bound to obey, as subjects were bound to obey in all their other capacities. The council had members of different kinds, all ultimately chosen by the sovereign. There were some magnates of the realm. There were the holders, whoever they might be, of great offices, the chancellor, the treasurer, the archbishop of Canterbury, and so on. There were also holders of much lower offices, and the old baronial complaint against councillors of humble birth was ceasing to be much more than a reactionary grumble. These lesser men, among whom the proportion of laymen to ecclesiastics grew steadily, were trained to administrative work, in which they found their whole careers. The council in 1536 had forty members, among whom were four bishops and fourteen temporal peers. The remainder were commoners. Two of them were the king's secretaries, whose office was rising in importance and would soon be called secretaryship of state. The council did work of every kind, the king attending only for some special reason, and it sat in secret. Its power of legislating was limited by the rule that it could not override an Act of Parliament. Its judicial powers were used to fill up deficiences in the working of the courts, especially in cases of great offenders. Much of its judicial work was done in a court, an offshoot of the council and composed of some of its members, called the court of star

The Court of Common Pleas in session. Henry VII, like many of his predecessors, took seriously the popular saying that 'a good king is a just king'. Though monarchs had delegated their judicial authority to judges, they kept their right to sit in judgement. Henry VII encouraged litigants to appeal to him for redress in the king's council if the courts of common law had been unable to reach a fair judgement.

chamber. This court sat in public, and its procedure was simpler and easier to understand than that of the king's bench or the common pleas. Its merits were appreciated, and the same is true of the court of requests, which had a similar origin and handled certain kinds of civil suits.

Under the Tudors the parliaments were not yet indispensable to the daily working of the government; the Tudors summoned them sometimes when they were necessary, as when direct taxation was needed, and sometimes because they were useful, of which the most obvious example was the ecclesiastical legislation which began after the fall of Wolsey. In the reign of Henry VII there were seven parliaments, six of them in his first twelve years, in the six of Edward VI there were two, in the five of Mary five, and in the forty-five of Elizabeth ten. Henry VIII began with six parliaments in six years, but in the fourteen years of Wolsey's dominance there was only one, and the next, which followed his dismissal, sat on and off for seven years. The sovereign decided not only when they were summoned and when dismissed, but in the main what business should be put before them. He could lawfully influence the composition of the House of Commons. No one thought it improper for lords of the council to write to sheriffs or others bidding them see to it that members of one complexion or another were returned. Public business could not be done satisfactorily without a sufficient number of fully informed men, that is of office-holders, in the Commons to guide their debates. The Crown could add to the number of members by granting charters to new boroughs, and some of the seats so created were easily filled by its own nominees. The statute of Henry VI confining election to residents in the constituencies had become a dead letter. Edward VI added twenty-two members, fourteen of them from seven boroughs in Cornwall; Queen Mary twenty-one members, returned by fourteen boroughs. It is reasonable to include justices of the peace among the holders of offices: although they were virtually unpaid their status meant a good deal among their neighbours. A large proportion, perhaps half, of any parliament were therefore predisposed to support the government. There might be degrees of willingness in their support, from free assent to subservience; but the House was likely to co-operate with the government unless some exceptional conditions roused opposition.

In the Tudor period there were six wars against France and Scotland, and, after the last of them, one against Spain; but they were unlike the wars of Edward III and Henry V. Four times the English sent expeditionary forces to France, and two of them made temporary conquests; but none of the four penetrated more than a day's march from the coast. The only war which lasted long and imposed a heavy strain on the national resources was the almost entirely maritime war against Spain. Compared with the early fifteenth century or the late seventeenth, the sixteenth century was comparatively peaceful; but this does not prove that the statesmen of the Tudor period were timorous; it was so because their national ends could be secured without committing the whole strength of the country to armed conflicts. The Tudors did something to organize both the army and the navy. Henry VII began his reign by providing himself with a bodyguard, which still exists as the Beefeaters. Henry VIII strengthened the defences of the coasts facing France by building castles, as they were called, forts with no high walls or towers, to make them less vulnerable to artillery, and with well-designed gun-emplacements. He took an interest in naval architecture. His own ships were few, but built for size and display; the fighting fleets consisted mainly of merchantmen requisitioned from private owners and navigated by their own masters; but the men-of-war set standards of design and equipment. The dockyard at Portsmouth, the principal naval base, was extended and equipped accordingly. Queen Mary's ministers took in hand the militia. The organization was based on the counties. A new and dignified officer, the lord lieutenant, was the county commander. The militiamen had to provide their own arms and armour, as in earlier centuries. The exchequer sent down coat and conduct money and the colonels, taking so much per man, supplied clothing and other necessaries, a system which in practice was both corrupt and inefficient. But the militia gave a good account of itself in action. The office of the ordnance, which supplied artillery to the army and navy, seems not to have been in good order. In 1598 it was reconstituted, with a suitable division of functions between the officers, and from that time there were periodical inspections of the artillery in the various fortresses and arsenals.

Henry VII had a Lancastrian claim of sorts to the throne, but forestalled a revival of serious Yorkist claims by marrying Elizabeth, the eldest of the children of Edward IV. The marriage did not entirely eliminate Yorkist claims, and one of them was backed by a considerable Yorkist party in England. With money provided by Margaret, widow of Charles of Burgundy and sister of Edward IV, Yorkist refugees in the Netherlands assembled 1,500 German mercenaries and took them to Ireland. There Lambert Simnel, a boy of obscure origin, had declared himself to be the earl of Warwick, the son of Richard III's victim Clarence. The true Warwick was a prisoner in the Tower and the king displayed him in public to make sure the fact was known. The conspiracy went forward. In Ireland the Yorkist Fitzgeralds were supreme. The earl of Kildare, of that family, was lord deputy and declared for Simnel. Within a month the rebels, with their Germans and some Irish, landed in north Lancashire. Henry was more than a match for them. He won an unqualified victory when they attacked his defensive position at Stoke on the Fosse Way, south of Newark. After the battle he showed the clemency which was habitual with him. He renewed the commercial treaty with Burgundy originally negotiated in 1478. More would have been needed to make him secure against a similar attempt. When it came, in 1492, it took eight years to stamp it out, but in the end no possibility remained of renewing the Wars of the Roses.

By that year France had to be taken into account. Before he came to the throne, Henry had found shelter in Brittany and he had come to England with French assistance. He had no firm peace with France, but only a treaty with a time-limit. Now, under the regency which acted for a new king, Charles VIII, a minor, France was advancing on two fronts. Brittany's autonomy was more seriously threatened than ever before, and the governor of Picardy was capturing towns on the Burgundian frontier. The duchess of Burgundy had married Maximilian, the son of emperor Frederick III, but the emperor's fortunes were at a very low ebb and he could offer no help. The French might soon possess themselves of the Breton shipping and harbours, and also of Calais. In Celtic Brittany there was a quasi-national feeling, and Henry allowed Lord Scales, the queen's uncle, to take an unofficial raiding force to its assistance. The French regular troops destroyed it. Henry apologized and negotiated, but with no success, and in 1489 he went to war in earnest. He sent 6,000 men to Brittany. A smaller force, which he sent ostensibly to reinforce Calais, won an important success by relieving Maximilian's town of Dixmude, in imminent danger of falling to an army of Flemish rebels. Charles VIII solved the problem of Brittany by marrying its duchess, so uniting it to the French crown.

A middle-class youth from Tournai, Perkin Warbeck, was in training for the part of Yorkist pretender, and he landed in Cork. In Ireland he made no headway but he decided to impersonate Richard, duke of York, the younger of the princes murdered in the Tower. Charles VIII invited him to France. King Henry made preparations for war on a larger scale, raising money by a benevolence. In October 1492 his large army sailed from Dover to Calais and sat down before Boulogne. But the campaign lasted only three weeks and was almost bloodless. Henry had no need to consider his allies, who had done nothing for him. The French offered large money payments for his expenses in Brittany, and for arrears under the Treaty of Picquigny in 1475, with commercial and maritime clauses, and a promise not to aid his enemies or his rebels. This Treaty of Étaples was an anticlimax. It was unpopular with the bellicose among his subjects; but the French kept their promises. The largest of the loose stones in Henry's political structure was firmly cemented in.

Perkin Warbeck had to leave France, but he found a welcome at Bruges from Margaret of Burgundy. The archduke Maximilian paraded him as far as Vienna in the character of duke of York, an aimless indiscretion. He corresponded with adherents in England, but Henry found informers, and a batch of lesser men were executed for treason, followed in 1495 by Sir William Stanley, reputed to be the richest subject in England, the same whose action had decided so much at Bosworth. Warbeck, however, appeared off Deal with fourteen ships. Two or three hundred of his followers landed without their leader, but the inhabitants set upon them and eighty survivors were taken up to London, where most of them were hanged. There was still Ireland. In the years since Lambert Simnel's appearance there Henry had made some progress, but not very much, in establishing his authority. The rivalries of the great families, especially of the Fitzgeralds and the Butlers, frustrated all attempts to govern through them, so that he appointed his infant son Henry as lieutenant, with an able and faithful soldier and administrator, Sir Edward Poynings, to be his deputy. Ireland was legally brought into the Tudor system by Poynings Law, which was not repealed until 1782. Actually there were two Acts of the Irish parliament. First, no parliament was to meet there unless the lieutenant and his council obtained the king's leave, and submitted a list of the Acts it was proposed to pass. Secondly all laws made in England should also apply to Ireland. Other statutes of the same parliament dealt with many administrative and financial matters, and Henry's able servants brought the Pale into the condition they aimed at. For the rest of Ireland Henry reverted to the most economical and the least hazardous policy: he put his faith in Kildare as lord deputy and was not disappointed. In the meantime Warbeck had failed almost as badly as at Deal. His eleven ships and the landsmen brought up by Desmond, like Kildare a Fitzgerald, failed to take the loyal town of Waterford, and he sailed away, this time to Scotland.

Warbeck was now no more than an insignificant adventurer. Burgundy had given him little enough help, and when Henry VII concluded the Magnus Intercursus (see p. 86) it contained a clause by which neither country should aid the other's rebels. Nor had Scotland any quarrel with England. The Treaty of Étaples had ended for the time being any chance of her being called upon to act under her alliance with France. But King James IV was young and all for action. He rashly gave his cousin Catherine Gordon to Warbeck in marriage and invaded England on Warbeck's behalf, but the invasion was an almost incredible fiasco. In 1497 Warbeck went back to Ireland. After a month news came of a rising in Cornwall. The Cornishmen, half foreign with the Celtic language which many of them still spoke, were so far from the Scottish border that they had more reason than anyone else for grudging the heavy taxation which the king raised, ostensibly for a punitive expedition against James. In May 1497 a mass of them, chiefly miners, set off, as they guilelessly believed, to petition the king. They had at least one lawyer with them, but their leader was a blacksmith. In Somerset a discontented nobleman, Lord Audley, joined them. They moved quickly, without violence, and they are said to have mustered 15,000 men; but they had few horses or firearms. The king had in hand the troops raised against Scotland, and he raised more. As the insurgents approached London from the west, finding their way barred, they bore right and made for Kent, the country of Wat Tyler and Jack Cade. They tried in vain to raise the commons,

The *Henri Grace à Dieu*, or *Great Harry*. This, the pride of Henry VIII's navy, was a vessel of 1,000 tons, and in its essentials (though not size) was little different from the line-of-battle ships of the early 19th century.

and their march was wavering when they encamped on Blackheath on 16 June. Next morning, Henry sent in his strong army to attack, and broke them to pieces. London had stood firm. There were only three executions, Audley, the smith, and the lawyer, and Henry exercised his clemency characteristically by inflicting no punishment except heavy fines.

Nearly three months after this hammer-blow Perkin Warbeck, with something like 120 men, landed at Whitesand Bay in the extreme west of Cornwall. That Cornishmen gathered to his standard is a fact most difficult to understand, but when he proclaimed himself at Bodmin as King Richard IV there were three or four thousand of them. Their numbers swelled, and they tried to fight their way; but Exeter, with gentry of Cornwall and Devon behind its walls, beat them off with heavy slaughter. They turned north to Taunton, with the county levies forming all round them and the king's army in motion. Perkin rode away secretly, but he was captured at Beaulieu in Hampshire and made to confess all his impostures before he was taken away and shut up in the Tower. Again Henry showed his clemency. A few ringleaders were hanged at Exeter. Counties, boroughs, and individuals who had failed in their duty, including some of the minor landowners, were heavily fined.

Warbeck's adventures had an evil sequel. After two years as a far from submissive prisoner, he was hanged, and he deserves no sympathy; but a harmless man, the earl of Warwick, Clarence's son, was also executed. The two had plotted to escape, and even if the plot was not a trap set by their keepers, Warwick's death was a judicial murder. That Henry should depart from his clemency so completely is explained by his foreign policy. In its main lines it remained simple and reasonable, to avoid wars and to open the widest opportunities for English trade, especially preserving that with the Netherlands. Scotland might have been a difficult neighbour, but King James IV had work to do in Scotland and was under no temptation to engage in a full-scale war. After border-fighting in 1497 and again in 1498, he agreed to truces which preserved the peace until 1513. He agreed to marry Margaret, the daughter of Henry VII. This was significant both as an encouragement and as a symbol of neighbourly relations. It was a fruitful marriage and almost exactly a century later the great-grandson of James and Margaret inherited the English throne and brought the two kingdoms into personal union.

Henry brought about another marriage, not fruitful but laden with fate, between the boy Arthur, Prince of Wales, and Catherine, the youngest daughter of the joint rulers of Spain,

Ferdinand, king of Aragon, and Isabella, queen of Castile. The personal union of Castile and Aragon, unlike the union of England and Scotland when it came, was not a single tie, but one link in an unparalleled series of political marriages. When it was formed in 1479 it created a new balance in European affairs. The two kingdoms, each with its own vitality and its own interests, in combination formed a single unit in international affairs, the great power of Spain. Most Spanish concerns were remote from English interests, but if Henry VII was to strengthen his dynasty in the manner of the time by a marriage alliance, none could be so advantageous as one with Spain. But the European marriage-network began to close in on England's one vital continental interest. In 1496 the Austrian archduke Philip, possessor of the Netherlands provinces married Joanna of Castile, the mentally unstable daughter of Ferdinand and Isabella. A new and incalculable possibility was added to the conceivable results of the Hapsburg marriage-alliances, the union of the empire and the Netherlands with Spain. If Spain were to bring the upstart Tudors into the network, she had to be satisfied that they were safe at least from pretenders, and it was to clear the way for the marriage of Arthur and Catherine that Warbeck and Warwick were put to death. Within half a year of the wedding Prince Arthur died at Ludlow Castle. Diplomatists and lawyers set about discussing the chances of obtaining a papal dispensation to enable Arthur's younger brother Henry to marry the child widow. Catherine stayed in England to await the outcome.

During the last years of Henry VII, in themselves quiet and prosperous years, there were small beginnings which pointed to immense uncertainties in the future. A French historian in the nineteenth century summed up this phase of the Renaissance by saying that three worlds were discovered, the New World, the ancient world, and the universe. The New World was discovered by Columbus, who was commissioned by Isabella of Castile. A pope had divided the whole globe into two areas for discovery respectively reserved for Spain and Portugal. England and France justifiably never accepted this exclusion, and the mainland of America was discovered by John Cabot, who sailed from Bristol under a commission granted by Henry. Cabot and his son made a long series of voyages, but they failed to establish either settlements or oceanic trade. With the revival of classical learning it was somewhat the same. Hints of it had been coming in from Italy since the early fifteenth century, and in Henry's time they multiplied. Eramus of Rotterdam, who was to become the leader of all Europe's classical studies, paid his first visit to England in 1499–1500 and, to his great benefit, came under the influence of two wonderful young men, John Colet and Thomas More. One of their older contemporaries was Thomas Linacre, a court physician and the first Englishman to make a European reputation as a humanist in the new manner. But all these four men had their greatest work still before them, and the ideas which they embodied were confined to a small number of pathfinders. So with the arts: England felt only ripples from the tidal wave of appreciation and creativeness which was converting Italy from the Gothic to something like a classical revival. The Florentine sculptor Pietro Torrigiano worked in England, and his tomb of Henry VII in Westminster Abbey is a masterpiece; but the splendid chapel in which it stands is medieval.

Except for the renewed strength of the central government, the England of Henry VII showed few outward symptoms of fundamental change. There were new social problems, but they did not attract general attention except where they intersected with old, recognized needs. The agrarian system of the lowland zone, the open-field system, was impaired by conflicting economic interests. Landlords and farmers tried to liberate themselves from the local common rights, sometimes increasing the hardships of the poor. The worst instances occurred when the old open ploughed fields were enclosed and put down to grass as individually owned sheep-pasture. The nation prospered from wool-production, but grazing employed few hands. Villages fell into ruin; the tithe would no longer support a priest; fewer militiamen were mustered. An Act was passed to check the depopulation of the Isle of Wight, vital for the defence of Portsmouth. Then, in 1489, came an Act for the whole realm, forbidding landowners to convert arable land into pasture or to allow habitations to decay. This was the first of a series of measures, lasting for more than a century, which were intended to reform agrarian abuses, and to do away with the causes of rural discontent.

King Henry VIII
1509–1547

1513	The defeat and death of King James IV of Scotland at Flodden.
1515	Wolsey becomes Lord Chancellor.
1529	The fall of Wolsey.
1532	The Church accepts that the king may veto acts of its Canterbury and York convocations (the 'Submission of the Clergy').
1533	King Henry VIII's marriage to Catherine is annulled.
1534	Act of Supremacy proclaims that the king '. . . is and ought to be the supreme head of the church of England'. The Second Annates Act imposes heavy taxation on the clergy, and confirms the monarch's practice of nominating the candidate for election to a vacant bishopric.
1535	Sir Thomas More and John Fisher are executed. Thomas Cromwell becomes the king's vicar-general.
1536	Anne Boleyn is executed. Dissolution of the monasteries begins. The Pilgrimage of Grace by northern rebels is suppressed.
1537	King Henry VIII permits publication of an approved English-language Bible (published in 1539 as the 'Great Bible').
1539	Statute of the Six Articles enforces adhesion to Roman Catholic doctrines.
1540	Cromwell is executed. Dissolution of the monasteries is completed.
1541	Henry VIII assumes the title of King of Ireland, with the assent of the Dublin parliament.
1542	The Scottish defeat at Solway Moss brings a short-lived peace with England.

In 1509 the accession of King Henry VIII changed the atmosphere of the court. He was young, accomplished, ambitious, extravagant, fond of display, but also masterful and ruthless. Erasmus and his friends hoped great things of him, and not without reason. During the first eighteen or nineteen years of his long reign they themselves did wonders, and they owed much to Henry's personal favour and to that of Thomas Wolsey, who became his chief counsellor about 1512. Erasmus made a long stay in England, his third, during which he published some of his most famous works. More wrote his *Utopia*, the most original political book of the century. Colet founded St. Paul's School, the most influential of the schools from which the new studies radiated through England. The foundation of new colleges in Oxford and Cambridge continued. A century earlier it had been stimulated by the fear of heresy. Now, and until King Henry's last years, it was associated with the study of Greek and Hebrew, mathematics and medicine. Voluntary societies were not to the liking of the Tudors unless they were under the eye of the Crown or the Church; but Linacre, with Wolsey's support, induced Henry to set up the College of Physicians of London, which lives to this day, having succeeded where a City foundation of 1423 had foundered almost without trace. During the second half of the reign, as we shall see, there were adverse conditions which hampered and distorted these movements of the mind; but the original momentum never died away altogether. In 1526 Hans Holbein came to England for the first time, the supreme northern painter of his day. He died of the plague in London in 1542, leaving behind him many portraits which enable us to know his contemporaries as we can know no earlier generation of English royalties, statesmen, and courtiers, and their ladies.

In public affairs Henry's later phase did not carry along with it so much of the earlier as it did in the arts: the change was abrupt. For the first eighteen or nineteen years Henry followed, if in a different style, the rhythm of the fifteenth century. In foreign relations he was chiefly concerned with France, Scotland, and the Low Countries, which last were now connected, inseparably but by no means simply, with Spain and with the Empire. Both France, the richest and most populous western state, and Spain, the most successful, had interests and alliances which did not concern England directly, but into which England was usually drawn as the price of friendship with one or other of the major states. The standard of good faith between allies was extremely low. The distinctive features of England's position were that she could afford to subsidize her allies, while they never had money to spare for her, that she was never in real danger of being invaded, and that her one standing link with the Continent was the commercial tie with the Netherlands. Under these conditions Henry fought two wars against the French. Early in his reign he played himself in by lending 1,500 archers to the regent of the Netherlands, who was at war with the duke of Gelderland, and

King Henry VIII. As a young and glamorous king, Henry was athletic, musical, and physically attractive. But he soon degenerated into premature old age. Popularly best-known for his succession of wives, he had a deep influence on British history: his break with the Roman Catholic church was a major event, while his contribution to British sea power bore fruit in later reigns and had great significance for the future.

then in the same year he joined the Holy League, which the bellicose pope, Julius II, formed for the purpose of expelling the French from Italy. Ferdinand of Spain and the emperor Maximilian were also in it, and Henry's plan was to attack Guienne. His first attempt failed completely, though there were some naval successes. Henry began building some very large ships of war. In 1512 he mounted an invasion of France from Calais, with an English force of 11,000 or so and 800 German mercenaries. He won a satisfactory, though not fiercely contested, battle which brought in ransoms, and he took the considerable town of Tournai by siege. The Scots had moved in support of their French allies. King James IV, with good artillery, seventeen guns, and all the men he could collect, crossed the Tweed and took the castle of Norham; but, south of the river, at Flodden, he was overwhelmingly defeated, and killed. It was not long before Henry discovered that his two allies were deserting him, and accordingly made peace.

Before his next war two of the actors, Louis XII of France and Ferdinand of Spain, died. The new French king, Francis I, and Charles of Spain, who became emperor in 1519, were contemporaries of Henry and committed to mutual rivalry. By the time they went to war in 1521 Henry had made an alliance with France, handing back Tournai, the only territorial gain he ever made, and getting nothing of substance in exchange; but that alliance wore out and Henry embarked on his second, comparatively uneventful, French war. He intended to finance it by unparliamentary taxation, pleasantly called an amicable loan, but riots in the East Anglian clothing districts and in London caused him to drop the plan, and he made peace without either gains or losses. Indeed he reverted to the French alliance on which Wolsey had founded new, but quite unsubstantial, hopes, and it was in this ill-defined position that the great crisis of his life overtook him.

In domestic affairs these earlier years had a character of their own, but here too the main elements were as they had been. Very soon after his accession Henry married his brother's widow Catherine of Aragon. He met parliaments in six of his first seven years and played for popularity by pardoning offences and excusing some unjust debts to the Crown. There were useful economic Acts, and some in other spheres, such as that which abolished benefit of clergy in cases of murder. One of the parliaments showed the familiar anti-clericalism of London in the case of Richard Hunne, who was found dead in Lambeth Palace, where he was imprisoned to await trial for heresy. That matter, however, was settled by the king. Against two kinds of men in high places he used the machinery of the law courts, and used it tyrannically. Richard Empson and Edmund Dudley, two detested financial officials of Henry VII, were unjustly executed for high treason, and so was the unfortunate earl of Suffolk, who had been recaptured after an escape, and whose only offence was his Yorkist descent. On the whole, however, Henry's rule in the early years was conservative, with the old ministers and without oppression.

In 1517 on the Evil May Day the London apprentices and roughs were incited to riot against foreign merchants and artisans. Troops put them down and there were fourteen executions; but Henry presented a dramatic scene in Westminster Hall, where he pardoned some 400 prisoners. By that time a personal change, the rise of Wolsey, had been completed and the daily working of government was more concentrated at the centre than ever before. Wolsey rose step by step as an administrator: beginning as a fellow of an Oxford college he became a chaplain to Henry VII and made himself useful in business. During the French war of 1512 he did well in matters of finance, transport, supply, and much else. In spite of the jealousy of senior men he won the young king's complete confidence. He was rewarded, as was usual, with ecclesiastical preferments. When he was hardly over forty he was archbishop of York, cardinal, and Lord Chancellor. Three years later he was made papal legate, for the purpose of promoting a crusade. Holding these and other offices in the Church and the government, he magnified them all. He worked closely with the king, whose favour was essential to him, but he controlled policy at home and abroad. No subject had ever been so powerful. It was power without popularity; Wolsey was overbearing and greedy; but there was only one occasion when the limits of this power were clearly discerned. In 1523 parliament was summoned to vote supplies for the second French war, the first session since 1515. London was already out of temper over a loan pressed out of it for the war. After stormy debates the Commons voted no more than half of what Wolsey demanded. Although this parliament did some useful routine legislation, Wolsey never faced another.

All through the period of Wolsey's greatness a dangerous problem in statecraft drew nearer. The king had no legitimate son, and no one could doubt that the Tudor dynasty and national security would both be threatened if a woman or a girl were to succeed to the throne. Henry, who was sincerely religious, connected his misfortune with the dubious circumstances of his marriage. The political marriages of the sixteenth century were often wrapped in sincere or insincere legal reservations. The queen, Catherine of Aragon, was the pledge of an alliance; but whenever the alliance was under strain it was remembered that, at least according to some credible jurists, there were technical flaws in the papal dispensation which enabled Henry to marry his brother's widow. At various dates from at least as early as 1514 there were secret speculations about the possibility of having the marriage annulled and so clearing the way for another union. In 1527 Henry and Wolsey turned over from the Spanish to the French alliance and made a treaty which envisaged a joint war against the queen's nephew, the emperor Charles V, king of Spain. Wolsey fell in with the plan of seeking annulment of the marriage. England declared war but all over the southern counties there was such refusal to co-operate that the government had to stop its preparations and make a truce with the Netherlands. Wolsey was unable to obtain the desired annulment from the pope, who was virtually in the power of Charles V after the latter's troops had taken Rome. After this failure Wolsey lost his offices of state, although remaining archbishop and cardinal. The king might have employed him if he had not made the elementary mistake of meddling in secret: he was arrested and died on his way to answer a charge of treason.

None of these events had any connection with the religious revolutions on the Continent which, we may almost say by a coincidence, went through their first decisive stages at this time. When Henry came to the throne northern and western Europe were Catholic. The kings of France and Spain stood up for their rights against the papacy, and now and again enlarged them; there were heretics, and inquisitors who put them down; there were some reforming bishops and reformers of religious orders; but, all things considered, the Church was stable. In 1517 Luther

BELOW King Henry VIII meets the French king at 'The Field of the Cloth of Gold.' Henry realised that his subjects' impression of the monarch was just as valuable as his power of patronage. He was a master of splendid public appearances, from the knights' tournaments in which he participated as a young king to his meeting with the Holy Roman Emperor in 1520. But, beneath the show, he was a skilled linguist and musician.

RIGHT Sir Thomas More, lawyer, scholar and member of parliament, who entered the service of Henry VIII. His efficiency led to promotion to the royal council, and in 1529, after the fall of Wolsey, he became Lord Chancellor. He resigned because he could not accept Henry's denial of the Pope's spiritual authority, and was executed. His book *Utopia* (1516) exposed the avoidable evils of English society.

put up his academic theses in Wittemberg. In 1522 Ulrich Zwingli began a radical reform of doctrine and church government in Zurich. By 1527 several German states, and also Sweden and Denmark, had renounced their obedience to the pope and rejected some of his central beliefs. Before long there were three main sections, Catholic, Protestant, and reformed or Calvinist, with the beginnings of more extreme, dissentient sects.

The ferment of ideas spread to England, especially by way of the Netherlands. The Wycliffe faction, Erasmus wrote to Pope Adrian VI in 1523, had been repressed rather than extinguished. In the universities and in the religious orders there were students of theology who were convinced by the new heretical writings. William Tyndale, a clergyman educated at Oxford who had visited Luther, translated the New Testament into English from the Greek, and copies printed in Germany were smuggled into England. Thomas Bilney, a Cambridge scholar, was orthodox in regard to the Mass and the papacy, but preached against image-worship and the invocation of saints: he was burned as a relapsed heretic in 1531. King Henry VIII was at first not unfavourable to Tyndale. But throughout his life Henry never departed from rigid orthodoxy in theology. He wrote a book against Luther for which the pope rewarded him with the title Defender of the Faith. He forced two bishops who held German opinions to resign their sees. He reaffirmed in a penal Act of Parliament the six main points which Luther and Zwingli denied. But he made profound and lasting changes in church order, without realizing that a new Church was taking shape.

It has been said that Henry made himself an absolute monarch by uniting his power as king with the powers which Wolsey had wielded; but this is only a half-truth. Some of Wolsey's power was based on his position in the international hierarchy of the Church, and some of Henry's on the support of parliaments. In 1529, when Wolsey fell, after six years of unparliamentary government, a parliament was elected which was not dissolved until it had completed Henry's ecclesiastical revolution in sessions spread over seven years. There were seven main statutes. They came one at a time, in accordance with the fluctuations of events and of opinion at home and abroad. Taken together they amounted to the severance of all the ties between the Church in England and the papacy. In future not the pope but the king was to receive the first year's revenue of the higher benefices. There were to be no more payments of Peter's Pence or any other taxes to Rome. No appeals from English courts were to go to Rome. The elections of bishops were so regulated that the electing body must choose the king's nominee. Anti-Roman opinions were exempted from some of the laws against heresy. These statutes involved penalties and, for that and other technical reasons, had to be enacted by parliament; but this did not mean that church matters were brought under the authority of the king in parliament. They were to be dealt with by the existing ecclesiastical machinery, with the king taking the pope's place, and exercising a closer control. The clergy in convocation were cynically told that, by recognizing Wolsey as papal legate they had incurred the penalties of praemunire, imprisonment and forfeiture of all their goods. They acknowledged that Henry was head of the Church, but they had spirit enough to add the qualification 'so far as the law of Christ doth allow'. They promised not to meet in convocation nor to pass new canons without the king's consent.

This was the constitutional side of Henry's policy of religious conservatism without the pope. It was accompanied by a few measures which seemed to presage generally acceptable reforms. For instance the parish clergy were not to live away from their parishes or to take secular employment, unless licensed. An English litany was published and an English Bible permitted. So far as these changes came to the knowledge of the laity they do not seem to have caused serious dissatisfaction. For those clergy, chiefly the higher clergy, who had to do with politics or the weightier matters of church administration, they posed disturbing questions. There were lawyers who justified them by the

BELOW Cardinal Wolsey, Henry VIII's favourite councillor from 1512 to 1529. His planning of diplomacy and of military campaigns was rewarded by promotion within the church. But, unlike some churchmen, he never held more than two bishoprics at any one time. His power and somewhat high-handed methods made him many enemies, and he failed to gain the sympathy of the parliament.

FAR BELOW Thomas Cromwell who, from 1532 to 1540, was the foremost minister of Henry VIII. After military, commercial and legal experience, Cromwell entered the king's service in 1529. His ability as a parliamentary manipulator helped Henry put through the reformation, and he himself planned many of these changes. But in 1540 he was executed for heresy and treason.

theory that the realm of England had always been an empire, not subject to any foreign jurisdiction, and that Henry was only revoking concessions which his predecessors had made to the papacy. Wolsey's successor as Lord Chancellor was a layman, Sir Thomas More, already the most eminent English man of letters, and also a severe controversial writer against the Protestants. As the official head of the legal system he had acquiesced in the Acts of parliament which had introduced some of Henry's changes. Behind them all lay the marriage question. One of the Acts empowered the archbishop of Canterbury to grant, for the whole realm including the province of York, all such dispensations as the popes had been wont to grant. Thomas Cranmer, who became archbishop of Canterbury in 1533, presided over a convocation which, doing what the pope had failed to do, pronounced the king's marriage with Catherine of Aragon invalid. The king married a court lady, Anne Boleyn, and parliament followed with an Act not merely affirming that this new marriage was lawful and that Anne's children should succeed to the throne, but empowering the king to exact an oath from any of his subjects to maintain all the provisions of the Act. Two subjects who refused the oath were John Fisher, friend of Erasmus and bishop of Rochester, and More, who had resigned his office in 1532 the day after the clergy formally submitted to the king. Neither Fisher nor More would accept the subjection of church to state, or the abolition of the Pope's spiritual authority. Both were executed.

In anticipation of more opposition, the king and his ministers added new offences to the list of those which counted as high treason; but in the next year they began to prepare for another revolutionary act which was certain to tighten the strain, the dissolution of the monasteries. There was no necessary connection between this and the royal supremacy. Either might have come about without the other. Not a few monasteries had been dissolved in the past, some of them as recently as Wolsey's time. Now, however, in two instalments, first the lesser and then the greater, all the religious houses were swept away, monasteries, nunneries, and friaries. The chief purpose of this revolution was to transfer the wealth of the monasteries to the king. Monastic property was put up for sale; the king's servants would have been overwhelmed by the task of managing these immense estates, property, and tithes. Moreover, those families which purchased (often after 'fixing' the market) thereby acquired a material interest in maintaining Henry's religious measures.

The government justified their action by grave, much exaggerated, and largely untrue accusations against the conduct of the monks. The great days of their fervour and influence were indeed over, with some exceptions like the austere Carthusian order; but they were a solid and respected element in the social structure, and they still made their own contributions to the arts and amenities of life. They were no longer the only writers of chronicles and treatises, but there was writing and reading and discussion among them. It is not far from the truth to say that, when they were dispersed, no societies of highly educated men existed anywhere except in London, Oxford, and Cambridge. The spoliation of their buildings was the worst destruction of beautiful things that has ever happened in England. Personally they were not treated harshly except for the few who died as Fisher and More died, or for overt acts of resistance. Some of the abbots and priors received high preferments in the Church. Many monks and friars became parish priests, and the remainder took pensions sufficient to support them. But the status of churchmen suffered. There were no longer mitred abbots to sit in the House of Lords, which for the first time had a majority of lay members. There were so many priests in search of livings that the

Anglici Matrimonij.

Sententia diffinitiua

Lata per sanctissimum. Dñm Nostrum. D. Clementem. Papã. vij. in sacro Consistorio de Reuerendissimorum Dominorum. S. R. E. Cardinalium consilio super validitate Matrimonij inter Serenissimos Henricum. VIII. & Catherinam Angliae Reges contracti.

PRO.

Eadem Serenissima Catherina Angliæ Regina,

CONTRA.

Serenissimum Henricum. VIII. Angliæ Regem.

Clemens Papa.vij.

CHristi nomine inuocato in Trono iustitiæ pro tribunali sedentes, & solum Deum præ oculis habentes, per hanc nostram diffinitiuam sententiam quam de Venerabilium Fratrum nostrorum Sanctæ Ro. Ec. Car. Consistorialiter coram nobis congregatorum Consilio, & assensu ferimus in his scriptis, pronunciamus, decernimus, & declaramus, in causa, & causis ad nos, & Sedem Apostolicam per appellationem, per charissimam in christo filiam Catherinam Angliæ Reginam illustrem a nostris, & Sedis Apostolicæ Legatis in Regno Angliæ deputatis interpositam legitime deuolutis, & aduocatis, inter prædictam Catherinam Reginam, & Charissimum in christo filium Henricum. VIII. Angliæ Regem Illustrem, super Validitate, & inualiditate matrimonij inter eosdem Reges contracti, & consumati rebusque alijs in actis, causæ & causarum huiusmodi latius deductis, & dilecto filio Paulo Capissucho causarum sacri palatij tunc decano & propter ipsius Pauli absentiam Venerabili Fratri nostro Iacobo Simonetæ Episcopo Pisaurieñ. vnius ex dicti palatij causarum Auditoribus locumtenenti, audiendis instruendis, & in Consistorio nostro Secreto referendis commissis, & per eos nobis, & eisdem Cardinalibus Relatis, & mature discussis, coram nobis pendentibus, Matrimonium Inter predictos Catherinam, & Henricum Angliæ Reges contractum, & inde secuta quecunque fuisse, & esse validum, & canonicum validaque, & Canonica, suosque debitos debuisse, & debere sortiri effectus, prolemque exinde susceptam, & suscipiendam fuisse, & fore legitimam, & præfatum Henricum Angliæ Regem teneri, & obligatum fuisse, et fore ad cohabitendum cum dicta Catherina Regina eius legitima coniuge, illamque maritali affectione, & Regio honore tractandum, & eundem Henricum Angliæ Regem ad præmissa omnia, & singula cum effectu adimplendum condemnandum omnibusque iuris Remedijs cogendum, & compellendum fore, prout condemnamus, cogimus, & compellimus, Molestationesque, & denegationes Per eundem Henricum Regem eidem Catherinæ Reginæ super inualiditate, ac fœdere dicti Matrimonij quomodolibet factas, & præstitas fuisse, & esse illicitas, & iniustas, & eidem Henrico Regi super illis ac inualiditate matrimonij huiusmodi perpetuum Silentium imponendum fore, & imponimus, eundemque Henricum Angliæ Regem in expensis in huiusmodi causa pro parte dictæ Catherinæ Reginæ coram nobis, & dictis omnibus legitime factis condemnandum fore, & condemnamus, quarum expensarum taxationem nobis imposterum reseruamus.

Ita pronunciauimus. I.

Lata fuit Romæ in Palatio Apostolico publice in Consistorio die. XXIII. Martij. M. D. XXXIIII.

The Bull of Pope Clement VII announcing the verdict in favour of Catherine and against King Henry VIII in the latter's divorce proceedings. Henry had waited six years for this decision, and the Pope's refusal to grant his petition, which was for no more than other European princes had been granted, was a crucial factor in his disenchantment with the Roman Catholic church.

entries of under-graduates in Oxford and Cambridge fell off.

The suppression of the monasteries was one of the causes of the only rebellion against Henry VIII, the northern rising to which, after it had begun, the name Pilgrimage of Grace was given. The other religious changes also helped to cause it, and, along with them the traditional hatred of upstart ministers and of recent unpopular acts. The list of demands is so comprehensive that it represents the grievances of all classes, and there were members of all classes among the rebels. The first to move were the poor, but as the movement gained strength others, up to the nobility, some from sympathy, others from fear, either joined in or came under suspicion because they remained neutral. The leader was Robert Aske, a landowner and a lawyer. Perhaps it was he who gave the rebellion a constitutional colouring by demanding a freshly elected parliament, and by summoning assemblies in York with something like a parliamentary form. It was nearer to being a regional rebellion than any other rising that ever happened in England; but it fell short of that. It was not planned or prepared throughout the region. It began in Lincolnshire, but it was past its peak there when Yorkshire and Lancashire rose. It was over when Cumberland and Westmorland stirred. The first disturbances were alarming because the government was taken by surprise; but troops were collected; the government gained time by negotiating and used the negotiations to create distrust between the classes among the rebels; it made delusive promises which induced some to disperse to their homes. There was no battle; indeed there was no fighting; it was more a demonstration than a rebellion. It was followed by repression. Two peers were beheaded: Lord Hussey, whose conduct in Lincolnshire had been ambiguous, and Lord Darcy, who surrendered Pontefract Castle. Aske was hanged. Hundreds of others perished. The north was effectively terrorized, and the council of the north was given its final form.

The Pilgrimage of Grace broke out when the first stage of the dissolution of the monasteries had been accomplished, but the second was still to come. Inevitably many of the clergy were compromised, and some who had openly offended paid dearly. The archbishop of York himself, Edward Lee, was under suspicion, but he managed to recover the king's favour. Several abbots were hanged. These severities no doubt facilitated the suppression of the larger houses, but the suppression revealed some who denied the royal supremacy. For that reason or others five more heads of houses far away from the scene of the disturbances were executed. The ungentle organizing mind behind these enormous events was that of Thomas Cromwell, formerly in the service of Wolsey, a layman of middle-class origin, who rose to power when Wolsey fell. He knew Italy and the Netherlands; had experience of commerce and finance and legal practice, and all-round ability which enabled him to carry out larger tasks of administration than any government in England had ever attempted before. His principal office was that of vicar-general, the king's deputy in the exercise of his ecclesiastical supremacy. In this capacity he even presided over convocation. But, like Wolsey, he took all policy for his province, including foreign relations and the king's conjugal affairs.

In foreign relations the annulment of Henry's marriage with Catherine was a rupture with the papacy and an affront to the king of Spain; but no foreign power intervened. The northern rebels corresponded with the Netherlands, and Pope Paul IV sent Reginald Pole, newly created a cardinal, thither as legate, with half-digested instructions to encourage the rebels and negotiate with the English government about the new ecclesiastical laws. He was too late to help the rebels and neither the king of France nor the regent of the Netherlands would so much as allow him to stay in their territories. Cromwell, however, watched the Continent with unnecessary attention. Like Wolsey he found that the succession to the throne was the most important matter of all. Anne Boleyn's marriage was a failure. She gave the king a daughter but no son, and after three years of increasing misery she was found guilty of adultery, which in the king's wife is treason, and beheaded. Her successor was Jane Seymour, a well-born lady, who died in giving birth to the much-desired son, Edward prince of Wales. For the fourth time Henry sought a wife. Cromwell chose, wrongly, Anne of Cleves, who was closely related to the princes opposed to Charles V in Germany. But there was no reason to fear Charles and no sense in provoking him. Queen Catherine had died. Trade with Charles's Netherlands was as valuable as ever to both parties. Cromwell was master of the machinery of government so long as the king trusted him, but he could never efface all differences of opinion in the council. It was not divided into parties, each committed to a policy, but some were more inclined than others to sympathize with continental protestantism, and some were less convinced than others that the king's religious innovations were well judged. One of these latter was the duke of Norfolk, the head of the great Howard family, whose vicissitudes are summarized in the fact that four times in the Tudor period they were attainted of treason and all their honours were forfeited, always to be restored. He had a long record as a soldier and statesman, and he had the chief responsibility in suppressing the Pilgrimage of Grace. He and his associates ousted Cromwell from his offices; the latter was condemned to death, not by trial at law, but by a parliamentary Act of Attainder. Convocation made use of evidence extracted from him to declare the marriage with Anne of Cleves null and void. With unbecoming haste the king married his fifth wife, the duke's niece, Catherine Howard.

Henry's ecclesiastical changes had no relevance to his relations with the Continent for the remainder of his reign; but they bore closely on relations with Ireland. While he and Wolsey were carrying on their expensive foreign adventures they had no money to spare for Ireland, and conditions there went from bad to worse. The earl of Kildare no longer gave satisfaction as deputy, but, when he was held in London as a hostage for two years from 1526, disorders in the Pale increased. In 1529 the emperor Charles V urged Desmond, the other head of the Fitzgeralds, to rebel. Kildare's own son, Thomas Fitzgerald, did rebel whole-heartedly in 1534, repudiating allegiance to England and appealing to the pope, Paul III, and to the emperor for aid. The chancellor, John Allen, archbishop of Dublin, was murdered; Dublin was besieged, and through the autumn and winter the rebels seemed to have full control. But English forces were landed, and the Irish army melted away. The English authority was restored by a mixture of force and deceit. In 1537 a parliament in Dublin imposed Henry's ecclesiastical settlement on Ireland, including, in spite of strong opposition, the dissolution of the monasteries. Soon the old, discredited policy of buying off Irish discontent was tried again, with some success. Some of the leading men accepted peerages and grants of monastic lands. To end the dependent status of the lordship of Ireland as a papal fief, Henry, with the assent of the Dublin parliament, assumed the title 'King of Ireland'. Before he died the first Jesuit mission was at work in Ireland.

For the time being Scotland, like Ireland outside the Pale, still adhered to Rome. In 1525 and 1527 the Scottish parliament forbade the importation of Lutheran, which meant rather anti-Roman than heretical, books. They continued to come in from the Continent, and a few travellers brought in ideas; but the authorities were watchful, especially James Beaton, archbishop of St. Andrews and cardinal. There was soon a Reformation movement but it did not rise to the level of political importance until the last years of Henry VIII. Anglo-Scottish relations continued on the beaten track. During the war with France which began in 1522 Scotland was at first held off with truces and negotiations, then attacked heavily on the Border, but without any profound effects. The English queen Margaret declared her son, the boy James V, king in his own right. When James was a man and a knight of the Garter, he married a French wife, and after her death he married another bride from France in 1538, Mary of Guise, a member of a family which was rising to leadership among militant catholics. By the time of Cromwell's fall, France was bidding for English support against the emperor, and, with or without it, was in no position to protect Scotland. King Henry would have liked to take this opportunity of winning Scotland away from its French alliance for good; but James V was by no means to be persuaded. Henry did not declare war, but first, in 1542, he sent raiding troops across the Border, and when they were beaten, reasserted the old claim to feudal superiority and sent Norfolk to march on Edinburgh. The invasion failed, and the Scots counter-attacked by the western road. They were divided, and there were Protestants among them who feared and distrusted the Catholics. They were disloyal to their commander. The king was ill and absent. At Solway Moss a shameful defeat left scores of the Scottish aristocracy as prisoners. James V died, leaving an only child, his daughter Mary.

The earl of Arran, the heir presumptive, favourable to friendship with England, became regent. When the Scottish estates met, they appointed ambassadors who concluded two treaties, one for peace and the other for the marriage of the Queen of Scots and the Prince of Wales. There was a short-lived reconciliation. Cardinal Beaton recovered his power; Arran was talked over by the French; the Scottish protestants lost ground, and the estates unilaterally revoked the treaties. Henry indeed gave the first offence, and he certainly gave the worst: he arrogantly renewed his claim to supremacy. After that he had no party to support him in Scotland. When he made peace with France in 1546 he refused to include Scotland. Three Protestants murdered the persecutor Beaton and defended themselves in his castle of St. Andrews by the sea, which they offered to Henry. He was planning another invasion when he died.

In England Henry maintained himself and his ecclesiastical laws against real and suspected dangers not without expenditure of his subjects' blood. Catherine Howard, more obviously guilty than Anne Boleyn, was beheaded. Henry's sixth and last consort, the estimable Catherine Parr, already twice a widow, survived him. In 1544 he made war on France for the third and last time, not in defence against anything, but for glory, conquest, and his fancied feudal right. He joined his army at Calais, but did not command it in person. A month later Boulogne surrendered, four days before Francis and Charles made peace. Henry also made peace, which was all he could do, on such terms as he could get. The French pensions to England were to be renewed, and Boulogne, quite useless in itself, was to be retained, but only until 1554 and only as the pledge for a further money payment. This ill-judged war added new force to the rivalries among the councillors of the ailing and prematurely ageing king. Hertford, the head of the Seymours, was the rising general. He was at odds with Norfolk, and with Norfolk's heir, the earl of Surrey, one of two poets who introduced Italian graces into English verse. Both these two Howards were condemned for treason. Surrey was beheaded after trial; and the two houses of parliament passed a Bill of Attainder against his father. In the hours while it awaited the royal assent, the monarch died.

Edward VI and Mary
1547–1558

1547	The death of Henry VIII. Somerset becomes protector for the young Edward VI. Statute of the Six Articles is repealed.	1553	The accession of Queen Mary.
1549	The first English-language prayer book is distributed, and prescribed for obligatory use by an Act of Uniformity. Kett's rebellion is put down.	1554	Wyatt's rebellion is suppressed.
		1555	The burning of heretics begins as orthodox Catholics are re-established.
		1558	Calais is lost to the French. The death of queen Mary.

The stages of the history of the royal family had been marked by Acts of parliament laying down the order of succession to the throne, and Henry filled in some details in his will, which also contained a scheme for the government during the minority of his son Edward VI, who was nine years old. This is an early attempt at preventing the undue concentration of power in any hand. There was to be no regent, but a body of sixteen executors, of mixed composition like the normal council, and another body of twelve councillors, composed of the same kinds of men, with purely advisory functions. This was transparently unworkable. Someone must carry out the formal duties of the sovereign, such as receiving ambassadors, so the executors offered a purely ceremonial primacy to the obvious man, Hertford, the brother of the king's mother and a successful commander in the French war. He accepted, and as most other men would have done, he thereupon assumed the full office of protector. He took the title of duke of Somerset.

The invasion of Scotland was already prepared. It ended with a military victory which brought no advantage whatever. Before Somerset's well-found army crossed the Border, with a strong fleet in support, St. Andrews had surrendered to guns brought from France. The Scots got together large, untrained forces with no adequate equipment, which they posted at Pinkie, on the Firth of Forth, only six miles east of Edinburgh. Rashly coming down from their strong position, the Scots were routed. The English took adequate military measures for controlling Scotland and withdrew. But the defeat threw Scotland into the arms of France. So far from waiting to marry King Edward, the little Queen of Scots went to France as the destined wife of the heir to that throne. For two years there was fighting in Scotland, from which in the end the English withdrew, though no peace was made, and France declared war. Boulogne withstood a French siege, but England was unable to carry on the war with vigour. Somerset's diplomacy had failed on both fronts.

This failure was, no doubt, partly due to the unwisdom of Henry VIII's last years, but it also followed from Somerset's failure to deal with two domestic problems, religion and social discontent. Henry's repressive policy of royal supremacy and orthodox belief had postponed the religious problem by keeping the continental Reformation at arm's length. The main outlines of the new religious map of Europe had been drawn. In Germany and Scandinavia there were Lutherans, well disposed towards kings and princes and satisfied to retain some of the old beliefs and observances. The more radical Swiss tradition was now represented by Calvinism, the great textbook of which, John Calvin's *Institutes*, was published in 1536. There was immense activity in controversial writing and preaching, excited partisanship in all classes, and confessional hatred in the wars of the western countries. There were contradictory opinions about the functions of lay and ecclesiastical authorities, but two inherited assumptions were still universally accepted, that there was such a thing as true belief, and that it was not merely permissible but a duty for the appropriate authority, whatever that might be, to enforce it, if necessary by the penalty of death.

The Protestant theologians approved of Henry's stand against Rome, but they regretted his conservatism. Their books impressed some English readers. Even Archbishop Cranmer was suspected of heresy, and many drank deeply of it besides the few who were detected and burnt; but the Lutheran and the Calvinist divines prudently stayed on their own side of the water. As it happened Henry died at the moment when the almost reactionary Howards were in eclipse. The first parliament of Edward VI completed a task left unfinished by his father: it confiscated the property of all the religious guilds and the chantries, foundations endowed for the saying of Masses. But it also repealed the 1539 Statute of Six Articles, with which Henry had stabilized the church on its Catholic foundations. It abrogated most of the statutes against heresy, and reduced still further the independence of the bishops. It permitted lay communicants to receive the cup, hitherto reserved to the clergy, as well as the bread in the Communion service. This last provision was, in at least one continental instance, conceded by the papacy; but it was a strong innovation for a lay assembly to grant it. The protector in council went further: commissioners were sent round the country to remove images and pictures from churches. Learned reforming priests came to England. The agitation of these years left behind it the first English Book of Common Prayer, written in superlatively beautiful prose, and prescribed for use in churches, by an Act of Uniformity which, it was vainly hoped, would halt the rising tide.

The people saw these innovations and were bewildered. Many were angry. The north was quiet, as well it might be, but in Cornwall a popular rising boiled up in 1549, different from that of 1497 in having many priests engaged in it; and in having as its main programme the restoration of religion as it had been, except only that the pope seems not to have been mentioned. There were some demands, not well thought out, which aimed at weakning the gentry, but the gentry of Cornwall and Devonshire did little to resist it. Some of them took refuge in or outside their counties. Two were among the leaders of the rebels. Exeter was surrounded and cut off for six weeks: the mayor and some other leading citizens showed firmness and good sense. In the end the city was relieved by Lord Russell, with a strong body of troops, including some foreign mercenaries who were diverted on their way to the war against Scotland. The rebels were broken in heavy fighting, and the punishment that followed was stern. Russell's mercenaries delayed on their march to the south-west because they were needed to check disturbances in Oxfordshire and Buckinghamshire, of which we know little except that priests and religion were involved.

The Cornishmen had wanted sheep and cloth to be exempted from some recently imposed taxation. Protector Somerset agreed to exempt flocks of sheep numbering less than a hundred throughout the country. There were complaints of high prices and scarcity in the south-west; but the economic aspects of the risings are confusing. There were disorders in many places in the Midlands and south, and these may be connected with enclosures. Enclosures and other economic matters, rather surprisingly, were the main grievances brought forward in East Anglia, where there was a widespread popular rising. The leader was Robert Kett, a tanner. Most of Norfolk was affected and part of Suffolk. Most of the rebels were countrymen, but there were some from Norwich, Yarmouth, and other towns. For six summer weeks Kett threatened Norwich from a large camp on Mousehold Heath, doing no harm. The government hesitated and at first was inclined to conciliation; but in the end threw in a strong force under the earl of Warwick which put an end to the movement with the usual battle and the usual executions. Historians have found no evidence that these rebels had any religious aims.

Somerset's hesitations and his liberal leanings brought him down: the jostling politicians turned him out of the office of protector. Warwick took his place, as the champion of order and strong government. He was not one of the old nobility, not a Beauchamp or a Neville, but the son of the financial officer Dudley who had been executed in the early days of Henry VIII. He began by ending the state of war with France and Scotland, neither of which had any need to prolong it. Boulogne was handed back, four years before the due date and for much less than the stipulated payment. The English withdrew altogether from Scotland, giving the French full liberty, which they exercised for the next ten years, to fix their tentacles there. This was inglorious, but England was disunited, and could not have supported an active war: expenditure on garrisons and fortifications was ominously reduced. Warwick, taking the title of duke of Northumberland, promoted his adherents and caused Somerset to be executed on a charge of felony. Then he set about building up his own power by pressing on with Protestant innovations. A second Prayer Book, authorized by parliament in

Thomas Cranmer. Unlike Henry VIII's other high advisers, Cranmer enjoyed the real affection of the king. Strongly in favour of church reform, he secured the royal authorization of the English Bible. His respect for royal authority dampened his moves towards reform, but did not save him from execution for heresy in Mary's reign.

Mary Tudor, Queen Mary I. Daughter of Henry VIII and Catherine, Mary succeeded to the throne in 1553. Her five-year reign was unhappy, largely because her staunch Roman Catholic beliefs were in conflict with the trend of rising protestantism.

1552, apparently without being laid be
fewer ambiguities than the first. A
which might be interpreted in a c
the Zwinglian (Swiss) doctrine that th
an act of remembrance, with no mi
Uniformity not only ordered the use of this
penalties on laymen who absented themsel
worship. Cranmer, whom Northumberland treat little consideration, wrote books in defence of these meas es, and drew up new articles of doctrine. But Northumberland's hopes depended entirely on the king. The king was educated for the part of a Protestant ruler. He began precociously to conform to the plan; but at the age of fifteen he fell ill of a galloping consumption. Northumberland made a desperate bid for a Protestant succession. He induced Edward to write a document devising the throne to his cousin and near contemporary, who is known as Lady Jane Grey. Her maternal grandmother was Mary, the younger sister of Henry VIII. After the illness of Edward VI began she was married to Lord Guildford Dudley, the protector's son. The protector did all he could to tie his supporters to the scheme: councillors and others gave their signed approval, Cranmer among them. Other political marriages were hastily arranged. The king died on 6 July 1553.

The power of the two protectors in the reign of Edward VI was derived from the impersonal power of the Crown, which was still the root as well as the emblem of unity and continuity. Northumberland's attempt to possess himself of that power was hopeless. When the king's death was known Princess Mary, the daughter of Henry VIII and Catherine of Aragon, wrote to the council declaring herself to be the true successor, and she had the country behind her. Jane the Queen, as she signed her name, received the Crown jewels and performed some acts of state but only an army could have upheld her, and Northumberland had neither the friends nor the money for that. No shot having been fired, on 19 July her own father told her that she was a prisoner and that her reign was over.

During the revolutionary days Queen Mary had refused to come to Court or to flee untry and she had made her way to
safety in the Howard ramlingham. She was a devout
Roman Catholic, a through her often insecure
existence. Many re had been explored, but
she was still ur d relied much on the
advice of h s master of the
Netherlan as no French party
in Engl en except Protestant
feelir stimate either the extent
or two of Northumberland's
r . The Lady Jane, Cranmer,
ed to death, but only kept as
ew council was indeed too large,
ward, seven old councillors of King
There were enough able men among
ions. Within a year the right conclusion
ne the custom for the more important
n by an inner ring, usually seven in number,
t some changes, but with a constant nucleus.
s the new chancellor, Stephen Gardiner, bishop of
under Henry VIII, who emerged from the Tower as
five years before, a steady, moderate, and clear-headed
ative. The forms of law were respected. The ordinary
of administration went on well. There were economies and
nsiderable financial reforms. Public borrowing, the customs, and the management of the Crown lands were all put into better order. Mary needed parliaments for religious legislation; but they did more than that. Meeting in every year of her reign they dealt with the militia, economic regulations, and many other matters. Opposition hardened as the reign went on, but the friction in parliament led to nothing worse than a brief detention of two members in the Tower.

No legislation was needed to reinstate the bishops who had been deprived of their sees, nor to prohibit preaching and refrain from prosecuting clergy or others who restored Catholic practices. When the first parliament met it repealed the ecclesiastical laws of Edward VI, thus putting the law back to where it stood in the last days of Henry. A deputation of members from both houses also waited on the queen to express a view on a great matter of state, and to be told, quite properly, that they were overstepping their bounds. Everyone thought that Mary's position would be insecure until she married. Many people in parliament and outside it believed that it would be safer and more wholesome for her to marry an Englishman than a foreigner. They may have been right, but they could not name any Englishman who combined the requisite qualities of rank, age, ability, and character.

Among eligible foreigners there was one of the highest possible rank, eleven year younger than the queen, a widower with one son, as devout a Catholic as she was. This was the emperor's son Philip, to whom his father had already handed over the kingdom of Naples and the duchy of Milan, and would soon pass on Spain, the Netherlands, and the Indies. Charles was again at war with France, and had good reason for prompting a proposal which might revive the English alliance. Mary secretly accepted Philip's proposal, assuming that it would need to be

The burning of the bishops Ridley and Latimer at Oxford in 1550. This is an illustration from Foxe's *Book of Martyrs* and shows the preliminaries of the execution, which included a sermon while the wood faggots were being laid.

approved by parliament. Some of the council, one of whom was Gardiner, were reluctant, and in the marriage treaty they insisted on conditions. Philip was to be titular king, and to assist in the government; but he was to have no share in conferring offices in the court or government. These were to be held only by Englishmen. England was to be governed separately according to its ancient laws and privileges. The marriage was not to engage England in the wars of Charles V, and the peace between England and France was to stand. If the queen died without children, Philip was to make no claim to the succession; but if they had a child, it was to succeed to the whole Burgundian inheritance in the Netherlands and Franche-Comté.

These conditions were publicly announced before parliament could meet, but not in time to prevent a storm-shower. News of the negotiation had leaked out, and there were demonstrations, trifling enough, in Kent and elsewhere. An excitable person of no importance, Sir Thomas Wyatt, made approaches to the French and Venetian ambassadors, to the queen's half-sister, the princess Elizabeth, and others and made plans of a sort for simultaneous risings in the west, the Welsh Marches, the Midlands, and his own county of Kent. He set up his standard at Maidstone in January 1554 and marched about 4,000 men as far as Southwark. The brave queen had appeared at Guildhall two days before, and roused the loyalty of the City. London Bridge was manned and Wyatt marched away to cross the river at Kingston and approach London from the west. His men were in sight of the queen's windows as they crossed St. James's Park; but there were soldiers on their flanks and when they found Ludgate closed against them they surrendered without fighting. Wyatt and about sixty others were executed, among them the earl of Suffolk, Lady Jane Grey's father, who had foolishly attempted a rising in Leicestershire and Warwickshire. There was no need for repressive measures, and Elizabeth was not compromised; it is uncertain what, if any, plans the rebels had beyond stopping the Spanish marriage; but the rising did harm to the queen's standing with her subjects. She could not justly be blamed for the execution of the 16-year-old Lady Jane Grey, which followed. Parliament, when it met, accepted the marriage, and confirmed the constitutional provisions. Philip would no doubt have encroached if he had found an opportunity, and once or twice he went indiscreetly near the line; but no real difficulty arose from that. What was more unsettling was that the queen's advisers and the bishops, or some of them, became more relentless in their attack on the Protestants.

Cardinal Pole came as papal legate to perform the mission which he had found impossible in the year of the Pilgrimage of Grace. Parliament submitted to the papal authority and the nation was absolved. Even at this solemn moment the owners of former church lands, among whom were many of the Catholics, were confirmed in their possession. The old laws against heresy were re-enacted, but heresy was already a crime at common law and the new severity rested not on a new state of the law, but on the spirit in which it was applied to individual cases. The bishops were enjoined to expel the married clergy from their livings. Those who had been monks or friars were to be divorced; secular priests who abandoned their wives might be granted

The mechanism of a turret clock made in about 1620. It is from Cassiobury Park, Hertfordshire, and is now in the British Museum. Such clocks were used in towers and turrets. Their design was strongly influenced by Dutch and Flemish clockmakers, though the English were not slow to make their own improvements. Flat wrought iron bars, easily obtainable and easily worked by blacksmiths, were used for the frames.

livings other than those which they had held. It seems that about one-fifth of the parish clergy, perhaps some 1,500 priests, were removed. Most of them found other means of support. They could not openly criticize the restored order; but their mere presence was a disparagement of it. A few of the abler and more prominent fled to the Continent, where, after the manner of refugees, they congregated in centres where they found sympathy, and sharpened their wits in controversies, sometimes among themselves, but more in preparation for counter-attack.

The main Catholic offensive was against the higher clergy. Cranmer, already condemned to death as a supporter of Queen Jane, was subjected to many interrogations and indignities, so that his admissions might discredit the reformers' cause, but in the end he died with an unrehearsed fortitude which undid the memory of his failings. At Oxford two other bishops, friends of the poor, Hugh Latimer and Nicholas Ridley, were burnt. Two more, John Hooper and Robert Ferrar, suffered in what had been their dioceses, Gloucester and St. David's. Nothing was spared that might bring home to the people the might of the drawn sword of authority; but each execution added to the number of those who believed the victims to be martyrs. Altogether something short of three hundred men and women were put to death in less than four years. In comparison with the numbers who died after judicial sentence in the same cause in France or Germany or the Netherlands, this number was small; but it was of a different order from anything that had been known in England before. The name of religious persecution has never been affixed to any other episode in English history. It was not due to cruelty on the part of individuals such as Gardiner, who died soon after it began, or Mary herself; but to rigorous beliefs on both sides. Many of the bystanders valued their human instincts above theology.

There was no open resistance, but much discontent, to which dissatisfaction over foreign affairs added. In 1556 and 1557 these were a couple of plots, too abortive to discourage the queen, or Pole who had become archbishop of Canterbury, and, after Gardiner's death, the principal councillor. For King Philip, England had indeed become more important than before. Two years after his marriage he had left England to take charge of the Netherlands on his father's abdication. He was away for two years but in 1557, he came back with the purpose of drawing England into a war against France. He succeeded. In July 1557 the earl of Pembroke led over a force of 7,000 men which helped to win the celebrated Battle of St. Quentin. But the victory was not followed up, and the English council had money neither to keep its troops on foot nor its fleet assembled.

It was not the fashion to fight in the winter, and the English commanders in Calais, although it was undermanned and in bad repair, with neither soldiers nor citizens in a proper state of mind, did not prepare to defend it. When the duke of Guise was suddenly at their throats on 1 January, they did their best, but surrendered on the 7th and, within a fortnight, when Guisnes fell, England had lost the bridgehead. It had held firm for more than two hundred years, and it had served as a base for invading France. It was so accessible and so well assimilated that it was almost part of England. Besides its practical usefulness it had the moral weight of giving England a visible footing in the continental state-system.

The queen and her ministers did what they could. Parliament made only a grudging money grant and a forced loan was collected. Another force was sent abroad and fought beside the Spaniards and Netherlanders in the victorious Battle of Gravelines; but Philip gave no help for recovering Calais. He used his successes to bring the French to negotiate, and the French were determined not to restore Calais as part of a bargain. The Spanish ambassador in England wrote that everything was wrong there except the queen's good will and stout heart.

Mary held on her course in spite of bitter personal humiliations. She had not borne Philip a child, and it was well known that she had built high hopes on deceptive indications that she would do so. Philip had many urgent preoccupations, and he had tried to behave correctly. He had even tried to moderate the policy of religious intimidation. But he had not been considerate, and he had cared nothing for English interests. The pope, the Neapolitan Paul IV, was an enemy of the Spaniards, and made himself disagreeable to Mary and Pole. The queen and the cardinal died, both on the same day in November 1558, abandoned by those who owed them most.

Queen Mary's end was tragic, and the tragedy was the greater because England was gathering new material strength and setting out on new creative adventures. The sixteenth century was a period of economic change for all western and central Europe. A long-continued inflation helped to make many industries more prosperous. In England revolutionizing new processes were introduced in mining, in the metal textile and other industries. Perhaps this wave of industrial development was started by the dissolution of the monasteries. Since some of the monasteries were great landowners in the coalfields, it may well be that the coming of new proprietors stimulated coal-mining. It continued during Mary's reign and was connected with the worldwide opening up of seaborne trade which followed from the Portuguese and Spanish voyages of the previous century. Although the British merchants had been very early explorers in the Atlantic, England was late in entering on oceanic trade. In the time of Edward VI Richard Chancellor sailed in a fleet under Sir Hugh Willoughby to search for a north-east passage to India. Willoughby died in Lapland, but Chancellor wintered by the White Sea, made a commercial treaty in Moscow and came home in Mary's reign to promote the Muscovy Company, the first English joint-stock company for foreign trade. Another overseas enterprise, of an entirely different kind, shows originality in its purpose. In Ireland Mary's government dropped the attempt to impose ecclesiastical changes, but sought to extend its control westwards from the Pale by colonizing the districts of Leix and Offaly. The Irish parliament duly constituted two new shires there, King's County and Queen's County, and gave authority to grant lands in them. Armed opposition presented much immediate progress; but this was the beginning of the policy of colonization in which the English persisted whenever they could until more than a hundred years later.

The Elizabethan Settlement 1558–1588

1558	The accession of Queen Elizabeth.
1559	A new Act of Supremacy is passed, in which Elizabeth takes the title of Governor of the Church. The Treaty of Edinburgh, by ending French interference in Scotland, assures the eventual triumph of Scottish Protestants. John Knox, forceful Scottish Protestant, returns from exile to Edinburgh.
1563	Statute of Artificers is passed, to regulate industry, agriculture, and employment.
1568	Mary, Queen of Scots, flees to England.
1570	The pope excommunicates Elizabeth.
1580	Drake returns after his voyage around the world.
1585	England joins the Dutch in their struggle against Spain. Raleigh founds the first English colony in America, on Roanoke Island.
1586	English Puritans hold a secret national assembly at Cambridge. The Treaty of Berwick repairs Anglo-Scottish relations; James VI of Scotland receives English pension.
1587	Mary, Queen of Scots, is executed.
1588	The Spanish Armada is routed.

There was no question that Elizabeth, the daughter of Anne Boleyn, was to be accepted as her half-sister's successor; but what that would lead to no one could imagine. The princess had at least steered her way through many dangers, most recently by conforming to Mary's Catholic reaction. She now had to take the responsibility for steering the country. It was at war with France and Scotland. The religious persecution was weakening the authority it was meant to reinforce. There was no archbishop of Canterbury, and nine of the episcopal sees were vacant. The nobility had not recovered from a century of civil strife: Norfolk was the only duke in England. Yet the enigmatic lady reigned for forty-five years during which there were only four occasions when persons of exalted rank suffered the penalty of death, and she lived into her seventieth year, which no English sovereign had ever done before. None of her predecessors had been what she became, the subject of eulogies which are still treasures of the national literature. Some of these are so fulsome that they can only be taken with a pinch of salt. Certainly, she was blessed with great ministers. The greatest of them was William Cecil, who became Lord Burghley. She appointed him secretary of state within a fortnight of Mary's death, and he never left her service until he died nearly forty years later. But even in collaboration with him she had more than the responsibility: she decided.

The central question was that of a new religious settlement. All other policy turned on it, and it had to be answered in the light of many and various considerations. It was reached quickly and with a minimum of public controversy. In choosing members for her council the queen discarded the Catholics who formed the majority there, retaining the moderates and adding seven of the Protestant element. The refugee reformers came hopefully back, though the foreign divines who had gone with them did not. A Supremacy Bill was put before parliament, and failed to pass. Only at the third attempt did the government produce a Bill which satisfied the Commons. This was no doubt because some of the members disliked royal supremacy more than papal supremacy, and possibly a majority of adult males in the country were of the same inclination; but the question was never put to any of them in that simple form. In the end they agreed on something very near to the supremacy as Henry VIII assumed it. Instead of the title Head of the Church, the queen called herself Supreme Governor, which gave less offence and perhaps implied that she claimed no authority to prescribe doctrine. She never appointed a vicar-general like Cromwell; but the Act authorized her to issue commissions for the exercise of jurisdiction over the Church. This was the origin of her court of high commission, a strong body, strengthened by subsequent Acts down to 1576, which had lay members, such as lawyers and the lord mayor of London, as well as the clerics. It could sit anywhere it liked, deprive clergymen of their livings and decide disputes between party and party which were only formally

Queen Elizabeth I. Once declared illegitimate by her father, Henry VIII, Elizabeth nevertheless succeeded to the throne in 1558 and reigned superbly for 45 years. Although it was chance which placed her on the throne at a moment in history when the English were poised for great things, her intelligence, strength of character and seriousness of purpose did much to enhance the achievements of her realm.

connected with the Church, for instance the question whether surgeons had the right to prescribe internal medicines. For at least the first ten years or so, this court, though active, does not appear to have been much complained of.

More delicate than the question of supremacy was that of uniformity. The government did not invite the clergy to discuss it in convocation, in which the clergy of Queen Mary's time were still sitting. Even in the House of Commons the government had difficulty in winning a majority of three. The Book of Common Prayer followed the arrangement and most of the words of the second book of Edward VI; but at the crucial points there were changes which were intended to widen the number of those who could join in Communion in their parish churches. That is to say words were chosen, sometimes two scarcely reconcilable sets of words side by side, which, it was hoped, both conscientious Protestants and conscientious Catholics could bring themselves to say. The clergy had to use this book on pain of imprisonment for life at the third offence. The laity had to go to church every Sunday and when they were absent without reasonable excuse, the fine was 1*s*. The rules about ceremonies, ornaments, and the like were drawn up in the same spirit. Heresy was still a capital offence at common law, but neither Catholics nor Calvinists as such were prosecuted. About 200 clergy were dismissed. There was no longer any law against clerical marriage. Some of the former married clergy came back, and younger clergy married. This added a new element to social life, especially in the country; the sons of the clergy came in time to make an identifiable strain in the middle classes, and the whole system became a support and also a restraint for the Church. Its ethos depended, of course, less on the laws and regulations than on the spirit in which they were administered. Queen Elizabeth's bishops were worthy men, almost all of comparatively modest social status to begin with, who did not give trouble. The archbishop of Canterbury, Matthew Parker, was appointed only a month later than Cecil. He did more than anyone of his generation to give the Elizabethan church its intellectual standing, by drafting the Articles of Belief and by working on a new translation of the Bible. There was little against him as a man; so hostile pamphleteers resorted to the fable that he had not been regularly consecrated.

England had thrown off the Roman allegiance for a second time, but this did not necessarily fix her international position. There was nothing to tempt either the French or the Spaniards to intervene against the ecclesiastical settlement. Weakened by their continuing war, they had their own Protestants to cope with, the Huguenots in France and the Calvinists in the Spanish Netherlands. The Council of Trent, sitting intermittently since 1545, had defined the Catholic doctrines, and was trying to restore international conformity in church order. The Calvinists feared that all the Catholic powers would combine against them, and the Catholic princes feared that the Calvinists all over Europe would make concerted rebellions. England was still at war with France, and France was refusing to give back Calais. The economic tie between England and the Netherlands was a mutual necessity. Philip II had many reasons for trying to preserve all he could of the co-operation which had been organized round his English marriage. He offered his hand to Queen Elizabeth. Even on the religious side the doors to peaceful coexistence might still be opened: in 1561 Pope Pius IV invited her to send representatives to the Council.

That both these overtures were refused was partly due to Protestant feeling among the English, but other events were causing England to resist the plans of the French. When Elizabeth came to the throne any legally minded person could question her title on the grounds that Anne Boleyn's marriage was invalid, and so forth. One possible claimant was Mary Queen of Scots, then in France with her husband the dauphin. Even if Elizabeth was the rightful queen, Mary, as the granddaughter of Henry VIII's sister Margaret, was her heiress presumptive. England and Scotland were at war, so Mary and her husband jointly claimed the English throne. For the moment this made no difference to anyone. The French king, the strong and successful Henry II, made the Treaty of le Cateau Cambrésis in 1559 with Spain. He recognized Elizabeth as queen, but she had to give up the claim to Calais under the transparently worthless condition that its status was to be reviewed after eight years. But King Henry II was accidentally killed and the dauphin, already king of Scotland, became King Francis II of France as well. Effective power passed to the militant Catholic and pro-Spanish house of Guise. During Mary's absence in France her mother, Mary of Guise, was regent in Scotland.

In Scotland, however, the French and Catholic interests were hard pressed. The reformers had made astonishing progress. Many people of all ranks had accepted their beliefs, and some of the nobility had taken the lead in dispossessing the churchmen.

John Knox, the Protestant who inspired the Scottish reformed church. His celebrated Pamphlet *First Blast of the Trumpet against the Monstrous Regiment of Women* was inspired by his belief that women were incapable of holding political power. In 1559 he returned to Scotland, where his preaching led to a successful revolt against the old order.

By 1557 the Lords of the Congregation were openly directing a movement to turn out the regent. Two years later John Knox came back from exile on the Continent to become the only Calvinistic divine who was the dominant figure of a nation. The lords declared Mary of Guise deposed and appealed for help to the queen of England. Her politic reaction was that she would help them to expel the French; but she did nothing to encourage disloyalty to Queen Mary. She moved slowly, but she sent a sufficient naval force to the Firth of Forth and, in spite of financial difficulties, she collected men and equipment for an army. The Scottish lords and people needed support against the French, but they attacked. The regent died. The English army advanced from Berwick and besieged the French in Leith, without taking it; but at Edinburgh an agreement was signed which corresponded more to the balance of forces than to the immediate situation in the field. The French were to leave the country. Their fortifications were to be destroyed. No foreigners were to be employed except by leave of the estates. Neither France nor England were to interfere in Scottish affairs. Francis and Mary were to renounce their claim to the English throne.

Francis and Mary refused to ratify this Treaty of Edinburgh; but events made that irrelevant. France was overwhelmed by civil wars and Francis II died. His young widow decided to return to her own kingdom which she had never known except as a small child. Her stormy experiences there for the next seven years were watched, sometimes anxiously, by the English statesmen, but they honoured their undertaking not to intervene. Queen Elizabeth did no more than mediate between the Scottish parties with good advice. Nor was Scotland in any way concerned with the war between England and France which broke out as a direct consequence of the religious troubles. The Huguenots were led by magnates of the highest rank, whose loyalty to their country was more patent than that of the Guises with their foreign intrigues; but for their own defence they needed allies, at least so long as the Crown had a chance of Spanish support. The English made a naval demonstration off the ports of Normandy; but they would give tangible help only at a very high price. The Huguenots handed over Le Havre, so that it could serve as the English base for a war in which the English objective was the recovery of Calais, or perhaps something even better. Instead of that the English found that the military operations of their allies inland went badly. The Huguenots were pushed back behind the Loire. Their patriotism reasserted itself, and they made peace, leaving the English garrison of 5,000 men to defend Le Havre. The defence was brave and well conducted; but fever was more deadly than the fighting; such reinforcements as arrived were of the poorest quality, and the remnant of the army surrendered. The Treaty of Troyes, of 1564, was as inglorious as the war. England took a money payment in exchange for the hostages whom she had held to guarantee the peace-terms of 1559, and thus renounced the ambition to recover Calais.

The expeditions to France and Scotland were so expensive that they were paid for partly by selling Crown lands and partly by borrowing in Antwerp. In ordinary times, however, revenue was more than enough to cover expenditure. Elizabeth's ministers kept expenditure down, sometimes even starving necessary services; but they extricated the country from its dependence on foreign lenders. By 1574 they accumulated a substantial reserve. Throughout the reign English public finance was far more stable than that of either France or Spain, which meant that England could count on carrying through a larger proportion of her military, naval, and economic plans. This was due to good management on the old lines rather than to new financial devices; but it was probably aided by a continued rise of the national wealth and production. Ministers gave much thought to economic policy in its different aspects, from the welfare of the labourers to the encouragement of foreign trade. From 1563 until 1601 there were Acts of Parliament which laid down the principles for dealing with poverty and the conditions of employment. Vagabonds, the undeserving poor, were to be punished; but the sick, disabled, and aged could now look to the parishes for relief, that is for food and shelter, where formerly they had depended on the chances of private charity. Locally elected, unpaid, part-time officers, more or less closely supervised by the justices of the peace, assessed and collected and distributed the poor-rate. This primitive system was beneficient or corrupt or even cruel as the local officers and local public opinion decided, but was much better than no system at all.

There was no such novelty of principle in the great codifying Statute of Artificers (or Statute of Apprentices) of 1563. On paper this was the most comprehensive legislative plan for the economic life of a country that any European government had made, and it paid more attention to agriculture than continental governments had yet begun to do. It co-ordinated the existing law and administration so far as they had to do with unemployment in the towns, the scarcity of agricultural labourers, and the rise in the cost of living. The aim of this codification was to stabilize the existing class structure, and with it the location of

William Cecil, Lord Burghley, Queen Elizabeth's secretary of state. A man of great talent, Burghley served Edward VI and Queen Mary as well as Elizabeth. His advice determined the Queen's policy and in general favoured moderation in foreign policy and firmness at home.

industry and the transference of labour from one place or occupation to another. The Act itself, however, allowed many exceptions and when the local magistrates came to administer it, they allowed many more. The judges acted on the principle that trade was not to be restrained except by explicit enactments, so that the restrictions in this Act applied only to the trades which already existed in the country when it was passed. The new industries which appeared in quick succession after that time were not hampered by limitations on apprenticeship, labour-contracts, or locality.

The progress of industrialization had probably not made the country very much richer by Elizabeth's early and middle years, but it was beginning to reduce its dependence on the importation of finished goods. For the time being this meant that its relation to the Netherlands was changing: the English business men, so long familiar with the textile districts of Flanders, were now welcome customers in the Antwerp money-market. In the early years of the reign we begin to hear of the 'new draperies', lighter and finer than the old English cloths, made by more highly skilled and better-paid workmen. Colchester became the centre for their manufacture and it spread westwards through Essex and Suffolk. Many of the craftsmen who introduced it came from the Netherlands. Some of them were Catholics, but the majority were religious, in fact Calvinist, refugees, who settled as communities in the towns, with their own churches and ministers. Until the early eighteenth century each new wave of persecution on the Continent sent its quota to England, as it did to other countries where they could find stable government and toleration. The Huguenot influx from France began in Elizabeth's reign. Not only craftsmen came, but experienced entrepreneurs and financiers. All played a part in lifting England out of its comparative economic backwardness.

Another migration of foreign labour, management, and capital into England was directly promoted by the government. The demand for metals of all sorts was increasing throughout Europe. The mining and metal-working industries were more highly developed, both technically and financially, in south Germany than anywhere else. England had undeveloped mineral resources, and growing metal industries. The queen therefore granted to some German capitalists, in conjunction with English partners, the right to work lead, copper, and other metals. They brought over engineers and miners, Catholics, and set to work in the Lake District and the Mendips. The export of the new metals as raw materials was prohibited, and they were worked up in Birmingham, Sheffield, and other places. The government also encouraged other new industries or foreign processes by grants of monopoly, not always wisely or profitably used, as in gunpowder, glass-making, and the extraction of sea-salt. The last two of these used coal as an industrial fuel.

All these new departures pointed to unlimited possibilities of growth in the future, but none made such an appeal to the imagination as the search for new markets. There was still more search than trading; the net profits of ocean voyages did not add appreciably to the national income; but there were substantial gains and prospects of much more. The Russian trade, extending overland to Persia, prospered. It was soon followed by ventures in every direction. Sir John Hawkins of Plymouth carried slaves from the west coast of Africa to Spanish America. Sir Humphrey Gilbert, more soldier than navigator, looked for a north-west passage to the Indies and planted the English flag in Newfoundland. Sir Francis Drake sailed round the world, and brought back a ring which he said was a present to Queen Elizabeth from the sultan of Ternate in the East Indies. In 1585 Sir Walter Raleigh founded the first, if short-lived, English colony in America. In 1600 the East India Company was incorporated, soon to become and long to remain the greatest English economic organization. These were only the most famous of many undertakings.

All this maritime enterprise went forward by its own momentum. The government made no great material contribution, though its approval and grants of privileges counted for something. The activity of the seamen changed the direction of English energy in many ways. It altered the map of England by bringing new life to the ports of the south-west, to which America and Africa were nearest. It brought a new theme into the ideas of educated men about the country and its place in the world. Year by year the voyages were recorded in print, from artless narratives to scientific studies. Propagandist geographers wrote for the reading public, and made known not only the travels of the English nation but, in translation, those of the Portuguese and Spaniards.

At every point the Portuguese and Spaniards were already in occupation of the most desirable and the most easily accessible points of trade and settlement. They made claims, which the English did not accept, to exclusive rights of trading and settlement in all the newly discovered countries. The English admitted that there could be sovereignty over narrow seas, and indeed they themselves claimed it in the North Sea and the Channel. They admitted that a colonizing power had the right to

An Elizabethan gentleman's garden. In medieval times monks cultivated gardens and alongside their vegetables and medecinal herbs sometimes planted flowers. By the Tudor period there were more formal flower gardens, with flowerbeds and trelliswork. Herb and fruit gardens were developing further, with some new species like blackcurrants and rhubarb being introduced from continental Europe.

exclude traders, but only from lands which it had conquered and civilized. International law permitted states to authorize aggrieved individuals to compensate themselves at the expense of co-nationals of those who had robbed or defrauded them. Seafaring newcomers discovered that, with luck and daring, small forces could break through to vast stores of treasure. They did not study international law. Francis Drake was the toughest and most resourceful of them all. He had some personal and religious motives which justified him in his own eyes in invading peaceful Spanish colonial towns. In 1573 he brought back treasure worth hundreds of thousands of pounds. Queen Elizabeth gave no satisfaction to the Spanish ambassador, though she was careful to express no open approval. From that time there was a state of undeclared war in Spanish America; but English piracy there did not bring about war between the powers in Europe. The Spaniards protested, and calculated the balance between these losses and the advantages of peace between England and the Netherlands. Some Englishmen drew their own conclusions from the stories of Spanish vengeance, and from reports of cruelties inflicted by the Spanish inquisition on English seamen. For the first time a mutual hatred grew up, and it was made fiercer by the religious indignation on both sides. But the long tradition of alliance, the consciousness of common interests, and the ambiguities of England's position in the religious schism were still realities which statesmen might use to restore co-operation between England and Spain.

On the evening of 16 May 1568 an open fishing-boat came into the harbour of Workington in Cumberland and Mary Queen of Scots stepped ashore. The warden of the West March courteously conducted her to Carlisle Castle. The English authorities, from the queen downwards, had to cope with a baffling responsibility. In the seven years since she returned to Scotland from France, Mary had lived through terrible adventures. Her vitality, her reckless impulsiveness, her inflexible Catholic faith had gained her some devoted friends and many unforgiving enemies. She had married, fittingly, a second husband and had borne a son; but her husband had been murdered. She had married the unprincipled ruffian who planned and managed the murder, and many of her subjects suspected that she was an accessary before the fact. The lords of the council had defeated her party, and this third husband had fled abroad. Queen Elizabeth's long-delayed but sincere proposals for reconciliation between Mary and her subjects had effected nothing. Mary had signed an act of abdication and her infant son had been crowned in her stead. She had escaped from captivity and had watched the defeat of her partisans in battle at Langside. Three days after that she had crossed the Solway Firth to England. She was a fugitive, but still belligerent. Her demission had been forced from her by threats and could be repudiated. She could still be divorced, and she could marry again. She was still heiress presumptive to the English throne, and she was a Catholic.

Her hopes of aid from her royal cousin were soon muffled in diplomatic procedure. Elizabeth discovered that it would not be proper for them to meet until Mary should have cleared herself of the accusations of the Scottish lords, and pending this she was virtually a prisoner, though treated with respect. Elizabeth and Cecil persuaded her to send commissioners to a conference which should examine the charges against her, and her counter-charges of treason against the lords. They offered to restore her in Scotland if she would renounce the French alliance and her claim to the English throne, which was reasonable enough, and also substitute Common Prayer after the form of England for the Mass. The commission, sitting first in York and then at Westminster, reported on all the evidence, and Queen Elizabeth concluded that nothing dishonourable had been proved either against the lords or Mary. This reads like the preamble to a reconciliation, but there was no reconciliation. The two queens never met, and Mary spent the rest of her life as a captive in one castle after another. She was neither passive nor powerless. Such correspondence and interviews as were allowed to her gave ample opportunities for intrigues in England and abroad, and when they came to be restricted, she fell back on deceptions which neither she nor her correspondents realized were easily penetrated by the government's expert intelligence service.

The first of the conspiracies which centred on Mary was the most dangerous because it called up the last aristocratic rising of the old territorial model; but it lacked the necessary foreign military aid. The Spanish ambassador in London took it upon himself to encourage his own master to take action. The ambassador had little grasp of Spain's existing troubles with the Dutch, or of France's with Huguenot rebels supported by English volunteers; his hopes of a French alliance were groundless. The Englishmen who supported Mary were not altogether disinterested. The first plan that leaked out was to seize Cecil and turn him out of office; the next to liberate Mary and marry her to the duke of Norfolk, who had presided over the late commission. Queen Elizabeth forbade the marriage. Norfolk was arrested, and his fellow conspirators were known; but in November 1569 the earls of Northumberland and Westmorland, Percy and Neville, raised the north. They celebrated Mass in Durham Cathedral and set off to rescue Mary from the castle of Tutbury in Staffordshire. The militia had not come forward in proper strength, and the president of the council of the North made no

A game of football. Football was played as early as the 14th century, and was a popular if bruising sport in Tudor times. Like shuttlecock, marbles, and tennis, it has descended from Tudor to modern times.

attempt to hold anything further north than York; but a royal army, assembled in Lincolnshire, Leicestershire, and Warwickshire, came up in support. A naval force turned the rebels out of Hartlepool, troops from Berwick made sure of Newcastle. The rebel earls turned back from Selby, their furthest south, and at Durham they disbanded their army and fled to shelter on the Scottish side of the Border. Borderers on both sides rose to their aid and there were ominous signs from Scotland; but Queen Elizabeth's cousin Lord Hunsdon won a fight that forestalled further trouble. The southern army looted and destroyed from Doncaster to the Tyne. Some 800 persons (including at a later date the earl of Northumberland) were executed summarily or after trial, and many more were pardoned but paid heavy fines. That the north, with some local exceptions, became in time a very Protestant region was due to persuasion, not coercion. In this Edmund Grindal, a Cumberland man exiled in Mary's time, made a beginning when he ruled tactfully but with purpose as archbishop of York from 1570.

Thus there was not, as many Protestants supposed, a common policy concerted for the taming of England by the Catholic powers. A further proof came when the pope, Pius V, acted by himself in 1570, when all was over with the rebellion. This was the last time any pope set the full apparatus of spiritual coercion in motion against any sovereign. Pius V was unaware that the papal power in international politics had fundamentally weakened. Without being provoked by any incident, and without seeking the approval of the continental powers, he issued a Bull excommunicating Queen Elizabeth and releasing her subjects from their allegiance. As an invitation to rebellion and invasion it fell flat; but the English government could not ignore it. Without rebellion and without invasion there was scope for conspirators and assassins. During the religious wars leaders on both sides were murdered by fanatics in Scotland, France, and the Netherlands; and killing an individual in the interests of the state without process of law was justified by a widely, almost universally, accepted political doctrine. As in the time of Henry VIII, parliament passed new laws making certain offences treason, especially those questioning the queen's title; but in 1572 there came another plot, the work of a Florentine banker, Roberto Ridolfi, who had moved in good society in London without acquiring common sense. His plan was that Mary Queen of Scots should be set free and should marry the duke of Norfolk. They both agreed, and the plotters indiscreetly scattered evidence right and left. Norfolk, the greatest nobleman in England, was tried by his peers and executed. Parliament petitioned for Mary to be similarly treated; but that would have been dangerous in an altogether different degree, and Elizabeth did no more than try ineffectually to hand over the responsibility to Mar, the regent of Scotland. There Mary's party had been in possession of Edinburgh Castle since 1570, and the possibility of a French landing in her support was her most promising chance; but in 1573 the English took advantage of an interval of French impotence. An army marched from Berwick; siege-guns were sent by sea to Leith; the castle was reduced; and Scotland was pacified.

The Bull had failed in its immediate effects; but it had committed both sides to a remorseless struggle which lasted as long as Elizabeth lived. Shortly before the Bull was published William Allen, a refugee priest who had been a fellow of an Oxford college, founded a college at Douai in Flanders. This became a seminary, and a base for missions to England, which reconverted some who had become Protestants, and stiffened Catholic resistance to practices, such as occasional conformity, permitting which the Church of England was drawing others away. In 1579 another pope, Gregory XIII, set up a Jesuit college in Rome from which missions to England were manned and instructed. The missionaries worked in secret: the existing laws made their activities, under one heading or another, capital offences; and the government had in its service agents, some of them of most unsavoury types, who often penetrated their secrets. The two most famous of the missionaries reached England in 1580, both of them formerly fellows of Oxford colleges. The hard controversialist Robert Parsons offended most of the English Catholics by working for foreign armed invasion. He died long afterwards in Rome. His companion Edmund Campion was captured, offered his liberty by the queen on conditions, then tortured, condemned on false charges of treason and executed. His character and conduct were saintly. Altogether the number of those who suffered death, on various charges but in fact for their faith, during the reign of Elizabeth, is reckoned, including those who died in prison, at some 250.

At the time of the papal Bull a threat to the Elizabethan settlement from the opposite direction was coming to a head. The extreme reformers went under the nickname of 'puritans', a word which has never fitted an exact meaning, nor denoted an organized society, but which is definite enough for ordinary purposes. Originally it was applied to men who wanted to purify the doctrine of the Church of England, then to those, no doubt largely the same people, who were in general rigorous in their theology and morals. The demand for strictness came from abroad, not through institutions, nor from any central authority, since there was no common organization of the non-Catholics, nor even of the Calvinist element among them. It was brought by the returning exiles of Mary's reign and by others who equated the demolition of Roman practices in the continental Reformation with the intentionally two-faced Elizabethan compromise. The Puritans began their protest by refusing to follow the Prayer Book in externals, such as vestments, even simple white surplices, or forms of words taken over from the older service books. Archbishop Parker tried to enforce discipline, but he could not carry with him all the ecclesiastical authorities, let alone the laity from Cecil downwards. Even the queen gave no support; she wanted to preserve unity against Rome and was comparatively indifferent to internal quarrels.

Growing quickly under these conditions the Puritan movement entered a new phase. In the fifteen-sixties the church in Scotland became not merely reformed, national, and established but a reformed church, unmatched elsewhere in its power over

Sir Francis Drake, the most celebrated Elizabethan seafarer, of fairly humble birth, he rose from apprentice on a coasting vessel to the rank of admiral, but most of his exploits were private enterprises. The Spaniards, on whose shipping and colonies he preyed, regarded him as a pirate. He was born in 1540, and set off on his famous voyage around the world in 1577. He died of a sickness while raiding Panama in 1596.

laity and policy. The key to this power was the parity of ministers, a system of church government in which there were no bishops, but assemblies, ranked one above the other from the parish to districts and then to an elected national assembly. Services of the Calvinistic type were secretly held in London and probably elsewhere as early as 1565. In 1570 Thomas Cartwright, a professor of divinity at Cambridge, and a Calvinist, openly preached against the constitution of the Church of England. He was deprived of his office, but, sometimes in exile, and then in England again he led a growing number of followers.

Parker died in 1575 and his successor Edmund Grindal, who was translated from York, appreciated the personal goodness of the Puritans, and did not exert himself against them. The queen took alarm at the growing divisions. The Protestants themselves were splitting as they had done on the Continent. There were now independents among them, who believed that there should be no bishops and not even any machinery of assemblies, but that the individual ministers and officers chosen by the congregations should be autonomous, like the little churches of the earliest Christian times. As yet there were no separatists, like those of

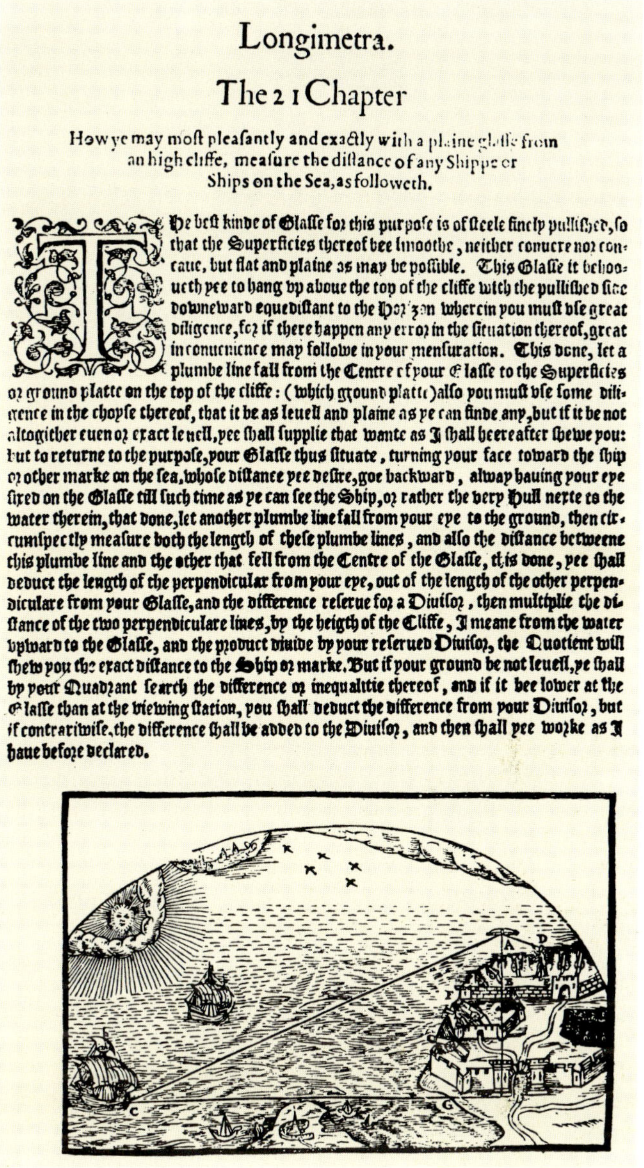
Longimetra.

The 21 Chapter

How ye may most pleasantly and exactly with a plaine glasse from an high cliffe, measure the distance of any Shippe or Ships on the Sea, as followeth.

The best kinde of Glasse for this purpose is of steele finely pullished, so that the Superficies thereof bee smoothe, neither conuexe nor concaue, but flat and plaine as may be possible. This Glasse it behoueth yee to hang vp aboue the top of the cliffe with the pullished side downeward equedistant to the Horizon wherein you must vse great diligence, for if there happen any error in the situation thereof, great inconuenience may followe in your mensuration. This done, let a plumbe line fall from the Centre of your Glasse to the Superficies or ground platte on the top of the cliffe: (which ground platte) also you must vse some diligence in the choyse thereof, that it be as leuell and plaine as ye can finde any, but if it be not altogither euen or exact leuell, yee shall supplie that wante as I shall heereafter shewe you: but to returne to the purpose, your Glasse thus situate, turning your face toward the ship or other marke on the sea, whose distance yee desire, goe backward, alway hauing your eye fixed on the Glasse till such time as ye can see the Ship, or rather the very Hull nexte to the water therein, that done, let another plumbe line fall from your eye to the ground, then circumspectly measure both the length of these plumbe lines, and also the distance betweene this plumbe line and the other that fell from the Centre of the Glasse, this done, yee shall deduct the length of the perpendicular from your eye, out of the length of the other perpendiculare from your Glasse, and the difference reserue for a Diuisor, then multiplie the distance of the two perpendiculare lines, by the heigth of the Cliffe, I meane from the water vpward to the Glasse, and the product diuide by your reserued Diuisor, the Quotient will shew you the exact distance to the Ship or marke. But if your ground be not leuell, ye shall by your Quadrant search the difference or inequalitie thereof, and if it bee lower at the Glasse than at the viewing station, you shall deduct the difference from your Diuisor, but if contrariwise, the difference shall be added to the Diuisor, and then shall yee worke as I haue before declared.

A page from a Tudor geometry treatise. The chapter gives a simple way of calculating the distance from the observer of a ship. More complex calculations, with instruments, were making navigation less haphazard, and the absorption of learning by seafarers was an important factor in the achievements of the Tudor navigators. The new printing presses facilitated the wider distribution of technical knowledge.

later generations who believed that any voluntary congregation could form a church. The Independents accepted the idea of a national church, though in a very attenuated form. The Presbyterians accepted it in a very rigid form. But confusion was coming in. 'Prophesyings' were held, that is meetings of clergy for the exposition and discussion of the Scriptures. They were not altogether new, but they increased and they were chiefly frequented by the Puritans. Queen Elizabeth enjoined Grindal to have them suppressed, and also to discourage preaching. He replied with a reasoned statement on the relations of church and state. The queen then sent orders to each of the bishops to suppress prophesyings, and she suspended the archbishop from exercising his jurisdiction. She allowed him to exercise his spiritual functions, and she reluctantly allowed him to stay in office even when his health failed; but by asserting her supremacy, she had lost something of her position above the contending parties.

After Grindal's death in 1583 the contention became more bitter. The new archbishop, John Whitgift, used his own powers and the high commission court not against Calvinism, for his own theological opinions were more Calvinistic than Grindal's, but against the attempts to alter church government. The high commission used a procedure of which many laymen disapproved: Burghley wrote to Whitgift that it smacked of the Roman inquisition. The court tendered an oath to clergymen which covered all the main points of the laws of supremacy and uniformity. If they refused or gave offending answers, they were punished. Over 200 ministers in East Anglia, Essex, Kent, and Lincolnshire alone were suspended. The laymen's distaste for clerical oppressiveness could put a brake on the enforcement of the laws. Justices of the peace were not under any supervision. Lay patrons of livings could present clergymen whom they knew to be Puritans. In parliament there were Puritan members: in 1571 one of them introduced a Bill for the reform of the Prayer Book. The privy council forbade him to attend parliament, on the ground that his Bill was against the prerogative of the queen, and the queen herself, through the Speaker, forbade the Commons to receive any bills concerning religion unless they had been approved by the clergy. The Puritans, however, advanced. In 1584 a petition was presented to parliament praying for relief from conformity, and the Presbyterian scheme was put into action. Whenever they were strong, the Puritan clergy assembled in a local court of elders, which they regarded as their rightful superior, In 1586 a national assembly was held in secret at Cambridge, and in the next year another actually in London. Another member of parliament braved the prerogative, and he was imprisoned. A third member, Peter Wentworth, broadened the attack, and tried to bring within the scope of parliamentary discussion not only religion but the succession to the throne. He was twice imprisoned in the Tower, for the second time in 1587. At that date the first Puritan movement had still not been effectively checked.

The internal affairs of the Church of England had no direct bearing on foreign policy. No foreign government formed connections with the Puritans. On the other hand, men in high office interpreted continental affairs in the light of their own religious convictions. Elizabeth and Burghley, though their religious convictions were not identical, agreed that after the Treaty of Troyes in 1564, they should avert any dangers that might threaten from abroad, but without indulging territorial ambitions. After the papal Bull of 1570 another line of thought appeared among those whose sympathies inclined towards the reformers. Sir Francis Walsingham, a zealous Protestant, who had been ambassador in France, became secretary of state in 1573. He believed that there was a 'common cause of religion' and he thought it was the duty of Queen Elizabeth to resist Catholic aggression not only if it were directed against England, but in itself. A younger generation of Englishmen, who could not even remember Mary's reign, took it for granted that the papalist powers were ill disposed. One of them was Philip Sidney, afterwards famous as a poet, statesman, and hero, one of the most radiant figures of his time. He married Walsingham's daughter. Men of this way of thinking could look for support, though not for positive leadership, to Sidney's uncle, the earl of Leicester. Leicester was a Dudley, the son of the wicked Northumberland, who had been protector at England's most Protestant moment. He was the queen's personal favourite, too grand to hold any ministerial office, and too unreliable a character; but influential at every level from the council to the Puritan clergy.

The particular matter in which these two conceptions of English policy came most clearly into conflict was the Netherlands revolt. The Dutch inhabitants of King Philip II's richest possessions were in revolt against Spain from 1567, led by Prince William the Silent of the province of Orange. The Prince sought aid abroad, but Elizabeth was at first unenthusiastic, while the

French Huguenots were crippled by the massacre in Paris on St. Bartholomew's Day, 1572. The Spanish Duke of Alva would have little difficulty, it seemed, in suppressing the Dutch rebels. But the wild and undisciplined Dutch 'sea beggars', who had been raiding the shipping of the Spanish Netherlands, pounced on the little seaport town of the Brill, commanding the entry to Rotterdam. The Spaniards never won it back, and from it there began a fanning-out of the revolt across the two maritime provinces of Holland and Zeeland. In the autumn the traveller Sir Humphrey Gilbert, half-brother to Sir Walter Raleigh, led 1,500 English volunteers who fought, neither very gloriously nor in complete harmony with their allies; but who were the first Englishmen since the crusades to go to war for their ideas.

For the next twelve years William the Silent, with unequalled constancy, fought and negotiated for his policy of uniting all the seventeen provinces under constitutional government with religious toleration. More than once, William seemed near to complete success. Although he sometimes tried to find a substitute, he always fell back on French assistance. In 1581 he held the two Dutch-speaking maritime provinces of Holland and Zeeland firmly, but they were Calvinist, while the Spaniards held the southern provinces, Catholic and equally intolerant. In 1584, just as the Duke of Anjou, to whom the Dutch northern provinces had sworn allegiance in exchange for his help, had proved a disappointing ally, Prince William was shot dead by a religious fanatic.

In England, at Leicester's suggestion, Burghley and Walsingham drew up for the privy council a bond of association, to be voluntarily signed by noblemen and others, pledging themselves to resist or avenge anything that should tend to the harm of the queen's person. This was unprecedented. For a voluntary body to take arms even for that purpose was a reminder of the Calvinist insurrections on the Continent, and the government may have given its authority in order to keep the movement within bounds. The words of the bond were amended to ensure a trial at law before any act of revenge. From the English point of view, the grave situation in Europe was growing graver. The Spanish ambassador had meddled with a plot against the king of Scots and had been expelled. Until Anjou went to the Netherlands, Elizabeth, over fifty years old, had negotiated for a French alliance with a marriage between herself and the duke. Now the Guises had made a league with Philip of Spain, obviously a menace not only to the Huguenots but to the Netherlands and to England. Ambassadors from the Dutch estates appealed to Elizabeth to save them in their extremity. They offered her sovereignty, but she declined. Antwerp, the greatest commercial city of Europe, had been surrounded for months and the Spaniards were pressing the siege. It fell before the Treaty of Nonsuch was signed. In this Elizabeth neither committed herself to a Protestant crusade nor endorsed the aims, whatever they might be, of the estates. She promised to send them an army and to maintain it at her own cost until they made peace; but she did not promise to declare war on Spain and she made conditions which would enable her to mediate between the parties if that became possible. She was to receive the Brill, Flushing, and the fort of Rammekens, west of Antwerp, as cautionary towns, that is as security for the repayment of all that she was to spend. These three places controlled the access to Rotterdam and Antwerp and the great rivers beyond them. Two English members were to sit on the Dutch council of state, and the English were to have a share in foreign relations and internal disputes which, on paper, amounted to a protectorate.

Leicester took command of the army, 6,000 foot and 1,000 horse, and the queen declared in a public print that she did not intend to govern the Netherlands either directly or indirectly. The estates with genuine enthusiasm, with a touch of guile, and with no judgement at all, offered to Leicester the position of governor general (*landvoogd*), with absolute powers in military and naval matters. In spite of the queen's justifiable anger, he accepted. Then everything went wrong. Leicester's two campaigns, in 1586 and 1587, were enormously expensive and achieved scarcely anything of value. He disagreed with the estates about a major question of policy: he wanted to cut off trading with the enemy and they wanted to permit it and to finance their forces by taxing the traders. Leicester misunderstood the elements of the constitution of which he was the figure-head. The central authority was far too weak, and he rashly tried to strengthen it. He favoured the Calvinist extremists, offending the religious moderates who had more to offer both in influence and in ability. In November 1587 he was recalled, leaving the Dutch to provide their own statesmen and generals, which they did with memorable success. The English regiments and the garrisons of the cautionary towns remained.

As England's chances of controlling the affairs of the Netherlands receded into the future, two other series of events drew her towards war with Spain. One was the tale of encounters by sea, not connected by any master-plan and almost self-generating, actuated by the simple motives of the seafarers. The other, in the region of high politics, revolved round Mary Queen of Scots. Scotland had been for years a centre of intrigues and conspiracies in which the purposes and acts of the principal actors are hard to understand, but in which religion and Spanish interests were involved to some degree. In 1586, however, this state of things

The execution of Mary Stuart in 1587. Although Mary was Queen of Scotland from 1542 to 1567, and queen-consort of France from 1559–60, she spent 20 of her 45 years as a prisoner. Tall, intelligent, and fond of reading, her Roman Catholic staunchness and her trust in unreliable friends and advisers impelled her to the execution block.

came to an end when King James VI signed the Treaty of Berwick. He and Queen Elizabeth each promised to maintain the religions professed in their respective realms, to assist one another with armed forces if invaded by a third power, and to make no incompatible alliance with another state. Nothing was written down about the English succession, but James was given to understand that the queen would not allow anything to be brought before parliament that would be detrimental to his right. That being so there was nothing shameful in his accepting a pension of £4,000 a year. The treaty did not refer to James's mother, who made a will bequeathing her crown to Philip of Spain. Walsingham, who knew everything, allowed yet another conspiracy to be formed on her behalf. When the required evidence was provided, she was tried by a special court in the hall of Fotheringay Castle and executed the next day. She died with all courage and dignity. Queen Elizabeth had hesitated for months before assenting to this course and made a pretence that she was not responsible. No one could tell what might be the consequences; but beyond doubt many Catholics would believe that Mary had died for her religion, and that Philip II was now by right king of England.

The collisions at sea and overseas culminated in 1585–6. Philip II, intending no more than an intelligible reprisal, ordered his officials on the Atlantic coast of Spain to seize all vessels in their harbours which belonged to the rebellious Netherlands or to England. They duly did so, and the English government not only replied in kind but dispatched Sir Francis Drake with thirty ships, mainly armed merchantmen, and 2,300 men, to release the confiscated vessels. He went for bigger game. He plundered Vigo, then the Cape Verde Islands, then San Domingo, the richest town of the West Indies, and St. Christopher. He destroyed a fort in Florida and touched on the coast of Virginia where he rescued the survivors of the colony which Raleigh had planted two years before. He brought home much treasure. Even in those days of slow travel and no newspapers there was such a thing as national reputation, and this news made many men confident that the Spaniards need not be feared.

England still negotiated in Brussels while one sign after another seemed to indicate that Philip was preparing to use all his resources against her. His broad strategic plan was formidable. The strongest possible fleet was to sail up the English Channel to the coast of Kent. It was to take on board the pick of the veteran army with which the governor, Alexander Farnese duke of Parma, had reconquered the southern Netherlands. A pamphlet was published in which the refugee William Allen, now a cardinal, admonished the English Catholics to rebel in support of the Spanish invaders, and only then did the queen break off her negotiations with Parma. But, though still technically at peace, the English seamen were already mauling the enemy. Drake left Plymouth in April 1587 and until June he operated against the Spaniards off their own coast. In Cadiz harbour he found the nucleus of the invasion fleet, not yet manned or equipped, and sank or burnt thirty-three of them large and small. Cruising to and fro he made many smaller captures, and in his dispatches he urged the council to strike hard against the Spanish preparations. The Spaniards had to make good the damage, which meant postponing their plans until the next year. Not everything went well with them. Their best admiral died, and the chief command was given to the duke of Medina Sidonia, a great nobleman in Andalusia, who had much to offer in matters of supply and co-ordination and could leave nautical matters to expert sub-ordinates. Parma was busy in collecting transport and clearing the waterways to bring his army to the coast; but his troops were suffering badly from disease, and there were no practical plans for embarkation. But there had never been a great expedition in which every detail was in order beforehand, and the fleet assembling at Lisbon was greater in tonnage and numbers of men than any that the western world had ever seen.

In England the council had good naval advice, which did not always coincide with Drake's, and it also made ready for defence on land if that should come. Cardinal Allen had misjudged his countrymen, as exiles usually come to do. The great majority of the English Catholics were loyal. Stopping a disciplined hostile force was another matter. There were beacons to spread the alarm; the militia were issued with firearms; the coastal defences were put in order; there was a mobile force, not very impressive, but posted at Tilbury to strike where it might be needed. During the months of waiting there were false rumours and false alarms; but the people were determined to resist. The merchants of London and the other seaports fitted out more than 120 vessels to join the queen's ships. But the organization behind them was bad. Whether from parsimony, or from mere negligence or wilful blindness, the council had not done nearly enough to provide ammunition or victuals, and the admirals failed to arouse even the queen to the danger of deficiencies which limited the length of time for which ships could keep the sea or maintain a battle. Unless there was indeed a vast difference of morale between the two fleets, the issue depended on skill. The Spaniards relied on size and numbers: their great ships were to pound their opponents at close quarters and then grapple and board. The English trusted to the speed of their manœuvrable smaller ships, and to their heavier guns. Their tactics were to hold off and harass, and to seize opportunities.

The first full-scale naval war between two Atlantic powers began on 19 July 1588, when Medina Sidonia sighted the Lizard. The grand fleet was in Plymouth Sound, where the commander-in-chief, Charles, Lord Howard of Effingham, had joined forces with Drake's western squadron. At the other extremity of the Channel English and Dutch squadrons were watching the Flemish ports where Parma's troops were waiting. For more than a week the two main fleets moved slowly up the Channel, as if they were demonstrating their two naval doctrines. The Spaniards were in close formation and kept their stations. The English plucked their feathers, disabling two ships. On 28 July the Spaniards were at anchor in Calais Roads. Howard sent in eight fire-ships, the torpedoes of that age, among the galleons, and the galleons hastily ran before the south-west wind. All day on the 29th the English followed them in the Battle of Gravelines (the first fleet action in which no oared ships were engaged, an off-fight) damaging every single one. Five big ships were incapable of further action; two were wrecks on the Flemish coast. The wind changed, and threatened to drive the rest ashore. They turned in worsening weather to make the hazardous journey northabout round the coast of hostile England and unfriendly Scotland, and the wild western rocks of Ireland. Ship after ship miscarried, until about half the Armada was gone.

After the Armada 1588–1603

1595 O'Neill, Earl of Tyrone, begins his Irish rebellion.
1598 The death of William Cecil (Lord Burghley), Elizabeth's secretary of state since 1558.
1600 William Shakespeare finishes his first great tragedy (*Julius Caesar*) and begins his second (*Hamlet*). The East India Company is incorporated by royal charter.
1601 The Earl of Essex is executed. A new poor law builds on the experience gained since King Henry VIII's pioneer poor law of 1531.
1603 O'Neill decides to end his Irish rebellion. The death of Elizabeth.

In bracing themselves to meet the Armada, in admiring their queen's courage as it approached, and in their relief and pride when it receded, the people had common experiences. When these experiences became history and myth they brought the national sense of community into sharper focus, the more so because they came at a time when English literature was coming to express a wider range of emotions than ever before, and with such a command of language that it appealed to a far greater number of hearers and readers. Many influences converged to furnish the Elizabethan mind, especially in its later years. The living tradition from Chaucer onwards was studied, and improved by themes and dexterities from French, Italian, and Spanish writers; but the central stream, which had been growing stronger for a century, was that of the ancient classics. In the grammar schools the grammar which was taught was not mere accidence and syntax, but literature in the widest sense in which schoolboys could absorb it, Latin everywhere and Greek for a minority. The universities taught the same subjects at a higher level, and university men were the experimenters in poetry and drama.

For the large and growing educated public there were translations. In almost every year of Elizabeth's reign some Greek or Latin book was translated either direct from the original or from some previous translation into French. Our language shows the result in many of the Greek words which have been absorbed into our vocabulary, including many of our scientific terms, but our thoughts and ideas show it too. For many Elizabethan readers the classical masterpieces of history, biography, and philosophy had the freshness of new English books. They abounded in stories, and arguments and memorable phrases, of which the moral was that the country, the commonwealth, had a supreme claim on the devotion of the citizen. English patriotism was enriched, and consolidated. We may say that for the first time it became fully independent and articulate. The two supreme Elizabethan writers, whose minds encompassed so many other realities, did their utmost for it precisely in these years: Spenser published the *Faerie Queene* in 1590–6 and Shakespeare's *Henry V* was performed in 1599.

Outside the sphere of imaginative literature there were many notable authors, and most of them were indebted to the classical renaissance, even the physician William Gilbert, whose *De Magnete* of 1600 is sometimes, not quite fairly, called the first English scientific book. Richard Hooker wrote an impressive and learned if difficult book on *The Laws of Ecclesiastical Polity* which, for the first time, put the principles of the Church of England on a philosophical basis. Puritanism also came under the prevailing influences. In the earliest English protestantism in Cranmer's time there are echoes of the stoics, and such echoes form a thread in the ideas of freedom and justice, which were spreading among Englishmen who were not theologians.

The universities were no longer places of education chiefly for

William Shakespeare, poet and playwright. In about 1585 Shakespeare began his career as an actor, and he later joined one of the actor companies which performed before the court. His plays were written for this company, and established Shakespeare as a master and innovator of the English language, and as a gifted portrayer of character.

the clergy. The professions of law and medicine, and employment in public business were ceasing to be clerical preserves, and laymen who aspired to them often started from an education at Oxford or Cambridge. We know a good deal about their purchases of books and their reading, both of which do them credit. The country gentlemen, who did not aim at offices higher than the commission of the peace, often did not stay at the university long enough to take a degree; but it was a frequent custom for them to continue their education in a practical way which had no foreign parallel. The legal faculties in the universities were small and narrowly specialized. They had never taught the English common law, which had to be learnt at one of the Inns of Court in London. Their field was the two kinds of Roman law, canon and civil; but when Henry VIII forbade them to teach canon law, nothing was left to them except the civil law, and that was useless except for practitioners in probate and divorce, and in admiralty cases because they were international. The country gentlemen therefore went over to the Inns of Court, where the common law was taught in a quite liberal spirit. Thus it was that a good many of the country magistrates were well qualified for their various duties, and that there were men available for election to the House of Commons who had a good grasp of legal ideas and procedure. In comparison with continental countries it came about that in England legal knowledge was less confined to the professional lawyers, and was exceptionally widely diffused through the governing class.

Although the twelve years of Queen Elizabeth's reign after the Armada saw so much organic growth, on the surface they were on the whole disappointing. The one considerable exception was in Ireland, where there were signs that new sources of energy might be brought to bear on the old problems. There was indeed no end as yet to the incursions into unsubdued territory which had no lasting results except to train the Irish in resistance and even in co-operation among themselves. Of the chief governors, the first who made his mark, in two terms of office, 1565–71 and 1575–8, was Sir Henry Sidney, the father of Sir Philip. Although he was badly supported from England, especially in the matter of money, he kept good discipline among his troops and used them effectively towards both the north and the west. In Ulster he fortified Derry. He rebuilt Dublin Castle. He constituted Longford and Clare, Sligo, Mayo, Galway, and Roscommon as new counties; he carried an Act for establishing schools, and he encouraged forty families of religious refugees from the Netherlands to settle in the ruined town of Swords, a few miles from Dublin. His successors were not all equally wise or successful. Sir John Perrot, an illegitimate son of King Henry VIII, went so far in dealing with his opponents by diplomacy that he was condemned to death for high treason. He had made some headway against the Scots and Hebrideans whose presence on the coast of Antrim had given trouble for generations. Sorley Boy Macdonnell, who lived from about 1505 to 1590, claimed to be lord of the Irish district called the Route. While he was fighting for and against Queen Elizabeth in turns, the Scots and islanders came over in large numbers, and King James VI of Scotland was powerless to stop them. As Essex had done before him, Perrot defeated Sorley Boy. The latter renounced his claims, and accepted lands and offices from Elizabeth. The one permanent memorial of Perrot's time is Trinity College outside the walls of Dublin, for which a small body of citizens obtained a royal charter in 1591. Ever since then it has been a bulwark of the European heritage of good learning.

Successes founded on something more substantial than victories in the field were to be seen in the province of Munster, in the south-west. Here there was colonization. It differed from the earlier attempts in King's and Queen's Counties and elsewhere because it had behind it the driving force of expansion, especially from the west of England, and because the English government organized and directed it. From 1579 to 1583 southern Ireland was devastated during the rebellion of Desmond, the head of the Fitzgeralds. The landing of Spanish forces at Smerwick in Kerry in 1580 had the same sort of significance as the Armada; but they were beaten, and Desmond was killed in 1583. Burghley and Walsingham devised and put through a scheme for repopulating Munster with gentlemen, tenant farmers, labourers, and townsmen. Large grants of land were made to 'undertakers', each of whom had to provide capital and contracted to bring over colonists of each function and grade in proportion to the extent of his seignory. The most determined and active undertakers were the same men who had ventured in America, including Raleigh, Gilbert, and Sir Richard Grenville, and they brought with them such outstanding men as Spenser the poet, and John White the artist famous for his drawings made in Virginia. Inevitably the scheme was not free from mistakes and defects. The grants went by favour, and even those settlers

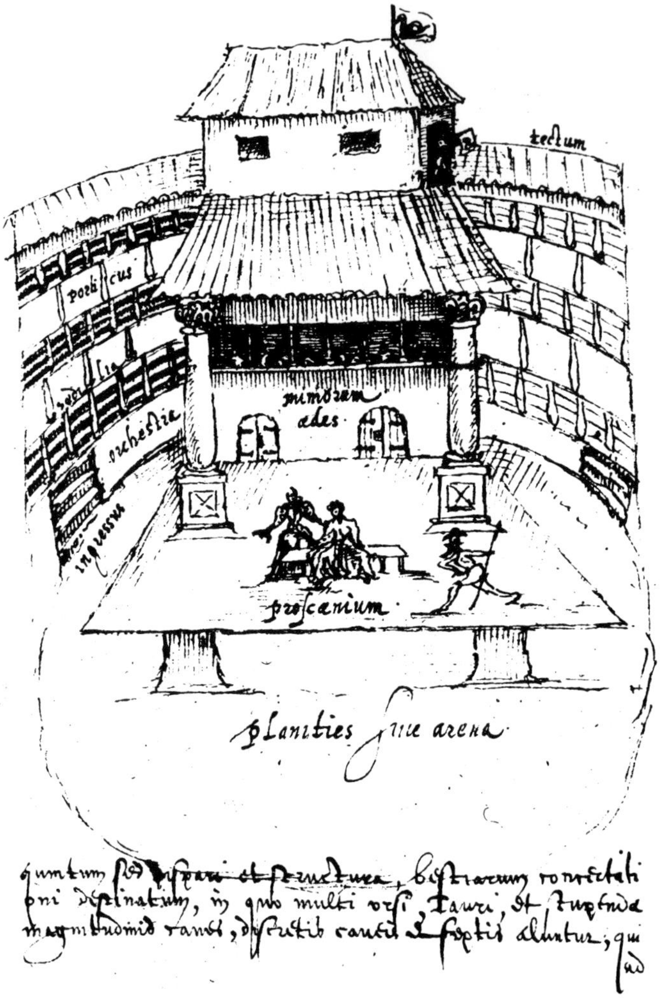

who had previous experience of Ireland were little qualified to establish tolerable relations with their new neighbours; but the next few years showed that colonization on these lines, whatever its inherent contradictions, could be made viable.

The next crisis began in the north. There Hugh O'Neill, who valued his inherited paramountcy much more than his English title of earl of Tyrone, had been active against a variety of rivals since 1568. In 1595 he turned against the English, in what they saw as a rebellion, but what the historian must regard as a war for the preservation of a way of life, which had not been deeply affected by centuries of contact with the Danes, the Normans, and the English and which was still distinct in its language, literature, and laws, and newly distinct in religion. O'Neill sought the help of Spain, and Philip II was glad to open a new theatre of war after his expensive failures in the Netherlands and the channel. In 1596 he sent money and munitions enough to keep the Irish in the field for eighteen months. If they were to liberate Ireland they must have Spanish ships and money; but the sea is a single theatre of war and the English broke up Philip's Irish enterprise in harbour at Cadiz. A powerful fleet, with soldiers on board, put out from Lisbon; only to be dispersed by a storm, and another failure in 1597 seemed to end O'Neill's chances of Spanish aid.

After a brief relaxation of the hostilities O'Neill's affairs took a turn for the better. He won some military successes. The parts of Ireland which had remained quiet now rose in his favour. The Munster colony was overrun and the colonists driven out. In 1599, to be sure, a Spanish fleet, setting out for Ireland, got no further than Brittany; but then the English counter-measures suffered a grievous set-back. Queen Elizabeth sent out, with the high rank of lord lieutenant, her favourite the young earl of Essex. He had many advantages. He was Leicester's stepson and he married Sir Philip Sidney's widow. He was an experienced, and in the opinion of some an expert, commander; at any rate in the eyes of the populace he was the hero of the raid on Cadiz. His father had been an unsuccessful colonist in Ulster, with a bad record of cruelty. He himself was unfit for high office. When he found the old obstacles in his way he suddenly left for England without the queen's leave, intending to demand stronger support. He deservedly forfeited his employment instead. His successor, Lord Mountjoy, was methodical and patient, exactly the man who was needed. In 1601 3,000 Spanish troops landed at Kinsale and fortified themselves. They had only succeeded in putting ashore enough stores and munitions for themselves, and so they could not raise the neighbouring country. An English squadron blocked their communications by sea and Mountjoy besieged them. Tyrone and O'Donnell approached from the north, but Mountjoy routed them and the Spaniards elected to go home on honourable terms. Mountjoy could go on with his pacification undisturbed; Tyrone was on the point of submitting in March 1603 when Queen Elizabeth died.

Little more need be said about the course of the war against Spain, which might have been altogether different if an attempt on Ireland had succeeded. The Spaniards and Portuguese were united against the English and the Dutch since the conquest of Portugal by Philip II in 1581. It gave Spain the magnificent base of Lisbon, and the Atlantic coast harbours of Portugal; but it exposed the trade of the East Indies and Brazil to English and Dutch attack. Regular English trade to the East Indies began with the foundation of the East India Company in 1600. Both the English and the Dutch had reached the height of their naval proficiency; but they suffered much from adverse weather and from sickness. For these reasons these twelve years of warfare were indecisive, each side in turn taking the initiative and neither driving home a success. The most famous English naval action of the time, the last fight of the *Revenge*, was an incident in an unsuccessful attempt on the Spanish treasure fleet returning from America. This was not the only occasion on which this rich prize eluded the English seamen. The most ambitious of their attempts on the mainland of Europe was the attack on Cadiz in 1596, in which Essex, commanding the land forces, won his reputation. This was the first expedition in which the Dutch co-operated with the English: they sent a squadron and good troops under Louis Gunther of Nassau. Spanish ships were destroyed in the bay; a force of 3,000 men captured the town; but the council of war rightly judged that they had not the means to push their invasion into Andalusia or to stay in Cadiz. Within a fortnight they sailed for England. A month before the expedition set out, the Spanish governor of the Netherlands, the archduke Albert, had suddenly captured Calais from the French, and the Cadiz expedition would never have started if the English had not reluctantly recognized that it was beyond their power to recover Calais.

Since the Armada the character of the war had changed. The Dutch were no longer mere rebels or merely one party in a civil war: the estates had formed a federal republic, with a regular army fighting behind well-defined frontiers. The Huguenots also had emerged from the stage of civil war. Their leader had become king of France as Henry IV. Queen Elizabeth had helped him with subsidies, and continued to do so even after he became a

An Elizabethan playhouse, the Swan in Southwark. In the 16th century new plays written in English were replacing the old morality plays. Although plays were still performed in the yards of large inns, by the end of the century there were several specially-built theatres in London.

Catholic as a means to uniting France, while tolerating his former co-religionists. In 1596, after the fall of Calais, England, France, and the Netherlands made a triple alliance against Spain, in which the new republic treated with the others as a full-fledged power. France was the power which needed help, but England gave it sparingly. Two years later Henry IV found that he could safely make peace with Spain. His defection did not materially weaken his allies; indeed it relieved them of a burden; but that burden, added to Ireland and the naval efforts, was weighing heavily on England. In 1600 tentative peace negotiations began at Boulogne, but they led to nothing.

Besides the disappointments abroad there were domestic reasons which made these years cheerless. One after another the great figures of Elizabeth's reign, the wise and the unwise, grew old and died, Leicester while the Armada was retreating, Walsingham in 1590 , Burghley in 1598. The best man now available was Robert Cecil, Burghley's younger son, who was secretary of state; but he had to hold his own among envious courtiers. The queen did not establish cordial relations with any of the three parliaments which met in these twelve years. She needed them for their grants of money; indeed she raised funds by extra-parliamentary methods such as sales of Crown lands, and loans without interest which were voluntary only in name. The conditions were unfavourable for raising money: during the fifteen-nineties, as in most of Europe, there was a disastrous run of bad harvests. There was very little open rural discontent. In 1596 there were disturbances in Oxfordshire about enclosures and other poor men's grievances, but only two gentlemen were implicated. In another economic matter, however, dissatisfaction ran high. In 1597 parliament presented an address against monopolies. The Crown had granted them, some to genuine inventors or promoters of new industries, others to mere outsiders who were given the sole right to sell specified articles, sometimes necessary articles of common consumption. All the recipients promised to pay the Crown handsomely, though many of them failed to do it. Some of their privileges infringed the legal rights of existing producers or traders; most of them tended to raise prices. In 1601 the grievance was still unredressed, and the Commons complained bitterly. The queen made one of her dramatic personal appearances and won all hearts by a magnanimous withdrawal.

But the background was gloomy. Even the religious divisions were becoming more irreconcilable. Two new statutes were passed in 1593 which confirmed the purpose of the government to repress dissent by force. The first heavily increased the fines for not attending church and, though it prominently mentioned Jesuits and seminary priests, virtually made any Catholic priest liable to the penalty of death. The second was called forth by the spread of separatism and by the clandestine circulation of savagely abusive pamphlets against the bishops and what they stood for. For the first time it was made a crime to attend dissenting assemblies for worship, a crime, if obstinately persisted in, to be punished with exile or death. Apart from this, fanatical Protestants could be charged, as the Catholics often were, with other offences, such as seditious words, and so a new tale of Protestant martyrs began, five of them at least.

The last armed insurrection of the Tudor period showed how far the system was out of repair, but it also showed that in all essentials it still stood firm. When Essex made his disobedient and unmannerly dash from Ireland he would not believe at first that he had ruined himself with the queen. As one attempt after another to regain her favour failed to move her, he and his friends toyed with some old tricks for getting power, such as flight to France, or a rising in Wales; and they actually began to edge towards a new kind of insubordination. Essex had to use such resources as he had, his friendships and a real, though perhaps not well-founded, popularity with the Puritans and some at least of the London citizens. In 1601 a plot was hatched at Essex House, in the Strand outside Temple Bar. Essex was to seize the Palace of Whitehall, and compel the queen to dismiss all her advisers and summon parliament. The council had information and sent for Essex, but he went on. The conspirators assembled at Essex House, and its master, with two hundred armed men, rode out to rouse the City. The City would not stir. Essex got back to his house by water, to find it surrounded by soldiers. He surrendered. He and four of his intimates were tried and executed, other's imprisoned and fined. That was all. The main lesson of his rising was that the country chose loyalty and understood it.

The Jacobean Peace
1603–1618

1603 James VI of Scotland becomes also James I of England, thereby uniting the Scottish and English crowns.
1604 James disappoints most Puritan hopes at the Hampton Court Conference.
1605 Guy Fawkes makes an unsuccessful attempt to blow up the king and parliament.
1607 English colonists found Jamestown in Virginia, destined to be the first permanent colony in America. The Midland Rising is quelled.
1611 Plantation of Ulster by English and Scottish settlers begins. The Authorised Version of the Bible is published.
1616 Edward Coke, Lord Chief Justice, is dismissed.
1618 Sir Walter Raleigh is executed.

In 1603 the great queen died. James VI of Scotland acquired the title of King James I of England. He had learning, steadfastness, intelligence, and a sense of humour. He liked to mix with people of all ranks, which gave rise to the criticism that he did not know how to keep his royal distance. In the last decade of the sixteenth century he had transformed both the kingdom of Scotland and the monarch's place in it. Hitherto, Scottish nobles had thought nothing of brandishing their swords in the king's bedchamber, or even, as in 1582, of kidnapping the king. But somehow, in ten turbulent years, with an execution here and a mark of friendship there, James had changed all that. Although in the Highlands he could not put an end to the feuds, battles, and murders which Highlanders seemed to regard as an essential part of their culture, he did reduce the number and scale of such outbreaks. He even achieved the dissolution of one large and troublemaking clan, the Macgregors. He tried to make it advantageous for nobles and chiefs to pursue their griefs in his courts instead of in ambushes, burnings, and other savageries. In general, he brought order and then law to the Lowlands but not to the Highlands. This had the unfortunate effect of perpetuating the differences between these two great divisions of the Scottish nation. In addition to all this, he muted the Presbyterians of the Church's General Assembly. Although a Protestant king, James had no love for the Presbyterians, while they in turn suspected him of harbouring tolerant feelings, or worse, towards the Catholics. James broke the Assembly's effect by fixing its meetings for times and places which he knew would deter his most dangerous critics from attending; its most troublesome members lived in St. Andrews and Edinburgh, and they were usually unwilling to travel more than fifty or sixty miles to its sessions. Five years before leaving Scotland for England he published his *Basilikon Doron*, which contained his ideas of how a monarch should behave. It is a book full of wisdom and tolerance. 'No kingdom lacks her own diseases', he writes in attenuation of the evils of Scottish society. In one line he describes the preoccupation of Scottish chiefs and nobles: 'They bang it out bravely, he and all his kin against him and all his.'

His accession to the throne of England was tranquil. His new subjects on the whole made him welcome, and he gave pleasure by scattering titles of honour much more freely than his predecessors had done. As was natural he brought some Scotsmen with him and a few of them afterwards became objects of jealousy to the English nobility; but he did not show any great preference for his other kingdom. He revisited it only once, for six months in 1617. Although he loved hunting, his personal qualities were not such as to make him popular with the English aristocracy, nor even with the legal and administrative office-holders whom he had inherited from the Tudors. He was no soldier, and he did not appreciate the military virtues in others. He prided himself on being a peacemaker and for England his

PREVIOUS PAGE King James VI of Scotland, later King James I of England. An intelligent man, James was too pedantic and insensitive to make good relationships with those whose cooperation he needed. He seemed both wise and inept, causing the Spanish ambassador to describe him as 'the wisest fool in Christendom'.

BELOW The Somerset House conference negotiating the end of hostilities between England and Spain in 1604. King James I realised that continued war was unproductive, but his peace with Spain was resented by many of his most influential subjects, largely because it meant that English ships could no longer trade with the Indies, and partly because it ended English support of the Dutch.

policy was to keep the country as he found it, but to reconcile the differences within it.

Until 1612 Cecil was the principal minister, at first as secretary of state and from 1608 as Lord Treasurer. Cecil became a peer at the beginning of the reign, and on his second promotion in the peerage took the title of Salisbury, which his descendants still hold. His steadying influence lasted until he died in office. There were, of course, some politicans who disagreed with Cecil, especially among the martial and adventurous men whom Elizabeth had encouraged, but an event at the outset showed that they had lost their prestige. Sir Walter Raleigh was one of them, a wonderfully gifted man with enormous failings. Queen Elizabeth had loaded him with presents and honours, though never with any responsible office in the state; but he was captain of the guard, warden of the stannaries, and governor of Jersey. Fairly or unfairly he was relieved of these offices, and he listened to the schemings of Lord Cobham, whose project was to depose James in favour of his cousin the Lady Arabella Stuart. There were two plots, this main plot and a by-plot on behalf of the Roman Catholics, both undoubtedly treasonable. Cobham and Raleigh were condemned to death for the former, and Raleigh's part in it was possibly less than guilty; but neither of them was executed. Without any pardon they were both kept in the Tower until 1617, and then there was a frightful sequel; but James's clemency reduced this treason to the level of an incident.

Whatever policy he might pursue, the union of the two Crowns had political consequences of the first magnitude. James at once became the most powerful Protestant sovereign in Europe. Moreover, since he personally had never been at war with Spain, and the international law of that time regarded war as a contest between sovereigns, England was technically no longer at war. Hostilities ceased. Ambassadors came from Spain and the Spanish Netherlands to Somerset House. The state of the European war was less critical and England was less closely involved than might appear. The Dutch, who were defending the detached stronghold of Ostend, had in their pay English troops with a nominal strength of 8,000, besides the garrisons of the Brill and Flushing. Their ablest statesman, John of Oldenbarnevelt, came over to dissuade James from his purpose, and Sully, the ablest minister of the neutral Henry IV, came over to back up the Dutch; but James made peace, leaving the auxiliary troops with the Dutch and retaining not only the garrisons, but also his quasi-protectorate over the republic. As it turned out the Dutch got on very well when he became a neutral like Henry IV. The English negotiators proposed a clause by which the Spaniards should permit trade with the Indies, East and West, in places where they had no 'regiment or property'. As was to be expected the Spaniards rejected this, and there was nothing about overseas commerce in the treaty; but during the next few years relations with Spain were not unfriendly; the English traded more

Part of James's first capital, Edinburgh. This engraving shows Moray House, in Canongate. Moray House was finished in 1628, just after James's death; the street activity suggests that the king's comments about his Scots' fondness for a fight remained valid.

vigorously than before and they succeeded at last, in 1607, in founding a successful colony on the mainland of America, Virginia, where the name of Jamestown still commemorates the king. And, more generally, his peace-making spelt opportunity. It gave England the longest period of peace with all her neighbours that she had ever enjoyed, longer than any she was to enjoy again until after the fall of Napoleon.

The two kingdoms also automatically formed a single unit in foreign relations, for which, very much in James's spirit, the name Great Britain was adopted. Legally indeed he was still entitled to make separate treaties for each kingdom, but he made scarcely any use of this right. He wished for as much unity as could be attained. But to most Scots, England was still very much a foreign country. Although the number of Scots living in England, especially churchmen and merchants, had been slowly growing, the wealthier Scots still sent their sons to France, not England, for education. Scottish trade, too, tended to be with the continent rather than with England. Trade with the Netherlands was so large that the harbour town of Veere in Zealand was very much a Scottish outpost. Nor were the English ready to treat the Scots as fellow-countrymen. Few followed James's recommendations to marry their sons and daughters to eligible Scots. The English continued to regard the Scots as undercutters in trade.

James expected that a common nationality would follow from common allegiance. The English judges stopped short of this, but conceded that it did follow for all Englishmen and Scots born after James's accession in England. The frontier organization on both sides of the border was dismantled, and it was brought under the normal legal rules and institutions. In 1606–7 the ministers laid before parliament a plan for union. James urged on the houses the principles that all laws providing for hostilities between the two kingdoms should be repealed, and that there should be one church and one king. The proposals were not well received; some genuine fears of Scottish competition were mixed in a mass of suspicion and prejudice. It must, however, be remembered that the ill feeling between the two nations was a fact of the situation, and also that, when constitutional union was achieved a century later, it took into account some primary factors, such as religious separation.

Few people could understand his position in the religious question. He wanted to promote peace and unity in this matter too, and he was a theologian, which means that he made a serious study of the intellectual issues on which his subjects were divided. Before his accession he had corresponded with continental Catholic authorities in such a way as to raise hopes that he would interpret the existing church settlement in a sense favourable to the recusants, those who refused to attend the English Church services. In England he announced that the statutory fines would not be enforced. He hoped that the papacy would co-operate with him to make the distinction between catholicism and treason clear and workable by authorizing the excommunication of extremists who overstepped the line. In theory this was a constructive proposal; but it was not accepted and there was no other positive action which James could take.

If the Catholics were deceived in their hopes of relief, the Puritans were equally disappointed. They too expected at least some relaxation of the laws. James had been brought up in the exemplary church of Scotland. He accepted its theology, but the English Puritans seem to have been strangely unaware that he had steadily pressed his royal rights in church government, and not without some successes. When James arrived in England the Puritans presented a petition, called the Millenary Petition, because it purported to represent the views of a thousand of the clergy. This stated their dissatisfaction, in a moderate tone. It mentioned in particular the inactivity of the parochial clergy, as exemplified in the scarcity of well-educated ministers, and the holding of livings by non-residents. The king was anxious to remedy this. He knew that one of the main reasons for it was the sometimes legal and sometimes illegal transference into the hands of laymen of tithe which had formerly been due to monasteries, and he wrote to the universities saying that he intended to return to the church his own revenues from this source. Up to a point he also agreed with the Puritans that the Prayer Book needed revision. It did in fact contain some small inconsistencies, and the Puritans hoped for concessions on points regarding the rite of confirmation and their old scruples about vestments, ceremonies, and the Articles of Belief. Lastly the ecclesiastical courts needed reform, either because in them judges who were laymen decided spiritual questions, or, more generally, because they did not satisfy normal standards of justice and effectiveness.

The petition suggested a conference on these matters. Overruling the bishops, the king granted the request, and he presided over the Hampton Court Conference, of bishops, members of the council, and Puritan divines, which occupied three days in January 1604. The time was short and some angry words were exchanged, but the proceedings were businesslike, and the result was not wholly unsatisfactory to the Puritans. There were to be some slight changes in the Prayer Book; the ecclesiastical courts were to be reformed, including the court of high commission; the abuses of pluralities (one priest holding several benefices) and non-residence were to be taken in hand, and preachers were to be planted, especially in Ireland, Wales, and the northern borders. These changes, however, were to be worked out in detail by six committees made up either of bishops alone or of bishops with members of the privy council. In their hands the reforms were whittled down almost to nothing, a foretaste of what was often to happen when James I, after a spurt of activity, left others to finish his work. The one result of the Conference for which posterity has been almost unanimously grateful was the commissioning of the Authorized Version of the Bible, one of the corner-stones of the English language, which was completed in 1611.

Well before that date the conservatism of the bishops and even of the king himself had produced results. They had blocked all

The Gunpowder Plot aroused great interest outside the British Isles. This, part of a German publication, shows the sequel of the plot: those of the conspirators who did not die in the course of arrest are being hung, drawn, and quartered.

Fires were frequent and very destructive in both town and village; houses were largely or entirely of wood, and densely situated. Firefighting apparatus like this was rare, and little more effective than the traditional buckets of water.

discussion of the doctrine that episcopacy was divinely ordained, and all proposals for restricting the autocracy of the bishops by associating them with assemblies. They had made no changes in ceremonies, and the clergy were still bound by the Act of Uniformity. In 1604 a new set of canons was passed by convocation. These required the clergy to subscribe to the Articles and to follow various practices to which the Puritans objected fundamentally. Some Puritan ministers, perhaps fewer than fifty, were deprived of their livings; but the Puritan movement was not checked. It continued to grow among the laity of all classes, in loose alliance with political discontent. The established church gained confidence from its greater uniformity and from the high intellectual standard of its best writers; but it never again came near to the Elizabethan aim of comprehending all Englishmen who did not acknowledge the pope. When the great poet John Donne, brought up as a Roman Catholic, finally became an Anglican in 1610, he was no more representative of the times than the French, Italian, Dutch, and Walloon theologians who clustered round King James to plan for Christian reunion. The nation was heading towards religious strife.

James met his first parliament in 1604. His previous experience did not include anything like this, and he never succeeded in working harmoniously with the 'commons in parliament assembled.' Queen Elizabeth's later parliaments had shown a spirit of opposition, and a tendency to pass on from particular grievances to a jealousy for the rights of parliament as such. Some points of parliamentary privilege needed to be defined, for instance the freedom of members from arrest for civil debts or for misdemeanours. In a way it was absurd that they should be even temporarily shielded against the operation of the law, but in those ill-regulated times it was easy for an official or a private enemy to clap a legislator into prison and deprive a constituency of its representative. This privilege was now established, and so was another which proved to be far more valuable than was foreseen. Elections were apt to be managed untidily and it was necessary for someone to decide whether a gentleman who came up to take his seat was properly qualified. This had been done by a subordinate of the Lord Chancellor called the clerk of the Crown, who issued the writs for holding elections; but in 1604 his decision between two candidates for Buckinghamshire was disputed, and the Commons successfully asserted the claim that it was they who had the right to decide disputed or doubtful elections. This cut off one means by which the Crown might have prevented its opponents from sitting. For the time being, however, the management of the Commons in session mattered more than the decision of borderline cases about membership, and in this James was badly served. Able privy councillors sitting in the house could have made sure that it had full information and could have given it legal and political guidance; but too few of them were available.

Altogether James had only four parliaments. The first met in 1604 and had four sessions spread over the next six years; the second, in 1614, was a total failure; the third met after six years of unparliamentary government and sat for three tumultuous years, to be followed closely in 1624 by the fourth. Their record of legislation was not impressive; they failed to rectify some admitted abuses, or to complete much routine business.

The first parliament addressed itself to religious questions and proved to be strongly sympathetic with the Puritans and hostile to the Catholics. Partly for this reason the king gave up his original leniency towards the Catholics, and took measures to banish priests and to levy the full fines on the richer recusants. Some priests were executed, apparently in the ordinary course of the law and without any special orders to the judges. When parliament was about to meet for its second session in the autumn of 1605, a small group of Catholic hotheads, men of good families, stuffed a cellar under the House of Lords with gunpowder. They arranged to have a fifteen-minute time fuse lighted by Guy Fawkes, to explode it while the king and both houses were together for the ceremonial opening. Lord Monteagle, a Catholic peer, received an anonymous letter warning him to keep away, and he showed it to Cecil. Two days before parliament met on 5 November Fawkes was discovered in the cellar; he and seven other conspirators confessed their treason and were executed after trial. There is no reason to suppose that English Catholics approved of the plot; but they were shocked and embittered by what followed. Henry Garnett, the superior of the English Jesuits, had a general and confused previous knowledge of the plot, and in confession he had been told of the plans. He was arrested, tried, executed, and afterwards revered by his own communion as a martyr for the secrecy of the confessional. Parliament passed a new Act against recusants and made sure that the country should remember the Gunpowder Plot. Special prayers were added to the Prayer Book. The anniversary was kept thus until 1859.

The first parliament left the religious problem worsening, and it failed to agree with the council on financial reforms. In 1606 the court of exchequer tried the case of a London merchant named Bate, who refused to pay the duty on currants at a new and higher rate demanded by the customs. The court decided for the Crown, and there were precedents from Mary's time onwards for the imposition of new customs rates without the consent of parliament. Lawyers were not unanimous about the grounds and limits of the king's right to do this; but the council took advantage of the judgement to bring in a new Book of Rates, with increased duties. Merchants were consulted, but they naturally disliked it, and parliament men were suspicious of anything which enabled the king to raise revenue without their approval. In 1610 the lawyers in the House of Commons debated the matter, and the debate is typical in one respect of the many debates in this and the following reign on the limits of the royal power. The speakers paraded much antiquarian learning, with little understanding of their circumstances or real significance; on this inadequate base there was created a persuasive picture of an English history composed of a succession of battles for freedom against an encroaching monarchy.

The atmosphere was unfavourable to the modernizing of the

Sir Walter Raleigh and his son. Thanks partly to his good looks, Raleigh attracted Queen Elizabeth's attention and was soon engaged in projects to colonize the North American coast. He later shifted his attention to South America, seeking the legendary but non-existent city of gold, Eldorado. He was the first well-known Englishman to smoke as a regular habit, and his example was widely imitated.

finances. In 1610 the council put forward a proposal called the Great Contract, the principle of which was as sound as could be. The revenue normally fell short of what was needed by some £50,000 a year. The nucleus to which the king was certainly entitled consisted of his feudal dues, but these were difficult to ascertain and collect, and highly inconvenient to the tenants-in-chief who had to pay them. In fact they were archaic. The king now offered to renounce almost all of them in return for £220,000 in compensation. The Commons unreasonably offered £100,000 and, with the king's consent, embarked on a further discussion of impositions. Salisbury, as a peer, could not appear in the House of Commons, but he screwed their offer up to £200,000, only to find that this was conditional on the granting of various concessions which James would only promise to consider. It may be that in the end the negotiation broke down because the king insisted on his own view of prerogative, which he sometimes expressed in needlessly provoking language, but which in essence was no more autocratic than the Tudor view. On the other hand, if the Commons had wanted to provide the Crown with an efficient and economical financial system, they would have made a beginning by discussing the Great Contract on a basis not of constitutional theory but of accountancy. James dissolved the parliament.

These questions of public finance were not closely related to economic changes. The general level of prices continued to rise, which was the justification for the new Book of Rates; the rise had become less rapid since about 1590, but this retardation had no pronounced effects. The new industries continued to grow, and so, as we shall see, did overseas enterprise. The population of England and Wales seems to have increased at a moderate rate throughout the sixteenth century, exceeding four millions by the end. The towns were growing, especially London. The City corporation looked with disfavour on the building of new houses, perhaps because great cities were hard to provision and were subject to epidemics, or perhaps because newcomers competed with the vested interests of the citizens. From the Armada year onwards the privy council tried and failed to stop the expansion of London, first by Acts of Parliament, then by proclamations, commissions, and legal proceedings. The growth of towns and trade promoted changes in agriculture, especially, for good and ill, enclosures. The last Act against depopulation was passed in 1597 and it was not effective.

There is evidence of rural discontent in a good many parts of the country from the beginning of James's reign; but there was only one serious outbreak, difficult to interpret. It began, in May 1607, near Kettering in Northamptonshire, in the heart of the country where arable land was being enclosed for sheep-pasture. Rioting by day and night spread to five neighbouring counties. The leader, John Reynolds (or Captain Pouch) stated that he was directed by the Lord of Heaven, but there is no evidence of any religious motive. The first objective of the rioters was to throw down fences, although they seem to have used the name of levellers in a wider, social sense. There was no real fighting. In the one recorded encounter a crowd of peasants without firearms was broken up and forty or fifty of them were killed by an irregular body of horse and foot hastily collected from the neighbouring gentry and yeomanry and their servants, under the command of two rich local squires of Puritan antecedents.

By July it was all over. Many poor people were executed by martial law or by civil justice. The government issued a proclamation, declaring that this Midland Rising was not caused by any famine or dearness of corn, which may be doubted, for the price of corn was high in 1607; but it also ordered an inquiry. One of the commissioners was the chief justice of the king's bench, a brother of one of the two militant squires. He wrote to the privy council in 1648 that these levellers were stirred up by others. Whatever the truth of this, it seems that the region was soon regarded as safe.

In James's first ten years there were no agreements or disagreements of much note with foreign powers; but there were shiftings in the international scene which concerned England's interests. The Dutch maintained their war on land and sea so successfully that in 1609, after difficult negotiations in which France and England mediated, the Spaniards agreed to a twelve years' truce, treating them as free states, and, if only in a grudging and complicated article, granting them permission to trade in the Indies. The twelve years of truce which followed enabled the Dutch to concentrate their energies in a many sided drive for economic expansion. Amsterdam replaced Antwerp as the commercial hub of Europe. Behind them old and new industries flourished, and through the whole remainder of the seventeenth century one of the propelling forces in English agriculture, industry, commerce, and finance was conscious imitation of the Dutch. There was also rivalry wherever the two nations sailed the same waters. Within a few years of the truce quarrels were engaging the attention of the two governments. One of these, over the large share of British coastal fishing taken by the Dutch, led the council to limit all fishing on the shores or seas of Great Britain to those who had bought a license. The Dutch agreed to negotiate after a year's respite.

Towards the end of that year the news arrived of an ominous occurrence in the East Indies, not the first. This time the Dutch, retaliating for the murder of their admiral, had built a fort in the Banda Islands and forbidden the English to engage in the spice-trade there. In effect, if on different legal grounds, they were making the same monopolistic claim as the Spaniards had made before them. But before negotiations could begin on either of these matters there was a crisis in Europe caused by rival Protestant and Catholic claimants to a pair of strategically-situated German duchies. Henry IV of France allied himself with the German Protestants and the British and Dutch. King James agreed to pay for 4,000 British troops in Dutch service. But the murder of Henry IV averted war. The English and the Dutch postponed their fishery negotiations for two years, thus for the first time acting on a principle which they followed on similar occasions until the middle of the century: in the face of a major political danger which threatened them both, they suspended their disagreements.

There were many Englishmen, not only veterans of the Elizabethan war but also adventurous young men, who would have welcomed a Protestant crusade. They had hopes of Henry, Prince of Wales, who set up house in 1610 at the age of sixteen. He was an admirer of Sir Walter Raleigh, interested in naval and military affairs, in horses and in tennis, outspoken and popular. Perhaps he had something in common with those who still believed that there was a common cause of protestantism in Europe. The king had not, and intended to advance his plan of general pacification by the one peaceful method of diplomacy which was open to him, that of royal marriages. So in 1611 and 1612 he had two complementary plans in mind. The Prince of

Wales might marry a Spanish princess: this idea was not altogether new, and an ambassador was sent to Madrid to propose it. James's daughter Elizabeth actually was betrothed to Frederick, the Elector Palatine, the leading German Calvinist prince. It was at this stage that the sagacious Salisbury died. Later in the same year 1612 another death seemed to cast a shadow on the future. Henry, Prince of Wales, succumbed to a fever. For the remaining years of James's reign difficulties multiplied, and his capacity to cope with them ebbed away.

Until about 1620, with Great Britain and all its neighbours at peace, the country was economically prosperous. The prosperity was, of course, neither uninterrupted nor universal. The cloth-trade underwent an unnecessary set-back, which had permanent consequences. William Cokayne, a London alderman who had grown rich in the Baltic trade, obtained a patent in 1613 under which he hoped to transfer to England some of the profitable industrial textile finishing processes for which English manufacturers depended on the Dutch. The plan failed completely. Cokayne could not organize dyeing and finishing on a sufficient scale, and the Dutch prohibited the importing of finished cloth. In 1617 Cokayne had to surrender his monopoly, but this fresh quarrel with the Dutch lasted on. Generally speaking, however, English commerce, industry, and population showed signs of healthy expansion. At home marshes were drained.

In Ireland a succession of chief governors pushed on the policy of colonization. Tyrone made his submission very soon after the death of Queen Elizabeth, and pacification continued, for the time being irresistibly. In 1607 Tyrone and Tyrconnel, the heads of the O'Neills and the O'Donnells, together giving up their own rivalries and the Irish cause, took ship for the Continent, to end their days in Rome. After the flight of the earls the British cleared their way by declaring all the land in six of the counties of Ulster forfeited for rebellion, and then colonized it more drastically and more systematically than any of their previous settlements. The union of England and Scotland meant that immigrants from Scotland and the Hebrides were no longer alien intruders; they were encouraged and, in spite of their Presbyterian religion, they seem for a time at least to have been less unwelcome than the English. The native Irish were indeed compulsorily removed from their freeholds and inadequately compensated. Estates of one, two, or three thousand acres were granted to undertakers, who were expected to build defensible houses and not to let farms except to Englishmen, Scots, or such Irishmen as had been in the service of the Crown. It was hard to find enough men of substance to carry out this plan, but the City of London was persuaded to form a company to manage large estates around their new city of Londonderry. The settlement did not fulfil the expectations of the promoters. Twenty years later there were 13,000 British men of military age, of whom only 7,000 were settled on land taken in 1607, and, as they had only 2,000 firearms among them they did not amount to a garrison or anything like it. The colonization of Ulster was, however, officially regarded as a success, indeed a matter for congratulation. In the prevailing conditions of unusual order it was imitated, less thoroughly, in Wexford, Longford, Leitrim, and King's County.

The numbers who moved to Ireland were much too small to constitute a drain on the population of Britain, and the same is probably true of the larger numbers who made their homes in North America. By the middle of the century these numbered about 100,000. The natural increase of numbers among the settlers seems to have balanced the deaths from all causes, and the number of emigrants of both sexes and all ages was also about 100,000. They had a slowly widening choice of destinations, and the motives for emigration were also becoming more various. Virginia offered to the adventurous, at the price of hardship and danger, the prospect of life in a society modelled on that of England. There were, however, Englishmen, Puritans, who abandoned England in search of a society where they could worship as they would. A group of families of Independents from Nottinghamshire, Lincolnshire, and Norfolk emigrated to tolerant Holland, only to find that in Holland they were still not in their own religious atmosphere and that their children would grow up as foreigners. With the support of English merchants, they formed a joint stock company, never incorporated, to found a New England. Just over a hundred landed at Plymouth, in the country of the Massachusetts Indians, thirty-five religious refugees from Holland, and the rest actuated not so much by religion as by the desire to better their material lot. Their hardships on the voyage and after it were terrible. It was a long time before they were more than a handful. They lived by mixed farming in an inhospitable climate. They began to trade with the Indians for furs, and to export these and maize to England. By a covenant signed on board the *Mayflower* they united in a political and religious society of the simplest direct democracy, with a governor chosen annually by the freemen.

From the economic point of view the settlements in themselves were unimportant, but they were growing and they were the fulcrum on which a great commercial movement turned. The American trade was not in the hands of a rich company like the East India Company, nor under the regulation of a company of the older type, such as the Merchant Adventurers. But it was no longer directed from west-country manor houses and quaysides: the outports complained that London was elbowing them away. There were plutocrats like Sir Thomas Smythe, who was governor of the East India Company and the Muscovy Company and treasurer of the Virginia Company, but most of the American trade was carried on by many small firms. America bulked far larger in Englishmen's imaginative geography of the world than in the accounts of imports and exports at the Custom House, no doubt because so many famous deeds had been done there against the Spaniards. There were many men of all parties who had personal links with it, and some of them, from Sir Thomas Smythe downwards, had leanings towards puritanism or to the Protestant policy of Walsingham.

After the death of Salisbury King James made changes in his methods of doing business. One was a short-lived and entirely unsuccessful attempt to take the secretary of state's duties into his own hands. Another, which he continued for the rest of his life at the cost of much unpopularity, was to govern with the assistance of a favourite. If he had chosen his favourites well there was much to be said for handing over correspondence and other troublesome detailed work; but the field of patronage, in which the favourites were especially involved, was the one in which jealousies and enmities were commonest. The first favourite was Robert Carr, who had come from Scotland as a royal page and was the first Scot to be raised to the English peerage. He does not appear to have done any definite harm; but three years after he rose to power, his wife pleaded guilty to a disgusting murder, and he disappeared from public life. His successor, George Villiers, who ultimately became duke of Buckingham, gradually built up a strong personal position, but played no part in major political decisions for several years. These were years in which the larger questions both at home and abroad were left unsettled. In 1613 the marriage of the Princess Elizabeth was celebrated with lavish display, and negotiations with the Dutch began in which there seemed to be a chance of settling the commercial disputes; but the English suspected that the Dutch offered concessions, including even a merger of the two East India Companies, with the intention of drawing them into hostilities against Spain. The negotiations trailed on for six years before they reached an inconclusive conclusion.

In 1614 James met his second parliament. He applied for money and ingenuously asked the members of the Commons each to present the grievances of his own constituency instead of combining them in general complaints against his government. They, however, debated a Bill against impositions, and almost succeeded in inducing the House of Lords to combine with them in opposition. Seeing no prospect of a money grant the king dissolved that parliament, which sat from April into June, and for the next six years he governed without one. It was, of course, hard to raise sufficient revenue. With unconcealed reluctance the country produced some £60,000 in response to an appeal for free gifts, which in its later stages was made by sheriffs and justices of the peace. Another £215,000 was obtained by accepting a lump sum in settlement of the old debt from the Dutch, coupled with the surrender of the cautionary towns, the garrisons of which cost money. This seemed discreditable and one councillor even said that he would wish the matter referred to a parliament; but the towns were useless as bridgeheads except in alliance with the Dutch, and it was more than doubtful whether they could any longer give Britain the power of holding a balance between the Dutch and the Spaniards in the Netherlands.

Sir Walter Raleigh was still a prisoner in the Tower, still under sentence of death. The public forgot his unpopularity and his offences. He was remembered only as an Elizabethan soldier and seafarer, and he came to be thought of as a champion of freedom. In 1614 he published a large folio *History of the World*, a compilation in stately prose, in which a recurring theme was the vengeance of God on wicked kings. His thoughts ran much on the riches of Eldorado, the country of the Orinoco, which he had explored. For years he had planned to obtain his liberty by leading an expedition thither, and in 1616 the Puritan secretary of state Sir Ralph Winwood, and Villiers, the rising favourite, prevailed on the king to let him go. The able Spanish ambassador, Sarmiento, protested, but Raleigh was strictly ordered not to engage in hostilities against the Spaniards, and he was plainly told that disobedience would cost him his life. He believed that if he disobeyed and brought back a booty worth millions, he would be forgiven. He attacked the Spaniards, and his expedition was a miserable failure. When he was executed under his old sentence the peace was saved; but he suffered alone, and many Englishmen believed that he had been basely sacrificed to an unworthy policy.

During the years with no parliament, antagonism in England between the monarchy and the common law grew and hardened. At the head of the common lawyers was Sir Edward Coke, a man of sharp, narrow intelligence, and combative temperament. In his writings he elaborated with unequalled learning his interpretation of the common law as a system guaranteeing rights of property and freedom, in many spheres, from arbitrary interference. As chief justice of the common pleas he resisted the view that the church should be exempted from the jurisdiction of the common-law courts; he judged that the king's right to issue proclamations had definable limits; and he set bounds to the authority of the court of high commission. Until this time the judges had been 'lions under the throne'. That phrase was coined by Francis Bacon, a man as opposite to Coke as any jurist could be. Bacon was a thinker of wide, rational genius, a pregnant and witty writer on many subjects. As Lord Chancellor he presided over the courts of equity, which in their special sphere were not bound by the rigidities of the common law. On his advice Coke was promoted to be Lord Chief Justice of the king's bench, where he would have fewer opportunities of asserting his principles. Coke did not become more pliant. He raised objections to the practice by which the king, before a case came up for trial, consulted the judges on the relevant law. He refused to recognize the king's right to order judges to postpone judgement in cases affecting the prerogative. In 1616 he was dismissed. For the first time a judge was dismissed mainly for reasons of policy, and so judicial independence became a new article in the creed of opposition to the Crown. And Coke out of office became a leader of the discontented legalists.

Discord Abroad and at Home 1618–1642

1618	King Charles I succeeds his father James I.
1620	The Pilgrim Fathers land in Massachusetts.
1627	Failure of the attack on La Rochelle.
1628	Buckingham is murdered. Parliament's Petition of Right, putting legal limits to royal prerogatives, is accepted by Charles.
1629	Charles begins to govern without parliament.
1633	William Laud becomes Archbishop of Canterbury. Thomas Wentworth (Earl of Strafford) becomes lord deputy for Ireland.
1635	John Hampden refuses to pay ship money.
1638	Scottish National Covenant is composed, to pledge Scotsmen to maintain their own Protestant worship.
1639	Charles moves north against the Scottish covenanters, but then agrees to respect Scottish religious and civil rights.
1640	Charles again moves north, but his army is defeated by covenanters. The Long Parliament begins, and commences to abolish royal prerogatives.
1641	Massacre of Protestants in Ireland. Strafford is executed. Parliament passes its Grand Remonstrance, a list of grievances.
1642	Charles fails to arrest five members of the House of Commons. Civil War begins.

It was not discontent at home, but events on the Continent which brought James's pacific policy to an end. There were signs that the general peace might soon break up. France was coming to the end of a period of Huguenot rebellions. Since the abdication of Charles V the Habsburg family had been divided into two branches, ruling respectively over Spain and Austria; both were considering the possible advantages of common action. In Holland, as the time grew nearer for the twelve years truce to expire in 1621, a sharp division appeared between those who wished to renew it, and those who wanted to let it run out, to be followed by a resumption of war with Spain. This division was entangled with another, in the region of theology. A Leyden professor called Jacob Hermans, in Latin Arminius, died in 1609 at an early stage of a controversy over his interpretation of Calvinist doctrine. He rejected predestination, which seemed to him irreconcilable with belief in a Light that lighteth every man coming into the world. This was not unwelcome to the governing oligarchy in the republic, the majority of whom were not rigid Calvinists, and James I, with his hopes of Christian reunion, was persuaded to write a letter, which was published, in favour of tolerating the new belief. But the orthodox Calvinist ministers feared that Arminianism was half-way to popery. They had always been among the closest supporters of the house of Orange, and they had the ear of Prince Maurice, the son of William the Silent, whom he had succeeded as stadholder. This eminent soldier is supposed to have said that he did not know whether pre-destination was green or blue. But he suspected that tampering with it might be a step towards prolonging the truce by offering to tolerate catholicism in the republic. James I, when better informed, withdrew his favour from the Arminians, although the states of Holland, in order to secure toleration for them, asserted a supremacy over all ecclesiastical matters, which was not altogether unlike his own in England. The states authorized towns to engage mercenary troops for the repression of religious disturbances; but this was a breach of constitutional law and a challenge to the stadholder. He acted suddenly. His troops disarmed the illegal levies. In 1619 Oldenbarnevelt, the one great statesman of the republic, and virtually its founder, was tried by a tribunal created for the purpose and executed. A national synod met at Dordrecht and condemned the Arminian belief as heretical.

This revolutionary episode had some consequences in British history which did not appear until later. Its immediate result was to weaken the internal and the international position of the Dutch republic. Not only was the truce running out: new dangers threatened from Germany, and the quarrels with the English overseas were growing worse. There was an unsettled dispute about the whale-fishery off Spitzbergen, and a new one about the cloth-trade. In Indonesia a ruthless Dutch governor-general, Jan Pieterszoon Coen, was putting into practice his

A pikeman of the 17th century. Despite firearms, the pikeman was the most important part of the infantry, although in the New Model Army an infantry regiment consisted of 420 pikemen and 780 musketeers. The pike was of wood, 3·5–5·5 m (12–18 ft) long, with a metal head; only the strongest men could wield it effectively. His helmet and plate armour were for protection against cavalry attack.

avowed belief that in the East the Dutch had no worse enemies than the English. Prince Maurice and his party needed British friendship. A Dutch mission came over, and made an agreement in 1619, not only for winding up the East Indian disputes, over which there had been negotiations for six years, but for active co-operation in the future. Some minor disputes were settled, but not the whale-fishery.

The British had to be content with this because they might soon come to need Dutch friendship, and they would not endanger that by pressing so hard for concessions as to weaken Prince Maurice in his own country. A crisis had developed in Central Europe in which Britain was indirectly, and might become directly, concerned. Bohemia had an elected king, and traditionally the head of the German Habsburgs (who was normally also the emperor) was elected. In 1618 the efforts of the Emperor Ferdinand II to enforce Catholic orthodoxy over the several national religious sects (mainly Protestant, some with roots in Wycliffe's England) led to revolution. The rebels declared the emperor deposed and the rising spread to his home country, Austria. He had no standing army. The rebels appeared before Vienna, and looked westwards, the only possible direction, for aid. They offered their crown to Frederick, Elector Palatine, and husband of King James's daughter.

Frederick asked the advice of his father-in-law King James. Like Queen Elizabeth James on principle sided with sovereigns against rebels, and Frederick was a subject of the emperor. In London there was not sufficient information about the state of Germany; but it was evident that, if Frederick accepted, the emperor would have no choice but to attack him, and that it would be hard for any armed German prince to keep out of such a war. James advised Frederick to refuse; but, before the dispatch arrived at Heidelberg, Frederick accepted. He was crowned in Prague and held court through the winter of 1618–19; but things went well for the emperor's diplomacy, and in August 1619 his army routed the Winter King. The latter had begun his adventure at a time when the Catholics of Germany were better able than they had ever been before to draw together in a united offensive. They were not content with expelling Frederick from Bohemia, and they were not alone. The archduke Albert, the Austrian-born governor of the Spanish Netherlands, believed that the war which would follow the twelve years truce would be the decisive struggle between catholicism and protestantism. In 1619 he persuaded the king of Spain to intervene, and in September 1620 16,000 foot and 3,000 horse crossed the Rhine at Mainz, to conquer the Palatinate.

The British king was indignant at the treatment of his daughter, but still pinned his hopes on some accommodation with Spain. He gave way to pressure so far as to permit the enlistment of volunteers for the defence of the Palatinate. Neither men nor money were forthcoming in anything like the expected quantities, but many of the younger nobility and gentry responded, and 2,200 men sailed for Holland under the best living English commander, Sir Horace Vere. The contrast between the excitement in political circles and this modest practical expression may be due to the general economic depression, which hung over the country from 1621 to 1624, though unemployment might have made recruiting easier. The continental upheavals were obstructing the markets for exports, and the government was blamed for real and imaginary extravagance, corruption, and inept interference.

Elections held in 1620 returned a House of Commons which, when it met in January 1621, was bent on trouble. Sir Edward Coke, though still a privy councillor, was the most prominent member. The Commons took the initiative. They raised the question of monopolies more obstinately than before. In spite of all that Queen Elizabeth had promised, and of all that had been said in James's parliaments, the abuses were as bad as ever. Now parliament brought out the old weapon of impeachment, against Sir Giles Mompesson who had a monopoly of gold and silver thread. They passed the Statute of Monopolies, which laid down the principles on which patents of monopoly have been granted until the present day. They are limited to cases in which they further the public interest, the best-known instances being those of new inventions. The same parliament passed half a dozen other statutes, but none approaching this in importance. Its time was occupied otherwise. It impeached another offender, no less a person than the Lord Chancellor, Francis Bacon, Viscount Verulam. Bacon had to admit the squalid delinquency of accepting bribes in his judicial capacity. This did not sound so bad in those days as it would now, but it put an end to Bacon's career, and it did no good to the king's dignity. In a committee to consider the state of religion a Somerset squire named John Pym recommended, no doubt following the Elizabethan precedent of 1584, that an oath of association should be taken by all loyal

A 17th century musketeer. Muskets were primitive and unreliable, accurate only up to about 50 metres, and not capable of firing more than two rounds per minute. A 'flash in the pan', when the detonating powder burned without setting off the main charge, was a frequent mishap. The musketeer carried in his right hand the wooden support needed when firing his long weapon.

subjects for the defence of the king's person and for the execution of the laws concerning religion.

It was for foreign affairs that the king had summoned the parliament, and they were enthusiastically in favour of supporting him in a Protestant line. We know now that they were mistaken in believing that protestantism could not survive without British support. That is what did in fact come about, but their grounds for believing the contrary were not contemptible. James did not agree, but he shrank from explaining his tortuous reasons. He imagined that the Spaniards, in order to keep him friendly, would restore his son-in-law to the Palatinate, and he wanted to keep clear of other quarrels. He announced that he intended to equip an army, but he did not say of what size, and instead of saying how he intended to use it, he warned the Commons not to meddle with state affairs. They made a grant for the immediate support of the troops in the Palatinate; but they addressed the king for a war against Spain, to save the Protestants and also to enrich Britain. The king lectured them for going outside their province, even reminding them of his right to imprison members. They composed a downright assertion of all their privileges, undisputed and disputed, as the birthright and inheritance of the people, and a claim to dicuss virtually anything they chose. The king dissolved parliament, dismissed Coke from the council and kept him shut up in the Tower for nine months.

The Dutch truce ran out, and almost on the same day Frederick and Elizabeth arrived as refugees at The Hague. Soon after this James began hoping to realize his aims in spite of everything by some scheme in which the marquess of Buckingham should play a part. This was now the title of the favourite Villiers. Starting as the younger son of a country squire, he had steadily advanced himself and his relations in rank, fortune, and influence. He had the airs of a grandee, and something like an ascendancy over the king. In 1618 commissions were appointed to inquire into the state of the Treasury and the Admiralty. The Admiralty was shown to be monstrously neglectful and corrupt. Buckingham leapt at the chance of distinguishing himself and was appointed lord high admiral. He had no experience of the navy, and no suitable experience of administration; he exerted himself, but without any noteworthy results.

The Dutch were uneasy when they heard reports that British ships were to co-operate with the Spaniards against the Algerine pirates in the Mediterranean. The king considered the idea of sending a strong naval squadron, with the lord high admiral carrying full powers as an ambassador, and with Charles the Prince of Wales on board in the capacity of expectant bridegroom for the sister of the king of Spain. James never understood how repugnant the proposal for marriage to a heretic was to the lady and to her countrymen, nor how serious were its implications for his own position in Britain. He saw, however, that in this form it was impossible both in its naval and in its diplomatic aspects. He therefore agreed to an utterly irresponsible escapade. Buckingham and the prince crossed France incognito and presented themselves in Madrid. The disconcerted Spaniards at first guessed that the prince must have made up his mind to simplify matters by becoming a Catholic; but they soon discovered that neither he nor the unmannerly Buckingham had anything more solid to offer than promises that the penal laws should be suspended. Charles asked whether the king of Spain would in the last resort use force to compel the emperor to restore the Palatinate to Frederick, and was told plainly 'No: we have a maxim that the king of Spain must never fight against the emperor.'

The two travellers came home not in the disgrace they deserved, but in triumph. Convinced that the marriage-negotiations had been a Spanish deception, they wanted immediate war with Spain. The committee of council rejected Buckingham's proposal; but the writs were out for a new parliament, and when it met it promptly voted £300,000 for war. The parliament, however, showed some sense of realities. It voted the money for preparations; it was to be expended by the direction of commissioners appointed in parliament, and for four purposes, home defence, Ireland, assistance to the Dutch, and equipment of the navy. The proposal to send an army for the recovery of the Palatinate was deferred, as it turned out for good. Parliament settled down to normal business and passed a considerable number of useful economic and other Acts. Buckingham, although miscast in the role of a popular leader, took the opportunity of instigating the impeachment of Lionel Cranfield, earl of Middlesex, who had risen from the City to be Lord Treasurer, and, while undoubtedly reforming the national finances, had enriched himself at the public expense.

The diplomatic preparations for the war with Spain met with some success. The power which had the strongest reasons for co-operating was the Dutch republic; but the colonial rivalry with the Dutch became more acute than ever. On the day when Charles and Buckingham departed for Spain, the Dutch at Amboyna in the Moluccas arrested the English principal agent there, Gabriel Towerson, with nine other Englishmen, one Portuguese, and nine Japanese soldiers. They were charged with plotting to seize the fort. The news of their torture, their, perhaps irregular, trial, and their execution reached London in June 1624. The massacre of Amboyna was an impediment to good relations with the Dutch for a generation and more. The statesmen, however, once again subordinated the merchants' grievances to the needs of the states. By a treaty with the Dutch, Britain undertook to pay 6,000 troops in their service.

Most important of the prospective allies was France, but the French price was correspondingly high. In December 1624 a treaty was signed by which the Prince of Wales was to marry the princess Henrietta Maria, who was just fifteen years old. It was stipulated on her behalf, as it had been for the Spanish infanta, that her household should be of her own religion and (secretly) that the penal laws should be suspended. As France had no navy, the French statesman Richelieu stipulated that James should

Francis Bacon, philosopher, politician, essayist, and Lord Chancellor. The 'Baconian Method' emphasized that theory needed to be preceded by the accumulation of observed facts. Though not infallible, this approach was the basis of the subsequent 'scientific method' with its emphasis on experimentation. As a statesman Bacon was less successful, and retired after being accused of corruption.

lend her a ship of the royal navy and seven merchant vessels. At the same time he hired ships from the Dutch for use against La Rochelle, which was held by the rebellious Huguenot leader the duc de Soubise. Men on board these ships were indignant when they found that they too were destined for La Rochelle. They refused that service, and Buckingham damaged his relations with France by giving them underhand support.

Neither the French nor the Dutch were concerned with an expedition which sailed from Dover on 31 January 1625 under the landless German professional soldier Count Ernst von Mansfeld. He collected 12,000 or so untrained British soldiers, and the obvious destination for them was the Dutch frontier-town of Breda, which was under siege. King James, contrary to the advice of the French, to say nothing of the Dutch, had intended them to make straight for the Palatinate. They landed on Dutch soil and James did not live to see their wretched dissolution there under stress of disease and hunger. He died in the month of March.

The old king's death made no difference to the conduct of affairs. During the last three or four years he had allowed Buckingham to override his will and ideas: his son's submission to the favourite was so complete that he had no will or ideas to call his own. In character Charles was utterly unlike his father, quiet, reserved, and refined; but his inherited beliefs about the divine right of kings and the unlimited duty of obedience were immovable. His first parliament met in a distrustful mood. The king's answers to a list of particular grievances, almost all economic, were reasonable and even conciliatory; but many members suspected that in the French marriage negotiations Charles had made some promise on behalf of the English Catholics. The government explained its military plans so badly that the Commons granted only two subsidies, and granted the customs duties only for one year, not for Charles's life. The royal marriage was celebrated in June, but the Commons wrangled on. Inconclusively but ominously they examined the theological ideas of Dr. Richard Montague, a self-appointed defender of the Church of England. Charles appointed Montague as one of his chaplains. Parliament was dissolved in August.

All this was a most inauspicious accompaniment to the military and naval preparations against Spain. These were lamentably slipshod. Buckingham, as lord high admiral, gave the command to his client Sir Edward Cecil, then raised to the peerage, who was ignorant of naval affairs and, in his meritorious service on land, had never held an independent command. He sailed from Plymouth in October with a fleet of requisitioned merchant ships, manned by discontented and untrained men, with too few officers of worth. He arrived off Cadiz, and it appears that if he had shown elementary decision and common sense even his force could have captured the almost undefended town, destroyed the Spanish warships stationed there and taken the treasure fleet which was approaching from America. In fact the fleet and the landing parties blundered in indescribable confusion. Nothing was accomplished and the fleet came home in November, the crews and soldiers rotting with disease.

Buckingham did what he could to improve the diplomatic position. France would give no further help. British ships were making prizes of French merchantmen trading with the Spaniards, and, contrary to King Charles's promise, the penal laws against Catholics were being enforced. Buckingham made a treaty of alliance with the Dutch and the Danes, promising heavy

Three views of King Charles I, engraved from a painting by Van Dyck. Like his father James I, Charles had many qualities but failed to use them to good effect in ruling his country. He was courageous, and with a certain competence in military affairs; he was a good family man; he was knowledgeable in the arts; he was pious. But Charles's inflexibility and his reluctance to listen to good advice proved ruinous.

subventions to the latter; but by this time the king was hard pressed for money. Forced loans were collected in England with very poor results. Buckingham failed to borrow in Holland on the security of the Crown jewels. The only remedy was to summon a new parliament, which sat for five weeks and achieved nothing except to inflame all the old and new discontents. They impeached Dr. Montague for his religious opinions. They impeached Buckingham himself in a long document covering all his misdeeds and, for good measure, some that were excusable. The king saved Buckingham by dissolving the parliament. That he was saved, and that none of his protégés such as Sir Edward Cecil were brought to book, proves both how high his ascendancy was, and how well the system of government hung together except when resolute members of parliament attacked it.

In 1627 Great Britain found herself absurdly at war with both France and Spain at the same time. The growing friction with France, and the popular feeling in Britain for the Huguenots gave Buckingham the idea of a great expedition to relieve La Rochelle. In the summer he set sail with about a hundred ships and 6,000 soldiers. With poor tactical judgement he made the unexpectedly difficult attempt to possess himself of the island of Rhé, outside the port. He had to call for reinforcements, and his troops suffered from disease. In October he had nearly 7,000 soldiers. After his total failure he brought back fewer than 3,000 to Portsmouth and Plymouth, leaving La Rochelle under strict French blockade.

After this second disaster attempts to raise money by unparliamentary means failed even more completely than after the first. Resistance to them became tougher. Five men of substance, all of them knights, were imprisoned for refusing to pay a forced loan. When they obtained a writ of *habeas corpus* the judges ruled that a prisoner incarcerated by the king's special mandate could not call on those who had imprisoned him to show any further cause. The king had won a point, but he had created a new grievance, and in his extremity he needed a parliament.

This third parliament of the reign reiterated all the old

complaints, and took notice of some new provocations, but it did much more. It did not shake Buckingham's position, and it had to leave most of the grievances unreformed; but it came to terms with the king and made him a handsome grant of money, five subsidies. He made a satisfying return. After tangled arguments in parliament he accepted the Petition of Right, which, purporting to declare what the law already was, tied the Crown down to a specific legal interpretation of its prerogatives on four points. Forced loans and benevolences without consent of parliament were illegal; so was imprisonment without cause shown; soldiers and sailors were not to be billeted in private houses, and martial law was to be abolished except, apparently, in armies in time of war. The last two points had arisen during the wars against Spain and France. These had still to be fought. While the parliament was sitting, a futile attempt was made to relieve La Rochelle. After it was prorogued Buckingham himself went down to Portsmouth, where fresh preparations were on foot. He made the suggestion to the Rochellese deputies who were there, that they should open negotiations with the king of France. That was his last political act. A man with a grievance, a discharged officer, stabbed him fatally.

The 'Triple Episcopacy', a Puritan cartoon satirizing Archbishop Laud and the court bishops. Cartoons, broadsheets, and pamphlets were by this time the usual ammunition in theological and political disputes. Ever since Henry VIII's reformation, disputants and ideologists realised that ideas could not be imposed by force; it was necessary to capture men's minds, and the printed word was already a means of doing this.

Parliament reassembled for another session, but the removal of Buckingham served to concentrate the protests of the opposition leaders on religion. The fear of popery had been reinforced by the co-operation of many Catholic states in the German wars, by the defeats of the Huguenots, by the French marriage of King Charles, and by the suspicion that he intended to tolerate popery or even to seek some compromise with it. The king and the ecclesiastics whom he favoured were absolutely loyal to the Anglican settlement, but the Puritans had a new ground for doubting them. By the irony of fate the Synod of Dordrecht, while it temporarily muzzled the Arminians in Holland, helped to spread their doctrine in England. One of the English representatives at the Synod was more than half convinced by their advocacy. Within a few years one English theologian after another was accused of Arminianism, that is of beliefs about grace and predestination which Puritans in general, as far as they understood them, detested. The religious disputes were sharpened in two ways: the Puritans had a new doctrinal bugbear, and the House of Commons began to assume the right to dictate beliefs. While Buckingham was still alive the king issued a declaration, which is still printed in the Prayer Book, forbidding controversy over the Articles of Belief, on pain of punishment by the high commission and other courts. After the assassination, the fiery orator Sir John Eliot proposed three resolutions, against those who should bring in innovations in religion, those who should advise the levying of tonnage and poundage without parliamentary grant, and those who should pay the same. The resolution on religion expressly mentioned popery or Arminianism, and like the other two it ended with a threat; anyone who contravened it was to be 'reputed a capital enemy to this kingdom and commonwealth'. The Speaker tried to leave his chair, but Eliot and two others held him while the protestation was read.

However it was described, this action was against law. Parliament was dissolved. The three members, with five others, were arrested. Eliot refused to answer before any tribunal except parliament, and so he was held in the Tower, where he died three years later, the first martyr for parliamentary claims. For the time being there was no prospect of successful co-operation with a parliament, and so the king tried to govern without a parliament, as his father and Queen Elizabeth had done with some measure of success. As it happened his two most prominent councillors were active administrators and strong disciplinarians who respected one another and worked closely together, the one in the church and the other in the state. William Laud, who was promoted from the see of London to that of Canterbury in 1633 and had done very well in the academic life of Oxford, was content to accept the royal supremacy, and hoped to exclude disruptive Puritan beliefs from the sphere of controversy, while restoring the traditional uniformity and seemliness of worship. He took part in secular business. He supported the not very effectual attempts of the council to enforce the law against uncontrolled enclosures, and the commission for depopulation, which stood up for the poor against the encroachment of landlords. So far as the council could invigorate it, the administration of the poor law became more active, and the other leader, Thomas Wentworth, ultimately earl of Strafford, throughout his career showed a similar and fearless regard for social justice. He was a rich Yorkshire landowner, who had sat in almost all the parliaments since 1614. In the session of the Petition of Right he occupied a very strong position at the head of those who might be called constitutional reformers. He was loyal to the Crown, but in favour of limiting the royal prerogative so far as that could be done by strictly legal means. Without in any way changing or sacrificing his principles, he entered the king's service as president of the Council of the North and was raised to the peerage, becoming a privy councillor in 1629.

The policy of Strafford and Laud had a defect of which they were both unconscious. Not only did they lack the communication between court and country which a parliament would have offered, if on barely tolerable terms. They also lacked the alternative on which authoritarian government might have flourished. Except for tax-collectors, defence departments, and a few unpopular inspectors of industries, the Crown had few paid, professional, civil servants. Across the Channel Richelieu was providing himself with means of surveying and organizing: without parliamentary grants no such thing was possible in

Britain. That the 'tyranny' lasted for eleven years was due to several different kinds of luck. First of all the Crown lawyers showed as much ingenuity as Coke and his followers in hunting for precedents. Gentlemen who had the necessary qualifications for knighthood, but did not undertake its few remaining obligations, had to pay money instead. The forest law was enforced in districts where it had lapsed into oblivion.

The one new exaction which was earmarked for a patriotic purpose was the most unpopular of all. A lawyer, John Selden, whose vast learning had been serviceable to the opposition, wrote a book for the government which claimed that King Charles was sovereign over the narrow seas surrounding Britain. The modern idea of territorial waters had not been worked out, and Selden's book gave a theoretical basis for various claims against the Dutch, such as the claim to levy toll on their fisheries and more substantial rights over commerce in time of war. To enforce the argument, Charles fitted out a fleet in 1634, which unintentionally enabled raiders from Spanish Dunkirk to damage the Dutch herring fleet. In the next year a fleet put out which was said to be the strongest that ever sailed from English harbours, but the results were poor. These fleets were paid for, at least partly, by an ancient but forgotten tax called Ship Money. At first it was levied on seaport towns in accordance with the principle that naval forces existed for the protection of maritime interests. When the tax was extended to the inland counties John Hampden, a very rich landlord in the Chilterns, refused to pay the trifling sum for which he was assessed. The judges decided against him, and rightly, but he was looked upon as a public benefactor.

Since there was no legislation, the government's most prominent acts of policy were done in the privy council and in the law-courts, especially the prerogative courts. Two of these, the courts of star chamber and high commission, though they could not inflict the death penalty, passed sentences which made them many enemies. The most notorious had to do with puritanism, or matters allied to it. Alexander Leighton was degraded from his Holy Orders and had his nose slit, his ears cropped, and his forehead branded. One of the great antiquarian lawyers, William Prynne, lost his ears and stood in the pillory. So did the physician John Bastwicke, who for two literary offences against the bishops was fined £6,000 and condemned to imprisonment for life.

The government was not afraid of the discontent which was stirring through the country, and it carried its energy into a new field when Wentworth became lord deputy in Ireland in 1633. There a strong hand was badly needed. There was an ill-paid, ill-equipped, and ill-disciplined army of 400 horse and 2,000 foot. The church was dilapidated in every respect. The finances were unhealthy. Wentworth summoned a parliament and a convocation, and through these and the law-courts he forced his programme. Offenders and opponents were beaten down without respect of persons. The City of London was fined £70,000 for failing to carry out the provisions of its charter for Coleraine, and the charter was forfeited. The Scottish Presbyterian ministers in Ulster had to subscribe to the Thirty-nine Articles or give up their livings. The earl of Cork, whom it was not wise to antagonize, was relieved of enormous sums by executive action without trial. At the same time Wentworth tried by every possible means to improve economic conditions. His ultimate aim was to extend colonies over the whole island, founded not only on English law but also on English religion, and he decided to plant (that is, colonize) Connaught immediately. In order to eliminate titles to ownership which might stand in the way, he stretched the law beyond its limits. The plantation was not in fact even begun. In smaller matters, such as encouraging the linen industry, Wentworth took some effective steps. At the end of his last stay in Ireland he wrote, with the optimism of the man of action, that the Irish were 'as fully satisfied and as well affected to his Majesty's person and service, as can possibly be wished for'.

The movement of population to America went on throughout these years, and the colonies there made healthy progress. There were new and permanent settlements in the West Indian Islands; Barbados in 1625, which was soon associated with Trinidad and Tobago; Nevis, Montserrat, and Antigua in 1628–36. The Spaniards were themselves peopling and fortifying the larger islands, and they were on the watch against the creation of any British base which might threaten their route for the transport of Mexican and Peruvian silver. A group of wealthy Puritans, including John Pym, the parliamentarian, and several peers, formed a company with aims like those of the Pilgrim Fathers. They planted colonies in two islands, one named Providence and the other, even more characteristically, Association. The company deliberately intended that these colonies should serve a strategic purpose, which the Spaniards suspected. The Associ-

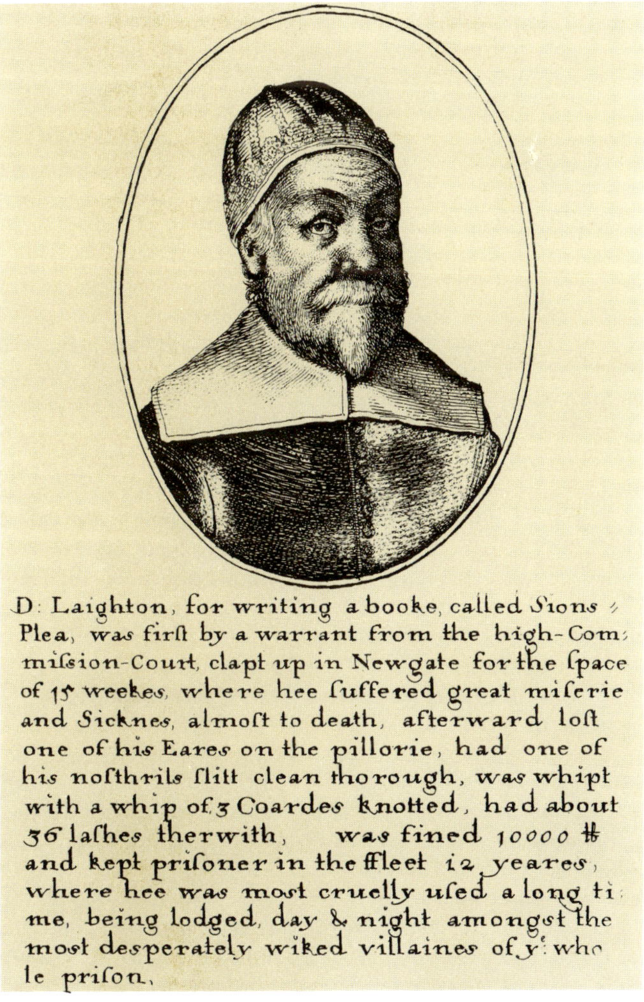

Alexander Leighton, a Scottish Presbyterian persecuted by Archbishop Laud in London, mutilated and imprisoned. In the reign of Charles II, Alexander's son Robert Leighton, a man of similar beliefs, accepted the Anglican archbishopric of Dunblane in the vain hope that this compromise with his conscience would be an example to be followed, thereby reconciling the Presbyterians and Episcopalians.

ation colony was short-lived, and the Spaniards broke up that on Providence Island in 1641.

On the mainland, however, the Spaniards allowed one new colony after another to go unmolested. The first was Maryland, in its name and nature characteristic of the elements in England which were least sympathetic to the Puritans, and least hostile to Spain. George Calvert, first Lord Baltimore, resigned the office of secretary of state, in which he had done good service, and declared himself a Catholic. He was not allowed to establish himself in Virginia unless he would take the oaths of allegiance and supremacy. Although he died before the charter was sealed; and although it was not until 1649 that his own religion, Jesuits and all, enjoyed more than connivance, he was the true founder of the first British colony with religious toleration. It prospered as a rural community modelled on the English social structure, gradually changing, like the other tobacco colonies, to the economy of plantation slavery.

The northerly colonies received the main stream of immigration, New England alone attracting about 20,000 between 1630 and 1643. As their towns and their commerce grew they developed new organs and conventions of self-government. The council in England had little or no power to control their day-to-day affairs; but it gave them charters which contained the outlines of written constitutions, adapted to their differing needs, to which charters they did not always conform. Their seaborne trade was also subject to regulation by orders in council which were meant to keep the profits as far as possible from falling into the hands of the Dutch or other foreigners. In return the importing of foreign-grown tobacco into England was restricted and the beginnings of tobacco-growing in England were firmly stamped out.

The leaders of the Church of England were regretfully aware that Englishmen overseas very often fell short of the prescribed standards of belief and behaviour. In 1633 Archbishop Laud proposed a general regulation of divine service in commercial and military establishments abroad, and the privy council gave orders accordingly. In 1634 for the first time a standing committee of the privy council was set up with wide powers over the plantations. It had, for instance, the right to provide for the endowment of churches overseas by tithe and other means. But it did not make much impression on the colonists.

Laud was not one of the few Englishmen who understood Scotland. As an English bishop and archbishop he was no more concerned with Scotland than he was with Sicily. He was, of course, aware that King James, after coming to England, continued his efforts to modify church order in Scotland. James made some progress in restoring the jurisdiction of the bishops and brought their appointment and promotion under the control of the Crown. In 1618 he induced the assembly to accept the five Articles of Perth, all of which, and especially one which prescribed kneeling at Communion, were obnoxious to the Calvinist majority. The ensuing outcry halted James in his tracks; but King Charles began his reign with an Act of parliament for the resumption of all Crown and church lands which had been transferred since 1542. As most of the Scottish nobility had enriched themselves from these sources, and also from tithe, this Act put an end to the alliance with the nobility on which the strengthening of the Crown had depended. It was not fully enforced, and the resulting compromise provided a better maintenance for parish ministers and fairer treatment for tithe-payers than they enjoyed in England.

In 1633 King Charles went to Scotland to be crowned, and five bishops took part in the ceremony, in blue copes braided with gold. Laud, who was one of them, had accompanied the king, and was shocked by the generally unecclesiastical appearance of the churches. He did not trespass on the preserves of the Scottish bishops, but he was informed of the steps which followed, and most likely he had some responsibility for them. In 1637 a Prayer Book for Scotland was ready, almost identical with the English book. When it was used at a service in St. Giles's church in Edinburgh, there was a riot. Almost the entire nation boiled over in excitement. The nobles appointed committees which in effect became a revolutionary government. In 1638 the Scottish National Covenant was drawn up, a long, historically argued, document which began by stating and justifying the confession of faith agreed upon in 1580. With strong expressions of loyalty to the king, the signatories pledged their means and lives to maintaining this true religion and worship. It was an association such as the English Puritans had talked of. The 'noblemen, barons, gentlemen, burgesses, ministers, and commons' who subscribed to it soon included an overwhelming majority of the literate population. The king withdrew the Prayer Book; but the covenanters began to arm. One of the subscribers, Alexander Leslie, had served for thirty years in Swedish armies on the Continent, latterly in the highest ranks. He obtained his release from the Swedish service, and in settlement of his claims for arrears of pay, he received two field guns and 2,000 muskets.

King Charles took the orthodox measures against a Scottish disturbance. He sent a naval detachment to the Firth of Forth, and went north to command in person. On 28 May 1639, encamped at Berwick in view of the Scottish army, he realized that he had led a badly armed, untrained, inadequately paid, and, in sum, useless force against the modern army which Leslie had created. On 18 June, without a shot fired, it was agreed that both armies should be disbanded. Charles gave his assurance that the Scottish general assembly and parliament should meet and determine, respectively, all ecclesiastical and civil matters.

When these two bodies met they each did something to limit Charles's authority. The parliament deprived him of his control over the composition of the lords of the articles, a committee to which almost all its authority was delegated. The assembly set to work to undo the innovations of Charles and his father. When it summoned the bishops to answer accusations before it and they denied its jurisdiction, Charles's whole conception of authority in church and state was at issue. He dissolved the assembly, but it stayed in session, abolishing the Prayer Book, the Articles of Perth, and episcopacy itself.

Charles decided that he must make war on Scotland in good earnest. In the committee of the privy council which advised him on these affairs, the clearest voice was that of Strafford, who did not underrate the factors of money and force that were involved, and spoke up for summoning a parliament. It would take time before any parliamentary revenue could be collected, so the councillors themselves lent the king the respectable sum of £230,000 for immediate use. On 3 April 1640 the parliament met and immediately proved the weight of the factors which Strafford did underrate. Only about a quarter of the Commons had sat in the parliament of 1628–9, but John Pym, by a review of the grievances of the eleven unparliamentary years, persuaded them

The execution of Strafford; a contemporary engraving. Charles's signature of the Bill of Attainder which permitted Strafford's execution was, in the eyes of his admirer, his one serious mistake. Thomas Wentworth, Earl of Strafford, was a Yorkshireman of demonstrated efficiency who had been his most intelligent adviser.

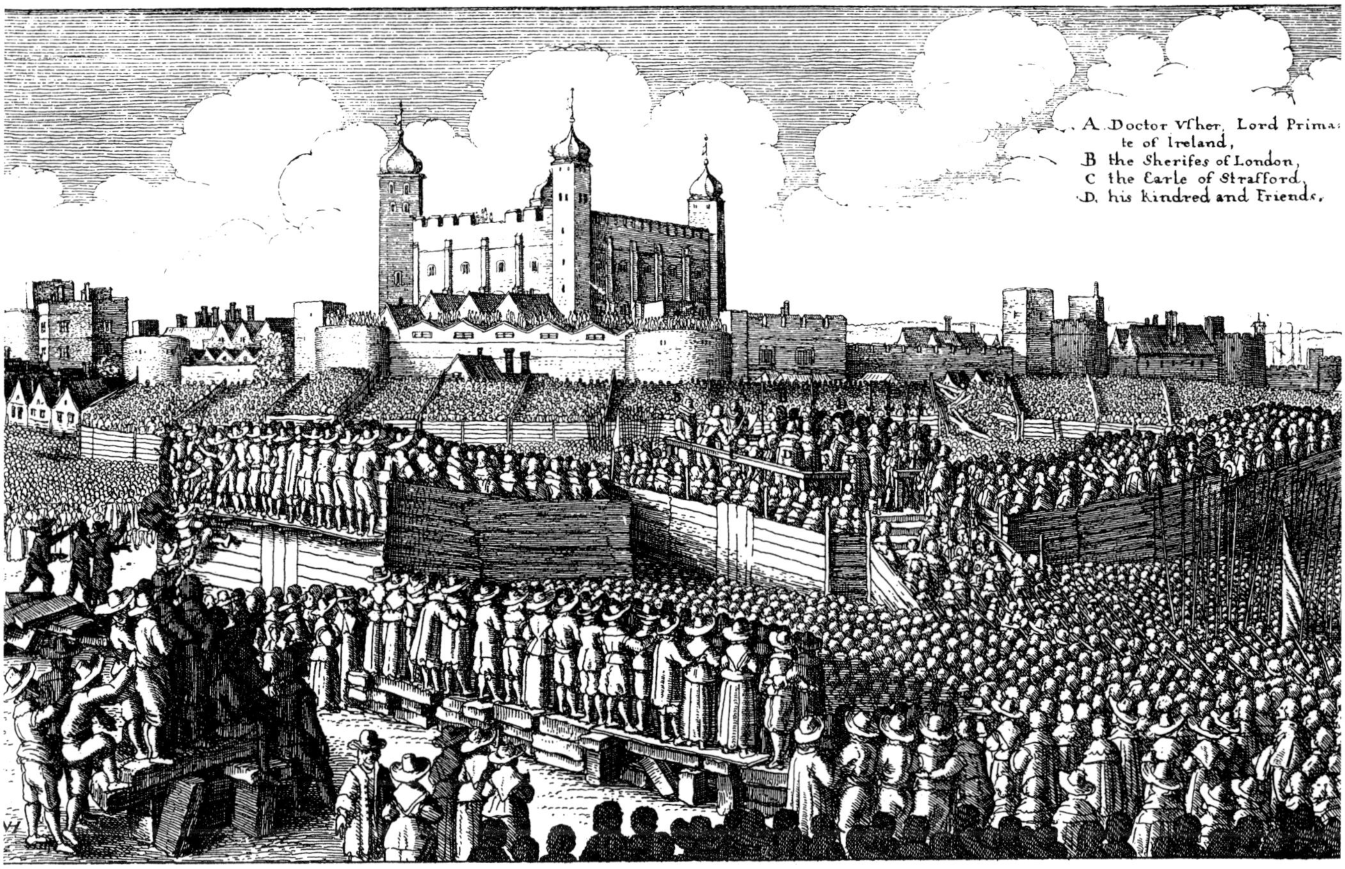

to refuse all supply until their own liberties and those of the kingdom were cleared. All that the government accomplished was to put forward very disputable evidence that the Scottish leaders had asked for assistance from the king of France. The king dissolved the parliament on 5 May. The convocation of the clergy, which customarily met and dispersed at the same time as parliament, was kept in being and passed a body of canons, the validity of which was at once disputed. These contained uncompromising assertions of the divine rights of kings and bishops; they gave orders, which were certain to be resisted, about the altar and bowing on entering and leaving a church; and they prescribed for the higher clergy and all schoolmasters and doctors of divinity, law, and medicine a very badly drafted oath undertaking to resist all innovations in the doctrine or government of the Church.

In August 1640 King Charles again went north, no more fit to meet his opponents than he had been in the previous year. The city of London refused to lend money, and so did the kings of France and Spain and the pope. The army was badly supplied, mutinous, and unreliable. Leslie crossed the Tweed unopposed. At Newburn on the Tyne the English army came under his artillery fire and ran. He took Newcastle, where he kept his headquarters for a whole year. His troops took possession of all the country as far as the Tees, and if they had chosen to move on to the Humber there was nothing to stop them.

Charles was reluctant to take the now inevitable course of summoning a parliament, but it was not long delayed by the device of a great council of the peers, who met at York and opened negotiations with the Scots at Ripon. In November a new parliament did meet, famous as the Long Parliament. By this time it was undeniably necessary to raise money, and, as tax-collecting was slow, money had to be raised by borrowing on the security of the revenue. But no one could be found to lend it unless the parliament was there to give the guarantees that the moneyed men required. It seems to have been genuinely for this reason that the Commons sent up a Bill, to which the king assented, that this parliament was not to be dissolved, or even prorogued or adjourned, without its own consent. No one foresaw that in consequence the parliament's legal existence would last through every revolution and counter-revolution for twenty years. In its first year the king assented to a series of Acts which declared one after another of his previous practices to be illegal. The Triennial Act laid it down that parliament should be summoned at least once in every three years, with or without the issuing of regular writs of summons and also that no parliament should last for more than three years. The court of star chamber, the high commission court, and other prerogative courts were abolished, dubious historical grounds being alleged against their legality. The forests were limited; fees imposed on knighthood were terminated; ship money was declared illegal. While it was occupied with this legislation, which ended most of the old controversies about prerogative for good, the House of Commons on its side reaffirmed the principle that its consent was necessary for the valid collection of tonnage and poundage, but made, for one year only, a sufficient grant.

These measures were not unanimously agreed on, but they did not cause any division of the parliamentary majority into parties. From the beginning the parliament also had other business on which emotions ran higher. First, outside the sphere of law-making, were the personal and political questions. Nine days after the opening of the parliament Strafford was impeached of high treason. It was believed that he intended to impeach Pym and the other parliamentary leaders of treasonable dealings with the Scots. Quite possibly they had overstepped the line; rather more probably Strafford was innocent of the intention that his accusers read into some words spoken by him in the committee of council on Scottish affairs. He had proposed that an army from Ireland should be used to subdue 'this kingdom', and he may have meant not England but Scotland. In neither case would any fine point of interpretation have affected the result. The charge was brought in order to destroy him. When the Commons saw that they could not be sure of his condemnation by the Lords, they dropped impeachment and followed the procedure of a Bill of Attainder, a naked use of power. This needed the royal assent, and Charles had promised Strafford protection; but he shrank before street demonstrations against his minister and assented. Charles's apologists in later times excepted this one decision alone from their thesis that the king had always been in the right; but Strafford's execution, although it left a shadow on Charles's reputation, and deprived him of his strongest servant, did also relieve him from the burden of Strafford's unpopularity.

Laud too was impeached, and on charges which only hatred could construe as treason. His trial was deferred for three years, and his execution for two years after that, but all this time he was a prisoner. Meanwhile the parliament debated religion, and as soon as they passed on from personal questions to issues of principle it began to appear that the Puritans and those who sympathized with them were only a section among the opponents of Laud. The Anglican lawyers, of whom the ablest was Edward Hyde, stopped far short of the Puritan position. Some of them defended the canons of 1641. Some tolerant and pacific laymen such as Hyde's friend Lord Falkland were willing to deprive the bishops of their political and secular functions. Even among the Puritans there were three tendencies. The central group led by Pym wanted a state church controlled by parliamentary lay commissioners; there were Presbyterians who wanted a church with assemblies on the Scottish plan and rigid Calvinistic orthodoxy; and there were Independents who combined the sectarian scheme with a leaning towards the toleration of all Protestant beliefs. In February 1641 the divisions came out sharply in a debate on the Root and Branch Petition for the abolition of episcopacy.

From August to November 1641 the king was in Scotland. The negotiations begun at Ripon had ended with an agreement that the Scots should be paid their late military expenses, and this promise had been fulfilled by a parliamentary grant of £300,000. The religious and constitutional questions were to be settled by the Scottish parliament and assembly, and, though this amounted to a surrender of Charles's claims, it was not unsuitable that he should do his part in person. Outwardly indeed his visit seemed to express reconciliation. The king drove through the plaudits of Edinburgh with Leslie, whom he created earl of Leven, beside him; but Leslie knew that Charles had a plan for seizing some of his opponents, and Charles tested the possibility of gaining Scottish support for his English plans. In England the parliamentary leaders were suspicious, and, while the king was away, black news came from Ireland which forced new decisions on all the leaders.

Under Strafford Ireland had been quiet. He never ceased to make new enemies there. He treated Ulster Presbyterians who signed the Scottish covenant as rebels, and some of them went over to join their brethren in Scotland; but a submissive parliament in Dublin granted money to raise the army to 9,000 men. It was this force, believed to be efficient, which Strafford had offered for service in Britain. The Irish parliament refused to support the plan and the army was disbanded. The Catholic majority in the Irish house of commons passed resolutions condemning many of Strafford's acts as illegal, and declared that the Irish were a free people to be governed only under the common law of England and the statute laws and lawful customs of Ireland. King Charles was suspected, probably unjustly, of bargaining to restore catholicism in Ireland in exchange for Irish Catholic support. But the resistance of Scotland proved that the English could be successfully defied. With speed and secrecy scarcely paralleled anywhere in the seventeenth century Irish patriots knotted together the strands of a national conspiracy. It broke out first in Ulster on 23 October, three months after Strafford's death, and it took the form of a massacre of Protestants. The reports which reached England were exaggerated; but at that moment of extreme tension even cool, impartial reports would have enraged many more of the English besides the opponents of the king.

The news from Ireland led Pym and his followers to harden their demands. No longer attempting to convince waverers, and before the king was back in London, they carried by a majority of only eleven the Grand Remonstrance, a portentous enumeration of all their grievances, personal, political, constitutional, religious, economic, and what not. It was accompanied by a petition, proposing, among other things, a general synod of divines 'of this island, assisted with some from foreign parts, professing the same religion with us'. The results of its consultations were to be confirmed by parliament.

All the hopes and fears which centred round this document were inseparably tied together with considerations on another plane. Ever since the last parliament of James I the Commons had tended to encroach on the functions of the executive and judiciary, not merely in great matters, such as the efforts to control the king's choice of ministers, but in smaller matters, such as the claim of the House of Commons to administer an oath to witnesses. During the troubles of King Charles's time the House of Lords was strangely inert, and the Commons sometimes acted alone. The Grand Remonstrance, which included pungent paragraphs about the bishops and the Catholic peers, was a case in point. Curiously enough the Lords, by ordering on 16 January 1641 that divine service was to be performed according to the law, set an example of action by one house alone. When the king was in Scotland the distrustful Commons quite properly appointed a committee to make any necessary representations to him there. They unanimously passed ordinances to deal with sensitive matters such as recruiting, and the provision of stores for the Tower and for the protection of Hull by the Yorkshire militia. In Hull the arms and ammunition for the Scottish wars were stored. The Irish rebellion came, and it would obviously be met by force. The Commons told the king plainly that unless he changed his advisers they would not provide him with that force, but that they would raise it themselves and commit it to the custody 'of such persons of honour and fidelity as we have cause to confide in'.

The king gave a reasoned answer to the Grand Remonstrance, but it was not of his own composition. From this time forward his most important pronouncements were drafted by Hyde, who continued to maintain his old point of view in parliament. He rightly considered that this was a better way for him to uphold legality than accepting office, which the king was willing to give him. Falkland and other like-thinking men made the other choice and accepted office; but on the king's side as on that of parliament there were others who thought that the time for conciliation had run out. The Commons ordered the printing of the Grand Remonstrance. A Bill was introduced to nominate a lord general, with powers to raise men and to enforce martial law. A threatening mob kept the bishops away from parliament. The king took action. On 3 January he caused articles of impeachment to be exhibited against one peer, Lord Kimbolton, and five members of the House of Commons, including Pym and Hampden. The peers declined to arrest them and, when the king sent a serjeant-at-arms to do it, the Commons replied that this concerned their privileges and they would consider the matter. Next day the king went down with three or four hundred armed men in company to arrest the members. They had executed a timely retirement into the fastnesses of the City of London and the Commons adjourned to Grocers' Hall. The City appointed Philip Skippon, an old soldier of Sir Horace Vere's, to guard them and to command the train-bands (citizen militia). The king and the royal family left London; and the five members returned to their places.

As late as 13 February Charles assented to an Act of Parliament which deprived the bishops of their places in the House of Lords, and indeed incapacitated all persons in Holy Orders from acting as members of parliament, privy councillors, justices of the peace, or judges of assize. He also assented to an Act authorizing justices of the peace and mayors to enlist men compulsorily for service in Ireland; but after that he was willing to make no more concessions. He refused his assent to a Bill appointing lords lieutenants for counties, who, or their deputies, were to be empowered to raise and command troops. In March he took the road from Theobalds in Hertfordshire towards the north, where his supporters were strong. The Lords and Commons turned their Militia Bill into an ordinance, under which the troops were to be employed as they, without the king, should direct. They duly raised an army of their own. In April Charles appeared in person before the gates of Hull. The governor refused to admit him, and was proclaimed a traitor, which parliament declared to be a breach of its privileges. The parliament sent troops and ships to make sure of Portsmouth, where the governor had declared against it. Little by little party strife had engendered or perhaps we should say had become, civil war. From the very first, and more evidently as year followed year, it was different in kind from any of the armed conflicts which had divided the country hitherto. A greater proportion of the people were engaged in it. The motives of the participants on both sides were more various and more complicated. The issues were less simple.

The Civil War and the Commonwealth 1642–1653

1642	Indecisive battle at Edgehill.
1643	The Solemn League and Covenant establishes an alliance between parliamentary and Scottish forces.
1644	The royalist army defeated at Marston Moor.
1645	Parliamentarians form the New Model Army. The royalists are defeated at Naseby.
1646	The Scots accept the surrender of Charles.
1647	Charles is seized from parliamentary custody by the army.
1648	The renewal of civil war; Scots and royalists are defeated by the New Model Army. Cromwell orders the exclusion of all unfriendly members from the House of Commons ('Pride's Purge').
1649	Charles is executed. The Commonwealth is established. Disturbances in the army are inspired by Levellers. Cromwell begins the re-conquest of Ireland with massacres at Drogheda and Wexford.
1651	The Battle of Worcester ends royalist resistance. The Navigation Act is passed to exclude Dutch ships from English trade. Thomas Hobbes publishes his *Leviathan*, advocating a strong government and state.
1652	War against the Dutch begins, the first of three before final peace in 1674.
1653	Cromwell dismisses parliament and becomes protector.

Like the revolt of the Netherlands against Spain, the armed conflict between king and parliament might be regarded as one incident in a contest between authority and freedom which convulsed half Europe for half a century. But the Civil War was exceptional because no other state except Scotland was involved. The French, the Spaniards, and the Dutch were all locked in the Thirty Years War, which began in Bohemia in 1618. Neither of the English parties could offer an adequate reward for armed intervention. Each side did receive some consignments of munitions from overseas, but not enough to affect the balance of forces. A handful of foreigners held high commands. King Charles's principal general was his young Calvinist nephew, Prince Rupert, one of the sons of the Winter King, who had learnt his soldiering in the Low Countries and Germany. There were some foreign engineers and other experts; but the whole affair was insular.

Even in the earliest stages it was not, like so many civil wars, a confused mêlée, and even in the latest stages there was very little guerrilla activity. Soon after the first encounters the king raised his standard at Nottingham, as he had raised it at York against the Scots, thus ceremoniously announcing not a punitive expedition against rebels, but formal war. There were some atrocities, as there always are in a war; but in general both sides respected the customary laws of war. The armament on both sides was for the most part reasonably up to date, the infantry carrying pikes and muskets, the cavalry swords and pistols. Drill and tactical formations were those which British volunteers and mercenaries had learnt in the continental wars. The parliamentary commander-in-chief was the earl of Essex, son of Queen Elizabeth's favourite.

The military movements conformed to the existing administrative geography of the country. To begin with, each side tried to establish control over the parts where it was stronger, and that meant taking possession not merely of terrain, but of the counties and their organization. Since the time of James I the armour and weapons of the militia had been stored in county depositories: these were objectives. At first the work of recruiting followed the old militia system of selective compulsion. Supply could be, and often was, carried out by justices of the peace. It was characteristic of the local power of the nobility and gentry that considerable numbers of troops were immobilized as garrisons of country mansions and obsolete castles which served little or no strategic purpose. There was too much dispersion of effort on both sides, and sometimes there were extensive troop movements which served no ascertainable purpose, so that almost every district had its skirmishes and small-scale cavalry raids, sometimes picturesque and sometimes heroic. But the main course of events turned on the operations of the field armies. These were small by continental standards. Probably the largest number which ever met in one battle was under 50,000, and the largest number who were under arms at any one time in England was between 120,000 and 150,000.

The parliamentarians began the war with two great advantages which they never lost. First, London was on their side. In the last months before the outbreak of war everyone could see that the civic authorities defended parliamentary privilege, that the capitalists would not lend money to the king, and that when riotous mobs assembled, as they did either spontaneously or under some hidden leadership, it was always to demonstrate against the bishops or the court. During the war the City did much more than play a political part, and man its defences: the trade and wealth of the port were the mainstay of the parliamentary cause. This was made possible by the second great advantage: the navy was on the same side. The officers and seamen were not separated by the social distinctions which prevailed in armies. They followed their own way of life together and thought alike. After some years of war disagreements in London gave trouble, and later there was a mutiny in the fleet, but the navy kept the friendly ports open throughout the war, hardly ever firing a shot.

These two inferiorities meant that Charles was never able to equip his army thoroughly. At the outset he was also inferior in numbers, and it seems that he could scarcely have fought at all if the parliament had not insisted that one of their aims was to punish every individual whom they marked out as a member of the 'malignant' party opposed to them. This made many moderate men think that their safety and the chances of a settlement depended on a royalist victory. A few of the nobility such as the duke of Newcastle were able to raise regiments on their estates, and Charles's supporters were strong in the north, the west, and the south-west. These, however, were the poorer and less populous regions. Parliament was in control of the regions to the north and south of London: East Anglia, Essex, Hertfordshire, Kent, and parts of the counties to the west of them. Most of the Midlands lay open to the operations of either army.

In the first year of the war, 1642, the king marched from Shrewsbury to strike at London. At Edgehill, overlooking the Warwickshire Avon, the parliamentary forces, superior in numbers, met him and failed to win the battle, but got away in good order. Charles went on his way, spending more than a fortnight on a week's march. When he arrived at Turnham Green the parliamentary army was already in London, and Skippon had the train-bands entrenched across his road. Drawing the unavoidable conclusion that his attack must be postponed, the king retired up the Thames to Oxford. There he rigged up a temporary capital.

In the spring he was to launch a new offensive with more adequate forces. One army from the north and another from the west were to unite with the small garrison of Oxford for the advance. This necessitated some preliminary fighting. In the north the clothing towns of the West Riding of Yorkshire formed a pocket of puritanism. The parliamentary commander Sir Thomas Fairfax, after some early successes, was defeated and had to give them up. The royalists held all Yorkshire except Hull, and Hull was besieged. In the west Charles's generals began equally well. After their army had won one battle near Bath and another near Devizes, Bristol, the second port of the kingdom, surrendered to Prince Rupert. Gloucester was the one strong point which interrupted the king's control of the Severn Valley. It was besieged; but the parliamentary army marched from London and relieved it. Charles marched to Newbury and blocked the return of Essex to London; but Essex fought, and Charles retired to Oxford. A few days later his affairs in the north took an unfavourable turn. During the summer the army of the Associated Counties (Norfolk, Suffolk, Essex, and Hertford – yet another association) had been fighting its way northward, bringing most of Lincolnshire under its control, and so clearing a way from London to Yorkshire. On the day after their last victory, the duke of Newcastle raised the siege of Hull. Charles's military position was no better than it had been a year before.

During this year 1643 the essential character of the war was changed. Having begun as a war within England, it became a war in all the three kingdoms. Once more Charles looked to Ireland for help, and by this time he had to treat with the Irish almost as a foreign power. In 1642 they formed a confederation which professed loyalty to the king, but was bound by oath to restore the Roman Catholic faith, and in each province they set up a general commanding the armed forces. Charles's representative, the marquess of Ormonde, afterwards lord lieutenant, made a truce for a year, called the Cessation, under which the Irish, though declining to send an army of their own to England, promised money which, in the event, they did not pay. Charles thus gained only the service of his own troops who had been serving in Ireland. They proved to be of scarcely any use. He had redoubled the worst suspicions of his enemies, and made it easier for the parliament to conclude their own agreement for mutual help with the Scots. The fundamental purpose of the latter, the Solemn League and Covenant was to reform the church in the three kingdoms 'according to the Word of God and the example of the best reformed churches'.

The Scots army under Leven crossed the border in January 1644. They besieged the duke of Newcastle in the town of the same name, but, failing to take it, they marched south and the duke, following them, took his army behind the walls of York. The Scots and a parliamentary army from the south besieged him there, but broke off when Rupert came over from Lancashire to join him. The two armies fought a pitched battle at Marston Moor on 2 July. The allies won a complete victory, taking 1,500 prisoners and all the royalist guns. Although there was still fighting, on and off, for six more years this day decided the issue of the war.

In February 1645 the House of Lords agreed to the formation of the New Model Army. It consisted of eleven regiments of horse, twelve regiments of foot, and 1,000 dragoons, mounted men armed with carbines, in all 22,000 men. The existing parliamentary armies supplied less than half, and the remainder were impressed from London and the eastern counties. The quality of the cavalry was high; the discipline and training sound, the pay ample and for a time regular. This army differed from its predecessors in several respects. It was paid by the parliament and so was free from county or other local ties. The officers were good, and, like the men in the ranks, were selected without regard to their religious opinions. In practice this meant that the religious zeal which was alive throughout Puritan England gathered into vigorous cells round officers and preachers. Before the New Model took the field, parliament passed the Self-Denying Ordinance, by which all members of either house, with a single exemption, were disqualified from holding military commands. There were good reasons for distrusting some of the

former high commanders. They seemed to be thinking that an outright victory over the king might not suit their personal prospects so well as a compromise peace.

Oxford was surrounded by flooded meadows and by earthworks, but it could not withstand a siege for any considerable time, and it could no longer be used as a pivot for the movements of armies. Fairfax, now the parliamentary commander-in-chief, sat down before it and lobbed in a few cannon-balls, but the king and Rupert rode out of the city. Without keeping all their available troops together they captured Leicester, and turned south. They unexpectedly came upon Fairfax at Naseby, near Market Harborough, and attacked. The battle cost the king almost all his infantry and all his artillery.

Fighting went on until Midsummer Day, 1646; but it consisted of the defeat of outlying royalist forces, and the capture of fortified places, Bristol, Chester, Exeter, and last of all Oxford. Even in Scotland, where the romantic Highland leader Montrose won victories all through the summer of 1645, the tide turned. Leven brought some cavalry back from England, and defeated him. He fled to Norway.

Before Oxford fell the king surrendered. Like his grandmother Mary Queen of Scots he exploited the advantages of his captivity. He began by surrendering not to the parliament, which had beaten him, but to the Scots, whose army was inactive, with advanced headquarters at Newark on the Trent. Montrose was still in the field, and Charles hoped that this would strengthen him in negotiating for a settlement with his Scottish subjects. He did not understand that the Scottish Presbyterians, like the English parliamentarians, would never trust his promises without guarantees. The parliament had captured his papers among the baggage at Naseby, and from these they had published damaging evidence of his correspondence with foreign powers. Later they published some documents, of doubtful significance, from his negotiations with the Irish. Whatever the detailed facts may have been, it is certain that he had tried to get Irish troops for England, and that in return he had offered not only a far-reaching toleration for the Catholics, but also indemnity for almost all offences since 23 October 1641. The papal nuncio in Ireland was alarmed by the general opinion there of Charles's inconstancy and bad faith.

The Scots did not express themselves so plainly, but they stuck immovably to their central demand, that the king should sign the national Covenant. The king tried in vain to tempt them with provisional compromises, but his principles forbade him to yield on the main point. The Scottish parliament therefore voted that the uncovenanted king was not wanted in that kingdom. They turned to the English parliament. That parliament had done something to fulfil the terms of their alliance, the Solemn League and Covenant of 1643. An assembly of divines, English and Scottish, had prepared the way for that alliance, and it debated theological profundities until after the battle of Naseby. Parliament adopted a presbyterian form of church government, and adopted a new *Directory* in place of the Prayer Book, but could not be induced to allow the church in England that

LEFT An impression of the Battle of Naseby, in which Prince Rupert's cavalry won initial successes for the outnumbered royalist army. But the New Model Army held firm, and a wing under Cromwell's command routed the weak left wing of the royalists, leading to a great parliamentary victory.

BELOW The Marquis of Montrose, a talented Scottish general and poet. In the Civil War he led his Highlanders in the royalist cause, winning several battles in Scotland. But he was finally defeated and executed in 1650.

freedom from state control which it had in Scotland. The alliance, however, was wearing thin. The Scottish army, with nothing to do, was unpopular among the English townsmen and villagers. It would gladly go home if its hosts would pay its expenses. Parliament was willing; it paid half the bill on account and the Scottish army, on its departure from Newcastle, handed over the king to English parliamentary commissioners.

The commissioners treated the king with the respect that was his due. He was accommodated, with unobtrusive military guards, at Holdenby House, the country-house which his father had bought for his mother. He resumed the familiar occupation of negotiating with parliament. In the seventeenth century it was usual for the two sides in a war to take one another's temperature by frequent, sometimes more and sometimes less secret, diplomatic exchanges. In the English civil war, thanks to the prevailing legalism and legal education, this practice took the form of exchanging lengthy argumentative proposals and replies. They were not so much overtures of peace as manifestos adapted to changing circumstances but reasserting the principles of the original cleavage. Now the circumstances had changed so much that parliament was discussing with the king the conditions on which he should be restored; but in the same unforgiving spirit. By way of making practical arrangements for that event it resolved that the army should receive part of its arrears of pay, that it should be reduced in numbers, and that no officer who refused to sign the Covenant should hold a commission. The army did not like this. First the officers expressed dissatisfaction; then the men in the ranks. The first objections were to the small amount of back-pay offered, and to the lack of a promise of indemnity. Other grievances followed, which were discussed by the council of officers, and by the agitators, elected representatives of the men. The men first showed unwillingness to volunteer for Ireland; then refused altogether to disband. Charles made his final offer to the parliament: presbyterianism for three years and parliamentary control of the militia for ten. An army council was appointed, consisting of the generals and, from each regiment, two commissioned officers and two soldiers chosen by election.

Everybody was taken by surprise on 4 June 1647 when a junior cavalry officer, Cornet Joyce, with no written instructions appeared at Holdenby accompanied by five hundred troopers. Nothing in writing passed between Joyce and the king, whom he escorted to the army headquarters at Newmarket.

So far from making the king's predicament worse, this seemed to play into his hands by dividing his enemies. The army issued a Declaration asserting the right to vindicate their own and the people's fundamental rights and liberties, and demanding a purging of objectionable members and a dissolution of the present parliament. The formal impeachment of eleven members was backed by a threat to march on London. London, however, both the civic authorities and the mob, began to support the Presbyterians in parliament against the army. Therefore the army marched, took possession of London, and installed Fairfax as governor of the Tower. On 1 August the army presented its proposals to the king: episcopacy was to be restored, but without coercive powers and with toleration for all Protestant sects; the judicial system was to be reformed; for ten years parliament was to control the militia and dispose of the great offices; parliaments were to be biennial and elected by reallocated constituencies. Among the other provisions was one that no one should be compelled to sign the Covenant. The king refused.

Whilst the king was corresponding secretly with those who were willing to help him out of his isolation, the army went through a crisis unlike any other that has ever arisen in England. During the war the unsettled conditions in hundreds of parishes had opened the way for the rise and multiplication of sects. Where a royalist clergyman could no longer prevent protests in church; where a justice of the peace took sides with the demonstrators; where there was already a zealous extremist group, new congregations formed, some of them linked together by travelling preachers and a rudimentary organization over a greater or smaller area. Few of these religious bodies survived for very long; but they began a lasting tradition of uncontrolled religious speculation and evangelism. Many of them drew, more or less consciously, on continental traditions of mysticism or enthusiasm. The one small body which won a permanent place in history was the Society of Friends, 'in scorn called quakers'. It combined these characteristics with an instinct for discipline. It came before long to hold pacifist opinions, and so its history has little to do with the army, but for the sects in general the parliamentary armies,

closely intermingled at many points with the general population, were a favourable environment. During the months with no fighting and very little pay, but endless opportunities for preaching and discussion, every religious idea and every political aspiration had been canvassed. Perhaps there were none that had never been heard of before: many of the political theories had been common among the continental enemies of monarchy, and the social ideas had grown from the age-long discontents which had shown themselves from time to time in popular revolts.

Inevitably, these ideas soaked into the army, probably many of them from London. With many minor conflicts they produced a deep division between the higher officers and the Levellers – a name heard long before in the Midland Revolt. The Levellers' manifesto, the Agreement of the People, demanded a completely new constitution. The sovereign body was to be an elected, single chamber, but many major matters were to be reserved for direct decision by the electors. Most of the senior officers were believers in the existing social system, but they took part in long debates in which they listened to extreme proposals, such as manhood suffrage, and apocalyptic announcements of the millennium. These were revolutionists that they dealt with, and that meant mutineers. Before the end of November 1647 the danger of mutiny was averted. It all flared up again, and was again put down in 1649, but by then the army had carried out its greatest historic actions and an internal crisis in the army had not the same significance as before. On both occasions the man who did most to restore discipline was Oliver Cromwell, second in command of the army under Fairfax. That Cromwell's position was unique had already been publicly shown by his being the one officer exempted from the Self-Denying Ordinance. He had the confidence both of the officers, who wanted to preserve the unity of the army, and of the men who wanted just treatment. With enormous force of character he combined intense religious conviction, of an Independent cast, but he had the humanity and tolerance which had grown up spontaneously among the Independents. The two outbreaks of mutiny were quelled with, for the times, extraordinary little bloodshed: altogether four ringleaders were shot. The spirit of the Levellers was not extinguished, either in the army or in civil life. Helped by their flood of pamphlets, the Levellers' ideas were absorbed into the stock of dissident thought.

In the last week of 1647 the king's diplomacy achieved its last success: he made a treaty called the Engagement with the loyalist Scots, mainly of the nobility, under which he was to establish presbyterianism for three years, denying toleration to the sects. This did not satisfy the constituted authorities in Scotland, and so it was not Leven's army but a hastily levied and imperfectly trained force that was raised there to support what was meant to be a general royalist rising throughout Britain. From April there were revolts in Berwick, South Wales, Kent, and Essex and, what was more serious, disorders in London and a mutiny in the fleet. Several ships defected, and in July the Scots crossed the border, perhaps twenty thousand strong. The operations of this summer are usually called the Second Civil War; but that is more than they deserve. As the Scots marched down the western road Cromwell crossed the Pennines and placed himself between them and Scotland. Near Preston he destroyed their army as a fighting force. The other outbreaks were put down in detail and severely. They caused deep resentment in the army, not only because they disturbed the peace and caused casualties, but because the Scots had come, and come with the intention of putting down Independency. Parliament, rescinding an earlier resolution to hold no more communications with the king, reopened its negotiations in September. It voted the king's concessions satisfactory. On the following day by Cromwell's order Colonel Pride picketed the House of Commons with his musketeers and prevented the Presbyterian members from taking their seats. These new royalists were about 140 in number. The remnant who were left, called the Rump because they were the sitting part, seldom mustered more than fifty or sixty, but they comported themselves as if they were a lawful parliament.

It was a matter of only a few days for the Rump to set up a high court of justice, with 135 members of whom as few as twenty were to make a quorum, for the purpose of trying 'Charles Stuart the now king of England' for prosecuting with fire and sword his design totally to subvert the laws and liberties of the nation. The lawyers took some pains to work juridical principles into the documents of this trial, but, of course, it was essentially a revolutionary act. There was no proposal to depose the king

A satirical playing card, showing a Scottish Covenanter and an English Puritan engaged in one of their endless doctrinal discussions. The Covenanters were Presbyterians who resisted Charles's attempted religious changes in Scotland. Their participation in the Civil War was a decisive factor in Charles's defeat; it was their army which precipitated the Battle of Marston Moor, a defeat the royalists never recovered from.

A Quaker meeting. The Society of Friends, whose members soon became known as Quakers, was one of many religious sects which appeared in 17th century Britain. Founded by George Fox, it was more lasting than most of its competitors. Believing that each pious individual can communicate with God through the inner light of his own heart, Quakers avoided all ritual, including sermons and ordained ministers.

before trying him for his life. He was condemned as 'a tyrant, traitor, murderer and public enemy to the good people of this nation'. On 30 January 1649 he was executed before his own palace of Whitehall.

Monarchy still cast its spell, and Charles's dignity in his last days abashed many even of those who thought ill of him. A shock of something like horror ran through all political Europe, and it seemed as if those who held power in England might have set every country against them. They had passed the point of no return. They made no attempt to evade their responsibility. The Rump abolished the monarchy and the House of Lords. It declared that England was a Commonwealth and free state. It appointed a council of state to carry on the republican government for one year. When it was first appointed there were 41 members, of whom 31 sat in parliament. After the first two years the membership was changed annually by making new appointments to 20 of the places. The standard of ability and devotion to duty was high: indeed the Council of State under the Commonwealth was more efficient and less corrupt than the privy council either in earlier or in later times. It worked through committees. Until September 1651 it was occupied almost entirely in making the government safe from its dangers in Scotland and Ireland.

Ireland came first. Divisions among the Irish had weakened the confederacy; Ormonde, as the head of the English interest, still held Dublin, and in 1647 he delivered it and the other places in his possession to commissioners who were sent over by parliament. They brought over two regiments of horse. The Anglo-Irish Michael Jones, commanding these and the English troops already there, defeated the Irish field army and enlarged the area under his control, but lost ground again in 1648 when Ormonde came back from England with a fresh commission from the king and operated with the Irish confederates. Ormonde took

LEFT Oliver Cromwell. An ordinary landowner, Cromwell rose to prominence only with the Civil War. After the victory at Marston Moor his prestige was enormous, leading eventually to his appointment as Protector. Strong in character, he was more moderate in his religious and political attitudes than many of his supporters. But his massacre of the defeated Irish at Drogheda is a dark blot on his reputation.

BELOW The beheading of King Charles I in Whitehall; a French depiction. This event generated great interest on the Continent, not only because of the sentiments aroused by the king's courageous and dignified last moments, but also because of its obvious future significance: that a people might execute its lawful king was a new and thought-provoking concept.

Drogheda and Dundalk, but Jones beat him on 2 August 1649. On the 15th Cromwell landed with 12,000 men, well equipped. He beat down all opposition that he met. His two great blows were the storming of Drogheda and Wexford. They had refused to surrender on summons and so, by the laws of war, Cromwell was technically justified in putting their garrisons to the sword. There is, nevertheless, a ferocity in his references to one class of non-combatant victims, the priests, which belongs to the darkest strain of the religious conflict. In the spring he returned to England, leaving his army in possession of a long strip of coast, stopping short of Waterford. His son-in-law Henry Ireton, the best brain among the more conservative army officers, took over the command, and the suppression of resisting towns and isolated parties ended with the surrender of Galway in May 1652.

The conquest of Ireland was followed by a settlement which carried the policy of colonization further than had ever been possible before. By Acts of Parliament in 1652–4, new masters were set over the tillers of the soil, to such an extent that perhaps two-thirds of the land of Ireland changed hands. A few Irish leaders and a few who were judged guilty of crimes were to die and to forfeit everything. The other landlords and farmers who had fought in the Irish armies were to lose two-thirds of their property. Those who had not manifested 'constant good affection' were to lose a third, and by one of the later provisions they were to remove themselves, on pain of death, to Connaught or to County Clare. English soldiers were to be rewarded with grants of their land, and immigrants were to fill in the gaps. A vast work of surveying and allocation began, and was still in progress when political changes made it necessary to revise these drastic decisions. Apart from colonization, and the energetic expulsion of priests, no small matters, the new regime did well for Ireland. In due course she was granted, like Scotland, thirty seats in the British parliament, and free trade with Britain; something was done for setting up schools; there was peace.

Scotland was more troublesome from the military point of view, but by right kept religious and political matters largely in her own hands. That England became a commonwealth was no impediment, legally, or morally, to the immediate succession of the late king's son as King Charles II of Scotland. He was in exile, and in 1650 Montrose lost his last fight and was executed as a traitor; but the new king paid the price which his father had refused and signed the Covenant. This brought all Scotland except the fanatical extremists to his allegiance, and the Presbyterians as a whole were implacably opposed to the toleration of sectarians to which the English army was committed. The Scots prepared an army to win the English throne for Charles. On the other side Fairfax, who had been detaching himself from the government since the trial of Charles I, refused the command. It went to Cromwell, newly returned from Ireland, and Cromwell, after some anxious days, shattered Leven's army at Dunbar. That did not amount to conquering Scotland. Charles was crowned at Scone and he had some troops about him in Stirling. In the summer of 1652 he made a dash for England by Carlisle and the western road. He had three days start of Cromwell, but he had 16,000 men at the most, and those irregulars. The English did not rise to support him and Cromwell, coming south by the eastern road from Berwick, picked up militia and other reinforcements so that he outnumbered the royalists by seven to four. When the two forces met, as far south as Worcester, the result was a foregone conclusion. The fugitive king was lucky to make his way to

France. The conquest of Scotland was completed by Cromwell's lieutenant, George Monck. The English administration was orderly and successful. It did not interfere in any important matters except that the national assembly was forbidden to meet and the church was deprived of all coercive jurisdiction. Needless to say the acquiescence of the Scots was sullen, and they were by no means grateful when Scotland, incorporated with England and Ireland, received free trade and representation in the common parliament.

When the council of state looked at Europe, its first impulse was one of revolutionary enthusiasm. The wars of religion were over but France and Spain were still at war, and Portugal was fighting for independence against Spain. Most important, the Spaniards had finally recognized Dutch independence. The prospect of organic union of the three kingdoms of the British Isles was coming near. If it could be extended to include the Dutch, the common cause of protestantism would be upheld by an irresistible maritime, federal republic. When the English made this proposal, the cautious Dutch calculated the probabilities. They knew a good deal about the open and latent divisions of England, if only because one of the last acts of Charles I before the Civil War had been to marry his daughter, the princess royal, to the young Prince William II of Orange, the grandson of William the Silent. They also had much in mind the economic friction between the two nations, which had grown worse and seemed to need clearing up before any joint action could begin. The English, in particular the strong committee of trade, were devoting thought to the same matter. This committee was in close touch with London merchants, notably those of the East India Company. It held the prevailing ideas of the time, which we call mercantilist. In accordance with these ideas the famous Navigation Act was passed in 1651. Its purpose was to encourage British shipping, and its method to exclude foreign, which in practice meant Dutch, ships from English and colonial trade. The Dutch protested against this as an unfriendly act. The English renewed all their old maritime and colonial demands, and were equipping a fleet. In the spring of 1652, cruising in the Channel under the command of Robert Blake, it met Admiral Tromp with fifty sail and he refused his salute to the flag. The English fired the first shots of a war that lasted two years.

This was a great turning-point in international relations. Economic and colonial rivalries had brought about a war in Europe. Because of them England had turned her back on the legacy of the Burgundian alliance. It was also a turning-point in the history of warfare. This war was fought entirely at sea: there were no land-operations. It was the first war outside the Straits of Gibraltar in which there was a succession of big battles between fleets. It proved that in the future only fighting ships would count: the hired and requisitioned merchantmen disappeared from the line of battle. In technique, in discipline, and in organization western European navies entered on a new era. The war itself was evenly balanced and hard fought, but the English had the advantage. Many writers think that the war and the power developed in it were characteristic of Oliver Cromwell, but that is an error. He had nothing to do with starting it, and as soon as he was in a position where he could stop it, he immediately did so. The terms were severe. The Navigation Act remained; compensation was paid for the massacre of Amboyna; the house of Orange, which had fallen out with the Dutch estates, was excluded from its hereditary offices, partly because of its Stuart alliance.

In Ireland and in Scotland the conduct of affairs by the council of state had been successful; in the Dutch war it had roused a sense of triumph which the English had scarcely felt since the Spanish Armada; but in all this there was an abnormality. The armed forces commanded all the support that they needed; indeed they controlled the government; but they were not integrated into the commonwealth. There was no legislature except a roomful of party-men with very dubious credentials. This was not the result of any deliberate policy. The council of the army had presented a revised version of the Agreement of the People to parliament on the first day of the king's trial, but the Rump procrastinated for four years without taking one step towards parliamentary reform, a dissolution, and a general election. This did not cause any acute inconvenience in the daily work of government, though the army and the parliament were far from agreeing about religion. The Rump did indeed move a little nearer to religious toleration by abolishing compulsory church attendance. In law reform and social reform it effected practically nothing. But the lack of any real constitution was an offence to everyone who understood that stable government must rest on some express consent, an offence to those who understood that there could be no real peace until the old and new royalists were conciliated and also an offence to those who had democratic ideas, in the sense that the consent ought to come from some body deserving to be called the people. Very few of the Rump were democrats in any sense. The members of parliament, under pressure from Cromwell and others, prepared a bill for a new representative body; but it was no more than a plan for perpetuating their own power. Instead of intermittent and periodically elected parliaments, the Rump wanted a self-perpetuating legislative and executive assembly in permanent session. It proposed that its own members should sit perpetually and should have the right to admit or exclude all persons elected in the future. Cromwell, being a member, listened to the debate on the third reading of this Bill until the Speaker was about to put the question. He made a speech, but then he called in a party of musketeers, who cleared the House. The same day he dismissed the council of state. Although excluded from public functions, these rigid republicans opposed every subsequent attempt to set up a new executive and legislature. For the moment the general and the army council believed themselves to be the only remaining authority with any right to make such attempts.

The Coming of Constitutional Monarchy 1653–1701

1655	Local government is administered by major-generals to thwart possible royalist resistance. The capture of Jamaica.
1656	Cromwell allows Jews to return to England.
1658	The death of Cromwell.
1660	The monarchy is restored with the recall of Charles II.
1662	The Act of Uniformity unintentionally encourages persecution of Roman Catholics and Nonconformists.
1666	The Great Plague in London reaches its climax, and is followed by the Great Fire. The Pentland Rising in Scotland is suppressed. Isaac Newton propounds his law of gravity.
1667	The Dutch raid Chatham, in the Thames estuary. Peace is made with the Dutch, lasting until 1672; the Dutch concede New York to Britain.
1673	Catholics and Nonconformists are forbidden to hold public offices by the Test Act.
1675	The Royal Observatory is established at Greenwich.
1678	Titus Oates fabricates the 'Popish Plot'.
1679	Covenanters' rising is defeated at Bothwell Brig. The Habeas Corpus Amendment Act is passed, giving some protection against imprisonment without trial.
1685	The death of Charles II and succession by his brother James II. Monmouth's rebellion is crushed at Sedgemoor.
1688	William of Orange, the future William III, lands at Tor Bay. James leaves England.
1689	The Bill of Rights is passed to confirm liberties established by the 'Glorious Revolution' of the previous year. William and Mary jointly accept the offer of the British crown. The Highland rising is quelled. First appearance of John Locke's *Two Treatises of Government*.
1690	William's forces decisively defeat James II in Ireland at the Battle of the Boyne.
1694	The Bank of England is founded
1695	Printing licences are abandoned, thereby creating considerable freedom for the press.
1701	The Act of Settlement is passed, thus securing an eventual Protestant Hanoverian succession.

The first attempt of the general and the army council to set up a legislative assembly was ridiculous. County by county the congregational churches chose God-fearing persons from whom the army council selected 129 for England, five for Scotland, and six for Ireland. For four and a half months these worthies wrestled with the tasks of reform. By the end of that time a majority of them saw that they were out of their depth. They surrendered their powers to Cromwell, the lord general. The army leaders, especially John Lambert, took the first and longest stride back towards normal government. They drafted the Instrument of Government, the first English written constitution, setting up a parliament for England, Scotland, and Ireland, to be held at least once in every three years. Parliament was to have the sole right to legislate and to impose ordinary taxes, and the chief officers of state were to be appointed with its approval; but monarchy, under some limitations, was to be restored. It was to be monarchy, but not quite kingship. The head of the state was to be called 'protector', the old title of the temporary heads in the minority of Edward VI and of others before him. He was to take the advice of his council of state for important steps; but he was to have a fixed revenue to pay the forces and the ordinary expenses of government. Oliver Cromwell accepted this office.

As protector, Cromwell gained great prestige for himself and for his country. In his first year he made what was considered an advantageous peace with the Dutch. He dreamed of a league of all Protestant states. Even in his actual policy religion played a part. When the great admiral Robert Blake showed the flag in the Mediterranean, one of his subsidiary purposes was to restrain the Moslem corsairs of North Africa. The protector used diplomatic influence with France to stop the persecution of ths Protestant Vaudois by the duke of Savoy. In 1654 he made war on Spain, from his own point of view a Protestant war, which he justified with the arguments current in the days of the Winter King. Europe had changed so much that these arguments were obsolete, and the protector rather presided over the policy than worked it out. There were men in the City who supported it for reasons of their own, men concerned with the East India Company, which lent money generously to this government, some of them also interested in the Caribbean, where the Spaniards had stopped them short in 1641. The greatest change in Europe since that time was that France had weakened Spain by unremitting warfare. By 1657, however, the superiority of France was not so complete as to make her indifferent to the attractions even of Protestant and revolutionary England, with its veteran army and victorious navy. The two powers formed an offensive alliance, and the results were such as Walsingham or Buckingham might have hoped for, even though the naval war was badly managed. In the second year of the fighting, the British force of 6,000 played a decisive part in the Battle of the Dunes,

King Charles II. Although beset by ideological enemies, Charles managed to retain his throne to the end of his life. With his encouragement the arts and sciences flourished. There were the Restoration plays of Dryden and Congreve, the achievements in astronomy, mathematics and chemistry linked with the names of Halley, Newton and Boyle, and the architecture of Wren.

which led to the surrender of Dunkirk. In the next year, the Treaty of the Pyrenees registered the end of the European primacy of Spain, and it was Great Britain which retained Dunkirk. Almost exactly a century after the loss of Calais, she had a strong point on the mainland of Europe. The same peace left her in possession of Jamaica, a most useful West Indian base.

At home the protector's personal religious opinions counted for much. Before the first of his parliaments met he dealt with church benefices on the principle of having the character and fitness, but not the opinions, of the clergy tested by boards of examiners. He left the constitution of the established church, including tithes and patronage, as he had found it. His government could not put an end to religious disorder, but it set an example of tolerance, even towards the papists. A representative of the Jews in Holland petitioned for those of his religion to be allowed to resettle in England, from which Edward I had expelled them. There was opposition on religious grounds; but the merchants wanted to receive these expert international traders, and the lawyers pronounced that there was no legal bar. Cromwell allowed them to come and to build synagogues. They did not gain full civil rights until 1858, but they began almost at once to render solid services. In spite, however, of its power and its ability and its virtues, the government of the protectorate was never solidly based. The first parliament was elected from an improved, though not radically rationalized, distribution of seats in England, Scotland, and Ireland; but the republican opposition was so pertinacious that the government expelled 100 members. The remainder set about to reduce the armed forces, so the protector dissolved parliament after the minimum time allowed by the law. Royalist risings, not very dangerous in themselves, led to an experiment in military government which heightened ill-feeling all round. Eleven major-generals (the title not of a rank but of their office) were put over the administration of large districts. Most of them used their authority to repress so-called profane and ungodly behaviour which, despite Puritan Acts of parliament, still persisted. The second protectorate parliament was elected in an atmosphere of growing and varied discontent: about a hundred members were prevented from taking their seats and fifty or sixty more stayed out in sympathy with them. To this unrepresentative body it appeared that the country could not be reunited except under a constitutional king, whose supporters might at the worst enjoy the protection of the De Facto Statute (an old Act making it as proper to obey a *de facto* king as a rightfully-installed king). They were prepared to gamble on crowning the protector. He would not cut himself off so completely from his past; but the Humble Petition and Advice of 1657 gave him the right to nominate his successor, and added a new hereditary upper chamber to parliament. His choice of the successor was inevitable and hopeless. In 1658 when he died no one could have been accepted except his eldest son Richard, an amiable man, quite futile in business, who in 1659 dissolved parliament to satisfy the army. The army recalled the survivors of the Rump, and Richard resigned.

Constitutionally the country was back where it had been in the spring of 1653. The royalists had been assiduously plotting; but the government had taken their measure. The nucleus of their rising was a force of 4,000 men under Sir George Booth, one of the excluded members of parliament and a recent convert to royalism. They took possession of Chester, but except there and in North Wales they never even assembled. The parliamentary general, John Lambert, disposed of Booth's force easily. Afterwards, like Cromwell, he expelled the Rump and the council; but he had no chance of playing a part like Cromwell's. He was just forty years old, with an excellent military record since the early days of the Civil War. For a long time he was Cromwell's most prominent supporter, and he was the chief architect of the Instrument of Government; but as a politican he inspired no confidence. There was no candidate for the vacant headship of state except the lawful heir, Charles II, and the practical problem was to create sufficient calm to enable him to take over. George Monck, commanding the army in Scotland, was of the opinion that the business of soldiers was to draw their pay and obey the orders of some legitimate civilian authority. Fairfax became active again in Yorkshire, organizing the county and the troops in the same spirit. Monck marched south, and London, the only nucleus of civilian power, came over to their programme. The members expelled by Pride in 1648 took their seats again; the reconstituted Long Parliament dissolved itself at last; there was a free general election; a new parliament (called the convention because there was no royal summons) met. The king returned.

For the next twenty years, 1660–88, the public affairs of the country were in a paradoxical condition not altogether without resemblance to that of Oliver's protectorate: the state acted with energy and sometimes with effect in economic and international affairs; but no stable foundation for national unity was laid, and the threat of a fresh revolution was never exorcized. King Charles II, however, started his reign with two great advantages. The first was that there was no need to pay attention to the wishes of any foreign power. None of them had helped Charles and so he was not bound by promises to any. A second great advantage was that his leading minister, Sir Edward Hyde, who became earl of Clarendon, based the settlement on respect for the law. This meant the law as it had been left by the last Acts of parliament passed by Lords and Commons with the assent of Charles I. The court of star chamber, the high commission, the councils of the north, of the Marches and Wales were not revived, nor were knighthood fines, ship money, and the abuses of the forest law. Only one Act of Charles I was repealed: the bishops were restored to their seats in the House of Lords. The treatment of the irreconcilable minority was politic and even generous. Only some fifty named individuals were exempted from an Act of Indemnity. Of those who were condemned to death, all but two had been prominently concerned in the trial and execution of Charles I, and of these two only one was executed. Lambert was held as a prisoner for the rest of his life.

During the six months of the convention in 1660 two urgent actions were taken. The first was to do away with the conditions which might bring about some new rebellion. The army and navy were disbanded, and money was scraped together to discharge their heavy arrears of pay. No troops were kept on foot except the First Foot Guards (now the Grenadier Guards), Monck's Coldstream Guards, and two regiments of mounted Life Guards. More than that parliament would not allow to the king. Although a good many castles and town walls were dismantled, many former soldiers still had arms in their possession, but parliament intended to rely for public order on the militia, the citizen force. In 1661–3 Acts were passed which fixed its numbers at not more than 90,000 men, including 6,000 horse. Except in emergencies its service was limited to a fortnight in the year. Its local commanders were seldom efficient and some went beyond their legal rights in taking action against real or suspected disorder. The king was not satisfied, and used his opportunities to increase and improve his army. He could reckon overseas garrisons, in Dunkirk and, later, in Tangier, as a reserve; but they depended for their upkeep on parliamentary votes. In Scotland and Ireland there were separate military establishments, supported by more manageable assemblies. In the last years of Charles's reign, as a result of steady pressure, he had a standing force of about 19,000 men, adequately organized and trained.

The other chief work of the convention parliament was to settle the land question. The usurping governments had confiscated and sold or despoiled many estates. Something had to be done for the original owners or their heirs; but it was impossible to disregard the interests of those who had lawfully acquired rights in such property. Any solution would have involved hardship to somebody, and the solution which was adopted was not perfect. The lands of the king and queen and the church were restored to them, and also those directly confiscated from their owners; but not those which had been sold, even under duress. This created some discontent; but it lasted.

In religion, which had been the most powerful threat to national unity, some practical questions were settled quickly. The bishops and deans and chapters came back to their cathedrals, and, as we have seen, took possession of their endowments. That was simple; but about a quarter of the parish clergy were intruders who must either submit to episcopacy or go out. At first there were moderate men on both sides who thought that the Prayer Book and episcopacy itself could be modified so as to meet the objections of the Presbyterians; but a conference held at the Savoy Hospital in 1660 failed to reach agreement on such a plan. Among the clergy the less tolerant party, who soon came to be called high churchmen, gained the upper hand, the more so because there were hare-brained plots for armed Puritan resistance, both in London and in the provinces. The king himself was not a religious man, but he had kindly feelings towards the loyal English papists, and he knew how the French monarchy gained from the support of the Catholic Church. He would not have been averse from a large measure of toleration all round; but his attempts in this direction, one of which was a Declaration of Indulgence in 1662, came to nothing. In 1662 the main lines of the settlement were laid down in an Act of Uniformity and it was completed by other Acts down to 1665. Unfairly to Clarendon these Acts have been known since Victorian times as the Clarendon Code.

The Church of England did not only return to episcopacy; it became more strictly episcopal than before: no one who had not been ordained by a bishop was to hold any benefice in it. There were many episcopally ordained clergymen among those who could not bring themselves to serve under the restored authorities. This latter body numbered about a thousand. They were not allowed to minister to congregations of their own. They were forbidden to teach in schools without a bishop's licence, which scarcely any of them were able to obtain. Since they were distrusted as much on political as on religious grounds, and the corporate towns controlled many elections to parliament, they were not allowed to live within five miles of any corporate town.

These laws were not always enforced, but ignorant or evil-minded judges and justices of the peace made enough use of them to justify the Nonconformists in complaining of persecution. In some points they were modelled on the even harsher laws against Roman Catholics, which were still on the statute book, but not rigidly enforced. The Roman Catholics, open and secret, at this time probably did not number much more than 100,000. The Protestant Nonconformists of all kinds may have been nearly as many as half a million men, women, and children, a tenth of the English people. The Clarendon Code was intended not to kill non-conformity but to cut its claws. It silently abandoned the historic claim of the Church of England to the allegiance of all the inhabitants of the country. The dissenters were already excluded from the English universities by the decisions of the universities themselves. Their opportunities were now still more restricted; but they maintained their traditions. The Quakers, in particular, insisted on such legal rights as remained to them. Among the great English writers of the Restoration, the most famous poet, John Milton, and the most famous prose writer, John Bunyan, were both Protestant dissenters.

The Church of England had preachers and theologians of whom it is still rightly proud and was refreshed by currents of attractive ideas. But it had no great success in ecclesiastical statesmanship. It firmly condemned resistance to kings, permitting in the worst provocation only passive obedience, or submission to the punishments inflicted by authority. The church courts were revived, though no one denied that they were much in need of reform, and the laity paid little attention to their rulings. Everyone knew that most of the clergy were too poor and a few of them were far too rich, but nothing whatever was done to rectify these evils. The taxation of the clergy had been voted for centuries by its own assemblies, the two convocations of Canterbury and York, and these had a general control over

BELOW John Bunyan dreaming about the pilgrim, and the struggle between Good and Evil, as depicted in the fourth (1680) edition of his *Pilgrim's Progress*. This was written while he was in prison during the Restoration; he had insisted on preaching at a time when only the established clergy were authorized to do so.

RIGHT The Great Plague in London 1665. This was the last of the really disastrous plagues which periodically appeared in British cities. It was of bubonic type and transmitted by the fleas of black rats; the latter travelled by ship, making seaports the commonest sites of these outbreaks.

church affairs. How much was to be paid in taxes by each benefice depended on a valuation made in 1535. A new valuation, though urgently needed, would have aggrieved innumerable clergymen of all ranks. In 1664 Clarendon and Archbishop Sheldon cut the knot by a private and unwritten agreement: in future the taxation of the clergy was to be done by parliament. Governments no longer needed the co-operation of the Church in finance, and its assemblies consequently declined. Soon they ceased to meet regularly, and there was no corporate debating or expression of the opinion of the Church of England.

In Scotland the king had no reason to expect any trouble from parliaments. There were economic and other problems, but for nineteen years business was done satisfactorily by a minister in London. From 1666 the minister was the very able, domineering, and theologically minded John Maitland, later duke of Lauderdale. The Scottish church problem was entirely unlike the English. Instead of bodies divided by schism there was the single Kirk, but irreconcilable parties within it tried either to extend or to abolish the authority of the bishops. At the moment of the Restoration things looked promising for the episcopal side, which hastily resumed possession; but between two and three hundred of the clergy, a larger proportion than in England, suffered ejection from their livings. Their strength was in the south-western counties, Ayr, Lanark, Dumfries, and Galloway. Repressive laws more severe than the Clarendon Code were enforced with the help of the soldiery. In 1666 came the Pentland rising. An ill-armed, untrained and deluded rebel force, of perhaps 3,000 to begin with, marched on Edinburgh, only to be miserably defeated and punished. After that Scotland was quiet.

Ireland too was quiet. The new regime reaped the benefits of the Cromwellian repression and met no resistance in its handling of the land question, which was far more complicated than that in England. After unsuccessful attempts to satisfy all reasonable claims for restitution, the Irish parliament in Dublin passed a pitiless Act of Settlement in 1665. The net result of the rebellion, the reconquest, and the Restoration was that the Protestants, who owned about a third of the good cultivable land of Ireland in 1641, now owned about two-thirds. This meant not only injustice but hardship for thousands of individuals; and it left a lasting legacy of hatred. The duke of Ormonde, who became lord lieutenant in 1661, did what he could to promote trade and industry, especially the linen industry. English economic policy in relation to Ireland was thoroughly illiberal, but perhaps mainly ineffective. The most ungenerous measure was the prohibition of the importing of live cattle from Ireland to England; but by a happy irony this did Ireland good. Since they could no longer send store cattle to England, the Irish fattened them at home and this was the foundation of the flourishing victualling trade of Cork. Whatever the reasons may have been, the only attempt at rebellion in Ireland in the whole reign of Charles II was the so-called Longford Rising of 1666, in which no one was killed except the rebel leader.

The Restoration made no break in the history of the British colonies. The conquest of Jamaica was completed in the summer of 1660, a commercial and naval base in the heart of the Caribbean. Some of the ablest of Charles's new men, Anthony Ashley Cooper among them, carried forward the enthusiasm for overseas ventures which had found scope under the protectorate. In 1660 two advisory councils were set up to prepare business for the privy council, one for 'foreign plantations', the other for trade. On them there sat together important councillors, including the secretaries of state, colonial officers, and City men. The Navigation Act was re-enacted and reinforced by other protectionist measures. A new proprietary grant was made for the colony of Carolina in 1663. Rivalry with the Dutch went on vigorously in the western and eastern seas. In 1662 the Royal Adventurers trading into Africa (the west coast, that is) received their charter. Their purpose was to supplant the Dutch in the lucrative slave-trade to the West Indian plantations.

Relations with the Dutch were involved with other foreign relations. The ministers were divided in their opinions about these, but Clarendon's influence, on the side of France against Spain, prevailed. France and Spain had made peace in 1659 after their long war; but Clarendon did the French two good turns,

Multituds flying from London by water in boats & barges
Flying by land
Burying the dead with a bell before them.
Searchers.
Carts full of dead to bury.

A scene during the Great Fire of London. Lath and plaster houses, crowded together, allowed town fires to spread rapidly. In the London fire of 1666 a misfortune became a catastrophe when a strong wind carried the flames through virtually the entire city. But when London was rebuilt the new brick structures were not only more fire-resistant but also less hospitable to rats and other disease-carrying organisms.

one of which seemed justifiable from the British point of view, though the other was more doubtful. The Portuguese were fighting their war of independence against Spain, and in this France was giving them indirect support, but they were also defending their overseas possessions against the Dutch. They offered King Charles the hand of the Princess Catherine of Braganza, with the handsome dowry of Bombay, Tangier, and more than £800,000 in cash. For the Portuguese the marriage had the solid advantage that it relieved them of part of their burden of imperial defence; but for the time being that was all. Even that relief was not all that it might have been. After two decades of effort at transforming Tangier into a valuable naval and commercial base, the British abandoned it in 1683 to the very Arabs against whom it had served as bulwark. Nor was this the only disappointment. As early as 1668 Charles found that Bombay was unprofitable. He gladly handed it over to the East India Company, the richest and most active of English economic groups. The new queen never gave birth to an heir. As a Catholic she was somewhat distrusted, though without reason, and she played no part in affairs. Charles wasted time and money on nearly a dozen ladies, mostly of poor intelligence, one of whom, however, Louise de Kérouaille, duchess of Portsmouth, was a capable agent of France.

The Portuguese marriage showed how complicated foreign affairs were, and in Charles's early years there was no unity of purpose among the ministers who dealt with them. Dunkirk was the symbol of the Cromwellian policy of military intervention on the Continent, and it was also expensive. The unadventurous Clarendon had no wish to fight in continental wars, and Englishmen in general did not want to maintain an army so near home. The town was sold in 1662 for about £400,000, and it was sold not to Spain but to France. No one in England foresaw that, as the principal port for French privateers, it would become a nuiscance, though not a great danger, to the British navy and merchant marine. The more enterprising men about King Charles were indeed enthusiastic for both the navy and the merchant marine. They thought the country was in fit condition to strike out at sea and in the colonies. The government had not run into serious difficulties with parliament. Finance, which had been a fatal hindrance for Charles I, was muddled, but it was not causing any bitter controversy. The whole system of taxing, borrowing, and accounting was badly in need of reform and modernization; but a beginning had been made. In the Civil War both sides had raised money by land taxes, and, except for an interval from 1660 to 1663 the taxing of land had come to stay. Another modern tax, the excise, was also continued. A direct tax, the hearth tax, proved to be difficult to administer and very unpopular with the payers. There were debts amounting to about one year's revenue. With encouraging memories of the navy's victorious services in the days of Blake, Ashley Cooper and other like-minded ministers allowed the always fermenting disputes with the Dutch to swell up into armed encounters on the West Coast of Africa and in North America, then into full-scale war.

This second Dutch war began early in 1665 and lasted two years and a half. Although the French were nominally allies of the Dutch, they succeeded in keeping out of the fighting almost completely, and although the English had an ally on land in the rear of the Dutch, the bellicose prince-bishop of Münster, he did nothing of importance, so that like the first Dutch war, this second was essentially a duel between the two maritime powers. The two powers were pretty evenly matched and pretty much alike in equipment. The first two campaigns brought hard fighting, with no decisive result. Then two heavy blows fell on England. The Great Plague swept the country, London worst of all. The government left the capital and so did many even of those who had duties there. In September 1666, when the plague was waning, the Great Fire destroyed 13,000 houses in the City. Some people thought it was due to the wrath of God; many held the baseless but poisonous belief that it was started by Catholic conspirators. For the moment it paralysed the national finances, and the government decided to start negotiations for peace. It also took the desperate decision not to set out a battle-fleet in 1667, but to rely on fortifications for coast defence and on commerce-destroying to weaken the enemy. In June therefore the Dutch sailed up the Thames estuary, broke through the defensive chain at Chatham, burnt four ships of the line and towed away the *Royal Charles*.

This was humiliating but it did not mean that the Dutch had won outright. They too were in financial straits, and the Treaty of Breda, which was signed on 31 July 1667, went a good way towards settling all the questions outstanding between the two powers. The British gained the New Netherlands, with its port of New Amsterdam, which was renamed New York, after the king's brother and heir, the lord high admiral. On the other hand, they gave up Surinam in South America, and they wrote off their claim to the spice island of Pulo-Run. Although they kept a station on the west coast of Sumatra, and for the time being also Bantam in Java, they were beginning to leave the East Indies to the Dutch. Except temporarily during the Napoleonic period, none of the territorial changes of the Treaty of Breda was ever reversed.

At home the war brought all the latent difficulties to a head. We have seen that there was trouble in Scotland during the war and a hint of possible trouble in Ireland: in neither case was this a mere coincidence. In England the disillusioned politicians made Clarendon their scapegoat, and although he had not been responsible for the war, the Commons impeached him, the king did not stand up for him, and he fled the country. That eased the state of feeling; but more was needed. After much unreasonable obstruction by the government and the Lords, the House of Commons appointed a committee, members of neither house, to investigate the public accounts. Their report revealed gross incompetence and fraud, and henceforth the Commons were justifiably reluctant to trust the government with money.

The ministers did not learn; they thought that they could fight the Dutch again with a better chance of success, especially if they had the French as allies. France had gone to war with Spain again and made easy conquests in the Spanish southern Netherlands. Although at the conclusion of this war Britain, the Netherlands and Sweden made a treaty, the Triple Alliance, to contain further French aggression, Britain's sincerity was doubtful. In 1670 by the Treaty of Dover a Franco-British offensive alliance was created. The new allies would heavily outnumber the Dutch fleet. On land the French would invade from the east with every prospect of success, while the British were to land in Zeeland. When the Dutch surrendered, their country was to be carved up, the British taking as their share positions commanding the estuary of the Scheldt, the highway to Antwerp.

Nothing need be said about the negotiations which preceded the third Dutch war except to quote the words of one of the secretaries of state, Lord Arlington: 'Our business is to break with them and yet to lay the breache at their door.' In March 1672 King Louis XIV of France was ready and war was declared, a war completely unlike the two preceding Anglo-Dutch wars. Britain was the ally, almost the satellite, of the power which made the heaviest attack and made it on land. The course of the war was completely unexpected. The French drove the Dutch back behind their inundations. The infuriated Dutch mob murdered the leading statesman of the republic, John de Witt. His political system fell in ruins, and William III of Orange was restored to the dignities of his ancestors as stadholder and captain and admiral general. An intelligent young man of twenty, who valued his recovered offices and happened to be the nephew of King Charles II, might be counted on to take a sensible view. Two ministers, the earl of Arlington and the duke of Buckingham, went to The Hague to talk William over, but William assured them that, rather than agree, he would die in the last ditch. That was startling, but not so startling as the outcome of the fighting. Winter came on with the French still on the wrong side of the water-line; in another campaigning season the Dutch found powerful allies. Year after year went by. The Treaty of Nijmegen marked the zenith of King Louis's power, but it left the Dutch republic intact, and it was not concluded until 1678.

By that time Great Britain had been at peace for four years. The two tough, indecisive naval campaigns that she fought were not the cause of her giving up. For the next fifteen years the government was holding at arm's length a revolution which overcame it in the end.

When the Treaty of Dover was made, a small inner circle of ministers knew that there were some secret clauses which would be worse than unpopular with a great many people in Britain, unless they could be disclosed in the glow of lucrative victory or at least in the enthusiasm of wartime. Charles declared himself convinced of the truth of the Roman Catholic religion, and he was to announce his conversion when the affairs of his kingdom permitted. Louis was to demonstrate his friendship by a money grant of about £166,000 and by lending 6,000 French troops if Charles should need them at home. Louis was to fix the date for declaring war against the Dutch, but only after Charles had made his announcement, and for this he was to choose his own time. This was Charles's personal policy. Judged by the standards of the time it was less anti-national than might appear to a modern eye. Aid in the form of subsidies from a foreign sovereign was scarcely objectionable in itself. Subsidies to allies were common enough. The Dutch promised in 1678 to aid the British in the event of rebellion at home, and in the eighteenth century they actually kept the promise. But the money which Louis promised and paid was meant to support Charles in a policy for which he could not expect parliamentary support, and the offer of troops was even more plainly made for the same reason. Of the two ministers who knew of these clauses, Arlington had become a Catholic, and the newly appointed Lord Treasurer, Clifford, was on the borderline between the Church of England and the Church of Rome. The others were hostile to Rome. Ashley Cooper, now earl of Shaftesbury, the most prominent opponent of Dutch trade and colonization, had served in the parliamentary army in the Civil War and was a friend of the dissenters. The unmanageable duke of Buckingham, the son of Charles I's favourite and the son-in-law of Fairfax, though zealous for the French alliance, was equally in favour of toleration for Protestants.

Two days before the formal beginning of the war, Charles, acting on his prerogative, issued a Declaration of Indulgence. He suspended all laws against 'whatsoever sort of nonconformists or recusants'. Places were to be licensed for public worship of Protestant Nonconformists under approved 'teachers', and Roman Catholics were to be allowed to exercise their religion in private houses. In principle this was what the country needed and what ultimately enabled it to settle down into mutual tolerance; but it immediately split the country in two. Parliament was not sitting. When the new session began the Commons voted three years' supply for the war only after the king had agreed to cancel the indulgence. But they were not satisfied yet. They passed the Test Act, under which every holder of office, civil or military, was to take the sacrament of Holy Communion according to the use of the Church of England, and in addition to the oaths already prescribed, to sign a declaration against transubstantiation which all conscientious Roman Catholics were bound to refuse. This ended the public careers of many loyal men, chief among them the duke of York, the heir to the throne and trusted lord high admiral. It deprived the state of the services of Roman Catholics until 1828, when at last it was repealed.

From about this time for many years many men of all classes believed that three things which they abhorred were closely allied: popery, France, and arbitrary power. Before the war was over Buckingham and Shaftesbury knew the secret of the Treaty of Dover, and new events hardened the suspicions of the country party, the party which was against the court. The duke of York married a Catholic Italian princess. Shaftesbury was dismissed from office. Still, when the peace came, the king had a chance of reuniting all but the irreconcilable. Neutrality in the continental war was favourable to British seaborne trade. The revenue from taxation went up accordingly. Among the new ministers the leading man was Sir Thomas Osborne, afterwards earl of Danby

Samuel Pepys. Known in his time as a very competent administrator of the navy, and as an intelligent participant in learned discussions, Pepys later gained greater recognition through his famous diary which, after being deciphered in 1825, provided a detailed and perceptive account of life in Charles II's time. Some of its details were so intimate that an unexpurgated version was not published until 1970.

and finally duke of Leeds, an old royalist and Anglican, and no lover of France. He made progress in reforming treasury procedure, and he tightened the government's control over its friends in the House of Commons. He went too far when he tried to impose on all office-holders a fresh test, a declaration that resistance to the king was unlawful, together with the undertaking already exacted from Nonconformists to refrain from all endeavours to alter the government in church and state. That would have brought in what is now called one-party government; the proposal was unsuccessful. Danby's most momentous act was the marriage in 1677 of the duke of York's elder daughter Mary to her cousin William of Orange. For some years it had looked as if this was a good plan for attaching William more closely to the Stuart family interest and for mitigating the unpopularity of the Catholic duke of York when he should succeed his childless brother as king. For William, in the five campaigns of his great coalition, had established himself as the champion of European liberties. He had fought on until an honourable peace was within the range of practical politics. Great Britain was ready to fight again on the Dutch side to bring this about, and in February 1678 parliament met in a warlike mood.

Suddenly the national unity fell to pieces. There were English statesmen on both sides who, unknown to one another, had put themselves in the power of Louis XIV. King Charles had made other secret agreements after that of 1670. He had not been punctilious about fulfilling them, but each time he had done more or less as Louis wished about parliamentary or foreign affairs. Altogether he had received the miserable total of £741,985, an average of £123,664 a year. But Louis was not such an innocent as to trust him; he followed the known principle that the interest of France was to keep England always divided. The opposition leaders feared the rise of French hegemony, but it did not immediately threaten British independence. Arbitrary government and religious intolerance seemed to them the supreme and most urgent dangers. They accepted money to spend in the cause. Parliament authorized Charles to raise 30,000 men and equip ninety ships. But the opposition grumbled, and the Commons suspected that the king wanted the ships and men for his own sinister ends. They passed an Act, which remained in force for seven years, severely restricting trade with France; but Britain exerted no influence on the settlement in Europe. The 1678 peace was on France's harsh terms.

Thus the materials for a crisis were already present when Titus Oates, a disreputable clergyman, revealed an imaginary Popish Plot. The core of it was that the papists were to assassinate the king and massacre Protestants in order to bring about the succession of the duke of York. Other informers backed Oates up with evidence, most of it rubbish. The king and a good many other shrewd men saw through it all and kept their heads; but parliament and the law-courts gave way to panic. From 1678 to 1681 about thirty-five innocent victims were executed. One of them was a Howard, condemned by his peers. The greatest was Oliver Plunket, Roman Catholic archbishop of Armagh and primate of Ireland.

Shaftesbury and some of his followers took advantage of this foul episode, with the result that for the next ten years the question of the succession divided Britain and made her impotent in European affairs. In 1678 Shaftesbury and Lord Russell, the earl of Bedford's heir, demanded the exclusion of James from the king's councils. Charles gave way and then he agreed to a parliamentary Test Act which excluded Roman Catholics from both houses. The Commons voted money to disband the newly raised troops, and they saw to it that this money did not come under the king's control. They proposed that sixty thousand of the militia should be embodied to keep order: the king refused. Blaming Danby as unjustly as they had blamed Clarendon, they impeached him. Charles knew that if he sacrificed Danby as his father sacrificed Strafford worse things would follow, and so in 1679, after it had sat for seventeen years he dissolved the parliament.

The general election went against the king, and before parliament met he persuaded his brother to leave the country. He dismissed Danby, who was lucky enough to survive in the Tower of London while his enemies quarrelled. The king tried to combine both sides in office, but the whigs were not placated. The first Exclusion Bill passed its second reading in the Commons: the duke of York, if the Bill became law, was to be excluded from the succession. Charles dissolved this parliament after it had sat for less than three months and dismissed Shaftesbury again.

From about this time the old names of court and country parties fell out of use, and people were distinguished as whigs or tories. Shaftesbury built up a primitive party organization in parliament and in the constituencies, especially in the City of London. He made a fateful decision. He might have united the exclusionists in some plan to make William of Orange the first man in the state. He was the ablest of the Stuart kindred, and the husband of the nearest in blood to the king and the duke. He might become regent, or even sovereign jointly with his wife. But

Shaftesbury preferred a showy lightweight, the eldest of the king's illegitimate sons, James Scott, duke of Monmouth. This choice was supported by the fiction that Charles had married the young man's mother before the Restoration.

Three parliaments, each newly elected, met in 1679–81. The first passed only three Acts, of which one, the Habeas Corpus Amendment Act, surrendered a point of prerogative and made it impossible for the Crown to imprison a subject without his ever appearing in a court of law. It is at least symbolic of one great principle of liberty. Whether it is the real foundation of liberty in this respect may be doubted: at any rate there is no Habeas Corpus in Scotland to this day. Charles's next parliament passed two Acts of no importance, and that of 1681 passed none at all. The business of all three parliaments was not to legislate but to deal with the crisis. In the first Shaftesbury brought in an Exclusion Bill in the Lords. In the second another passed the Commons, but they rejected a resolution to name one of James's daughters as next in succession. The Lords threw the Bill out. Lord Halifax, a statesman of much weight, holding central opinions, had a great part in persuading them; but although he wanted James to succeed, he was for limiting the constitutional powers of a Catholic monarch. In the third parliament, which met in Oxford away from the London populace, Charles even offered a regency of Mary or Anne on lines suggested by Halifax; but the Commons thought this was a mere trap and they refused. Charles took them by surprise and dissolved the parliament.

He was able to do this because he had fallen back on his secret dependence on France. For the remaining four years of his reign he governed, like his father, without a parliament. Good trade and French subsidies relieved him of any need to extort money from unwilling subjects. And he pressed his advantage home. Shaftesbury was accused of high treason, but the London grand jury set him free. He fled to Holland and died. Monmouth, arrested and released on bail after foolishly disturbing the peace, compromised himself with some plebeian but reckless plotters. When they were arrested he went into hiding; but the government struck hard not only at the plotters but at the whig leaders. Lord Russell and Algernon Sidney, though not conspirators, were executed, the one for refusing to deny and the other merely for believing that there are cases in which it is right to resist the powers that be. Titus Oates was brutally punished, but left alive. The Crown lawyers set to work to undermine the municipal liberties on which whig juries and many whig borough members of parliament depended. Boroughs were deprived of their charters and received others which left no loopholes for admitting malcontents. The City of London was brought to heel like the rest, and not only the City itself but its constituent guilds. The authoritarians did not limit their attentions to the political world. They distrusted all corporations as independent centres of opinion; but the church and the universities, where corporate feeling was strong, were firmly on the side of prerogative. There was no opposition left.

Charles II died in 1685. His brother's accession went off smoothly, indeed auspiciously. A parliament was elected and proved more friendly to the Crown than any parliament since the early years of the Restoration. Its loyalty grew all the stronger when the whig refugees made a desperate appeal to force. Argyle appeared in his own country and failed to raise it against the king. Monmouth landed at Lyme Regis with about 150 followers. Something like 4,000 ill-armed and untrained rebels gathered round him in the west country. The militia was not equal to the situation, but made itself useful when the regulars took charge. The whole affair was over in six months. Besides those who were killed in action about 150 rebels suffered death after trial and about 800 were sent as slaves to the plantations.

James himself provoked opposition. He continued the policy of friendship with France and dismissed Halifax, his only anti-French minister. In the same month Louis XIV revoked the Edict of Nantes, the only guarantee of toleration for the Huguenots. When parliament reassembled after the defeat and execution of Monmouth, James asked it for three things, more money, 'a well-disciplined standing force . . . to guard against all disturbances from without and from within', and freedom to give any office, military or civil, to a Roman Catholic. He might have been given a reform of the militia as an alternative to a standing army and he might have been given an Act of parliament opening certain offices to non-Anglicans. Rather than compromise he did without a money grant. He prorogued parliament and then dissolved it. He never met a parliament again.

An army of 16,000 or so camped on Hounslow Heath for summer training in each year from 1685 to 1688. Ten out of twelve judges decided in a test case that it was lawful for the king to give Catholics dispensations to hold military commissions. The Tower of London, and the chief commands of the army in Ireland and of the fleet were all entrusted to Catholics. Others sat at the treasury board and in the privy council. The purging of corporations went forward. The Inns of Court were pressed to admit Catholics. In Cambridge the vice-chancellor refused to admit a Benedictine monk to a degree and was deprived of his offices. In Oxford the Catholics gained a foothold; but Magdalen College refused James's nominee as president and the king expelled twenty-five of the fellows. At first he hoped for support from the Protestant dissenters, and he had some supporters among them, including the Quaker William Penn, the founder of Pennsylvania; but most of them held back in alarm. In the spring of 1688 the king's chances of success were improved by an event which almost everyone had assumed to be impossible: the queen was with child. James took the final step in reverting to the programme of 1672: he issued a Declaration of Indulgence.

Now was the time for the Church of England to act on its doctrine of passive obedience. An order in council commanded that the Declaration should be read out in all the churches. The archbishop of Canterbury and six of his brethren politely declined to do their part. The king had them charged with seditious libel, committed to the Tower, and arraigned in the court of the king's bench. The jury aquitted them, but this, though of great moral effect, was unlikely to stop the drift towards toleration. Lay opposition was unorganized, so armed intervention from abroad seemed the best chance to those who feared a Catholic recovery. William of Orange was no believer in limited monarchy. As the principal servant of the Dutch republic he knew the advantages of a republican constitution, but he judged that in monarchies, and particularly in Britain, the king should have 'the necessary powers'. But he made no secret of it that he was against James's policy of removing the religious tests. The birth of an heir apparent reduced almost to nothing his prospect of taking a leading part in British affairs. A few days after it William received an invitation secretly sent over to him by

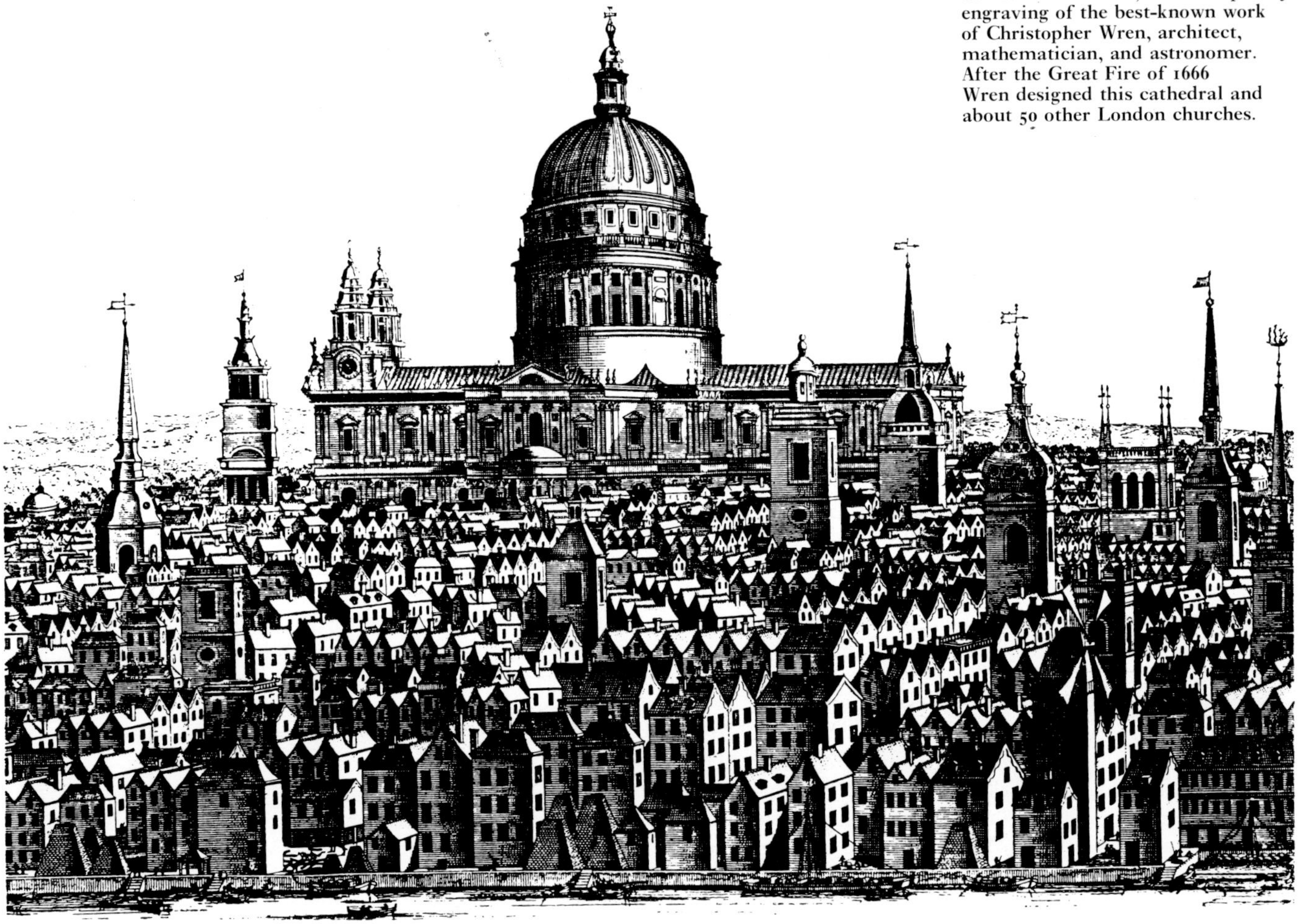

St Paul's Cathedral; a contemporary engraving of the best-known work of Christopher Wren, architect, mathematician, and astronomer. After the Great Fire of 1666 Wren designed this cathedral and about 50 other London churches.

seven men. One was Danby; others were the suspended bishop of London, Compton, and five great members of the nobility. They offered to attend William, that is to join him in rebellion, if he could arrive with a sufficient force before the end of the year.

With his own unequalled energy and ability William collected an army of Germans, Dutch, Swedes, Swiss, and French Huguenots, persuaded the Dutch republic to support him, and allayed the suspicions of the Catholic opponents of Louis. Four months after receiving the invitation, he landed in Torbay at the head of the largest disciplined force that ever invaded England, about 11,000 foot and 4,000 horse. The English fleet, which in any case was full of disaffection, missed its chances of intercepting him. King James's army far outnumbered his: it was the largest concentration of trained regular troops that had ever stood on English soil; but its morale was patchy; some of its best commanders deserted, and it never came into action. By Christmas the king and the infant prince were in France, and William was provisionally in charge of the government.

This revolution was almost bloodless; in London and elsewhere disorders broke out but they were easily repressed. There was an end to the hesitations and uncertainties about foreign policy which had lasted since the Dutch wars. Louis declared war on the Dutch in November, but he regarded his guest James II as king, so the two countries were not legally at war until William and Mary as king and queen declared war in May 1689. In fact the war was an inseparable concomitant of the revolution. This was the beginning of the system of European relations to which, with only one major interruption, Britain remained committed for the next sixty years. She fought a succession of wars against France, five in all, with various continental allies of whom the Dutch and the emperors were the most constant.

The wars, and most of all the Nine Years War of William III, dictated the main lines of the new constitutional settlement. They imposed moderation. When there was a political dispute, neither side pushed it to the length of endangering defence. When William and Mary came to the throne they assented to the Bill of Rights, which condemned as illegal the most disputed pretensions of James II. It condemned outright his claim to suspend laws, and it condemned dispensations to exempt individuals from obedience to particular laws, except such as were authorized by Act of parliament. It left the remedying of many other grievances to the ordinary process of legislation.

One of the most conspicuous, the lack of fairness and system in the parliamentary franchise and in the distribution of parliamentary seats, was left alone for nearly a century as too hot to touch. Some were pressed by the whigs. They introduced Bills, for instance, to revive that provision of the Triennial Act of Charles which limited the duration of any parliament to three years. One of them passed both houses, but the king refused his assent. Rather than lose the services of the whigs he gave way and accepted a later Bill. Altogether he used his veto three times, and his relations with parliament were seldom smooth or tidily adjusted; but the mere fact of the war did away with two of the largest openings for conflict. Every year much urgent business had to be done in parliament, especially the voting of large sums of money. Annual meetings of parliament were an unquestioned necessity, and the volume of parliamentary business has remained so high ever since that they have never been interrupted. The other great field of disagreement was the army. The Bill of Rights declared that the keeping of a standing army in time of peace was illegal. There was no historical justification for this, and when peace did come it led to difficulties; but peace was exceptional for many years, and the military machine stood firm. James II had tried to overawe London with his camp at Hounslow Heath. In 1694, when the state of the war was critical, William III encouraged the loyal citizens with a strong force in Hyde Park. The militia, 'the constitutional force', was neglected, but neither the country levies nor the London train-bands were quite without responsibilities.

The final touches were given to the constitutional settlement by the Act of Settlement of 1701. This provided for the future succession of Protestant heirs to the throne, and 'the better securing of the rights and liberties of the subject'. It had an abortive clause which was meant to do away with the system which had gradually become established, of government by a committee or 'cabinet', by putting the main control of business back into the hands of the privy council. Two other clauses did become permanent law. The judges were to be removable by the Crown only upon an address by both houses of parliament. The King's Pardon could not be granted after an impeachment by the Commons. The defence of the constitution against arbitrary government no longer depended on new Acts of parliament, but increasingly on the mutual dependence of the executive and the legislature. There were still to be a few impeachments; but impeachment was a slow and uncertain process. In the future ministers stood or fell when they could or could not command majorities in the House of Commons. They became parliamentary leaders, and they were beginning to lead parliament by forming and combining parties.

The means of doing this were still tentative. Several times in William's reign parliamentary committees undertook administrative duties for which experience showed them to be ill fitted. Another abortive clause of the Act of Settlement excluded all holders of paid offices under the Crown from sitting in the Commons. Many of the politicians could be broadly classified as whigs or tories. In forming his cabinets William had to take into account which of these types, or which of a good many sub-types, they belonged to; but what he mainly had to consider was their usefulness in their several offices: as yet there was only a vague notion of ministerial unanimity. The ultimate solutions of these questions were influenced by two tendencies in the management of business. First, mainly in consequence of the demands of the war, the scale of administration increased. The existing departments employed more men in every grade, and new departments grew up beside them. Secondly in some departments there were great reforms. This was specially true in finance. Taxation became more efficient; permanent long-term public borrowing was established; the Bank of England was founded, and financial technique was modernized. The reformed administration needed able men, and found them.

There was a liberating growth of tolerance. The Protestant Nonconformists were rewarded for their support of the Revolution by the Toleration Act of 1690 which gave them freedom to worship so long as they did not meet behind locked doors. It is true that there were new penal laws against Roman Catholics, including one in 1700 by which their priests were made liable to life imprisonment for saying Mass; but this was a dead letter. Within a short time prejudice against them declined and the law was interpreted favourably to them, so that, although their disadvantages were irksome, they could profess their faith openly. The law against blasphemy was sharpened and threatened the growing tendency among Protestants towards unitarianism; but in practice this too had little effect. The nonjurors, the small minority of Church of England clergy whose consciences forbade them to take oaths to William and Mary, were deprived of their offices but left in peace. In 1695, when the Act for licensing printed books and papers expired, after discussion, it was allowed to lapse.

In this last discussion John Locke gave advice to some of the politicians on the liberal side. His writings, which had helped to prepare people's minds for the new settlement, came to be so widely accepted that, having begun as the creed of the party, they became almost a national orthodoxy. In the century after his death in 1704 Locke had more influence abroad, notably in France and America, than any previous English political writer, and he owed this influence to the national experience of which he was the interpreter. He also wrote in a comparatively timeless way about philosophy and a variety of other subjects, including education; but in politics and to some extent in theology, his ideas were of and for his times. Although he had a retiring nature and a preference for anonymity, he touched the active world at many points. His father was a lawyer who served as a cavalry captain on the parliamentary side in the Civil War. He himself was educated as a physician, and in that capacity became acquainted with Shaftesbury, whom he came to serve as secretary and adviser. After Shaftesbury's fall he went into exile in Holland, where he came into contact with venturesome liberal thought. In England after the Revolution he had official employment in connection with trade and 'plantations', and other public business. He taught that the purpose of government was the preservation of liberty and property, and that this purpose could not be fulfilled under absolute monarchy, but only if there were a legislature with supreme power to make laws, and

The musician Henry Purcell, whose death at the age of 36 in 1695 was a misfortune for native English music. Purcell composed much church music, some of it in traditional English style, but some in the light French style enjoyed by Charles II. His work, which was sometimes spirited and sometimes of a gentle delicacy, is believed to have influenced Handel.

BELOW Sir Isaac Newton, best-known of the scientists who enlivened the reign of Charles II. Newton showed that white light could be divided into a spectrum of colours, he developed a theory of gravitation, and was co-inventor of the calculus which enabled natural forces to be studied quantitively. For 24 years he was president of the Royal Society, the forum of experimentalists chartered by Charles in 1662.

RIGHT The Battle of the Boyne. Not for the first time, the Irish Catholics marched under the Stuart banner to defeat. King William's victory not only spoiled James II's attempt to regain his throne; it provided a taunting battlecry for the Irish Protestants in their centuries-long conflict with the Catholics.

an executive, distinct from it, entrusted with a power to act for certain definite purposes. If the executive subverted the whole legal structure, it forfeited the right to obedience, and revolution was the ultimate guarantee of legality. This reasoning provided a theoretical basis for renewing political co-operation through representative institutions.

Locke was one of the writers who brought the scientific movement into association with the humanities and with practical affairs. That movement had been checked by the Civil War. William Harvey's discovery of the circulation of the blood had made him the most famous of English experimentalists. His accumulated scientific notes disappeared when the parliamentary troops took over the palace of Whitehall, where, as a royal physician, he had quarters. William Gascoigne, the inventor of the screw micrometer, was killed on the royalist side at Marston Moor. But as soon as London and Oxford settled down, scientists began to gather for experiments and discussion. Two years after his restoration King Charles II granted a charter to the Royal Society and so became the figure-head of the movement in England. The activity continued into the eighteenth century in almost every branch of natural science. Newton earned an even greater fame than Locke. In his lifetime his discoveries in mathematics and optics were more admired than his law of gravitation and its application to the solar system. Even Newton became a man of affairs: he was master of the Mint and sat in parliament. The typical man of large affairs who threw off germinal ideas in the sciences was Sir William Petty. As a young man he taught anatomy in Oxford, and he coined the phrase 'political anatomy'. Another of his phrases, 'political arithmetic' became the regular name for statistics, and remained current for more than a century. Except in commercial calculations statesmen and economists made little use of it for some time to come; but a beginning was made in vital statistics, and various kinds of insurance were brought into relation with a reliable actuarial framework.

The scientific movement, which inspired changes in technology and ideas, was fully international, but it was influenced, favourably or adversely, by the rivalries of states. In the economic history of Europe there is a great turning-point somewhere about the middle of the seventeenth century. Until then there had been all-round expansion and inflation, of which one aspect was that prices rose, another that distant lands were explored and colonized, a third that capitalism spread through industry and commerce. That phase ended. The rise in the level of prices was halted or reversed. No new lands were discovered. Instead of exploring, the trading powers fought one another for the overseas possessions which they had already acquired. States consolidated their political and economic power behind the ramparts of protective tariffs. But much of this was less true of Britain than of the continental states. Here the rise in prices slowed down but, at a more moderate pace, it continued. Once the civil disturbances were over, overseas expansion began again and gathered force. There were still anomalies which hampered development; but in many departments of life the island now had individual characteristics which gave it a new standing in the world, and one especially. It had created a constitutional monarchy. Britain was the only country in the world where an elected assembly shared the work of government with a king, in accordance with mutually acceptable principles of co-operation.

At first the immense value of this invention was not appreciated either at home or abroad. The unconcealed virulence of party feeling seemed to amount to a continuation of civil strife, and the prospects in Ireland and Scotland seemed even less happy. In both countries the new regime had been established by force. In Scotland the Stuart reaction had been more successful than in England. In 1679, the year after the Popish Plot, the Covenanters of south-west Scotland started demonstrations which grew into an unplanned rising. Loyal Scottish militia under Monmouth put them down; but they were treated with comparative clemency. Lauderdale dropped out. The duke of York, prudently withdrawing from England, took up residence as the king's representative in Scotland, where he procured two Acts of parliament which ensured his unopposed succession to the throne. He could not indeed either crush or conciliate the resistance of the religious extremists; but when Argyll landed in the west Highlands with about 300 followers, his rebellion failed even more miserably than Monmouth's in England. In Scotland James, as king, almost succeeded in his policy of tolerating both Catholics and dissident Protestants; but when the crisis came in England he had to summon his troops southwards and leave Scotland to shift for itself. The main lines of a settlement for Scotland were worked out in London, and accepted by a convention in Edinburgh. Unlike the English Declaration, the Claim of Right roundly declared that the estates had a legal right to depose the king. Episcopacy was declared illegal. From 1690 onwards free general assemblies of the Kirk regularly met and gained more authority over Scottish opinion than the unrepresentative parliament. John Graham of Claverhouse, Viscount Dundee, collected an irregular force of Highlanders and at Killiecrankie inflicted a check on the regular troops who marched against him; but it was only a check. For the next twenty-six years the Highlands did not disturb the peace of Scotland.

Relations with England were, however, made more difficult by the Revolution. The Stuarts had many supporters in Scotland. One incident of the repression of Jacobites, the massacre of

thirty-three men, two women, and two children at Glencoe in 1692, was a cruel injustice, and, at least technically, King William had some degree of responsibility for it. Hitherto the Scottish parliament had been amenable to royal control through the lords of the articles; but the Claim of Right did away with this body, and the parliament became a new factor in national affairs. These, especially matters of commerce, inevitably included friction with the southern neighbour.

In Ireland the Revolution was more violent and more decisive. James II gave the command of his army in Ireland to Richard Talbot, earl of Tyrconnel, who later became lord lieutenant and worked whole-heartedly to build up the royal power in Ireland on a Catholic basis. When the king fled to France, Tyrconnel held Ireland for him, while the Protestants proclaimed William and Mary and prepared to defend themselves in the north. After less than three months in France, James landed at Kinsale, intending to make Ireland his stepping-stone for a reconquest of England. He summoned an Irish parliament which was overwhelmingly Catholic, and at once set about legislating away the land settlement of Charles II and the constitutional subordination to England. The patriot parliament sharpened the fears of the Protestants, and accomplished nothing. The fate of its Acts depended on the movements of the two armies. In August 1689 the Catholics, after a siege of 105 days, withdrew from before Londonderry. A mixed army, British and foreign, of 20,000 in nominal strength, landed in the north-east and worked its way southwards. The winter halted operations.

Seven battalions of French troops came to reinforce the Irish and in June 1690 King William came over to take command of his army, which was now strengthened to nearly 40,000 and outnumbered his opponents. His victorious crossing of the Boyne gave him possession of Dublin and ended the Jacobite revolution in Ireland. James retired again to France; but William's generals could not end the war until the surrender of Limerick in the autumn of 1691. The terms were meant to include all the Irish who were still under arms, and to cover all the questions over which they were fighting. The English did not keep the promises which, it is true, were ambiguous, but all Irish Catholics had to accept them and were not in a position to object. Instead, in the course of the next few years, they imposed a code of penal laws, resembling the French laws against the Huguenots, by which the Catholic majority was excluded from public life and from many of the avenues to prosperity and influence. Its freedom of worship was accompanied by restrictive conditions, which, however, were largely ignored. Individuals who had fought against William forfeited their estates, with the result that Protestants now owned three-quarters of the rural land and nine-tenths of the property in the towns. In its immediate purpose of preventing Jacobite or Catholic risings this policy succeeded. Politically Ireland was quiet again for many years. The war was not even followed by guerrilla fighting, for which the country was so well suited. This was due in large measure to the policy which allowed young men to follow the garrison of Limerick into exile and foreign service. But this appearance of tranquillity did not conceal a fundamental weakness in the English ascendancy. The English colonization of Southern Ireland had failed and no attempt was made to push it further. The governing minority could not bridge the gulf which separated it from the subject people and its subject religion.

Thus at the beginning of the eighteenth century England faced four great political uncertainties, in the succession to the throne, the hostility of France, the new relations with Scotland and with Ireland. All these, and the standing problems of economics and domestic government, were to be handled by the new device of constitutional monarchy.

Wars and Politics 1689–1763

1702	William III falls from his horse, fatally. War of the Spanish Succession begins against France.
1704	Admiral Rooke captures Gibraltar. Marlborough defeats the French at Blenheim.
1707	The Act of Union establishes a common legislature for England and Scotland, while preserving Scottish law and worship.
1713	The Treaty of Utrecht (signed 1715) ends the War of the Spanish Succession.
1714	Queen Anne is succeeded by the first Hanoverian, King George I.
1715	The Jacobite rising in Scotland is frustrated.
1716	The Septennial Act establishes seven instead of three years as the maximum interval between parliamentary elections.
1721	Robert Walpole begins his two-decade ministry.
1733	John Kay invents the flying shuttle, which revolutionizes weaving, Jethro Tull publishes *The Horse-Hoing Husbandry*.
1740	War of the Austrian Succession begins, against France and Spain.
1743	King George II leads the British army to victory at Dettingen.
1746	The Jacobite rebellion is defeated at Culloden.
1748	War of the Austrian Succession ends.
1756	Seven Years War begins against France.
1757	The Battle of Plassey leads to the British conquest of Bengal.
1759	Britain's 'Year of Victories' (Quebec, Quiberon Bay, Minden, Lagos), Actor-manager David Garrick celebrates it all with his song 'Heart of Oak'.
1763	Peace of Paris confirms most of Britain's overseas gains, notably in Canada and India.

The Nine Years War of King William III was the first of four which together occupied almost half the years between 1689 and 1763. The second is known as the War of the Spanish Succession (1702–13), the third as the War of the Austrian Succession (1740–8), the fourth as the Seven Years War (1756–63). In their military and naval aspects these wars were very much alike. The armies were much larger than those in former wars; they consisted as before of long-service regular troops. Those of the greater powers were not national armies, but included contingents hired in foreign countries, some of which merely permitted recruiting within their borders, while others, particularly small German states, let out their own forces to hire and so were able to maintain much stronger armies than they could have afforded otherwise. At first the French army was the model which the others imitated, but later the Prussians surpassed it in drill and in battle. Their temporary superiority was typified by what was called the Prussian manœuvre, the method of deploying a marching column into a line facing its front: it is still performed on ceremonial parades. The new large armies came to be organized in divisions, formations of all arms within the army. In armament there were neither major differences between the nations, nor major inventions, and this is true also of the navies. One invention which changed the appearance of the battlefield, and to some extent tactics, was that of the bayonet. The pike was completely superseded by the early eighteenth century.

Sea power was the key to British strategy. The song 'Rule, Britannia!' dates from 1740. The British always had continental allies, whom they supported by sending expeditionary forces to the Low Countries or Germany or further afield. Beginning on a small scale which increased from each war to the next, they also contributed money subsidies. In none of the wars did the French land a force on British soil, and only once, in 1759, did they attempt anything more menacing than a raid. In all the wars, fighting extended to America and Asia. Two of them ended with treaties in which the French ceded some of their overseas possessions.

Until Ireland was conquered, William III could only spare for the Continent about the same military forces as he needed in Ireland. He failed to prevent the French from landing troops in the south-west of Ireland, just as they failed to prevent his army from landing in the north-east. Within a few days of the Battle of the Boyne the French defeated the British and Dutch fleets off Beachy Head; but disease among their crews, always in those days a greater cause of casualties than enemy action, prevented them from following up their victory. In 1692 at Barfleur (also called La Hogue), on the coast of Normandy, the English won the first of the battles which, from time to time, gave them command of the Narrow Seas in their French wars. For the remaining five campaigns the French set out no battle fleets, but did much damage to British commerce. In 1694–5 for the first

PREVIOUS PAGE Queen Anne. Although Anne was not overflowing with talent, her good intentions and a fortunate choice of favourites ensured that her reign (1702–1714) was marked by achievement: the Union with Scotland, the victories of her favourite Marlborough, while Vanbrugh was building great country houses, and literature was being enriched by the work of Swift, Defoe, Pope and Addison.

time a British fleet wintered in the Mediterranean. On land there was plenty of hard fighting and it was not until 1695 that the British won a success. This was not a battle in the open field, but it was even more significant because it was a success in siege-warfare, the most expensive, the most scientific, and the toughest kind of action. In conjunction with troops from Brandenburg and Bavaria the British invested the great fortress of Namur. After nearly three months it surrendered, the first notable defeat of Louis XIV. The three main belligerents were all impoverished by the war and they made peace in the Treaty of Ryswick in 1697.

This peace lasted only five years; but it must not be imagined that the French and the British were predestined, irreconcilable enemies, or that the statesmen of either nation normally regarded the defeat of the other as an end in itself. In the tangled diplomacy of the succeeding years they were capable of co-operating for common ends, and twice they even fought side by side as allies. At Ryswick, by recognizing William as king, Louis XIV satisfied the primary British purpose in the war. The Dutch, whose security was also aided by that recognition, were granted a reduction in the French tariff on their goods. The emperor's interests were less simple, and he was still at war with the Turks on his eastern frontiers; but for him as for the other powers, peace with France made it easier to cope with the problem of the Spanish Succession.

This problem had its roots far back in the past, and it seemed certain to demand a settlement very soon. The unhappy invalid King Charles II of Spain could not live long, and there was no generally acknowledged heir to his vast possessions in Europe, North Africa, the Caribbean, South America, and the Philippines. Three claims were to be expected, each based on an arguable but disputed chain of legal and genealogical reasoning, one French, the second imperial, and the third Bavarian. The inheritance was so great that reasonable men might agree to avoid war by a partition, and that was the solution which the powers did accept when twelve years of fighting had reduced them to reason. Before the war began Louis XIV and William III agreed in good faith on a Partition Treaty which they were prepared to press on their neighbours. The death of the Bavarian heir frustrated this first plan, but they succeeded in the harder task of devising another. This second agreement too was futile. The Spaniards asserted themselves: they would have no partition. King Charles II bequeathed all his possessions to the French claimant, Louis's grandson, Philip duke of Anjou. If Louis refused this legacy it would fall to the family of his old opponent the emperor, and there was no chance that this would be peacefully accepted by the rest of Europe. After anxious deliberations he accepted.

Even that decision did not precipitate war in the west. Louis, however, was not careful to respect British and Dutch commercial susceptibilities, and when, by a fateful coincidence, the exiled King James II died, Louis publicly addressed the boy his son as his successor. The British and Dutch therefore had to fight again with the same aims as before. William also died, after fighting began on the Continent but before Great Britain was actively engaged. He was succeeded by his sister-in-law Queen Anne, the younger daughter of James II. Her English birth was one of the factors which brought about a gradual weakening of support for the Stuart pretender: another was the national feeling roused by the French war. The process was obscured by bitter party divisions. Until 1710 ministers committed to strong prosecution of the war remained in power, but only by making concessions to the sectional demands of the tories and the whigs. The tories, who cared much for the interests of the Church of England, and comparatively little for continental war, first lost most of their offices and then took control entirely, when, as we shall see, the political aims of the war assumed a new aspect.

To complete their new grand alliance the British and the Dutch had to adopt a new war-aim: the emperor would join only if they supported the claim of his younger son, the archduke Charles, to the Spanish throne. The war ran a very different course from the previous war. The armies and fleets were larger and more expensive; both sides showed greater determination, so that the war lasted longer; the operations were more destructive of life and property; they moved at greater speed and over greater distances. This last change was partly due to the military genius of John Churchill, duke of Marlborough, who never lost a battle and never failed to take a fortress that he besieged. But his victorious armies were the composite forces of a coalition. The imperial general, Prince Eugene, was a commander of the same highest order, and Marlborough was well supported by statesmen and administrators, not to mention the navy. Together they destroyed the predominance of France which had lasted since the humbling of Spain. The victory of Blenheim in 1704 extinguished the ambitions of the French in Germany; that of Ramillies in 1706 swept them out of the Spanish Netherlands. The French were willing to accept these accomplished facts as the basis of a settlement; but the maritime powers were committed to the emperor's war in Spain. There, after deceptive early successes, they were defeated. They obstinately held out for 'no peace without Spain', a policy so costly and so impracticable that Marlborough's support in Britain crumbled away. A new ministry took office in 1710 with the purpose of making peace.

There were no longer any obstacles in the way of partition. The old emperor Leopold had died in 1705; his elder son succeeded him, but in 1711 he also died, to be followed by his brother Charles. No one had supposed that Europe would allow him or any other man to rule in both Vienna and Madrid. The peace of Utrecht, which was embodied in six treaties between the major and minor powers in 1713, was distrusted and resented in many quarters. It was not completed until the last subsidiary treaty was signed in 1715. But it was the most successful and most comprehensive pacification of Europe that had ever been negotiated. Europe still did not form a single system of states; but for the main European system, in which Great Britain's chief interests lay, this peace marks an advanced development of the technique and machinery of diplomacy, and, more than that, of the capacity of statesmen to register and further common purposes by diplomatic means. For nearly thirty years Europe suffered no war on the grand scale.

France no longer supported the Stuart claim to the Crown. She allowed the Dutch to strengthen both their commerce and the artificial system of defence by which they maintained garrisons in advance of their frontiers. Philip was indeed to be king of Spain; but the French and Spaniards undertook that their two crowns should never be united, and they never were. All the other advantages which Great Britain gained were in the sphere of commerce and overseas possessions. English ministers and the business men who gave them advice had never lost sight of the objectives which had seemed desirable in the days of Charles II; but there was no chance of moving towards any of them until the

John Churchill, first Duke of Marlborough. A military commander of great talent, Churchill gained influence not so much by ability as through the friendship of his wife with Anne, princess and later queen, and by his skill in deserting friends at the most opportune moment. He was over 50 when King William made him commander-in-chief. There followed a brilliant career, with several famous victories over the French.

year of Blenheim, when Sir George Rooke captured Gibraltar. The capture was no great matter; but magnificent feats were needed to hold the rock against the combined French and Spanish forces. In 1708 Minorca was taken, and after the war the British held it. Port Mahon, an admirable harbour, was in the best possible position for a naval base within the straits. Besides ceding these places, the Spaniards made what was expected to be a mutually advantageous bargain with Great Britain by selling the right to import 4,800 African slaves within the next thirty years into the Spanish colonies in America. The French surrendered their territorial rights in four not unimportant scenes of recurrent attacks and counter-attacks on the fringe of their American possessions: Hudson Bay and Hudson Straits, for the fur-trade; Newfoundland, for the land establishments of the fishermen; Nova Scotia, a mainland settlement, originally colonized from Scotland, and St. Christopher or St. Kitt's, a West Indian island. In Newfoundland the French retained fishing rights which have been causes of disputes within living memory.

Both in Britain and in France there were local, temporary, and personal reasons which strengthened the inclination to keep the peace. In England there was a change of dynasty. When Queen Anne died in 1714 the Act of Settlement took effect and she was followed by George I, who was a grandson of the Winter Queen and so a great-grandson of James I. He was a Lutheran, in no way personally implicated in anything that had happened in England, unable to read or speak English, but a man of importance in his own right. As elector of Hanover he was the absolute ruler of a not inconsiderable state and a member of the body of nine which

elected the emperors. He was well versed in international affairs and an able military commander. His private life was far from edifying, and several constitutional safeguards had been erected to prevent him from subordinating British to Hanoverian interests. James Stuart, James II's son, the Stuart pretender, landed in Scotland in 1715. In the absence of French support his attempt was a dismal failure: the number of those condemned and executed after it was substantially smaller than after Monmouth's rebellion; but it was obviously advisable to give the new king time to play himself in before risking unnecessary excitements at home or abroad. In France also there was a new king, a child, and the regent had strong interests in maintaining the dynastic arrangements of Utrecht.

Spain was the dissatisfied power. There were other rulers with whom Spain might make common cause, chief among them the emperor. By the Treaties of Utrecht he had received, as an addition to his hereditary dominions, the southern Netherlands, from which the Spaniards had derived nothing but trouble for generations past. This made him not exactly a neighbour of Britain, but the landlord of an important property on the opposite side of the street. When he tried to unbolt the front door, the closed port of Antwerp, his old British and Dutch allies insisted on keeping it shut.

The diplomacy of this peaceful interval in Anglo-French relations was very complicated. It broke down in 1718, when the Spaniards reoccupied their former possession, Sicily; but the French, British, and Dutch coerced them in a brief and economical war. Five years after their failure, the Spaniards tried again, this time in alliance with the emperor. At the end of this second minor war of 1727–9 the Spaniards as a nation gained nothing, though they were placated with the granting of three Italian principalities in reversion to their king's stepson, whom they had made their protégé.

Down to this point the conduct of international affairs may be considered tolerably successful. It was, however, based on a principle and this principle, the Balance of Power, had inherent defects. The Utrecht treaties were supposed to embody it in a comparatively advanced form: power was distributed among all the states, both great and small, in such proportions that, with judicious combinations among themselves, they could meet any aggressor or aggressive combination in sufficient force to deter it from action. But any change of balance called for revised combinations, and every new precautionary combination might be mistaken for a threat.

There was constant and growing friction between the Spaniards and British traders in America. The Utrecht settlement had been beneficial there in many ways, but it was based on pretences. Nominally the British were admitted only to a strictly limited trade; but they expected the Spanish customs officers to connive at unlimited smuggling. The trading elements in London were acquiring greater influence with parliament and the politicians, as commerce grew and as governments concerned themselves more effectively with its growth. By 1738 there was a popular outcry against the Spanish claims and proceedings, which sometimes were undoubtedly arbitrary. The two governments submitted their complaints to a joint commission, whose award fell far short of the British estimates of damage, and left over for future consideration the main questions, the right of search at sea and the boundaries of the new British colony of Georgia. The British government gave way to the outcry, which was now a cry for war, and so the country was drawn by the commercial men who cared nothing for the mainland of Europe into a major continental war in which the Utrecht settlement at last broke down.

This was the war of the Austrian Succession. The main issue at stake was whether the empire and the Austrian dominions should be kept together or broken up on the accession of a woman, Maria Theresa, as the heiress of the emperor Charles VI. France and Spain, this time in alliance, pressed the British hard. In 1743 at the victorious Battle of Dettingen, King George II in his sixtieth year fought gallantly on foot, the last British reigning sovereign to go into battle. In 1745 the British and their German allies lost the Battle of Fontenoy in the Netherlands and the Young Pretender, Charles the grandson of James II, landed in the Hebrides. In a year of romantic vicissitudes he occupied Edinburgh, proclaimed his father as King James VIII of Scotland, and reached Derby with a small and dissolving army. Back in Scotland, his army was defeated in the Highlands at Culloden. His subsequent flight to France meant that the Stuart cause was lost for ever. At sea the navy did more than hold its own. In the treaty which concluded the hostilities the French and British conquests were restored to their former owners, and so nothing was added to the overseas dominions; but in this war the British system of using the national resources for warlike purposes was brought to completion, and the results confirmed the more aggressive of the merchants and politicians in their confidence. The financial reforms which began under William III with the Bank of England, the national debt, and improved taxation had been carried much further. Each war cost more than its predecessor, but the debt which remained could now be carried as a normal part of the economy. It was managed on modern principles, for instance, with a sinking fund for reducing it, and with periodical conversions to lower rates of interest. The stock was no longer held only by the privileged trading companies: members of the general public invested according to their means, and the security appeared so good that foreigners in the friendly countries held considerable and increasing amounts. In spite of losses inflicted by enemy warships and privateers, the merchant marine was greater in tonnage at the end of each war than at the beginning.

In North America and India there were local rivalries with the French which broke out in fighting whether the authorities in London and Versailles wanted it or not. They were far more expensive than the seventeenth-century rivalries with the Dutch, because in America they involved the hundreds of thousands of settlers, while in India the trading companies or their allies could hire armies of indigenous troops. After the war of the Austrian Succession these rivalries went on unabated. The French had to return Madras, their conquest, to Britain; but, by the skilful co-operation of their civil and military officers, they acquired a dominant position among the states of south India. A competent British governor of Fort St. George attacked the French post of Pondicherry unsuccessfully, but in this attempt Robert Clive, a clerk holding a temporary commission as ensign, confirmed his military reputation. In 1757 he was back in the East India Company's army, and distinguishing himself again. Three years later the French government, tired of the financial drain of these operations, recalled its ablest servant, Joseph Dupleix, and peace was made between the French and British companies.

While these events were going on the American conflicts came to a head. Here it was the British who had to restore a conquest in the peace-treaty of 1748: Cape Breton Island, between Newfoundland and Nova Scotia, at the southern entrance to the St. Lawrence river. But the French had ambitious strategic plans for the American colonies. Their governor in Canada built a chain of forts which were intended to link Canada with Louisiana, penning in the thirteen British colonies along the seaboard and leaving the Mississippi basin and the further west open to French expansion. There were collisions on the frontier between French troops and colonial militia, and in 1755 the British government sent out a general with two regiments of troops, and an admiral who was ordered to intercept French reinforcements on their way out.

Once again colonial rivalries culminated in a major war, but, as before, the combination of powers which was necessary to oppose the French could only be brought together by supporting continental allies in their several aims. This time the combination was novel, because the French had succeeded in making friends with their longstanding antagonists, the Austrians. The British system had to be correspondingly adjusted: subsidies went to Prussia instead of Austria. The adjustments fell short of perfection: the Dutch were ceasing to believe that their interests, scattered though they were all over the world, needed to be upheld by great-power politics. They remained neutral. It was in the second year of the Seven Years War (1756–63) that the British eighteenth-century system of war-making reached its highest effectiveness. The conduct of the war had been a matter of parliamentary disputes in which the personalities of half a dozen leading statesmen were mixed up with strategic issues; but in this year William Pitt, afterwards earl of Chatham, took control. As a politician he was passionate and unmanageable; in choosing men he was sometimes, but not always, brilliantly successful; but in his day he was irresistible as an orator. He surpassed all other men in decision, and in the power of inspiring generals, admirals, and the rank and file of the forces and of the nation with the will to win. On the Continent there were alternate victories and defeats for the coalition, and the Russians came in against it; but both sides could have fought on longer. At sea Minorca was lost, and in 1759 the French collected landing-craft in the Channel ports; the British fleet destroyed those at Le Havre. The two French fleets, Mediterranean and Atlantic, tried to unite, but the Toulon fleet was defeated and when the Brest fleet set out alone to escort an invading force, Lord Hawke frustrated it in the Battle of Quiberon Bay. Overseas there were unexampled British victories. In India the surrender of Pondicherry marked the end of French power. In the West Indies

Edinburgh Castle. The birthplace of King James VI of Scotland (James I of England), this castle was successfully defended by its English garrison when the Jacobite rebels were in control of the rest of Edinburgh in 1745.

Guadeloupe was captured. In North America, Cape Breton Island was taken for the second time and then, one after the other, Fort Frontenac on Lake Ontario, Fort Duquesne, on the site which was renamed Pittsburgh, Fort Niagara, and, last of all, the capital of Canada, Quebec.

These were not the only conquests. When it came to negotiating the peace of Paris in 1763 various islands and coastal forts up and down the world were restored to their former owners, Guadeloupe and Minorca among them; but Britain's gains were worth more, from any point of view, than the whole of her previous overseas possessions. The king's possessions now deserved the name of an empire if the earlier seaborne empires of Spain, Portugal, Holland, and France deserved it; but it was a composite assemblage of territories with no central organization. They had in common their allegiance (which in India was the allegiance of a trading company and not of the inhabitants) and their being included in the war or peace that alternated between Great Britain and other states. Economically they were believed or expected, to various degrees and each in its own way, to be profitable to Great Britain.

The navigation laws and the tariff constituted a commercial system, one of the instances of the 'mercantile system' or mercantilism, by which trade was directed into the channels which orthodox opinion considered to be most profitable for the country. The regulations were easily evaded, often inconsistent, and encouraged crimes like smuggling, but they did something to promote seaborne commerce and British manufactures, including shipbuilding. The West Indian islands were regarded as the most profitable colonies, because they provided raw materials which could not be grown at home and absorbed British industrial products. Some of the mainland colonies had industries of their own, such as iron, and steps were taken to prevent them from becoming competitors. In 1750, for instance, there was an Act of parliament which freed colonial pig and bar iron from all duties in Great Britain, but prohibited rolling and slitting, power-driven forging, and steel making. A series of reforms in the customs tariff, mainly carried out by Sir Robert Walpole in the seventeen-twenties, changed its general emphasis: formerly intended to control the balance of payments, it now aimed at protecting industries. Agriculture, by far the largest industry, was protected by the corn-laws, which paid bounties for the export of corn when it was abundant and cheap. In exchange for this favour, landlords had to submit to heavy taxation. The land-tax was the main elastic element in public finance, regularly lowered in peacetime and drastically raised to meet the expenses of war. Economic thinkers were still chiefly occupied in writing for particular interests, such as the East India Company. The available information was so scanty that no one could trace the social effects of individual measures at all exactly. There were differences of opinion as well as of interest: elements of free-trade doctrine made their appearance; but on the whole the business world believed that the combination of colonial wars with protectionist policy was successful.

As it happened some other factors contributed to a rise in prosperity which seems to have reached a peak, at least so far as it was symbolized by high real wages, before the Seven Years War. None of them were entirely disconnected with the international economic relations, but they had also separate sources of their own. In the seventeenth century England was the most populous area in Europe within which trade was not obstructed by tariffs or other artificial barriers. All through that century there were statesmen who saw that both countries would benefit economically if Scotland could come into this market. The dynastic union in the time of James I brought a common citizenship. It enabled Scotsmen to buy land in England and vice versa. But English conservatism, then and thereafter, except during the short-lived and unstable union under the Protectorate, blocked all attempts at removing the remaining barriers. During the war of the Spanish succession the political inconvenience of separateness became intolerable to the English. They saw, however, that, if they left the Scots in possession of the two inheritances which they valued most highly, their own church and their own law, it would be possible to set up a common legislature. This was the principle of the Act of Union of 1707, by no means a flawless document, but in the circumstances of the time a triumph of common sense and mutual concession. The English were content to reduce the Jacobite danger, and the temptations which the French could dangle before the Scots: they did not anticipate that by admitting the Scots on equal terms to their home trade and their colonial trade, they would strengthen their own economy. In the belt of land between Edinburgh and Glasgow manufactures, including linen, soap and sugar-refining, grew up. The population rapidly increased. Glasgow became a great port for the Atlantic trade. The flow of Scotsmen into England brought fresh brains and energies where they were needed. Hundreds of graduates who came south from the new and soon famous medical school of Edinburgh were the most valuable among a host of workers. At the same time the Scottish officers and regiments, including from Pitt's day Highland regiments, were winning their fame in the British army.

The union with Scotland was the greatest among many movements which unified the island and bound it together in social and economic co-operation. Religious toleration on the whole had this effect. The Nonconformists, being excluded from public life, applied their abilities to private business and a good many of them became powerful in it. Churchmen ceased to regard them as dangerous, and as the old controversies subsided they took part in various philanthropic movements, in aid of the poor and the sick and for elementary education. The Jews were still excluded from many opportunities in business, for instance by their inability to take the Christian oaths required by the City companies; but their services to the state went back as far as the Revolution. It must, however, be admitted that in 1745 a government Act of parliament to simplify the procedure for naturalizing Jews caused the first recorded anti-Semitic agitation after the resettlement. The government repealed the Act, and there was nothing more of the same kind for more than a century. The incident was isolated and had no deep significance: it was like the reactionary spasms which now and again interrupted all the other unifying movements.

Essentially these were movements of men's minds, but some of them had a material groundwork. Improvements in transport opened up the provinces to the influence of London, and brought the villages nearer to the towns. From 1663 onwards private entrepreneurs were authorized by Acts of parliament to build turnpike roads, roads with toll-gates. A hundred years later England had constructed its first new road-system since the Romans. After the rebellion of 1745 General Wade planned the roads and bridges which began the opening of the Scottish Highlands. No sooner were the roads there than the coaches came, with a large organization behind them for providing horses. The royal mail coaches, steadily multiplying in numbers, regularly covered their forty or fifty miles a day. They carried not only letters and passengers but books and papers. The first newspaper had started on a French model in the times of Charles II. In 1702 London had the first daily newspaper in the world. By 1714 nine or more provincial towns had their own local journals. Literary journals, with a full range of reviews and articles of intellectual and imaginative content, were read by the educated public throughout the island and beyond it.

These changes were closely related to a social change which ran through all classes, almost a convivial revolution. As a bonus from their long struggles for other freedoms the British peoples had received a capacious freedom of association. The Tudors and the early Stuarts had suspected and repressed attempts to form societies outside the circle of those which openly carried on innocuous activities under the authority of royal charters. Even the ale-house, where many people said what they liked, was a public house and licensed. But from the middle of the seventeenth century, beginning in London, voluntary societies grew up for all kinds of purposes which owed no account to anyone and never attracted the attention of government informers. Freemasonry of the modern type is first heard of in England during the Civil Wars. When the poet Dryden and the essayist Addison flourished, the literary life of London was concentrated in the coffee-houses. The eighteenth century was the golden age of dining-clubs. In 1709–10 there was founded the Gentlemen's Society of Spalding in Lincolnshire, the first of hundreds of societies in which neighbouring squires, clergymen, doctors, lawyers, and others met to exchange civilities and ideas. In the provinces, as well as London, there came to be more specialized societies, including professional voluntary societies, such as those of the medical men, which published scientific periodicals. Later in the century various kinds of less mature societies crystallized in the clubs, with buildings owned and managed by their members, providing centres for the male social life of special bodies, political, social, sporting, or what not.

This is not a mere byway of social history: it is one of the indications of a quality which also helped to form British institutions and to distinguish them, for some generations to come, from those of other countries. The strength of British institutions, we may almost say the most wholesome elements of British public life, came from below. Local interests, local reputations, and local initiative counted for relatively more than in the countries which had centralized administration, trained professional administrators, and effective paternalist intervention in business. The counties were virtually free from day-to-day control except in matters of taxation and the militia. Quarter sessions, the chief administrative authority, consisted of local justices of the peace, now appointed normally for life by the lord chancellor. No small part of the always increasing business of parliament consisted in local Acts. The county feeling which grew out of business, sport, and hospitality, was also active in some of the philanthropic movements. Among these movements one of the most beneficient was the building of new hospitals. It began with Guy's, the Westminster, and the London; but by the middle of the eighteenth century Bristol, York, Winchester, Northampton, Worcester, and Liverpool had hospitals paid for by local funds and managed by local voluntary workers, some of whom were nonconformists.

It would be misleading to suggest that this spontaneous vigour of institutions which touched the common man directly was democratic. The middle class or middle classes, the people between the governing class and the wage-earners, became more numerous, more differentiated, and, generally, more necessary than before. Both the increase in state employments consequent on the wars, and the growth of trade and manufactures had these effects among lawyers, accountants, surveyors, and professional men in general. But so far from acquiring political power or influence they had proportionately less of it in the middle of the eighteenth century than in the middle of the seventeenth. At the earlier date, for whatever reason, the aristocracy had taken a fall in the Civil Wars. Some of its members had parted company with the majority (in itself a failure for the class), but most of them, to the general astonishment, had undergone military defeats, followed by expropriation and political impotence. If their fall is hard to understand it is even harder to explain their recovery. Perhaps it would be nearer the truth to say, not that they recovered but that the main body of the survivors, with the main bulk of their property, were gathered up into a new, stable, governing landed class.

Many independent causes converged to form the eighteenth-century aristocracy. Economic changes favoured the building of great estates. In the late seventeenth and early eighteenth centuries the continued enclosures and associated changes turned England into a country where the greater part of the land was farmed for the purpose of obtaining money returns. Even in the unenclosed parishes over most of the country there was no longer an independent peasantry. The agricultural middle class of farmers were few in numbers, but they owned or rented most of the land, employing wage-labour to cultivate it for the market.

The musician George Handel, one of the many great continental Europeans who practiced their arts in London. Born in Saxony, Handel composed oratorios and operas which could be enjoyed by large audiences. His oratorio *Messiah* is his best-known composition and, just as in his lifetime, is still frequently performed.

The same times were bad for the small landowners of higher social standing. The land-tax pressed heavily on them. They had to pay it in cash which was hard to come by, especially if there was a run of bad harvests when the tax, as in the sixteen-nineties, was at a high wartime level. Land was still the most favoured of all investments, and there were always rich men ready to buy. A great and growing proportion of the larger landowners had other sources of income besides their rents. Some of the proudest of the nobility married their daughters to the sons of City magnates. Some of those magnates themselves bought estates, as their predecessors had done for centuries. The landowners as a whole, with the expert assistance of lawyers but without new legislation, moulded the technicalities of ownership so that an estate could be kept together as a unit through financial adversities which might otherwise have forced them to sell.

In various ways many landowners ceased to be mere countrymen but came into the public view. They and their families had a recognized claim to commands and promotion in the new standing army. The great admirals, enriched by prize-money, joined their company. Young men came back from the grand tour sometimes bringing Italian painters or architects with them. They vied with one another in building palaces in town and country. They were not, strictly speaking, as aristocratic as some of the continental aristocracies: King George I was disappointed with their pedigrees. Few of them were experts in their own private business. The English universities did not pay any attention to social studies as the German universities were beginning to do. But the governing class was secure and self-confident, able to supply the men who were needed for the many public positions of power and responsibility.

There is some reason for thinking that, perhaps as a natural reaction after the troubled times of the seventeenth century, people in many walks of life became more willing to submit to government by their 'betters', to agree that, as Dr. Johnson put it, there is a mutual satisfaction in governing and being governed. Freedom was a national boast, and, as we have seen, everyone was at liberty to do many things which had once been forbidden; but there was a tendency to sharpen privilege and to restrict opportunities. For instance the modern game-laws began in the reign of Charles II and became steadily stricter all through the century. The principle was that only landowners and their guests might shoot game: even yeomen might not do it if they had less than £100 a year. No one has ever pretended that these laws were not hated in England, like the parallel laws in France; but there is little trace of resentment against some other changes which were enacted, if perhaps often evaded. In 1697 the City of London limited the liveries, the governing elements, of its twelve great companies to those with £1,000 and of the inferior companies to those with £500 a year. In 1711 an Act of parliament imposed a qualification on county members of £600 and on borough members of £300 a year in landed property. In 1732 the qualification for justices of the peace was raised from £20 to £100 a year in land.

More than once it was proposed to make the peerage into a closed hereditary caste, or to give special protection to the landed property of peers. The best known of these occasions was Stanhope's Peerage Bill of 1719, which was meant to limit the power of governments to control the House of Lords. It was meant to prevent any repetition of what happened in 1712, when a majority of the peers were against the policy of making peace, but the government overcame it by creating twelve new peers, who turned the balance. The great parliamentarian Sir Robert Walpole, however, persuaded the Commons to throw out this Bill, which would in fact have limited their own powers. The legal relations between the two houses had been settled, mainly by a series of disputes and compromises in the seventeenth century. The Commons had abandoned any claim to act as judges in any matter except the defence of their own privileges. The Lords had not entirely given up any claim to control finance, but in practice they had conceded two points: only the Commons might initiate a money Bill, and, though such a Bill had to pass through the Lords like any other, they might not amend it. A third principle, embodied only in two standing orders made by the Commons themselves in the early eighteenth century, affected the relation of parliament to the country: only the government could introduce money Bills. This made it difficult or impossible for Bills to be promoted to raise taxes or spend public money on behalf of merely local or sectional interests. It meant that parliamentary alliances and hostilities would be more likely to start from national questions and less likely to accentuate geographical divisions. It is characteristic of the time when local and regional differences within Britain had ceased to disturb the course of politics.

Thus Great Britain was the first modern state in which the government had to carry out its tasks with the general consent of a governing class. That class had, as the principal organ for expressing its wishes, an assembly with hundreds of members, meeting regularly for several winter months in each year to review all the activities of the state. It would have been much more difficult if there had been legislation on major constitutional and domestic problems; but the main lines of the Revolution settlement were not challenged, let alone disturbed. The tory government which put through the peace of Utrecht had also passed two Acts against the Nonconformists. The Occasional Conformity Act of 1711 prohibited a simple method of evading the Test Act: mayors and other members of corporations who were chapel-goers had qualified for office by taking the Sacrament, as prescribed in the Act, once a year. The Schism Act of 1711 forbade Nonconformists to keep schools. Early in the reign of George I the whig government very naturally repealed these Acts; but the more cautious among them would not risk provoking extremist opinion by repealing the Test Act itself. They only ventured so far as to relieve nonconformists, under certain conditions, from the penalties for breaking it, giving Roman Catholics no relief at all. Thus the Protestant dissenters built up a considerable and educationally progressive system of schools; but they declined in activity and in numbers.

Generally speaking it was a period of dullness and laxity in social institutions. Pluralism and absenteeism among the clergy, indiscipline among schoolboys, and idleness among their masters were symptoms in their respective spheres of maladies which spread widely. In 1725 the Lord Chancellor was impeached and convicted of accepting bribes and of other malpractices in his office. Although some municipalities and such corporations as the East India Company and the College of Physicians had long practised voting by ballot, the voting both in parliament and in parliamentary elections was open. So, in the elections, was bribery. In the houses of parliament straightforward bribery could effect very little, but there were similar methods of persuasion. In the main the composition of the House of Lords

A label used by the South Sea Company for its commerce. The 'South Sea Bubble' which engulfed this company led to stricter regulation of all joint-stock companies. The so-called Bubble Act made a royal charter – a prerequisite for the formation of a joint-stock company – difficult to obtain. This made uncontrolled speculation less likely, but it also raised difficulties for promising new industries.

was fixed by heredity: the government controlled only the small number of recruits who came in to fill vacancies in the twenty-six bishoprics, or who, by promotion in the law or by acquiring exceptional wealth, became acceptable as recipients of new peerages. But men in power could tempt even the richest peers with higher rank, or with lucrative offices, or, to some men most desirable of all, with participation in power. Out of more than 200 peers, there were usually about fifty who were closely attached to the government by such ties as these. Most of the high ministerial offices were normally held by peers. As late as 1783 there was only one cabinet minister, Pitt, in the House of Commons.

The House of Commons controlled finance, and therefore the business of the state could only be carried on, and the ministers keep their places, if year by year it voted supplies. To compass this required masterly skill and elaborate standing arrangements for managing men. The king, on the advice of his ministers, could dissolve parliament at any time. This meant not only that in the event of extreme disagreement the government could appeal from the Commons to the electorate, but that this possibility might restrain members who were against risking the loss of their seats. Actually no eighteenth-century parliament was prematurely dissolved with this intention. Under the Triennial Act there had to be a general election every three years, which gave the House, even with a normal proportion of members who had sat before, too little time to settle down into a routine of docility. A general election fell due in 1718, soon enough for the government to allege that the country had not recovered sufficiently from the upset of the Jacobite rising in 1715. Accordingly the Septennial Act, which remained in force until 1911, prolonged the maximum duration of a parliament to seven years.

Every government desired to have as many as possible of its supporters elected, and it had enough direct means at its disposal, such as finding seats for civil or military servants of the Crown, and influencing the voters in dockyard towns, to provide normally a reliable nucleus of some 150 members. For carrying on business in ordinary times, when comparatively few members attended, this was very useful; but for a majority in critical times the government depended not merely on its power of convincing argument, but on the support of a sufficient number of the few men who controlled bodies of voters and so of members. The counties had a certain independence. They nearly always elected residents from within their own borders. The franchise was fairly wide: a freehold worth 40*s.* a year was no longer a substantial holding; but the county magnates kept the choice of candidates in their own hands, and were able to influence or to intimidate many of the electors. The counties returned eighty members, and the representatives of the cities and larger towns were not much more numerous. More than 300 sat for small boroughs which, as a Swiss observer wrote in the 1720s, were biased in their elections by money, or promises, or threats. A complex and in parts unsavoury world of borough-owners, borough-mongers, and party managers, of all ranks from peers to aldermen, ensured the ultimate subservience of the machinery of freedom to the aristocracy. No eighteenth-century government ever lost a general election.

Nevertheless the personal composition of the House of Commons was partly a matter of chance. Governments had to make sure that, once elected, it would behave coherently. The first guarantee that it would do so came from the party system. The division into whigs and tories reached a climax of mutual bitterness in the last four years of Queen Anne. The tories made the peace; passed the Occasional Conformity and Schism Acts; and clapped the ablest of the whigs, Sir Robert Walpole, into the Tower. The Queen died; out went the tories and in came the whigs. Some of the tories had compromised themselves with the Pretender; the tories as a parliamentary party were ruined; the party existed chiefly as a frame of mind among some of the country clergy and squires. Some of their leaders were in exile; some discredited either politically or personally or both.

After this violent bout of party strife, the party divisions under the first two Georges seem relatively pointless. All the competitors for office were whigs, agreed on all the main domestic issues. For a few years there was a disagreement of principle between the more warlike and the more pacific wings of the party. The first Lord Stanhope, who had been a general in Spain during the war of the succession there, was the dominant minister during the little war of 1718–20. His ministry fell at the time of the South Sea Bubble, an international financial crisis in which the South Sea Company was involved, and after that there was no division of principle. Walpole stayed in power from 1721 to 1742, steadily on the side of peace at home and abroad. There were many politicians and pamphleteers who attacked him, fairly or unfairly, but in comparison with his earlier days the parliamentary eloquence and even the satire of Dean Swift appeared factious and personal. For all that, to turn a ministry out and fill the vacant places was more constructive than merely to impeach the ministers. Walpole was still in office when the War of the Austrian Succession began; but he was in no way fitted to direct it. The most vigorous personality in the government which took office in 1742 was Lord Carteret, whose interest was concentrated on foreign affairs. Some of his colleagues feared that his diplomatic combinations might commit the country too closely to the interests of continental allies, and many people distrusted, in particular, the influence of the king's private concerns in Hanover. Half way through the war Carteret, by then called Earl Granville, lost office. For the next twelve years, 1744 to 1756, a succession of governments followed in which electoral and parliamentary policy were managed by the duke of Newcastle, a great organizer of voting, and his brother, Henry Pelham, whose capacity lay in the regions where Walpole had been the master. It was under the shelter of this domestic leadership that William Pitt came over from opposition to office, and rose step by step until his great days in the Seven Years War, when he was secretary of state, and Newcastle, unheroic but indispensable, was prime minister.

It was not only governments that operated in the market of parliamentary influence, and, strange to say, it does seem on balance that this competitive wire-pulling, even with its element of corruption, contributed something of value to public life. The good party man has his own kind of loyalty, and he may well be a good and loyal citizen.

The obvious disadvantage of this, as of any party system, was that there had to be outs as well as ins, and so the state lost the services of valuable men for long stretches of years together; but, even in opposition, they assisted parliament in its function of bringing the collective common sense and judgement of the governing class to bear on affairs. Parliamentary proceedings were by no means secret. From 1689 the votes were published daily at a very low price. Reporting of debates was not allowed, and strangers could be excluded from the House of Commons if a single member demanded it. These were survivals from the days, not very distant, when the houses had protected themselves against the pressure of riotous mobs; but they were no longer strictly maintained, and the country in general had a good idea of what went on behind the closed doors. To that extent the government acted in view of a wide public.

By degrees constitutional monarchy grew to be what was afterwards called responsible government. The machinery by which it did so was the cabinet system. Under Queen Anne and for a generation before her time interdepartmental business and general policy had been discussed at regular cabinet meetings, sometimes with the sovereign present and sometimes not. These gatherings were nominally committees of the privy council, and other dignitaries, such as the archbishop of Canterbury, attended more or less regularly with the ministers. A smaller body, an inner cabinet, acting more efficiently, grew in importance. By Walpole's time this cabinet was still a meeting of ministers each of whom was in undisturbed charge of his own office, but it had acquired new characteristics. It worked by unanimity: ministers no longer opposed or criticized one another outside it. The unanimity centred round one minister, usually holding the office of First Lord of the Treasury, which ceased to be a financial office. The cabinet was unanimous in agreeing with his line. The sovereign never attended, and so the prime minister, as he came to be called, presented the sovereign with the collective advice of his servants. This included advice on who these servants were to be. After the first ministry of Queen Anne there was none which could be regarded as freely chosen by the unguided will of the monarch. As we shall see there were occasional departures from this system, and attempts to upset it, but in these main points it has lasted from that day to this.

The purposes of government were still limited to the preservation of justice and public order, the conduct of war and, more remotely and indefinitely, promoting the national prosperity; but to fulfil these purposes the state had to exercise more control over the social structure and over the daily lives of the people. The new constitutional balance proved to be well fitted at least for raising a great revenue, and for spending it on the pay and equipment of armies and navies. In many ways the standards of achievement were still imperfect. Everyday life was disorderly. There were street-fights and duels, elections riots round the hustings, workmen's disorderly assemblies and, at least in London, apprentices' riots. Even in London the police were not equal to their responsibilities, nor the magistrates; the military were often summoned and their action was sometimes insufficient and sometimes too harsh. But there was no rebellion except the two Jacobite risings, neither of which roused popular support in England, and economic depression, when it occurred, never led to organized national or regional protest.

There were some well-intentioned improvements in poor law administration, mainly due to local initiative and embodied in local Acts of parliament. The poor law had no central administration, and the government had no organ which made plans for it or collected more than scraps of information about it or any other social phenomenon. In 1696 Locke wrote a report on the Poor Law for the Board of Trade, emphasizing in the manner of the time the vice and idleness of the poor; but the only means available to the Board for discovering the cost of the poor-rates to the nation was a very defective return made by the parish clergy. Even in 1801, when the Home Office called for information about the acreage under various crops, it applied to the incumbents of parishes. The governing class as a whole was not sufficiently concerned with the state of the legal poor, the recipients of poor relief, to create adequate organs of inquiry. When problems arose from the state of the next higher stratum of the unprivileged it tended to disclaim responsibility. Early in the eighteenth century complaints were heard in parliament against combinations of skilled workmen to raise their wages. Employers asked for the continuance or revival of the old Tudor system by which justices of the peace regulated wages. By the middle of the century parliament began to find industry too complicated for such a simple procedure. An Act on the old model was passed for the woollen industry in 1756; but when the Gloucestershire justices took action under it, the employers protested that in the face of Yorkshire competition they could not pay the rates prescribed. Parliament accepted their argument for freedom of contract, and abolished the fixing of wages by the justices. Harmony between classes seemed to be as well established as constitutional equilibrium.

Change and Stress 1763–1783

1764 John Wilkes is expelled from the House of Commons.
1770 Captain Cook lands in Australia.
1774 Joseph Priestley discovers oxygen.
1776 American Declaration of Independence. Adam Smith publishes his *Wealth of Nations.*
1782 A naval victory over the French at The Saints confirms the British hold in the West Indies. Britain acknowledges American independence.
1783 William Pitt the Younger begins his ministry.

In the year 1776 the thirteen colonies on the mainland of North America unilaterally declared themselves independent, and seven years later Great Britain recognized their independence. Looking back we can all see now that these events opened new chapters in history. The liberated states formed a union which has acquired greater wealth and armaments than have ever before belonged to a single political organism. In English history, however, these events fall into a different perspective. While they were being enacted British opinion was fiercely divided. Some thought of the Americans as rightly fighting for their freedom; others condemned them as rebels; no one doubted that the secession of the thirteen colonies would be a disaster. Within a very short time everyone could see that it had not been disastrous in the sphere where the worst consequences had been expected. Commerce with Britain, so far from diminishing, actually increased when the old mercantile system ended and the new American sovereign states traded as and where they pleased. It is not a mere coincidence that 1776, the year of the Declaration of Independence, was also the year in which Adam Smith, a Scottish professor, published his book *The Wealth of Nations.* It was the first book which raised economics to the status of a major branch of knowledge; its authority was practical as well as academic, and its message was that the nations would grow in wealth if they would release the energies of traders and producers from the restraints of protectionism. As we shall see, the next phase of British economic policy after the American crisis was a successful reduction of trade barriers.

It is even more remarkable that British ill feeling against the seceders died away rapidly. The king, George III, not surprisingly had been most obstinate in resisting their demands; but when the first American diplomatic representative, John Adams, arrived in Britain, the king said that as he had been the last to consent to the separation so he would be the first to meet the friendship of the United States as an independent power. He was actuated only by the same royal courtesy that he showed to his Roman Catholic and Nonconformist subjects at home; but if he had been endowed with foresight he would have had another reason for acting so. The problems which faced the United States in the next eighty years, some of them already dimly visible, were new, enormous, and beyond the capacity of the most far-sighted of European statesmen. If the governments which grappled with them had also been faced by the equally formidable problems of Europe and Asia, their difficulties would have been intolerably multiplied. In a world of sailing ships and horse-transport on land it is unlikely that any constitutional device could have for long bound together self-governing communities on both sides of the Atlantic so as to produce a joint and harmonious policy. Edmund Burke, the most eloquent of the parliamentary sympathizers with the Americans, gave his reason for not proposing a scheme for a representation of the colonies in parliament: 'A

The Scottish economist Adam Smith. *The Wealth of Nations*, Smith's best-known work, was virtually the beginning of the study of economic history and of economics; its explanations of the advantages offered by free enterprise are still quoted. Smith was of fairly humble birth; in Scotland it was easier than in England for bright but impecunious pupils to obtain university scholarships, and be sent to Glasgow University.

great flood stops me in my course . . . I cannot remove the eternal barriers of the creation.'

If this is so there is less profit than might otherwise appear in tracing the exact course of the events which brought it about and still less in apportioning praise and blame among the statesmen who succeeded or failed in directing the course of events. It would be more valuable to estimate the ties which held the colonies to their connection with Great Britain until they had reached such relative maturity. Up to a point, of course, they were similar to the ties which held the Spanish, Portuguese, and French colonies; but there is no exact parallel. The colonists knew that they depended on Britain for military and naval defence against large European forces, but this dependence ceased to seem real when the French lost Canada and gave up their plans for western expansion. There still remained genuine old-fashioned loyalty, so much of it and so steady that, after the surrender, thousands of families opted to remain British subjects and left their homes for a new life in Canada, where their descendants still have the title of United Empire Loyalists. Another sentiment, probably commoner, and in its nature far from uniform in depth and content, was pride and satisfaction in a common inheritance of language, culture and ways of life. Colonial learning, poetry, and journalism had their merits; colonial architecture in town and country was very good; but they had sprung from British arts, with little direct inspiration from elsewhere. The ideas and phraseology of political life were the same on both sides of the ocean, and patriotic feeling in times of war was equally a common possession.

The public business that had to be transacted between Westminster and the colonial capitals grew steadily greater. Most of the colonies maintained able full-time agents to manage it. One of them was the most prominent American of his time, Benjamin Franklin, scientist, author, and politician. Business did not always run smoothly: it seldom does. The first main area of difficulty was economic. The mercantile system was embodied largely in prohibitions and restrictions: the officials and judges who tried to enforce them had to contend not only with unpopularity, but with legal subleties and outright resistance. More impersonal grievances arose in some colonies which failed to maintain a stable currency because of a fluctuating balance of trade; such fluctuations were at least partly the result of British action or inaction. A very large question which became more immediate after the retreat of the French was the treatment of the Indians as the colonial settlements were pushed forward into their hunting-grounds. Many influential Americans, including Benjamin Franklin, were personally interested in developing land beyond the eastern mountains; but British politicians and officials tended to require irksome guarantees for fair treatment of those who sold their immemorial rights in the land. Then, in addition to the specific grievances, there was a proneness to take offence. The British parliament tended to assert itself in American, as in all other, affairs. At the same time, and for similar reasons, the colonial legislatures did the same. They contended with the executive and the judicature much as the British parliament did; but for the colonies the higher executive and judicature were in London. In the legislative assemblies a school of eloquence flourished in which pugnacity was a short cut to applause. The structure of discontent varied with the varieties of social system from the predominantly middle-class colonies in the north to the southern colonies which were aristocratic. In the seaports highly respectable merchants and professional men had means of inciting mobs to riot and destroy. This sounds ugly, but it was much the same in London and Amsterdam. This social phenomenon had been of less account in Walpole's London than in Pym's; but it seems to have come to the fore again in London about the time when it began to give concern in Boston.

Although there was friction there was no separatism or American nationalism before 1775. From the British point of view this was unfortunate. If there had been an articulate party demanding independence, conservative elements would have drawn together to oppose it, and at the same time British statesmen would have tried not to play into its hands. As it was they assumed that the American opposition was rational and practical, and that in the last resort excesses there could be put down as they could in Britain. So they stumbled forward, alternately making and withdrawing demands, the more liberal among them resisting coercion and the less liberal resisting concession.

In 1765 they had to deal with a particular problem which seemed to have ascertainable limits of pounds, shillings, and pence. The Seven Years War had been victorious for the Americans and for them the gains were near at home. They had done their share of fighting, and the British exchequer had contributed, not ungenerously, to their expenses. For Great Britain, however, this war, again more expensive than the last, had added so much to the national debt that the country needed some new source of revenue. Hitherto the Americans had never contributed anything to the overhead expenses of their local wars, the services of the navy in keeping the seas open, and the services of the armies on the European continent. It seemed reasonable that they should do so, and it seemed inoffensive to pass an Act of parliament in 1765 extending to America the familiar system of stamp-duties, which the British had copied from the Dutch. Certain classes of legal documents were not to be valid unless they bore inexpensive stamps bought from the government. This was the first tax other than customs duties ever imposed on the colonies by Great Britain. It was greeted with arguments that it was illegal and with perorations about Brutus and Cromwell, also with riots. There was a change of government in Britain, and the new liberally minded ministry of Rockingham repealed the Act in 1766. They also passed a Declaratory Act, affirming that the British parliament had the right to tax America. The Americans did not demand the repeal of this Act, nor did the British ever take any action under it.

For three years they tried to raise new revenue by the old system of import duties, only to be met by determined opposition both in America and in England. In 1770 they repealed all the new duties except that on tea. The East India Company needed urgently at that time to dispose of surplus tea in the American market, and, by a special arrangement, the price to the Americans, even with the tax, was to be attractively low. Without either constitutional or economic justification the importation of tea was resented as a symbol of British oppression. In Boston rioters emptied chests of tea into the harbour. The British chose this moment to begin coercion. They closed the port of Boston to all imports; they suspended the constitution of Massachusetts. They made legal provisions for military government there, and they increased their forces in the vicinity.

The rest of the colonies rallied to the support of Massachusetts. In 1774 the first American Congress met in Philadelphia, a revolutionary assembly, but the predecessor of the present legislature. Fighting began in the next year. The Americans still kept in mind the possibility of some sort of agreed settlement, and the British still thought that the Americans might return to a modified allegiance. Every armed encounter necessarily deducted something from these hopes. At first this civil war was on a small scale. Both sides had successes and reverses; but, when the Declaration of Independence followed, the British had greater resources, better troops, and a larger number of seasoned officers. They commanded the sea, and they had good bases at Halifax in Nova Scotia, and New York. When hostilities began they had 28 warships and 4,000 men in North American ports. The expense of supplying these forces and a land army at a distance of thousands of miles from their home bases was of the same order of magnitude as European war; but in the long run the British could have counted on winning the war if they had not made one huge miscalculation. In 1778 France made an alliance with the Americans.

The war which followed was entirely unlike the four preceding French wars. Once more, to be sure, the French attempted no invasion; but neither did the British strike against France in Germany or the Low Countries. There was no Grand Alliance; Britain had no allies at all. France had not fully recovered from the last war, especially in her finances. She saw an opportunity of winning back some of her losses without committing herself to unlimited war, and she aimed at a more manageable and defensible empire than the world-wide possessions which she had failed to keep together. American independence for its own sake meant little or nothing to the French statesmen. It appealed to the liberal ways of thinking that were fashionable at that time among French intellectuals. American diplomatists, especially Benjamin Franklin, were popular in France, and French volunteers went across to support the cause; but the ministers would have withdrawn official support in exchange for material concessions by the British to France. A year after the Franco-American alliance the Spaniards declared war on Britain, for quite different reasons of their own. They did not like the prospect of American independence at all. It would put ideas into the heads of their own American subjects, and they did not recognize the American republic until after the war was over. But they attacked Gibraltar and Minorca, with powerful French assistance.

Britain's burden was now so heavy that other powers saw chances of snatching advantages. For more than a generation Russia had been finding her way into the diplomatic affairs of western Europe. The empress Catherine set up as the champion of the northern neutrals whose commerce with France was, as usual, interfered with by the British navy. The Dutch also were neutrals. Politically they were sharply divided between the Anglophil supporters of the stadholder and a liberal, oligarchic, and middle-class element who sympathized with French ideas and supplied the Americans with munitions. This party won the upper hand and, giving way to French and Russian arguments, joined the Armed Neutrality. Great Britain's strength was fully taxed by the American rebellion. She now had to fight two European powers, with a combination of unfriendly states looking on and demanding that she should keep her naval pressure against French commerce within limits which they prescribed.

Great Britain returned blow for blow. She declared war against the Dutch, whose weak and neglected navy was able to sustain only one indecisive encounter. The Dutch merchant marine was still comparable with the British in size. The British rounded up practically the whole of it as prizes. They captured Dutch posts in America and Asia with no effective resistance except here and there from the French. Gibraltar held firm through three years of blockade and siege. In the naval war against the French and Spaniards in the Atlantic and Caribbean the British had reverses and made mistakes, one of which in 1781 led to the surrender of their army which was operating successfully in the southern American colonies. This surrender of 7,000 men under Lord Cornwallis, at Yorktown in Virginia, strengthened the desire for peace in parliament and in the country. Then Minorca fell. Lord North, who had been prime minister for twelve years, went out of office; Rockingham and the whigs came in. Their ministry, however, fell to pieces when Rockingham died within the year, and the peace was made by Lord Shelburne, with whom the others refused to act. Sir George Rodney won the Battle of the Saints, off the West Indian island of Dominica, a victory which at last gained command of the sea, too late to change the course of the negotiations to end the war, but in time to mitigate the losses in which the British had to acquiesce. They acknowledged the independence of the United States. In a mutual restoration of conquests with France, they lost Tobago and conceded further fishing rights in Newfoundland. To Spain they relinquished Minorca and Florida. The treaties, however, also registered some gains. Negapatam, near Madras, was of little value to the Dutch, who gave it up; but the right to navigate in the Moluccas, to which they had held on through their three previous English wars, was still valuable.

The ending of the imperial ambitions which had radiated out from the thirteen colonies did not imply that Great Britain renounced her seaborne empire. For the moment indeed the unprecedented exertions of the war had overstrained her finances, and indeed her whole organism. But, although no one understood it at the moment, the second most important fact of this peace-settlement, in the long run perhaps as important as American independence, was that of all the powers it was France on which the strain had told most heavily.

PUNCH CANDIDATE FOR GUZZLEDOWN

PREVIOUS PAGE Electoral bribery, as depicted by William Hogarth. Hogarth's satirical paintings were sold to the public as engravings. He specialized in series of narrative pictures, showing topical aspects of society, as in his series of parliamentary election pictures. His particular genius lay in portraying the harsh morality of the first half of the 18th century, sharply but with humour.

BELOW The Industrial Revolution bore its most spectacular fruits in the 19th century, but its foundations lay in the previous century. One monument of those preparatory years is the iron bridge at Ironbridge, near Shrewsbury. This was the world's first all-metal bridge, and was completed in 1781. Cheaper iron-smelting, using coke instead of charcoal, made this engineering advance possible.

Some of the ideas and attitudes characteristic of the movement for American independence were not peculiar to America, but also showed themselves in various parts of Europe. Both in Holland and in Ireland, for instance, there were men influenced by the French liberal ideas who called themselves 'patriots', and in both countries, in spite of the extreme differences of social and political institutions, they represented educated middle-class elements who were excluded from some civil rights by ruling oligarchies. The American events encouraged and strengthened them. Some of their proceedings resembled those of the Americans; for instance, first in Ireland and then in Holland, they enrolled corps of armed volunteers. In due course this cosmopolitan wave of unsettlement became a factor in general history. The first European country where it influenced political events was Ireland.

Ireland had probably a population of four millions or so, much greater than that of the thirteen colonies, about double that of Scotland, and about half that of England and Wales. Dublin was a shining capital, and there was fine Georgian architecture both there and in country houses. Most of Ireland's overseas trade was with Britain. Some hundreds of absentee landlords who lived there drew perhaps an eighth of the rent of all Irish land. However detrimental this was to Ireland, they had a direct interest in its economic welfare. The Irish parliament could not legislate except with the approval of the British government, which also appointed the heads of the Irish executive. The British parliament could, and occasionally did, legislate for Ireland, sometimes to keep Irish trade and industries within the bounds of the mercantile system. Pamphlets had been written early in the eighteenth century proving on the principles of Locke that this subjection was unjust. In 1719 the British parliament, by a declaratory Act, affirmed its right to make laws for Ireland. After that the desire of the governing Protestant minority to manage its own affairs expressed itself only in incidents, not in a movement. Whether the country was permanently in a state of economic depression is a controverted point. On the whole it seems that, although there were years of famine, as in 1728–9 and in 1740–1, and also industrial and commercial crises, there were improvements in the home market, and at least periods of relative prosperity.

How and when there began a great rise in the agricultural population it is impossible to say, but it was probably a complication in Irish problems from the middle of the century. From 1771 the linen industry seriously declined. Even before that, the public revenue diminished and the public debt increased. The American war brought these troubles to a head. Trade with the revolted colonies became illegal. In Ireland agitation for 'free trade' began. The British government was by no means ill disposed. In spite of some concessions to the woollen and fishery industries there was great distress. Lord North would gladly have gone further, but the protests of English manufacturers, afraid for their exports, brought him up short. In Ireland therefore non-importation leagues were formed. The Ladies' Association for the Encouragement of the Manufacturers of Ireland resolved: 'We will not wear any article that is not the product or manufacture of this country, and . . . we will not permit the addresses of any of the other sex who are not equally zealous in the cause of their country.' The newly formed volunteers, Protestant, highly respectable, and originally intended as a supplement to the reduced forces available for defence, proved to be equally zealous. The government was faced by a demand for free trade with a threat of force. It gave way and extended to all Irish industry the policy formerly applied to the linen industry, that of bringing it inside the British protective enclosure. The viceroy, the earl of Buckinghamshire, who was a great landowner in Ireland as well as England, wrote 'the satisfaction of Ireland seems final and complete'. He wrote prematurely. There were still uncertainties about whether the new economic system would be permanent; there was a growing feeling, as in Holland, that the Catholics deserved relief from their disabilities. Two concessions were made. The inoperative Act of 1700 which prohibited the celebration of Mass was repealed. Catholics were permitted to hold long leases. But more was demanded and the volunteers declared for legislative independence.

None of the European events of the Seven Years War affected such great masses of people, either immediately or in their remote consequences, as those in India, and after the war Indian affairs became matters of high concern in British politics. The East India Company was one of the oldest and by far the richest of the joint stock companies for overseas commerce. Its monopoly of trade between the British empire and India extended also to the China trade and to south-east Asia. In the seventeenth century the latter had been one of the chief arenas of Anglo-Dutch rivalry, but that episode was closed and in the eighteenth century India proper was the centre of British interest. In theory the constitutional basis of the Company was simple. It was a body of private traders with a charter. Its charters were not perpetual, but were granted for terms of years, and at each successive renewal the government stipulated for an annual payment from the Company's profits. Loans from the Company, as from other trading companies, were a major resource of public finance even after the rise of the Bank of England and of private investment. In return the government promised to protect the Company against the competition of British and foreign interlopers and against oppression or unlawful interference by foreign, whether Indian or European, states.

There the functions of the British government ended. The Company made its own treaties with Indian rulers; but from the beginning these were more than trading bargains. Like the Portuguese and the Dutch before them the British discovered that they could not trade profitably unless they leased permanent 'factories', where they stored their goods to wait for favourable market conditions before they bought or sold. In most places the ruling authorities could not firmly guarantee that a factory would be safe from aggression, and so it was a short step from stocking a factory to fortifying it. In the eighteenth century the Company took another step: from local, passive defence it moved on to maintaining military forces of its own which could ensure the safety of the factories by taking an active part in local wars. The British government did not step in to share the new responsibilities which partook of the nature of government, not of trade. When the Crown took over Bombay as part of the dowry of Catherine of Braganza it failed to derive any benefit from it, and soon handed it over to the Company. The directors recognized before the end of the seventeenth century that the Company was 'in the condition of a sovereign state in India'; but this was only a fleeting mood. By the middle of the eighteenth century its

Charles James Fox. Entering parliament at the age of 19, Fox held office only for brief periods but won a reputation as a leading statesman. As a prominent whig, he supported liberal causes like American independence, the early stages of the French Revolution, and parliamentary reform. But his active participation in the impeachment of Warren Hastings bore the taint of unscrupulous opportunism.

relations with India and Britain were in a state of planless and almost lawless confusion.

About this time the Company reached a peak of prosperity. It chartered twenty ships for each year's trade, the imports and exports each running at about £1,000,000. In India its servants were divided among nearly a score of factories, mostly on the coast, divided into the three presidencies of Bombay, Calcutta, and Madras. Each presidency was an autonomous unit, pursuing its own policy in relation to the Indian rulers. There was no effective control over the British military and civilian administrators. Nearly all of them made the long voyage to India and its unhealthy climate in the hope of enriching themselves, and few kept clear of the temptation to use force and fraud. They engaged in illegal private trade; in financial transactions, official and personal, with traders and rulers they were oppressive lenders and dishonest borrowers. Some made enormous fortunes and came back to England to live ostentatiously and to acquire influence in politics. Perhaps the most conspicuous of them was Pitt's adventurous father, to whom the regent of France paid £135,000 for a diamond which is still among the French state jewels. For these 'nabobs' political activity in England might be a luxury; for the Company, depending as it did on periodical grants of privileges, it was a necessity. The Company had so much patronage at its disposal, so many possibly lucrative jobs to offer, that it could easily make friends among the great, and its influence could be a useful crutch to a politician.

It resulted from the condition of India that the Company added political power there to its trading wealth. When it began its existence the Moslem empire of the Moguls with its capital at Delhi held together, by a wise and tolerant bureaucratic rule, all the provinces from the Hindu Kush to the coast of Coromandel. From the middle of the seventeenth century it was in decline, and after the death of the emperor Aurungzeb in 1707 it fell to pieces. Foreign invaders and rebellious governors fought one another, not merely to set up kingdoms of their own but to conquer without any limit.

In this chaos the Europeans could not keep their footing except as belligerents. Only two European nations were still in a position to do this as principals, the French and the British. The British had two advantages. They had more factories and more trade to start with. They were more consistently supported by their home government, and in particular they drew on better types of men in the subordinate ranks. They were also beginning to acquire a third advantage which made their possessions something different from a string of beachheads along the coast. Their allies ceded territory to them, and instalments of political control. This was most important in Bengal, a fertile province which provided a solid basis of strength. The French were beaten out of the field, as we have seen, but the Company was still involved in Indian rivalries. In 1764, through the faults of its own officers, it found itself at war not only with the nawab of Bengal, originally its puppet, but with a coalition which he had formed to assert independence from all European control. Major Hector Munro, with twenty guns and 7,000 men, of whom 1,500 were Europeans, met them at Buxar in Bihar. In one day he made the Company the paramount power from Calcutta to Delhi and beyond. Clive, who came out as governor of Bengal, made a treaty by which the Company received the *diwani*, the control of revenue and expenditure, in Bengal, Bihar, and Orissa, with the right to maintain an army of British and sepoys. These dazzling advances, accompanied by a boom in the Company's trade, turned the eyes of British statesmen to India.

At that time, in 1767, Pitt, now earl of Chatham, was a member, though not the head, of a weak and ill-assorted cabinet. He saw to the heart of the Indian problem, and proposed that the Company should retain its commercial functions but that all its acquisitions of Indian territory should be taken over by the Crown. This was not such an impossibility as he believed the remote control of America to be. It meant only that the lives and fortunes of a population greater than that of Germany should no longer be at the mercy of a body in no way fitted to govern them, but instead should be the concern of those who represented, even if it was corruptly and incompetently, the honour and the interests of the British nations. The Chancellor of the Exchequer did not see it in that light, and others of Chatham's colleagues were politicians without imagination. The prime minister persuaded them all to agree on a more pedestrian scheme. For two years nothing was to be decided except that the Company was to pay to the exchequer £400,000 a year, and its dividends to the stockholders were to be limited to ten per cent.

The two years ran out and the scene changed. In Bengal there was famine. The military expenses of the Company rose, but its revenue from the *diwani* fell. Its trade needed public assistance. It could not deny that both sides of its administration, commercial and territorial, needed reform. When Lord North came into office he had to cope with ungenerous opponents in parliament, who accused him of wishing to control the Company's patronage for sinister ends, and with others in the Company, who used their exclusive knowledge of Indian affairs to drive a hard bargain with the government; but his Regulating Act of 1773 ensured the solvency of the Company, and began the consolidation of British India. More than that, it began a new era by making Indian affairs a national responsibility of Great Britain. The Company received a loan of £1,400,000 and its tea re-exported from Britain was freed from customs duties. The governor-general of Bengal was to have authority over the governors of Madras and Bombay. He was to be advised by a council with four members besides himself. The first members were chosen by the government. Incoming dispatches were to be communicated to the government. There was to be a supreme court, with a chief justice and three other judges appointed by the Crown. All these constitutional arrangements were to be reviewed in 1780.

The need for revision became urgent before then. After a revival of its trade the Company again fell into financial difficulties. In India fresh wars drained its resources. Personal incompatibilities have always to be reckoned with, but the Regulating Act had not provided against them, so the governor-general and his council neither worked well together nor established satisfactory relations with Madras and Bombay. Two attempts at new legislation were baffled by the same kind of opposition as had obstructed Lord North. In 1783 Burke and Charles James Fox enjoyed a brief period of office along with North, and they piloted a Bill through the Commons which was meant to transfer the powers of the directors, except in purely commercial business, to a new board of seven commissioners in London, with security of tenure for a term of years, and so independent of day-to-day interference by parliament, but not independent of the ministers, who were to appoint its members. The House of Lords threw out this Bill, and the new prime minister, Chatham's son, the younger Pitt, devised a plan in closer conformity with the known preferences and aversions of British politicians. At the first attempt, when he had no assured majority behind him in the House of Commons, it was rejected by 222 votes to 214. A general election gave him command of the House, and his Bill, slightly modified, passed in 1784. Two years later it was supplemented by an Act which gave the governor-general power to override the will of his council. That completed the constitution under which British India was governed until 1858.

Its two principles were autocracy in India and parliamentary oversight at home. The board of control differed from that proposed by Fox and Burke primarily in this, that its president was a parliament-man, a privy councillor, and sometimes a member of the cabinet. Appointments in India were left in the hands of the Company, but subject to veto by the Crown. The office of governor-general at once acquired great dignity. It was held by a succession of noblemen of whom none fell below a high standard of ability and some touched unquestionable greatness. The long history of their wars and their law-making falls outside our subject; we can only notice here that from this point it was controlled by responsible British efforts to carry out what were believed to be public duties.

Each of the two men whose handiwork withstood all the storms and dangers combined heroic virtues with tragic faults. Clive, the soldier, spent only a few years of his short life in India. He cleared the field for constructive statesmanship, but he sometimes used ignoble weapons. Warren Hastings went out to the East only six years after Clive, and he lived in Indian affairs for thirty years. As governor-general, he forged the privileges of the Company into a system of government, for which he needed immense courage and strength of will as well as judgement. He was not insensitive to the damaged splendours of the old Indian civilizations. He did something to promote Oriental studies. But he, too, sometimes dealt unjustly. His career was scrutinized by British politicians, one of whose mixed motives was the rising humanitarian sympathy with the oppressed. Burke and his friends, who had learnt much about India, and some of it from tainted sources, decided to make an example of Hastings, or rather a scapegoat, and in 1788 the House of Commons impeached him on charges of corruption and cruelty. After 145 days of Ciceronian eloquence the Lords acquitted him. To impeach him at all was an error; to drag out the proceedings for seven years was abominable, and so the world in geneal understood it.

In addition to trade and government there was a third point of contact between British and Indian civilization, a growing British concern for the spiritual welfare of the peoples who were coming under British rule. From the late seventeenth century it had been advancing in two directions. On the one hand missionaries went out to make converts. In 1649 the Long Parliament passed an Act for a body which still exists, the New England Company for the Propagation of the Gospel in North America. Other societies for other parts of the world followed after it. They did not employ many evangelists, nor draw on wide classes of subscribers for their funds. Besides the missions, the religious motive gave an impulse to linguistic studies. Oxford became a centre of Oriental learning, which was endowed, among others, by Archbishop Laud. Some students took up Arabic, Persian, and other eastern languages only for the practical purpose of translating into them the Scriptures and other edifying works; but others desired to know the Oriental literatures and religions, and then, as a natural consequence, to study every kind of Asian institution and custom. British missionaries did not go to India as the Roman missionaries came to Britain, carrying with them a civilization which they claimed, and the islanders admitted, to be higher than what was there already. The great scientist Robert Boyle was a devout man and he was also, partly because of his interest in Christian missions, a director of the East India Company. He wrote of the Chinese and Indians as the most civilized nations of the world.

One type of Christianity which had appeared from time to time in many ages and countries was that which paid little or no attention to institutions, whether ecclesiastical or secular, or indeed to the social environment in general, but concentrated its force on the relations of individual men with their God. This spirit was bringing new life into the English Nonconformist tradition in the late eighteenth century and it was in this spirit that the Baptist Missionary Society was founded during the trial of Warren Hastings. Its hero William Carey owed nothing to the governing class or to university learning. He was the son of a village schoolmaster, and before he became a minister of religion he worked as a shoemaker. In his early days in India he supported himself and his wife and family from his earnings as foreman of an indigo factory. He was a born linguist. His grammars and dictionaries and translations represent almost superhuman labours. The government of Bengal cautioned him against the dangers of over-zealous proselytizing. He and his fellow workers withdrew to the Danish settlement at Serampur, a little to the north of Calcutta. He was one of the pioneers of a new kind of contact between civilizations, unrelated to the arts and the

The Bridgewater Canal, opened in 1761. This picture shows the Barton Aqueduct, a celebrated innovation by the canal-builder James Brindley to carry his waterway over a river. The ambitious engineering of this canal, and its commercial effect – it brought coal to Manchester – inspired many other canal projects in the late 18th century.

sciences or to social, economic, or political organization, but addressing itself to the individual soul, of whatever race or station, as an end in itself. It did not occur to anyone to accuse him of spiritual imperialism.

While Britain was wrestling with these problems in America, Ireland, and India it passed through some of the most innovating stages of the Industrial Revolution. The term may be inexact, but it conveys that there were fundamental economic changes, and that, however each of them came to pass, they were all connected together, each being more or less a cause or a consequence of all the others. Whenever they began the way was prepared for them by previous events, and if ever they stopped they prepared the way for what has happened since.

From about the middle of the century the increase of the population of Britain, hitherto moderate, accelerated. Perhaps England and Wales had about six million inhabitants in 1700 and something approaching seven millions in 1780. There was no national census until 1801, so that our knowledge of the facts is imperfect and speculation about the causes is insecure. There appears to have been a fall in the death-rate. One factor which almost certainly favoured this was an improvement in nutrition. The supply of fresh meat increased as winter-feed kept greater numbers of cattle alive. More fruit was eaten, and a greater variety of vegetables. Some of the improvements in medical knowledge and medical services may have helped survival even at this early date: the one obvious example is inoculation against smallpox. There is no reason for thinking that sanitation improved in other ways, and no certainty about the influence of changes in human fertility or in social customs. The difficulty of answering these questions is greater, not less, because a similar growth of population occurred at about the same time not only in many parts of Europe, notably in those parts which most resembled Britain socially and economically, but also in Ireland, China, Java and other very different countries.

The population grew, but the growth was not evenly distributed over the country. On the contrary some of the towns grew quickly, and the industrial districts became more industrialized; but some of the country districts were, to a greater or smaller degree, depopulated. Improved methods of farming spread gradually over the country, and the average yield of crops to the acre increased, as did the average weight of animals destined to become meat and the average weight and quality of the fleeces on the backs of sheep. Larger farms made efficient agriculture commoner. Some of these changes created fresh employment, but as a whole they probably created redundancy. Many rural workers found their way into the growing towns, but there were also other sources on which these towns grew. Small towns and villages, some of which had not been purely agricultural, declined and sent their contingents. The process of urbanization meant that people were concentrated in the places where there was work to do, and where work paid both the employer and the workmen better than it did in the old days when the workers were dispersed. That such places became more numerous and exercised a more powerful attraction resulted from two sets of changes, each closely involved with the other at every point, changes in commerce and changes in industry.

Britain had gathered in more than its share of a great growth in European commerce. That commerce probably more than doubled between the late seventeenth century and the late eighteenth, mainly because of the rising trade with America and Asia. Imports and exports both increased, and that meant more ships and bigger ships. Britain came to have the largest merchant marine in Europe. Shipbuilding increased, and all the ancillary industries for equipping and victualling ships. Inland transport had to keep pace with seagoing transport: the cargoes of exports had to be collected from the farms and workshops all over the country. So Britain's already improving system of roads and waterways became still better. More roads were built; better services of coaches and stage-wagons ran along them; strings of packhorses were becoming scarcer. But only the waterways could shift the bulkier merchandise. The area within a day's haul of navigable water was greatly increased. By this time it included all East Anglia, the Thames valley up to Lechlade, the Trent as far as the Burton breweries, the Derwent to Derby, and the Don to within three miles of Sheffield. Hundreds of thousands of pounds had been spent on these and other rivers, nearly always remuneratively; but more was needed. The next step was to the more costly system of cutting canals. The West Riding woollen manufacture already had its outlets by canal to the Humber when, in 1759, the duke of Bridgewater began a great undertaking which linked his coalmines at Worsley with industrial Manchester six miles away. By the early nineteenth century the whole lowland zone had a close network of waterways. To be on it or near it was an advantage to the traders at both ends of the inland journey, to the producers at one end, and to the shipmasters at the other, and so some seaports, such as those on the estuaries, which were already the larger, gained at the expense of others, and the changes in transport tended to concentrate population in the greater ports.

Other causes had the same concentrating effect. A clothier's costs could be reduced if the weavers who supplied him were all near at hand, not scattered round in the cottage industry of the putting-out system. Early in the eighteenth century there were some large productive units, but only where the nature of the work dictated it. When a big ship was built, scores of men had to work together. There were some mines and some iron-foundries which needed large and compact labour-forces. In the industries which produced goods for the individual consumer there had been attempts to collect workers under one roof, but, in spite of their obvious advantages in saving transport and tightening supervision, they were only sporadic. A new era began when many machines could be driven by a single central force.

The first power-driven factory in Britain was set up in 1719 on an island in the River Soar at Derby. Its business was silk-throwing, the process corresponding to spinning wool or cotton, and the machinery had been invented long before in Italy. The power was water-power. In a very short time British technology pointed the way to new uses for such factories, first in spinning then in weaving, and simultaneously in several subsidiary processes. Textile mills were built by the streams and rivers; but already a new source of power was available. The first steam engine in industry started to pump water from a mine in Staffordshire in 1712. By 1760 there were certainly scores of them at the same kind of work: whether the number was approaching 100 or approaching 200 is not certain. Before the end of the century everyone could see that the steam engines, as improved by James Watt, could be applied to almost any industrial process. They not only made larger factories possible; they were not dependent on the weather as watermills were, and

they could be erected anywhere. Steam accentuated all the tendencies of change, first of all in the textile industries.

The 'factory system' developed in England and the Scottish Lowlands before it took hold on the Continent; but on one very important side it was the product of a European, not merely a British, movement. Scientists had made and were making indispensable contributions to technology, and the new activity of the scientists was part of a revival which also affected continental countries, especially France and Germany. In 1754 the Society for the Encouragement of Arts, Manufactures and Commerce (now usually called the Society of Arts) was founded; but another society, small, wholly private and provincial, was more typical of the period. It could not have existed either much earlier or much later. This was the Lunar Society, a body of men concerned with science and industry in the Midlands, who met once a month, each entertaining the rest in turn at his house. Some were Nonconformists; some had studied at Scottish universities; there were physicians, manufacturers, ministers of religion. There was not a single member of the landed class, and yet there were half a dozen men in this small body who were powerful in their own day and are still famous in ours. Josiah Wedgwood the potter sat down with James Watt and his partner Matthew Boulton, with William Withering, who introduced digitalis into medical use, with Erasmus Darwin, the first eminent member of his family, and with the great Joseph Priestley, physicist, chemist, unorthodox theologian, philosopher, and political scientist.

The ideas which the members of the Lunar Society exchanged at their meetings, applied in their businesses and disseminated about the country, were bold and fruitful; but they belonged to the characteristic rational thought of the eighteenth century and they shared its limitations. In so far as they dealt with the structure and welfare of society they were, like the ideas of Adam Smith, in a sense individualistic. They favoured the liberation of the individual from the hampering restrictions of corporate bodies and from legislative interference with supply and demand. They thought of society as an aggregate of individuals, and Priestley used a phrase which later became a battle-cry, 'the greatest happiness of the greatest number'. They did not include any concept of an organic welfare of society as a whole. This deficiency was normal in Britain at that time. Even in France, where there was a strong, centralized administration, with a tradition of paternalism, individualist ideas were in fashion, and the German states, where state-management was taught in the universities, were remote from industrial progress.

So it came about that the Industrial Revolution in Britain brought about not only the greatest but the least controlled social changes that the country has ever seen. The immense increase of production needed banks in London and in the country, specialized houses for insurance, for buying and selling stocks and shares, and for new kinds of professional services; but the government was not called upon to do more than to lay down broad lines of law within which the promoters and managers had to act. The vast new population concentrated itself in the places where there was a demand for labour. London spread out to the east for the poor and to the west for the rich; but the centre of gravity of Britain changed. The Midlands, Lancashire, Yorkshire, and the north-east became the most urbanized regions of Europe. In South Wales, by 1800, there was a flourishing new industrial belt based on local coal. From the already sparsely populated countryside men came to work in the mining towns, ensuring that up to 1914 Welsh would be the language of Wales's new industrial region. In the Scottish Lowlands, too, there was the beginning of the industrial age. By the end of the century the factory textile industry was developing, James Watt's steam pumping engines were enhancing the prospects of the Scottish mines, and the Carron ironworks had achieved a great technical reputation with their 'carronade' guns for the navy. Britain as a whole underwent cyclical fluctuations of prosperity. Capitalism had multiplied its scale of operation without developing such organs as would have raised it to the full status of an economic system.

The preliminaries and the most active periods of the Industrial Revolution fell within the period of the unchallenged power of the governing class. It might seem that the landed aristocracy were bound to lose in power and even in wealth as the towns grew. It is easy to find examples in the nineteenth century of conservative and rural resistance to industrialization; but in the eighteenth century, and for a few years after it, there was nothing of the kind. For generations the landowners, rank by rank, had made alliances, either by marriage or by business contracts, with the new rich. They had profited from mining under their estates; they had built and managed docks and harbours; as we saw, they now cut canals. At no point did they draw a line and say that it would be beneath their dignity to take up shares in some new kind of venture. Nor did any except a diminishing remnant attempt to ostracize the City man or even the millowner who bought an estate. Some of the classical expressions of snobbishness belong to this period; but the governing class as such neither opposed the greater changes nor attempted to regulate them. Whether for that or for other reasons, although parliament inquired into many of the economic aspects of commerce and industry, governments did not concern themselves with the wider social issues of the time.

It was indeed well known that from time to time discontent among the wage-earners ran dangerously high. The efforts of

An early British railway. Railways (more usually, plateways, using flanged plates) were in use in the 18th century, before the appearance of the steam locomotive. Usually they were used in mining, to take the coal or ore to the nearest wharf. This meant that, as in this picture, the loaded wagons had the advantage of a downhill run and horse power was needed only for hauling back the empties.

The Scottish engineer James Watt. Though not the inventor of the steam engine, and at times so jealous of his patents as to hinder its development by others, Watt's horizontal 'quick-acting' steam engine (bottom) was certainly superior to previous designs, and made the use of steam power commercially more attractive. No longer would steam engines be limited to pumping duties in mines.

public-spirited individuals were spreading knowledge about the misery, bad housing, and bad health of the towns, old and new. The concentration of workpeople in factories made it possible to see what were the hours and conditions of labour, facts which were inaccessible under the domestic system. One example among many will show how some of the men of the new world applied their minds to these questions. Dr. Thomas Percival, a Nonconformist physician, was one of the founders, in 1781, of the Manchester Literary and Philosophical Society, in which he and like-minded men surveyed the social conditions around them, and discussed possible remedies. This led to immediate results in local philanthropy; but it did not yet contribute as it might have done to any national movement. As it happened Manchester was not represented in parliament. There were no government inspectors or administrative officials to bring these matters to the notice of ministers. No existing public authority could survey this field.

In other fields the social conscience was increasingly active. A good many wealthy men had negro servants whom they had bought in one or other slave-market. A private worker, Granville Sharp, promoted one legal action after another to establish the principle, which was finally laid down in a judgement of Lord Mansfield in 1772, that the status of slavery was inadmissible on English soil. This judgement was widely applauded, and there were examples in parliament of a willingness to put things right when they were obviously wrong. In the same year, 1772, an Act abolished the cruel *peine forte et dure* by which accused persons who refused to plead guilty or not guilty were pressed to death. Two years later there came an Act for the registration and

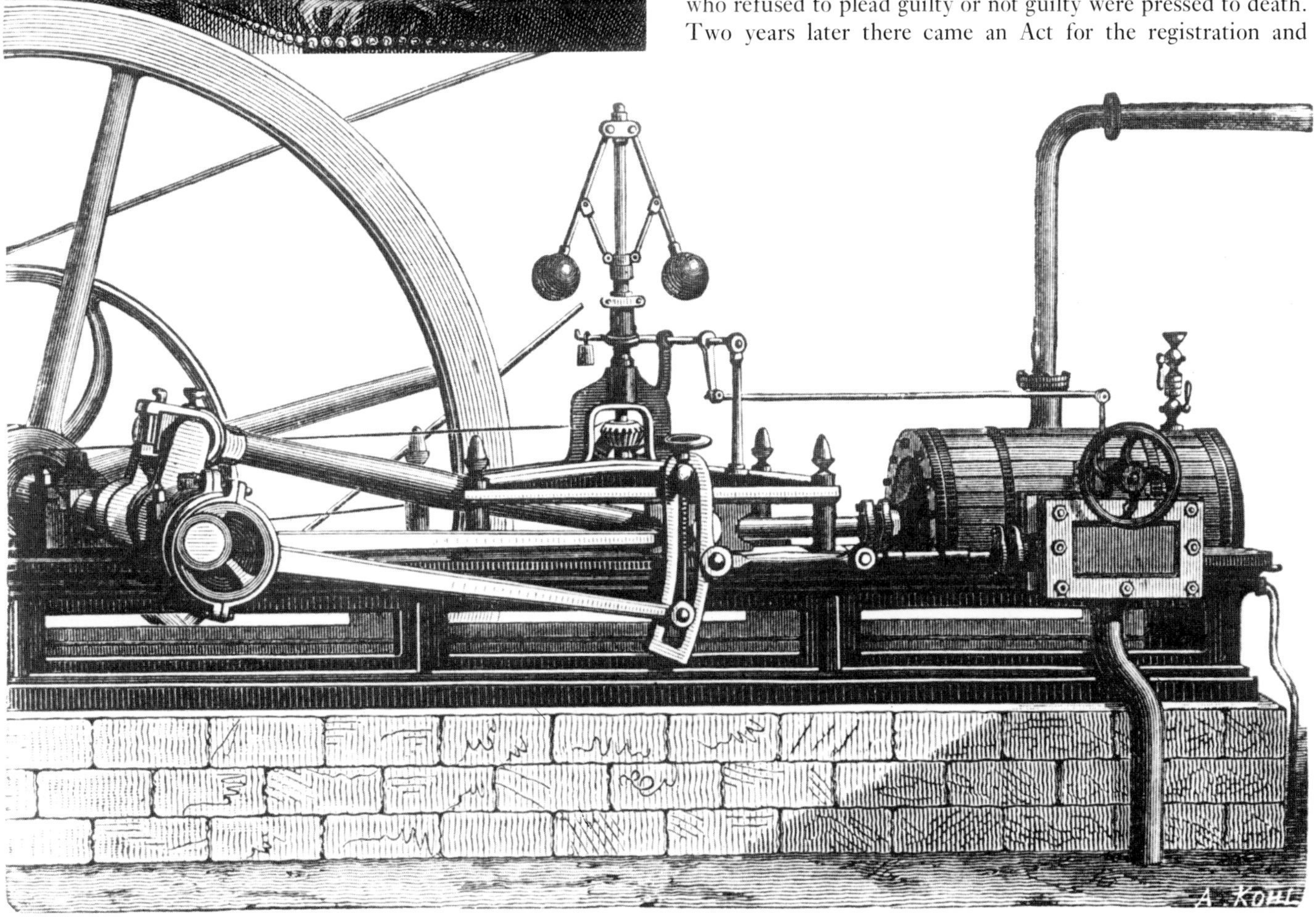

John Wilkes. Like so many who bring about long-needed change, Wilkes was in many ways an unpleasant character, gaining popular support by a carefully-staged and conspicuous defiance of established authority. He played a great part, however, in establishing a relative freedom of the press in Britain. This picture shows him indulging in his favourite occupation, oratory, while on trial before the King's Bench.

inspection of private madhouses, and another to begin the reform of the abuses in prisons, which had been exposed by the researches of John Howard. But the social problems of Manchester and the whole new industrial world remained beyond the horizon of parliamentary vision.

The long reign of George III, from 1760 to 1820, was the classical period of English parliamentary oratory and political intrigue. When he succeeded his grandfather at the age of twenty-two King George was tolerably well educated, but he knew nothing about public affairs. He announced himself to parliament: 'Born and educated in this country, I glory in the name of Briton.' The general public soon came to like him for his clean living, his honesty, and his country ways. He never lost their respect, though its quality changed with time. He suffered from a defect of health which affected his mind, at first briefly and at long intervals but with growing severity until, for the last nine years of his life, with the added affliction of blindness, he was shut away in Windsor Castle. There he underwent the barbarously uncomprehending treatment meted out in those days to the mentally deranged. At his accession nothing of this could be foreseen. The politicians saw him uneasily as a newcomer who took his position seriously. The Seven Years War had passed its most victorious year, and the ministry had to make decisions in the spheres both of the war-leader Pitt and the manipulator of parliaments, the duke of Newcastle. Had enough been spent already or could the money be found for complete victory? Would it be wise to leave Frederick of Prussia to resist the Russian invaders of his country without support? Ought war to be declared on Spain, which seemed about to attack? The cabinet split over Spain, and Pitt resigned. The king had been taking counsel with his intimate friend the earl of Bute, and it was appropriate that constitutionally Bute took public responsibility for his advice by becoming a secretary of state for six months preceding Pitt's resignation. He was an accomplished man, married to an heiress with high political connections and a large income from the coal under her estates. His character and intelligence carried him through as a courtier; but as prime minister he was distrusted by the stage-hardened repertory company of politicians as a Scot and an intruder. War was declared against Spain after all, and the fleet won rich islands from both her and France, but the peace-negotiations of 1763 brought on new controversies at home. Bute could not bear the public and often unfair jibes directed against him, and resigned.

In the next five years there were five ministries. The first two followed the traditional pattern of combinations among the whig families, the chief differences being that the duke of Bedford and his allies were in opposition to the first and joined the second; but the American question came to a head when this second ministry passed the Stamp Act, and so the next men in office were a party with a principle. The prime minister, the marquis of Rockingham, was an estimable figure, but his name is chiefly remembered now for the china-factory set up on one of his Yorkshire estates. His private secretary was Edmund Burke, whom he started on his political career, and who wrote with a wealth of argument that parties with principles, preferably in office, were good for the common interest. Having done his best by repealing the Stamp Act, Rockingham could not keep his cabinet together for the next stage of American policy and he had to go. The next attempt was a combination of able men grouped round the dynamic Pitt, now earl of Chatham; but Chatham fell ill and dropped out of active business. One of the ablest of his colleagues, Charles Townshend, died and the rest quarrelled. Chatham resigned and in 1770 the ministry collapsed; but the instability came to an end, and the next prime minister, Lord North, stayed in office for twelve years.

Although the American question dominated politics, the instability of governments was partly due to events at home. Opposition outside parliament became almost unmanageable. It was directed not simply against this government or that but against whatever government happened to be in power, and it did not spare parliament itself or even the young king. Law and order had never been safe from occasional riots and disturbances; but since the times of Queen Anne and the Septennial Act they had given little cause for alarm. The Riot Act of 1714 laid down rules for the action of magistrates and the use of the military. Governments had been careful not to provoke irritation, and, as long as any Jacobite danger remained, many people had an additional reason for preserving quiet. But the men were still there who could form a mob, and as London spread out their numbers grew. Something had been done to improve the petty justice of London, but nothing to strengthen the police. In spite of occasional prosecutions there was no effective restraint on libel and misrepresentation by journalists and pamphleteers.

It happened that in the seventeen sixties John Wilkes burst into politics. He was still young, a member of parliament, and a militia colonel in Buckinghamshire, witty and completely shameless. He became the most extreme supporter of Pitt and Temple in their campaign against Bute and the peace-terms of 1763. He jeered at Bute and the court in a most objectionable article, and a secretary of state issued a warrant for the arrest of the author and publishers. Wilkes was imprisoned. A judge first ordered his release as a member of parliament entitled to privilege, and later declared that the warrant was illegal because it was general, that is because it did not specify the names of the persons to be arrested. The government had Wilkes dismissed from his colonelcy and expelled by parliament. These were incidents in a furious struggle of more than a year in which the government took several knocks in the law-courts, but deserved them for its high-handed imprudence and lost much of the confidence of its supporters in parliament. Wilkes on his side lost most of his aristocratic backers, and for the time being the government won. By dubious means a fresh prosecution was started against him for reprinting his libel and, to make good measure, for printing another work, not his own, *An Essay on Woman*, which had nothing to do with politics but was obscene. Rather than face the charge he withdrew to Paris and was declared an outlaw. He was deeply in debt and his career appeared to be finished.

While Wilkes was abroad the Stamp Act was passed and repealed. He came back during Chatham's government and immediately went into battle again on all fronts. His outlawry was declared void on technical grounds, but he served a term of imprisonment on the old charge, and a new charge of libel was brought up. Four times he was elected to parliament for the county of Middlesex, and four times the Commons rejected him. The fourth time they declared Colonel Luttrell elected, though he had 296 votes to Wilkes's 1,143. That provided Wilkes with a constitutional case which some politicians and many other people thought worth fighting for: the Commons had flouted the right of the people to choose their own representatives. In 1771 Lord

North's government was in and it gave way on this principle by allowing Wilkes to take his seat.

He was a member for eighteen years and did nothing of importance in the House; but he continued to be a political idol, the first British demagogue. He became an alderman of London and served his year as lord mayor. He appealed to the mob: in 1768–9 there were grave labour troubles in London, and strikers in a dozen trades took him for their hero. When he went to prison a riotous crowd came to release him. Troops fired on them and a spectator was killed. At a by-election for a second member for Middlesex there were fights between rival gangs and a Wilkite was killed. Incident followed incident, with passions rising on both sides; but Wilkes had new allies who helped him to score point after point. After Chatham's resignation the anonymous *Letters of Junius* appeared. No one knows who wrote them, but it was someone who knew politics from the inside and wrote with the skill of a master and with unsparing rancour. He weakened Wilkes's opponents at a time when the lawyers among them were growing uneasy about the government's feud against him.

In the end his victory followed from an encounter in which the City stood up against the Commons. The government, deciding to protect its independence from the populace by enforcing the secrecy of parliamentary debates, caused the Commons to summon the editors of three newspapers which had published reports. One of them refused to appear. The Commons sent a messenger to arrest him and the City authorities had the messenger arrested instead. The lord mayor, with Wilkes, and another alderman who was a member of parliament, were summoned for their insolence. Lord North wisely cheated Wilkes of the opportunity of stating his case, but the other two languished for a month in the Tower. Nothing was altered in the law regarding parliamentary reports; but it was a triumph for Wilkes to have lured the Commons into attacking the ancient stronghold of liberty the City.

Parliament as well as successive governments had in fact behaved tyrannically. The courts of law had more than once put a stop to their measures, but the judicial decisions had not been consistently on the side of freedom. It was Wilkes, and those who, at different times and for different reasons, supported him, who had conjured up a new force in politics. They had no economic policy. They offered no material benefits to the strikers and the unemployed. They demanded inquiries into the past measures against Wilkes and improvements in the legal system. They wanted shorter parliaments, laws against placemen and against Crown influence in parliament, and the redress of grievances all round; but although there were twelve Wilkite members of parliament in 1774 they did very little to further these causes. Their significance is that they created British radicalism. They set it in motion on the political, not economic, rails that it followed during its hundred years or so of effective existence. They built its first organization, with a committee in London, travelling organizers, and subscribers up and down the country. Their society split before long, and if some of its members yielded to temptations from guileful politicians, this also was to become a radical tradition. But, in spite of many interruptions, some of them long, there was now a popular element in the constitution, or rather looming behind it.

The good temper and common sense which enabled Lord North to put the radical agitation to sleep were not his only good qualities. He was intelligent, witty, loyal, and industrious. It was no accident that he held for twelve years the office of prime minister, an office which, as he maintained in the old-fashioned way, did not exist. His great misfortune was that his twelve years saw the beginning and almost the whole course of the American war. An additional misfortune was that the groups of whigs who were out of office opposed his American policy tooth and nail. Entering parliament when he was twenty-two as a protégé of his kinsman the duke of Newcastle, he rose by merit. By 1770 he had seen sixteen years of parliament and eleven of office. The enormous demands of the American troubles strained every part of the constitution, and North had to carry out repairs while the machine was running. He made some improvements in the methods of raising money for the war. In relation to Ireland, as we have seen, he was as liberal as the circumstances of the time allowed him to be.

The opposition chose as their ground for attacking him the plausible untruth that North was the king's instrument for setting up personal rule on the basis of parliamentary corruption. Burke produced abortive plans for limiting the numbers of men in the government's pay (placemen and pensioners) in parliament, and a rising whig lawyer, John Dunning, carried a motion 'that the influence of the Crown has increased, is increasing, and ought to be diminished'. These demonstrations of 1780 had two good sequels. First a commission on public accounts began a thorough survey of all the government offices. Once the facts about all the sinecure offices, unjustifiable pensions, duplications, and negligence were set down in writing, men who wanted economy and efficiency, irrespective of party agreed on particular reforms. And, although they were often extravagant and irresponsible, the criticisms of North's government gave impetus to a more sober demand for reform which was maturing in the country. It was about this time that 'reform' became a household word. An organized movement for financial, administrative, and electoral reform spread through a dozen counties, beginning from Yorkshire, and set up a central organization in London. It attracted politicians as Wilkite radicalism had done, but more of them and of better quality. For the time being it achieved no reforms, but it began the reform movement which carried its objectives half a century later.

Very closely after this beginning a warning came that either delays or false steps in the march of reform might be disastrous. It came as a complete surprise. In 1778, to give the army the benefit of the services of the king's Catholic subjects in England, an Act was easily passed by which recruits were relieved from the duty of making religious declarations. In 1779 the proposal to extend this Act to Scotland sparked off riots there. Extreme Protestants in England formed an association, and a Scotsman in

Newgate burning during th Gordon Riots of 1780. Quite savage, and expressing long-standing discontent, the Gordon Riots were ignited by a proposal, passed by parliament, for improving the position of Roman Catholics. The mob, which seemed likely to take over the whole of London, was dispersed after a few days, thanks to an unexpected and bizarre alliance between the king and John Wilkes.

parliament, Lord George Gordon, became their leader. That he was scarcely sane did not impair his power of rousing no-popery hysteria in London citizens, and then in the mob. For thirteen days London was in chaos. Newgate Prison was thrown open and the prisoners let out; the Catholic chapels of foreign embassies were burnt and then private houses, including that of the Lord Chief Justice, Lord Mansfield. To begin with, the government misunderstood its powers; but it kept its head, and once it grasped that it had a legal right to use troops without pedantic formalities, it acted sternly. Altogether 458 people were killed or wounded, and twenty-one rioters were executed after trial.

The Gordon riots recalled parliament to realities; but North could not remain in office after the worst failures in America and at sea. A new ministry undertook the winding-up of the war. Rockingham was prime minister again, with Burke in minor office and two outstanding men, Lord Shelburne, formerly a follower of Chatham, and Charles James Fox. They did two wise things. One was to carry out some reforms in pensions, the rights of placemen to sit in parliament, and the control of expenditure. The other was to take a step forward in relations with Ireland. The Statute of 1719 was repealed at Westminster and Poyning's Law was repealed in Dublin. The Irish parliament passed a series of protectionist laws and a good many others. For the time being it left the Catholics without the franchise and did not disturb the control of the Irish executive by the British government. Its leader was Henry Grattan, who was always liberal-minded and consistent within these limits; but the constitutional relations of England and Ireland were still in a stage of transition.

Rockingham died before the peace-talks with France and Spain began. His colleagues could have formed a great ministry, but they had lived too much by faction. Burke, the believer in party connections, and Fox, the gambler for freedom, would not serve under the sagacious and wide-minded Shelburne, who made the peace. Shelburne, a great-grandson of Sir William Petty, with a distinguished early record as a regimental officer, was qualified both by experience and by his intellectual powers to be prime minister; but they did not suffer him to hold that office for as much as a year. They even turned him out of office by carrying a resolution against the peace-terms, though they did not reject the terms. Lord North was public-spirited enough to take office with them under the not very congenial duke of Portland, but the only notable event of their few months of power was the failure of Fox's India Bill. It was beaten by the king, who let it be known to the peers that he wanted them to reject it. The Commons voted that there had been a scandalous breach of privilege. The king dismissed the ministry and chose a first lord of the treasury who served him for the next eighteen years.

Nine Years of Peace and Two French Wars 1783–1815

1793	Revolutionary France declares war on Britain.	1804	The first steam railway locomotive makes its successful run in south Wales.
1797	The Royal College of Surgeons is incorporated by royal charter.	1805	Nelson's naval victory off Trafalgar secures Britain from a French invasion.
1798	Nelson wins a decisive victory over the French fleet at the Nile. The Irish rebellion is quelled.	1807	The slave trade is abolished within the British empire. The first national census of the population is taken.
1799	Income tax is introduced.	1808	British troops begin the Peninsular campaign.
1800	Parliamentary union of England and Ireland is established.	1815	Wellington directs the British army to victory over Napoleon at Waterloo. Corn laws are introduced to combat falling grain prices.
1802	Short-lived Peace of Amiens. The steamship *Charlotte Dundas* runs successful trials on the Clyde.		

William Pitt the younger was the strongest man in British public life from 1784 to 1806, nine years of peace and thirteen years of war. He was only out of office for four years towards the end, and even then not powerless. He was a practical realist, with an appetite for facts and a wide view of their significance. When he saw that something needed to be set right in policy or in administration he did his best without hurry or fuss or heroics, but if opposition seemed too strong he waited for a better opportunity. He knew that the general cry for reform was justified by the inefficiency and unfairness of the constitution. He also understood that day by day the Industrial Revolution was creating new problems and altering the balance of interests in the country. Though the first national census, in 1801, one of the pillars of social science, was not his personal work, it is characteristic of his time and spirit. Equally characteristic was his remark that any man with ten thousand a year was fit for a peerage. He left parliamentary management largely to colleagues, who did it competently, and in his time the old party distinctions lost much of their meaning. Although he regarded himself as an independent whig, in his later years the Pittites were a new species of tories. It was also sympatomatic of the changing structure of society that one reform of the highest importance was brought about by an organized movement which cut clean across both the old party differences and still older social differences.

This was the abolition of the slave-trade. From the late seventeenth century, humanitarians, most of them prompted by religious feelings, drew attention to one or other of the evils of negro slavery. Their central idea was respect for the dignity of human beings as such; in their phraseology, as creatures to whom the lamp of life should not be denied. They prevailed on the law-courts to declare that slave-owning, and its consequences such as the recapture of runaways, were illegal in England. They worked for the abolition of the British trade in African slaves.

In 1787 William Wilberforce, who had entered parliament seven years before at the age of twenty-one, became the parliamentary leader of the abolitionists. He was a friend of Pitt, with all the advantages of wealth and personal charm, but he dedicated himself to this cause and persisted against the unyielding resistance of the vested interest which it challenged. Not until 1804 did the House of Commons pass one of his Bills; not until 1807, after Pitt's death, did another Bill finally become law. By one of the ironies of history the result was at first to increase the slave-trade from Africa to North America: the British having renounced the traffic, the liberated Americans took it up for themselves. Wilberforce deserved the unique respect which surrounded him for the rest of his life, and the body of his supporters in parliament and the country also deserve respect and gratitude. They could not have succeeded without persuading men of many different types, but the driving force of the whole movement came from the evangelical Christians at its centre. The evangelical movement was the British phase of a revival which also made itself felt in Protestant countries on the Continent about the middle of the eighteenth century. It was akin to the Methodist movement.

The Methodist leader, John Wesley, a man of prodigious energy, lived through the whole eighteenth century except for two years at the beginning and nine at the end. As a fellow of an Oxford college before he was thirty he began to organize strict religious practices among his acquaintances, and ended with an immense following among all classes, especially among the poor. They were organized into local 'classes' with an annual conference to decide policy and doctrine. After Wesley's death Methodism broke away completely from the Church of England. The Methodists in the end did without episcopal ordination for their ministers, and so more or less unintentionally became Nonconformists. The old Nonconformist bodies had undergone various influences since the seventeenth-century summer of Puritanism. Many of the Presbyterians and Independents had followed the rationalist stream to become Unitarians; but some of them and some of the Baptists had been touched by the religious individualism which we have noticed in William Carey. Although the different persuasions co-operated for such purposes as had to do with the state, there had been lively theological divisions between and within them; but these were dying down. When Wilberforce underwent an experience of religious conversion he was strongly influenced by a book of Dr. Philip Doddridge, a learned, tolerant, and distinguished Nonconformist divine. The evangelical movement, insisting on personal religion, brought about a new, mutual respect between some of the Nonconformists and some of the Anglicans. Nonconformism had been especially welcomed in Wales. The Methodist revival there had begun in the 1730s and, helped by the existence of a literate middle class, made rapid progress. So did other revivalist movements; the poor standing of the Anglican church in Wales must have been a contributory factor in this.

Evangelicals of all kinds continued to influence conduct and opinions far outside their own immediate circles. It seems to have been partly due to them that from about the time of Pitt and Wilberforce the tone of public life began to improve. There were, however, many converging influences, as in the philanthropic and humanitarian movement generally. The Quakers played a considerable part as abolitionists, and their contribution had sources of its own, as it had in such matters as education and the care of the mentally sick. No doubt there were also purely secular streams of thought which helped to advance all these good causes; but it is difficult to identify them. The Industrial Revolution may well have favoured the rise of the typical virtues of the businessman, such as honesty, sobriety, good temper, and kindness, while also encouraging the typical vices of the inhuman master and the ill-treated man.

Once he had a large parliamentary majority behind him after the general election of 1784, Pitt dealt with unfinished business to such purpose that he put nearly all of it into tolerable order. As we have seen he settled the constitutional questions about the future of the East India Company. He allowed the impeachment of Warren Hastings to go forward. He set up a new committee of the privy council to take the place of the old Board of Trade, which Burke had unwisely suppressed. In some directions where commercial and territorial power were beginning to expand there was little for the state to do. One of the most imaginative of all overseas undertakings was the formation, decided upon in 1787, of a settlement in Sierra Leone for liberated slaves then stranded in Britain; but the Crown merely negotiated with the chiefs for the territory that was needed, and the organization was done voluntarily by a British committee. Almost at the same time another overseas settlement began, for a very different purpose, and with little or no understanding of the future which awaited it. This was the penal colony at Sydney, which provided the first population for New South Wales, the oldest Australian state.

The main concerns of policy were nearer home. Pitt made some changes in taxation, including the lowering of some export duties, on grounds which were purely British; but he went on to plan complicated commercial negotiations with several countries, which, if they had all been completed, would have rearranged British overseas commerce in accordance with the ideas which Adam Smith had systematized. Commercial diplomacy was never easy, and most of the world was not prepared to welcome British exports as heartily as Great Britain hoped in the expanding phase of the Industrial Revolution; but Pitt succeeded in his commercial treaty with France in 1786. This treaty,

William Pitt the Younger. Pitt became a member of parliament in 1781, Chancellor of the Exchequer in 1782, and prime minister in 1783. He resigned his office in 1801 when the king proved unwilling to support further his policy of conceding rights to Roman Catholics. He returned to office in 1804, when he devised the Third Coalition against Napoleonic France, but died in 1806.

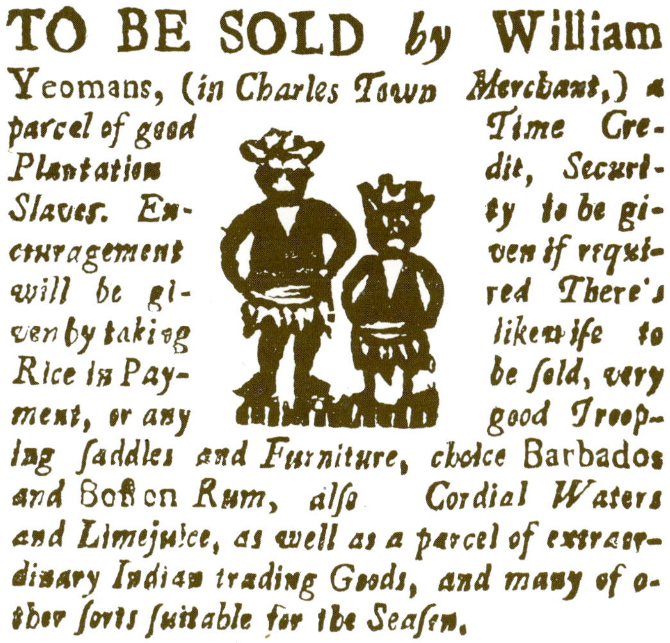
TO BE SOLD by William Yeomans, (in Charles Town Merchant,) a parcel of good Plantation Slaves. Encouragement will be given by taking Rice in Payment, or any Time Credit, Security to be given if required There's likewise to be sold, very good Trooping saddles and Furniture, choice Barbados and Boston Rum, also Cordial Waters and Limejuice, as well as a parcel of extraordinary Indian trading Goods, and many of other sorts suitable for the Season.

The slave trade, carrying Africans to the Americas, was one of the most lucrative fields for British shipowners until the 1807 Act which ended British participation. Incoming shipments of slaves would be sold on arrival, and were the subject of advertisements like this, published in the Charlestown Gazette in 1744.

sometimes called the Eden Treaty from the name of the ambassador who signed it, put an end to the mutual exclusions of trade which the tories had unsuccessfully tried to terminate in their commercial Treaty of Utrecht in 1713. France lowered her tariff and received the benefits of the new and better British manufacturers. It is said, for instance, that there was never hot soup in the palace at Versailles until King Louis XVI was served in Wedgwood china, which did not crack.

Josiah Wedgwood was not always on the side of removing the impediments to trade. He had a considerable share in frustrating another part of Pitt's commercial policy, that which related to Ireland. Here Pitt had to consider other factors besides the economic factors. When he came into power Grattan's parliament was discovering the limitations of its new legislative independence. It failed to agree on a measure of electoral reform which should still exclude Catholics from the franchise. It started on a course of protectionism, including corn-laws; but many Irish manufacturers were still shut out by the British tariff, and there was much unemployment and discontent. In the north disturbances were caused by organized Protestant and Catholic gangs. Pitt proposed a bold and reasonable remedy. He caused resolutions to be drawn up for reciprocal free trade between the two countries, and for Irish contributions to defence. The Irish parliament accepted the proposals. In the British parliament they were bitterly opposed, and behind the parliamentary opposition stood the General Chamber of Manufacturers, arrayed for this purpose by Wedgwood. The resolutions were amended, plainly to the disadvantage of Ireland. The Irish parliament rejected them, and Pitt did not, indeed could not, persist.

On another great question, not yet so urgent as it became after his time, he gave way to opposition and never found the opportunity for a new initiative. This was parliamentary reform. The weight of argument was overwhelmingly on the side of reform; but none of the possible schemes could be carried out without depriving the Crown and the political magnates of powers over the electoral machinery, which they regarded as a sort of inherited or lawfully purchased property. Rotten boroughs (where depopulation had reduced the electorate to a handful) and pocket boroughs (whose voters were securely under the control of a local patron) were also profitable to the small fry who had votes to sell, and the whole mass of anomalies, besides supporting these vested interests, were shielded by a timid but obstinate conservatism. Almost everyone spoke of the British constitution as an object of admiration and the envy of other nations. If one part was tampered with there was no knowing where reform would halt: the municipalities and even the established Church lay open to many of the same criticisms and had good reasons to fear that their turn would come. Nor could it be proved that the unreformed state of parliament was a bar to reform in other members of the body politic. To look ahead for a moment we may notice that unreformed parliaments had a creditable record in dealing with religious intolerance, the criminal law, commercial policy, the protection of factory labour against exploitation, and many minor matters. Pitt brought in a very moderate Bill, which, if it passed into law, was to be followed by other steps in the same direction. He proposed to disfranchise thirty-six rotten boroughs and to transfer the seventy-two seats to the larger counties and to London and Westminster. In the counties he proposed to widen the franchise by extending it to those who held land to the same value as the 40*s.* freeholds, but held it by copyhold or certain kinds of long leases. This would have enfranchised many small land-holders, but not the mass of the farmers, who were tenants at will. Pitt proposed to pay compensation to the borough-owners. Some objected to this and others to the other provisions: the Commons threw the Bill out by a large majority.

Once or twice in these years of peace there were reminders that continental affairs might easily work out to the disadvantage of Great Britain; but uneasiness in two separate directions was dispelled by a single diplomatic success. After its humiliation in the American war the Dutch republic, not surprisingly, found that its internal dissensions grew sharper. On one side was the stadholder William V of Orange, whose mother was a daughter of King George II. Against him were most of the governing class; but their enthusiasm for reducing his powers diminished as the patriot party grew stronger and better able to press the liberal ideas which they shared with the French intellectuals. In 1787 an armed detachment of the patriots stopped the stadholder's wife on a journey towards the frontier. Her brother, the king of Prussia, sent an army to avenge this insult and to clear up the local situation. It occupied much of the country, including Amsterdam, and the stadholder was restored. Sir James Harris, the British ambassador at The Hague, saw his chance and persuaded the Dutch and the Prussians to join in a triple alliance. Two years later, in 1790, all three states had good reason to be satisfied with this combination. They were nervous about the possible consequences of Russian successes in war against Turkey and Sweden: none of them wanted to see Russia dominant in the Baltic or intruding into the Mediterranean. There was a critical moment when the Danes joined Russia and invaded Sweden. The three allies forced them, by a threat of war, to return to neutrality.

The diplomacy of these years was abnormal because France was temporarily unable to play her part as the greatest of the continental powers. She had ended the American war victoriously, but she could not find the money to pay for it. Her monarchy still provided the most splendid spectacle in Europe. But one minister after another failed to put the finances straight, and the whole system of government was brought under destructive criticism by irreverent malcontents. Here and there all over Europe observers were convinced, not all for the same reasons, that France was on the brink of some kind of disaster. In

A social evening, as depicted by Thomas Rowlandson in an illustration for Oliver Goldsmith's *The Vicar of Wakefield*. This novel, published in 1776, remains a classic of English literature, being an ironic commentary on upper-class life of the time.

May 1789 the long-dormant states general met, and in August the Bastille fell. Whatever it amounted to, the French Revolution had evidently come.

As seen from Britain it appeared at first to mean that France was in course of exchanging authoritarian government for representative institutions and constitutional monarchy. This was something that whigs could welcome: it seemed like a movement similar to the Glorious Revolution of 1688, but even less subversive. It appealed to the liberal-minded as the dawn of a new age. Its ideals became part of a certain unrest which stemmed from economic distress in some localities and the hope of parliamentary reform. This unrest was most marked in Scotland, which is why the government's reaction was so strong there. In 1795 a 'British Convention' assembled in Scotland. Its aim was universal suffrage, annual parliaments, and the restoration of the suspended Habeas Corpus Act. The Convention was forcibly broken up and three of its delegates were sentenced to transportation. Whereas the political trials in England often resulted in the acquittal of the accused, this never seemed to happen in Scotland. But as the years passed the French revolutionaries by their acts seemed less and less appealing. With massacre, regicide, and the influx of French refugees the word 'revolution' in Britain ceased to mean a turn of the political wheel and gathered permanent associations of cruelty and violence.

By 1792 most of the British governing class, both ministers and opposition, were shocked by the excesses of the revolutionists, and afraid that their infectious ideas might inflame discontent in Britain. France was at war with both Austria and Prussia, and the French successfully invaded the Austrian Netherlands, the region which could be regarded as the natural frontier of England. Pitt took diplomatic steps with a view to an agreed settlement between all the parties. It soon appeared that the French did not regard the matter in such simple terms. In order to confirm their military success, and in defiance of the treaties of Utrecht, their assembly declared open the navigation of the River Scheldt. This involved a violation of the sovereignty of the Dutch republic over the mouth of the river, and also commercial and strategic dangers against which Britain had been shielded by the stopping of egress from Antwerp. Shortly afterwards came another act of the assembly, the Edict of Fraternity, which promised friendship and assistance to all peoples wishing to recover their liberty. This was meant to summon collaborators to assist the French in every country they might invade; and it was not unduly alarmist to imagine that in time Britain might be on the list. Pitt's government made it clear that it would be useless to negotiate for a settlement in the Netherlands so long as these two decrees remained in force. No one in France could stand up against the warlike enthusiasm of the extremists. On 1 February 1793 France declared war against the two members of the triple alliance of 1788 who were still neutral, Great Britain and the Dutch republic, or rather its stadholder William V, whose fellow citizens were assumed to wish for liberation.

The British government, merely through behaving correctly according to the traditional principles, had become engaged in war. For war on the traditional lines Britain was not in perfect readiness, but was in a position to make ready. The Admiralty had recently been usefully reformed, and a strong fleet was available, needing only to be equipped. The army was indeed very weak. For reasons of economy it had been reduced by degrees until

John Wesley, founder of Methodism. A travelling preacher, he had the gift of inspiring the uneducated. He emphasised the value of Sunday schools and of hymn-singing. The break with the Anglican church was not his intention, and occured after his death.

there were only 13,000 men under arms. The worst deficiencies were in the higher direction of the war. Not only was there no commander-in-chief; there was no organization worth the name either for supply or for strategy. It was only under the stress of fighting that some inadequate measures were taken to make good these deficiencies. At first it was expected that in Europe Great Britain's main task would be to subsidize as allies the other powers opposed to France. To this she was equal, and before joining in the hostilities she prevailed on her allies to keep the war within the traditional limits by dropping from their proclaimed intentions the restoration of the French monarchy. Pitt expected a short war, and he believed, like his father before him, that the security and advantage of Great Britain was to be furthered in the West Indies, the Baltic, and the Mediterranean. Instead of such a war as this he had to spend the rest of his life in a struggle of which he did not see the end. Except for one delusive peace of barely more than a year and another of nine months, it lasted until 1815, twenty-three years after he embarked on it.

Nobody was culpably unaware of the facts of the situation. There were some facts which were not properly appreciated. The French army had been disorganized by the revolution. Many officers had joined the emigration and many others had been dismissed or guillotined. It was not understood outside France that by this time the remnants of the old army were being fused with newcomers of all ranks and that the army now combined revolutionary impetus with the high professional competence of the reformed and well-equipped army of the previous decade. Again it was excusable for the allies to think that they could profit from the fierce royalism and conservatism of some regions of France. This too was an illusion. Neither of these errors lasted long. Both were exposed in a British operation of the first war year. At intervals for more than a century past there had been plans, which could never be put into effect, to invade France from the Mediterranean coast. In 1793, when the royalists in Marseilles invited British help, the time seemed to have come. The British and Spanish fleets took possession of Toulon unopposed. They occupied some of the heights behind it, and waited for Austrian, British, and Sardinian troops, of which only a few Sardinians arrived. Three months after the landing the French came in force and the allied navies could do nothing but burn the French ships in the harbour and evacuate their bridgehead, carrying with them a few refugees. The tactical handling of the French artillery was excellent: it was commanded by Napoleon Bonaparte, a lieutenant with nine years' service.

Misunderstandings such as these, and incompetence, contributed to prolong the war, but there were, as there nearly always are, misunderstandings and incompetence on both sides, and the reason why it lasted so long was that it was different in kind from the wars of the preceding century. The difference was not in the fighting. Armies and navies increased in size and improved in efficiency as the years went on, but there were no fundamental innovations in weapons or even in the structure of the battle on land or sea. The great changes lay in the relations of the armed forces to the nations behind them, to the people in town and country and to the kings and governments and constitutional systems. France introduced the principle of the *levée en masse*, selective compulsory service in which, though there were limits to the possible size of armies, their numbers increased enormously. In 1792 the French had 200,000 men in the field; in 1794 nearly 750,000. In 1812 the numbers assembled for the Russian campaign were reckoned at 540,000. In Europe generally the war had two phases, of which the first was announced by the Edict of Fraternity. The old governments had no deep roots among their subjects. In carrying out their limited functions they were hampered by the accumulated abuses of unearned privilege and irresponsible authority. When Bonaparte, a general at the age of twenty-seven, marched through Italy, he met no army that gave him any trouble and no government that was not as much afraid of its own people as of the invader. Like other French generals in annexed or merely occupied countries, he encouraged such changes in the laws as did away with feudal restrictions and class-relations, and so built up a body of supporters and a system for feeding and supplying his troops. Changes like these, many of them genuine reforms, went on in one part of Europe and another as long as the war lasted. Bonaparte, even when he became an emperor, was 'the revolution in jack-boots'.

In the later years another set of changes grew up within or beside these and ultimately formed ramparts against them. The old states of western Europe had crystallized round solid national nuclei. The unassimilated national minorities on their outskirts, such as the Welsh, the Bretons, and the Frisians were ruled by assimilated upper and middle classes. When the French people had cleared away the provincial and corporate divisions which stood between the state and the individuals, a spirit, with its own ideas and its own literature, inspired it as a whole whose only unity was the unity of the state. By clearing the undergrowth in the occupied countries the French prepared the way for a like spirit to grow up among them, and, for at least the last seven years of the wars, Napoleon fought against national indignation at the

A Martello tower at Bexhill in Sussex. Many such towers were built as defence against Napoleon's threatened invasion of Britain. Situated along the south coast, several of these structures can still be seen.

loss of freedom. This wave of opinion was expressed in their own ways by poets and philosophers; it prompted constitutional changes in some countries, and in some others it aided the effort by which the opponents of France increased their armies to match the new scale of warfare.

These changes can be traced in Britain, but only in weakened forms. The island was still further insulated by the state of war on land and sea. There were already radical and reforming movements in existence; there were already channels for discontent to run in, and there were neither inarticulate subjects nor apathetic rulers. There was already a stubborn, if unreasonably boastful, national pride. The French ideas and the reaction against them deeply influenced domestic parties and events, but there was only one occasion when they even came near to changing the course of the fighting. This was in 1797, when Great Britain's allies were hard pressed on land, and her financial stability was in greater danger than at any time before. In the Channel Fleet, lying at Spithead, the lower deck put forward justifiable complaints, and backed them up by a refusal to obey orders which was mutiny in law, but orderly and rational. The cabinet granted the demands; but then, in July, the North Sea fleet at the Nore, whose business was to blockade the Dutch, was led into mutiny by men whose aims were political. This second mutiny was sternly crushed before the enemy heard of it, and in October the admiral, Adam Duncan, led the fleet in the Battle of Camperdown, where the small Dutch navy was annihilated as a fighting force. The British community held together through the severest test since the Civil War of Charles I.

During this war the navy was at its zenith. As the mutinies showed, its administration had grave shortcomings, and there was no lack of errors in the strategical use of fleets; but there was an unparalleled series of victories, and the navy did its main tasks successfully all through the wars. Neither the French, nor some of the other powers who joined them from time to time, were unequal opponents except in numbers. The French ships, for instance, were better in some ways than the British, and the British copied improvements from captured French men-of-war. The French had tactical methods of their own, such as firing at the masts of ships instead of the hulls. Taking it all round the British had to rely on skill and discipline. They succeeded once more in preventing invasion. Several times the French made plans or preparations or preliminary movements to attempt it. In 1797 the French meant to unite their fleet with the Spaniards and the Dutch to cover invasion, but before Duncan fought at Camperdown, Jervis had defeated the Spanish fleet in the Battle of Cape St. Vincent. A French force of 1,500 wretched irregular troops was put ashore in 1797 on the open coast near Fishguard but the Pembrokeshire militia easily made them surrender. Both sides understood that there could be no effective invasion unless the invaders had command of the sea: as Nelson wrote in 1801 when troop-transports were assembling in the Channel ports: 'This Boat-business . . . may be a part of a great plan of Invasion; but can never be the only one.' Three or four years later similar preparations were made on a greater scale; but Napoleon marched his army away to attack the Austrians. Two days after the Austrians capitulated, Nelson's last and greatest victory of Trafalgar established the British command of the sea for the remainder of the war. Nelson was a national hero for many reasons, not all of them pertinent, and the Admiralty did not entirely concur with the public in admiring his glorious disobedience to his superiors; but he was the greatest of the admirals. Besides his infallible judgement in action he had three great qualities. He was a tremendous fighter, fleet against fleet, ship against ship, or hand to hand. He was a keen student of his

BELOW In the 19th Century the steam railway and the steam ship changed, in a sense, the dimensions of human life. This picture shows the launch of the *Great Britain*, the first of the iron-built, propeller-driven, transatlantic liners. Built at Bristol in 1843, this vessel is now preserved in the same drydock in which she was constructed.

OVERLEAF The Menin Road, by Paul Nash. Despite progress in action photography, Britain employed official war artists in both world wars. This painting shows part of the Western Front in 1918. The muddy shell-scarred landscape is no artist's nightmare, but a portrayal of reality.

profession, reading everything that was published about naval science. His relation with his captains, 'a band of brothers', is one of the classical examples of leadership.

In its other standing duties, protecting commerce and troop-movements, and operating against the enemy, the navy did equally well. The army, in contrast, though capable of rendering good service, was used to little purpose until after the Battle of Trafalgar. During the first three years of the war a coalition of powers, stronger in numbers than any of its predecessors, began operations on the time-honoured plan of moving against France through the Austrian Netherlands. Russia, Austria, and Prussia, however, the three strong military powers, were too much occupied in partitioning Poland to use their full forces in the west; Spain, Portugal, Sardinia, and the Dutch had little to offer. By 1795 the French were not only out of danger, they had annexed the Austrian Netherlands. They had set up a satellite republic in the territory of Britain's former allies the Dutch, who thus became an enemy nation. Prussia and Spain made peace. Britain had to realign her hopes on a new alliance with Austria and Russia; but by 1797, the year of the mutiny at the Nore, these hopes too had foundered, and Britain stood alone, without an ally and protected only by her ships.

This was the situation when General Bonaparte made one of the greatest of all recorded miscalculations. Ever since the time of Louis XIV ingenious writers had toyed with the idea that France, already powerful in the Mediterranean and its commerce, might enrich herself by conquering Egypt. The rise of British power in India had added the inducement of opening and commanding a new route to India overland. In 1798 Bonaparte embarked 35,000 men at Toulon, slipped past the British blockading squadron, captured Malta, landed his army in Egypt and mastered the country in a single battle. Thirteen days after that battle Nelson sailed his fleet alongside and won the most complete of all naval victories. The French army was marooned without the least chance of relief. It went on fighting with diminishing numbers until 1801, when it capitulated to a British general. Long before that Bonaparte had secretly left it. In France, instead of being court-martialled, he brought off a conjuring trick which made him, under the title of first consul, head of the government. He had to face a second loosely united coalition, this time of Britain, Austria, and Russia, but without Prussia. Two years of startling chances and changes followed. Russia dropped out of the coalition and revived the armed neutrality of the North, only to see the Danish fleet destroyed by Nelson in the harbour of Copenhagen. The pro-French tsar, Paul, was murdered, and danger from the North was at an end; but the exhausted Austrians made peace. With this peace, in 1801, France reached undoubted ascendancy in Europe. Between the subject republics of Holland and Switzerland its frontier ran along the Rhine. In Italy there was no truly independent state north of Naples and there were French troops in that kingdom. Britain again had no ally.

As it happened, for reasons not connected with the conduct of the war or foreign policy, Pitt resigned his office at this juncture, and did not return to it until after two eventful years. He did not go into opposition and his successors saluted him as 'the pilot that weathered the storm'. His resignation did not change the course of policy. Napoleon needed to reorganize France. He had already attempted to begin negotiations for peace before his most recent victories, and in 1802 the peace was made by the Treaty of Amiens. France was to withdraw her troops from Naples and the Papal States, to acknowledge the independence of Corfu and the other Ionian Islands off the western coast of Greece, and to restore Egypt, which she no longer controlled, to the Turks, who could neither control nor defend it. Great Britain handed back all her miscellaneous conquests except three. She kept Ceylon, which she had taken from the Dutch in 1795, and Trinidad, which she had taken from the Spaniards in 1797. She promised to restore Malta to the knights of St. John, who had been in no condition to take charge of it when the French there surrendered in 1800. This promise she never kept. The treaty left French power on the mainland of Europe untouched. Bonaparte refused to discuss commercial relations, let alone to revive the Eden Treaty, and in the result British seaborne commerce actually began to decline. Even before the new treaty was signed Bonaparte used diplomatic pressure in Italy to exploit the advantages which he had gained in the war. Very soon he began to do likewise in Germany, and his proceedings in the West Indies, in the Near East, and in the restored French posts in India aroused British suspicions. His position in France became even stronger: he was made first consul for life. He made no attempt to conciliate Great Britain, and the British Government concluded that he meant to renew the war when it suited him. In all probability they were right. They declared war on France in 1802.

The Napoleonic war lasted longer than the revolutionary war, and it cost all the powers greater exertions. At first it seemed to most Englishmen a mere continuation. Pitt came back into office, and in the same week Napoleon crowned himself emperor of the French. The new coalition, Britain, Russia, Austria, and Sweden, had divergent purposes; Great Britain could not be sure that the others agreed with her in aiming at the reduction of France to its former frontiers. For her, the war began auspiciously. Nelson won his historic victory over the combined French and Spanish fleets at Trafalgar. For the rest of the war the French navy never recovered. Four figures, for the whole of the two wars, summarize the results of the naval operations. By shipwreck the British lost 101 warships, the French, because they spent less time at sea, lost 24. The British lost 10 ships captured or destroyed to the French 377. The French preponderance on land became, however, soon after the beginning, equally overwhelming. Before the end of the year 1805 the Austrians were knocked out of the war. In that dark hour William Pitt died. Charles James Fox, Foreign Secretary in the reconstructed government, tried in vain to make peace. The solitary British military success was on a peninsula: the French were defeated at Maida in Calabria. But Prussia came into the war and suffered a heavy defeat. Finally Russia was forced to make peace, and virtually accepted freedom to dominate eastern Europe in exchange for leaving France mistress of the west and centre. The third coalition was dissolved, and Britain again stood alone.

In the end there was a fourth coalition, more closely knit and, as it proved, irresistible; but it came together gradually, after great unforeseen events. Napoleon tried to use his European hegemony to ruin British commerce: the main principle of his 'continental system' was to exclude British exports and re-exports from every port in Europe. The British not only smuggled in their goods on a gigantic scale, but they retaliated, so that the two powers were soon trying to enforce a mutual self-blockade. It had little effect on the military operations. An

American diplomatist indignantly described the British captures of American ships as 'robbing one nation to starve another'. Friction increased until the United States declared war in 1812. They unsuccessfully invaded Canada, and the British burnt their capital, Washington; but this was only a distant sideshow, simultaneous with the great events of Napoleon's decline. Another side-issue of the continental system was that Napoleon planned to bring Denmark into his system, and in 1807 a British fleet, without any declaration of war, forced the surrender of the Danish fleet by bombarding Copenhagen.

The first great French thrust was across the Pyrenees. In 1807 Portugal was invaded and its king withdrew to his colony Brazil. In the next year Napoleon set up his own brother as king of Spain. Both he and the British were slow to see that Spain and Portugal, as a peninsula, were the next best thing to an island from the point of view of a naval power. The British sent forces there, but on the small scale and in the unenterprising spirit in which they had sent forces to France and the Low Countries in the revolutionary war. When Austria was goaded into resuming war against the French the British sent a more ambitious expedition to the Dutch island of Walcheren, but it was dreadfully mismanaged and accomplished nothing. By that time, however, the Peninsula was becoming an important theatre of war. When things went wrong an outlying British force could be evacuated by sea, as was Sir John Moore's after his death at Corunna in 1810. Nothing interrupted the shipments of men and supplies to Lisbon. The British had two great advantages besides this of geography. No one doubted that they were on the side of the populations in their spontaneous resistance to France. And they had found a commander of the highest quality in Arthur Wellesley, who ultimately became duke of Wellington.

Wellesley was born in the same year as Napoleon, and born to high opportunities. He was a younger son of an Irish peer, and he was elected to the Irish parliament when he was twenty-one. He had already become a professional soldier, and he took his profession seriously. He was twenty-nine and a colonel in India when his elder brother came out as governor-general. When he took command of the force in Portugal in 1808 he knew war well, both from long experience of campaigning and from the point of view of the statesmen. He had even held office for two years as chief secretary for Ireland. But every step in his career was marked by industry and character. He has been called the greatest man who has ever been sincerely content to serve. In the Peninsula he advanced, retreated, dug himself in, advanced again, fighting battles and sieges on his way until, after six years of it, he crossed the Pyrenees, marched up to the line of the Garonne and won a battle at Toulouse. His army by this time was a secondary force, attacking France in the rear while the great allies bore down from the north and east. They were in Paris already. The drama which began with Napoleon's march to Moscow in 1812 had ended when Prussians, Russians, and Austrians converged on his army at Leipzig. Napoleon abdicated and was set up in a miniature monarchy on the Italian island of Elba. An elderly brother of the unhappy Louis XVI came to rule as Louis XVIII over a France reduced almost to the frontiers of 1792. The allies settled some minor matters in Paris and then the diplomatists assembled in Vienna to lay down the frontiers, the dynastic affairs, and the international law of a pacified Europe.

They soon discovered that they had to overcome deep disagreements among themselves. They were even relapsing into the old diplomatic habit of forcing peaceful change by threats of war. A thunderstorm broke. Napoleon had drawn the moral from

Lord Nelson, mortally wounded, on the deck of HMS *Victory* at the Battle of Trafalgar. A truly great commander and a truly great victory together made this battle an inspiring memory for later generations of British seamen.

their quarrels. On 1 March 1815 he landed at Golfe-Juan on the French riviera. Military France rose with him again and Louis XVIII ignominiously withdrew to England. On the Belgian frontier Wellington was building up an army of Belgian, Dutch, and Hanoverian troops, and Blücher another of Prussians. Once they were united they would invade France; but, if Napoleon could keep them apart and defeat them separately, he would be great among the great powers again. He concentrated his army and went forward with his own bewildering speed. By 14 June he had 120,000 men at Charleroi and neither Wellington nor Blücher knew that he was on the move. Next day the first shots were fired. On the 16th the Prussians were checked, and Wellington retired to a strong defensive position at Waterloo. Then Napoleon and his marshals began to make mistakes. Wellington stood up to a long day of hard fighting on 18 June; the Prussians came back into battle and the French were routed.

It was, as Wellington said, a very close-run thing, and not only on the battlefield but for the whole hundred days of Napoleon's reappearance. That episode left its mark on the peace-settlement, which was to restore the old states and their governments, with alliances and allocations of territory which should prevent any new military threat from France or from revolution.

British statesmen took a great part in this settlement, but it was seven or eight years before British policy was seriously involved in maintaining or modifying any of the detailed arrangements for the Continent. It will be best not to describe these now, but to take them up point by point as they become matters of dispute. For the present we need notice only those clauses in the Vienna treaties which affected Great Britain directly.

The period of the revolutionary and Napoleonic wars was the only one in which British governments resolutely aimed at expansion overseas and had the means to effect it. This was not a policy of colonization. The wars themselves stopped emigration. The policy was to use sea-power to acquire naval and commercial bases, the framework of a maritime empire, which might well entail annexations of territory, as those of the Dutch and Portuguese and of the British in India had already done; but for which colonization, if it were to come as in time it did come, was not a considered aim but an unplanned increment. So at every favourable moment of the wars there were offensive operations overseas, and their principal gains were confirmed by the peace.

In Europe there were three acquisitions, but two of these were of negligible importance. The little rock of Heligoland, originally Danish, facing the mouths of the Elbe and the Weser, had been a useful smuggling post in the time of the continental system, and it was retained, for no serious reason, until 1891 when it was traded to Germany in a negotiation about Zanzibar. After that, when Germany built a great navy, this transaction took on a different appearance. The Ionian Islands were under a British protectorate until 1863. Then they were amicably handed over to Greece, which was still part of the Turkish empire in 1814. Malta, the third acquisition, had a very different history. Its strategic value was always great; its naval dockyard brought employment and prosperity and in the war of 1939–45 it was a vital and fiercely assaulted link in the British strategic chain.

When the French revolution began the British were reforming their judicial and financial systems in India and following the policy of not interfering with the Indian states; but they had trouble on their hands from Tipu Sahib, the aggressive sultan of Mysore. For some time he was treated with indulgence; but when the elder Wellesley arrived as governor-general, an arrogant man and a stranger to such ideas, Tipu was found to be in communication with the French governor in Mauritius, and to be intriguing with self-constituted French agents. Wellesley and some of the members of the British cabinet regarded India as an outlying theatre in the French war, and gave up the policy of restraint. Napoleon's Egyptian expedition made them more determined, and by 1805 there was no longer any French influence in southern India. Tipu had died when his capital, Seringapatam, was stormed; the Company had taken the Malabar Coast, and handed over other rich areas of his dominions to his feudal superior, the nizam of Hyderabad.

The Company's dominions grew by an often-repeated sequence of events, provocation, coercion, annexation. Short of outright conquest there were degrees of subjection, of which the commonest was a 'subsidiary' treaty. A prince would accept a garrison of the Company's troops in his state or close to his frontier; in exchange for protection he would promise, or even pay, an annual tribute, and he would renounce the right to carry on relations with other states independently of the Company. Every clause of such a treaty left openings for disagreement when either side was ready to pick a quarrel. By 1805 the Company controlled or protected the whole of north-east India from Delhi to Calcutta, the whole coast from there round by Tanjore and Travancore, and the vast inland regions of Mysore and Hyderabad. Its army had destroyed the military power of the Mahrattas, between those regions and the north-east. The mogul emperor in Delhi accepted its protection. It was unquestionably paramount over the whole of India. Its servants, who were in control of administration and justice, had to rely on self-confidence, improvisation, trial and error: a good many of them were keen-eyed observers, but few had real knowledge of Indian society. There was no uniform system for the three provinces either in the constitutional relations of the administration and the law-courts, or in the financial and economic system of extracting revenue from the land. The differences were in no way related to the differences between the regions and their peoples.

In 1813 the time came for one of the periodical renewals of the East India Company's charter, and changes were made which foreshadowed new kinds of British influence on the future of India. The renewal of the charter in 1793 had been opposed partly because the Lancashire manufacturers feared the competition of Indian textiles. Even then their fears were ill founded: they were underselling the Indians in Africa and America. By 1813 the Industrial Revolution had gone so far that they and other exporters had good prospects of selling in India itself and beyond. Their opposition took a different direction and succeeded: the Company was deprived of its monopoly of trade with India, and that great market was thrown open.

At the same time new attitudes to missions and education were announced. The Company had chaplains who ministered to Europeans, but, not altogether without reason, it distrusted the missionaries, who had no respect for the susceptibilities of Hindus or Moslems. The evangelicals, however, were strong enough to have a clause of their own embodied in the charter. A bishop of the Church of England was to have India for his diocese, with an archdeacon for each province. In 1814 the bishop arrived, a good classical scholar, energetic but discreet, Thomas Fanshaw Middleton by name. He aimed not at making

Ships of the East India Company defending themselves against French warships in 1804. The Company, richest of the trading monopolies, had its own military forces in India, and its merchant ships were well armed.

converts but at educating missionaries and schoolmasters, so that conversions might follow from the spread of knowledge and the example of the European inhabitants. Education, however, was not to be left only to the clergy, and it was not necessarily to be limited to the importation of European knowledge and ideas. Every year the East India Company was to set aside at least 100,000 rupees (say £12,000) for 'the revival and improvement of literature and the encouragement of the learned natives of India, and for the introduction and promotion of a knowledge of the sciences among the inhabitants of British India'.

The wars opened the way for extensive conquests in and around south and south-east Asia by expeditions from India. Mauritius was taken from the French in 1810: it had given some slight trouble; it was a commercial centre, and it could be a useful stage on the voyage to India. But the main acquisitions were at the expense of the Dutch. The old rivalry with them had been asleep for more than a century, and the British had no foothold left in what is now Indonesia except Bencoolen, an unhealthy station on the west coast of Sumatra. They were, however, turning their attention that way again. In the peace-treaty of 1784 the Dutch had abandoned their claim to exclude all shipping but their own from ports of the Malay Archipelago. The neighbouring sultan of Kedah ceded the island of Penang to Great Britain. The Dutch were apprehensive that the British would establish themselves in other harbours. The French conquest of Holland made all the Dutch possessions legitimate booty for the British Crown, even if they were taken by the East India Company's forces; and the Crown proceeded to take possession. Ceylon, still only partially subdued, but rich and with an old-established Portuguese and Dutch civilization, was permanently held. So were St. Helena and the Cape of Good Hope, where the Dutch had ports of call for their East Indiamen. At the Cape, where water, vegetables, and fresh meat were to be had, a colony had grown up, mainly of its own accord. Farmers had settled for more than three hundred miles along the coast to the west of Cape Town, further than that to the east and to comparable distances inland. Their economy was based on Malay and Bantu slavery, and the white population amounted to sixteen thousand. Some of the remote pastoral Boers regarded themselves as independent of any allegiance to the authorities in Cape Town, and engaged in warfare against the tribes whom they pressed back.

For some years the British occupied and governed, too much on the same lines that they followed in India, the eastern possessions of the Dutch, especially Java, most fertile of all agricultural countries in the tropics, and the smaller islands which were rich in tin. But the British were not merely greedy. Their plans for expansion were part of their plans for peace and prosperity all over the world. One of their devices for hindering French aggression in the future was to set up the prince of Orange as king of a new state, combining what had been the Dutch and the Austrian Netherlands. This bulwark against France needed the means to fortify and organize its defences, and so, in a comprehensive revision of Anglo-Dutch relations, the Dutch recovered their island empire, and also, less important, their West Indian colonies. Not that the British meant to renounce their oriental trade. Some of their men on the spot even urged the government to keep back at least something from the Dutch. When that was refused, they found a substitute. Singapore was acquired from a new rajah of Kedah, an empty island on the straits of Malacca, which in due course became the greatest trading city between Calcutta and Hong Kong.

Even with this we have not named all the overseas advances that resulted from the wars, but this is enough to show what immense horizons had opened, what unprecedented tasks had been undertaken, and with how little foresight.

Sooner or later the French Revolution and the French wars were bound to alter British relations with Ireland. As it happened it was the war which brought about the first legal changes, the precursors of others leading on to a new constitutional system. After the failure of Pitt's commercial proposals in 1785 discontent and internal divisions in Ireland were as bad as before, but there were some years of relative prosperity and the most urgent problems were religious and political. In 1792 the radicals in Ulster formed the United Irishmen, with a programme for Irish independence based on French republican ideas. In the months before and after the outbreak of war the government pressed through the Irish parliament a Catholic Relief Act, granting what seemed to be the most practicable immediate step to conciliation. The Irish Catholics received the franchise on the terms on which the Protestants already held it. They were allowed to serve on juries, and to hold some minor offices, and junior commissioned ranks in the army. They were not, however, allowed to sit in parliament. The measure was acceptable to the Anglo-Irish governing class and its British friends because it seemed to preserve their ascendancy. Some of the whig members of the British cabinet wanted to go further, and they saw to it that the steady-going lord lieutenant was superseded by Lord Fitzwilliam, Rockingham's nephew and heir. Fitzwilliam was a great landowner in County Wicklow as well as in Yorkshire, but his virtues did not include either caution or submissiveness to his instructions. He dismissed three of the principal ministers, was overruled by the British government, and sent in his resignation after less than a month in Dublin.

This made it harder for Pitt to go on with his still undisclosed plans for gradual but drastic changes; it sharpened both the demand for concessions and the fear of what they might lead to, the more so because at this stage of events the French revolutionary ideas were making headway in Ireland. The United Irishmen revived after a brief suppression, and there were collisions between Protestants and Catholics in the north. The Protestants formed the Orange Society; the United Irishmen allied themselves with agrarian terrorists, and prepared to arm for rebellion. In 1796 Theobald Wolfe Tone, one of several Irish Protestants with sympathy for the Catholics, went by devious ways to France as their emissary. The French sent a squadron of forty-three sail, including fifteen ships of the line, with Tone on board and about 15,000 soldiers. After many mishaps some of the ships entered Bantry Bay, but a storm prevented any landing. So far as Ireland itself was concerned the French probably miscalculated as badly as the British more than once miscalculated the chances of royalist risings in France; but they still kept open the possibility of intervening. In the next year the Dutch fleet which was defeated at Camperdown was earmarked as part of a force for another Irish attempt. In the end the rebellion exploded in 1798 without foreign aid. The British attempted to forestall it. In the six northern counties the yeomanry were called up to assist regular troops in disarming the population: they acted brutally but largely succeeded in their task. A plot for a *coup d'état* in Dublin was frustrated, but to the south and south-west there was savage civil war. A rebel force estimated at 15,000 captured Wexford, with its garrison, and Enniscorthy. Near that town, at Vinegar Hill, a strong force of regulars destroyed it, and the remnants of the rebellion were stamped out with much severity. Even so, 900 good French troops were put on shore in the far north-west, at Killala.

Parliament House, Dublin. The old, corrupt, Irish parliament lost its role when the Union with Ireland was promulgated during the Napoleonic wars. The Union was not a great success, and had Gladstone succeeded with his Home Rule Bill in 1886 a new Irish parliament would have again sat in Dublin.

They crossed the Shannon before they had to surrender to superior forces.

Pitt had a plan for solving the Irish question which was simple and statesmanlike. He proposed that Ireland should unite its parliament with the parliament of Great Britain, in which those of Scotland and England were already united. Thus the executive, the cabinet, would be responsible to a body representative of all the three old kingdoms. The right to sit in parliament, which would have produced a House of Commons with a Catholic majority if granted to Ireland alone, could safely be granted if the members were to form only a minority in a united parliament. Pitt carried the union without holding out any open promises of completing Catholic emancipation. He overcame conservative reluctance in Ireland by using the normal methods of parliamentary management on a large scale: peerages and offices were granted, and dispossessed borough-owners were compensated at the rate of £7,000 for a seat. The necessary adjustments in finance, including the combining of the public debts, were by no means unfair to Ireland. These arrangements having been negotiated, the Bill passed and Pitt moved on to the Catholic question. A substantial body of his cabinet refused their support, and the king would not be argued out of his belief that if he assented to the further measure of Catholic relief, he would break his coronation oath to defend the Church of England as by law established. A prime minister, though dependent on a parliamentary majority, was still in law and in popular belief the king's servant. Pitt respected the king's motives, as the king respected his; so the minister resigned. During the interval of his absence from office an undistinguished but not incompetent cabinet carried on the war, made peace, and returned to war, without reopening the Catholic question. In Ireland neither the conservatives nor the revolutionaries resisted the union. Only one incident reminded the politicians that, so long as the French wars lasted, there might be dangers there. In 1803, soon after the renewal of the war, Robert Emmet, a gifted and idealistic young man of twenty-five, found his way back to Dublin after interviewing Napoleon, and led a gallant but futile and murderous attempt to seize the government. The union was unshaken.

In its social and religious implications it was entirely unlike the union with Scotland. Nothing was preserved from change by future parliamentary action. Ireland gained the freedom of trade which had recently been refused, and was admitted to the British protective system; but this did not mean that new economic forces would find a needed and otherwise impossible outlet. The union added to the British economy a fine capital city, minor ports and market towns, an active linen industry, and thirty-two agricultural counties, most of them much less productive than the average of the British lowland zone. For the time being this did not disturb the affairs of either party to the bargain.

The resignation of Pitt was the only event in British parliamentary politics during the war which raised issues of great importance. As a landmark in the history of the monarchy it lost much of its significance, because from 1810 until his death in 1820 the king's illness completely incapacitated him from taking part in public work. His son, the Prince of Wales, took his place with the title of 'regent', derived from France, the traditional English 'protector' having been contaminated by Oliver Cromwell. As regent, and afterwards until 1830 as King George IV, he was a man of pleasure and of some taste in the arts, but he made no impress on the constitution. Nor did the four ministries which carried on the war in succession to one another, after the death of Pitt. There were able men among them; they worked steadily and made some improvements in the machinery of government; but the war overshadowed every other activity. Reform movements did no more than stir in their sleep.

LEFT Vaccination against smallpox; a cartoon by Gilray of 1802. Edward Jenner, an English doctor, introduced the technique in 1798. As it could be regarded as interference with God's will, however, it was resisted.

RIGHT Robert Burns, regarded as the greatest Scottish poet. Of humble birth, Burns used conversational rhythms. His lyrics on peasant life, patriotism, nature, and love were written in the Scottish vernacular.

Ministers, even prime ministers, came and went as their capacity for business improved or deteriorated and in particular their capacity and that of their intimate groups to work harmoniously with other groups and other men. There was no practical alternative to prosecuting the war, except when everyone agreed on the Peace of Amiens. The differences of opinion which arose from intellectual grounds had to do with subsidiary matters such as finance. In 1797 there were monetary difficulties, and the Bank of England suspended cash payments for its notes, a suspension which lasted until 1819. Prices rose, and in 1810 a parliamentary committee recommended the drastic remedy of deflation by a return to gold currency; but the government, rightly fearing unemployment and a fall in standards of living, was not convinced. The war was the most expensive ever known, and the national debt rose from 400 to 834 millions, which caused general but unnecessary consternation. The management of loans was not very skilful, but taxation entered on a new era with the introduction of the first income-tax in 1799. By the end of the wars this tax raised more than a fifth of the whole revenue; but it was regarded as an invasion of privacy justified only by an awful emergency. After the peace it was abolished and all lists and records relating to it were ordered to be pulped. Financially the nation muddled through, and there was a general, if confused, belief that this was owing to commercial prosperity. The Industrial Revolution proceeded on its course. From an early date in the revolutionary war exports rose. They reached a high level in 1802; and though they fluctuated during the Napoleonic war, in its later years they were higher still.

Behind the humdrum business of parliament there were tendencies which were destined before long to change the ethos of the national institutions. The Welshman Robert Owen, who had made a fortune as a manufacturer, introduced strikingly generous treatment for his workers at New Lanark, and began to work out a socialist theory of society. In 1802 Sir Robert Peel, a Lancashire cotton magnate, a supporter of Pitt, and the father of the great prime minister of later years, carried the first of all factory laws, a modest Act for preserving the health and morals of apprentices employed in mills and factories. Previously the maintenance of public order had been mainly a matter for local authorities. The influence of French ideas at various social levels created a national problem. It was similar to that of the dissenters at the Restoration of 1660, but on the whole it was handled with better judgement. Little was done to interfere with intellectual subversiveness: Pitt thought it unnecessary to prosecute William Godwin for his *Political Justice* because it was priced high at two guineas. There were some prosecutions of seditious writings but no martyrs for them. Some were acquitted. The only death penalties were inflicted on undoubtedly guilty persons, such as 'the Unfortunate Colonel Despard', the perpetrator of a crazy attempt remarkably similar to Robert Emmet's in the same year. But the government needed to watch for conspirators, and, neither the profession nor the name of detective having been invented, it did this by means of 'spies'. It also began to give more frequent and direct instructions to the counties and boroughs in matters of police, in fact to feel its way towards the creation of efficient police-forces under some measure of central control. There were signs that members of the professions would no longer tolerate the extreme confusion of the law about their qualifications and privileges. In 1797 the Royal College of Surgeons was created by royal charter, and the surgeons began to overcome the many abuses which had grown up under their earlier incorporations. In 1815 the apothecaries, who with some of the surgeons more or less constituted the body of family doctors, had their position regulated by Act of parliament.

Not far removed from these practical creations and from political affairs in general, but not yet in regular contact with them, was the intellectual movement which, as we shall see, became powerful after the peace under the name of utilitarianism. Jeremy Bentham's book *The Principles of Morals and Legislation* was published in 1789, and controversial writings for and against the French revolutionary principles began a new era of activity in political thought. It was indeed partly from those principles and partly from the wars, horrible and burdensome as they were, that English literature of all kinds drew new inspiration. What is called the romantic movement can be traced back to anticipations, British among others, in the eighteenth century. The force of continental, especially German, examples came into play in the early years of the revolution. The movement, widespread through all the arts and infinitely variegated, broke away from the reasonable, the harmonious, and the normal to emphasize contrasts, conflicts, dangers, and defiance; that is, the individuality of nations and people. English poets again became interpreters of the history of their times. The lives of Wordsworth and Coleridge were involved in every stage of the long tragedy of the European mind; Wordsworth at first was an enthusiastic supporter of the French Revolution. Byron and Shelley grew up during the Napoleonic war, and every generation of Englishmen from their time to our own, in forming its own notions of liberty, nationality, democracy, and duty, has repeated ideas and phrases from those days, and especially from their poetry; Shelley's pamphlet *The Necessity of Atheism* earned him expulsion from Oxford University and *Queen Mab*, a long poem against orthodox Christianity, soon followed. In Scotland, learning and the arts continued to take a course of their own. Scottish doctors were renowned not only in London but further afield; several Russian tsars, including Peter the Great and Alexander I, chose Scotsmen as their personal physicians. Edinburgh was the great intellectual centre, with its concentration of churchmen and professors. Its reputation was solidified by the appearance in 1775 of the first *Edinburgh Review*, a journal of intelligent discussion. Robert Burns, whose most familiar but not greatest work is *Auld Lang Syne*, is reckoned to be the greatest of those who built their poetry on Scottish popular speech. It is also well to remember that *Rule Britannia* was written by an expatriate Scot.

Recovery 1815–1846

1819	Troops fire on a demonstration in Manchester, in favour of parliamentary reform (the 'Peterloo Massacre').
1825	The first public steam railway is opened between Stockton and Darlington.
1827	A British naval squadron intervenes at Navarino in favour of the Greek liberation movement against the Turks.
1828	The Test Act repealed, allowing Nonconformists to hold public office.
1829	Catholic Emancipation Act allows Roman Catholics to hold almost any public office. The London Metropolitan Police force is established.
1830	The last agrarian rising in Britain.
1831	Riots flare up in Bristol after the defeat of the parliamentary Reform Bill.
1832	The parliamentary Reform Bill is passed.
1833	The Twelve Hours Act is passed, the first of several major factory acts.
1834	The Poor Law Amendment Act is passed. The Tolpuddle Martyrs are transported to Australia.
1835	The Municipal Reform Act provides for elected town corporations.
1836	The Chartist movement for electoral reform begins.
1840	Penny postage is introduced. Queen Victoria marries Prince Albert. Canada is granted responsible government.
1846	Irish potato famine. The corn laws are repealed.

The statesmen gathered again at Vienna after the final defeat of Napoleon, doubly aware of the complexity of their agenda. They had to draw the frontiers of Europe, and to distribute territories, restoring so much as could be restored to the rightful owners, if such there were, but also providing for stability in the future. Stable frontiers could not be contrived unless the states behind them were stable. Within most of the countries, the old regimes which were being restored were in open or latent conflicts with the institutions and the ideas of the abnormal years since 1789. The result was, at least in the most important respect of all, a settlement. There was no war between any of the great western and central powers until 1854, the longest peace that the European state-system had ever enjoyed. This peace was not the automatic consequence of the dispositions made in 1814 and 1815. It was in jeopardy several times, and it was preserved partly because the powers improved the style and machinery of their diplomacy. In 1818, 1820, 1821, and 1822 there were regular congresses in which the great powers agreed on measures against revolutionary tendencies which threatened to spread from centres of discontent and to upset the newly recovered equilibrium. Different statesmen and different nations interpreted this balance in very different ways. Conservative or reactionary sovereigns, investing their own status and their own ambitions with a religious sanctity, roused suspicions among their neighbours. But the concert of Europe was a reality. It lasted after this period of congresses into a much longer period during which, even after the interruptions of major wars, conferences or full congresses were efficient instruments for settling or tiding over major international differences.

In this phase of European relations the position of Great Britain was unique. She had no direct interest in any of the contentious questions about frontiers or dynasties. The personal link of her sovereigns with Hanover no longer counted for anything in policy, and in 1837 it came to an end altogether because Queen Victoria, who succeeded to the British throne, was excluded by the Hanoverian law of succession from inheriting the electorate. Indirectly, of course, these questions touched British interests when they affected the balance of power, and so did the underlying antagonism of 'liberalism' (a new word, spreading from France or Spain in the twenties) and conservatism. Immediately after Waterloo the British and Russian royal families were the only two which could look back on the previous twenty years without recalling either some actual fall from power or some narrow escape. Great Britain was the only monarchy in the world in which the ministers were in practice responsible to an elected assembly. Even the new Dutch monarchy, with a parliament of one chamber, was framed on an autocratic model. To this extent British policy never coincided with pure continental conservatism; and, as reforming legislation made the British constitution more liberal, the difference

Lord Byron. The sixth baron of that title, Byron captured the popular imagination both by his poetry and his death in the Balkans while helping the Greeks in their fight for independence against the Turks. As one of the romantics, his influence was felt more in continental Europe than in Britain.

widened. It was, however, chiefly geographical insularity that kept Great Britain from fully participating in continental affairs. She reduced her land forces to a modest establishment; but she maintained her naval predominance, and this no other power had any reason to challenge. It enabled her to press an international scheme which one section of the public earnestly believed in, the suppression of the slave-trade all over the world. In this she found support from some states and opposition from others. Sea-power also enabled her to push forward colonial enterprises. There was no longer a thorough-paced policy of expansion as there had been during the wars. There were no European rivals, and as much had been gained as could well be managed; but there was no hesitation about using force when it could clear away a local obstruction. So there were wars and annexations in Asia and Africa in the eighteen-twenties and thirties and forties; but none of the continental states objected to them.

On two occasions, the navy went into action in Mediterranean waters. North Africa, west of Egypt, had not been a theatre of war, but during the wars its corsairs interfered with shipping somewhat as they did in the seventeenth century. In 1816 Lord Exmouth, with a squadron, was ordered to visit Algiers, Tunis, and Tripoli and to call on them to release all British subjects whom they held as prisoners. This they all did. Tunis and Tripoli agreed that they would no longer treat their Christian prisoners as slaves, but over this the dey of Algiers made difficulties. Exmouth agreed that the point should be referred to the sultan; but while he was sailing home Algerians murdered a party of coral-fishers who were under the British flag. The government ordered Exmouth to turn back. With five sail of the line, and a Dutch frigate squadron co-operating, he anchored off Algiers and demanded the abolition of Christian slavery and the release of all Christian slaves. When this was refused a bombardment of eight hours forced compliance. About three thousand slaves, mostly Spanish and Italian, were freed.

The other naval action, the battle of Navarino in 1827, resulted from a crisis which put all Europe on the alert. Even before Napoleon's Egyptian expedition Great Britain was sensitive to any movement which threatened either of the two overland routes to India, that by the Gulf of Suez and the Red Sea or that by Asia Minor and the Persian Gulf. When the French threat was removed, there were opportunities for the Greek-speaking subjects of the Turkish sultan to enrich and strengthen themselves, and a national movement began among them. This appealed to many people in Britain and all over Europe, to some as a national rising, to some as a Christian movement against Mohammedan rule, and to yet others because it called up memories of the glorious freedom of ancient Greece. In 1821 the Greeks rebelled. The sultan crushed the revolt in Asia Minor and the islands by ruthless massacres; but on the mainland the Greeks proclaimed their independence, and the sultan had to wage war against them. This he could not do without the help of the pasha of Egypt. The Greeks, in great danger and divided among themselves, sought foreign help. Lord Byron, the romantic poet who was admired on the Continent even more than in Britain, went out as a volunteer, behaved magnificently, and died of malaria in the town of Missolonghi.

For the British government and for the future of Greece, Byron's death was more than a symbolic episode; it was decisive. Until then it had appeared that British interests would be best served by neutrality and by watching the Russians and the Turks as Queen Elizabeth had watched the French and Spaniards when the Dutch rebelled. George Canning, the Foreign Secretary, brought Russia and France together on the side of complete Greek independence. The Turks refused to grant an armistice; British and French squadrons shut the Turkish and Egyptian fleets in the Greek bay of Navarino, and were joined by Russian ships. The allied admirals, without being ordered to fight, but under real provocation, destroyed the two fleets and virtually ensured Greek independence. The British government did not approve this action, since the Turkish power, whatever its iniquities, still seemed to be needed as a counterweight to Russia; but the Russians attacked European Turkey from the north; the French drove the Turkish troops out of the Morea, and the sultan gave in. The Greek state was recognized as independent. Its territory was much smaller than the areas of Greek population. From its foundation until our own times it has contended with political instability at home and with the ambitions of unstable but warlike neighbours. One of these, Rumania, or rather its southern province, Wallachia, began its independent career about the same time. The great powers always watched the Balkan peninsula anxiously, and also the wider Eastern question, as it came to be called, the problematical future of the Turkish dominions. But none of the great powers intervened in that region with a fleet or an army until 1854, by which time many of the conditions which made the long peace possible had been undermined.

The Duke of Wellington passing through Rugby railway station in 1843. Like other notables, the Duke had his coach loaded on to a railway flatcar for his rail journeys. At this late stage of his career he was remembered by many as the victor of Waterloo, but others saw him as an elder statesman blocking urgent political reforms.

The British public took no interest in these distant affairs. Even in parliament they were seldom debated, and for the remainder of the nineteenth century Great Britain was insular in mind. The few self-appointed experts on foreign countries spoke and wrote, sometimes ably, but, except on commercial matters, to a very limited audience.

The domestic problems which had to be solved after the return to peace, by contrast, were urgent and absorbing. The first years after the peace were black and difficult, and the tory ministry of Lord Liverpool, which had been in office during the last years of the war and stayed until 1827, had to cope with such emergencies that it could not undertake large constructive measures. For a few months after the peace there was all-round economic prosperity; but the demobilization of 300,000 men, the falling-off of European demand for exports, and a run of bad harvests, produced severe poverty and unemployment. Now that foreign corn could be imported, a new measure of protection for home-grown corn was enacted, so strong in appearance that it caused dissatisfaction out of all proportion to its effect. In 1817 riotous outbreaks in London and in northern industrial areas caused justifiable alarm, and the government knew no remedy but repression. The Habeas Corpus Act was suspended, but prosecutions of offenders failed, and then economic conditions became easier. Discontent turned mainly into a political channel: its leaders organized mass demonstrations in support of the movement for the reform of parliament. In 1819 the magistrates tried to disperse such a meeting at St. Peter's Fields in Manchester. They sent in the yeomanry and the yeomanry lost their heads: two women and nine men were killed, and about 400 injured.

The memory of 'the Manchester Massacre' or 'Peterloo' rankled for generations; but the remedy of repression was tried again. It was planned more intelligently than before; though many contempories and many historians failed to recognize this improvement. Of the six Acts which parliament passed, two were just and necessary, one to prevent delay in bringing offenders to

A cartoon urging King William IV to make his influence felt on the side of parliamentary reform. Eventually the king did help the reform pass through parliament, by agreeing, under pressure, to create enough peers to vote the measure through the House of Lords, should that House, spurred by the Duke of Wellington, maintain its hostility.

trial, the other 'to prevent the training of persons in the use of arms and the practice of military evolutions'. Two were local and temporary, to authorize justices of the peace in sixteen disturbed areas to seize arms, and, with some exceptions, to prevent outdoor meetings for the next five years. Only two could justly be held to interfere with reasonable liberties. Of these the first tightened the law against blasphemous and seditious publications, and the other made political journalism more difficult by extending the scope of the stamp-duty on newspapers. But in the same session parliament also passed a second Factory Act. It was a limited measure, a further step in the protection of specially vulnerable classes of workers. Economic arguments were paraded to show that even the shortest steps in this direction would be harmful to the poor; but they did not succeed as they had done a few years before, and it was no negligible advance that this Act limited the working week of children in cotton factories to 72 hours, and fixed at nine the age at which they might begin work.

None of this legislation affected the two primary facts of social misery and sporadic disorder. Arthur Thistlewood, a former militia officer, had imbibed revolutionary ideas in France and frequented various radical associations in England. Most of his friends did not know, but government agents were fully aware, that he was also a conspirator in the style of Brutus and Guy Fawkes. He was arrested during the suspension of the Habeas Corpus Act, unsuccessfully prosecuted for treason and afterwards imprisoned for a year for threatening a breach of the peace by challenging the Home Secretary to a duel. After his release he made plans for a revolution, in which the first act was to be the murder of the entire cabinet as it sat at dinner. The police swooped while the conspirators were arming. Thistlewood and four others were hanged. There was no more of such reckless violence, and the tentative ameliorations went forward.

In 1825 there came the first of the cyclical crises and depressions which upset commerce and industry every nine years or so throughout the century; it brought extreme poverty and unemployment. In that same year there was another and bolder Factory Act, still applicable only to cotton mills and to workers under sixteen, which also forbade mill-owners and their fathers and sons to sit on juries for the trial of offences against it. Even more important, in 1823 Sir Robert Peel, the new tory Home Secretary, began the much-needed reform of the criminal law by abolishing the death penalty for several far from heinous offences. William Huskisson, who had served under Pitt, became president of the Board of Trade, where he began a long series of skilfully co-ordinated measures to facilitate commerce and to cheapen articles of ordinary consumpion. They fell short of bringing in free trade; they gave preferential treatment to the empire and to countries which made reciprocal treaties, but they followed the economic ideas of the time in adapting the tariff and navigation laws to the new conditions. In another sphere old restrictions were done away with. An Act of 1800 had forbidden all combinations of masters or workmen. It had failed to extinguish either trade unions or associations of employers, but had made certain acts unlawful which, nevertheless, went on. In 1824 and 1825 the law was modified on the principle of defining and limiting lawful combinations. In theory the purpose was to check intimidation; in fact the new law had a one-sided effect in favour of the employers; in due course it needed revision; but it was a better starting-point for rational improvement.

In 1827 Lord Liverpool was mortally ill and resigned. Two tory ministries followed which held office each for only a few months. In the first the prime minister was George Canning, a man of lively mind and by no means typical of his party, who died in office. His successor, Lord Goderich, failed to combine the tory groups in one cabinet, and after this failure the duke of Wellington took office. He was faced by two problems already of long standing, which turned on large and simple issues and were bound to involve both popular emotions and political manoeuvrings, namely the Catholic question and the question of parliamentary reform. Both dragged on for years, and neither was solved without dangerous excitements. The Catholic question, the first to come to a head, affected the whole United Kingdom but particularly Ireland. The presence of Irish Protestant members in the union parliament did have the effect that Bills for Catholic relief made better progress than before in the House of Commons; but none could pass the Lords. And nothing was done to relieve poverty in Ireland: the prevailing economic ideas discountenanced direct grants of public money, as they did for England, and it was even believed that the workhouse system, as England knew it, was more than Ireland could afford. So agrarian discontent and endemic agrarian outrages went on, and unrest spread into the towns; but the Catholic disabilities affected the whole of the population except only a small minority, and they provided a basis for the first political movement which drew its strength from the Irish masses. It was led by Daniel O'Connell, a lawyer and an orator born, who knew his people and understood by instinct what few popular leaders have known, that the way to success was to concentrate every energy on a single, intelligible purpose. In 1823 he formed the Catholic Association. It was supported by the Catholic clergy, who had never taken political action before, and it was financed by the 'Catholic rent', a penny a month for every member, which soon totted up to £1,000 a week. The authorities in Dublin Castle thought the Association threatened law and order, and dissolved it.

O'Connell, the lawyer, founded a new association which collected the same rent from the same membership. In 1826 there was a general election and O'Connell discovered that the forty-shilling freeholders of the counties, whose proper function was to vote as their landlords told them, could be told by this new and greater power to vote the other way. In 1828 O'Connell himself, though debarred as a Catholic from taking his seat in parliament, put up for County Clare, and was elected and re-elected like John Wilkes before him. It was evident that at the next general election most of the Irish counties would go the same way, and the best observers believed that Ireland was on the verge of civil war. At that moment the United Kingdom was fortunate in its men. The two heads of the cabinet were the Anglo-Irish duke of Wellington and Sir Robert Peel. Both had been consistent opponents of Catholic emancipation. Both saw that in this crisis they must change their minds. They had to deal with the king, and that was not easy; but in the last resort his conscience was not obstinate like his father's. The Catholic disabilities were repealed; Catholics might sit in parliament, O'Connell among them; all offices were opened to them except those of regent, Lord Chancellor and lord lieutenant of Ireland. Only an amendment, successfully moved in the House of Lords by a bishop, prevented the Act from relieving the Jews of the same disabilities; the latter had to wait until 1856.

This was a milestone on the sorrowful road of British relations with Ireland, and also, in the development of Irish society. In Britain it was scarcely less significant. Here the Catholics were a minority and were mainly landowners, with their dependants, and growing bodies of ill-paid Irish immigrants in the industrial regions. In the same sessions of parliament, and before Catholic emancipation, another measure had been carried which heightened the symbolic effect of emancipation when it came. This was the repeal of the Test and Corporation Acts. For many years Protestant Nonconformists had been protected by annual acts of indemnity from the penalties of breaking these laws. Their repeal thus made little or no practical difference and, in order to secure the agreement of the bishops the old oaths were not simply done away with. Ill-considered declarations were required instead; but this repeal, taken with Catholic emancipation, plainly ended the system by which full citizenship had been reserved to members of the Church of England. It did this at a time when the question of parliamentary reform was coming to a head.

Parliamentary reform reconstructed the electoral machinery through which the aristocracy had controlled the House of Commons, reducing the inherited muddle to comparative coherence; but it was even more important as a symbol of the reforming spirit. It came about in such a way that it seemed first as if the reformers would not stop short of violent revolution, and later as if only reform could avert it. When parliament had disposed of the Catholic question a skilful politician could have contrived a plan of moderate readjustment and won support for it from a sufficient combination of the divergent groups which made up the two main parties of tories and whigs. That, however, was beyond the capacity of Wellington, who could not keep together the different elements of his cabinet.

Changes outside parliament altered the conditions of the final struggle. On 25 June 1830 the unreliable King George IV died, and was succeeded by his brother William IV, an elderly naval officer, in some ways eccentric, but good-hearted and not incurably unfriendly to reform. On the Continent there was a sudden run of startling events which looked as if they might bring down the whole Vienna settlement in ruins. In July the reactionary Charles X of France made a very incompetent attempt at a *coup d'état*. Three days of barricades and shooting in the streets of Paris were enough to send him packing: he abdicated and found asylum in England. His cousin Louis Philippe, duke of Orleans, the head of a branch of the French royal family which had a footing in the revolutionary camp, had well-prepared followers and stepped into the vacant office in alliance with the middle classes, with a vaguely liberal programme. But this French revolution touched off another.

In August the Belgians, the people of the former Austrian Netherlands, broke into rebellion, demanding independence from the kingdom in which they were yoked with the Protestant Dutch. It was a matter of immediate importance to the United Kingdom to make sure that these neighbours of the French, Catholic, and governed by French-speaking upper and middle classes, did not revive the subordination to France which had been broken off by the fall of Napoleon. The French government proposed that the British government should act jointly with it in the Belgian crisis, and Wellington accepted this as the best means of avoiding war.

In England itself there happened in this summer the last of all agrarian risings. The labourers in the southern and eastern districts had grievances: low wages, winter unemployment, and the introduction of threshing machines. They rioted and burned ricks but did no murder; they had no common aims or conspiracy. One of them was killed by the yeomanry, but they were put down easily. After it was over, nine of them were hanged, about 450 transported, and 400 imprisoned. Wellington drew back from any attempt to work with the moderate reformers at home. When he plainly declared that he would oppose any measure of reform, the populace in London began to show hostile feeling. His parliament majority fell to pieces, and on 15 November he resigned. A fortnight later Poland broke out in insurrection against Russia.

The new government in Westminster with Lord Grey as prime minister consisted of aristocratic whigs and was supported by the radicals. It was united on parliamentary reform and led by able men. It brought in a strong Bill, which passed the Commons by a majority of one. If none but the English and Scottish members had voted, it would have been lost: the Irish members tipped the balance. In April 1831 the tories defeated the government and the king agreed to dissolve parliament. The whigs, returned with a large majority, brought in a second Bill, and when it was before the Lords they accepted an amendment, which was liberal in appearance but in fact strengthened the power of the landowners in the counties. It was to grant the franchise, hitherto reserved for freeholders, to tenants who held land worth £50 a year or more at the landlord's will. Thus all substantial farmers would have the right to vote in public at the hustings, and risk losing their farms. If none but the lay peers had voted on the Bill so amended, it would have passed; but 21 bishops voted against it.

Disorder broke out in many places, much more menacing in temper than the usual political disturbances, and backed or fomented by new radical associations. In Bristol, when the tory recorder arrived to hold quarter sessions, the mob sacked the Mansion House, threw open the prisons, and burnt down the bishop's palace. A cavalry charge restored order; but there were ugly portents in many places, including London. The government held on its course firmly and introduced a third, somewhat modified, Reform Bill. In order to get it through they asked the king to create a sufficient number of peers to overcome the adverse majority in the upper house. When the king boggled over

A textile factory in the 1830s. The cotton industry was the first of the large trades to be industrialized. Only in a factory could steam power be effectively used to drive machinery. The labour force, in which women and children predominated, worked very long hours for rather low wages, but successive factory acts brought a steady improvement.

the number, they resigned, and the king tried to find tory ministers who would put through a moderate reform. That could not be done without Peel, and Peel had the sense to stand out. The country waited as if on the verge of revolution. The whigs refused to take office again without the promise they needed from the king. The king gave his promise, but he did not need to fulfil it. He persuaded Wellington to drop his opposition and on 4 June 1832 the Bill passed its third reading in the Lords.

Thus was it proved once and for all that in the last resort the king and the Lords could not withstand the express will of the House of Commons if resistance would imperil elementary law and the conditions of normal living. It did not mean that the constitution had become democratic or even that anyone in the political world except the many-coloured minority of radicals believed that a step towards democracy had been taken. Most of the whigs hoped that this Act would be final, and they believed that they had preserved the best of the old constitution, in which a property-owning and tax-paying minority enjoyed in various degrees the right of voting for representatives in parliament. Only in one substantial principle did this Act embody the result of French revolutionary thought and practices. Until this time in most of the boroughs the members of parliament were elected by the municipal corporations, so that the representation of the burgesses was indirect. Now all elections were made by individual voters.

This was a sign of the transition by which, for the purpose of electing members, the boroughs and the counties became aggregates of individuals, or as we say 'constituencies', a new and to some people odious word in 1831. In some boroughs there had been a wide franchise which included some householders who were artisans or labourers. Now there was a uniform franchise for all the English boroughs (Scotland and Ireland being covered differently in separate Acts). It was not a wide franchise: the voters were householders whose houses were worth £10 a year or more, and £10 was the rent of a lower middle-class abode. In the counties the qualification for freeholders was 40*s*. (£2), for copyholders and long leaseholders more, for tenants-at-will £50. Altogether there were about 214,000 electors in England before 1832, and 435,000 in the United Kingdom. The estimate of the government, made in 1831, that the first Bill would add half a million to this number seems not to have been far wide of the ultimate result. In a few boroughs with a previously wide franchise the Act reduced the number of wage-earners who were entitled to vote.

In its traceable effects on the work of parliaments the redistribution of seats was much more influential than the systematizing of elections. Fifty-six despicable little boroughs, returning 111 members, were disfranchised; thirty others each lost one of their members. Forty-four populous places, hitherto unrepresented, most of them busy industrial centres, became parliamentary boroughs returning sixty-six members. For many years the social character of the House of Commons appeared much the same as before; but from the first the House was better informed about the interests and needs of the world of business,

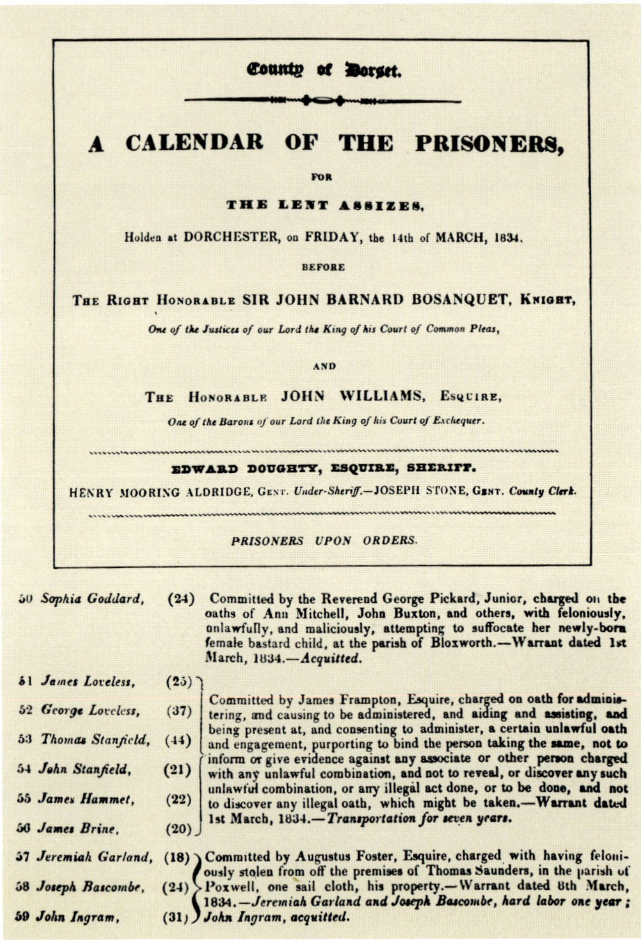

County of Dorset.

A CALENDAR OF THE PRISONERS,

FOR

THE LENT ASSIZES,

Holden at DORCHESTER, on FRIDAY, the 14th of MARCH, 1834,

BEFORE

THE RIGHT HONORABLE SIR JOHN BARNARD BOSANQUET, KNIGHT,

One of the Justices of our Lord the King of his Court of Common Pleas,

AND

THE HONORABLE JOHN WILLIAMS, ESQUIRE,

One of the Barons of our Lord the King of his Court of Exchequer.

EDWARD DOUGHTY, ESQUIRE, SHERIFF.

HENRY MOORING ALDRIDGE, GENT. *Under-Sheriff.*—JOSEPH STONE, GENT. *County Clerk.*

PRISONERS UPON ORDERS.

50 *Sophia Goddard*, (24) Committed by the Reverend George Pickard, Junior, charged on the oaths of Ann Mitchell, John Buxton, and others, with feloniously, unlawfully, and maliciously, attempting to suffocate her newly-born female bastard child, at the parish of Bloxworth.—Warrant dated 1st March, 1834.—*Acquitted.*

51 *James Loveless*, (25)
52 *George Loveless*, (37)
53 *Thomas Stanfield*, (44)
54 *John Stanfield*, (21)
55 *James Hammet*, (22)
56 *James Brine*, (20)
Committed by James Frampton, Esquire, charged on oath for administering, and causing to be administered, and aiding and assisting, and being present at, and consenting to administer, a certain unlawful oath and engagement, purporting to bind the person taking the same, not to inform or give evidence against any associate or other person charged with any unlawful combination, and not to reveal, or discover any such unlawful combination, or any illegal act done, or to be done, and not to discover any illegal oath, which might be taken.—Warrant dated 1st March, 1834.—*Transportation for seven years.*

57 *Jeremiah Garland*, (18)
58 *Joseph Bascombe*, (24)
59 *John Ingram*, (31)
Committed by Augustus Foster, Esquire, charged with having feloniously stolen from off the premises of Thomas Saunders, in the parish of Poxwell, one sail cloth, his property.—Warrant dated 8th March, 1834.—*Jeremiah Garland and Joseph Bascombe, hard labor one year; John Ingram, acquitted.*

The sentencing of the 'Tolpuddle Martyrs'. The calendar of the Dorchester Assizes, recording the case and sentence of six (nos 51–56 in this list) would-be trade unionists, charged with administering illegal oaths.

and it was not long before men who were products of the Industrial Revolution stepped into leading places in parliamentary politics.

After the Reform Act, parliamentary politics, with its ups and downs and its ins and outs, was watched by a larger and more critical audience than before. Division lists were published; reporting was encouraged. The radical movement outside was not satisfied with what it had gained, and its parliamentary representatives, though neither many nor united, were able to hustle the reluctant whig leaders into further advances; but for the first ten years or so there was never a situation in which one party claimed to stand for progress and the other was admittedly against it. Both parties were composite, and the divisions of opinion on many important matters cut across party lines; besides which there were many more or less technical reforms on which members of parliament were willing to accept expert opinions if the experts agreed. So the stream of remedial legislation flowed on. In 1833 slavery in the colonies was abolished. The large sum of £20 million was paid to the slave-owners in compensation; but even so this was an unprecedented inroad on the rights of property. In the same year came a new and somewhat stronger Factory Act, the Twelve Hours Act, which included the small beginnings of factory inspection and of schooling for employed children. In 1847 the Ten Hours Act, still only for textile industries, carried the same principles further. Controversy over factory legislation became entangled with larger problems of employment; and there was even one occasion, in 1858, when an association of factory occupiers promoted an Act to reduce the strictness of the rules for fencing machinery.

Bit by bit the factory laws became not merely humanitarian restrictions, but a part of the growing structure of provisions for public health. In the building of that structure several purposes converged. Governments had concerned themselves from time immemorial with epidemics; but there was no epidemic on the largest scale between the Great Plague in Charles II's reign and the Asiatic cholera of 1831. That emergency began the creation of the modern sanitary institutions which were finally merged in the Ministry of Health. Their development was supported by a network of associations in which politicians, medical men, and social scientists worked together.

The reform of the Poor Law ultimately aided the public health movement, even though at first the two movements were directed by two sets of men who disagreed about many fundamental questions. Except where it had been locally reformed by Act of Parliament the old Poor Law was a branch of local government, slipshod, wasteful, corrupt, and without any central control or supervision. During the Napoleonic war parish officers formed the habit of supplementing wages, especially agricultural wages, by payments of 'out-relief' from the rates. All these defects were drastically tidied up by the Poor Law Amendment Act of 1834, the most ambitious piece of social legislation which parliament had ever enacted. Poor relief was still paid for by local rates, but England and Wales were mapped out into unions of parishes, each with its local board of guardians elected *ad hoc*. These boards were supervised by a small central board of commissioners sitting in London. The Act was intensely unpopular, chiefly because it did not admit mere poverty as a ground for public relief; but also for harshness in many smaller matters. The moving spirit among the commissioners, Edwin Chadwick, was passionately in earnest about preventative medicine, and had his own philanthropic associations behind him; but he was dictatorial and he despised and starved the medical services which he controlled. It was not until well on in the twentieth century that the Poor Law was integrated into the health services.

Another important statute was the Municipal Reform Act of 1835. If it had come earlier it would not have been easy to deprive the municipal corporations of their functions as electors to parliament. The corporations were now to be elected by all male ratepayers, and whether a place was incorporated as a borough was to depend on relevant circumstances, of which population was the most important. The better boroughs soon showed themselves competent and useful, steadily extending their activities and their legal functions. There were other directions, such as law reform, in which lasting improvements were made, but some where there was little or none. In 1834 a notorious blow was struck against the workmen's right to combine. Six perfectly well-conducted labourers of Tolpuddle in Dorset were transported to Australia as convicts, for administering illegal oaths to their fellow members of a union. A mighty petition brought their release and return two years later; but from 1867 to 1869 eleven reports of a royal commission and much patient work in parliament entirely failed to produce any reform of the law. Nor had politicians relaxed their severity in keeping down public expenditure, though the state had plainly recognized widening responsibilities for the material welfare of the people.

Two popular movements, very unlike in their motives and composition and results, began in the late eighteen-thirties and soon rose higher in the numbers of their supporters than any organized movements in Britain had ever risen before. Chartism took its name from the People's Charter, published in 1838, which, besides general sentiments such as a complaint of high taxation, contained siz demands, all of which were meant to make parliament representative of the popular will, and all of which except one were realized between 1858 and 1911. That one which has never come to pass was a sign that the promoters had no experience of the working world of politics: it was a demand for a general parliamentary election every year. Of the other five the most significant were manhood suffrage and vote by ballot. Equal electoral districts were demanded as a subsidiary precaution against undue influences; the property qualification for members of parliament, which it was proposed to abolish, could be evaded; and the payment of members, while no doubt it would make it easier for poor men to enter politics, was not the only way by which they could maintain themselves. Taken altogether it was a reasonable programme carrying on the original character of British radicalism with a slight French infusion, essentially a bid for power, not an economic or even a political programme. Its supporters could not have agreed on any programme except the outline of a democratic constitution and that only for parliament. Some of them were revolutionists, openly advocating physical violence; some were steady, chapel-going Nonconformists. Some were for agrarian reforms such as splitting up large estates; some were socialists with plans for the control of industry. The movement, with its monster petitions and monster meetings,

BELOW Thomas Telford, Scottish civil engineer. Although a builder of notable bridges and canals, Telford is best remembered as a builder of really good roads. His foundations and drainage, the use of his fellow-Scot Macadam's impermeable road surface, combined to create a road which was smooth and longlasting. He died in 1834, at the beginning of the railway age.

THE

Stockton & Darlington Railway Company.

CLASS A PREFERENTIAL 5 PER CENT SHARES.

No 15415

£25 Share

ACT OF 1858.

This is to Certify that Edward Godman Kirkpatrick of Barham Court, in the County of Kent, Merchant; Luna Saul, of Brunswick, Cumberland, and Charles John Rennell, of No. 62, Eaton Place, Middlesex, Esquire, are the Proprietors of the CLASS A PREFERENTIAL SHARE Numbered 15415 in the STOCKTON & DARLINGTON RAILWAY COMPANY, subject to the Rules, Regulations and Orders of the said Company.

Given under the Common Seal of the said Company. Dated the Twenty Fourth day of September in the year of our Lord one thousand eight hundred & fifty eight.

Secretary

FAR BELOW A share certificate of the Stockton & Darlington Railway. This was the first public-use steam railway. It was a commercial success and encouraged new schemes elsewhere. The resulting boom in railway shares, the 'railway manias' of 1835–47, resulted in many investors losing their money, but nevertheless gave Britain the beginnings of a railway network.

A scene from the Irish potato famine. When the peasants' staple food, potatoes, was blighted in three successive years, 1845–47, the deaths of thousands followed. This was one of the first social crises to be exacerbated by economic theorists: relief would have been prompter if the prevailing ideological orthodoxy had not condemned the idea of state action interfering with the free activity of economic forces.

alarmed the propertied classes. There were strikes and riots. At Newport in Monmouthshire a dozen or so Chartists were killed in an abortive rising. The year 1848, even more than 1830, was a year of revolutions on the Continent; again a French king hurriedly crossed the Channel and there were outbreaks in Germany, the Mediterranean countries, and Poland. The greatest of all Chartist demonstrations assembled on Kennington Common and trudged towards the Houses of Parliament. The police told the leaders that they would not be allowed to cross the bridges. Everyone knew that there were troops in readiness. The procession turned back, and Chartism was dead.

One of the many causes of its failure was the success of the other movement, well led and better organized than any previous political agitation, the movement for the repeal of the corn laws. This was started by middle-class leaders and, though they were political radicals as well, its aim was economic. It was a single aim, and it could be put forward in very simple terms: if import duties on foreign corn were abolished, bread would be cheaper. Other, more complex, arguments could be found, but they had to be skilfully managed if they were to make it appear that cheaper corn would not mean ruin for landlords, farmers, and agricultural labourers. In 1838, the year of the People's Charter, a group of Lancashire manufacturers founded the Anti-Corn Law Association, afterwards called the Anti-Corn Law League. Their task was difficult because the price of corn was not uniformly high, but they succeeded equally well in hard-hitting platform propaganda and in persistent debate in the House of Commons. Two leaders with complementary gifts, both mill-owners in Lancashire, were the lucid and statesman-like Richard Cobden and John Bright, a Quaker with a commanding oratorical style of his own invention.

The parliamentary attacks on the corn laws took place during the second ministry of Sir Robert Peel, which began in 1841. Peel, whose own wealth came from Lancashire mills, was the son of that Sir Robert Peel who had introduced the first Factory Act. A tory in the succession to Pitt, he had made his mark first by his law reforms, then by the establishment of the Metropolitan Police. This demonstrated that the best instrument for maintaining law and order was an efficient civilian force for which central and local authorities shared responsibility. After ten years it was extended over the country. When the Reform Act had passed, Peel did another signal service by regrouping the defeated tories on the basis of accepting parliamentary reform as an accomplished fact. This was the beginning of the change by which the tories became conservatives, a word which had already been used for those who resist or scrutinize change instead of regarding it as desirable in itself. It was soon after Peel's time that the two main parties came to be commonly called Conservatives and Liberals. Except for a few months in 1834–5 Peel was out of office until 1841, but even in opposition he had great authority. None of his contemporaries equalled his skill as a party leader or his grasp of interdependent social and economic realities. Not that he was always right. He opposed the Ten Hours Bill. Nor was he rigidly consistent: he was strong enough to abandon a policy when it ceased to satisfy his test that the constitution should be preserved. In his second ministry he began the reform of taxation which was completed, according to his principles, twenty years or so after his death. He abolished the import duties on a great number of articles, including foods, raw materials, and partly manufactured articles, and reduced the duties on many more. In order to do all this and to carry the small income-tax which was needed to balance the budget, he let off income from land lightly and retained the corn law. There were other measures which buttressed this liberal commercial policy. The keystone was the Bank Charter Act of 1844. This ended a long-drawn currency controversy by setting an almost completely self-regulating gold standard for the pound sterling, in the sense that, in relation to the currency, the function of the Bank of England was only to exchange notes for gold and gold for notes. It provided the merchants and financiers with 'sound money', confidence in which enabled British commerce and the London money market, with British manufacturers behind them, to grow still greater.

The first shock to the rising confidence came from Ireland. After Catholic emancipation there was no whole-hearted attempt to uproot the causes of the Irish grievances. It was not easy for governments to co-operate with O'Connell; but he held back from the extreme course of agitating for the repeal of the union. there were still coercion Acts; but three solid reforms were accomplished. The collection of tithes for the Protestant Church of Ireland had been little more than an annual ritual of argument and violence. the 1838 Tithe Commutation Act converted tithes to a properly administered land tax. In the same year the Poor Law was extended to Ireland. In 1840 the municipal corporations were reformed. In that year died Thomas Drummond, a

Scotsman who adopted Ireland as his country, and beginning as an engineer officer and a scientist, ruled for five years as under-secretary in Dublin. He founded the Royal Irish Constabulary and the stipendiary Resident Magistrates who presided over the amateur justices of the peace. He is remembered for writing to the magistrates of Tipperary that 'property has its duties as well as its rights. To the neglect of those duties in times past is mainly to be ascribed that diseased state of society in which such [agrarian] crimes take their rise.'

It was after Drummond's death that Peel's great ministry began, and Peel was not expected to make concessions to discontent. O'Connell demanded repeal of the Union without plainly intending to use force; but Peel drafted troops to Ireland, and prohibited a mass meeting. O'Connell told his followers to obey. Although his movement had failed as Chartism had failed, he was prosecuted and found guilty, by a Protestant jury, of contriving by intimidation to procure changes in the government, laws, and constitution. After a few months in prison he succeeded in an appeal to the House of Lords. The leadership of Irish nationalism passed to a new generation, moved by the mature national spirit for which continental revolutions had set their examples. For the present the Young Ireland movement was in the stage of obscure beginnings. Peel pushed through some tentative steps towards conciliation, and appointed a strong commission to examine the agrarian question. Then came the irreparable disaster which cuts modern Irish history into two parts, before and after.

Ireland was overcrowded. The population, taking the country as a whole, was the densest in Europe, rather more tightly packed than that of the Netherlands. In 1841 it reached its maximum, eight millions, one-third of the population of the British Isles. Its economy was backward. There were no railways, and in hundreds of thousands of homes there was no money, because the people grew their own food and needed no coin except to pay their rent and buy a few inexpensive necessaries such as tools. A larger proportion than in any other country depended for food on the potato, and the potato was subject to a blight, already known in America and Germany, which appeared in England in 1835 and again in 1845. The scientists knew next to nothing about crop-diseases. In July 1846 three-quarters of the Irish potato crop rotted in the ground. The Irish governing class, with scarcely any officials and only a rudimentary system of local government, did what it could to improvise food supplies and relief-works which would enable the workers to pay for food. Many landlords remitted rents, spent generously and did their best for their tenants, of whom some were bewildered and some recalcitrant; but only the government could do anything to match the need. No British government had ever coped with famine, and it was the more baffling because the economists believed that state action was at bottom inimical to economic welfare. In spite of opposition Peel spent public money on buying and distributing American maize and in subsidizing relief-works. He decided to throw the ports open to imports of foreign food by repealing the corn laws. There were mistakes in the details both of the policy and of its execution; but there always are mistakes, and there can be no doubt that Peel made the right choice in the emergency.

Calamity followed calamity. There was a second bad potato harvest. Starvation was followed by disease. In the years 1846–50 very nearly a million people died in Ireland. Emigration from the ruined country rose to dreadful proportions: from 1852 to 1861 more than another million people left it, two-thirds of them for America. By 1911 the population of Ireland was half what it had been in 1841, and from one-third it had fallen back to one-tenth of the population of the United Kingdom. What that meant in terms of human suffering can never be estimated. In a narrower perspective it led on to the decline of the Irish landowners, to the financing of nationalist movements by embittered exiles especially in America, and to new complications in the relations between Ireland and her neighbours.

An agricultural upheaval of a different kind was transforming the Scottish Highlands. Agricultural progress and rising population towards the end of the eighteenth century had meant that small-scale crofters' farming was no longer sufficient. Not enough food was produced. Landowners' estates faced insolvency. The first reaction was a wave of emigration, with Highlanders from particular localities tending to settle in their 'home' colonies in Canada. In 1811, with the best of intentions, crofters in Sutherland were moved from the glens to the coast, where economic prospects seemed better. Later transfers, however, were resisted, and tenants were forcibly moved from their ancestral homes and land. Thus began the Clearances, which would culminate in the Glengarry Clearances of 1853; entire families were uprooted, put on ships, and despatched to the colonies. The land they left behind was then farmed according to the latest principles.

Victorian Prosperity 1846–1870

1848 The climax and decline of the Chartist movement.
1849 Navigation acts are repealed. Britain annexes the Punjab.
1851 The Great Exhibition is held. A Dover-Calais telegraph cable is laid.
1854 The Crimean War begins, continuing to 1855
1857 The Indian Mutiny begins at Calcutta.
1858 The Indian Mutiny is mastered. The Jews gain full civil rights in Britain.
1859 Charles Darwin's *Origin of Species* is published.
1865 Joseph Lister practices antiseptic surgery in Glasgow. The Salvation Army is founded.
1867 A second Reform Act extends the franchise.

Peel's great decision about the corn laws and Ireland was also a turning-point in British party politics. He had all the whigs and radicals with him in repealing the corn laws; but a substantial body of Conservatives voted against him. They were led by a theatrical and incongruous figure, Benjamin Disraeli, whose middle-class origin and Jewish descent did not prevent him from infusing into their landowners' self-interest a devotion to chivalric values which were supposed to be sacrificed by commercial and industrial materialism. Unable to save the corn laws, they split the party and turned Peel out of office. For the next twenty years there was no strong government with a united party behind it. But this did not interrupt the set of commercial policy towards free trade. The cyclical fluctuations did not vanish as they had been expected to do after the Bank Charter Act, but the trend of growth and prosperity continued. After a few years Disraeli gave up protectionism. One government after another chipped away restraints on trade, the navigation laws, some of the colonial preferences, import duties on hundreds of articles. Both imports and exports increased. Between 1846 and 1850 more than £150 million were invested in British railway companies, mainly by the middle class. From 1855 onwards there was a marked and increasing excess of imports over exports; but this was financed by invisible exports. Britain's share of the world's carrying trade was rising, and British capital was earning greater dividends by financing developments overseas, especially in South America, China, Africa, Canada, and Australia where British engineers built whole railway systems, and also in Europe. Continental visitors were impressed, not always pleasurably, by the concentration of the national energies on wealth-getting. It was from the Continent that this gratifying progress sustained a second shock.

On the Continent the revolutions of 1848 had subsided, leaving behind them so many ambitions and fears that the great powers could not be trusted to maintain for very long the peace which began with the Vienna settlement. Liberal German nationalists had tried to unite their country under the Prussian king as emperor; but the king had refused and Prussia set itself against the liberal ideas. The Austrian empire was threatened by the national movements which it had suppressed for the time being in Italy and Hungary. In France a short-lived republic had elected as its president a nephew of Napoleon, who with very little difficulty had set up as emperor with the title Napoleon III. He was all for free trade and prosperity; he announced that empire, or his empire, meant peace; but his military men were active, and the oppressed nationalities beyond his frontiers looked upon him as a potential saviour. In the inner circles of British politics there were some who sympathized with one side or the other in each of these antagonisms. The queen and her serious-minded consort, Prince Albert of Saxe-Coburg-Gotha

PREVIOUS PAGE Queen Victoria and Prince Albert. This photograph was taken in 1859 at Osborne House, the Queen's residence in the Isle of Wight. Two years later Albert, who had done so much to guide the queen, was dead of typhoid fever. Victoria's mourning was intensely genuine, leading to a long seclusion through her middle age.

RIGHT One of the naves of the 1851 Great Exhibition. Essentially, this exhibition displayed the wonderful possibilities of the new age of industry and science. The building itself, the Crystal Palace, with its broad expanse of brightly illuminated covered area, was an example of what new technology could achieve.

followed German affairs intently. The French emperor had lived in England for years as an exile, and had friends here. But political Britain as a whole was still indifferent to continental affairs. The radicals, many of the liberals, and most of the business world believed that civilization and progress were inseparable from free trade and peace. In 1851 the whole nation celebrated the blessings of industry and international friendship in the Great Exhibition, housed in the Crystal Palace erected in Hyde Park. The duke of Wellington, over eighty years old, was a frequent visitor to the Exhibition, more gazed at than any of the exhibits; but when he died in the following year, to be entombed 'with rare magnificence', people thought of him as the hero of an epic which had come to its conclusion.

A few perceived that this magnificence expressed another, not pacific, side of human nature. Both the political world and the wider public were shocked and disillusioned to find, very soon, that war was imminent. The trouble came in the remotest corner of Europe, and from causes which seemed to be entirely outside British control or responsibility. The Turkish empire, already weakened by rebellions, seemed certain to lose more territory whenever the Greeks and others saw opportunities. Its internal government was so corrupt and incompetent that it seemed unable to hold its heterogeneous territories together. Russia was the one great, independent country in which the established form of Christianity was the Orthodox, or Eastern, Church, and the Russians had gradually become patrons and protectors of the millions of Orthodox who were still under Turkish rule in Europe and Asia. Russia could use this as a means of influence and even of extending its frontiers in the Balkan peninsula and further east. Austria, also a neighbour of the Balkan provinces, would resent such action. The French had their links with Arab Christians who were not Orthodox but Catholics. British interests in the region were less definite and less localized; but traditionally Britain was unwilling to see a strong European power in control of that part of the Mediterranean which lay on one of the routes to India. A dispute arose in Turkish Palestine between Orthodox and Catholic priests, each claiming the right to look after the Holy Places associated with the presence of Christ. Tsar Nicholas I of Russia and the Emperor Louis Napoleon of France took opposing sides on this issue. Nicholas vainly proposed that the great powers, notably Britain and Russia, should prevent future trouble by partitioning the Turkish Empire between themselves. The Turkish sultan rejected Nicholas's demand that the Russian tsar be recognized as protector of the Orthodox Christians within the Turkish Empire. Negotiations failed. In 1853 the Russian army crossed the river Pruth into Moldavia and the Turks declared war on Russia.

In the Russo-Turkish war there were victories and defeats on both sides, but France and England vacillated between intervening and keeping clear, each sometimes urging the other on, and sometimes holding back. When the Greeks joined the Russians, the British and French fleets blockaded the Greek coast and so forced them into neutrality. The fleets moved towards the Dardanelles, then went through into the Black Sea and then began to concentrate off the Russian port of Sebastopol at the southern end of the Crimean Peninsula. The tsar sent an ultimatum. The war began in March 1854 and lasted less than two years. It was not a war to the finish for either party. The British sent out fewer than 100,000 men, the French more than three times as many. They did not repeat Napoleon's error of invading the Russian land-mass. Apart from bombarding some forts on the Baltic coast and from some minor raids even further away, they concentrated their whole effort against the Crimea, on which the Russian naval threat to Constantinople and the Turkish empire was based. This was perhaps a month's voyage from Portsmouth, but it was three months' march from Moscow. There were no modern means of communication except an electric submarine cable from Balaklava to Varna in Bulgaria. All the armies suffered hideously. Of the British 2,755 were killed or died of wounds but 21,000 died of disease. For the first time in history there were newspaper correspondents in the theatre of war, and they told the whole British public the truth about the unpreparedness, and the official incompetence and worse which had led to this breakdown. There were only two popular heroes on the British side. Florence Nightingale brought organization and compassion to the care of the sick and wounded. Lord Cardigan's Light Brigade, due to confused orders, made a successful but very costly frontal attack on a strong Russian position at Balaklava. There were enormous blunders in tactics and strategy, in supply and reconnaissance, in discipline and administration. The allied troops won a pitched battle at the Alma; then they laid siege to Sebastopol and won another battle outside it at Inkerman. The siege went on through the Russian winter and Sebastopol was captured in September 1855. By that time negotiations for ending the war were far advanced.

The ineffective ministry which drifted into the war was a coalition of whigs and Peelites, under Lord Aberdeen, which held office from 1852 to 1855. It resigned before the fall of Sebastopol, and the new prime minister was Lord Palmerston, an Irish peer who sat in the Commons and was, among other things, an outstanding parliament man. For the whole period between the eclipse of Peel and his death in 1865 he appealed to the public imagination more vividly than any other statesman. He had held office before the fall of Napoleon; he had been Foreign Secretary for sixteen years, and he had been a necessary member of whig cabinets since Grey and Melbourne. In home affairs he was no ardent reformer; in foreign affairs he was on the liberal side, and he was apt to assert his views in provocative language; but there were few occasions when his actual influence made foreign relations more thorny than he found them.

The terms agreed upon in the Peace of Paris were such that Russian aggression against Turkey was suspended for more than twenty years. Neither England nor France has even been officially at war with Russia since. The Danubian principalities were made independent states under Turkish suzerainty. The independence and integrity of the Ottoman empire were guaranteed, and the rights of other states to interfere on behalf of its Christian subjects were extinguished. Turkey at last became formally a member of the European state-system. The fleets of the powers outside the Dardanelles were forbidden to enter the Black Sea.

Great Britain had learnt some hard lessons. The army and navy had come under the searching eyes of reformers, and in the ensuing years there were improvements. The pace was leisurely, but medical and nursing services were organized. Partly as a reply to French competition, naval architecture and armament were efficiently taken in hand. But neither service acquired a sound higher organization or an adequate system of training. At the emotional level the Crimean War was a great historical event, but it made no corresponding impression in the public attitude to

policy. It cost £70 million, of which more than half was paid by taxation and less than half had to be borrowed. In the upward course of material prosperity it was scarcely even an interruption.

The public could not be as indifferent to the colonies as it was indifferent to foreign countries. Many families kept in touch with their cousins overseas by letter-writing and some even by occasional visits. Increasing numbers travelled to and fro on business. There were strong links of sentiment. One was the interest in Christian missions. This was closely allied to the suppression of the slave-trade, and of slavery in the British possessions, which occupied the philanthropists and parliament and the navy. In nearly all the colonies the white settlers grew in numbers by immigration and by natural increase; in some of them there were unmistakable signs of future wealth. Major constitutional decisions had to be taken; but, as it happened, even when the colonists were divided by ill feeling or by overt violence, relations with the mother country were conducted with cool deliberation. British statesmen and administrators had the warning of American independence before them, and many considerations restrained them from asserting their authority. They openly admitted that they did not and could not know enough about the local conditions in the colonies to lay down anything but the broad principles of policy. They were not prepared to spend large sums on development; they grudged expenditure on anything beyond defence. Some of the radical politicians watched over this page of the estimates as they watched over government expenditure in general, with the prevailing ideas of public finance on their side. It had come to be generally believed that European countries could not derive any economic benefit from colonies. Most people assumed that, sooner or later, colonies of settlement would become independent. No British government had a policy of expansion. Some projectors worked out schemes for assisted emigration and for planned settlement; but with little practical result.

There were indeed a few annexations; but they were made for limited purposes and not with the aim of finding outlets for the new wealth or alleviations for the new poverty at home. The Cape Colony, with its few English-speaking inhabitants among the Dutch and the African majority, was already hard enough to govern. A new and more difficult problem arose there, which had parallels on a greater scale elsewhere, for instance in Russia and America, the problem of spontaneous movement forward from the frontier. British governments wanted no new territories; but when farmers ventured into the neighbourhood of warrior tribes like the Zulus, and traders established themselves to the north-east in Natal, disturbances resulted, and demands for protection. These were refused; larger bodies of the Dutch, dissatisfied with their opportunities under British rule, set out for the north. From 1835 to 1837 some 5,000 men, women, and children crossed the Orange River in the Great Trek. They made it clear that they wanted to be independent; but an unforeseen consequence of their heroic movement and the resistance to it was the diversion of some of these migrants into Natal. This brought lawlessness and insecurity intolerably near to the old centres of population, and in 1843 the government reluctantly annexed Natal. It did not decide whether or in what legal form it would, if necessary, extend its authority over the other new settlements.

Two other acquisitions, Aden in 1839 and Hong Kong in 1842, were incidental, intended for safeguarding eastern trade. The sultan of Aden had a reasonably good bargain when he

The charge of the Light Brigade. This incident of the Battle of Balaklava was the most renowned event of the Crimean War. Due to a misunderstanding the small Light Brigade was sent against the main Russian positions. The latter were captured, but about a third of the Brigade's cavalrymen were casualties. Tennyson celebrated the event in verse: 'Theirs not to reason why, Theirs but to do and die.'

accepted British protection and a detachment of troops from India: Egypt at the time was in rebellion against its Turkish overlords and he was in danger from both sides. Hong Kong was the one gain which Great Britain made for herself in the first China war, the Opium War of 1839–42. In this war the British aim was to gain admittance for trade, but it discreditably included the illicit trade in opium from India. Great Britain shared equally with other European powers the other rights and privileges which China then and afterwards conceded. Aden and Hong Kong were not evidence of deep-laid imperial schemes, though some continental observers soon suspected that they were.

The French, in the first phase of their revival, were easily tempted into adventures overseas, and it was to forestall a move which they were expected to make that the British, in 1840, proclaimed New Zealand a colony and incorporated it with New South Wales. For years indignant missionaries and advocates of systematic colonization had drawn the attention of parliament to the evils of uncontrolled white immigration, and especially to the demoralization and oppression of the Maoris; but even this annexation was made reluctantly. Almost at once it became evident that New Zealand must be separated from Australia. The early years of the colony were troubled by collisions with the Maoris and by divergences of policy between the government and the New Zealand Company, organized to carry out the ideas of the systematic colonizers. The company was dissolved and the executive was made responsible to the local assemblies. Between 1847 and 1850 the European population doubled; but its expansion and its absorption of land inevitably led to serious hostilities, which did not end until 1869. They were caused by ruthless land-grabbing, but they were far from being the most savage of frontier wars. Even before they were over wise measures had been taken for conciliation, and from 1871 the small indigenous population ceased to decline.

It was in this period that Australia was launched as a social entity, with the makings of a nation. At the beginning there were settlements in New South Wales, but only on the coast. The interior was unexplored. There was no programme of expansion: other posts occupied as a precaution against Napoleon had been abandoned after 1812. Before wholesome conditions for the development of the region could be established, it was necessary to put an end to its use for penal settlements. Transportation to the West Indian colonies had been used as a punishment for political offenders in the seventeenth century and later. New South Wales was founded in 1788 to be peopled by convicts and their keepers. As a part of the humanizing of British criminal law it might have been possible to devise a scheme for such offenders as could build a community overseas; but nothing of this kind was thought out. Neither on the voyage nor when these men and women were landed as prisoners, nor when they were set free to seek their own livelihood, was anything ensured except that they were bundled out of sight. It soon became known in Britain that the results were alarming and disgraceful. Yet further penal establishments were founded in Tasmania, Norfolk Island, and Western Australia. In 1837 a committee of the House of Commons recommended the abolition of the whole system; but it was not until 1868 that it was finally done away with.

This chapter in the record of man's inhumanity to man is rich in lessons for the study of society. Great Britain expelled altogether some thousands of its people. Some of them, but for the stupidity of the laws, could have lived useful lives: such were

Lord Palmerston. An Irish viscount who sat in the House of Commons for 58 years, Palmerston had two long spells as Foreign Secretary. In the first he was constructive, and played a key role in the emergence of an independent and friendly Belgium. Later he began to strike aggresive anti-foreigner postures, often based on ignorance, which appealed to the man-in-the-street but did little good for Britain.

the Tolpuddle 'martyrs'. Others were villains who, in earlier years, would have been sent to the gallows. Among the millions who now populate Australia there are descendants of convicts of either kind, and these include men and women of whom any country would be proud.

Even if British opinion had not turned against it, transportation could not have survived in the growing population and wealth of Australia. The first half of the century saw the rise of the Australian wool-industry. Exports of wool grew rapidly, and, although sheep-farming does not directly employ many men, they provided a basis for all-round prosperity. The first railway was opened in 1850, and by that time the university of Sydney was coming into being. In the next year a transformation of the Australian economy began with the working of gold in Victoria and in New South Wales. Between 1850 and 1860 the population nearly trebled.

Because this economic growth was spontaneous, and because it sprang from conditions unlike those in any other part of the world, Australia was not hampered by well-intentioned supervision from Westminster. Systematic colonizers rightly believed that in principle the occupation of land should not be left to haphazard private enterprise; but they could not prescribe for a country where the optimum area for a farm might be hundreds of thousands of acres. A gold rush always upsets everyday business, but only the men on the spot can put it right. So, although institutions had to be adapted quickly to the changing scene, the necessary constitutional progress did not provoke conflicts. the indigenous people were too few and too harmless to raise problems like those of New Zealand.

The main decisions related to the division of the country into states and the allotting of powers to elective assemblies. For the latter there were useful precedents, especially in Canada. The whole continent was declared to be British territory in 1826. There were already settlements in Queensland, and within ten years in Western Australia, Victoria, and South Australia. In 1842 New South Wales was granted a legislative assembly, with two-thirds of the members elected and the rest officials and official nominees. In 1850 the Australian Constitutions Act laid down the broad lines on which the five colonies, New South Wales, Tasmania, South Australia, Victoria, and Queensland were to exercise responsible government. Western Australia had to wait longer, and the idea of a legislature, executive and judiciary for the whole of Australia, though it had already been mootted, was not practicable until the twentieth century.

Canada, the oldest, the most populous, and the most complex of the colonies of settlement, had more disturbances; but its affairs were essentially in Canadian hands, and by an early date it was freed from any effective subordination. In the huge area of Canada, besides small trading posts on the Pacific and around Hudson's Bay, there were three blocks of population. The French-speaking province of Quebec was Catholic, conservative, and self-contained. Beyond it, reached by the St. Lawrence river, was Upper Canada, which had begun to grow when the United Empire Loyalists came as farmers and opened up Ontario. In the early days it was too remote to attract as many immigrants from Britain as the maritime provinces, Nova Scotia and New Brunswick, south of the St. Lawrence, which prospered by the timber-trade, fisheries, and shipping. In 1791 Upper and Lower Canada were constitutionally separated and given each its own elected assembly, though with very restricted powers. Each had a governor and a nominated legislative and executive council. Each, however, came, as was virtually inevitable, to have grievances, and friction arose between the two. Upper Canada was the more restive. It was dominated by an oligarchic combination of rich families. The Church of England was endowed with large areas of land although many of the people, especially the Scots, did not belong to it. Quebec had some positive complaints, financial and other; but its discontent in the main arose from a developing national feeling.

By 1837, in the eyes of the law, both provinces were rebellious. The British government sent out Lord Grey's radical son-in-law, Lord Durham, to act and report. As a man of action he was a failure. The Report which he signed scarcely deserved the status of a political classic which was conferred on it sixty years or so later by a school of British politicians who thought that it embodied principles of universal validity. It applied the traditional British idea of promoting the interests of two adjacent countries by a union, like those unions which had formed the United Kingdom. So Upper and Lower Canada were united in 1840, and remained so until 1867, when everyone recognized that the geographical extent of a single government should be decided by common sense in the light of the people's wishes. Durham also recommended that the principal demand of the rebels should be granted. This had come to be called 'responsible government', which meant that the officials in Canada should be responsible, except in matters of imperial concern, to the representative body. It was never defined in strict legal terms, and it was never granted by any Act of parliament; but British governments conceded it step by step in practice. From 1847 Canadian ministries depended on a parliamentary majority like British ministries. In 1853 the clergy reserves were handed over. The Canadians framed their own tariff and in 1858 laid protective duties on British goods. Great Britain was still responsible for defence and for the conduct of Canadian foreign relations; but the growth and transformation of Canada and the federation of 1867 were achievements of a free nation.

The affairs of the Indian peninsula were more completely separate from the affairs of the United Kingdom than those of any other subject peoples had ever been from their masters. With sailing-ships, and even in the early days of steam navigation, the journey round the Cape lasted four months. Most of the British in India went out as young men to spend their working life there, seldom if ever visiting the home country to which, if they survived the climate and other hazards, they would retire when they could afford it. The Europeans in the East India Company's army numbered about 40,000, the Asians more than three times as many. The Europeans engaged in commercial and administrative work were few, European women much fewer. Except in the highest ranks there was scarcely any movement to and fro between employment in Indian administration and any kind of public service at home. Government in India was authoritarian. It had to overcome immense obstacles in an uncharted multiplicity of unknown languages and misunderstood religions, customs, and institutions. A serviceable literature in English about these things was slowly accumulating; but the British reading public had neither elementary knowledge nor imaginative grasp of anything Indian.

In this period British influence brought about decisive changes in India, but mainly through the traders and engineers who brought the gifts of the Industrial Revolution and through individual administrators who put liberal ideas into practice. From the time when Wellesley claimed for Great Britain the status of the paramount power, it was certain that more territories would be annexed, and more independent states brought under protection. This process went forward until it was halted by reaching natural barriers or lands too poor and difficult to be worth attention. There is no need to summarize here the developments of political doctrine, such as the rule that if a native dynasty died out, its legitimate successor was the British Crown, nor the campaigns, in Afghanistan, towards the Himalayas, into Burma, and elsewhere. Except in the direction of Burma British rule virtually reached its full extent.

The spirit and purpose of this British rule was still uncertain until the eighteen-thirties, the years of confident reform in Britain. A wide choice of possibilities lay open between respecting Indian civilization, preserving it as the basis of society, while associating Indians with the work of government at every level, and, on the other hand, maintaining the separateness of the Europeans as the surest way to keep them free from entanglement in Asian conflicts, and to introduce order, material progress and the diffusion of knowledge on the western model. The two most influential groups of thinkers in British political life, the evangelicals and the utilitarians, firmly adhered to the latter view. Almost all of the senior military officers and civil servants were strong believers in Christian ethics and missionary endeavours.

Indians who were reformers looked on education as a means to prosperity and eventual self-government. In 1835 Thomas Babington Macaulay, the great historian, then a member of the supreme council in India, drew up a scheme for higher education in which English was to be the language of instruction, and its content was to be western and progressive. The Act for renewing the East India Company's charter, passed two years earlier, laid it down that no native of India, nor any natural-born British subject was to be disabled by religion, descent, or colour from holding any place, office, or employment; but the future was not to be what these two documents, taken in conjunction, foreshadowed. The educational system grew rapidly and provided many efficient subordinates for the administration; but, more from neglect and inattention than from any positive policy, very few Indians reached responsible, and none reached high, appointments. The government took charge of social welfare in spheres which no government in Great Britain had ever touched. The Indian tax-payers bore the charges, but the public works were beneficial to all classes, and the civil servants were free from corruption to an unheard-of-degree. Road-making, bridge-building, forestry, the training of engineers, and many other social services were carried on as efficiently as private enterprise could manage them anywhere in the world.

In this hopeful phase the Indian Mutiny suddenly broke out. In January 1857 four regiments at Barrackpore, near Calcutta, gave trouble. Disorder spread until about a third of the Bengal army was fighting against its commanders. The mutineers, though they had no plan and no organized leadership, moved up the rivers until they captured Delhi. The country did not rise to support them, nor did the most dangerous of the native princes. But it seemed as if the existence of the British power was at stake. The European troops were dispersed, wrongly posted, and slow to move. In spite of heroic resistance by isolated groups commanded by soldiers or civilians, the rebels committed atrocities worse than Europeans had ever suffered in India before. At the beginning of 1858 the relief of Cawnpore restored British authority, but fighting went on throughout that year. It ended with military victories, not with any agreement or terms of settlement. There was indeed no one with whom such terms could have been made, nor any possible agenda for negotiation. this was not a national rising, indeed there was in no sense an Indian nation. It was a military revolt, ignited by complaints of the soldiery which could be, and were, satisfied by administrative remedies. Its explosive force was hatred of foreign rule and religion. The mutineers had no conception of the available British strength. When it was suppressed the government resumed its policy of welfare with energy and conviction; but, for all that, the memory of these years impaired the chances of progress on the westernizing line that had been chosen. During the fighting British troops had avenged their massacred women and children by fierce reprisals; and in spite of the efforts of a magnanimous governor-general, Lord Canning, severe punishments were meted out. The British could never regain their full sense of security, or their confidence in the prospect of a westernized India.

In Britain the news of the Indian Mutiny brought horror, and at first intense anxiety; but it did not lead to any lasting change of policy. The East India Company was deprived of its last

George Stephenson. A self-educated mechanic, George Stephenson so improved the steam locomotive as to make possible the railway age. Between the opening of the Stockton & Darlington Railway, which he engineered, in 1825, and his death in 1848, Britain's main railway links took shape. Many of them were built by himself or by his son Robert.

remaining political functions; but that was irrelevant to the causes of the Mutiny, and hardly amounted to a change of policy, since the Company had already lost its power of making appointments when the examination system was introduced a few years before. In Britain the Mutiny appeared, like the Crimean War, to be a distant disaster, scarcely detracting from the benefits of progress. In 1867 a Conservative government stole a march on the Liberals by extending the franchise. France and some of the states of the American Union had experimented with manhood suffrage and come to no harm; in Great Britain, but in the boroughs only, roughly speaking, the well-paid artisans were given votes. Both parties in parliament agreed that this advance from the compromise of 1832 was justified by the prevalence of religious influences and 'the civilizing and training powers of education . . . so far as the mass of the people is concerned'. Statisticians were soon to be equally satisfied from their point of view. They described 1871–5 as a 'period of record prosperity, as testified by a rising birth-rate and average wage-rate and a falling rate of pauperism and unemployment'. It was not only that the British congratulated themselves: the strongest evidence came from other countries. The assembly at Westminster had become the mother of parliaments. Not only Canada and the Australian States made it the model for their legislatures. The two new European states, Belgium and Italy, with the world to choose from, in drafting their constitutions, had followed the same pattern as closely as they could, a constitutional monarchy with two legislative chambers and responsible government. Belgium's first king had learned his trade in England.

In 1845 Benjamin Disraeli published a political novel, *Sybil*, with the sub-title *The Two Nations*, and the idea of this sub-title has become almost proverbial as a summary of society about that time. The rich and the poor were separated not only by the primary material differences in diet, clothing, housing, and so forth; they lived in segregated systems of knowledge and ideas. This interpretation does account for much of what happened; but it leaves much unexplained. Before there was any change in the political position of the wage-earners, their agitation for political rights subsided. Before their violent protests against machinery had achieved anything whatever, they ended, and an orderly trade-union movement developed. These two phenomena were partly due to the general increase of prosperity, which included an improvement in the standard of living for many urban workers. But another great social change which underlay them was the rise of the nineteenth-century middle classes as economic development demanded more professionals.

The notion of the middle classes was and is indefinite, but, wherever the lines are drawn which separate them from the classes above and below, they had other things in common besides their intermediate position. Among them were nearly all the highly educated and the creative artists of all kinds. The more prosperous of them kept horses. Some amused themselves expensively out of doors or in their homes. Others devoted their leisure to the things of the mind. They were all to some extent free to follow their tastes, whatever these might be, because many thousands of domestic servants, mainly women, were available for employment in their homes at inexpensive wages. Within this body, proportionately more numerous in Britain than in the continental countries, there were great variations of skill and social opportunity, from the specialized heads of large staffs in mansions or institutions to the untrained casual helpers. The relationship of employer and employed might be one of mutual respect and considerateness, but at the other extreme it might mean cruel exploitation. From the point of view of society as a whole no one surveyed it and considered whether these domestic workers did not deserve, in their totally differing circumstances, some such protection as workers in the mines and factories were beginning to enjoy as of right.

The middle classes needed far more than the aristocracy did to appear respectable. Even those of them who had inherited their wealth or their gainful occupations were exposed to competition and needed to guard their reputations. Therefore they tended to conform to social conventions and to common standards of education and manners. Social satirists dissected their snobbishness, but as a body they were seldom praised as they deserved for their energy, their courage, and their sense of responsibility. They were not a political class with common interests. They were not a caste nor anything like it: there was a constant flow of newcomers mainly from below, and a less conspicuous wastage in a downward direction. The middle classes grew in numbers, and probably in proportion to the rest, because they were needed to

Charles Dickens. A master of story-telling, Dickens was a prolific novelist who achieved great popularity. He did not shrink from realistic description of the social evils of Victorian times, especially the mistreatment of children and of the poor, and thereby helped to bring about reforms.

fill thousands of posts which the wars, the overseas expansion, and the Industrial Revolution created. In two distinct ways they mitigated the harshness of the conflict between the two nations. First, although some of them were oppressors of the poor, it was to middle-class men that the workers looked for help in the difficulties of daily life. The illiterate often needed the help of the literate; the inexperienced needed the help of someone who was approachable. A village schoolmaster or a shopkeeper, or a country banker or doctor, could explain some point of law or business practice. Most of the prominent radical leaders themselves came from these classes. Secondly the nation became better equipped to deal with its social problems, and the equipment was largely devised and mainly operated by such men.

The progress of the middle classes was clearly visible in the history of the professions. The members of the old professions increased in numbers, and submitted to regulation of their qualifications, their discipline, and their privileges. Among the lawyers the tendency was to restrict entry to the bar, the higher branch, and it was believed that this raised the standard of education and character. The solicitors combined in the Law Society in 1831. The physicians and surgeons engaged in controversy about their professional organization from the late eighteenth century until 1858, when many anomalies were tidied up by the Medical Act. The civil engineers were a new profession, and their Institute was founded in 1818. The Royal Institute of British Architects came in 1834. On the borderline between the professions and 'business', was the Pharmaceutical Society of Great Britain, of 1841. Books of reference helped people to find their way about in the increasingly complex society. Roadbooks became bigger and better, giving the market-days, coaching-inns, and the times of stage coaches. George Bradshaw began to publish railway time-tables in 1839, and kept pace with railway-building at home and abroad. Commercial directories improved. In London they were no novelty, but Birmingham had the first of all provincial directories in 1763, and it was quickly followed by many others. Then came the professional directories: the *Law List* in 1839, medical directories regularly from 1846. The neatest and most comprehensive of the British books of reference, *Whitaker's Almanack*, began in 1869.

There were parallel changes in the public institutions, the state. There had been inquiries into economic evils at intervals from 1621 or earlier. Some were conducted by parliamentary committees, and some by the privy council or the Board of Trade. As time went on they improved in thoroughness and in intellectual quality, and in 1789 the report on the slave trade by the privy council's committee on trade inaugurated the modern succession of authoritative government reports. In 1815, as before, the privy council dealt with any business that required the issue of proclamations, and the Home Office dealt with all domestic business that did not specifically belong elsewhere; but there was no standing machinery for collecting social information or exercising social control. Step by step such machinery came into existence, partly, as in the instances of public health and education, under the privy council, partly, like police and factory inspection, under the Home Office, and partly under neither of them but in separate government offices, of which the type was that of the commissioners who supervised the new Poor Law of 1834. The permanent officials came to possess fuller and better information than had ever been collected before; they set in motion the activities of inquiry and policy-forming, often in the old forms of royal commissions or parliamentary committees. Great Britain, by imperceptible degrees, acquired a bureaucracy, not on the large scale that was already usual in countries on the Continent, but sufficient to transform the style of administration. Changes in the design of the administrative machinery became an important element in constitutional history.

The bureaucrat is one of the types of middle-class men, and this was more or less consciously recognized when the civil service was reformed so that it came to resemble a profession. It had indeed not been a single service at all: each office had its own separate staff, appointed by nomination, in which personal and party and family influence weighed heavily, with consequent inefficiency and unfairness. The system of entry by examination was introduced first for the East India Company's service, and after 1853 for the service at home. About the same time, the phrases 'civil service' and 'civil servant' came in from the same source. It still took a long time before the system was extended to cover, as it did by 1900, most of the servants of the Crown. The new system brought into existence not a profession, whose members in dealing with clients used their individual judgements, but a hierarchy giving and obeying orders. The service also bore traces of having begun from the admittance of outsiders by the abolition of privilege. Young men were given secure posts for all their working lives, as though they were a kind of aristocracy. But from the first the service maintained very high standards of integrity and public spirit.

Its virtues were closely bound up with those of educational institutions. The administrative reformers worked in consultation with academic reformers, especially in Oxford, and the civil service examinations were framed to test the abilities of those who had recently completed university courses. In the course of time a regular staircase of examinations was formed, by which students were classified and ticketed at every stage from childhood; but this was still far in the future and each institution examined with a view to its own requirements. University degrees did not confer the right to practise any profession. At Oxford no one could matriculate without signing the Thirty-Nine Articles. At Cambridge the religious tests were different but almost equally effective: Nonconformists might not hold scholarships or fellowships, nor take degrees. Outside the universities there was a movement for their reform which naturally drew support from opponents of the privileges of the Church of England: not until 1856 did parliament begin to do away with the tests, and even in 1871, when the process was completed, there still remained a legal obligation for each college to maintain Anglican services in its own chapel, with a few other shreds of the old church monopoly.

A new relation grew up between the universities and the state: little remained of the old theory of academic freedom, descended from medieval opinions about the church and corporations, according to which each university and each college within it was independent of the state. The reform of the government and teaching of Oxford and Cambridge was, however, mainly done from within. Progressive university dignitaries explained their plans to royal commissions, but the plans were carried out by the governing bodies of the colleges and universities. Sometimes they received princely financial support from benefactors, but never a penny from the Treasury. Cambridge had led the way in the middle of the eighteenth century by introducing periodical written examinations for honours in mathematics. Oxford

followed with its own system from 1801; and, by the time when the religious tests disappeared, both universities, besides pass examinations at a more modest level, had competitive examinations not only in mathematics, classics, and other humane subjects, but also in natural science. Each had its home-grown and elastic arrangements for instruction. Both recruited their undergraduates from widening social circles, though not yet from the widest circles of all, those which did not regard the typical employments of the middle classes as their birthright, or even as practicable objects of ambition. A new ideal of academic freedom grew up, new at least in England: every teacher should be free to teach and to publish what he believed to be true.

Since Oxford and Cambridge were powerful enough to keep their development so much under their own control, the main positive achievements of the movement for university reform lay in the creation of new universities. These could not afford and did not desire expensive plans for residence and tuition. Most of them followed the models which had yielded admirable results in Scotland and Germany. The obvious place for a beginning was London. A strong combination of liberal and radical politicians, philanthropists, and authors obtained a charter in 1828 for a college, now University College in Gower Street, which provided lectures of high quality in the arts and sciences and medicine. It was actually called a university, but it was unwelcome to Oxford and Cambridge, to the medical corporations, and to churchmen, and so it neither examined nor gave degrees. A parallel and similarly incomplete Anglican institution, King's College, was set up, and the real beginning of London University did not come until 1836, when these two colleges were brought together under a new body which examined and gave degrees, but did not teach. Its growth and constitutional history were indescribably complicated. At first the examining body had some of the marks of a government department. It was not until late in the nineteenth century that London became one of the most influential academic centres in the world, the mother of many universities.

Only one other university was founded in England before 1884, that of Durham. In 1832 the excessively wealthy governing body of Durham Cathedral set aside a sum from its revenues for a university which was mainly intended to educate men for the clergy. In 1852 the medical school which had grown up in connection with the Newcastle Infirmary was added to this university, which, however, remained small and unambitious. Another early foundation did not outgrow its original purpose. University College, Lampeter, began to train clergy for Wales in 1827, was empowered to give the bachelor's degrees in arts and divinity, and was affiliated to Oxford and Cambridge. The Church of England had not sufficient roots in Welsh life to support it in wider growth, even if that had been possible in its remote situation among the mountains. But in the populous towns of England, local enterprise, local pride, and such local conditions as the prevalence of nonconformity, created many colleges of different types which in time were to become components of universities. Besides the medical schools, of which there were a good many besides Newcastle, there were colleges which taught the arts and scientific subjects, technical colleges, and sectarian theological colleges. Fortunately for their intellectual standards the University of London obtained the power to admit all comers to its examinations, and so men reared in these provincial centres, and even self-taught men, were certified by an impartial authority as having acquired such knowledge as universities transmitted.

Higher education went its own way, and for the present little or nothing was done to co-ordinate it with school education. The older universities had no entrance examinations. Some schools had special links, usually in the form of scholarships, with colleges, and some were annually inspected by visitors from the universities; but with such exceptions as these the schools were worlds to themselves. Among them in the first half of the nineteenth century a great deal was done by and for the middle classes, and something for the wage-earners. It was in this period that most of the public schools either came into existence or assumed the characteristics which qualify them to be so described. Their origins were various. The two medieval residential colleges, Eton and Winchester, and some other old-established schools such as Westminster and Charterhouse were the most eminent. Some old grammar schools changed their function when their headmasters, supplementing their incomes by taking boarders, made them into regional or even national institutions. Among these the greatest was Rugby. From 1828 to 1842 its headmaster was Thomas Arnold, who impressed on the school, and ultimately on many other schools, a combination of scholarship, religion, organized games, and training in responsibility. He also drew his boys not only from the old society of the lowland zone, but also from manufacturing families in the Midlands and the north.

The other schools which resembled or imitated Rugby had naturally characteristics of their own, and they varied in constitution. Some, such as Uppingham, were adapted grammar schools; others, such as Marlborough, were new foundations with defined social and religious purposes. What they all had in common was that they were made by private initiative. The state kept an eye on them; but the royal commissions and the few parliamentary discussions were concerned with them primarily

as charities, whose endowments ought to be applied according to the purposes of their founders. Except when a charter mentioned that Latin or some other subject must be taught, the content of education was not a concern of the state. If it had been, the public schools might not have lagged as they did behind the growing demand for modern studies, the sciences, and modern languages; but the freedom of the public schools was the basis of their success in imposing their chosen qualities of character.

Elementary education was generally thought to be all that manual workers and the humbler clerks required, and in it no problems about curriculum arose. Here again the state kept its intervention to a minimum. Reformers sometimes rescued some misapplied endowment for elementary teaching; but there were no state schools. Free education, or very cheap education, was provided on a large scale by charitable religious societies, the most important being the National Society of 1811, which was Anglican, and the undenominational British and Foreign Society of 1814. Their aims were limited and their methods, it would appear, neither inspired nor inspiring; but they did teach reading, writing, and arithmetic to many thousands of boys and girls, probably a majority and an increasing majority of their age-groups. From 1807 onwards reformers pressed for grants of public money to aid them. In spite of squabbles between the denominations the first government grant, a modest £20,000, was made to the two societies in 1833. After that came the inspection of schools, the authorization of educational expenditure from local rates, the creation of an education department under the privy council, and other piecemeal improvements. By many different channels the public became aware that Great Britain, and especially England, was below the best continental standards, and even for material reasons strong bodies of opinion favoured the reform which many of the grammar schools still awaited. The greatest obstacle was religious dissension; but by 1870 agreement was reached that education should be compulsory up to the age of thirteen, either, as the parents chose, in board schools under local boards, with unsectarian religious instruction, or in denominational schools, or in purely private schools which were not even inspected. As yet the board schools still charged fees.

These developments of the social organism were accompanied, as causes and consequences, by active thought about every province of social study. There was no hard-and-fast line between intellectual and imaginative literature. Poets and novelists set themselves to interpret the life about them and not only observed and felt, but studied. Some writers, like the Brontë sisters, carried on the unadulterated romantic impulse; but many others, for instance their own biographer Mrs. Gaskell, mingled it with social criticism and protest. Wordsworth, living on into advanced old age, and coming to value the historic and the established, moved far away from his early enthusiasms. Coleridge, not quite a philosopher after he ceased to be an inspired poet, but still original and profound, worked out principles for a religious conservatism. Early in the eighteen-thirties various writers, of differing education and antecedents, found that thousands of readers responded to criticisms, indeed denunciations, of the idols of the age of reform. Thomas Carlyle passed on his fierce sincerity to many who found his arguments confused. John Ruskin made the middle classes aware of the arts and their history, and in the same books revealed the ugliness of industrialization and its cruelties. Charles Dickens, a self-taught genius, not only awoke among his contemporaries of every station sympathy for the down-trodden, but hit hard, if not always shrewdly, at the workhouses and the debtors' prisons, at religious and philanthropic cant and at the comfortable acceptance of social injustice. Not that he destroyed the indestructible complacency of the fortunate. There were other authors who flattered it, and it derived some nourishment even from writers who were fundamentally against it. Tennyson wrote grave and musical poetry expressing many moods, amongst them the belief in progress and pride in the national freedom and power. Browning, few of whose poems were known very widely, could be quoted in support of a shallow optimism which was alien to his own hard-earned faith.

In several ways the social machinery for maturing and disseminating systematic thought was better than it had ever been before. So many excellent minds were concentrated in London that men of letters, public men, and business men could associate and act together at a high intellectual level. In these circles thought and its expression could be completely free from extraneous pressure or influence. All through the eighteenth century newspapers and periodicals had improved in quality and had become more specialized. Miscellanies had been followed by literary periodicals, learned periodicals, and scientific periodicals. The nineteenth century was the great age of the reviews. The revived *Edinburgh Review* dated from 1802. The tory *Quarterly* began in 1809. They were both made up of authoritative and, at least formally, anonymous articles. Other groups of men with ideas in common could imitate these august examples.

The most prominent group to take advantage of these opportunities were the Benthamites, who were also called utilitarians, from their central doctrine, or philosophical radicals, which meant not so much radicals with a philosophy behind them as scientific radicals, radicals whose policy was based on consistent principles. Their period as a school coincided with the

Charles Darwin, whose *Origin of Species*, published in 1859, caused a sensation far beyond the boundaries of biology. His suggestion that species developed through the natural selection of their most viable members seemed to many little short of a refutation of the Bible. His theory, evolved during a five-year trip to the South Pacific and then matured for a further twenty years did, however, become generally accepted.

working lives of James Mill, a leading disciple of Jeremy Bentham, who published his *History of British India* in 1817, and his son John Stuart Mill, whose *Autobiography* appeared in 1873, the year of his death. Their writings covered almost every subject except natural science and technology, and there were scientists, especially psychologists, medical men, and sanitary reformers, who drew copiously on their ideas. John Stuart Mill himself wrote on logic, ethics, political economy, the position of women, representative government, and even religion, and all his works were treated as serious authorities even by those who disagreed with them. His opinions, and those of the school in general, of course underwent development with the changing times, but it was a continuous development, preserving the central ideas.

The principle of utility, already formulated before Bentham's time, was the idea that social institutions or proposals were to be justified not by natural or any other rights, but by their contribution to the greatest good of the greatest number. In this assessment every man was to count as one and none as more than one. Another basic idea was that of freedom, and this broadened and deepened, from economic freedom as Adam Smith had conceived it and political freedom as the French revolutionaries had imagined it, to an ideal of freedom as the end of man. In their many applications these ideas provided the cutting edge to much reforming legislation, for the utilitarians all believed in parliament as an instrument of utility. John Stuart Mill himself sat there for a few years as a member; but the influence of these ideas spread beyond that of the radical parliamentary groups and became an element in the general outlook of the time.

One peculiarity of that general outlook was the lack of positive influences from the old English universities. In both of these there were men highly distinguished in their special studies, but the only new enterprise which made itself felt outside was the Oxford Movement, and that concerned only the Church of England, and, within that church, the clergy far more than the laity. It began when a small number of clergymen combined to rouse opinion against the interferences with ecclesiastical endowments which formed a necessary part of the reforming of public institutions. In the eighteen-thirties Peel and the whigs in agreement removed some of the worst inequalities in the incomes of the higher clergy, prohibited the holding of more than two livings by one incumbent and eliminated some of the causes of friction over the payment of tithe. Instead of admitting the need for reform and trying to direct or control it, some ecclesiastical conservatives stood out for the independence of the church from the state. They reverted to the Anglo-Catholic doctrines of the Laudians as they understood them, and along with doctrines about the church and its government, they also revived related theological doctrines and religious practices. The university authorities in Oxford were displeased by what seemed to be romanizing tendencies, but they were embarrassed because in its early phases some of the leaders of the movement were learned like Edward Bouverie Pusey, some were reverenced for their personal holiness, like John Keble, and all professed attachment to the national Church. Outside Oxford the movement made some converts. It was akin to such outgrowths of romanticism as the Gothic revival in architecture, admired by Ruskin. Its progress, however, was always hampered by the difficulty that the high claims now made for the Church of England had originally been put forward for the Church of Rome. Every Puseyite who seceded, as some did, to Rome strengthened suspicion that the movement was unfaithful to the Reformation. In 1845, to the consternation of many, John Henry Newman, the subtlest mind and the one enchanting writer among the leaders, confessed himself convinced by the Roman case. A few of his friends went with him, and, after many troubles, he was at last appreciated as the carrier of precious gifts. The rest of his companions closed their ranks and worked together to bring the Church of England over to their way of thinking. For more than a century the division which then began was a determining factor in the internal history of that church, as in its relations with other churches and with the world.

The year 1858 saw the beginning of a revolution in the biological sciences. From it immediately arose the second of the two great intellectual movements of British origin which have convinced the whole western world, and have made the greatest of all the changes in popular beliefs in Britain. The biological discovery was a solution, not finally perfected, but determining the main lines of future thought, of the problem of the origin of species. For many centuries most of the world believed that the species of living beings had come into existence ready made, each with its distinguishing characteristics and each incapable of interbreeding with any other so as to produce fertile offspring. The version of this belief given in the biblical book Genesis was closely woven into the fabric of Christian theology and ethics. Numerous ancient and modern scientists and philosophers had questioned one or other of its articles, and in the eighteenth century some tried to demonstrate that life had developed from lower to higher forms, the diversity of species being established in the process. The line of thought was assisted by geology, when it traced the formation of rocks through a far greater period of time than anyone had thought possible, and sought to place the fossil remains of life in the chronology of the world. Now two naturalists, Alfred Russel Wallace and Charles Darwin, simultaneously but independently arrived at an explanation which covered all the facts then known. They showed that species could have originated by natural selection, that is by the survival of the fittest in the struggle for life. Fitness for survival meant the possession, among the infinite variations which always diversify living individuals, of those which are favourable to survival and reproduction.

This was more than a technical hypothesis. It did away with the accepted ideas of the creation of the world and of man. Man ceased to be unique, at least to the extent that he was shown to be organically related to lower, and even to the lowest, forms of life. Under the name of evolution this idea was accepted remarkably quickly by the educated people of the western and westernized countries, bringing with it a new, radical criticism of theology and ethics. Much, perhaps the whole, of human history seemed to be a mere chapter in the struggle for life. Anthropology and ethnology fitted, even more easily than the history of civilized peoples, into the evolutionary framework. Some theologians and some scientists tried to rebut the whole train of reasoning; others exerted themselves to distinguish the dogmas which it disproved from those which, perhaps in some new formulation, remained untouched. During the next half-century popular Christian beliefs were remodelled to meet this emergency; but, to different degrees in different social environments, the intellectual ascendancy of the churches and sects grew weaker.

The Great Society
1870–1902

1870	Gladstone's government makes elementary education available to all children.	1888	County and district councils are established.
1871	The Trade Union Act legalises trade unions.	1889	A month-long London dock strike wins increased pay.
1872	The secret ballot is introduced for elections.	1898	Kitchener's army defeats the Sudanese at Omdurman. Germany's new Naval Law challenges British sea power.
1882	The British bombard Alexandria, occupy Cairo, and temporarily station troops in Egypt until 1954.	1899	The Boer War begins.
1884	The Fabian Society is founded. A third parliamentary Reform Act extends the franchise to virtually all male householders.	1900	The Commonwealth of Australia is proclaimed.
1885	General Gordon is killed in Khartoum.	1902	An Anglo-Japanese alliance is initiated. The Boer War ends. The Education Act places secondary and elementary schools under the control of county and borough councils.
1886	Gladstone's Home Rule Bill is defeated.		

The year 1870 saw the outbreak of war between the France of Napoleon III and the Prussia of Bismarck. The war turned the relations of European states into new courses, but it made no such break in the main underlying theme of European history, the spreading of the industrial revolution over large continental areas. As was to be expected, other countries, one after another, overtook the lead which Britain had established. By imitating British technology and organization, and by improving on them, France, Germany, Belgium, Switzerland, and Italy, and some less central regions, came to enjoy the same prosperity, with rising population, growing trade and industry, and higher standards of living. Real wages rose in all these regions until after 1890. Then, as in France and Germany, the rise in Britain slowed down and there seemed to be an actual decline after about 1903, but this appearance was partly deceptive. Parallel to the rise in real wages there was a rise in social services, and, with wide variations between different countries, it was generally true that the workers received, without paying for them all, substantial benefits from public education, medical aid, and insurance.

Continental states could not and did not promote industry and commerce by the British principles of free competition, free trade, and free markets. They relied on protective tariffs, state subsidies, and limited, tentative state control. But their competition did not cause Britain to retaliate. British prosperity was not, indeed, unbroken. The trade cycles were inexorable, and they brought with them bankruptcies, unemployment, and every kind of economic misery. Twice there was something worse than merely temporary depression. In the eighteen-sixties the breaking-in of the North American prairies and the building of railways across them brought immense new supplies of wheat at prices far below the cost of growing it in Britain, and, for most purposes, wheat of better quality than could be grown here. Not long after the Canadian and American wheat, came meat from North and South America and from New Zealand. In England thousands of farmers were ruined; many thousand acres of arable land were put down to grass.

The agricultural depression had profound social effects. It started a decline in the power of the landowners, and in the independence of the countryside from the towns. In the end it was merged in a more general depression which lasted into the early nineties. In 1879 British exports were less by a quarter in value than they had been at their peak in 1872: the woollen and metal industries were hard hit. In the middle eighties there was a less extensive slump, notably in metals and cotton. It is not surprising that some politicians began to ask for a protective tariff; but they made few converts. The liberal economic policy was in its nature adaptable; the shocks of change were distributed among many self-regulating units, and so, in spite of everything, Britain held her own in manufactures, commerce, and finance. The industrialized nations, in their mutual dealings and in their

W.H. Smith, one of the many Victorian businessmen who prospered by providing for the new needs of a maturing society. Growing literacy, and the urge to read among ordinary people, gave him the chance to develop his father's newspaper business; his establishment of a chain of railway bookstalls made his name and fortune.

trade with the countries of primary production, built up a complicated interdependence. But, as we shall see, the cumulative effect of thousands of such small responses to market-opportunities, if it did not cause, at least powerfully promoted, two positive movements in the action of the British state. These were social reform and imperialism, neither of them essentially novel, but both dominant in this period as never before.

Nothing was changed in the main lines of the constitution; but in many spheres the reforming movements were carried further for the same reasons and in the same spirit as before. In 1873 the Supreme Court of Judicature Act rounded off the long process of reorganizing the principal courts of law, so that only minor alterations have been made since then. In local government the countryside needed different arrangements from those of the towns. A reasonable plan of elected authorities at two levels, county and district, was introduced in 1888 and supplemented in 1894 by the less useful addition of parish councils with very restricted powers. The allocation of powers to the different councils, the degree of control that the central government was to exercise over their action, the drawing of their boundaries on the map and such-like niceties directly affected the welfare and convenience of the population. On the whole they were handled with good sense and a good measure of public spirit. The machinery for parliamentary and local elections was adjusted to keep pace with the new conditions. In 1872 voting by ballot was at last adopted in place of the more manly and perfectly absurd system of open voting. In 1884 there came a uniform franchise for counties and boroughs. In principle the qualification was residence for one year, from which it resulted that a vote was as easy to acquire in the country and small towns as it had been in parliamentary boroughs. Thus agricultural labourers were enfranchised. The number of electors in Great Britain was raised from about three million to about five million. These and other changes did not make the constitution effectively democratic; but they cleared the way for the population to become a democracy if it so desired.

The great body of legislation of which these measures were specimens was enacted by means of parliamentary divisions and party conflicts; but in the main, once passed they were accepted; none of them was repealed. The years from 1868 to 1880 had a character of their own in the political education of the British peoples. The most influential medium of expression was speech-making, in parliament or, increasingly, on public platforms. This remained so until the coming of broadcasting and television. The orator's power did not depend only on his performance: like a preacher or an entertainer he gained from conforming to the idea of his personality which his hearers brought with them. The two party leaders, both very fortunate in this respect, were both first-rate politicians. Gladstone was an expert in finance and in departmental management; Disraeli not a man for detail but imaginative and inspiring. Neither of them was simple enough to be at all easily understood, but their sharply contrasted characters made their antagonism seem to each set of followers like the war between good and evil. Gladstone believed instinctively in religion and in freedom. He was a high churchman, moulded by the Oxford movement, but his elaborate mental processes enabled him to work with and for the Irish Catholics and the Nonconformist middle classes. Disraeli kept on good terms with the still dominant moderate churchmanship, without pretending to be anything other than a patriotic man of the world, and he used the language of national self-assertiveness, display, and adventure. This contrast concealed from most people's eyes the fact that neither party was irrevocably for or against any single course of political action.

Gladstone's first and greatest ministry lasted from 1868 to 1874. Its three most lasting achievements were the Judicature Act, the Elementary Education Act, and a series of army reforms. This last was partly prompted by the spectacle of Prussian efficiency in the war against France and in the war of 1866 against Austria. It reorganized the War Office, replanned the recruitment of the line infantry on the basis of counties, shortened the soldier's term of service from twelve years to six and (this last by prerogative, not by Act of Parliament) abolished the sale and purchase of officers' commissions. It stopped short of introducing a general staff and a satisfactory high command; but as far as it went it was wholly good.

There was nothing distinctively liberal in the reform of the law-courts or of the army, or even of education, and the same may be said of the Trade Union Act of 1871. This legalization of trade unions indeed marked a departure from the old liberal reverence for freedom of contract. A related willingness to permit interferences with the rights of property may be traced in some of this government's legislation about public health and local government. A new strain of liberalism, critical of the utilitarians and of *laissez-faire* economics, arose among academic writers, particularly in Oxford, at this time, and began to influence

William Gladstone, the grand old man of late Victorian politics. Gladstone, a Liberal, was often portrayed as slow and unadventurous compared with his Conservative rival, Disraeli. But as time passed he seemed to stand out from the mass of 19th century statesmen by his integrity and fairmindedness.

politicians a few years later. The older liberalism was continued in Gladstone's disestablishment of the Protestant Irish church, and other measures; but it was not because the electorate wanted a change from liberalism to conservatism that a Conservative majority was returned at the general election of 1874. The government's impetus was wearing out. Before the dissolution it was defeated in the Commons on a Bill for setting up new universities in Ireland, which roused many-sided opposition out of doors, but was not a characteristically party proposal.

Disraeli stepped into power as the only possible alternative, and retained it until 1880, the year before his death. His cabinet was strong in ability, and after a few years included a Conservative of a new type, W. H. Smith, the head of the great firm of booksellers. It added several notable statutes to the body of social legislation. In 1875 alone, besides a Trade Union amending Act, there were the first serious attempts to deal with the problem of housing, the first comprehensive measure for setting standards in the sale of food and drugs, and a great consolidating Public Health Act. The government paid attention to the agricultural depression but, through no fault of its own, invented no remedy. Almost throughout its existence, however, it was occupied with foreign and overseas questions, and in these Disraeli's way was to emphasize the elements of power and spectacle. His most famous acts were dramatically effective, but from a practical point of view it is not certain whether they effected anything worth mentioning. By Act of Parliament the queen received the title of empress of India, which subtly altered her relation to the Indian princes and to her own subjects, while at the same time drawing attention to the unique constitutional status of her Indian dominions. In 1869 the Suez Canal was opened. It shortened the sea-route to India, and not only for Britain, for it was followed by the beginning of direct trade between India and the continental countries. A French company and French engineers had built it; but the French defeat by Prussia checked the ambitions that might have developed around it. The pasha of Egypt, who had recently received the title of khedive or viceroy from the sultan, owned seven-sixteenths of the shares, but he was wasting his resources in imitation of European progress and was well on the way to insolvency. He offered Gladstone's government a chance to buy, which it declined. The khedive's finances went from bad to worse, and Disraeli, against strong opposition in the cabinet, bought him out. Britain thus acquired influence, though not power, over the policy of the company, for instance in preventing it from charging unduly high fees for shipping. Whether it ever enabled Britain to avert any grave danger to her interests may be doubted; but the purchase was regarded for many years as a master-stroke.

Events in the Near East intensified the local rivalries and the divergences between the great powers, which could support, but could not often restrain, the rivals. Since the Crimean War Russia had moved in the direction of internal reform and modernization; Turkey had gained new assertiveness without any real reform. Britain was to learn that her own internal changes had altered her character as a member of the European concert: her governments had to allow for the opinions of the newly enfranchised thousands. In 1875 the people of the province of Herzegovina rebelled. Some of their Christian and Slavonic neighbours in the Turkish empire and in independent Serbia acted with them, and the Turks set in motion their cruel and clumsy organs of repression. Gladstone suddenly appealed to British sentiment in a pamphlet which demanded the removal of the Turks 'bag and baggage' from their Bulgarian provinces. He roused fierce moral indignation among all classes, and not only in his own party; but the Russians also reacted in their own way to the Turkish atrocities: they declared war and invaded Turkey. Now there were two popular excitements in Britain, one against the Turks, the other the old hostility to Russia. The government knew that neither of them was well informed, but it yielded some ground to each. It sent the fleet to Bezika Bay outside the Dardanelles. When the Russians occupied Adrianople, it came so close to war as to send part of the fleet to Constantinople, and to carry a vote of £6 million for military purposes. But Austria was more closely concerned than Britain in the Balkans; Germany, Austria's ally, was not concerned at all, and peace was a European interest. Bismarck summoned the powers to a congress in Berlin, where the old diplomacy achieved one of its greatest successes, and one of its last. The map of the Balkans was redrawn, with a belt of liberated kingdoms between Turkey and the great powers. Austria gained a protectorate over Herzegovina and Bosnia; Russia took Bessarabia and also the Armenian districts of Kars and Batum. Germany, the honest broker, took no territory; but Disraeli, who went to Berlin in person, did not come back empty handed. He had accepted the cession of Cyprus from Turkey. This was one of his plans for committing Britain to advantageous alliance with a reforming Turkey; but nothing came of Turkish self-reform, and, as things turned out, Cyprus was not of the slightest use. Disraeli returned to a triumphant welcome.

His dreams and schemes of empire did not amount to an imperialist policy. There was indeed British activity all over the world in his time, but it was not co-ordinated. Fiji was acquired from friendly native chiefs, and its governor became high commissioner to a protectorate over various other Pacific islands. There were three wars, in 1874 against Ashanti, in 1879 against the Zulus, in 1878 and again in 1879 against Afghanistan. All three arose from the affairs of old-established possessions in those regions, and only the Afghan war, against a neighbour of Russia in Asia, had anything to do with large strategic considerations. All of them were preliminaries to unexpectedly serious wars of later times. They were unintentionally steps towards assuming greater responsibilities. There was no wide public interest in them, and they did not involve anything like a national effort. Afghanistan was India's affair and the other wars were not expensive. British budgets rose steadily, but only from £74 million in 1874 to £82 million in 1888. Sir Garnet Wolseley's military successes in West and South Africa won him a high reputation with the public; but the popular heroes of overseas adventure were the missionaries and the explorers. David Livingstone, who was both, died in 1873. His marvellous career began at the age of ten, when he was a piecer in a cotton-factory near Glasgow and bought a Latin primer with his first earnings. His motive force was religion, but he did much to discover the geography of East and Central Africa. In his last years his name came to be associated with that of H. M. Stanley, another 'self-made' man, an explorer of immense determination, whose motives were simpler and less exalted.

Disraeli's tenure of office ended for good with a heavy defeat in a general election in 1880. However this is to be explained it was due in part to Gladstone's action, unprecedented among statesmen of his standing, but soon to become a normal practice: he attacked the government in campaigns of platform speeches. He

Sunday in a worker's home. The condition of the working class aroused the interest of many reformers but, in general, living standards rose throughout the Victorian period. At times and places, as was inevitable in the boom-and-slump of economic progress, hardship was suffered by the poorer families especially.

spoke for the rights of small peoples and against aggressive foreign and colonial action; but when he was back in office he was unable to stop expansion or limit responsibilities which grew out of earlier territorial advances. In 1884 protectorates were declared over Somaliland, over the Lower Niger, and over South-East New Guinea; three more acquisitions of the familiar kind. In two parts of Africa, the Transvaal in the extreme south and Egypt in the extreme north-east, the new departures were of the highest importance, though few understood this.

South Africa had four component but separate parts. The old Cape Colony and Natal were under the Crown; the Orange Free State and the Transvaal Republic were not. The Free State and Natal were threatened by the warlike Zulus, and molested from time to time by other Bantu tribes. Defence was a common interest of all four regions, the more so because in the eighteen-seventies the Transvaal government showed itself incapable of maintaining it alone. At the same time the northern regions were ceasing to be purely pastoral: the Kimberley diamond fields were discovered. The purpose and nature of the northward migration made complete political union impossible, but, short of that, British experience elsewhere suggested that the four areas might come together in some sort of federation. Disraeli moved prudently in this direction. The British administrators on the spot acted with courage and in good faith, but they took false steps which created a new problem. They annexed the Transvaal, with the consent of its government; but they unwisely allowed that government to pretend in public that its consent was unwilling. They launched a war against the Zulus, which was very likely necessary for the survival of the Transvaal settlements, and was ultimately victorious; but in the course of the war there was one perilous defeat. Disraeli neither blamed these subordinates nor exposed the unfairness of Gladstone's charges of wanton aggression. In office Gladstone neither cancelled the annexation, nor supported the efforts which the administrators still made to bring about federation. The Zulu threat having been eliminated, most of the British troops were withdrawn. The Boers believed they had been cheated. They proclaimed their republic and took possession of their country. Sir George Colley advanced from Natal to relieve the few isolated British posts in the Transvaal. He discovered something hitherto unknown: that the Boers, who lived in the saddle and shot as well as they rode, were the most dangerous enemy in Africa. At Majuba Hill, on 27 February 1881, he was decisively beaten and killed.

Gladstone could have continued the war, with what result no one can guess; but he accepted defeat. Great Britain recognized the right of the Transvaal to complete self-government, subject to British suzerainty, which included the control of its foreign relations. 'Suzerainty' was a new word in official documents, and three years later in an amending convention it was dropped. Great Britain kept the right to control the treaty-relations of the Transvaal except with the Orange Free State.

The defects of Gladstone's handling of foreign relations were equally visible in Egypt, and Egypt was an object of many sided interest to the great European powers. It had a population of nine millions and an army of 4,000. The khedive's wasteful attempts

Trongate, Glasgow, at the turn of the century. Glasgow was one of the many cities which grew rapidly in the age of industrialization. First came the cotton industry, and later heavy engineering and shipbuilding. Victorian prosperity was expressed in new imposing buildings, better transport and urban services.

to imitate the externals of European civilization had resulted in oppressive taxation, in failure to pay the interest on foreign loans, and finally in the appointment of an international commission to control the finances. France, which was the principal creditor country, took the leading part in the early days of foreign control, not without exciting the jealousy of other powers; but, when a new and more alarming difficulty supervened, France drew back. The new difficulty had been partly caused by the French themselves. Tunis, adjoining their colony of Algeria, was following the same road to ruin as Egypt, but there a Moslem rising broke out against the dey and against foreign influence. It might have spread into Algeria, and the French prevented this by invading Tunis and declaring a protectorate over it. This unplanned adventure both drew on France's resources and increased her anxiety about the attitude of other powers. Great Britain was reluctantly taking part in the financial control, mainly because of the Suez Canal.

In 1881 there came a series of nationalist *coups* in Cairo, led by the Egyptian-born Colonel Arabi, and directed impartially against the Turks and the foreign financial mentors. When Arabi's followers rioted and killed some fifty Europeans, French and British naval squadrons anchored off Alexandria, but the French ships were recalled. The British admiral destroyed the fortifications by a heavy bombardment, which settled nothing. But Gladstone's cabinet promptly sent Sir Garnet Wolseley with an efficient and well-equipped force of 13,000 men. Less than a month after he left Britain Wolseley defeated Arabi completely at Tel-el-Kebir. The British thus found themselves the only power that could provide Egypt with its elementary needs of government and order, to say nothing of solvency or welfare. They notified the other powers that they had undertaken the duty of advising the khedive until a satisfactory and stable condition of affairs should be established. They sincerely intended to go as soon as possible, but their entirely informal rule lasted until 1936 and their army did not disengage itself until 1954.

Egypt is a Mediterranean country, facing Turkey, Greece, Italy, France, and, less directly, Britain and Russia. That was its significance in the international politics of 1882–3; but behind it lay Africa. It misgoverned a vast, largely desert area known as the Sudan, or south country, of which the principal town was Khartoum, a thousand miles from Cairo on the Nile. A fanatical leader proclaimed himself the Mahdi or Messiah, and raised the country in rebellion against the Egyptians. The British government, oblivious of its new responsibilities, allowed the khedive to send an absurdly inadequate force to suppress the rising. The force was destroyed, and it was rightly decided that the Egyptians must evacuate all the Sudan south of Wadi Halfa. This meant extricating numerous small and isolated garrisons from the southern area. One, at Suakim on the Red Sea, was reinforced with British and Indian troops and held; but the rest had to be collected by an expedition up the Nile. Mistake followed mistake in London and Cairo. General Gordon, the unmistakably heroic commander of the expedition, neither adequately supported nor adequately controlled, was surrounded in Khartoum, Wolseley was sent out, and worked his way up the Nile with just such a force as was needed; but he had started too late. On 26 January

A soap advertisement of 1887. Soap manufacture made several fortunes in the 19th century; as was frequently the case, the high profits enjoyed by the original businessmen were associated with great public benefit, in this case personal hygiene. This particular advertisement also reflects the link between colonies and commerce – the 'trade follows the flag' theme.

1885 Gordon's Government House was stormed and he was killed. From the queen downwards great numbers of people placed the blame for this disaster on Gladstone and his colleagues. Slowly the irresistible resources of the empire were brought into play but it took thirteen years to recover the Sudan.

In the light of later events parliamentary politics may seem to have been completely out of perspective, but actually they reflected the true proportions of the time, in this, that they were dominated by Ireland. From the time of the Irish famine there had been variations between worse and better times, shiftings of alliances, hopes, and disappointments; but there was no change in the immovable ill will between the two bodies of extremists. On the one hand agrarian outrages, including murder, never ceased, and there were revolutionary conspiracies, sometimes with more and sometimes with less well-educated leaders. Against them were evictions by landlords, and attempts to combine repression with the removal of the causes of discontent. No real progress was made with agrarian legislation. The law was altered so that landowners could override the claims of heirs and creditors and sell their estates; but ninety per cent of the land thus released was bought by a new class of Irish landlord, no more efficient and no less harsh than the old. In 1879 the House of Lords rejected a Bill to improve the position of tenants. The Union had not opened the way for the settlement of Irish questions by the joint deliberations of British and Irish members at Westminster. Every year the leader of the Irish Nationalists moved a resolution for the repeal of the Union, with no chance of success.

In the new parliament which brought Gladstone into power the outlook for Ireland changed. Partly because strong support came from America and from the parish clergy, and partly because its fractions co-operated, the Nationalist party won 65 seats. It elected as its leader Charles Stuart Parnell, a Protestant landowner with an American mother. He united all the nationalistic forces inside and outside parliament and he ruled them in a spirit of undisguised hostility to Britain. When the cabinet tried to end the agitation by the customary mixture of reforms and coercion, the parliamentary party blocked its measures by

The eviction of an Irish peasant family in the 1890s. It was said in the mid-19th century that only in Russia did the peasants receive worse treatment from their landowners; by the 1890s the lot of the Russian peasant had improved but in Ireland many landowners maintained their needlessly cruel and uncaring attitude towards their tenants.

obstruction, and the leaders, imprisoned for conspiracy, issued a No Rent Manifesto from their gaol. They plainly had the upper hand and they were released. In 1885, after the death of Gordon, Gladstone's difficulties multiplied. He had to invent new taxes to wipe out a large deficit; but his budget proposals were defeated in the House of Commons, a reverse which happened only on one other occasion in the nineteenth century (1852). Gladstone resigned and for eight months, with the same parliament, there was a Conservative government. The new prime minister, Lord Salisbury, carried on the dual policy of coercion and concession, firmly and with conviction, but with no better results. When the general election came in 1886 the Liberals won 335 seats, to the Conservatives' 249, a majority of 86. The Nationalists won exactly 86, so that they held the balance and, apparently, with a little luck could dictate their terms. But they were not lucky.

Gladstone, without disclosing his conversion, came to the conclusion that the time had come for home rule; but he knew from the criticisms and secessions of his own colleagues since 1880 that it would be enormously difficult to hold a Liberal cabinet together to carry home rule into law. He saw that such a measure would be most firmly established if it were carried, like Catholic emancipation and the repeal of the corn laws, by the party which had steadily opposed it. To suppose that the Conservatives might take some such action for some sort of home rule was not to count on their deserting their principles; there were at least some influential Conservatives whose minds were moving as his own had moved. But Gladstone would need to be both more trusted and more dexterous than he was if he were to hand over this responsibility without either splitting his own party or seeming to intend to split his opponents. He had scarcely begun the manœuvre when news of his change of mind leaked out. Salisbury, still in office, made it clear that he would not consent to home rule. He was duly defeated by a combination of Liberals and Irish Nationalists. Gladstone had to take office in adverse circumstances. Some of those to whom he offered high places refused, among them Lord Hartington, the heir to the great whig dukedom of Devonshire and to large Irish estates, whose brother, as chief secretary for Ireland, had been murdered in 1882. Gladstone worked on the draft of his Home Rule Bill. It proposed an Irish parliament and executive in Dublin with power over everything except the very wide field of 'imperial' matters: defence, foreign and colonial relations, customs and excise, trade and navigation, the post office, and currency. Although this field was so wide, there were to be no Irish members at Westminster, unless they were summoned for the special purpose of revising this Act. This provision was indefensible: it could not have lasted. When the Bill was before the cabinet the two leading radical ministers resigned. It was debated for sixteen days in the House of Commons. John Bright was there. He did not speak but he had published his opinion, which was flat against any parliament in Dublin. A new, dour strand of opposition came from Ulster. The Bill was thrown out by 343 votes to 313, nearly a hundred Liberals voting with the majority.

This defeat was final: neither parliament nor the electorate ever reversed it. When an Act which purported to give Home Rule to Ireland was passed nearly thirty years later, it made special

BELOW A cartoon published just as the Irish Party was splitting into pro-Parnell and anti-Parnell factions. Parnell, an Irish landlord and Protestant, made bitter enemies. Forged letters implicating him in murder and published by *The Times* failed to bring him down, but his involvement in a divorce case finished him. In this picture he is the left-hand tug-of-war contestant.

RIGHT The Marquis of Salisbury. A true-blue Conservative who had little taste for democracy, Lord Salisbury found his main interest in foreign affairs. As prime minister he almost always kept foreign policy in his own hands, and it was under his auspices that Britain drifted into the Boer War.

provision for six counties of Ulster, which remained a part of the United Kingdom. The course of events was so confused that many observers failed to appreciate this finality. Soon after the parliamentary decision Gladstone resigned. The Conservatives in alliance with the dissentient Liberals gained a majority of 118, and except for one Liberal interlude of three years this combination remained in power for nineteen years. The Liberal unionists became more closely assimilated to their allies as time went on, until in the end it needed a sharp eye to tell the difference. The Nationalists as a party kept their old sources of strength and much the same number of seats in parliament, but their luck ran out.

In 1890 *The Times* newspaper accused Parnell of complicity in agrarian and political crimes. The government appointed a judicial tribunal. Officials in Ireland tried to rake up evidence against Parnell, but the tribunal reported that the original evidence bought by the newspaper was forged. Parnell was not entirely vindicated on all counts, nor was it revealed how malignant the attack on him had been; but the incident left him stronger than before. Within the year his career was cut short. He was cited as co-respondent in a suit for divorce. Not only liberal Protestants in Britain but also the Irish Catholic clergy thought this a disqualification for public life. The Nationalist party split and quarrelled.

Two years later there was another general election, to which we shall refer in a moment. Gladstone returned to office for the last time with a majority of 40, at the age of 83. There is no reason to suppose that his supporters in the country had been moved principally, or even to any great extent, by enthusiasm for Home Rule. Many other questions were discussed in the election campaign. But Home Rule was still an aim of the Liberals, and Gladstone introduced a second Bill, providing for Irish representation at Westminster, but only for matters of Irish and imperial, not of solely British, concern. It made no provision for the special needs and character of Ulster. Having duly passed the Commons it was thrown out by a majority of 419 votes to 41 in the House of Lords. From then until 1906 Home Rule was a dormant issue. The Conservative governments, with strangely little trouble from Ireland, pursued the policy of killing nationalism by kindness. They passed measures for social amelioration and public works. The last and most important of them, the Land Purchase Act of 1903, weakened the governing class. Aided by government loans, tenants bought holdings which the landlords were compelled to sell. Ireland, not excluding Ulster, became mainly a land of peasant proprietors. No one was reconciled.

One of Gladstone's worst miscalculations at the time of the first Home Rule Bill was that he underrated the importance of one of the two radicals who resigned from his cabinet, Joseph Chamberlain. Chamberlain reached the age of fifty in that year, and in many ways he was typical of the newly rising political class. He caught the public eye with his monocle and his orchid as Disraeli and Gladstone did with their less showy make-up. He had retired from business in Birmingham, well off but not very rich, to become the leader of a political connection, with a family and Nonconformist nucleus. He was a good speaker, quick in retort; but more a man of action than of ideas. His radicalism, audacious enough in his early days to question even the value of the monarchy, followed the old political pattern; but in Birmingham he set an example of using the public authorities to promote civic welfare. He and his supporters made it a model for British cities, not only in the old services, but in new fields such as housing. He did much for education, in the end promoting the foundation of the university there. He took the lead in reorganizing the Liberal party, and consequently all political parties, to fit the requirements of the new wide franchise. Instead of leaving the choice of candidates and the planning of electoral campaigns to the old haphazard operations of influence, he first set up party committees in his own neighbourhood, to which Disraeli in 1878 opprobriously applied the American word 'caucus'. Both the word and the thing had come to stay, and Chamberlain's National Liberal Federation also became a model which every national political party had to imitate. His opposition to Home Rule was in no way inconsistent with this liberal and radical record. Of that the concurrence of John Bright is sufficient evidence. But even if Gladstone had made full use of his talents by giving him higher office than that of president of the Board of Trade, and even if the two had agreed on an Irish policy,

Chamberlain at the centre of power might well have turned policy into a new course.

He was an imperialist. That is, he believed British overseas expansion, in all its different manifestations, to be valuable in itself, and to be more valuable, both in Britain and to the world, the more intimately the component parts of the empire were linked together. In his opposition to Home Rule he expressed this wider view, and in succeeding years he became the leader, so far as it ever had a single leader, of the overt imperialism, in which many formerly separate ingredients combined. This was not only a British phenomenon: between 1880 and 1900 something of the sort appeared in all the industrialized countries of Europe and in the United States. Its most visible expression was the annexation of tropical territory, especially in the partition of Africa. Of the entire British Empire (excluding India) at its greatest extent, more than a third of the area and more than a quarter of the population were acquired in those few years. One reason why the pace was so fast was the rivalry between the powers. Sometimes British governments were still reluctant to annex, but overcame their reluctance because they feared that some other expanding power would threaten a British colony or head off a possible future British advance.

Behind this rivalry were many motives for expansion, but one was common to all the greater states. As each country became industrialized it became an effective competitor in its own home market, and in export markets, even in the home markets of the other industrial countries. The latter therefore turned their thoughts to their own colonial markets. Great Britain, which kept its colonial ports open to the commerce of other nations nevertheless had an advantage over foreigners in the internal development of its colonies and their trade. British exports to and imports from the self-governing colonies (as they were still called) rose decidedly from 1894 to 1900; exports to India rose, but less sharply; imports from India fell until 1898 and then did no more than recover. The other possessions taken together had a smaller share of commerce, which increased substantially. In overseas investment in all parts of the world Britain was the largest lender, perhaps having more than double the stake of France, which came next. About half the British overseas investments were under the British flag, and only about 6 per cent in continental Europe.

There was a current maxim that trade follows the flag, and objectors who said that it followed the price-list were held to be sordidly materialistic. There was indeed much more besides economic calculation in the imperialistic movement. It inherited a good share of the popular enthusiasm for the missionaries and the explorers. Some of the prophetic voices of the Victorian age were unmistakably British: Cecil Rhodes imbibed some of his ideas from Ruskin's lectures. Intellectually the movement was not contemptible. Its textbook was published in 1883 by an eminent historian, Sir John Seeley, with the title *The Expansion of England*. The reading public knew it from the stories and verses of Rudyard Kipling, alternately the genius and the journalist. It did something to further the practical colonial studies which were obviously useful at the time, such as language-studies. Chamberlain personally did stalwart work for the study of tropical medicine. The anthropologists and ethnologists who were investigating African and Asian society were less directly affected. Their stimulus came from science, and British administrators overseas showed, on the whole, less interest in these matters than some foreign colonizers. The officials, like the missionaries before them, saw their task in the very simple terms of an absolute contrast between civilization and barbarism. If they were to build up respect for human life, to say nothing of making it healthier and better worth living, the foundations of society as they knew it were so utterly lacking that there seemed to be no need for minute study of the existing conditions. Law and order must be introduced, and if necessary imposed. Chamberlain did not disguise his belief that British lives were 'more precious' than those of Africans.

The indigenous inhabitants must be lifted out of their poverty. The invaders came from a country where the economic function of the state was to clear the way for private enterprise, and where it was generally believed that if a man would not work, neither should he eat. This meant that the invaded peoples should be taught to work. Teaching was not a sufficient inducement in itself. Hitherto they had worked only under some kind of compulsion; but the British had to invent new incentives without approaching slavery, which they abhorred and intended to abolish wherever they had the power. This dilemma was the more difficult for the officials because, whether the primitive countries were legally under British rule or not, they were being penetrated and opened up by European traders, often brutal and unscrupulous, to whom they were nothing more than sources of potential wealth from agriculture and the forests, or from mines. Annexation might be the best means of protecting them against oppression by Europeans.

Imperialism was not a party matter: there were imperialists among the Liberals, though fewer in proportion than among the Conservatives. Lord Salisbury, whose second and third periods of office as prime minister, from 1886 to 1892 and from 1895 to 1902, covered the main stages of expansion, was a man of intellect and principle, firm in his loyalties but not prone to enthusiasm. He was an authority on foreign affairs and he saw the colonial problems in their international and ethical setting. Before 1880 Africa, as it was said, was a coast, not a continent. Round the

coast were innumerable European trading-posts, and, at intervals, larger and smaller colonies. The British navy patrolled the whole coast-line and its services were at the disposal of native chiefs or European business men who needed protection. The explorers altered all this. As the interior became known, and it was seen that there were expanding possibilities of trade, the European governments began to assume the responsibility of protecting their own subjects. At the same time the partition of independent Africa (except only Ethiopia) began, the greatest change in the political map of the world that has ever been made in a single generation. This revolution was unique in another respect besides its physical extent. It was made without a single act of war between any of the European powers. If there was a point of time at which this astonishing fact was ensured, it was at the Congo conference in Berlin in 1884, when Gladstone was in office. There, little heeded by the British public, the diplomatists agreed on the broad outlines of the distribution of African territory. The states were not ready to move into the lands which they coveted for the future. They even agreed to exempt one vast territory from competition between themselves: what afterwards became the Belgian Congo was handed over to a company under the personal presidency of Leopold II, king of the Belgians.

When Salisbury came into power he found the colonial world entering on this new phase. Besides the emergencies of Egypt and the Sudan, there were local problems needing attention in many parts of the world, and in several of them Salisbury's cabinet authorized forward movements. In three, partly because of the example of the Congo company, and in spite of the discouraging past experience of the East India Company, the new territory was not brought directly under the Crown but entrusted to a chartered company. In 1886 the Royal Niger Company obtained what was to become Nigeria; in 1888 the British East Africa Company, the future Kenya and Uganda; in 1889 the British South Africa Company, Rhodesia [later Zambia and Zimbabwe]. These companies were meant to carry out colonial development by private enterprise. The administration was in the hands of their servants, and their finances, commercial and governmental, were under boards of directors in London. There were no tariff or other barriers against foreign traders, who, however, were encouraged by their own governments to resort to their national colonies. All three British companies attracted to their service, in all ranks, able men of high character who made the welfare of the Africans one of their purposes.

The other colonial measures of Salisbury's second ministry were equally circumspect, and none of them was seriously challenged. When there was a general election in 1892 it turned on domestic questions. In one respect it marked a stage towards the completion of democracy: for the first time one of the parties in its annual conference agreed on a detailed programme for legislation. It was the Liberal opposition which took this step, afterwards a normal preliminary for all parties, tending to restrict the freedom of ministers and of parliament itself, but on the whole making their dependence on their constituents more open and reasonable. In this case it helped to bring Gladstone back into power for the episode of the second Home Rule Bill. After that he retired, to be succeeded by Lord Rosebery, a very different sort of man, who won the Derby twice running while he was prime minister and understood almost everything in politics, but vanished for good from regular public activity once he had lost an election in 1895. Rosebery was an imperialist, and in his short time there were developments in both kinds of colonies. Uganda became a protectorate. The Australian states began to negotiate for federation. It was, however, after his resignation that the country began to see imperialism as a guiding force in policy.

Lord Salisbury, on returning to power, appointed Chamberlain Secretary of State for the Colonies. Chamberlain roused the somnolent Colonial Office to a sense of mission. Every year there were incidents overseas to interest or to excite the public. South Africa became a danger-point. Ten years earlier great discoveries of gold in the Transvaal had begun to increase its importance for the rest of the world, and by 1896 its exports of gold were so great that they became an important factor in the monetary affairs of Europe. The mining industry brought an influx of many thousands into the territory of the old-fashioned and hitherto sequestered republic. There were African workers and cosmopolitan, but mainly British, capitalists, speculators, and engineers. The president of the republic, Paul Kruger, a strong character and a rustic hero, led his people in refusing to assimilate the newcomers. Their industry was heavily taxed and they were denied the franchise except on virtually prohibitive conditions.

In Cape Colony there was another strong man, Cecil Rhodes, the prime minister. Rhodes had acquired great wealth, first in diamonds and also in gold. Though he never relinquished his belief in co-operation between the British and the Dutch, he was the moving spirit in the British South Africa Company, and in its successful rivalry with the Transvaal in the northward drive against African tribes. His courage and his grandiose ambitions gave him a pre-eminence among all the queen's subjects overseas. In 1895 the Colonial Office granted some, but not all, of Rhodes's demands for territorial changes in connection with a projected railway to Kimberley, and, with good legal justification, checked a design of Kruger to penalize imports from the Cape in favour of imports through the Portuguese port of Delagoa Bay. Then came the news that Rhodes's friend Dr. Jameson, with a force of police from the Company and Bechuanaland, had violated the Transvaal frontier, to make a dash for Johannesburg. It was scarcely a secret that a rising of the immigrants in the Transvaal was brewing. Jameson had 470

A scene from the Battle of Omdurman: a Scottish brigade prepares to repel an attack by the Dervishes. Although photography was well-established by this period, war artists still travelled to the more important campaigns.

mounted men, 8 machine-guns, and 3 guns, with 180 miles to ride. He defied an order to stop, sent in the queen's name by the high commissioner for South Africa. There were only twenty miles still to cover when he was trapped. He surrendered, having lost sixteen killed. The Johannesburg rising never started. The Boers behaved magnanimously. Rhodes resigned as prime minister. A select committee of the House of Commons heard witnesses and rummaged among minutes and telegrams for five months. It censured Rhodes severely and historians have disputed ever since whether it ought also to have censured Chamberlain.

This was the first black mark against British imperialism and it had grave consequences; but for the next few years South Africa was not in the political foreground. The confident mood was soon restored. In 1897 in the queen's diamond jubilee celebrations, what most impressed the populace, after Queen Victoria herself, was the multi-coloured procession of detachments from the armed forces of every part of the empire. Some of their comrades were actually fighting in West Africa and on the north-west frontier of India. A large Anglo-Egyptian force under Sir Herbert Kitchener, commander-in-chief of the Egyptian army, was working its way from battle to battle into the Sudan. In 1898 at Omdurman, across the river from Khartoum, the Sudanese flung their whole fighting force against it. Six thousand of them are said to have been killed, most of them by machine-gun fire. This victory made Great Britain morally and practically responsible for the government of the Sudan, as the active partner in an Anglo-Egyptian condominium. The system lasted until shortly before the Sudanese became independent in 1955, and the constructive work which made this independence possible surpassed the highest hopes of those who first undertook it. The Battle of Omdurman had an immediate result in another sphere. A French expedition had completed a two years' march from the west, leaving posts on its route. Major Marchand, with seven other French officers and eighty African troops, raised the French flag at Fashoda, on the Nile 200 miles south of Khartoum. Kitchener met him in person, and convinced him that he could not do this on the khedive's territory. There was friction enough with France already about African boundaries, and now the dream of a French highway across the continent from west to east was dispelled.

In the meantime the British government supported the demands of the immigrants in the Transvaal. They were entitled to diplomatic support, and the British claimed on historical grounds to have a fuller right to give this support than would have belonged to a mere foreign power. Kruger retracted some proposed alien laws to which the British objected, but they demanded drastic reforms. They did not threaten war; but their negotiators knew, and the press made it clear to the world in general, that if the republic refused, it would be invaded. Kruger armed: he fortified Johannesburg, imported weapons, including heavy artillery, and engaged European officers.

The simplicity of the position was obscured by a cloud of incidents and negotiations, until on 9 October 1899 the republic sent an ultimatum and war began. With its ally the Orange Free State it had about 50,000 mounted infantry and it could count on something more than sympathy from the Afrikaners of Cape Colony. Against it, in the long run, were the gigantic resources of the British empire. The braggart imperialists of the British popular press screamed out hatred and contempt for the Boers. But Great Britain was unprepared. There were 14,750 regular troops in South Africa, and 10,000 arrived from India the day before the war began. A field force of 47,000 was ordered out from Britain. Canada, New Zealand, and the Australian states sent contingents of volunteers, many of them better suited for the conditions of this war than the regulars. But before the first of these reinforcements arrived, the Boers had taken the initiative, won battles, and shut up most of the British forces in three towns, Kimberley, Mafeking, and Ladysmith, which, unwisely, they besieged. When the main army had all landed in December, it numbered 70,000, the largest British army which had ever been sent abroad. The commander-in-chief and some of his subordinates made mistake after mistake and suffered reverse after reverse. In December Lord Roberts was sent out to take over the command, with Lord Kitchener as his chief of staff. Their energy and professional common sense restored the position quickly and by the end of February 1900 the Boers were defending their own territory and incurring losses.

The war went on until May 1902, altogether two years and eight months. First the two republics were invaded and annexed in proper form. When the towns and the railways had all been captured, Kruger fled into Portuguese territory. But the Boers betook themselves to guerrilla warfare and did all the damage that mobility and marksmanship could inflict. Roberts having gone home in triumph, it was Kitchener who had to spend more than a year, with heavy losses of life, in building blockhouses and stretching barbed wire, and, also, to the accompaniment of fierce if sometimes misdirected criticism, in rounding up and providing for the women and children in concentration camps. The British press and public had gone through moods first of gloom and then of elation, now they became irritable and impatient. The peace-terms settled the immediate pressing questions. The republics accepted British sovereignty and a grant of £3 million towards rebuilding and stocking farms. The major problems of South Africa were left to be settled in the future. It may, however, be said that the price which Britain had paid for this conquest was a governing condition of policy in the years to come. In money it was £250 million, which the nation could afford. Two-thirds of it was paid for by loans, and the necessary taxation was scarcely felt to be burdensome. The loss of lives was heavy: 5,774 were killed, to be compared with the 2,755 lost in the Crimea; but 16,000 died of disease, as against 21,000. Florence Nightingale was still living, much honoured and in complete retirement. She closely questioned young men returning from South Africa about the medical and hospital services. What they had to tell was a small part of a lamentable tale of inefficiency, over-confidence, and ignorance. On the other side there were stories of heroism, adaptability, and even statesmanship; but nothing in the policy or the social system of the late nineteenth century was any longer exempt from searching scrutiny.

Queen Victoria died in the first month of the twentieth century. Her successor, Edward VII, was chiefly known as a man of pleasure. His genial example influenced the social habits of the wealthy even in wartime, and people of all kinds felt that they were living in a new era, in which a good many taboos were relaxed. At the level of public business circumstances prevented the public from understanding that the war had indeed been the prelude to a new era, not of enjoyment but of conflicts and hardships. In 1901, when the fighting in South Africa had taken its turn for the better, the government dissolved parliament and,

The railway bridge across the Firth of Forth, opened by the Prince of Wales in 1890. Built by the North British Railway to shorten the route between Edinburgh and Aberdeen, the long, high, cantilever design was necessitated by the Admiralty's stipulation of generous clearances to allow the passage of all conceivable future warships.

in patriotic mood the country confirmed it in power with a large majority. This parliament sat for the next five years, prolonging a relation between the parties which soon ceased to correspond with what the electorate thought of them. Once the peace-treaty was signed Lord Salisbury, who had only a few more months to live, resigned the burden of office; but the continuity of the cabinet seemed almost complete. The new prime minister was Salisbury's nephew Arthur Balfour, who had been leader of the House of Commons for several years. With him sat his brother as president of the Board of Trade. The strongest man was still Joseph Chamberlain in his old office as Colonial Secretary, his power underlined by the presence of his son Austen Chamberlain as Postmaster-General. The Chancellor of the Exchequer was a successful merchant, but all the other members of the cabinet were members of the governing class. The prime minister was a reputable writer on philosophy, and as chief secretary for Ireland he had shown earlier that he was not a weak man, but like his uncle he never made it his practice to supervise his colleagues in their departmental duties. The result was a very creditable record of legislation in the familiar domestic fields. Ireland, as we have seen, received its last main agrarian law. In 1902 a great Education Act was passed. This determined the whole future of secondary and technical education, and for their good, by bringing them under the county and county borough councils, which also took the place of the old *ad hoc* school boards as the authorities for elementary education. As education was not the province of a separate cabinet minister, the difficult parliamentary task of piloting this Bill, especially through the reefs of bitter sectarian opposition, fell to Balfour himself. It was a sign of the times that the civil servant who planned the Bill, Sir Robert Morant, earned a very high reputation with the informed public.

The two groups of problems left behind by the South African war did not yet involve legislation: they had to be thrashed out by investigation, largely out of the range of public attention. First were the purely military questions. The army was controlled partly by a commander-in-chief, partly by the secretary of state for war, always a civilian, who was the head of the war office and responsible to parliament. The division of functions had never been satisfactory and the war had shown that in the last resort it occasioned much inefficiency and even some unpardonable corruption. Two remedies which have ultimately been adopted, and are now accepted as matters of course, are the creation of a ministry of defence for purposes common to all the services, and the provision of a staff organization for each service. Both had been advocated long before the South African war, the latter, which was the prior need, in two short and masterly books by Spenser Wilkinson, called *The Brain of an Army* (1890) and *The Brain of the Navy* (1895). Balfour missed his chance of making these reforms. Instead he rearranged the functions of a hitherto disregarded committee of imperial defence, under the chairmanship of the prime minister, and, terminating the office of commander-in-chief, set up an army council on the model of the existing admiralty board. But by giving the committee of imperial defence an office with a professional secretariat, he created a nucleus from which the imperial general staff developed. In the main the internal reorganization of the army was scarcely begun in his time.

The other set of problems directly resulting from the war related to the future of South Africa. Whatever the permanent constitutional arrangements were to be, it would not conduce to either harmony or prosperity to leave the Cape Colony, Natal, and the two former republics under four separate governments. While the conquered territories were still in military occupation there were men on both sides who had enough political sense to make considerable progress towards agreement on aims. Cecil Rhodes had died before the end of the war, too soon to elaborate his warning to the British against making the mistake of thinking they had beaten the Dutch. The most influential of the Afrikaners were the generals Botha and Smuts, the latter a lawyer and a skilled handler of ideas. They had to deal with the high commissioner, Lord Milner, who had been appointed by Chamberlain and was his strongest instrument.

The imperialists believed in unities and unifications, with some sort of unification or federation of the whole empire as a goal. Milner regarded South Africa as eminently suitable for this treatment, and he inspired the very able young men, his 'Kindergarten', who worked under him in rehabilitating the country. They worked towards a unitary, as distinguished from a federal, constitution for South Africa. Experience has shown that in this they judged well; but they made no adequate study either of the Dutch Afrikaners or of 'native affairs'. Milner, within his limits a first-class administrator, had little or none of the politician's indispensable art of understanding and managing opinion. In education, assisted immigration, and other matters he openly worked for a British future for South Africa. He publicly approved a petition for suspending the Cape constitution, a policy which Chamberlain had already rejected. He consented to the plan of making good the deficiency of African labour in the gold mines by contracts for the import of Chinese labour. This had the result of reuniting the British Liberal party, which had been distracted during the war by disagreements between its two wings, represented at one extreme by the Liberal imperialists and at the other by those, stigmatized as pro-Boers, who regarded the war as unjust. Their opponents declared that the outcry against 'Chinese slavery' was an insincere party dodge; but it aroused the basic hatred of oppression, however justifiable on economic grounds. The scheme was withdrawn, but not before 47,000 Chinese immigrants had been signed on.

From Colonial War to European War 1902–1914

1904	The *Entente Cordiale*: Britain and France move towards alliance.
1906	The Liberals gain a landslide victory; 29 Labour members are also elected, making the Labour party a serious force.
1907	New Zealand becomes a Dominion.
1909	Old-age pensions are introduced.
1910	Outbreak of strikes; troops are sent to calm riotous miners at Tonypandy.
1911	The power of the House of Lords is reduced by the Parliament Act. Payment of members of parliament is instituted. A scheme of national insurance against personal illness and unemployment is adopted.
1914	Gun-running in Ulster. Britain declares war on Germany and Austria in August, and against Turkey in November. The British Expeditionary Force lands in France.

Joseph Chamberlain was not involved in the incident of Chinese labour. He had spoken in South Africa against the proposal, and he was no longer Colonial Secretary when it was accepted. For a variety of minor reasons of policy he was not altogether comfortable with his colleagues and, while he was away in South Africa, they made a change which meant more to him than to them. During the war a small amount of revenue had been raised by a duty on imported wheat. The cabinet, most of whom were orthodox free-traders, did away with it. To Chamberlain they seemed to be knocking down the first courses of a structure which he hoped to build high. He believed that a customs union within the empire might prepare the way, as a customs union in Germany had prepared the way, for closer constitutional bonds. He knew that this would not be easy: the self-governing colonies had given assistance during the war, but they had also made it plain that they intended to increase their control over their own affairs. Chamberlain, however, also wanted to give up the old economic principles for domestic reasons. As a manufacturer he favoured this method of meeting state-aided foreign competition. His old radicalism was still alive, and as a social reformer he had promoted the intervention of public authorities, especially but not solely municipal. When he resigned from the cabinet he set himself free to appeal to the public on all these grounds. With support from well-chosen economists, business men, and journalists he began a campaign in the country in favour of protectionism, under the easily penetrated alias of 'tariff reform'.

For two years, 1903–5, the campaign went on and its entrenched opponents made an unexpectedly stout defence. The regions which were politically most mature were those in which industry and nonconformity were most fully developed: Scotland, the old highland zone, and the Midlands from Northampton northwards. This time was the zenith of the skilled workman, and the standards of argument needed in platform speeches by both sides was probably higher than at any earlier time, when education was backward, or in the later times when unskilled and semi-skilled labour counted for more, and the mass media of communication superseded platform oratory. In the narrower circle of politics Chamberlain's action split the Conservatives and Unionists into protectionists and free traders. Balfour understood the arguments on both sides so well that neither could believe in him as a leader. Instead of dissolving parliament he resigned from office, hoping that no Liberal government, divided between the imperialists and anti-imperialists, could hold its own with a parliamentary minority. He underrated the Liberal leader, his elderly and genial, but far from imposing, fellow Scot Sir Henry Campbell-Bannerman. The new prime minister began by neatly frustrating a conspiracy of the three leading Liberal imperialists to claim three principal offices for themselves. He shepherded them into the places which

The Rolls-Royce car, in Edwardian times and later, was a symbol of perfection in British engineering. This 10-horsepower prototype was photographed during army manoeuvres in 1904, when it was being tested for military use. C.S. Rolls, one of the two men who created the enterprise, is at the wheel.

he considered suitable and then dissolved parliament and fought a general election.

This general election was notable not only for the issues and the result, but also because it was the first in which organized labour was one of the contestants. The labour movement had been gathering strength for generations, and drawing together contingents from widely differing recruiting fields, with assorted weapons. The old individualist radicalism had something in common with religious nonconformity: neither of them respected the rich or reverenced the state. In each generation there were educated men of the middle class, and even a few of the aristocracy, who had no patience with the committee-methods of the social reformers and their step-by-step advance which looked, from in front, exactly like marking time. They were attracted by theories, and they had many theories to choose from, most of which were socialistic, favourable to state action and not alarmed by the prospect of class war. Karl Marx lived in London from 1849 to his death in 1883. In the year of Marx's death William Morris, the poet and artist, declared himself a socialist and began to write pamphlets and make street-corner speeches for the cause. In the same year the Fabian Society was founded, soon to be joined by George Bernard Shaw and Sidney Webb. It was named after Fabius Cunctator, the delayer who won a war for the Romans by a gradual wearing-down of his opponents' strength. Its members rejected the Marxist doctrines, and worked for the nationalization of the means of production, distribution, and exchange by permeating the minds of all those, preferably influential, people who were willing to listen. All the time the trade unions were growing in numbers and experience: their objectives and their successes were in the field of wages and conditions of work and their leaders were not socialists.

In 1886 the schism in the Liberal party over Home Rule had a result which brought all these labour movements into a closer relation with party politics. Until then each of the two historic parties had been stratified by classes on much the same lines as the nation, dukes at the top and others rank by rank below. Now, although the separation came over Home Rule, the upper classes mostly ranged themselves on one side. The unions were reaching the point where they needed men of their own, not philanthropic sympathizers, to watch their interests in parliament, and where, with improving organization and good leadership, they could find the money to finance trade unionists as candidates and members. There were already some Liberal members of working-class origin, and in the general election of 1886 their numbers rose to eleven, of whom six were miners.

Very soon the idea of a separate Labour party emerged. At a by-election a Scottish journalist and unpaid union official, originally a miner, James Keir Hardie, stood against both the Conservative and the Liberal. In 1892 he was elected to

James Keir Hardie, virtual founder of the Labour Party. Keir Hardie founded the Scottish Parliamentary Labour Party in 1886, and by 1892 was an Independent Socialist member of parliament for a London constituency. He helped form the Labour Representative Committee in 1900, and from 1900 to 1915 was member of parliament for Merthyr Tydfil, in South Wales.

parliament with Liberal support, and in 1900 without it. In that year the new tendency was confirmed by the setting-up of the Labour Representation Committee, combining trade unions and socialist societies, with James Ramsay MacDonald as its secretary. As fate would have it in the next year there was a strike on a railway in South Wales. The Taff Vale Railway Company sued the Amalgamated Society of Railway Servants for damages. Almost everyone who had thought about the subject supposed that trade unions were legally immune from actions for damages; but this company won its case, and the final court of appeal, the House of Lords, upheld the judgement. This as good as prohibited industrial action by trade unions. The Conservative government was by no means perturbed: it appointed a royal commission. The membership of the Labour Representation Committee more than doubled, and before parliament was dissolved three of its candidates won heartening victories at by-elections.

At the general election of 1906, 158 Conservatives and Liberal unionists were returned, against 374 Liberals, 84 Irish Nationalists, and 54 Labour members, these three parties together giving the government a majority of 354. The cabinet reflected the changed composition of the political class. The prime minister himself and about a third of his colleagues were not members of the Church of England; eight of the nineteen were professional men, and one was a former trade union leader. It would in any case have been difficult to keep such a great majority together. In the event it did hold together for eight years, surviving two more general elections, which diminished its numbers, and this is the more remarkable because from an early stage a new problem came to the fore which had been increasingly present to the minds of the political leaders, but which they had scarcely mentioned in their constituencies. This was the problem of Britain's international relations. That the time had come to strengthen the national defences was brought home indirectly to the House of Commons by the army reforms on which the new Secretary of State for War began to work as soon as he was appointed. Richard Burdon Haldane was another Scotsman, a barrister and one of the Liberal imperialists. Though he was not allowed complete freedom, especially in finance, he succeeded in creating a comprehensive and coherent new model, without antagonizing either the military professionals or the far from militarists majority of the Liberal party. In the main he followed the lines of the inquiries consequent to the South African war. The imperial general staff was created, to carry out some of the essential functions of general staffs as they were known on the Continent, though still without a finally satisfactory relation to command and to political control. The regular army itself was brought to a very high degree of efficiency. It was to have a force of six infantry divisions and one cavalry division, with the necessary specialist troops, and this force was to be ready at short notice to serve abroad, as British expeditionary forces had served for centuries, if necessary in Europe.

All this was done without legislation; but another part of the reforms, which needed the authority of parliament, in its nature caught the attention of the civilian population. The old militia, which since 1867 had been partly trained and could be embodied as a regular force, was given a more useful standing as a special reserve, additional to the reserve of time-expired men who were liable to be called up. The old yeomanry and volunteers were civilians who underwent training in their spare time. They had grown up piecemeal and without much supervision, especially in times of anxiety, from 1859 onwards, and in 1863 the government had been empowered to call them out in the event of apprehended as well as actual invasion. Now they were to be called the Territorial Army, with fourteen divisions and fourteen mounted brigades, properly equipped, inspected, and commanded. They were not necessarily liable for service abroad, though men willing to undertake it might volunteer beforehand. Haldane's army reforms would have been well timed in any year from the Crimean War onwards, but it was coming to be understood that they were specially relevant to changes that had altered British relations with the Continent since 1880, and still more since 1900. Since the Franco-German war there had been peace between the great powers, but it had been an armed peace, and it became less, not more, stable as time went on. There was such a thing as militarism, a belief in the value of armed might in itself and apart from its specific purposes. A great army is a focus of tradition and enthusiasms, and it is also an interest, with an inherent tendency to grow greater. An armed state, even when it does not back up its policy and threats, is a latent menace, and other states will take their precautions. All the great European powers used their resources, to the limit allowed by their social development, in training mass-armies, and in building railways to mobilize them quickly and to transport them, fully supplied, to strategic points. Even the strongest might conceivably have to meet alone an overpowering combination of enemies, and so the balance of power was maintained by alliances. Great Britain had remained consciously, sometimes uneasily but more often with self-congratulation, outside all this.

In 1880 there was no ground for expecting that she would become involved. The only power which she watched with apprehension was Russia. From time to time, as in 1885 when the Russians grabbed a town on the border of Afghanistan, the fear of a Russian march on India revived. The British governments and their advisers probably overrated the strength of Russia all through this period, and suspected it too easily of hostile intentions. Distrust of Russia did indeed die down; but not until better-founded anxieties had taken its place. In the eighteen-nineties Germany, a late-comer, joined in the quest for colonies, especially in Africa, only to find that Great Britain sometimes prevented the moves and always expected to have her approval sought. In the years when British pressure on the Transvaal republic was increasing, the Boers not only obtained lawful military supplies from Germany but entertained hopes of political support. The young German emperor, William II, congratulated them in an open telegram on the defeat of the Jameson raid. Everyone knew that this was an empty demonstration, because, without a fleet, Germany could take no action against the British anywhere; but even then, and still more three years later, after Fashoda, which enraged the French, British statesmen became uncomfortably aware that naval supremacy alone might not be enough to rely on in a world where she had not a single treaty of alliance.

The first formal step away from this isolation did not amount to entering the European system of alliances. It was a defensive alliance with Japan, and it had to do with the Far East. The Japanese coveted more territory to relieve the pressure of population; but in 1897 the Russians had established a protectorate over Korea, which they were peacefully penetrating, and their trans-Siberian railway was approaching completion. Great Britain, like France, Germany, and Russia, had already acquired footholds in China, and diplomatic action with Japan seemed to be a useful way of warning the Russians. In the event it had a considerable effect in Far Eastern affairs, when it was concluded in 1902, though no one foresaw what the general course of those affairs was to be.

When the Conservative government made the Japanese treaty, not long before Lord Salisbury's retirement, some politicians already favoured the idea of finding an ally in Europe. Chamberlain was attracted by the idea of joining hands with Germany. Germany was the most populous of the purely European states; in industry and commerce it was advancing rapidly; it set an example in many branches of education and social policy. British thinkers as well as business men on the whole found it easier to understand and appreciate the ideas and customs of Germany than those of France. It seemed that colonial questions could be solved by negotiation, and on the German side there was some

The London suburb of Raynes Park in Edwardian times. The electric tram, swift and cheap, made it easier for the lower-paid workers to live further away from their place of employment.

King Edward VII with the French president in Paris. Though the trend of events brought the 'Entente Cordiale' between France and Britain, Edward's visit to Paris in 1903 and his tactful but warm behaviour did much to speed the development of the new alliance.

support for the idea 'to Germany the army, to England the fleet'. With hopes, like those of Cecil Rhodes, for co-operation of the two European powers with the United States, Chamberlain twice in 1898 and again in 1901 induced the Foreign Office to make written proposals to Germany. The German response was completely negative. However it is elaborated, the reason amounts to this, that the Germans had decided to become a great power at sea. For some years private groups had been urging the causes of colonial expansion, and of naval expansion in support. In 1898 a naval law was passed, the first of a steadily expanding series, and in the eyes of those who drafted it the first step towards building a navy strong enough to challenge the British.

For several years after the German naval dockyards set to work there was no counter-action on the British side, but there was a change in foreign policy which afterwards provided a basis for counter-action. Without ulterior aims the British government entered into an agreement with France which, by give and take, put an end to the friction over colonial questions. Great Britain recognized the right of France to intervene in Morocco, France recognized the status of the British in Egypt. In Newfoundland the French gave up their rights in the fisheries, which went back to the Treaty of Utrecht. In West Africa, Siam and Madagascar the British dropped their objections to French claims, and in the New Hebrides a joint Anglo-French authority was set up. But this bargain could not have been struck if the mutual ill-feeling which had lasted, especially on the French side, since Fashoda, had not been exorcized. That was achieved, and so far as magic played a part in the achievement, it was supplied in the form of pageantry by King Edward VII, who was already personally popular in Paris. The *entente cordiale* was quickly accepted on both sides of the Channel.

The ignorant British public thought of foreign countries one at a time, but to the few who were well informed they were units in alliances. Germany was bound to Austria-Hungary and Italy; both much inferior to her in power. Austria's nationalities made her both vulnerable and ambitious; Italy also had territorial ambitions and she attached more importance to these than to co-operation with Germany. Since 1895 France had been in alliance with Russia. She was doing much by government action and private investment to bring Russia's forces and industry up to the standards that would be needed if eventually Germany were brought to fight on an eastern as well as a western front. But this prospect was shattered by the Russo-Japanese war of 1904–5. The Russians were soundly beaten on land and sea, and at home they were divided by a prelude to revolution. The Germans raised objections to the French absorption of Morocco, to which Great Britain had consented. The Liberal cabinet, taking office at this juncture, found that they had to pick their way through an international crisis. The French ambassador explained how grave it was. The new Foreign Secretary, Sir Edward Grey, was one of the Liberal imperialists, scarcely trusted by the pacific majority of his party, but his experience, and his rare personal dignity fitted him well to represent the nation. He said that he could not commit Great Britain in advance to support the French in arms if the Germans forced them into war over Morocco. The ambassador suggested that, without any commitment, it would be wise to begin military conversations to settle the technical character of Anglo-French co-operation if it should ever prove to be necessary. The two other Liberal imperialist leaders, Asquith and Haldane, agreed, and so did the prime minister. No one else was consulted. The soldiers were already talking on their own; staff talks went on until the outbreak of war eight years later.

All through these eight years the international question, or more simply the German question, was by far the most

David Lloyd George. Raised in North Wales and elected Liberal member of parliament for Carnarvon in 1890, Lloyd George soon attracted attention. During the Boer War, after making anti-war speeches, he was accused of being 'pro-Boer'. He was Chancellor of the Exchequer by 1908, and the force behind the social reforms which followed. In his wartime premiership his intelligent lack of scruple was valuable.

important for the future of Britain, but it was only by degrees that this came to be understood first in political circles, then by large bodies of opinion, and at last by everyone. One reason for this was that excitement ran high over other questions. In Campbell-Bannerman's time besides the army reforms, there was a Trade Disputes Act, which undid the results of the Taff Vale decision; there were useful minor enactments about agricultural holdings, workmen's compensation, and the like, and the government announced its intention of instituting non-contributory pensions for the aged. One South African question was settled in a liberal sense: instead of merely representative legislating bodies, such as the former government had intended, the annexed republics received full self-government. Campbell-Bannerman, already old when he took office, held it for little more than two years. His successor, Herbert Henry Asquith, belonged to the less democratic wing of the Liberal party; but, as Chancellor of the Exchequer, he had shown commanding parliamentary abilities, and he had taken the first step in graduating the scale of income-tax in accordance with incomes. He was a firm free-trader, and not an ardent social reformer; but in his first year as prime minister the promise of old-age pensions was made good. In the following year, 1909, there was an admirable opportunity for removing the many shortcomings of the existing system for dealing with poverty. The Conservatives had appointed a strong royal commission to inquire into the Poor Law. This commission now reported. The minority published a report signed by Mrs. Sidney Webb, one of the members of the commission and her husband's close collaborator, which advocated drastic changes on the principle which was in fact followed a good many years later, the principle of distributing the work of the Poor Law among appropriate authorities for health, education, and personal relief. The majority were more timid; but there was so much common ground that an energetic minister or even an energetic civil servant could have done a great work of construction; but such men were wanting. The notable reforms, large and small, of this government, were in other fields.

In India the time seemed ripe for some considerable advance on the lines of Gladstonian liberalism. As early as 1861, and in some places even earlier, provincial legislative councils had been set up, composed partly of official members, and partly of non-officials nominated by the provincial government. Forty years of educational and material progress made many Indians both desirous of going further and capable of working usefully in representative assemblies. In 1885 came the modest beginning of the All-India Congress, which at first was far from radical in spirit. It inevitably promoted a spirit of co-operation and a desire for greater participation in government throughout the subcontinent. By degrees it became a centre of dissatisfaction with British rule as such. At the same time, however, obstacles to co-operation revealed themselves clearly: the Hindu predominance in Congress was answered in 1905 by the foundation of the All India Moslem League. By then in practice most of the unofficial members of the provincial councils were virtually elected, since the advice of bodies which recommended appointments was normally followed. In 1909 the British government introduced the measures which were called, from the names of the secretary of state and the viceroy concerned, the Morley–Minto reforms. There was to be an elected element in all the legislative councils. This, with nominated non-official members was to out-number the official element, and in Bengal the elected members were to be in a clear majority. But Hindus and Moslems were to form separate electorates. This was the first firm step towards parliamentary government in Asia, and it was not ungenerous.

David Lloyd George, the new Chancellor of the Exchequer, understood contention and enjoyed it. In his budget of 1909 he proposed to raise a far larger sum than had ever been raised before. Some of it was needed for the navy, but new liabilities were to be incurred. A road fund was to be raised, and the money for it was to come from new taxes on petrol and motor-licences. Children's allowances were to be deducted from income-tax. At the modest cost of £100,000 a year, there was to be a national system of labour exchanges. Heavy new taxation of the regular kinds was needed, but there was a provocative scheme for the future. The whole of the land in the country was to be valued, a gigantic and perhaps impossible operation, and on this basis the unearned increase in the value of land at any future sale was to be taxed at the rate of twenty per cent.

This budget started a constitutional crisis. The House of Lords had been almost comatose throughout the long years of Conservative rule, but it woke to activity as soon as the Liberal government began to send up Bills. One of the first was to improve the 1902 Education Act, notably by ensuring that teachers were appointed for ability rather than for their religious affiliation. This the Lords amended so severely that the government dropped it. One of Asquith's early ventures was a Licensing Bill, to expedite the process of reducing the number of public houses. The Lords threw it out. Constitutional authorities, both politicians and professors, took it for granted that the Lords could not reject a money Bill. In 1860, when the Lords rejected a Bill for a duty on paper, the Commons had affirmed this very clearly without being contradicted. In 1909, however, the exasperated peers thought they could appeal to the people as they had done over Gladstone's second Home Rule Bill. Against the advice of some of their wisest heads they threw out the budget.

Asquith had no choice but to dissolve parliament: someone must have authority to raise the taxes. The general election gave him a majority of 124 to do it with, and he passed the budget. But he had to do more: the Lords had deliberately staked their constitutional powers on one throw without calling the odds. The Parliament Act of 1911 made three great changes. It denied to the Lords any right to reject any Bill certified by the Speaker of the House of Commons to be a money Bill. Every other public Bill, even if rejected by the Lords, was to become law if the Commons sent it up in three successive sessions, provided that two years were to elapse between the first and third of these sessions. This increase in the power of the Commons was made more acceptable by a shortening of the maximum duration of a parliament from seven years to five, which meant that the Commons could not override the Lords except for Bills introduced in the first three years. The preamble to the Act promised a reform in the composition of the upper House; but any conceivable reform would have strengthened its reputation, and it was many years before anything was done to redeem this promise. The circumstances of the passing of the Act touched, though they did not alter, the position of the Crown. The Act needed the assent of the Lords themselves, and as some of the Lords talked of refusing, the only way to make sure of this was to follow, on a far greater scale, the precedent of 1832, when the king promised to create sufficient peers to pass the Reform Act. Asquith had a draft list of some 250 names, many of them very good names indeed, which he was ready to submit. When it was made clear that the king was willing to create new Liberal peers, 500 if necessary, the resistance collapsed and the Parliament Act was passed.

In spite of the constitutional crisis, 1911 was a memorable year for social legislation. Several of the more prosperous of the smaller states, and Germany among the great, had wholeheartedly adopted the principle of state provision for social needs. Like all forms of protectionism and all forms of socialism it implied diverting the natural channels of economic life; but it respected capitalism itself, and, at least in Germany, was meant to strengthen it by removing the causes of discontent. In Britain the way had been prepared for it intellectually by the new collectivist liberalism, but only short steps towards it had been taken in practice. The National Insurance Act of 1911 set up a new administrative machine, affecting the daily life of millions and bringing permanently the same type of social organization to which Germany had led the way. It provided for compulsory health insurance of all persons employed at what may be called a high working-class wage. It also instituted compulsory insurance against unemployment in certain selected trades, an experiment which was afterwards extended and modified in principle. The civil servants who planned and executed these measures, such as Sir William Beveridge, an economist who was brought in from outside, reached the highest standards of ability, the reward of a generation of reforms in government and the universities.

Another measure of 1911 was symptomatic of the changing character of the public institutions, namely the introduction of payment for members of parliament. This had been an item of the Liberal programme for a good many years; but it was brought on at short notice by a judicial decision, the Osborne judgement. Most of the Labour members of parliament depended for their livelihood on grants paid to them by trade unions; but the Walthamstow branch of the Amalgamated Society of Railway Servants did not see why their money should be spent on a political party. A chancery judge ruled that no one had a right to compel them to subscribe for such purposes. Sixteen members of parliament lost their salaries, and attempts to make do with voluntary levies on trade unionists were unsuccessful. The House of Commons therefore voted £400 a year to each of its members. This did not make them any more professional politicians than they were before; but it was a visible sign of a mainly invisible transition. The proportion of members of parliament who owed their importance not to eminence in business, or in society, or in thought, but to sitting in parliament at the will of some paymaster, was growing. There were such members in all parties, and the modern parties themselves were among the paymasters.

Contemporaries were puzzled by the acute labour troubles of the years 1910 to 1912. They were part of a movement which was not confined to Great Britain: France had similar experiences, and French writers, being more articulate, explained them by a theory about the social value of proletarian violence in itself and apart from its objectives. In Great Britain, however, there were tangible causes. The excited, often ignorant, and ultimately futile opposition to the Parliament Act and the Insurance Act heated the whole atmosphere of public affairs. The social legislation seemed to bring no immediate benefits to the workers. The Labour members in parliament seemed to be effecting very little, and in the election of January 1910 their numbers dropped to forty. There were dogged strikes on the railways, in the ironworks, in the coalmines, in the textile trades, and among the dockers. The government, as a precaution, several times moved troops into the areas of disturbance. In 1910 at Tonypandy in South Wales their arrival probably put a stop to rioting and

The South Wales miners' strike of 1911. These events at Tonypandy were exagerrated by propagandists of both sides. Nevertheless, the situation was tense. The top picture shows mounted police demonstrating their potential to a far-from-impressed but far-from-violent gathering of strikers. In the centre, police protect non-strikers, while the lower picture shows a crowd of miners at their pithead.

looting: they did not fire a shot, though their commander afterwards wrote a jocular passage in his memoirs implying that they did use some force. On two occasions of mob violence in 1911 rioters were killed by musketry fire: two in the Liverpool dock strike and two at Llanelly in a railway strike. But the floods receded in the end, and there followed a time, we may almost say an age, in which industrial relations, though often bad, were bloodless and never ungovernable. No other country in Europe, perhaps in the world, had such a record.

It might be an error to suggest that another kind of disturbance, which reached its height a little later than the industrial unrest, was related to it. This was the outbreak of militancy in the agitation for women's suffrage. Several different kinds of feminism advanced steadily all through the nineteenth century. In some British communities, for instance among the Quakers, women had enjoyed complete equality with men for centuries: but they were not propagandists. The propelling ideas developed from those of the French Revolution: John Stuart Mill gave them a reasoned and moderate expression. The legal disabilities of married women as owners of property, a grievance mainly of the upper classes, were removed. There were many rich and a few very rich women, just as there were many cultivated women and a few great women artists, such as the women novelists from Jane Austen to George Eliot. It was of a piece with the general progress of the nation that there should be more and better girls' schools. The rise of the public schools had its imitators, but the most influential movement was the rise of well-managed day schools, usually called high schools. To provide these with adequate teachers, and for other purposes, higher education for women was needed. In 1869 Girton College, which afterwards moved to Cambridge, was founded; in 1871 Newnham College at Cambridge, after which, little by little the number of women's colleges increased, their performances in examinations improved, and the universities began to admit them first as listeners and then as members.

The higher education of women did not meet with organized or suffocating opposition. Its progress was slow, but by the time of Edward VII it was, on a modest scale, an integral element in the national life. With the admission of women to the professions it was otherwise. The professions had grown great by exclusiveness. They used their power, and disseminated a great deal of pseudo-scientific twaddle, to keep the women out. But by 1900 women doctors were a fully accepted part of the community, growing in numbers. As the state assumed new social functions its activities increasingly affected women and increasingly opened questions in which some women were better informed than men. Inevitably the demand for women's suffrage came into the range of practical politics. Women were eligible for seats on district and parish councils from their foundation in 1894. In 1907 women who had a property qualification were accorded the right to vote in elections for county and borough councils and to be elected to them. There was still a long way to go before they could hope for the vote in parliamentary elections; but the stage of resolutions by the Commons in its favour was reached. By that time, however, militancy had begun. The inventor was Emmeline Pankhurst, the widow of a radical barrister, herself exercising the minor office of registrar of births and deaths. Beginning with annoying pranks she and her followers, the suffragettes, moved on to breaches of the law. They harassed ministers and members of parliament, regardless of their opinions on the suffrage, on the curious principle that only the party in power could legislate. Their fanatical exploits went on until the outbreak of war.

The constitutional crisis over the House of Lords left behind it something even graver, a new Home Rule crisis. The second general election of 1910 returned exactly equal numbers of Liberals and Unionists, 272 of each, so that the Liberal government depended on the support of the eighty-four Nationalist and forty-two Labour members. Early in the spring of 1911 the government introduced two controversial Bills to satisfy national aspirations in two countries. In Wales the Church of England was to be disestablished, for reasons as cogent as those for the similar treatment of the Church of Ireland forty years before; but it was also to be partly disendowed, the proceeds being destined for a Welsh national library, university, and museums. This measure had unforeseen effects. The liberation of the church from its links with the state, and even the need to make the best of its straitened finances, give it new vigour. By ceasing to be English it took its place beside the Nonconformist bodies as a Welsh national institution.

This controversy was fought out as a regional and ecclesiastical matter. The Irish question, by contrast, was no less divisive throughout the kingdom than it had been in Gladstone's time. The new Home Rule Bill was indeed more statesmanlike than its two forerunners, in the sense that it embodied the federal conception which had germinated in imperialist thought. It was so drawn that at some future time parliaments might be set up in England, Scotland, and Wales on the model of that now proposed for Ireland. The imperial parliament at Westminster was still to be supreme, with forty-two Irish members in it, and the Irish parliament was to have exactly that degree of autonomy which was possessed after 1920 by the parliament of Northern Ireland. Much had changed in Ireland. Lively literary activity in prose and poetry, and the drama, had diversified and enriched the nationalist movement. A crusade to revive the almost extinct Gaelic language and ways of life began among scholars and took hold of the imagination of some who found the Nationalist party tame and unenterprising. Its leaders followed some of the tactics of the Czechs in the Austrian kingdom, a parallel to which the British politicians paid no attention whatever. But the enmity between Catholic Ireland and the north-east, with its Protestant society of all classes and of comparatively recent Scottish and English descent, had not been softened. It had grown harsher. Belfast, where a great shipbuilding industry had grown up almost from nothing since the eighteen-fifties, had become the largest city in Ireland, and the business community there had practical reasons for resisting any attempt to give Dublin authority in its affairs. Before the Home Rule Bill was brought in, both the Nationalists and the Liberals were prepared to make concessions of some sort to these feelings; but they did not understand that the Protestants of Ulster would not be satisfied with anything short of exempting them from Home Rule and retaining their province in the United Kingdom.

This was as plain as a pikestaff before the end of 1911. Led by Sir Edward Carson, a Dublin-born Protestant who had been attorney-general in England, the Ulstermen drafted a constitution for a provisional government, to be set up in the event of the passing of the Bill. In the first week of 1912, without breaking

Emmeline Pankhurst in dignified custody. Married to a barrister who was a strong believer in women's rights, Mrs Pankhurst's exploits gained publicity for the cause but her activities in the First World War, when she advised women to enter the armed services and industry, were probably more productive. She later joined the Conservative Party.

the law, they began to form the first private army in the British Isles since the Civil War. It was lawful because the local magistrates gave their permission. By the spring 80,000 Ulster Volunteers were on parade together. That they might ultimately break the law was shown by the words of the Covenant by which in the autumn thousands of signatories declared that they would hold themselves justified in taking or supporting any action that might be effective in preventing the operation of the Bill if passed, and more particularly to prevent the use of the armed forces of the Crown to deprive the people of Ulster of their rights as citizens of the United Kingdom.

This was a revolutionary situation, the more so because these proceedings were countenanced and openly supported by the leaders of the Conservative party in parliament. Asquith, the prime minister, entirely failed to take control. His government refused to accept an amendment to the Bill excluding Ulster from its scope, and his own nearest approach to compromise was to offer exclusion for a limited period of time. The House of Commons began to discuss the intricate details of drawing a frontier through the outlying counties where the Protestant and Catholic populations were even more mixed than elsewhere in Ulster. The Bill passed the Commons twice, only to be rejected twice by the House of Lords. Under the Parliament Act a third veto by the Lords would not prevent its becoming law. Some people still believed that Ulster was bluffing and others that without Ulster an autonomous Ireland could not be viable. Behind the scenes all the leading personalities, from the king downwards, took part in negotiations, without the smallest chance of reaching agreement.

In Ireland the situation became more dangerous. The Ulster Volunteers went on with their training. In 1912–13 there was a long and disorderly strike movement centred in Dublin, the last sequel of the British labour unrest, and the strikers, failing to find support from the Nationalist party, made friends with extremist elements. A small volunteer force was set up, with the purpose of keeping order, and this gave a hint that something more ambitious was possible. A movement to enrol Irish volunteers was publicly launched. The Covenant itself had referred to the possibility that the armed forces might be ordered to coerce Ulster, and Bonar Law, the leader of the Conservative party, in a speech in Dublin appealed to the army to disobey any such orders. In March 1914 Asquith for the third time moved the second reading of the Home Rule Bill, giving in detail his useless proposals for Ulster. There were other possible purposes, short of general coercion, for which the armed forces might be used, for instance the defence of scattered posts in Ulster where there were stores of arms and ammunition. A cabinet committee on 12 March sanctioned the transfer of the Atlantic fleet from the coast of Spain to the Isle of Arran, opposite Belfast, and the concentration and reinforcement of troops at certain points in Ulster.

Then came an incident which at last opened the eyes of the British public to the truth. At the Curragh camp near Dublin, the not very sagacious general officer commanding in Ireland announced with the authority of the Secretary of State for War that officers in his command who were domiciled in Ulster might 'disappear', and that any others who were not prepared to take part in active operations against Ulster might resign their commissions. Many of them did so, some with heavy hearts, for instance those who lived in Southern Ireland and wanted Home Rule. The news of this caused confused excitement. The Secretary of State and the chief of the general staff had both been personally responsible for giving this assurance and they had to resign. Although not a single order had been disobeyed by anyone, unless it were a cabinet memorandum forbidding officers to ask for written assurances; many Liberals in parliament, and newspapers, tendentiously spoke of the 'Curragh Mutiny'. It seems curious that the whole incident concerned only officers.

On 24 April the Ulster Volunteers, without let or hindrance, landed 30,000 rifles and 3 million rounds of ammunition at Larne. The government then made it clear that the import of arms into Ireland was illegal. By the middle of May the numbers of the opposing private army had risen to 100,000. On Sunday 26 July a cargo of arms was landed for them at Howth; but the police told the triumphal procession which escorted the arms into Dublin to stop. They called on the military to help. The crowd threw stones and a major gave the order to fire. Three civilians were killed.

Except when they added to the burdens on national finance, foreign affairs had scarcely any point of contact with domestic policy. They were still regarded as the domain of specialists, who were not obliged to take parliament into their confidence. Many of the supporters of the government were strongly pacific. Some of them were doubtful about the imperialist tendencies of Sir Edward Grey, but all agreed that he was an upright man and a skilful negotiator. He had a series of successes in bringing diplomatic conferences to agreement, and these successes in comparatively small things diverted attention from great realities. The struggle for power in Europe was moving towards open war. Germany was determined to be powerful at sea as well as on land. One separate thread in British diplomacy, formal and informal, consisted of direct invitations to Germany to halt or postpone the competitive building of warships. They began in 1910 and ended in 1913. They could only have succeeded if Great Britain had made some concession which would strengthen Germany very materially in some other direction, and that Great Britain was not prepared to discuss. In the international crises of Europe she always aimed at diminishing tension and eliminating causes of quarrel, but step by step she was drawn into co-operation with the opponents of Germany. In 1907 Russia, weakened by defeat in the Far East at the hands of Japan and by consequent troubles at home, made, with little difficulty, an agreement to end her quarrels with Great Britain in Asia, as

King George V and Queen Mary at the Coronation Durbar ('audience') in Delhi in 1911. From Queen Victoria to King George VI British monarchs were styled Empress or Emperor of India.

France had ended her colonial quarrels. Although the British government had no definite long-term policy, France and Russia began to count on it that this co-operation would continue in some form or other.

The crisis over Morocco, with which the Liberal government had to deal in its first days of office, ended with agreement; but in 1908 another arose in the Balkans. A revolution in Turkey, carried out by a nationalist and reforming party called the Young Turks, opened various possibilities of self-assertion for the Slav nationalities under Turkish rule and for the liberated states surrounding Turkey. Whatever the consequences of the revolution might be, it would not leave the Slavic subjects of Austria-Hungary exactly as they were. The Austrians had administered their protectorate in Bosnia and Herzegovina for thirty years, to the economic advantage of both sides, but now, with ambitious views for the future, they annexed the two provinces. The prince of Bulgaria declared Bulgaria independent, and Crete demanded union with Greece. The break-up of the Turkish empire had begun at last. In 1911 it went further. The Germans, ostensibly to protect trading interests in Morocco, sent a warship, the *Panther*, to Agadir. This intrusion on what was supposed to be a French preserve raised fears of a Franco-German war, but Germany accepted compensation in West Africa and left the French alone. The Italians, however, judged that then or never was the time for ensuring their own North African designs. They invaded Tripoli and Cyrenaica, and a year later obtained them in full sovereignty.

By that time the Turks were hard pressed in Europe. Bulgaria, Serbia, Montenegro, and Greece drove them back across Thrace. Austria, with Germany behind her, and Russia, the ally of France, were ready at need to intervene on behalf of their clients. A conference in London, with Grey presiding, stopped the war by devising a just partition of the conquered territories. In the next year, 1913, the victors quarrelled among themselves: the Bulgarians made a surprise attack on the Serbs, who were helped by their Balkan neighbours. This episode of two months was settled without a conference of the great powers; but, when the fighting stopped, the rival ambitions of both great and small remained as they had been. Both Germany and France brought their preparations for war to a height at which they could not be maintained for more than a very short period. Germany's finances were stretched to the utmost. France, to meet the German superiority in man-power, raised the period of compulsory military service to three years.

On 28 June 1914 the archduke Franz Ferdinand, heir to the aged Austrian emperor and a man with strong sympathies towards the Slavic nationalities, paid an official visit to Sarajevo, the capital of Bosnia. There two Bosnian nationalists shot him dead. The Austrian government, justifiably imputing guilt to the government of independent Serbia, sent an ultimatum on 23 July – three days before the gunrunning at Howth – with a list of demands, tantamount to the surrender of Serbian independence. This the Serbs refused and Austria-Hungary declared war; Russia mobilized; Germany declared war on Russia.

The British cabinet was divided. Some of its members hoped, even when the next step was taken and Germany declared war on France, that Great Britain might remain neutral. There were also Germans who hoped for this, and Grey exchanged communications to see whether the German government would make any promises to limit their action so as to keep clear of any threat to the Channel. The French ambassador knew that no commitment was implied by the Anglo-French military conversations; but there had been more than conversations. The British had removed their battleships from the Mediterranean to British waters in 1912 and the French had withdrawn their own from their west coast to the Mediterranean. The cabinet now guaranteed the defence of the exposed French coast. The diplomatic action of the *entente* might be thought to have created a moral obligation. The cabinet was divided. When Grey addressed the House of Commons on 3 August many of his Liberal and Labour hearers heard his review of past events with uneasy surprise. The climax of his speech turned on the friendship with France: 'how far that friendship entails obligations, let every man look into his own feelings, and construe the extent of the obligations for himself'.

But this self-examination was not needed. In the same speech Grey warned the House that the Germans might take a short cut into France by violating the neutrality of Belgium. They did so within hours of his warning. That was part of their previously fixed strategic plan. It made three changes in the minds of the British public. First, it was a downright breach of an international treaty; secondly, it was an attack on that point in Europe which had been regarded for centuries as vitally important to Britain; thirdly, it was an unprovoked attack on a small state. This last made a deep impression on public opinion. Great Britain declared war on Germany. King George V spoke for the great majority of his subjects when he said to the American ambassador: 'My God, Mr. Page, what else could we do?'

The Great War
1914–1918

1914 The British conduct a skilful retreat at Mons. Trench warfare begins. A naval victory off the Falklands compensates for the defeat off Coronel.

1915 Germany adopts, then abandons, unrestricted submarine warfare. The Dardanelles campaign begins. The Germans use poison gas at the second Battle of Ypres. A Liberal-Conservative coalition government is formed. An Anglo-French force lands at Salonika.

1916 The Dardanelles campaign is abandoned. The first conscription bills are passed. Disappointing naval battle off Jutland. The Battle of the Somme brings heavy losses. The British use tanks for the first time. Lloyd George becomes prime minister and forms a war cabinet.

1917 The Germans recommence unrestricted submarine warfare. The British adopt the convoy system. British troops capture Baghdad. Russian Revolution; withdrawal of Russia from the war begins. America declares war on Germany. The village of Passchendaele is captured after horrific losses. Balfour accepts the concept of a 'national home' for the Jews in Palestine.

1918 The Germans launch a spring offensive against the British near Arras. Electoral reform extends the vote to virtually all adult males and to most women. Austria and Turkey surrender. Germany agrees to an armistice.

The war transformed the conditions of daily life for the whole country and brought about deeper, if less measurable, changes in people's minds. When it began, Great Britain could claim to be closer than any other country to the idea of a liberal state. Its commercial system was almost unlimited free trade. With negligible exceptions it allowed freedom of speech, association and assembly not only to its citizens but to all who chose to enter as immigrants. The proportion of the inhabitants employed by the state was far smaller than anywhere else in industrial Europe. Except that women had no votes, the parliamentary system responded to public opinion as smoothly and promptly as any that had ever been tried. The armed forces were recruited on a voluntary basis. Local government was largely free from central control. The education of almost the entire middle and upper classes lay outside the state system. There were no identity cards, and no national register of individuals' age, parentage, employment and so forth. A man's home was his castle. August 1914 did not mark the end of all this; but it was the beginning of the end for much of it.

By mid-August the British Expeditionary Force was taking up position in the sector of front line allocated to it in Northern France. Advancing into Belgium, it met the advancing German thrust at Mons. Though outnumbered, it made a not unskilful retreat. The Germans broke through here and elsewhere to advance on Paris in the hope of defeating France before the Russians had completely mobilized their forces. However, in the Battle of the Marne, outside Paris, the Germans were held and forced to withdraw several miles. After this the opposing armies literally went to ground, digging themselves into ever more elaborate systems of trenches. The combination of trenches and guns made a defensive line which could be breached, and then but temporarily, only by the most expensive attacks.

At the close of the summer exercises the First Sea Lord, Prince Louis of Battenberg, had decided that in view of the international situation the Royal Navy's reserve ships should be kept manned. So when the war started, the navy was ready. In the Mediterranean, however, the German battlecruiser *Goeben* managed to reach Turkey and helped to induce that country to join the war as Germany's ally. The *Goeben* had been shadowed by British cruisers but bad luck and confused instructions resulted in the chase being given up without a fight. Troubridge, commander of the cruisers and bearer of one of the most distinguished names in British naval history, was thereupon condemned by a court of inquiry and summoned to a court martial: in 1914 (as well as in 1939–40) the Admiralty tended to divert blame for its own mistakes on to local commanding officers. Soon afterwards, at the Battle of Coronel, off the coast of Chile, a weak British cruiser force encountered a powerful German squadron, attacked in unfavourable conditions and was sent to the bottom. This engagement was followed by the Battle of the Falklands; the

Herbert Asquith, prime minister during an exceptionally hectic period of British history (1908–15). A former barrister, he became a Liberal member of parliament in 1886, Home Secretary under Gladstone in 1892, and Chancellor of the Exchequer in 1905. The split between Asquith and Lloyd George was the vital factor which reduced the Liberal Party to impotence soon after the war.

same German squadron was confronted by battlecruisers sent out by the Admiralty and was destroyed. At the close of 1914 the Admiralty could take pride in its safe transport of soldiers to France, its protection of British trade, and the stifling of German trade by its blockade, whose effectiveness was limited only by an unwillingness to offend neutral shipowners with a too rigorous enforcement.

At the outbreak of war Lord Kitchener, very much a conquering general in the eyes of the public, was brought into the cabinet as Secretary of War. Not only did he direct the war effort in the sense of providing men and material for the army, but he also directed strategy. His experience was valuable, but made it even more difficult for mere politicians to argue with him; he was not always right. He was correct, nevertheless, in dismissing the general view that this would be a short war, and he set in motion a recruiting drive, aiming for half a million new volunteers. Some reinforcement would in any case have become necessary; the British Expeditionary Force, after its retreat from Mons and useful participation in the Battle of the Marne, was almost spent; after heavy fighting around Ypres in early winter it could only hold 21 miles of the 450-mile Western Front. Voluntary recruitment was easy. Although many members of the government, and especially Grey, abhorred wars and this one in particular, the masses accepted it willingly. Many young men took a romantic attitude to the conflict, responding enthusiastically to the war poems of men like Rupert Brooke, who spoke of death in action as man's friend, and thanked God 'who has matched us with His hour.' Britain's best young men, the skilled, the idealistic, the selfless, the leaders, threw themselves into a war in which casualties were high. Their quality and competence were badly needed on the home front, and were missed after the war. Despite this flood of volunteers, some Britons who had no thought of entering the services, by reason of sex or age, did their inglorious best to rally others round the flag. A few women, indignant at the thought of healthy young men staying out of the army, sent white feathers, symbols of cowardice, to male friends and acquaintances or even to complete strangers in civilian clothing. Often they did not realize that the latter might be soldiers on leave. Thoroughly disreputable men, such as the politician Horatio Bottomley, were paid to make demagogic speeches shaming young men to come forward.

Another unpleasant manifestation, fanned by the popular press which had blossomed so dramatically in the pre-war decade, was mindless anti-German agitation. Mobs attacked shops whose owners had German names. The kennels of animal welfare societies filled up with unwanted dachshunds. The king later decided to change the too-German name of the royal house to Windsor. Battenberg, however, found that hostility could not be averted by changing his name to Mountbatten; to the Navy's loss, he was obliged to quit his office.

Only in 1915 did it come to be generally realized that this might be a long and arduous war. In that year, lack of military success, coupled with the emergence of several defects in handling the war, caused criticism of the government. The main setback was the failure of the Dardanelles venture. This operation was initiated by Churchill, the First Lord of the Admiralty, who throughout the war belonged to that group which favoured opening up new fronts in the east rather than pouring men and material into the destructive yet stagnant Western Front. The idea of landing to seize the straits leading to the Black Sea was so bold that many believed it was reckless. With many military and naval figures opposing the operation, it was impossible to divert much of Britain's effort from France to this new campaign. The appointment of commanders who were cautious in their approach was fatal for an operation whose success depended on drive and forcefulness. To make things worse, confidence that battleships alone could force the straits led to an abortive naval attack in February. This was foiled by mines, and merely alerted the enemy to Britain's interest in the area. When the first landings were made on the Gallipoli Peninsula in April, the Germans had had time to strengthen the Turkish defences. A second landing in August was similarly costly and failed to secure more than a vulnerable beach-head. In November Kitchener paid a visit and promptly ordered a withdrawal. The latter was the best part of the campaign, conducted skilfully and safely. In the Gallipoli operations the Australian and New Zealand contingents suffered grievously, a tragedy subsequently commemorated in their home countries by Anzac Day. In 1914 the Dominions had accepted almost as a matter of course that if Britain was at war, so were they. Large contingents were also sent from India. In South Africa, after a group of Afrikaners who sought to take advantage of 1914 to reverse the result of the Boer War had been suppressed, Botha and Smuts swung their Dominion behind the British cause. Smuts later became a valued, if part-time, member of the British war cabinet.

When the Dardanelles operation ran into difficulty, the First Sea Lord, Admiral John Fisher, resigned to demonstrate his opposition to the way it was handled. Fisher was by now an old, probably tired, man with a weakness for dramatic gestures; but he was regarded as the virtual creator of the modern Royal Navy,

HMS *Audacious*, a Dreadnought-type battleship, sinking after striking a German mine in 1914. This was the first serious loss suffered by the Royal Navy, and was initially kept secret; so much material and psychological capital had been invested in the Grand Fleet that evidence of its vulnerability to new kinds of weapons was regarded as potentially demoralizing.

having sponsored, during his earlier term of office, such innovations as the Dreadnought-type battleship. Churchill was blamed by many for squandering thousands of valuable lives at the Dardanelles. This situation, together with press criticism of shell shortages on the Western Front, reinforced the call for political changes. Hitherto, Asquith's pre-war Liberal government had ruled alone. At the beginning of the war the Conservatives readily entered into a kind of electoral truce, as did the Labour party. More surprisingly, the Irish Nationalist members of parliament also swung behind the government, partly because they sympathized with Belgium, regarded as a small Catholic country, like their own, which had been trampled by a powerful neighbour. In May, however, it seemed that the Conservatives would no longer support a government which was showing public evidence of incapacity. Asquith thereupon felt obliged to offer to take the Conservatives into a coalition government which would yet remain strongly Liberal. In the new coalition cabinet Asquith and Grey retained their offices of premier and Foreign Secretary, but Churchill was switched to a less prominent post and Haldane, whose military reforms had done so much to modernize the army, lost his job. Too many Conservatives had persuaded themselves that Haldane was 'pro-German'; he had studied philosophy at a German university. Churchill's replacement at the Admiralty was Balfour, the only Conservative to gain a really vital post. At the same time, because of the munitions shortage, Kitchener was relieved of responsibility for military supply, which was transferred to a new Ministry of Munitions, headed by Lloyd George. The Labour party received recognition by the appointment of its leader, Henderson, as Minister of Education, on the informal understanding that he would devote himself to labour problems.

Meanwhile the war continued. At sea the decisive clash with the German High Seas Fleet, expected by the Royal Navy and prescribed by naval textbooks, seemed no nearer, because the German ships stayed safely in their bases. In 1914 the British Grand Fleet had hastily been withdrawn to the Atlantic after the fanciful sighting and reporting of submarine periscopes in Scapa Flow, the main base in the Orkneys. However, the battleships returned in 1915. In the meantime, English east coast towns had occasionally been bombarded by a German battlecruiser squadron. In January 1915 the British battlecruisers at last caught up with this squadron and the Battle of the Dogger Bank ensued. Unquestionably a British victory, the triumph was marred by a confusion of signalling which caused the British ships to concentrate on the oldest and slowest German vessel, which was sunk, instead of pursuing the others.

Protection of British shipping had always been a first purpose of the Royal Navy, and it had notable success in this endeavour during 1914. Not only was the English Channel kept secure for the shipment of men and material to the Western Front, but German ships preying on trade routes throughout the world were effectively dealt with. In 1915, however, the German command realized that the submarine, or U-boat, offered great opportunities for damaging Britain's sea communications. The range of U-boats, especially of those based in Belgium, was sufficient to allow them to patrol the western approaches of the British Isles. As the sinking of unarmed ships without warning was contrary to internationally accepted standards for the conduct of war, the U-boats, after sighting a freighter or liner, would come to the surface, order the crew to take to their boats, and sink the vessel. Great losses were inflicted on British merchant shipping in this way. The Royal Navy had no means of detecting submarines under water, and even if a periscope were sighted, very prompt ramming or a very lucky shot were required to sink the U-boat. The submarine's underwater invulnerability could be exploited to full advantage only if it remained submerged and delivered a surprise torpedo attack. The Germans were therefore faced with the choice of violating the rules of war by attacking non-combatants without warning, or of maintaining moral standards at the price of hindering the operations of a potentially war-winning weapon. In early 1915 they chose the less moral path, a choice made easier by Britain's evident intention of starving

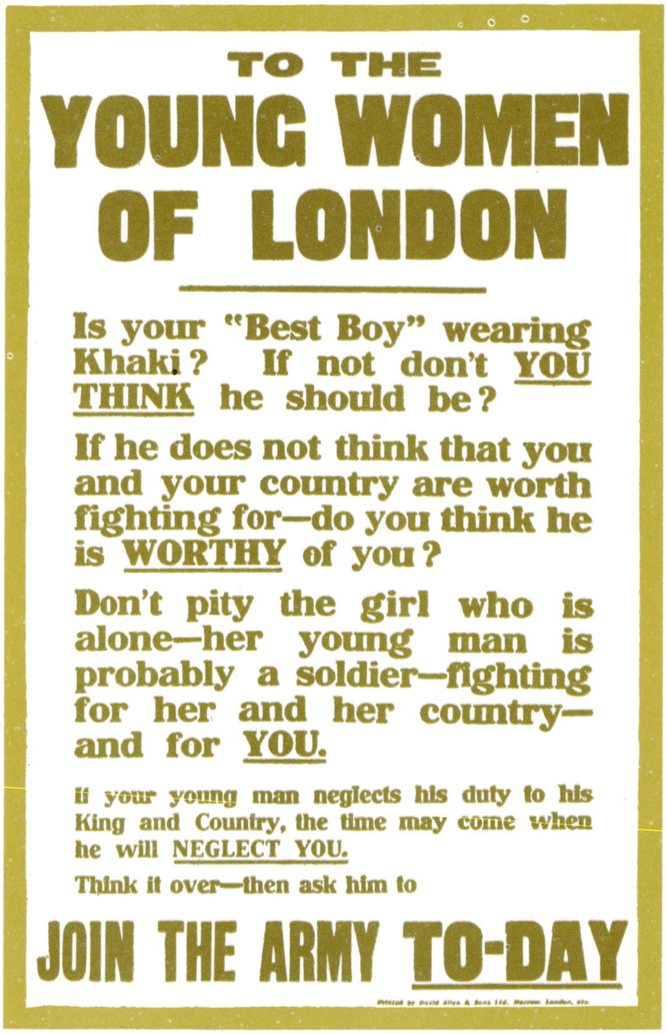

Part of the recruiting drive: a poster urging women to act as the great persuaders. The association of love with death was a favourite theme of 19th century poets and novelists, and some might regard this poster as a grotesque though unconscious repetition of the idea. But it was not only in Britain that wartime patriotism was taken to extremes.

German civilians by the naval blockade. In the following weeks the U-boats began to inflict such losses that the starvation of Britain could no longer be regarded as an impossible fantasy. But this 'unrestricted' submarine warfare aroused protests from influential neutrals which were so strong that the German government did undertake to cease attacking innocent merchant ships without warning. This change came after protests by the American government at the sinking of the British transatlantic liner *Lusitania* in May 1915, when, out of a total of almost 1,200 victims, 159 American citizens died. It was not revealed at the time that the liner's cargo included munitions, but this would probably not have made any difference to the American outcry.

On the Western Front, early 1915 brought massive British casualties in two offensives which made hardly any headway. At the same time, reluctance to abandon a very exposed British salient near Ypres entailed heavy losses in the defence of a doubtful asset. The technical problem was evident: attacks on properly entrenched positions were costly to both attackers and defenders, and almost always failed; surprise was vital, but was precluded by the heavy preliminary bombardment considered essential to weaken the defences. Insistence on heavy gunfire preparation caught short the munitions industries of Britain (and of Russia, France, and Germany as well). Some, but not enough, interest was aroused by a British offensive which, because of shell shortages, went ahead without artillery preparation; the Germans were taken by surprise and their lines were pierced, but the attack petered out (like all such breakthroughs) after only a few miles. The Battle of Loos, which began in September as a British offensive, was more typical, although it was said later that if the British commander, Sir John French, had thrown in his reserves at the time of the breakthrough there would have been a marvellous victory. Whether this was true or not, the consequent dismissal of French was the most important result of the Loos failure. His replacement as Commander-in-Chief of the British forces in France was Douglas Haig, a former corps commander.

In resolving to maintain a million British soldiers in France, Britain had virtually abandoned her generally accepted role as a naval, rather than military, power. This decision does not seem to have been discussed in any democratic sense; it was simply allowed to happen. Together with the heavy casualties, it meant that recruitment statistics acquired a vital interest to the government. So far, all the British who fought and died in France had been volunteers; the question was whether enough volunteers would continue to come forward. Britain was still liberal Britain, where government interference in the life of the individual was regarded as a social evil. Conscription was almost the ultimate interference; it involved the government ordering men to leave their families, put on uniforms, and kill or be killed. Kitchener was against conscription, although during 1915 an increasing number of military men and ministers became convinced of its necessity. Those who favoured it had mixed motives. The Army Council was concerned simply with getting as many troops as possible, and was not at all interested in the needs of the British economy. Most Conservatives took the same view, although a few entertained fantasies of introducing military and civil conscription at the same time; that is, the government would have the right to direct workers to certain kinds of work, and at government-fixed wage rates. When, towards the end of 1915, Kitchener's authority seemed to be waning, the pressure for conscription grew. As a kind of rearguard action, Asquith initiated a new voluntary recruiting drive: men of military age were invited to agree to serve when and if asked, on the condition that unmarried men would be called first. This campaign, as might have been expected, did not obtain great results, so in January 1916 Asquith brought in the first Conscription Bill, which called up unmarried men for service; but it was not long before another bill called up married men as well.

In the final years of the war, therefore, the army's numbers were maintained by conscripted men. Yet in total, more volunteers served during the war than conscripts. That two and a half million young men could actually volunteer for the horrors of trench warfare was a phenomenon to intrigue future generations. Clearly it said much about the mentality of pre-war Britain; what exactly it said is another matter. At the time it was regarded as quite normal for millions to volunteer. What was abnormal was to protest against war. Conscription immediately raised the problem of what to do with the pacifists. Pacifism was not a particularly strong movement in Britain, but it was strong and talented enough to be noticed. Public opinion could not be expected to tolerate men of military age evading war service simply by declaring that they were pacifists. On the other hand, the country was said to be fighting for its freedoms, its liberal freedoms, and those freedoms included the right to be pacifist. In the end, some arrangements were made, which was creditable; but some injustice was perpetrated too. Special tribunals readily found useful if arduous work for young men who opposed the shedding of blood, if their scruples were based on provable religious beliefs. Escape from military service was harder for those of no recognized religion, and for those who simply

Trench warfare on the Western Front was one of those grim situations where the only response was to laugh or to cry. *Punch* chose to laugh in a series of cartoons which enlisted the British sense of humour to cope with the unimaginably horrible. For those in the front line this kind of humour might well have helped morale; but for those at home it did nothing to bring reality closer.

declared that this war was immoral. Many such pacifists were conscripted; the unluckiest and least compromising faced the prospect of front-line execution for refusing to obey orders; the more fortunate simply went to prison. Questions of conscience had already troubled the Labour party. A few of its leaders actually believed in their phrases about the brotherhood of man. Keir Hardie was a fervent pacifist, and opposed the war; when he died in 1915 he was still member of parliament for Merthyr Tydfil. But Ramsay MacDonald was obliged to resign the leadership of the party in 1914; he was not a pacifist, but opposed Britain's entry into the war. Back in the patriotic fastnesses of Scotland, he was expelled from his golf club.

One of the supporters of conscription had been Lloyd George. As Minister of Munitions, he was all too conscious of the effect of skilled workers leaving their factories to volunteer for the army. He thought, rightly, that conscription would help to bring some ordered rationality into the system. Lloyd George was a successful and forceful minister and his appointment soon resulted in improved and prompter deliveries of military supplies. He was realistic enough to accept that the trade unions, already flourishing before the war, would become stronger and more influential in the course of the conflict. The key to munitions production was a willing labour force, and trade unions were seen as a valuable liaison between government and workers. There had already been some labour troubles, one factor being the rise of prices without a parallel rise of wages. Lloyd George was quick to recommend wage rises where dissatisfaction seemed likely to lead to strikes; his alacrity was not diminished by the circumstance that it was the employer, not he or the government, who would have to foot the bill. Still, when all too many industrialists were obviously doing well out of government war contracts, it would have been impossible in a free society to prevent workers demanding, and getting, wage increases. Trade union leaders and officials had to be careful in their dealings with the government; any excess of support for the government's policy ran the risk of workers seeking more aggressive men to represent their interests. In some factories this did happen; an influential shop steward would by-pass the official union channels to present his fellow-workers' demands. During the war a few shop stewards, regarded as troublemakers and harmful to the war effort, were deported to other parts of the country. The government could take this action under its all-embracing Defence of the Realm Act which, since the outbreak of war, had enabled it to do many unpalatable things by means of a mere Order in Council. Workers seem to have been relatively undisturbed by the internal exile of shop stewards; the same cannot be said of Orders in Council limiting the opening hours of public houses (restrictions which survive to the present day) and providing for dilution of the beer. Both these measures were intended to counter excessive drinking, which was said to have a bad effect on production.

Apart from wages and conditions, the trade unions also negotiated temporary agreements which enabled unskilled labour to do skilled work. A similar agreement permitted the entry of women workers into trades previously limited to men. Again, it was stipulated that this was only for the duration of hostilities, and that the women should receive the minimum wage; otherwise the unthinkable might occur, with a woman worker earning more than a man in the same job. By the end of the war women were not only working in engineering factories but were on public view as bus conductresses, railway porters, and farm labourers. Some came from jobs as domestic servents; (during the war the total number of domestic servants fell by a quarter), but probably most of them were at work for the first time in their lives. Many women thus gained a sense of economic independence, just as many men, working alongside them, realized that women were not so different after all. The suffragettes had abandoned their cause-losing exploits at the beginning of the war, and the success of new women workers provided a real reason for men to reconsider the justice of votes for women. In 1918 women over 30, and with minimal property qualifications, were accorded the vote. The age limitation, dropped, with the property qualification, in 1928, was to ensure that women voters would not outnumber men. The 1918 Act also extended the vote to all men, irrespective of property qualification, who could claim a few months' fixed residence.

If 1915 was a disappointing year for the British, deprived of expected victories and a triumphal termination of the war, 1916 was even more depressing. The war had evidently settled down into routine, dreary for most people, yet only too horrifying for others. The Battle of the Somme, in which one per cent of Britain's entire population became casualties for no purpose, and the unsatisfying performance of the Royal Navy at the Battle of Jutland, enlivened without brightening the general picture. Armchair strategists did find some interest in the new technologies of war: gas, tanks and aeroplanes. All had appeared before 1916, but it was in that year that they really seemed to become significant. Poison gas had been introduced by the Germans in 1915. It was contrary to the rules of war and its

Trench warfare on the Western Front in 1916: *above left*, advanced observers, prepared for a German gas attack, *above centre*, men of the Lancashire Fusiliers fix bayonets as a preliminary to 'going over the top' against the German trenches; *below left*, machine-gunners at the Battle of the Somme, wearing anti-gas helmets; *below right*, a section of the Welsh Guards awaits its turn in a reserve trench; *above right*, the tank promised to end the deadlock of trench warfare but it did not arrive in sufficient numbers to achieve this in the First World War.

A German Zeppelin. This unit, No. L277, made an air raid over Essex in September 1915. Transferred to the Western Front, it was forced down by gunfire in early 1916 in France, where this photograph was made.

introduction on the Western Front, where the prevailing wind blew towards the German lines, confirmed the popular British belief that the Germans were too clever by half. Soon the French and English retaliated in kind, but gas did not break the deadlock of the entrenched Western Front; had it done so, its use would have been an act of mercy. Much more promising for breaking through entrenched defences was the tank. The idea of a tracked armoured vehicle was neither new nor solely British, but it was the British who brought the idea to fruition; in effective secrecy, moreover, the name 'tank' itself being part of that secrecy. Understandably, the number of tanks employed in battle was not sufficient to cause a strategic revolution; the tank arm was never quite strong enough to change the course of the war. During the war British military aircraft increased from 63 to many thousand. At first used for reconaissance, aircraft soon carried offensive weapons, guns for use against other aircraft and bombs for dropping on enemy positions. Their use was not decisive, but they achieved enough to convice everyone that they would be a key factor in a future war. In the early months of the war German airships, the Zeppelins, dropped bombs in night raids on Britain, but they soon became too vulnerable to defensive measures. They were followed by German bombers, which carried out several raids before British defences, organized by the Royal Navy and its air arm, made such attacks too costly.

The domestic scene was further disturbed by events in Ireland. Since 1914 the Irish question had so receded in peoples' minds that it was a great, even demoralizing, shock when the Easter Rising occurred in Dublin. The more determined Irish nationalists had not relished the Home Rule party's support of Britain, nor the enthusiasm with which Irishmen had joined the Irish regiments of the British army. Led by Paidrig Pearse and James Connolly, the revolt was suppressed after a few days of bitter battle, although not before Pearse had been proclaimed 'President of the Irish Republic.' The ringleaders were executed almost summarily. One of them, De Valera, only escaped this fate because he had the good fortune to be an American citizen. Lloyd George responded by a sincere attempt at another Home Rule scheme. He persuaded the Ulstermen and the Home Rulers to get together, but the big Irish landowners, who were represented in the cabinet, refused to compromise.

The Battle of Jutland, the first and last encounter anywhere between complete battle fleets of Dreadnought-type ships, occurred at the end of May. Thanks to British decoding of German radio transmissions, the enemy fleet was intercepted in the North Sea. Twice the German ships blundered into the British line, and twice they succeeded in turning back before suffering serious damage. During the night, a failure of the Admiralty to provide the British commander, Jellicoe, with vital information, together with the failure of certain British commanders to inform Jellicoe that they had sighted enemy ships, enabled the German fleet to regain port. In the sporadic engagements that had taken place British losses had been serious, much heavier than the German. This was because of defects in British armour protection and in gunnery techniques. The Germans could claim a victory, but their commanding officers were shaken by the narrow escape. Even allowing for technical deficiencies, it was clear that in a full engagement the size and armament of the British battle fleet would have devastated the German battleships.

A few days later a British cruiser was mined. This would have been merely one of many similar occurrences had it not been for the presence of Kitchener on board. He was drowned. He had been losing authority in the cabinet, and this trip to Russia was probably a device to get rid of him for a while; if so, it succeeded beyond all expectation. He was replaced as War Secretary by Lloyd George; the Conservatives had objected to Asquith himself taking over that post. Asquith was considered too gentlemanly, a charge which could not be levelled against Lloyd George. The latter arrived too late to prevent the British offensive, later known as the Battle of the Somme. The battle, which poured successive waves of infantry against firm German defences, continued for four and a half months before the attempt to break through was abandoned. On its first day alone, 1 July 1916, 20,000 British soldiers were killed.

Although Haig was not the overbearing, obstinate, and unimaginative man portrayed by later generations of historians, Lloyd George was probably right to distrust the judgement of the military establishment. As the Somme offensive indicated, the soldiers in command seemed to have no idea of how to win the war apart from continuing to fight costly battles on the Western Front, in the hope that Germany would be exhausted before the Allies. Lloyd George concluded that strategy must be changed; total war must be waged, but not only on the Western Front. There ensued, in November, negotiations involving Lloyd

George, the Conservatives, and the newspaper proprietor Max Aitken (later Lord Beaverbrook). Lloyd George's intention of waging a war for the total defeat of Germany won him much support among those who were dissatisfied with the war record of the Asquith government. Eventually, Asquith was manoeuvred into a situation where he was obliged to resign. A new government was formed headed by Lloyd George. This split the Liberal party into Asquith and Lloyd George factions.

Lloyd George reconstructed not only the government's membership, but also its structure. Previously there had been a war committee to run the war, which reported to the cabinet. This had meant that decisions were slow. The new prime minister appointed a small war cabinet consisting only of himself, the Conservative leader Bonar Law, Curzon, Milner, and Henderson. Henderson was there because he represented the Labour party (or, more important, labour). Milner and Curzon were chosen because they were men accustomed to taking big decisions. Milner appears to have been the leading personality in this group of five, after Lloyd George, often acting as a useful brake on the premier's sometimes fanciful imagination. At this stage of the war the fact that Milner had been born in Germany of a German father was not counted against him. This war cabinet devoted itself to the big questions, and called in professional advisers, especially generals and admirals, to help in its deliberations. It had its own secretariat, keeping proper records and enabling it to function efficiently. On the next lower level, Lloyd George established new ministries and departments to deal with wartime problems; food, shipping, agriculture, information (the euphemism for censorship and propaganda), and national service. There was also a new Air Board. This was headed, as were several other ministries, by a successful businessman; this type of man hitherto had rarely been seen in ministries, but proved invaluable as the government widened its intervention in economic and industrial affairs.

1917 was a grim year. Lloyd George's faith in 'eastern' campaigns proved unrealistic. Allied troops already landed at Salonika still made no headway and did not divert German strength from the Western Front. In the Middle East, there were successes throughout the war against the Turkish empire; a force from India marched into Iraq; and Arab leaders were incited to revolt against the Turks as the British gained a new popular hero in Lawrence of Arabia. But British involvement in Palestinian affairs created long-term problems. In 1917, before General Allenby marched into Palestine, the 'Balfour Declaration' stated (or seemed to state) that Britain accepted that Jews should have a 'national home' in Palestine. It included a proviso that the non-Jewish inhabitants should not suffer; this was plainly ambiguous, and Jews and Arabs each interpreted it to suit themselves. Earlier, the British had ejected the khedive of Egypt, claiming he was a Turkish vassal; his successor they called king, and they established a protectorate to ensure that he stayed on the right side of the fence.

On the Western Front, Haig's offensive at Ypres was planned on the basis of all kinds of incorrect assessments. It began in August, and three months and thousands of dead later culminated in the mud of Passchendaele, a few miles down the road. But it was not the war on land which was significant in 1917. That year was marked by a successful U-boat campaign which almost starved Britain into submission but helped to persuade the USA to make war on Germany; and the war situation was transformed by the revolution in Russia.

In 1917 the German High Command was well aware that another unrestricted submarine campaign would risk bringing the USA into the conflict. But it calculated that there was a good chance of defeating Britain before the American war effort could make itself felt. In 1915 about a million tons of British shipping had been sunk by U-boats; in the first half of 1917 the unrestricted campaign inflicted losses two and a half times greater, a rate of loss which Britain could not bear for long. Those responsible for dealing with this crisis were very much men in the wrong place at the wrong time. The Minister of Food was against food rationing, and for long contented himself with issuing statements about how much food people ought to eat, advice which the population failed to observe. It was not until 1918 that his successor introduced ration cards for the main food items; by that time the worst of the crisis was over. The First Lord of the Admiralty was equally ineffective. This was Carson, appointed perhaps because of his valuable support for Lloyd George's 1916 grasp of the premiership. He lacked the intellect and character for dealing with the Whitehall admirals, who assured him that there was little they could do about the submarine problem. They asserted that the convoy system would not reduce losses and was in any case impracticable because merchant navy officers would not be able to keep station. At this, the most perilous period of the war for Britain, Lloyd George's ungentlemanly qualities proved invaluable. Scorning time-honoured etiquette, he burrowed beneath the heads of the Admiralty and discovered other naval officers who disagreed with their superiors. Convinced that the convoy system was the only answer, Lloyd George announced that it would be introduced. As a result, shipping losses were reduced to a tolerable level.

The Russian Revolution of March and November 1917 resulted in a total Russian withdrawal from the war by March 1918. The emergence of a self-proclaimed worker's government in Russia caused some concern in Britain, especially because 1917 was a year when war-weariness really set in, and there was a growing public interest in a negotiated peace; this seemed more feasible and less expensive than a total victory. The feeling was particularly strong in the Labour party, probably reflecting the mood of industrial workers. It was on this issue that Henderson resigned from the government in 1917. Another representative of labour replaced him, but as Henderson remained leader of the Labour party his resignation was a serious rupture.

The 1917 U-boat campaign had, as anticipated, brought the USA into the war in April of that year. In spring 1918 the German command made its final effort on the Western Front, knowing that it had to strike its blow before the American troops were fully installed in France. After considerable initial success, gained by surprise tactics which broke the British-held sector of the line in northern France, the German attack petered out and was followed by a retreat which threatened to develop into a rout. The German High Command realized that defeat was imminent, and at 11 a.m. on November 11 the Armistice came into force. Britain had suffered two and a half million casualties. Of these, three quarters of a million were dead. Their names can still be read on war memorials in every town and village.

Between the Wars
1918–1939

1921 The Irish Free State is created, but Ulster is excluded.
1924 The first, short-lived Labour government, under Ramsay MacDonald, takes office.
1926 The General Strike fails, but leaves a lasting impression.
1931 The Home Fleet goes on strike. The economic depression deepens. MacDonald forms a coalition National government. The Statute of Westminster offers independence to the Dominions. Britain abandons the gold standard.
1932 The neutron, and technique of 'splitting the atom', are discovered at Cambridge.
1933 Hitler becomes Chancellor of Germany.
1936 King Edward VIII abdicates. Spanish Civil War begins.
1938 Germany annexes Austria. Neville Chamberlain, at Munich, sacrifices Czechoslovakia, and much else, in the hope of preserving peace. Hitler declares his friendship for Britain.
1939 Peacetime conscription into the armed forces begins. Britain and France declare war against Germany.

The peace treaty and economic readjustment were the most pressing problems facing Britain after the Armistice. The political atmosphere was cleared by the election of December 1918; until then the 1910 parliament had extended its own life by special emergency legislation. In the election campaign Lloyd George presented himself as the winner of the war, and as a man determined to make the Germans pay for it. He and his coalition of Liberals and Conservatives received an overwhelming majority. The Asquithian Liberals were reduced to only 26 seats, which meant that the Labour party (57 seats) became for the first time the official opposition. Of the 81 Irish Nationalists elected, 73 were of the new militant Sinn Fein party, and these refused to take their seats. But the leaders of the Labour party failed to win seats, because of their pacifist leanings; for a time a hitherto unknown miner led the parliamentary Labour party. The heavy Conservative vote meant that, Churchill excepted, Lloyd George's leading colleagues were of that party.

Although it was called an Armistice, the document which the Germans signed in November 1918 was really a surrender, for it gave the Allies custody and supervision of German armed forces until the signature of a final peace treaty; the German High Seas Fleet steamed to the British base at Scapa Flow for safe-keeping. The peace terms could therefore be virtually dictated by the leaders of four victorious powers, Britain, France, America and Italy. When all the delegations assembled at Versailles it became evident that the US president, Woodrow Wilson, was concerned above all with a 'just peace': no annexations, the creation of new states to accommodate formerly subject nations, and a League of Nations to prevent further world wars. France had reason to be more fearful and therefore less generous; Clemenceau was insistent on German disarmament and heavy reparations payments. Lloyd George's intentions fell midway between these two. He, too, wanted Germany to pay reparations; beyond that he was flexible. The main provisions of the 1919 treaties included the creation of new nations like Czechoslovakia and Yugoslavia as well as the reconstitution of Poland from former German, Russian, and Austrian territories. The League of Nations was established. Former German and Turkish colonies and territory were not granted outright to the victors, but entrusted to their administration 'under Mandate' of the League of Nations. Britain received mandates for former Turkish territories, including Palestine, and for German East Africa (Tanganyika) where a campaign had been fought throughout the war. German South-West Africa was mandated to South Africa. Germany was obliged to pay war reparations to the victors; the amount was fixed later and was so large as to be unpayable. She also agreed to unilateral disarmament. Her land forces were to be sufficient only for maintaining internal order; she was to build no submarines and was to have no warships above 10,000 tons (contemporary battleships were of around 30,000 tons). This was a peace treaty

William Cosgrave, president of the Irish Free State, raises the Irish flag over City Hall, Dublin, in 1922, when the Republic was declared. Cosgrave, after a brief but bloody civil war, accepted dominion status for Ireland.

which was going to cause as many problems as it solved. A foretaste came when the German skeleton crews left on board their ships at Scapa Flow scuttled the vessels in protest at the terms being forced on Germany. More important, the American senate rejected the Versailles Treaty, signed by the US president. This meant that American guarantees, so precious to France, of cooperation to prevent Germany again becoming a menace, were void. American non-participation was also a serious blow to the new League of Nations.

The frontiers of the new revolutionary Russia were yet to be determined. In 1917 Allied troops had landed at Archangel to protect supplies there, and the following year British troops entered the Caucasus to protect oil wells from possible Turkish occupation. Soon these Allied troops were fighting sporadically against the Bolsheviks in the Russian civil war. In the Baltic, the Royal Navy sank several Bolshevik warships. Churchill and Milner advocated a kind of crusade against Bolshevism, with the sending of strong forces, but Lloyd George put an end to this. He feared the reaction of war-weary troops sent to fight in a doubtful cause, and internal disaffection at home. In fact, British workers were more interested than inspired by the Bolshevik revolution, but dockers did refuse to load a ship with munitions destined for anti-Bolshevik Poland. In later years, fear of Soviet strength or moral influence reappeared, occasionally to the accompaniment of 'red scares' ignited by the popular press and some Conservative politicians. But real communist influence in Britain was negligible. The British Communist party remained tiny. Socialist ideas, in a watered-down form, were already being expressed by the Labour party and it seemed likely that one day the party would put them into practice.

The anxiety in 1919 that the 'Bolshevik spirit' might find its adherents in Britain persuaded the government to speed the demobilization of impatient soldiers. As the men returned, women workers were dismissed to make way for them; by 1921 the number of women workers was less than ten years before. In the later stages of the war Lloyd George had established a Ministry of Reconstruction; the intention was 'to build a country fit for heroes'. That the heroes returned to something rather less than this intention was more the result of circumstances than of politicians' insincerity. The war had been financed partly by increased income tax, a burden which the upper and middle-income classes shouldered cheerfully, partly by internal loans, partly by foreign credit and partly by sales of assets abroad. With assets lost by war activity, these sales combined to reduce British investments abroad by one-fifth. More serious, and not immediately realized, was that Britain's trading position had deteriorated. Overseas customers had been lost, especially for such traditional industries as textiles and coalmining. It was true that new industries were developing, their products including vehicles, aircraft and radios; but they were not sufficiently advanced to compete in overseas markets. With exports in the 1920s usually only around 80 per cent of the pre-war level, there was little chance of Britain amassing the funds to restore her overseas investment position. Internally, economies had to be made. One of the first casualties was the Fisher Education Act. This had been passed in the war, and was designed to provide free elementary education for all children up to 14, with provision for part-time education up to 18, and corresponding improvements in higher education and nursery schools; it was not implemented. To avoid a repetition of the expensive pre-1914 naval race, Britain was a party to the Washington naval treaty of 1922. This stipulated that Britain and the USA would be allowed to build fleets of equal size, with Japanese tonnage 60 per cent of the British and American allowance, and France and Italy each 35 per cent. Battleships were to be limited to 35,000 tons. Strictly speaking this was an abandonment of the earlier British philosophy of the 'two-power standard', the maintenance of a navy which was at least equal to the combined navies of any other two powers. It also implicitly acknowledged that America was to be supreme in the Pacific, and that war between the USA and Britain was unthinkable.

Central government control over the economy had been extended during the war to a degree unimagined in 1914. Moreover, this control had been effective; there were frequent absurdities, but the era of free competition had not been without its absurdities either. Rationing, introduced in the final months of the war, but continuing, for sugar, until 1920, had at least shown that government control might make the best use of limited resources. The merits of nationalization were appreciated by many more people, and it had been expected that some industries would indeed be nationalized. But this did not happen; both public and political enthusiasm waned. National war-built factories were sold off; wartime controls were allowed to lapse. During the war, central control of the more than 100 different railway companies had ended wasteful competition and facilitated the transport of enormous quantities of war traffic. But a plan to take the railways under permanent state control was shelved. Instead, there was a compromise. Britain's railway companies were divided up on a territorial basis and four large companies created to absorb the old ones. The case of the mines was different. They too had been under government control, and the miners confidently expected nationalization. Mining was a grim business and mine-owning was grimly competitive; consequently there was considerable animosity towards the private owners who, in order to maintain their markets, had extracted the maximum effort from their men for the smallest possible provision of wages, facilities and safety measures. A commission of enquiry recommended nationalization, but its recommendation was rejected. Wage increases kept the miners quiet until 1921, but the government then found that shrinking export markets meant that the industry would become an enormous drain on government finance. So the mines were decontrolled and their owners, to meet competition, decided to cut wages. The resulting strike, during which the miners were deserted by their allies the railway and transport unions, lasted three months and was a failure.

Cessation of hostilities was followed by a renewal of nationalist pressures, especially in Ireland. The Sinn Fein members of parliament formed their own unofficial Dail ('assembly') of Ireland in Dublin. The formation of their own army, the Irish Republican Army (IRA), made a crisis inevitable. To deal with the IRA, the Royal Irish Constabulary was reinforced by auxiliaries, and by war veterans whose piebald uniforms earned them the name of the 'Black and Tans'. These soon degenerated into undisciplined bands whose acts of terrorism were as bad as those of the IRA. Barbarous incidents and guerilla warfare persuaded the government to act decisively. The Irish Free State was formed with its capital at Dublin, possessing complete autonomy, but remaining within the British Commonwealth. The six mainly Protestant counties of Ulster remained part of the United Kingdom, with their own parliament for local affairs at Belfast, and sending just 13 members to the House of Commons. Nationalism also asserted itself in Egypt. In 1922 Britain recognized Egyptian independence but retained the Suez Canal and control of defence arrangements; passage of oil supplies had become a British priority. India, whose peculiar status was emphasized by its separate representation in the League of Nations, had been promised in 1917 that it would eventually be granted responsible government. This was not enough for the nationalists, especially after a British-commanded company of Indian troops had opened fire on an unarmed crowd at Amritsar, killing hundreds. The Indian National Congress, flag-bearer of nationalism, was inspired by Gandhi and his campaign of non-violent civil disobedience.

A general election was held in 1922. The coalition had been weakened by the ill-health of Bonar Law and by differences over unemployment and trade protection. The 'Chanak crisis' of that year hastened matters, causing Lord Curzon to resign from the government. The Chanak affair originated in the refusal of the new Turkish government to accept the peace settlement, because it meant handing over a large area of Anatolia to Greece. Lloyd George took a strongly pro-Greek attitude. British forces at Chanak were threatened by a possible Turkish attack. Lloyd George issued an unnecessarily strong ultimatum and the Turks held back. The situation disturbed both the Conservatives and the Dominion governments; most of the latter did not agree to contribute troops in the event of a war against Turkey. These events split the coalition. Bonar Law formed a Conservative government with Curzon as Foreign Secretary and the Midlands steel industrialist Stanley Baldwin as Chancellor of the Exchequer. The election which followed was won by the Conservatives. The Asquithian Liberals did better than the Lloyd George Liberals; but the Labour party, with its reinstated pacifist-inclined leaders, outnumbered all the Liberals with 142 seats. A few months later Bonar Law, mortally ill, resigned. The choice of successor lay between Curzon and Baldwin. On the advice of other senior Conservatives, the king chose the second best. It was argued that Curzon would be unsuitable because his seat was in the House of Lords, in which the opposition party, Labour, had no effective representation. Soon afterwards Baldwin precipitated a general election on the issue of free trade. He lost. The free-trading Liberals and the Labour party improved their vote, the protectionist Conservatives were reduced to 258. As Labour had more seats than Liberals, the first Labour government was thereupon sworn in. Winston Churchill had made a well publicized remark that Labour was 'not fit to govern'; but the new administration, with Ramsay MacDonald as premier, easily disproved this. As the party was short of experienced men, it included some Liberals and non-party figures in the government; Haldane became Lord Chancellor and a former Viceroy of India went to the Admiralty. As everything depended on Liberal support, a plainly socialist policy was impossible. This was a moderate government, modestly seeking to do useful but unspectacular things.

The weakness of the Labour government was its desire to conduct a civilized relationship with the Soviet Union. It reestablished diplomatic relations in 1924. This made it vulnerable to 'red scare' attacks. After one of these the government resigned. Just before voting took place in the ensuing general election of October 1924 the *Daily Mail* published a letter from the head of the Comintern, Zinoviev, to the small British Communist party, urging the latter to engage in subversive propaganda among the armed forces. This letter was a forgery, but it helped to win the election for the Conservatives. With 424 seats they formed the next government, Baldwin's second. The most remarkable feature of this new administration was the appointment of Churchill as Chancellor of the Exchequer; he had now returned to the Conservative party which he had left in 1903. The new government promptly abandoned a commercial treaty which the Labour government had been negotiating with Russia. Later, in 1927, it achieved its ambition of breaking diplomatic relations with Russia. A prelude to this was a police raid on the Russian trade delegation in London. This raid, which was contrary to diplomatic protocol, did not produce the damning evidence of Soviet plotting that had been hoped for.

Churchill had agreed with the Treasury that Britain should return to the gold standard, which had been abandoned in 1914; the pound was to be convertible to its value in gold. The exchange rate of the pound thereupon rose, causing British exports to become less competitive. Some exporting industries, notably mining, sought to mitigate this by lowering their costs; that is, they again required wage reductions. The trade unions were already more militant; their coordinating body, the Trade Union Congress's General Council, threatened a general strike on the issue. Baldwin appointed a royal commission and meanwhile prepared measures to deal with such a possibility. The leaders of the Communist party were arrested; more

The General Strike of 1926. Armoured cars escort essential supplies in London. The strike was non-violent and shows of force did nothing useful, apart from keeping up the spirits of the fainthearted.

relevantly, an organization to recruit voluntary substitute workers was set up. In March 1926 the Royal Commission reported, recommending wage reductions for the miners. The miners appealed to the General Council of the TUC, which called for a general strike. This, the General Strike of 1926, lasted nine days. Despite bitter feelings, it was remarkably peaceful. Both sides were firm but well-disciplined, and there were few ugly incidents. Volunteers who manned buses, trains and other essential services were assaulted vocally rather than physically. Workers' councils issued permits for essential supplies to be delivered. But the TUC leaders were divided. Some thought the strike might get out of hand, because extreme militants were gaining popularity. In the end, against the miners' wishes, the TUC agreed to end the strike in exchange for somewhat vague government promises. Since the strike had been going well there was a natural feeling of betrayal among many strikers. The trade union movement was weakened, a fact reinforced in 1927 when the triumphant government introduced a Trade Disputes Act making general strikes and 'sympathetic' strikes illegal, and attacking Labour party finance. Trade union members would in future 'contract in' to pay the political contribution, which went to the Labour party, instead of 'contracting out' of the otherwise automatic payment of their contributions.

Churchill was one of the more vociferous and militant anti-labour members of the government, although subsequently he did cooperate with the Minister of Health, Neville Chamberlain, in introducing new social welfare measures. These included a new Pensions Act, and a Local Government Act which transferred the old Poor Law guardians' work to local authorities. This Conservative government also extended state control in the generation of electricity; the Central Electricity Board was set up, and soon there was a national electricity grid. The conversion of the British Broadcasting Company to the state British Broadcasting Corporation was also a nationalizing measure even though the old company's managing director, Reith, stayed on, and even though elaborate and remarkably successful provisions were included to prevent governmental influence being brought to bear on the content of radio programmes.

Baldwin's government managed to last five years, a new election being called in May 1929. From this, the Labour party emerged the winner, but not with an overall majority. MacDonald's second Labour government therefore had to rely on Liberal support. The party now had more experienced men, so there was less need to call in outsiders. But its ministers were unenterprising. Only Oswald Mosley had any trace of brilliance, and he soon left to form his own party. Philip Snowden, as Chancellor of the Exchequer, was unlikely to undertake any radical measures for the growing problem of unemployment. Unemployment was not new; throughout the 1920s there were usually about a million men out of work. But the so-called Great Depression was at hand; the New York stock market crash of 1929 soon had its repercussions on the financial stability of Europe. Each country took emergency measures to protect its currency. Trade barriers suddenly appeared. By the end of 1930 there were two and a half million unemployed in Britain. Snowden, in accord with the general spirit of the time, had no intention of incurring a budget deficit by easing the slump with increased government spending. Because of the gold standard, there was nothing to prevent an accelerating flow of gold out of the country. An attempt was made to obtain a large loan from foreign banks, but the New York bankers stipulated that a condition of such a loan would be considerable cuts in government spending. Such cuts would have meant reducing, among other things, unemployment pay; neither the TUC General Council, nor several cabinet members, would agree to this. The government was split and MacDonald resigned. But, on the urging of the king, MacDonald agreed to form a 'national' government of the three parties. This was for long felt by Labour party members as a betrayal, so much so that MacDonald and the Labour ministers were expelled from the party. Both MacDonald and the king felt that this national coalition government would only be a short-term emergency administration, to deal with the economic crisis; yet it lasted in various forms until 1945. Within days unemployment pay had been reduced, government salaries were cut and taxes were raised. The government and its supporters, anxiously awaiting industrial protest strikes, ignored hints of a blow from an unexpected quarter. In September units of the Home Fleet went on strike. Technically it was a mutiny. In fact it was not; the officers, whose pay had also been cut, sympathized with the striking sailors. It was a quiet,

One of the many demonstrations against unemployment. These are the workers of Southampton making their feelings felt in 1932. One placard reads 'Share out the work'; this was an apparently reasonable suggestion which neither managements nor unions, in the 1930s and later, seemed to relish.

A cartoon likeness of J.M. Keynes, the Cambridge economist whose *General Theory of Employment, Interest, and Money* of 1936, though not quite as original as sometimes claimed, was a major and significant work which helped persuade governments to intervene in the economy in pursuit of full employment.

peaceful affair, handled gingerly and settled by government concession. Nevertheless, a strike in the Royal Navy was a blow to international confidence in Britain. That same week the gold standard was abandoned. The pound was allowed to float, or rather, to sink. Stark necessity had at last triumphed over financial orthodoxy and pride. Export prospects improved. In the autumn MacDonald's government won approval in a general election; the 'official' Labour party formed the opposition, its number of seats reduced to 46. MacDonald was head of a government whose strongest party was the Conservatives. A Conservative, Neville Chamberlain, became Chancellor of the Exchequer.

Chamberlain, very much a representative of industry, like Baldwin, now had no difficulty in introducing trade protection. Tariffs and quotas were introduced on a wide range of imports. With a few exceptions, since 1919 British industrialists and their political representatives had sought to solve chronic difficulties not so much by enterprise, initiative, and the taking of hard decisions, as by adopting the easiest available remedies. First came wage reductions as the simplest means of reducing costs, then tariffs and 'Buy British' campaigns to damage the prospects of better and cheaper competing products. It was in these years that the British economy was confirmed in its downward course. Nevertheless, in the 1930s the situation was not wholly bleak. True, there were towns and cities in South Wales, Scotland and the northeast where two-thirds of the labour force was unemployed. Traditional industries such as mining, textiles and shipbuilding had been hit hard. But in the southern part of England especially, new industries and new technologies were being exploited by a new generation of enterprising industrialists. The car industry flourished, and the motor car spread to the middle classes. Luxury cinemas were built in every city, providing cheap entertainment for everyone; the attraction of the cinema was an important reason for Britain's falling beer consumption, from 35 million barrels in 1920 to 27 million in 1940.

Although domestic servants had become scarce, housewives found they could buy a whole range of labour-saving household devices, mostly electric. According to some statisticians, even families of the unemployed had as good a standard of living with their unemployment pay as they would have enjoyed with the wages of a pre-1914 wage-earner. Moreover, from 1932 onwards unemployment slowly declined from its peak of 2.7 million. In the later 1930s rearmament helped in this; earlier, the government's encouragement of the housing boom had also to some extent alleviated unemployment while bringing supply and demand for housing closer together.

In the Unemployment Insurance Act of 1934 the government accepted the final responsibility for looking after the unemployed. It assumed, pessimistically enough, that relief would need to be assured for 15 per cent of the work force. One feature of the Act caused long-lasting resentment. This was the 'means test', which stipulated that after a worker had come to the end of the unemployment benefit period his entitlement to public assistance would be established only after his affairs had been examined; any savings he might have, or any member of his household with a job, could mean that he would receive less assistance or none at all. This measure, penalizing the old Conservative virtues of thrift and close family life, aroused such resentment that when new welfare schemes were proposed in the 1940s it was unquestioningly assumed that every member of the population, even foreigners in some cases, would be entitled to benefit, without having to demonstrate poverty to an official.

The economist J. M. Keynes had for some years been making convincing assertions that at times of industrial depression governments should promote recovery by accepting a budget deficit; greater demand for goods could be encouraged by reduced taxation, and employment created by public works such as road-building. In 1929 the Liberals, united under Lloyd George following Asquith's retirement, had included Keynes's economic policy in their election manifesto, but gained little support. In the 1930s financial orthodoxy, the emphasis on a balanced budget, was challenged but not overthrown. Here and there, however, the government intervened to help the economy. British agriculture flourished as never before, with guaranteed prices supported by subsidies. Clydeside shipbuilding was also subsidized, enabling the giant liners *Queen Mary* and *Queen Elizabeth* to be built. The government sponsored schemes whereby companies in declining industries cooperated to reduce productive capacity. By 1937 unemployment was down to about 1.5 million, not much higher than the 1920s average.

Protective tariffs may have enabled one or two industries to survive and flourish, although by and large protection merely postponed the evil day when nettles had to be grasped. But tariffs had an imperial function as well. The concept of an Empire trading bloc cemented by preferential tariffs was old. The new British protectionism enabled the idea to be carried out. But when the long-awaited tariff conference between Britain and the

The Abdication Crisis: the wedding of the Duke of Windsor, formerly King Edward VIII, and Mrs Wallis (Duchess of Windsor) in France in 1937.

Dominions was held at Ottowa in 1932, the British negotiators discovered what they should have known all along, that the Dominions would not discuss trade in a spirit of cousinly generosity; they would bargain aggressively in a spirit of commercial advantage. The Ottawa conference was just one event in the rapidly developing empire. The 1931 Statute of Westminster spoke of a British Commonwealth of Nations and offered each Dominion full equality with the United Kingdom, under the same king, who would be represented by his Governor-General. The Dominions began to appoint their own ambassadors to foreign states, but they varied in their response to the Statute. New Zealand did not even ratify it. To ease the fears of French Canadians the British North America Act remained in force despite the Statute, thereby making it impossible for a Canadian government to make constitutional changes without approval from the British parliament. Ireland took the greatest advantage of the new liberties. The course of Irish history had been uneasy since the declaration of the Free State in 1922.

There had been a bitter civil war, launched by those who opposed the agreement. Those rebels who survived their defeat continued to agitate, especially about the existence of Ulster. In the late 1930s some of these, the IRA 'irregulars', carried out several bomb outrages in England as part of their protest. In 1936, under De Valera, the Irish Free State was renamed Eire, and became a republic in all except the very formal sense; formal republican status came in 1949. In India the British government, as always, envisaged eventual independence but could see only obstacles ahead. However, the 1935 India Act gave the Indian provinces almost unrestricted self-government, and looked forward to an independent Indian federal government; the latter, however, was blocked by the growing intransigence of the Indian National Congress. The basic problem was seen to be the hostility between the two dominant communities, the Hindus and the minority Moslems. Churchill bitterly opposed anything approaching independence for India.

MacDonald retired in 1935, and was succeeded as prime minister by Baldwin. The latter did not stay long. He received considerable public esteem for his handling of the abdication crisis of 1936. The newly installed Kind Edward VIII wished to marry an American divorced woman. Baldwin, after a good deal of tension, persuaded the king that he had to choose between marrying a divorcee and retaining his crown; the British people would never accept both. Edward abdicated, to be succeeded by his brother as King George VI. This was the top society sensation of the decade, if not the century. Interestingly, the greater British public could only experience the climax, for the press exercised its freedom by not mentioning the matter until the final days; for weeks earlier, only foreigners and the very top of British society had known about it.

When Baldwin went, Neville Chamberlain succeeded him. It was unfortunate that both Baldwin and Chamberlain came to power at times when their best qualities could only be disadvantageous. Baldwin was a serene, uninterfering man, in office at a time when major decisions about the economy, foreign policy and rearmament should have been made. Chamberlain's mind was one-track, and narrow-gauge as well. As Minister of Health his narrowness of vision and his concentration on the administrative side of things, combined with a strong wish to do good in the world, produced an excellent record of beneficial and useful progress. As the prime minister confronted with a completely new phenomenon, the problem of Adolf Hitler, he was doomed. But after 1939 he was a convenient scapegoat, not only for many politicians and journalists, but also for that sizable if not major part of the population which had given a sign of relief at his grasp of a dishonourable peace in 1938.

British interwar foreign policy was dominated mainly by a fear of communism. Later came a distrust of fascism, a term embracing a variety of regimes, the most threatening of which were the Japanese and German. Fascist Italy was regarded as unpleasant but relatively harmless. For Germans, Hitler's national socialism seemed to promise an end to international humiliation, inflation and unemployment. The western Allies' relaxation and subsequent abandonment of the reparations provisions of the Versailles Treaty, and the association of Germany in international agreements, came too late to save the moderate German 'Weimar' government; by 1933 Hitler was in power and popular. He immediately announced his intention of rearming. The British government accepted the need for a matching British rearmament but, conscious that public opinion was not in favour, did little about it. In March 1935 Hitler reintroduced conscription and announced the existence of the German air force. The League of Nations seemed powerless against these breaches of the Versailles Treaty. Japan, having occupied Manchuria in 1931, had been condemned but not punished by the League. In 1935 Italian troops were sent to invade Abyssinia. The League agreed to impose economic sanctions, but Italy's most vital import, oil, was not touched. British weakness meant that a simultaneous war against both Italy and Germany became the great fear of military planners. At the same time a war in alliance with one of these against the other seemed feasible, although unwelcome. There was a good deal of muddled thought, as well as cowardice, evident in British decision-making circles at this time. It is difficult to explain otherwise that abysmal foreign policy venture of the 1930s, the Anglo-German Naval Treaty of 1935. This allowed Germany to build a fleet up to 35 per cent the size of the British navy, and as many submarines as Britain. This was a clear repudiation of the Versailles Treaty, and was made against the wishes of France.

In 1936 Hitler marched his troops into the Rhineland, which had been demilitarized by the Versailles Treaty. French alarm was acute and justified, but without British support strong action was impossible. In February 1938 the Foreign Secretary, Anthony Eden, resigned because Chamberlain was pursuing his own initiatives, such as the courting of Italy, without consulting him. The following month Hitler's troops annexed Austria. In September it was obvious that Hitler intended to invade Czechoslovakia, which happened to be France's ally but not Britain's. Chamberlain, still conducting his own foreign policy with the aid of low-quality advisers, flew to Germany to intercede with Hitler. The latter seemed to raise his terms after each concession by Chamberlain. At the end of the month the Prime Minister was back in Britain. Air raid precautions were taken. Children were evacuated from the cities. The fleet was alerted. Then Hitler suggested a meeting between the British, French, German and Italian heads of government at Munich. The Munich agreement which followed seemed to have preserved peace, but at the expense of the Czechs. Czechoslovakia was forced to surrender the Sudentenland to Germany. This territory, until 1919 part of the Austrian Empire, was mainly German-speaking. It was vital for Czechoslovakia's defence, because it contained the Skoda armaments works, and its frontier with Germany was mountainous and well-fortified. In return for this acquisition and the consequent crippling of the hitherto powerful Czech army, Hitler declared his friendship for Britain. Chamberlain flew back to a warm, even adulatory, welcome in Britain. Hitler, a few months later, was able to march into the rest of Czechoslovakia, meeting little resistance. Duff Cooper, the First Lord of the Admiralty, resigned in protest at the Munich agreement. This resignation caused more stir at the time than Churchill's condemnations from the sideline. Churchill, after all, had an unfortunate record behind him: the Dardanelles, the gold standard, the General Strike, resignation over India and opposition to Baldwin in the abdication crisis.

The emotional and political temperature was rising in Britain. The Spanish Civil War brought closer the realization that soon everyone would have to take sides. The government knew quite well that Germany and Italy were helping Franco's insurgents in Spain, but it had no desire to intervene. Politically-

The official photograph marking the Munich Conference, which decided the fate of Czechoslovakia. Chamberlain is standing on the extreme left of the front row, Hitler in the centre, with Mussolini on his left.

conscious Britons, on the other hand, urged intervention. Left-wingers, in particular, were prompt in responding to the call for volunteers to help the Spanish government forces. The eventual defeat of the latter left bitterness in Britain as well as in Spain.

Bitterness, too, came to Chamberlain; he realized after Hitler entered Prague that the precious piece of paper he had brought back from Munich was worthless. Rearmament went ahead. The Labour party no longer opposed it; its pacifist leader Lansbury had been ousted for that very reason in 1935. Lansbury's successor was Clement Attlee, among the first of those who had fought in the 1914–18 war to gain high political office. Meanwhile Britain and France took the step of negotiating, unenthusiastically, for a common front with the USSR. But the countries of eastern Europe, especially Poland, which were threatened by Germany, distrusted the USSR so much that agreements for the common defence of eastern Europe seemed unlikely. The obvious weakness of France and Britain must also have been a factor in persuading the Soviet leadership in August to sign an agreement with Hitler instead. This sacrificed Poland, brought the German army closer to Moscow, but at least promised Russia a breathing space. Meanwhile the British government abandoned all its previous caution, and gave guarantees of assistance to small countries facing the possibility of aggression. One such country was Poland. So when Hitler attacked Poland in September 1939 Britain declared war, followed an hour later by France. The Dominion governments, in their new independence, deliberated carefully; with the exception of Ireland, all joined in to support the mother country.

World War 1939–1945

1940 Britain fights an unsuccessful Norwegian campaign. Churchill forms his coalition government. British troops are evacuated from Dunkirk. The Royal Navy attacks the French fleet at Oran. The German air force narrowly fails to win the Battle of Britain. British aircraft carriers cripple the Italian navy at Taranto.

1941 Roosevelt signs the Lease and Lend Bill. British military aid to Greece ends in a costly evacuation from Crete. British and Soviet forces occupy Iran. In the Malayan campaign Japan inflicts serious defeats on the British army and navy.

1942 Singapore is surrendered to the Japanese. A British counter-attack at el Alamein opens the final victorious campaign against the Germans in Libya. British and US forces invade French north Africa. The Beveridge Report recommends greatly enlarged post-war welfare services.

1943 The British capture Tripoli. British and US forces land in Italy. Churchill, Roosevelt, and Stalin confer at Teheran.

1944 British and US troops land in Normandy. The Japanese thrust towards India is defeated. The Germans launch rocket attacks against Britain. The Education Act proposes free education up to 15 years of age (effected in 1947).

1945 The Yalta Agreement defines Allied spheres of interest worldwide. Germany surrenders. The British recapture Rangoon. Attlee's Labour party wins a landslide election victory. Japan surrenders after the dropping of atomic bombs on Hiroshima and Nagasaki.

This war had been foreseen. On the home front, the government was well prepared. Gas masks and identity cards were ready. In anticipation of lethal bombings, children were quickly evacuated out of the cities. The more comfortable families who received the evacuees realized, often for the first time, that city children could be undernourished, poorly clothed, and perhaps insect-ridden. Chamberlain immediately took Churchill back into office, as First Lord of the Admiralty. The Emergency Powers Act gave the government power to act like any dictatorship. One of its first measures was to intern German residents. Many of these were refugees who had entered Britain to escape Hitler; it was some time before they were released. On the whole, though, mindless anti-German feeling of the 1914 type did not recur. Although the government had dictatorial powers, its conduct was tempered by the knowledge that parliament still functioned; the Emergency Powers Act could not prevent its ejection from office by a vote of no-confidence. During the war there were several occasions when the government was attacked by members of parliament, but only once did this result in a change of government. The main parties agreed that in by-elections the candidate of the previous member's party should be given a clear run. But this did not prevent the new Common Wealth party, founded by an ex-Liberal, Sir Richard Acland, and somewhat socialist in tone, from entering and winning a number of such by-elections.

Britain and France could do little to help Poland. The French army had followed the post-1918 doctrine that defence could always beat attack; it was installed in its Maginot Line, a powerful, largely underground, line of fortifications. For seven months Europe settled down to the 'phony war', in which nothing very much seemed to happen. At sea, the stirring event for Britain was the destruction of the powerful German 'pocket battleship' *Graf Spee* by three cruisers at the battle of the River Plate. On the other hand a British battleship and an aircraft carrier were lost, unnecessarily, to submarine attack. In November 1939 Soviet forces attacked Finland. Although a nominal ally of Nazi Germany, the USSR feared an eventual conflict with it, and attacked Finland to improve her defences. In Britain, public opinion was aroused by the gallant and effective Finnish defence and the government played with the idea of scorning Swedish and Norwegian neutrality to send forces to help the Finns. Luckily, Finnish resistance collapsed before any such ideas were put into practice. In April 1940 the war intensified, with Hitler's invasion of Denmark and Norway. British forces were sent to Norway, but they were too weak to achieve anything and were quickly evacuated. Norwegian coast defences, and the Royal Navy at the two battles of Narvik Fjord, inflicted crippling losses on the small German surface fleet.

The failure of the Norwegian campaign reduced confidence in the Chamberlain government's ability to win the war; in May a vote of censure resulted in many Conservatives turning against

Winston Churchill visits Battersea, in London, after a heavy air raid in September 1940. Visits by ministers and royalty to bombed areas were frequent and well-publicised, and probably had the intended effect on public morale.

BELOW The evacuation of London children in 1940. Toddlers from the working class suburb of Kentish Town, each carefully labelled, are marched to their train at Euston Station for despatch to the north.

RIGHT London under air attack. At night, Londoners used the Underground's stations as shelters; shown here are, presumably, late arrivals who were unable to find a place on the platforms.

the government. To this assault was added the Labour party's decision that if a coalition government were formed it would refuse to serve under Chamberlain but would agree to serve under Churchill. Chamberlain, although not yet defeated in a parliamentary vote, took the appropriate decision and resigned in favour of Churchill. In his last year of office he had served his country better than that country realised. He was the ideal politician for organizing the home front; here the policies and philosophies he had adopted were retained right through the war. The wartime concept of a benevolent dictatorship with a controlled economy and egalitarian society belonged to the Chamberlain period. The Sterling Area was created to embrace those countries still using the pound in their international transactions; its first aim, successfully achieved, was to avoid a disastrous capital outflow from Britain. Food rationing began in January 1940. This was timely, and organized on principles which became the envy of other belligerent countries. Food coupons were not exchangeable for fixed amounts of the various foods, but were merely valid for certain periods. This meant that for each rationing period the allocated ration per person could be different, according to the supply situation, which usually depended on the merchant shipping situation. The British housewife always knew that her shop would actually have in stock the food to which she was entitled. Later a 'points' system for tinned food enabled her actually to choose which tins she would buy. Almost simultaneously, the Chamberlain govern-

The Dunkirk evacuation: arrivals at a British channel port. The troops are mainly British, but include some French (recognisible by their helmets). The contrast between the crowded deck and the underpopulated gun platform suggests that even in the direst crisis the British would preserve their social distinctions.

ment introduced subsidies to keep down the price of basic foods like bread and milk. Rationing and subsidies together meant that everybody could buy enough food, and those with high incomes could not buy more than their fair share. This put an end both to undernourishment and overeating, and represented a dietary improvement which was reinforced by the abolition of white bread. To avoid the 1914–1918 phenomenon of 'war-profiteering', a crushing excess profits tax was levied on industries doing well out of war production. The egalitarian approach was emphasized by allowing the combined income tax and supertax rate for those with high incomes to reach 95 per cent. Moreover, a new sales tax, Purchase Tax, was levied at a high rate on luxury items. Rents were frozen. Chamberlain also made a number of wise appointments. That he elevated Churchill, a man whom he had no reason to like and every reason to fear, might perhaps be attributed to the force of public opinion. Churchill's popularity had risen when the war he had long forecast actually broke out; his calls for rearmament were remembered. But the appointment of the non-political Woolton was an act of inspired judgement. As Minister of Food Woolton almost succeeded in making food rationing fun. His ministry issued intelligent and intelligible advice on what to eat, so that the housewife could take full advantage of whatever foods were in good supply. Perhaps the most celebrated of his ministry's recipes was 'Woolton Pie', a steak and kidney pie made without steak or kidney.

The Liberal Foreign Secretary Grey, decades earlier, had described Churchill as a man who would be a failure in every political office except that of prime minister. When Churchill became premier, a very square peg at last found the square hole it was seeking. In May 1940 he had everything in his favour, apart from the not unimportant circumstance that Britain was facing defeat. He knew about the waging of war, and he possessed the inspiration and the gift to uplift the British people. That the Labour party and industrial workers were glad to have him as leader, despite memories of the General Strike, illustrates both Churchill's worth and the depth of the crisis which Britons realized they were facing. His speeches, both in the House of Commons and over the radio, were masterpieces in form, substance, inspiration and language. Even his enemies had to admit that this was something more than a superior journalist, something more than an ambitious politician. On the other hand, his choice of advisers was often poor, and this meant that his frequent interventions in the conduct of the war could be ill-informed.

Like Lloyd George in 1916, Churchill formed a small inner war cabinet, initially of five. Besides himself, there were two Labour representatives, of whom Attlee was one, and two Conservatives, including Chamberlain almost until his death late in 1940. Bevin and Beaverbrook joined later in 1940. Bevin, a powerful and intelligent trade union leader, was in charge of vital yet delicate labour affairs. Beaverbrook had distinguished himself as Minister of Aircraft Production in the Battle of Britain,

BELOW Spitfire fighters over Britain. The small technical superiority of these machines over corresponding German aircraft in 1940 was an important factor in the defeat of the German air force during the Battle of Britain. The Spitfire carried eight machine guns, was very manouevrable, and marginally faster than the German fighters escorting the attacking bombers.

FAR BELOW A coastal defence observation post. Such posts, manned by the army, were established along southern coasts when a German invasion seemed possible in 1940. The apparatus is fairly simple: binoculars, telephones, and a small rangefinder are the main items.

working miracles in the production of fighter aircraft.

Churchill's appointment coincided with Hitler's invasion of Holland, Belgium and Luxembourg. The Germans then swept around the northern end of the Maginot Line and put the French and British forces in disarray. While the French were retreating, the British forces, less their equipment, were taken from the beaches of Dunkirk by naval and private ships. Air attacks caused heavy losses, but about 335,000 British soldiers, and some French, got away safely. Hitler's decision not to send strong land forces against Dunkirk was probably mistaken; he wanted to use maximum strength against the French, but had he prevented the evacuation he would have deprived Britain of a trained nucleus around which to build her new army. Italy declared war against France and Britain at this time; for Britain the main threat arising from this was the powerful Italian fleet which, on paper, could dominate the Mediterranean. When France agreed to an armistice it was again naval considerations which seemed most alarming. There were powerful French squadrons based in North Africa. The British feared that these ships would be taken into the Germany navy, thereby transforming the naval situation. At Oran, Royal Navy ships bombarded the French squadron, putting it out of action and causing great losses of life which the French remembered for long afterwards.

The final weeks and days of French resistance had given Britain valuable time to organize herself for the next logical step, a German invasion. The amateurish Home Guard enrolled male civilians. Churchill had exerted the strength of will to resist the French appeal to allocate the fighter aircraft reserve to the ill-fated battle for France. This was important because, in order to invade, Hitler had to secure the English Channel, and he could

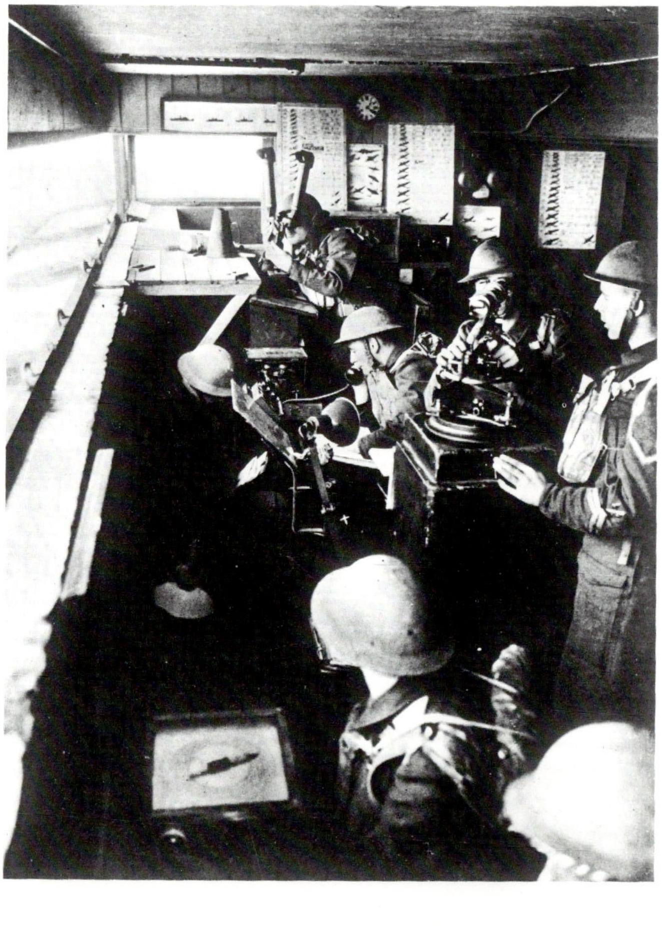

Scottish fruit-farmers support the war effort with raspberry jam: a local advertisement for seasonal workers. The war brought labour shortages, hence this appeal. How much of the resulting jam would actually go to brighten the lives of servicemen is unclear. It had become normal for every appeal to the public to be linked with the war effort, even when much imagination was needed to see the connection.

do this only with air power. There began, in the summer of 1940, the Battle of Britain, the first campaign fought with air forces only. British advantages, compensating for German superiority in numbers, included a superior High Command, and the circumstance that the battles were fought over Britain; control of aircraft from the ground was easier and pilots who were shot down might live to fight another day, as might their aircraft. Britain also had a number of technical advantages. Radar – the location of objects by radio waves – was more advanced in Britain than anywhere else in the world; this meant that advance warning could be given of approaching aircraft. British rearmament had started late, so that although weapons were in short supply they were often of a more modern design than those of Germany, where series production had started earlier; thus the Spitfire fighter was superior by a small but all-important margin to the corresponding German fighter. Thanks to the work of Polish and French intelligence experts, Britain inherited the key to one of the German High Command's most important ciphers. A whole organization, 'Ultra', was devoted throughout the war to deciphering German messages; advance warning of German intentions was therefore available for many of the war's operations, including the Battle of Britain. At first the German air force fought for command of the English Channel. Having damaged shipping but not defeated the British Royal Air Force, it shifted its attacks to radar stations and aerodromes. This was the most perilous time for Britain. With few available aircraft and pilots, the ability to ensure that aircraft were placed just where the Germans were approaching was vital. Equally essential was the ability to refuel without being taken by surprise on the ground. By September the situation was desperate. At this point the Germans shifted their attack to London, and lost their chance of victory. Daytime bombing was costly, so night bombing was substituted. During the winter nights London and other cities came under heavy air attack, but the fighter arm had time to recuperate. Bombing was not as effective as air force spokesmen had claimed before the war, but damage from incendiary and high explosive bombs was appreciable. By the spring of 1941 the German air assault had plainly failed. This had a great effect on neutral opinion. When the American ambassador in London forecast imminent British defeat, Washington no longer believed him. British prestige was further enhanced by victories against Mussolini. Italian soldiers and sailors were not keen on fighting this particular war. Thousands of Italians surrendered to British forces in Italian North Africa; British troops advanced from Egypt into Libya and captured Cyrenaica. Italian East Africa, including Abyssinia, was captured by the British during 1941. Despite a shortage of aircraft carriers, the Royal Navy crippled the Italian battle fleet by air attack in the harbour of Taranto. A few months later British naval supremacy was confirmed at the Battle of Cape Matapan, in which an Italian squadron was put to flight with heavy loss.

By this time the American government felt able, without political risk, to help Britain. Churchill had made an appeal, 'Give us the tools and we shall finish the job'. Roosevelt responded with the Lend-Lease Act; this enabled Britain to import supplies and arms from the USA with no immediate requirement to pay for them. At the end of hostilities in 1945, 20 per cent of British war supplies came from the USA; another 10 per cent came from Canada. By 1943 Britain was totally at war, with no able-bodied person wasted. In the end, because of labour shortages, Bevin had to conscript workers for certain jobs. Some men called up for military service were sent to work in the coalmines instead. At the same time, he ensured that factory conditions were improved. Worker's canteens were provided, as well as 'Music While You Work' transmissions. The munitions flow from North America meant that in Britain fewer industrial workers were needed for the same war effort. This flow depended on sea communications. In 1941 the submarine was causing losses to shipping, but the convoy system, British success in underwater detection of submarines, and development of underwater explosive weapons made the U-boat seem a manageable problem. The picture soon changed, when the Germans began massing submarines for night attacks on the surface. In 1942 the U-boat was as great a menace as it had been in 1917, but new defensive measures, especially the use of aircraft equipped with very sensitive radar, saved the day. On the surface, the naval event of 1941 was the excursion of the new German battleship *Bismarck* into the Atlantic; the intercepting British battlecruiser *Hood*, like her predecessors at the battle of Jutland, blew up after her magazine had been detonated. However, enough ships were available to intercept and sink the *Bismarck* as she hurried towards safety in one of the French Atlantic ports.

In 1941 events turned against Britain. Hitler's attack on the USSR in June gave no immediate reason for optimism, for the Red Army's potential was under-estimated. Despite Churchill's previous animosity towards communism, he promised full support for the Soviet Union. Supplies were sent to Russia by the Arctic sea route, and later through Iran, which Soviet and British forces occupied for the purpose in 1941. The Arctic convoys, passing close to German-occupied Norway, were very perilous; of 800 freighters which were sent during the war, 85 were sunk, as well as several warships. But in 1943 and 1944 two German battleships were sunk in this area.

Britain was more or less honour-bound to the hopeless endeavour of sending troops to help the Greeks when the Germans invaded in April 1941. The troops were soon evacuated to Crete. This island was defensible, but German air superiority and tactical competence gained them a victory in which many British soldiers were taken prisoner and several warships lost. Moreover, the British troops had been transferred from Libya; so when German forces entered the North African campaign they found only weak British forces and soon drove them back deep

A German submarine is brought to the surface by depth-charge attack. As in the First World War, the U-boat was Germany's most effective weapon against Britain. Only the development of radar, especially airborne radar, and of new underwater projectiles, saved British shipping from a total disaster.

into Egypt. By late 1942 the British had retreated to El Alamein. But here, reinforced and under new leadership, they made their counterattack. This was a complete success. General Bernard Montgomery's Eighth Army drove the *Afrika Corps* not only out of Egypt but out of Libya as well.

The Japanese assault on the US Pacific fleet at Pearl Harbour in December 1941 brought America into the war; this assured a victorious outcome. Britons had hitherto assumed that they would avoid defeat, but had very vague ideas of how they would bring the war to an end. But Japanese intervention also brought initial humiliating defeats. Hong Kong was known to be indefensible, but when the Japanese army swarmed through Malaya and forced the surrender of the naval base of Singapore, the low point of the war seemed to have been reached. Britain lost prestige, and consequently power. Henceforth Australia looked to America, not Britain, for defence. The spectacle of an Asian army defeating the British stirred Asian nationalists everywhere, not least in India. The Indian National Congress, given Hitler's racial pronouncements, could hardly have opposed Indian participation in the war against Germany. Now, with Japanese troops advancing to the borders of India through Burma, it was a different story. There was an intensive campaign of civil resistance, mainly non-violent. Britain reacted strongly, gaoling hundreds of Congress members. Unrest in India was quelled, and eventually the British, under the leadership of General Slim, succeeded in mastering the Japanese armies and the techniques of jungle fighting. The defeat of the Japanese at the Battle of Kohima, in 1944, was a great triumph of persistence and willingness to learn. By 1945 the Japanese were being pushed back; Rangoon was recaptured in May 1945.

The Royal Navy suffered badly in the Far East. In 1941, two capital ships, *Repulse* and *Prince of Wales*, despatched to protect Malaya, were sunk by air attack; they had been unprovided with air cover. After further losses in the East Indies and off Ceylon, the British Far Eastern Fleet was withdrawn to Mombasa, in East Africa. In the same period came a further naval humiliation. Two German battleships, having endured months of ineffective bombing in the French port of Brest, sailed up the English Channel in daylight to the safety of a German port. As with the disaster off Malaya, the basic cause of this failure was inadequate provision of aircraft for naval use. Too many resources had been devoted to building and crewing bombers, wrongly believed to be the key war-winning weapon.

Britain was the base both for the 'free' forces of nations under

PREVIOUS PAGE Bombing-up a Lancaster at a base in Britain prior to a raid during the Second World War. Night after night these aircraft took part in raids over Germany, particularly over the Ruhr. It was the Lancasters of 617 Squadron that were responsible for the highly successful Dambusters raid in March 1943, where Barnes Wallis's revolutionary bouncing bomb was used.

The active participation of women in the war effort was accepted as a matter of course in the Second World War; *left*, the Minister of Food, Lord Woolton, addresses members of the Womens' Land Army, an organization established to replace conscripted farm workers; *below*, women workers assemble the fin of a barrage balloon.

British forces land near Rangoon in 1945. The campaign against the Japanese in Burma was fought with great tenacity and growing competence. The prevailing jungle, and the problems posed by a monsoon climate, meant that new techniques of warfare were required.

German occupation, and for the coordination of resistance movements inside those countries. British agents were especially successful in their liaisons with the French resistance and with Tito's partisans in Yugoslavia. The terms of the Franco-German armistice in 1940 had divided France into the German-occupied north and west and an independent but impotent central and southern zone with its capital at Vichy. Britain was in a neither-peace-nor-war relationship with Vichy France. There were few hostilities, but the Free French movement under de Gaulle was the strongest of the exiled Allied forces in Britain. The French colonial empire was not taken over by Germany, but remained under the control of the Vichy government. Efforts to persuade colonial Frenchmen to declare themselves for de Gaulle were usually unsuccessful. In Syria the British fought Vichy French forces to secure a stronger position in the Middle East. In late 1942 there was an Anglo-American landing in French North Africa. This was a useful exercise both in large seaborne landings and in Anglo-American cooperation. A combined chiefs of staff organization was established in Washington to help this coordination. In July 1944 there was another joint venture, a landing in Sicily. This was quickly successful and led to Italy's surrender. German forces continued to fight a sturdy rearguard campaign among the mountain ridges of the Italian mainland. A landing in the German rear at Anzio, in early 1944, helped the Allied advance, but Italy did not prove to be a short cut to victory. The idea of creating a 'second front' with a landing in France had already been raised. The Russians blamed the British for delaying this, and the Americans would have preferred to attempt it in 1943. But Churchill and his advisers were probably right; the proper equipment was not then available, and a failure could have been exceptionally serious. The Anglo-American landings were made in northern France in June 1944. This was a well-planned operation under the overall command of the American General Dwight Eisenhower, with the British General Montgomery in operational command. It provided good scope for British inventiveness. Since a major port was unlikely to be captured intact, a concrete prefabricated harbour was towed across the Channel and assembled. To ensure the supply of motor fuel, an undersea pipeline was laid. One of the reasons why the British had fewer casualties than the Americans during the landing operation was that a variety of devices had been provided, including tanks which exploded mines ahead of them, and tanks which provided bridges for other tanks to climb over.

The Normandy landings coincided with a last trial for the civilian population. German self-propelled V1 and V2 missiles were directed against British cities. The V1 was slow and easily dealt with. The V2 was a rocket and unstoppable. Luckily its launching sites were captured before it became too dangerous. After a temporary reverse, when the Germans launched their counter-offensive against the Americans through the Ardennes, and another when Montgomery's scheme of using paratroops to capture vital bridges well inside the German lines just failed to succeed at Arnhem, the Anglo-American forces advanced into Germany. Meanwhile the Red Army, which had been fighting the bulk of the German army for the previous three years, captured Berlin in May 1945. Hitler committed suicide. His successor surrendered to the Allies near Hamburg.

During the war Churchill had several meetings with Roosevelt and Stalin. At Casablanca in January 1943 the American and British leaders had decided to announce that they would demand unconditional surrender from Germany. At the August 1943 Quebec Conference Roosevelt and Churchill came to certain agreements about the sharing of atomic secrets. By 1940 scientists at the universities of Cambridge and Birmingham had satisfied themselves that production of an atomic bomb, though expensive, was possible. Later that year, when the Battle of Britain was still being fought, atomic and other scientific secrets were transferred to the USA. At Quebec it was agreed that British physicists could participate in the programme which the Americans had started. Thus Britain would be kept up-to-date with the techniques of construction and manufacture being developed by American scientists. The two leaders met with Stalin at Teheran in November 1943 and at Yalta in February 1944, for further discussions on the conduct of the war and the shape of the postwar world. In late 1944 Churchill was in Moscow. It was agreed that the USSR would have a dominant role in certain eastern European countries, but Greece was accepted as a British sphere. Stalin stuck to this agreement a few months later; when communists began a rebellion in liberated Greece, the USSR stood back while British forces helped to suppress it. Later, in Poland, Stalin went somewhat further than had been agreed, installing a pro-Russian Polish government instead of the London government of exiled Poles. At Yalta plans were agreed for a United Nations Organization to replace the ineffective League of Nations, and it was decided to divide conquered Germany into British, French, American, and Soviet occupation zones.

In the campaign against Japan, most of the spadework had already been done by the Americans; the British role was relatively small. In 1945 the army continued to fight a creditable campaign in Burma; the Australian army brought its long and arduous struggle in New Guinea to a victorious conclusion; the Royal Navy sank a couple of Japanese heavy cruisers. Soon, however, the war was out of Churchill's hands. He had dissolved the coalition government after the German surrender and called an election in July. In this his Conservative party was thoroughly beaten by Labour. Attlee was the new Prime Minister.

Probably Britain voted against the Conservatives rather than against Churchill. It remembered unemployment and it remembered Munich. In the election campaign the Conservatives were less concrete in their proposals for a better world than were the Labour spokesmen. Much interest had been aroused by reports commissioned to study certain social problems. The most important was the Beveridge Report of 1942. William Beveridge had been one of the architects of the welfare schemes introduced by Asquith's government before 1914. His 1942 report proposed the extension and improvement of government services offered to the population. He proposed that free health treatment, unemployment benefit, retirement pensions and family allowances should be combined in a simple scheme. There would be no means test; everyone would have an entitlement by right. The Beveridge Report was a point of departure that was discussed throughout the war. The Conservative members of the government were noticeably lukewarm. But in 1945 the coalition government did introduce family allowances; these were smaller than the sums proposed by Beveridge, but were balanced by the provision of free school meals, directly benefiting every child. The coalition government could also claim credit for the 1944 'Butler' Education Act, which proposed free education for all children up to a school-leaving age of 15, separating them, however, at the age of 11 into those who would attend grammar schools and those who would go to less prestigious secondary schools, both free. In the 1945 election campaign it was the Labour party which seemed to take most seriously the discussion about the welfare state and government planning. Possibly it realized better than Conservatives that the British people had developed into a very thoughtful electorate. The war was largely responsible for this, but there had been earlier signs. Penguin Books had made a great success of selling serious paperback books at sixpence a copy. The illustrated weekly *Picture Post* and its imitator *Illustrated* discussed serious issues but attracted a wide readership. During the war paper rationing had meant that newspapers had space only for serious matters. The BBC found that programmes with a high intellectual content, like the 'Brains' Trust', appealed to a large and not necessarily educated audience. In the forces the government had insisted that time be spent on current affairs discussions. Political awareness, memories of the past, and a clear idea of a desirable future, impelled many people to vote for Labour, even though they had never done so before and would never do so again.

The Britain which the Labour government inherited was in need of change; but this change would be accomplished at a most difficult period of British history. Resources had been spent in the war which could never be recovered. Although casualties in the war had been far fewer than in 1914–1918, 303,000 British servicement had been killed, together with 109,000 from the Empire and Commonwealth. 60,000 civilians had been killed by bombing, and 30,000 merchant seamen had been lost at sea.

Labour in Power 1945–1951

1947 The coal industry is nationalized. India is granted independence.
1948 The railways are nationalized. The British leave Palestine. The National Health Service begins.
1949 Britain becomes a founder-member of the North Atlantic Treaty Organisation. US bombers are stationed in Britain.
1950 British forces join in Korean War.
1951 Iran nationalizes British oil installations. The Festival of Britain is held. Churchill forms a Conservative government.

The achievements of the 1945 Labour government bear comparison with those of the reforming Liberal government of 1906. But whereas the latter conducted its reforms at a time when Britain seemed prosperous and all-powerful, Attlee's government had to attempt its social transformation at a time when Britain was plainly relinquishing her great-power status, both politically and economically. Attlee was an unassuming man; as is so often the case, he had been elected to leadership of his party not because of his ideas but because of his apparent lack of ideas; the candidate whose views offend the fewest receives the most votes. Possibly Attlee did have his ideas; he certainly had his principles; and he was firm. But as leader of the cabinet he acted more as a very efficient chairman, encouraging his ministers to develop their own initiatives.

Wartime expenditure, much of it on the basis of foreign credit, internal loans, savings and the sale of overseas investment, was one main reason for economic weakness. Wartime damage and losses, especially of shipping, was another. Loss of pre-war markets made prospects worse. Government planners estimated that, to recover, Britain would need to raise her exports to 175 per cent of the pre-war level. This she grimly did within five years, but by then circumstances had changed, and more was required. Britain's decline, and her apparent loss of political importance with the emergence of the USSR and the USA out of their pre-war isolation, accelerated the trend towards independence in the Commonwealth. American goodwill, called patronage by some and 'the special relationship' by others, was all-important.

War conditions had made the life and standards of the working class somewhat better, and the life of the middle class somewhat worse. This is a broad assessment; at the extremes were certain skilled factory workers who had prospered remarkably, and some middle class people, notably those who were retired on fixed incomes, who had suffered disproportionately. The country was roughly divided into those who wanted to return to the good old days, when incomes could encompass certain luxuries and servants could be found, and those who wanted to escape from the bad old days, when unemployment was always a possibility, when an illness in the family meant financial catastrophe, when factories were simply cheerless places of work, and a large family could not properly feed itself. In 1945, to a large degree, the Conservative party represented those who wanted to return to 1939. For people who decided they could not face life in Britain, emigration provided a useful safety valve. Those who, by 1945, longed for a little luxury, tended to move to southern and eastern Africa; those who felt that hard work and intelligence would find better prospects, away from the controls and restrictions of Whitehall, often preferred to settle in Canada; those who were not quite sure what they wanted went to Australia.

American Lend-Lease assistance came automatically to an end when the war finished. It was replaced by a large American loan.

Ministers of the incoming Labour government in the garden of Number 10 Downing Street in 1945, led by Prime Minister Clement Attlee (front, sixth from left). Three stalwarts of socialism whose names lingered long beyond the life of that government were Aneurin Bevan, Health (back, first left); Emmanuel Shinwell, Fuel and Power (front, first left); and Ernest Bevin, Foreign Secretary (front, fifth from left).

This was at a very low rate of interest, 1.6 per cent, but there were conditions. Britain could not extend her system of preferential tariffs for the Commonwealth. The pound had to have a fixed exchange rate; this was established at 4.03 dollars, a figure chosen virtually by guesswork. After one year the pound was to become convertible into dollars. Holders of the so-called 'sterling balances', mainly countries that had extended credit to Britain during the war, would thus be able to claim repayment of these debts in sterling, which could then be presented to the Bank of England for exchange into dollars. Such dollars could, among other things, be spent on replacing imports from the Sterling Area, chiefly from Britain, with imports from outside the Sterling Area, notably from the USA. Probably neither the American nor the British negotiators realized the full significance of this. But the outflow of Britain's foreign exchange reserves in 1947 led to emergency measures, including high import duties on tobacco and films, designed to reduce the expensive imports of these two American products. The main decision, however, was to end convertibility of the pound. The American loan was exhausted faster than expected. Fortunately, Britain had a substantial share of the Marshall Plan, an American scheme for massive financial aid to help put post-war Europe on its feet. The fixed value of the pound was much too high, making exports too expensive. In 1949 the Chancellor of the Exchequer, Stafford Cripps, announced its devaluation to 2.80 dollars. The British still regarded the pound sterling as sacred, and its devaluation a matter of deep shame. They vented their wrath, through press and parliament, on Cripps. To prevent speculators making a vast profit, he had maintained up to the last moment that there would be no devaluation. He was accused of deception, and took the accusation to heart, being a man of austere principles. He retired in 1950, worn out.

The achievement and suffering of the Russian people had made a great impression during the war, and there was much goodwill for the USSR. In the 1945 election, the British Communist party had even managed to win two seats. In that election the slogan 'left can speak to left' had been used to help persuade voters to choose Labour. The government's attitude was a little more cautious. It felt that Russia would have to be handled in a firm but friendly manner. Bevin was appointed Foreign Secretary because he was not the kind of man to be pushed around by the Russians. On the other hand, the export of jet aero engines to Russia was permitted. Britain ended the war with a clear lead in this new technology, and those engines helped Soviet engineers catch up; subsequent Soviet claims that the Labour government had always been hostile hardly corresponded with this circumstance. There was little the government could do about the Soviet takeover of eastern Europe, except to make known its disquiet. What was to be known as the 'cold war' probably began in 1948, when the Czech government was overthrown by a communist coup; but Britain had already introduced peacetime conscription in 1947. In July 1948 the USSR tried to force the British, French and American forces out of West Berlin by cutting the latter's communications with the west. Probably Stalin was surprised to find that a western airlift succeeded in keeping all West Berlin supplied. There were ugly incidents, in one of which a British airliner crashed as a result of threatening manoeuvres by a Soviet fighter, but after ten months the Russians lifted their blockade. Partly in response to this crisis, the North Atlantic Treaty Organization, NATO, was established in 1949. Britain was a member, along with Canada, the USA, and those western European nations which agreed to coordinate their armed forces. Meanwhile Britain quietly set about making its own atomic bomb. The two bombs dropped by the Americans on Japan in 1945 had shown that any power aspiring to conventional ideas of greatness, as Britain still did, would have to possess nuclear weapons. In America the McMahon Act had repudiated the promises made to Britain at the Quebec Conference; America would offer no assistance and would refuse to supply bombs to Britain. The first British-made atomic bomb was successfully tested in Australia in 1952. It came as a surprise to the British people, who had not been informed of the project. Nor were the people told that the main reason for the bomb's existence was less military, against Russia, than diplomatic, against the USA; a British bomb, giving Britain the possibility of starting an atomic war, was thought to make it less

India's Legislative Assembly, the seat of parliament in New Delhi, in 1947. Lord Mountbatten, Viceroy of India, made independence a reality in August of that year and became the country's first Governor-General. India remained a British dominion but soon sought republican status. This was achieved in January 1950 but India remained within the British Commonwealth.

likely that the USA would neglect British interests in any future international crisis.

The Labour party was committed to granting independence to India. During the war, Cripps had been in India, trying to negotiate an agreement with the two nationalist parties, the mainly Hindu Indian Congress and the Moslem League. He failed, but at least gathered an impression of how difficult it would be to arrive at a solution which would satisfy both Moslems and Hindus. In 1946 Louis Mountbatten, who had distinguished himself in the war and had royal connections, was appointed Viceroy. He had the task of making independence a reality; Britain no longer had the will or the capacity to hold India by force against strengthening national feeling. To help concentrate minds, the government announced that, whatever happened, Britain would leave India by mid-1948. Mountbatten, seeing the situation at close hand, advanced this to August 1947. The second-best solution of partitioning India into mainly Hindu India and mainly Moslem Pakistan was more or less unavoidable. The result was that after independence many Hindus had to leave Pakistan for India, and many Moslems had to travel in the reverse direction. Rioting broke out, and there occurred some of the most horrific religious massacres ever seen in India. All the same, a knot had been cut. Britain quit India and there was goodwill on both sides. Mountbatten stayed on as the first Governor-General. Later, India became a republic but arrangements were made for her to remain a member of the Commonwealth. A minor consequence of this was that the formal title of the British monarch as Emperor or Empress of India was relinquished, being replaced by the description 'Head of the Commonwealth'. More important, India, as a member of the British Commonwealth was able to exert a pacifying influence in international affairs, through Britain and the latter's relationship with the USA. In 1950 the Commonwealth governments adopted the Colombo Plan, designed to channel economic aid from the richer members to the poorer; it worked quite well, but never had enough funds to do all that was needed.

In 1948 Britain quit Palestine amid worldwide criticism. In retrospect, the evacuation was probably wise, for it shifted an intractable problem from Britain to the world community acting through the United Nations. After the Balfour Declaration of 1917, acknowledging that the Jews should have a national home in Palestine, Britain permitted limited immigration into that territory, which she administered under League of Nations mandate. Between 1922 and 1939 the percentage of Jewish inhabitants in this predominantly Arab territory rose from 11 per cent to 29 per cent. Arab resentment grew, as had been feared. In general, Britons preferred Arabs to Jews; they still visualized the former as dignified camel-riding and date-eating nomads. The government recognized the importance of Arab goodwill for the security of oil supplies. In 1939, therefore, the British restricted

British forces in charge of an arrested ship carrying illegal Jewish immigrants to Palestine in 1947. The passengers are displaying the bodies of two casualties suffered when the immigrants resisted arrest.

immigration just at the time when Nazi Germany was creating a flow of Jews seeking refuge. After the war the problem was still there, with the added factor that the Jews' experience in Nazi-occupied Europe had gained them enormous sympathy. Bevin could see the dangers of further unrestricted Jewish immigration into Palestine. The Royal Navy was instructed to intercept ships carrying illegal immigrants; this it did, in a generally humane manner for which it received no thanks. The US government, mindful of the votes of American Jews, pressed the British government to relent. Meanwhile, Jewish organizations, called guerilla by their friends and terrorist by their victims, began to kill British soldiers and administrators – and subsequently a high United Nations mediator – in Palestine. There were reprisals, as well as outbreaks of Arab counter-terrorism. But although Jewish violence, and especially the activities of a terrorist fringe in Britain itself, diminished the sympathy which Britons felt towards the Jews, it did help to persuade the government to refer the Palestine problem to the United Nations in 1947. In 1948 the United Nations proposed a plan for the creation of a State of Israel. Britain refused to administer this plan and withdrew from the territory. The new State of Israel was accordingly established under United Nations auspices and was immediately attacked by its Arab neighbours. This conflict would continue for decades.

The Labour government's foreign policy was probably little different from that which a Conservative administration would have adopted. The two parties differed mainly in their attitudes to home affairs, although both the parties and the press had their own reasons for exaggerating such distinctions. What the Labour party described as its socialist programme included the welfare state, based in the first instance on the proposals of the Beveridge report. Then there was the taking into state ownership of certain important industries. The Conservatives, despite their vocal opposition to such nationalization, had in the past themselves been nationalizers; in 1939 they had amalgamated two loss-making airlines, Imperial Airways and British Airways, to form the state British Overseas Airways Corporation. Finally, as means to their various socialist ends, the Labour party believed in government planning, with government controls in the form of licensing or other restrictions to ensure that those plans were effectively observed.

There was little trouble nationalizing the Bank of England; nobody noticed any difference. That longstanding ambition, nationalization of the coal-mining companies, came next, in January 1947. This coincided with one of the worst winters in

BELOW The winter of early 1947. This was one of the worst winters in living memory. The resultant disorganization, and especially the breakdown of coal supply, was blamed by much of the press on the Labour government. This was unfair, but politically very effective. and, as a Conservative election theme, lasted many years.

FAR BELOW Nationalization of the coal industry. On 1st January 1947 at collieries all over Britain the new bright blue flag of the National Coal Board was raised. This was the first major nationalization measure of the Labour government, and was easily accepted by the general public, which for decades had been aware of the troubles of the coal industry.

memory. The government persuaded the miners to abandon temporarily their recently won five-day week. Most of them did work the extra Saturday half-day, but there was still insufficient coal. This led to transport breakdowns and further shortages. Gas and electricity cuts were skilfully exploited by the Conservative press to suggest that nationalization meant shortages. This was unfair, but the criticism seemed to stick in people's minds. In January 1948 the railways were nationalized. As with the mines, former shareholders were compensated with government stock. In retrospect the terms were generous, although described at the time as niggardly. Both the railways and the mines faced enormous problems of readjustment and com-

The National Health Service. The NHS was both the pride and joy of the British socialists and an enormous improvement in the lives of most of the population. No longer was it necessary to postpone hospital operations or the acquistion of spectacles or false teeth because of financial considerations. In this picture, free NHS spectacles are being dispensed at Moorfields Eye Hospital in London.

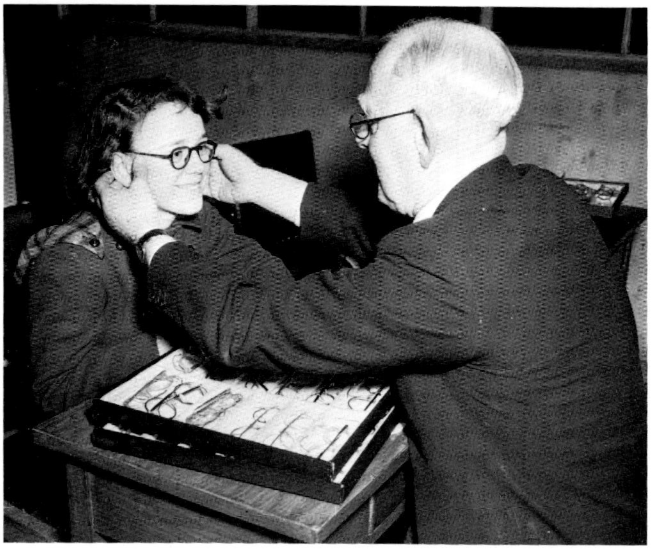

The general election of 1950: a Liberal candidate sticking her own posters. This publicity photograph emphasizes how the Liberals were at a disadvantage because their financial resources for campaigning could not match those of the other two parties. The Conservative and Labour parties, strongly representing sectional interests, could obtain much money from, respectively, industrialists and trade unions.

petition; their shareholders did better from the nationalization settlement than they would have done from continued ownership. But, because these two industries had great problems, they could not become shining examples of the merits of state ownership. British Railways, in particular, with its slow, dirty, unpunctual trains made a bad impression on the public. Later the gas and electricity industries were nationalized, with little difficulty and probably with little effect. More controversial was the nationalization of the steel industry. This was taken into public ownership, but little change was made in its structure or operations. At first the nationalized industries received cooperation from their workers. The latter felt that the government was on their side, one of its first acts having been the repeal of the disliked Trade Disputes Act of 1927. When the financial crisis of 1947 occurred, and Cripps introduced his policy of austerity, wage claims were held back for about 30 months. This was despite a manpower shortage which should, in theory, have raised the price of labour. Unemployment had practically vanished; the return to the economy of a million or so pre-war unemployed was absorbed by the 400,000 extra servicemen taken by conscription, and by the additional 650,000 civil servants who were recruited for nationalized industry, planning, and controls administration.

Controls were required not only as part of the socialist concept, but because resources were short. Rationing had to be continued. Bread rationing, avoided during the war, was imposed for two years from 1946 with the laudable aim of diverting wheat to starving Germany and India. Keynesian economic policies, which recognized that by running budget deficits or surpluses the government could control the level of activity, had been adopted during the war, and these were continued. As unemployment was still greatly feared, it was usual to budget for a deficit, so as to encourage activity. This meant that businessmen had a ready market. They could not all expand to satisfy this market because materials and labour were short. Government planners allocated materials to individual industries in accordance with what they thought to be the national interest. This infuriated businessmen. In time, consumers were persuaded that controls prevented them obtaining what they wanted. Labour leaders did not help their case by insisting that 'the man in Whitehall knows best'.

As might be expected, it was the most inept example of government planning which attracted the most attention. This was the grandiose groundnuts scheme, supervised by the Minister of Food, John Strachey. In the 1930s Strachey was very much the idol and ideologist of young marxist intellectuals, thanks to his publications which convincingly proposed a brand of marxism that would be applicable to what was seen as the British situation. His groundnuts scheme was carefully planned. Any expert and specialist, provided he supported the scheme, was listened to with respect. A vast area of Uganda was chosen for the cultivation of the groundnuts, with the aim of providing a new source of edible oils for Britain and a new source of income for Uganda. Unfortunately, neither the soil nor the rainfall was suitable for groundnut cultivation. It took some years for this to be admitted, after millions of taxpayers' pounds had been devoted to the scheme. This scandal made an enormous and long-lasting impression on public opinion. Possibly the wrong lesson was learned. It was not that government planning was proved useless and wasteful, as the Conservatives asserted; the lesson concerned the perils of entrusting executive power to ideologists.

This government passed bill after bill designed to improve society. Butler's Education Act came into force, with the so-called '11-plus' examination selecting, or claiming to select, the academically gifted at the tender age of eleven years. Legal aid,

British troops in the Korean war: a field regiment of the Royal Artillery relaxes in an interval during a battle. As the photograph indicates, this war was fought with the equipment and methods of the Second World War.

enabling the needy to finance court cases, was introduced. Many partners in broken marriages were at last able to afford a divorce; legal aid was therefore blamed for the consequent rise in the divorce rate. Flogging was virtually abolished for criminal offences. An attempt to abolish capital punishment was blocked by the House of Lords. Agricultural subsidies and marketing boards were made permanent and improved. There was a new Town and Country Planning Act. National Insurance against old age and unemployment was enhanced. But the gem of the welfare state was the National Health Service. This was planned with loving care by the Minister of Health, Aneurin Bevan. He managed to overcome the resistance of doctors or, more accurately, their representatives, by allowing doctors to treat private, paying patients in addition to their NHS patients, with beds for the former reserved in hospitals. Everything in the NHS was to be free, even false teeth and spectacles. It was indeed a model for the whole world in its early years, but successive governments were more and more reluctant to finance its needs, which grew as the possibilities of medical science expanded. Decades later, it still ensured that the seriously ill should have good treatment without financial worries, but in many respects it did not provide the best possible service.

After five years, in 1950, there had to be an election. Labour won it, but with a majority of only six seats. It could only struggle on until 1951 when, in a new election, the Conservatives won a workable majority. The last phase of the Labour government was not happy. Much of the original verve and optimism was gone. It had little fresh to offer. It joined in the Korean war, in which British troops fought and died under the United Nations flag. Rearmament was accepted. Pacifism had once been strongly represented in the Labour party, and it was certainly not belligerence that had caused defence expenditure after 1945 to remain at the high proportion of 7 per cent of the national income. After the Korean War started this rose to 10 per cent. Then, in 1951, a rearmament programme bringing defence to 14 per cent was adopted. This imposed a severe strain. Bevan resigned from the government when it was decided to impose charges for spectacles, teeth and prescriptions under the NHS. Harold Wilson resigned from his presidency of the Board of Trade because he believed 14 per cent to be impossible. He proved to be right; the percentage was later seen to be economically disastrous and was reduced. In its final months the government lost prestige because it seemed to be impotent in the face of Iranian nationalization of the British refinery at Abadan. Eventually that problem was solved with the help of the big oil companies and a Teheran coup organized by the American Central Intelligence Agency. The settlement involved a greater share for American oil companies in Iranian oil, but was otherwise satisfactory. But it came too late to help the Labour government.

Painful Readjustment 1951–1986

1952	Identity cards, introduced in 1939, are abolished. A British atomic weapon is tested off Australia.
1953	Sugar and sweet rationing ends, bringing wartime rationing virtually to an end.
1956	The first nuclear power station, at Calder Hall, begins operations. An Anglo-French force invades Suez Canal zone, and then withdraws.
1957	The Gold Coast becomes independent Ghana.
1958	The Campaign for Nuclear Disarmament (CND) is launched. First women peers enter the Lords.
1960	Nigeria becomes independent. Conscription ends.
1965	Oil is discovered in the North Sea. Unilateral declaration of independence by Rhodesian government. The Race Relations Board is established.
1967	The decision is taken to withdraw British forces from east of Suez by the mid-1970s. The Scottish National Party wins the Hamilton by-election.
1968	Police violence in Londonderry marks the beginning of a prolonged crisis in Northern Ireland.
1971	Strikers protest against the Industrial Relations Act.
1972	Troops fire on demonstrators at Londonderry. Massive expulsions of Asians from Uganda, who immigrate to Britain.
1973	Britain joins the Common Market. Oil producing countries begin the first phase of large price increases, thus intensifying wide-ranging inflation.
1974	Miners and railwaymen strike. Edward Heath's Conservative government fails in general election.
1978	The upsurge of strike action, characteristic of the 1970s, culminates in the 'winter of discontent'.
1979	Referenda on home rule in Wales and Scotland disappoint the nationalists. The Labour government is heavily defeated in the general election. Margaret Thatcher, Britain's first woman prime minister, heads the new Conservative government.
1980	Announcement that ground-launched cruise missiles are to be deployed at two bases in England.
1981	The Social Democratic Party is launched. Social unrest in Brixton gives rise to serious disorder. Argentinian forces occupy the Falkland Islands, which are retaken by British troops. A Briton pleads guilty to spying for the Russians and is sentenced to 35 years' imprisonment.
1983	The Conservatives are re-elected to power, with an increased majority, in a general election.
1984	Trade-union membership at GCHQ is banned in the interests of national security. A year-long stoppage in the coal industry begins.
1985	A serious disturbance occurs in Tottenham, north London, during which a policeman is murdered.
1986	The GLC and six metropolitan county councils are abolished.

Except for one lapse in 1956, Britain's slow retreat from the old imperial greatness was accomplished with neither an undignified rout nor a purposeless last stand. Different Britons came to terms with the new realities at different speeds. In 1962 the American statesman Dean Acheson declared that Britain's problem was that she had lost an empire but not found a role. The anguished protests that this remark aroused in Britain suggested that, for many, a highly sensitive nail had been struck on its head. But although greatness was gone, renown and good repute was still achievable. Renown, when it came, was rarely the result of the spectacular projects in which governments invested public money. However, run-of-the-mill government grants for education and research must have been a factor in Britain's lead (among countries of large or medium populations) in that crude but respectable measure – the number of Nobel prizewinners per head of population. A high reputation was won in the arts, especially those which attracted a popular audience. Among many other successes, British television, or much of it, could be enjoyed by intelligent adults. In fashion and entertainment 'swinging Britain' set the international style in the 1960s. Superficially, the new pop music of the Beatles, and the miniskirts of young women, were just part of a young people's craze. But they were also part-cause and part-consequence of a profound change in attitude. One manifestation of this change was significant, yet seldom mentioned: servility, especially that between the generations and the sexes, was becoming archaic.

In these three and a half decades Britain had six Conservative and two Labour prime ministers. First came Churchill, restored to office in 1951 at the age of 76 and continuing through a carefully concealed illness to 1955. When it regained power the Conservative party was still not entirely reconciled to the abandonment of the past. Nevertheless, Churchill's government reversed very little of the Labour government's legislation. The steel industry, which had been half-heartedly nationalized by Labour, was half-heartedly denationalized by the Conservatives. This shuttlecock performance would be carried on by subsequent governments, to the delight of their more ideological supporters but not to the benefit of the industry. Road transport, which had been nationalized with the railways in 1948, was also sold back to private enterprise, even though private enterprise

The Festival of Britain of 1951 was a much-cherished project of the Labour government. It commemorated the centenary of the Great Exhibition, and also was designed to express the progressive spirit of post-war Britain. London's Royal Festival Hall (centre) is one of the permanent legacies of the Festival. The shot tower (left, now demolished) was used in past centuries for the manufacture of musket and cannon balls.

was not quite so willing to grasp this supposed prize as had been anticipated. Controls and restrictions were lifted; food rationing, bit by bit, came to an end. More freedom encouraged greater production, but this brought fresh problems, later to become familiar. The economy 'overheated' as resources of material and labour became short; this tended to raise wages and prices. As the economy became busier, both industry and consumers tended to buy more from abroad, threatening the balance of payments. This could have been countered by lowering the international value of sterling, but governments still shrank from devaluation. Hence the phenomenon of 'stop-go' policy, with the government first encouraging and then discouraging economic activity with such Keynesian methods as adjustment of the rate of interest, restrictions on credit and changes in tax rates. Britain, and the Sterling Area, continued to feel an acute shortage of dollars, the so-called 'dollar gap'. The growth of American tourism in Britain, and the stationing of American forces in Britain after 1949, did bring in dollars, but not enough.

One triumph of this period was the increase of house-building. In the previous government, Bevan had been entrusted with both housing and health. In transforming the nation's health, he had been forced to neglect housing. The Conservatives managed to achieve a rate of 300,000 new houses annually. Perhaps more transforming, in the longer run, was the decision to end the BBC monopoly in broadcasting. This was done when a skilfully conducted campaign persuaded the government to establish an independent television service, financed by its own advertising.

Both Churchill and Eden were in favour of easing the cold war by conferences with the post-Stalin Soviet leaders. At Geneva in 1954, at a conference which the US government declined to attend, Eden played an important role in helping the French extricate themselves from their difficulties in Viet Nam. This was followed by another Geneva conference attended by President Eisenhower, Eden, and the French and Soviet premiers. This produced little that was concrete, but was a step towards getting East and West on speaking terms.

Churchill retired in 1955 and his successor Eden almost immediately became entangled in the Suez Canal problem. Regarded, quite wrongly, as Britain's main artery, the Canal had long been guarded by British troops. After the ousting of the Egyptian King Farouk by army colonels, the demand for British evacuation was intense and sometimes violent. The British left peacefully enough in 1954. But the Egyptian leader, Colonel Nasser, nationalized the Canal in response to the sudden withdrawal of American and British financial support for the building of a new Aswan dam. This created some alarm in Britain; Eden, in addition, saw a parallel between Hitler and Nasser. After seeking other ways out, the British and the French governments planned an invasion of the Canal Zone, in conjunction with Israel. In Britain, the operation, when it was started, was described by the government as an attempt to impose peace between Israel, which had already started to advance towards the Canal, and Egypt. British opinion was deeply split; the BBC was criticized for reporting both sides of the argument. International pressure, especially American, forced the British and French to abandon the operation when they had almost captured the entire Canal. Eden was blamed by half the country for pursuing an aggressive policy and by the other half for abandoning a successful military enterprise when it was on the brink of success. The Suez episode persuaded many people that Britain could not, after all, behave like a major military power. Mistaking an Egyptian colonel for a German corporal cost Eden his reputation as a cool statesman, and he resigned. The Canal was closed for some years, with little noticeable effect on Britain.

The Suez affair could be regarded as an aberration amid a general policy of withdrawal from worldwide commitments. In the 1950s the granting of independence to former colonies accelerated. The Gold Coast became Ghana, a self-governing member of the Commonwealth, in 1957. Almost all the other colonies gained independence in the 1960s and 1970s. In Kenya independence was delayed until 1963 by the emergence of the Mau Mau terrorist movement, which preyed on white farmers and demanded independence on terms which Britain deemed unacceptable. In 1960 Eden's successor Macmillan visited southern Africa and made himself unpopular among whites by acknowledging that 'winds of change' had to be heeded. In 1961 South Africa, whose racial policies were disliked by other

BELOW For Brian Epstein (centre) and the Beatles the future looked very rosy in 1963. A combination of Epstein's astute management and the group's genuine talent, particularly as composers, soon gained international renown for the Beatles. This, in turn, helped to create the 'Swinging Britain' image in the 1960s when world attention focused on British style – particularly in music and fashion.

FAR BELOW Post-war reconstruction afforded considerable scope to town planners. This early model of a scheme for the redevelopment of Croydon, however, has none of today's high-rise office blocks.

RIGHT Sir Winston Churchill, pictured here in 1960 at Hyde Park Gate, had retired from being prime minister in 1955 but remained a Member of Parliament despite his advanced age.

members, was eased out of the Commonwealth. Cyprus was a problem, because a strong Turkish minority resisted the Greek majority's alleged wish for eventual union with Greece. British forces in Cyprus were attacked by supporters of such a union; the Greek Cypriot leader Archbishop Makarios was deported. Later, Makarios was restored and an agreement for independence patched together. But a subsequent Turkish invasion ensured that the Cyprus problem would be long-lived. The British-created federation of the two Rhodesias and Nyasaland proved a failure. Northern Rhodesia finally became an independent member of the Commonwealth as Zambia, and Nyasaland as Malawi. Southern Rhodesia remained a colony until the white population made the mistake of taking matters into its own hands. Malaya, where in post-war years British troops and administration had quelled a very menacing communist guerilla movement, formed the basis of another federation, Malaysia, which was created within the Commonwealth. Indonesia resented the inclusion of Borneo in this federation, and adopted a policy of armed 'confrontation'. British troops therefore stayed there for some time, until the exertions of confrontation brought down the Indonesian president himself. Later, Singapore left this federation to become independent.

Britain's hydrogen bomb was ready in 1957. By that time it was evident that rockets, not bombers, were the delivery system of great powers. Macmillan persuaded the American government to make available its imminent Skybolt missile. When this was cancelled, British nuclear strategy was left in mid-air, but President Kennedy offered to supply Polaris missiles, which were fitted in British-built submarines.

The proportion of families owning cars, refrigerators, televisions, and washing machines rose dramatically in the late 1950s. In 1959 Macmillan was telling the British that they 'had never had it so good'. Holidays abroad became attainable for all except the lowest income families. More higher education institutes were created. For decades Britain had been behind other industrial countries in technical education; many ascribed the slow rate of economic growth to this undeniable fact. Colleges of Advanced Technology were established, and also some new universities, which soon became fashionable.

Britain began to look towards Europe. A decision was taken to join the European Economic Community – the 'Common Market'. Previously, Britain had refused to join because her commitments to the English-speaking world seemed too binding. In 1963, however, the French president, de Gaulle, vetoed the British application because he felt Britain was and would remain a satellite of the USA. That was a bad year for Macmillan, whose old-fashioned mannerisms at last began to attract the shafts of satire, not least on television. His Minister of Defence was found to be having an affair with a girl who was simultaneously making her favours available to the Soviet naval

FAR BELOW The Suez crisis, 1956. British paratroops (red berets) greet the first contingent of United Nations troops on their arrival in Port Said, Egypt, soon after a ceasefire had been declared. Both British and French paratroops had been successful in their missions, but international pressure and a severe run on British gold and currency reserves forced the British and French governments to end the operation.

attaché; this had not resulted in any breaches of security, but Macmillan was regarded as negligent in this matter. Then, when politically weak, he had to have an operation. He resigned.

His successor, Alex Douglas Home, was the last Conservative leader to be selected by a small clique. He had hitherto been an earl. In previous years, a successful Labour party member in the House of Commons, Anthony Wedgwood Benn, had been aware that on the death of his father he would become a peer and therefore ineligible for membership of the House. He had fought a persistent and intelligent campaign, and finally obtained an Act enabling peers, under certain circumstances, to resign their peerages. Home, too, took advantage of this to become a member of the Commons, where prime ministers were expected to sit.

Home's government did not last long. In the 1964 election the Labour party gained a majority of just five seats. Harold Wilson, the new prime minister, did exceptionally well to govern with this small margin, and then increase it to 66 in the 1966 election. In their years out of power the Labour party members had been engaged in internal struggles, conveniently described as conflicts of left versus right. The nuclear bomb had aroused great misgivings. The Campaign for Nuclear Disarmament (CND) succeeded in engaging people of all classes and political views in non-violent acts of opposition against atomic weapons. Its demand for unilateralism – the abandonment by Britain of nuclear arms irrespective of what other powers might do – was echoed by the left wing of the Labour party, which one year succeeded in persuading the Labour party conference to accept the philosophy. Further confict had arisen over the right wing's more or less successful bid to remove from the party's consti-

tution the commitment to nationalize industry; nationalization might inspire stalwarts of the Labour movement, but it lost votes in general elections. Wilson had been regarded as sympathetic towards the left, but as premier he soon removed that impression. Economic problems took up much of this government's time. There was a new commitment to centralized planning,

BELOW **In the 1948–57 struggle against Communist guerillas in Malaya, the British succeeded in gaining the cooperation, or at least the acquiescence, of the population, and gradually reduced the guerillas to small remnants deep in the jungle. This picture shows a Chinese resident returning to the British forces a questionnaire about local guerilla activity. The British transferred power to an independent Malaya in 1957.**

which by now was also acceptable to the Conservatives, Macmillan having established his National Economic Development Council for this purpose. Under this Labour government there were successive short-term measures to deal with economic crises, but finally, after years of resistance to the idea, the pound was further devalued to 2.40 dollars. Meanwhile other very fundamental decisions were made. The cancellation of the TSR-2 military aircraft, inherited from the previous government, implied several things: Britain could not afford to design and build complex military aircraft, and the British aircraft industry could no longer expect the taxpayer willingly to fund huge and very often wasteful projects. On the other hand the costly Concorde jet airliner project was allowed to go forward, partly because it was regarded as important for the future of Anglo-French cooperation. Further relief for the economy was obtained by the decision to abandon the 'east of Suez' role; British naval and military strength was to be withdrawn from Asia.

This government enacted several useful, if unspectacular, changes. In 1967 a Road Safety Act as last went some way towards reducing the number of unnecessary deaths and injuries caused by road vehicles; it provided for the alcohol level of offending motorists to be tested on the spot. Another Labour innovation was the establishment of the parliamentary commissioner, or Ombudsman, who had power to investigate the cases of citizens who felt that they were badly treated by

FAR BELOW **Queen Elizabeth II and the Duke of Edinburgh are presented to chiefs of the Central Region of Ghana (formerly the Gold Coast) during a royal visit in 1961. As with some other former colonies, the Westminster pattern of government bequeathed by the British did not fit easily into the local culture; political development was punctuated by coups, one of which deposed Ghana's President Nkrumah in 1966.**

FAR BELOW **Prime minister Jomo Kenyatta of Kenya inspects a guard of honour during the independence ceremonies in 1963. Perhaps because it takes decades for a people to learn how to combine proper respect for parliamentary institutions with a proper disrespect for their members, British-style democracy made an uneasy beginning in Kenya, but Kenyatta's authority held firm.**

BELOW **Harold Wilson, Labour prime minister during the 1960s and 1970s. Regarded by some as a shallow opportunist, but by others as a man who could quietly secure agreement between opposing interests, Wilson was well-intentioned and flexible. His resignation at a time when he was firmly in power was unusual.**

government officials. In 1969 the voting age was reduced from 21 to 18. In 1968 theatre censorship was removed. The Open University was founded; this enabled adults of all ages who had the right qualities, but not necessarily the right school-leaving certificates, to work for a degree. Other Acts made life easier for homosexuals, for those wanting to end their marriages, and for those who did not want a baby. In 1965 the death penalty was virtually abolished. In education, Labour had always regarded the schools as shapers of society; Conservatives tended to regard them as investments for the future. The division of children at the age of 11 into the favoured few and the rest was distasteful to Labour principles and also educationally unsound. The Labour government set about the nationwide introduction of comprehensive schools. Instead of children being sent to different types of school according to their performance in the 11-plus examination, they were all sent to the same type of school, known as comprehensives. Many local authorities, especially those of Conservative majorities, resisted this measure, but gradually the change came about. Neither the educational nor the social advantages of comprehensive schools became self-evident. Children still did not have an equal chance, because some comprehensive schools were good and some were bad, and because private schools were still available. But possibly a useful foundation for genuine progress had been laid.

Britain continued to withdraw from her colonies. In Southern Rhodesia, however, the routine was rejected. Rhodesia had a responsible, white government elected by the large white population. In 1965 the government led by Ian Smith, a former Battle of Britain pilot, made a 'unilateral declaration of independence'; this was a drastic way of avoiding the imposition of an eventual 'majority' (that is, black) government. Several meetings were arranged between Wilson and Smith, but no compromise was reached. Britain was handicapped because no black Rhodesian leader seemed to have enough support to carry the burden of heading a black government. British armed intervention had been ruled out by Wilson; his public admission of this seemed

BELOW The anti-nuclear movement. Most effective of the popular movements against atomic weapons was the Campaign for Nuclear Disarment (CND) which, among other things, made an annual Easter march from the atomic weapons establishment at Aldermaston to London. This is the 1960 march, led by the Canon of St Paul's Cathedral, passing through Chiswick.

FAR BELOW Mid-morning break at Barclay Secondary Modern School, Stevenage, Hertfordshire in 1949. The school building programme that continued during the 1950s and 1960s was substantial and of great social benefit even though design and construction were sometimes imperfect. By the 1980s it was realised that many of the post-war schools were expensive to maintain and inconvenient in use.

unnecessary. Economic sanctions were applied both by Britain and the United Nations. Thanks to collusion by South Africa and by certain Western companies, including British firms, the Rhodesian economy held out. It was not until 1980, after the development of strong and active black guerilla movements, that the British government was able to negotiate a settlement allowing for the establishment of a majority government, at which point the country became Zimbabwe. Elsewhere in Africa, the Nigerian civil war of 1968–1970 was an embarrassment because British public opinion favoured the breakaway regime of Biafra, whereas the government saw the political necessity of backing the Federal government. It was only the victory of the latter that enabled the issue to recede.

National problems inside Britain itself became obvious during this Labour government, and remained to trouble subsequent administrations. Not only did the Irish, Scots and Welsh assert their independence in ways which were sometimes violent and always politically disturbing, but there was the additional difficulty caused by the resentment felt by many native Britons towards the very numerous immigrants from the West Indies, East Africa and the Indian sub-continent. Immigration from the West Indies had become a flood in the 1950s. The newcomers arrived at a time of labour shortage and seemed willing to do the least agreeable kinds of jobs. Only in the localities in which they most densely settled did they arouse resentment; such resentment was probably not racial, but the natural consequence of residents having to share scarce resources, like housing, with strangers. However, there were disturbances in Nottingham and London which did have racial overtones. The Macmillian government had passed an Act in 1961 that severely limited immigration, and successive governments took their own measures, usually seeking to show that they were reducing immigration without being racialist. A Race Relations Board was established in 1965 and one of its principal tasks was to monitor the actual observance of anit-discrimination laws passed by parliament. In general, it became unlawful to discriminate against anybody on account of colour, race or national origin. Some Britons resented this kind of legislation. The British Union of Fascists founded by Oswald Mosley before the war was by this time only one of the several fascist groups operating in Britain; opposition to immigration, even outright opposition to immigrants, was part of their policy, and they gained members in this

The University of Surrey, one of the 'new universities'. University expansion in the 1960s provided wider opportunities for bright school-leavers, but also helped to ensure that in the world of learning academics would continue to outnumber scholars. A decade later the aims and even the competence of the universities was beginning to be questioned.

A North Sea oil rig. With almost fairy-tale good fortune, Britain discovered large off-shore oil deposits shortly before the energy crisis of the 1970s. It remained to be seen whether the British would make of this resource better use than they had made of other post-war assets.

West Indian immigrants arrive at Southampton Docks. The photograph was made in June 1962, just before the Commonwealth Immigration Act came into force. This Act was the first of several seeking to limit the number of immigrants. Nevertheless, immigration continued at a slower rate, generating alarmist slogans to arouse the timorous.

period. The National Front, the most significant fascist party, was founded in 1967. Yet the most sinister prophecies were not fulfilled. Immigrants did not swamp the native population; even in London they only accounted for 3 per cent of the population in 1966. Fascist parties remained as splinter groups; their main threat was that they stimulated equally extreme left-wing opponents. Violent clashes between rival demonstrations were damaging for British society but welcome to both sides, simply because they gained publicity and therefore recruits. But it was not only fascists who pointed out that Britain had become a multi-racial society without any proper consultation of the public.

The British electoral system was unfair because it gave the two largest parties a disproportionate number of parliamentary seats. The small Liberal party was badly affected by this; its share of parliamentary seats was far smaller than its share of the vote at general elections. Naturally enough, the two major parties blocked electoral reform, even though the existing system was said to be responsible for the alleged inability of the British to elect the kind of government they really wanted. Parties whose supporters were concentrated in just a few constituencies were better placed than those, like the Liberals, whose support was diluted throughout the country. This circumstance favoured the election of Welsh and Scottish Nationalist members of parliament.

In its early years the Labour party had committed itself to Scottish home rule, but as soon as it gained power it found ways to avoid this commitment. In its own, rather limited, way the Conservative party seemed to do more for Scotland; between the wars it had established Scottish departments in Edinburgh, and as early as 1928 had introduced a Secretary of State for Scotland. The National Party of Scotland had been formed in 1928. Electorally unsuccessful, it joined a smaller party in 1934 to create the Scottish National Party. In 1945 a candidate of this SNP won its first parliamentary seat, in a by-election. The seat was lost in the general election of that year, and it was not until 1967 that the SNP won another, at the Hamilton by-election. Success followed success, and by 1974 it had 11 members of parliament. Both the main parties by this time realized that Scottish national feeling could no longer be ignored, although some observers suspected that some of the SNP voters were inspired not so much by the desire for home rule as by a feeling that both the Labour and Conservative parties were unresponsive to local needs, preoccupied with irrelevancies and, in short, rather tedious.

The Welsh Nationalist Party, founded in 1925, wanted a self-governing dominion status for Wales. But its existence was not taken seriously until the 1960s when the apparent upsurge of Welsh nationalism was unexpected if only because initiatives had already been taken over previous decades to meet the local wish for special treatment. In 1942 the Welsh language was given official standing in the courts, thereby finally reversing the language provisions of King Henry VIII's Statute of Wales. Churchill in his 1951 government had created a Ministry of Welsh Affairs, and by the mid-1960s there was a Secretary of State for Wales with a seat in the cabinet and a Welsh Office in Cardiff. This city had been chosen, not without bitter opposition from the north, as capital of Wales in 1954. For some years the Ministry of Education had been pressing for the establishment of more Welsh-speaking schools. The Welsh Region of the BBC had devoted more time to Welsh-language broadcasts than was actually welcome to the average listener in Wales.

The Welsh Language Society was founded in 1963. It had a simple aim, the elevation of Welsh to at least equal status with English. Its methods were militant; although it turned its back on the use of violence against people, it did not favour constitutional means of advancing its cause. Attacking English-language road-signs, with paint brushes, demanding that documents be bilingual, it was sometimes crude and sometimes witty. It was an embarrassment to the Nationalist party, yet it did succeed in extending the official use of Welsh. In these years the Welsh Nationalist Party (Plaid Cymru) turned its attention away from the traditional Welsh-speaking areas, which were in decline anyway, and towards the more heavily populated and largely English-speaking south. In South Wales the people seemed ready to listen. In 1967 the president of the party won a parliamentary by-election at Carmarthen, and this success was repeated in subsequent general elections. Three Welsh Nationalists won seats in the 1974 election.

The importance of the Nationalist members of parliament was enhanced by the small majorities which governments usually had in the 1970s; James Callaghan's Labour government foundered in 1979 when it lost the support of the Nationalists. In 1973 a commission recommended devolution for Scotland and Wales; that is, the provision of national assemblies to deal with their own affairs, with only a bare minimum of provisions for preserving the unity of the United Kingdom. The Welsh and Scottish electorates each voted in a referendum in 1979; in Wales a majority voted against devolution, while in Scotland the majority

From 1968 onwards Northern Ireland has been a deeply troubled province. British troops were originally sent in to prevent direct conflict between the Protestant majority and the Catholic minority. Violence from both communities, however, has been directed at the troops, who have had to contend with violent demonstrations, bombs, booby traps, sniper fire and the like – much of it instigated by the Provisional IRA. In the main picture, soldiers watch as colleagues in an armoured vehicle attempt to force a way through a burning barricade. During an eight-month period in 1981, a number of republican detainees in the Maze prison went on hunger strike. When ten fasted to death, soldiers on duty had to be extra vigilant (inset).

in favour was so narrow that in view of the large number of non-voters it could hardly be claimed that the Scots wanted devolution. These referenda seemed to mark the end, at least temporarily, of the nationalists' progress.

In 1968 yet another period of disturbance began in Ireland. The position of the Catholic minority in Northern Ireland had been unhappy. The Protestant majority had found ways to discriminate against Catholics in such vital matters as housing and employment. From 1963 a Northern Ireland government had begun reforms, but soon came under attack from the more extreme Protestants. Simultaneously, there were stirrings of a civil rights movement among Catholics. In 1968 a civil rights march went ahead in Londonderry, even though banned by the Northern Ireland Home Affairs Minister. It was attacked by police with unnecessary brutality. From this point onwards violence from both sides increased. In 1969, following outbreaks at Londonderry, where Catholics hoisted the flag of the Irish Republic and where there were several deaths, British troops intervened. Gradually the crisis deepened, with the British government proposing one expedient after another. The IRA was itself split, between its official wing IRA and the 'provisionals'. It was the provisionals who initiated and maintained the campaign of terrorism in Northern Ireland and later extended their operations to England. Bombs in public houses, particularly, caused several deaths; but the English did not vent their outrage on local Irish residents in England. With the Catholic minority in fear of Protestant domination within Ulster, and the Ulster Protestants similarly fearful of Catholic domination in Ireland as a whole, there seemed little prospect of a compromise. British governments seemed unable to escape this financial and military burden, explaining that a withdrawal of troops from Ulster would be followed by copious bloodshed as Catholics and Protestants came to grips with each other. As time passed, however, more and more mainland Britons felt that in some way Ulster should be linked to the Irish Republic, and questioned both the necessity and the morality of the use of British troops in a role which, in several areas, was becoming uncomfortably close to that of an army of occupation. In 1968–1978 about 2,000 civilians and soldiers died in this inglorious struggle.

Heath's Conservative government of 1970–1974 intended to reduce government intervention in the economy; it had plans for selling off some parts of nationalized industries. But within a few months the collapse of the Rolls-Royce company was followed by its nationalization; like its predecessors and successors, this government had been forced to react to circumstances and abandon its earlier intentions. The Irish and Rhodesian problems continued to exercise the minds of ministers, to little effect.

BELOW The Concorde jet airliner. A product of Anglo-French co-operation, this was one of those projects into which the taxpayers' money was channelled with little hope of commercial return. At the time, those who doubted the project's commercial prospects were derided as pessimists, but Concorde never approached the economic success promised by its proponents.

FAR BELOW, LEFT In 1973 the signature of premier Edward Heath makes Britain a member of the EEC. A previous application had been blocked by President de Gaulle of France.

FAR BELOW Leicester Square, in London, during a dustmen's strike in 1979. Such strikes in the late 1970s were said to have contributed to the 1979 election victory of the Conservative Party.

A scandal over the paying of bribes by an architectural group to influential local government officials involved the Home Secretary, who resigned. A number of Labour party local government dignitaries were also accused, and some went to prison. In 1973 Britain entered the European Economic Community (the 'Common Market'). Later, the Wilson Labour government obtained marginal improvements in the conditions of Britain's membership. Both major parties had been split on the issue of whether or not to join, or to remain in, the EEC, so the proposal, by opponents of membership, that the public should be allowed to express its opinion by the hitherto un-British device of a referendum, was accepted. In this referendum two-thirds of the electorate voted, and there was a majority for staying inside. In 1973 the oil-producing countries began to introduce drastic price increases; these threatened the growth-based economies of the western world. Luckily, oil had been discovered in the North Sea in the 1960s, and work on exploiting these deposits went ahead quickly. In 1975 a Labour government set up the British National Oil Corporation to supervise this operation. The world oil crisis implied a renewed role for coal and for coalminers. In 1974 the miners and the government failed to agree about a wage claim; a big increase for miners was regarded as a threat to the current effort to hold down inflation with a pay policy. There was a miners' overtime ban; the government introduced the three-day working week to save fuel; after a period of adjustment industry managed to turn out almost as much in three days as it had produced in five days. The conflict was put to the test of a general election. Heath's slogan was 'Who rule Britain?'. Labour won four more seats than the Conservatives. A new Wilson Labour government took power, relying on support from the minor parties, notably the Liberals with their 14 seats and the Scottish and Welsh Nationalists.

Born in 1925, Margaret Thatcher first experienced executive power as Secretary of State for Education during the 1970–74 Conservative government led by Edward Heath, and took the leadership of the Party over from Heath in 1975. As a result of the convincing Conservative win in the 1979 general election, Mrs Thatcher became Britain's first woman prime minister.

Britain was still in grave economic difficulty, with rising inflation, high unemployment, and an imminent balance of payments crisis. Remedies continued to be hasty and superficial. The state of industrial relations was known to be a fundamental weakness. Some thought the trade unions were too strong, seeking to use the threat of strikes to impose their views on society. Others thought they were too weak, insufficiently capable of preventing strikes. Collective wage bargaining in Britain, where a given industry or plant would have members and officials of several competing unions, was anarchic. It contributed to the situation where bargaining was inflationary and took little account of the true value of a man's labour. Irrationality was by no means confined to industrial relations. In central and local administration and in much of industry, policy-making and decision-making was weak; the number of wrong decisions was greater than could be attributed to bad luck. Too often, it seemed, the requirements for obtaining a managerial, administrative, or even educational position were far removed from the qualities required for doing the job well. Frequently, in personnel selection, pedigree carried more weight than performance, and connections more than competence. This was shown, to little ultimate effect, by the Fulton Commission of 1968, which implied that key positions in the civil service were filled not so much on the basis of candidates' capabilities, as on the schools and universities attended. The practice of election for political office and selection (typically by examination and interview) for other posts had once seemed progressive and foolproof, but evidently it could be circumvented by the second-rate. Meanwhile, neither elected nor selected, Queen Elizabeth II reigned from 1953 with the sureness and assiduity that were so often lacking elsewhere in her realm.

The previous Wilson government had failed to agree about an industrial relations bill. The Conservative Heath government had actually carried through its Industrial Relations Act. This was well intended but trade union opposition caused it to create more problems than it solved. The 1974 Labour government adopted a highly conciliatory approach to the unions, announcing what it called a 'social contract'. The unions would abate wage demands, and in return the government would repeal the disliked Industrial Relations Act and introduce measures favoured by the unions. But what seemed good for the unions was not good for management. Even more than in the immediate past, managers exhausted much of their daily energy in picking their way through the minefield of labour legislation backed by union militancy. Meanwhile, inflation continued. Among its effects was the impoverishment of one part of the community to the apparent benefit of another, that part whose bargaining power had obtained wages and pensions which rose with the cost of living. Much else seemed wrong. Unemployment grew at the same time as those in work were profiting from long hours of overtime. It became difficult to dismiss workers; it could happen that the inactive and incompetent stayed in their jobs while the active and competent wasted in unemployment. Although the degree to which compassionate legislation had benefited the parasitic rather than the needy tended to be exaggerated in the public mind, this problem certainly existed, a nettle that governments hesitated to grasp.

One of the remedies for inflation, it was thought, was a so-called wage guideline which formed part of the unwritten 'social contract'. The government set a norm for annual increases and the trade unions were invited to hold to it. This worked reasonably well for two years. But in the 1978–1979 wage-bargaining season the government, now led by James Callaghan, tried to impose a 5 per cent norm. The worst-paid workers seemed likely to suffer under this. In general, members of the strongest unions and the best-paid groups had not suffered appreciably under this kind of wage restraint. But the poorer-paid, like the hospital workers, had. When these poorer categories of worker went on strike for higher pay, joined by better-paid workers with their demand for what they called a 'living wage', the winter became grim for Britain. Hospital patients were neglected. Grave-diggers went on strike. There was a national strike of firemen, and of ambulance drivers. The Labout party was split on the issues. Callaghan, aware that events were destroying the Labour party's claim to have a special and fruitful relationship with the workers, seemed ineffective. The crisis passed but was not forgotten. In May 1979, in a general election, the Labour party was soundly defeated by the Conservatives.

The new government was headed by Margaret Thatcher, Britain's first woman prime minister. She was committed to fairly drastic, though not always well-informed, policies and had the advantage that by 1979 the British people were more willing than previously to face the realities of their situation. More of them suspected that what for a decade had been termed Britain's economic crisis was in reality a political crisis. They believed that Britain still had assets requiring, but not getting, competent and wholehearted utilization.

Many people therefore welcomed the government's programme of cuts in public expenditure and its concerted efforts to reduce the rate of inflation, which, including all items in the general index of retail prices at the end of 1979, was 13.5 per cent rising to 17.9 per cent at the end of 1980; but then it began to fall steadily and this achievement was claimed as a vindication of the new policies of cost efficiency in the national economy.

The early 1980s seemed to be a time of purposefulness and determination, a mood reflected in the new government's policy of avoiding 'U-turns'. In 1980, it was announced that 160 US ground-launched cruise missiles were to be deployed in Britain at RAF Greenham Common, Berkshire, and RAF Molesworth, Cambridgeshire. This move was claimed as part of the modernization programme of long-range nuclear forces that was needed in view of the large missile capability of the Soviet Union. A 'peace camp' of women outside the perimeter wire at Greenham Common could do nothing to stop the deployment of the missiles, which were flown in by military transport aircraft. Britain was also seen to be taking a stand on terrorism, and an armed siege at the Iranian Embassy in London was skilfully ended in its sixth day by members of the SAS (Special Air Service regiment) who shot dead five of the six gunmen.

The SDP (Social Democratic Party) was launched in 1981, headed by four former Labour ministers. It aimed to represent those dissatisfied both with the drift towards extremism in the Labour Party and with the sterile and rigid framework created by the two major parties during the previous two decades. During the summer an intended political and electoral alliance between the SDP and the Liberals was announced. At this time, however, the clouds of urban unrest began to gather in several areas where some degree of friction was usually present between the police and disadvantaged communities of West Indian origin and descent. Following disturbances in St Paul's, Bristol, in 1980, a year later there was disorder for some days in Brixton, south London, arising from the style of police investigation. This was followed by conflict between youths and police in Toxteth, Liverpool. The government asked Lord Scarman to set up an enquiry into the Brixton troubles and his report in late 1981 highlighted the need for improvements in the local police force, the housing policies of the local authority and the quality of education received by the ethnic minorities.

A serious international development in 1981 took the nation – and the government – by surprise. Impatient at the alleged lack of progress made during negotiations on the question of sovereignty of the Falkland Islands (a British dependent territory), which the Argentinians disputed, the then Argentinian military regime sent a force that invaded the islands on 2 April and established a military governorship there. On the following day, the UN Security Council called for a cessation of hostilities and withdrawal of Argentinian forces from the islands. A British task force of some 5,000–6,000 troops was swiftly assembled and dispatched to the South Atlantic to reclaim the islands. The ensuing conflict was short, frequently bloody and fought in extremely cold and wet conditions. The Argentinian occupying force was overwhelmed by the sheer professionalism and tenacity of the British troops, but the Argentinian formal surrender on 14 June was not achieved lightly. With a loss of 254 British and some 750 Argentinian lives, the cost of the war to Britain was estimated at £700 million. Seven British ships were sunk or severely damaged. Although the government remained resolute in having no doubts about its sovereignty over the Falkland Islands, in 1985 the frontier between Gibraltar (another British dependent

Arthur Scargill, president of the National Union of Mineworkers, addresses miners during the 1984–85 miners' strike. He was found to be in contempt of court for declaring the strike official in Yorkshire and Derbyshire, in defiance of a judge's ruling, and was fined heavily. After the strike had ended, his best efforts failed to prevent dissident miners forming the breakaway Union of Democratic Mineworkers.

FAR BELOW **Following the announcement in 1980 that cruise missiles were to be deployed at two RAF bases in southern England, the membership of the Campaign for Nuclear Disarmament increased dramatically. Marches and rallies took place, and the General Secretary of CND, Monsignor Bruce Kent (centre, in dark raincoat), became a prominent figure in the peace movement.**

BELOW **Clive Ponting, an assistant secretary in the Ministry of Defence, was charged in 1984 with communicating information to an unauthorized person (Tam Dalyell MP) regarding the sinking of the Argentinian battle cruiser *General Belgrano* during the Falklands conflict. His acquittal in 1985 only served to inflame the controversy surrounding the government's stance on national security.**

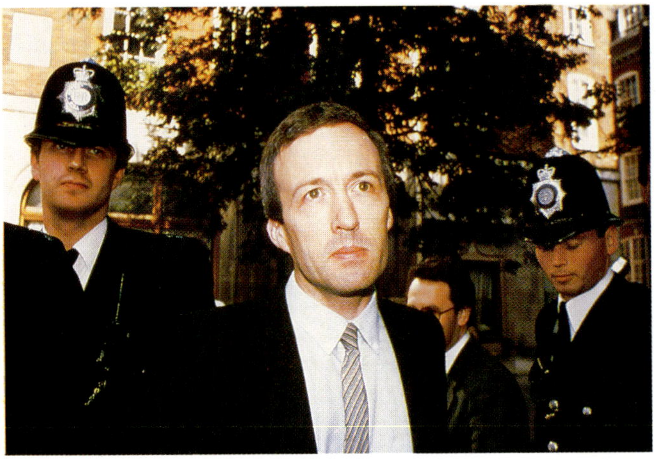

territory) and Spain was fully reopened and Britain undertook for the first time to discuss sovereignty. It was also confirmed in 1985 that British sovereignty over Hong Kong would end in 1997.

The House of Commons and the establishment were rocked in the 1980s by a number of confessions and allegations concerning spying activities, which highlighted serious imperfections in internal security. Starting with disclosure in 1979 by Mrs Thatcher of Sir Anthony Blunt's admission that he had passed information regularly to the Russians between 1940 and 1945, the most serious damage was done by Geoffrey Prime, who had previously worked at GCHQ (Government Communications Headquarters) at Cheltenham – the centre of the British intelligence network. In 1982, Prime was found to have disclosed to the Russians information of the utmost secrecy and was sentenced to 35 years' imprisonment. Despite these embarrassments, Mrs Thatcher's personal image in the first half of 1983 remained considerably buoyed up by the successful outcome of the Falklands campaign, and the wisdom of the decision to hold a general election in June was borne out by a greatly increased majority for her party. The new government did not delay long, however, in attempting to strengthen national security by imposing a ban on trade-union membership at GCHQ. But there was to be no government intervention in a major stoppage throughout almost the entire British coal industry, which started in March 1984 over opposition of the NUM (National Union of Mineworkers) to pit closures. In certain areas NUM members defied their union's instruction and continued to work. Mass picketing of pits occurred and there was often violent confrontation between miners and police. The strike ended in March 1985 because less than 50 per cent of miners remained on strike. The rift between sections of mineworkers widened when dissident miners, principally in the Nottinghamshire area, left the NUM and formed the Union of Democratic Mineworkers. More than 26 million working days were lost as a result of the year-long dispute.

In spite of appearing to stand for law and order, the government continued to have little success in stemming the rising crime rate. Violent crime, in particular, gave cause for grave public concern. British football fans blackened their already tarnished reputation abroad when, in 1985, a stadium wall collapsed at the Heysel Stadium in Brussels under the weight of spectators fleeing from charging Liverpool supporters, many under the influence of alcohol. Most of the 39 dead were Italian supporters of the Juventus team from Turin. As a result of this tragedy, English clubs were indefinitely banned from participating in European football competition. Later that year, inner-city violence flared up in Handsworth, Birmingham, in Brixton and in Tottenham, north London, where a policeman was murdered during a large and violent demonstration against the police.

In 1986, the GLC (Greater London Council) and six metropolitan county councils were abolished – they had consistently exceeded government expenditure targets and had increased their expenditure significantly more than other local authorities in England. During both Conservative administrations, the programme to 'privatize' certain government concerns went resolutely ahead. The oil and gas exploration and production activities of BNOC (the British National Oil Corporation) were taken over by Britoil in 1982 and 51 per cent of Britoil's shares were offered for sale by tender. 1984 saw the flotation of British Telecom, which was to run the telecommunications and data-processing services of the Post Office. The net proceeds of the sale of British Gas in 1986 was £3,600 million.

By the end of 1986 the annual average rate of inflation had dropped to 3.4 per cent, but the seasonally adjusted level of unemployment (excluding school-leavers) in March remained a great cause of concern to the nation as a whole: at 13.2 per cent, representing 3,197,700 people, it had never before been so high. Was this the sort of price Britain would have to pay for a continuing preoccupation with combatting inflation through reductions in government spending?

When Britons looked abroad they could find much to envy, but they were reluctant to imitate foreign practices and concepts. Their attachment to British civilization (and especially to the British civilities) may have had its price, but it expressed long-standing aspirations. Exactly when the British first realized the values of their cultures, first realized that they enjoyed a civilization that was worth defending, is arguable. Perhaps it all began in Tudor England. But certainly it reflected the circumstance that the British, on the whole, had been very lucky in their history. Much of this good fortune they had reinvested in the world, to help make it a better place for themselves, and for others too.

Following a conclusive British victory in the Falklands conflict in 1982, the requisitioned liner *Canberra* comes home to a joyful welcome. The campaign to recover the islands took place largely in barren and inhospitable terrain (inset) and in wet and wintry conditions; the conflict was short and bloody but the British troops ultimately proved to be better trained and more highly motivated than the Argentinians.

Index

This index includes references to pictures, captions, and date tables as well as to the main text. To avoid too complex a notation the following system is used:

Page numbers in normal type indicate one or more references in the text on that page, with or without an illustration of the subject or a reference in the caption of an illustration (the caption may sometimes be on an adjacent page).

An italicised page number indicates an illustration and/or caption reference only.

It will be noted, therefore, that where a page contains both a textual and a pictorial (or caption) reference, the page number nevertheless figures in the index once only and is in normal type. Secondly, an italicised number does not necessarily mean that the subject is illustrated – it may be mentioned merely in a caption.

Where a date table includes information on a subject not found elsewhere, a page reference is given, with the suffix 'd'.

Individuals' names are usually entered according to their surnames, but there are exceptions, especially in the earlier periods where, for example, Robin Hood and Julius Caesar are entered under R and J respectively.

Where an individual changes his name in the course of the narrative (typically when he becomes an earl or lord) the alternative name may be given in brackets.

Acknowledgements

The Publishers would like to thank the following for their kind permission to reproduce the photographs in this book.

Aerofilms Limited 44, 47, 61

Art Directors Photo Library 304

Bodleian Library, Oxford 121, 135

The Bridgeman Art Library 17, 185

The British Library 97, 123

Reproduced by Courtesy Of The Trustees Of The British Museum 28, 32 below

Camera Press 307 below right, 311 and inset

Collectors Photographs Limited 312, 219 below, 223, 227, 229, 231, 232, 235, 236, 243, 249, 250, 251, 252, 256, 257, 260

England Scene (Andy Williams) 303

Robert Estall Photographs 14, 36, 80, 186

E. T. Archive 29, 122, 124, 131, 155, 156, 157, 192, 217, 225, 241, 242, 269

Mary Evans Picture Library 2–3, 4, 6–7, 9 overprint, 21, 23, 32 above, 33, 46, 62, 70, 71, 91, 114, 120, 133, 134, 142, 143, 144, 145, 147, 153, 164, 168, 176, 183, 191, 193 above, 195, 196, 199, 206, 209, 211, 214, 215, 219 above, 220, 239, 246, 262, 271, 272, 273

Vivien Fifield 25, 56, 57, 64, 66, 83, 98, 104, 113, 117, 118, 127, 140, 141, 154, 160, 162, 166, 170, 175, 180, 188, 193 below, 198, 200, 201, 208, 263

Fox Photos Limited 285

John Freeman 203

The Frick Collection, New York 107

The John Hillelson Agency, Erich Lessing/Magnum 1, 14 inset

Michael Holford Photographs 9, 13, 15

Robert Hunt Library 261, 265 above, 287, (Imperial War Museum) 264 above right, 264 below, 265 below, 266, 284

The Illustrated London News Picture Library 240, 274, 276, 278–9, 280 below, 281, 282 above and below

Imperial War Museum 204, 264 above left, 283

The Mansell Colletion Limited 24, 34, 39, 40–41, 42, 55, 58, 59, 67, 73, 74, 82, 92, 93, 96, 99, 101, 106, 108 above and below, 109, 112, 119, 128, 132, 137, 152, 163, 171, 202, 210, 218, 226, 238, 244, 254

The National Maritime Museum, London 78–79, 59

National Portrait Gallery 78, 89, 169, 173, 178

Popperfoto 286 above and below, 290, 291, 298 above and below, 299 above and below, 300 below, 301 below, 302

Rex Features 301 above, 306 and inset, 307 below left, 308, 309, 310 above and below

Rolls-Royce Limited 248

Ronald Sheridan's Photo-Library 18 above and below left, above and below right, 35 above and below, 45, 49, 72, 115, (J. Larkin) 26, 48

Spectrum Colour Library 77

John Topham Picture Library 280 above, 292, 293 above and below, 294 left and right, 295, 300 above, 302, 305

Trinity College Library Cambridge 54

West Air Photography 53

George Wright 75

Jacket pictures:

The Bridgeman Art Library, bottom left, bottom right

Camera Press, centre back

Oscar and Peter Johnson Gallery Ltd/The Bridgeman Art Library, top left

The John Hillelson Agency, David Hurn/Magnum, above right

Michael Holford Photographs, below left

Rex Features, below right, above left, bottom centre

Thyssen Bornemisza Collection/The Bridgeman Art Library, top right

ZEFA Picture Library, top centre